A Restorative Justice Reader

A Restorative Justice Reader brings together carefully chosen extracts from the most important and influential contributions to the literature of restorative justice, accompanying these with an informative commentary providing context and explanation. It includes works both by well known advocates of restorative justice and by some of the key critics of the restorative justice movement.

The new edition has been thoroughly revised to take account of the rapid expansion of the literature of restorative justice over the last decade. Classical readings are accompanied by more recent literature representing the most significant contributions to research, discussion and debate concerning restorative justice.

Gerry Johnstone is Professor of Law and Research Director of the Law School at the University of Hull.

A Restorative Justice Reader

Second edition

Edited by Gerry Johnstone

 Routledge
Taylor & Francis Group

LONDON AND NEW YORK

First edition published 2003 by Willan

This edition published 2013
by Routledge
2 Park Square, Milton Park, Abingdon, Oxon, OX14 4RN

Simultaneously published in the USA and Canada
by Routledge
711 Third Avenue, New York, NY 10017

Routledge is an imprint of the Taylor & Francis Group, an informa business

British Library Cataloguing in Publication Data
A catalogue record for this book is available from the British Library

Library of Congress Cataloging-in-Publication Data
A catalog record has been requested for this book

ISBN: 978-0-415-67235-1 (hbk)
ISBN: 978-0-415-67234-4 (pbk)

Typeset in Times New Roman
by Cenveo Publisher Services

Contents

Preface to the second edition

A Restorative Justice Reader was first published in 2003. Since then, the literature of restorative justice has expanded rapidly. As a result, a new edition of the *Reader* seems due: both to provide more up-to-date readings representing particular themes/authors and to represent new themes and issues which have emerged since the first edition. The first edition combined classical and contemporary readings. Whilst most of the classical readings have been retained, a significant proportion of the contemporary readings have been replaced by more up-to-date material. There has also been some adjustment to the structure and range of the book; in particular, a new section on evaluation has been added.

Selecting material has been difficult. For every piece included in this Reader, many other important and interesting readings could have been included. My hope is that *A Restorative Justice Reader* will – whilst serving as a useful volume for busy students, practitioners, policy-makers and others seeking to engage with some of the key literature of restorative justice – serve as a stimulus to further exploration of the rich literature on the topic.

I am extremely grateful to authors and publishers who have allowed their work to be reproduced, sometimes in edited form, in this text. I would also like to thank Brian Willan, who encouraged me to start working on this second edition, and Nicola Hartley, who with enormous patience encouraged me to complete it.

Preface to the first edition

Amongst the most important developments in contemporary crime policy and criminal justice is the emergence of a vibrant international campaign promoting restorative justice as an alternative to conventional ways of viewing and responding to crime. Proponents of restorative justice contend that, in responding to crime, our main concern should not be to punish offenders; rather, it should be to ensure that offenders account for and repair the harm they bring about. They also maintain that, rather than entrusting the task of dispensing criminal justice entirely to state officials and professionals, modern societies should create processes in which ordinary people, including the perpetrators and victims of an offence, resolve collectively how the harm created by the offence should be repaired and how reoffending is to be prevented.

Restorative justice policies and programmes are usually offered as a progressive alternative to the increasing use of imprisonment and other exclusionary measures to control crime and dispense justice. Many penal reformers and professionals interested in developing constructive ways of dealing with people whose lives are somehow affected by crime have found restorative justice appealing. Moreover, the idea has recently started to influence government thinking and policy, especially but not exclusively in the realm of youth justice. With official encouragement and support, restorative justice schemes are now proliferating rapidly around the world. Such has been the success of the restorative justice movement that, today, anybody interested in the future of crime policy and criminal justice – indeed anybody interested in the development of more constructive forms of conflict resolution and crime control – has to understand what it is about. One problem they may encounter is simply getting access to the diverse international literature on restorative justice. However, even if this difficulty is overcome, there is the problem of knowing where to start and how to work one's way through a rather bulky, diverse, international literature. Nor is this simply a problem of separating the wheat from the chaff. As numerous commentators have pointed out, restorative justice is not a single coherent theory or perspective on crime and justice, but a loose unifying term which encompasses a range of distinct ideas, practices and proposals. The danger with a random browse or trawl through the literature is that one could spend a lot of time reading repetitive materials on a few aspects of restorative justice, whilst failing to encounter other aspects of restorative justice thought and practice which are of equal or greater importance. An even greater danger is that one will encounter literature advocating and supporting restorative justice, or evaluating it in terms of its effectiveness in achieving its declared goals, but not encounter the extremely important critical literature which highlights the limitations and potential dangers involved in developing restorative justice.

It was partly in order to address such problems that I wrote my recent book *Restorative Justice: Ideas, Values, Debates* (Willan, 2002, 2nd edition Routledge, 2011). However, those whose interest in the subject has been whetted (either by reading that book or in other ways) will want to read some of the key 'original writings'. But, for the busy student or practitioner, constructing an appropriate reading list – one which will enable him or her to encounter a range of key writers and a range of key ideas, processes and critiques in a manageable way – remains a daunting task. Hence, this book contains an edited selection of key literature on restorative justice, encompassing a range of authors and topics from a number of continents. The hope is that the reader will benefit from the effort I have put into: (1) *selecting* a suitable range of writing on restorative justice; (2) *editing* the selected material, so that the most important ideas and topics are covered and so that repetition is, if not entirely avoided, at least reduced considerably; (3) *organising* that material so that one can work through it in a systematic, logically structured way; and (4) introducing the material so that the contexts in which it was produced and some of its most significant features can be better understood.

I would like to record my thanks to Brian Willan for originally suggesting this book. I also wish to thank a number of people who made extremely valuable comments, concerning both the structure and content of the book. Inevitably, I have not been able or willing to incorporate all their suggestions, but a significant number of them have been taken on board. Thanks, therefore, to John Braithwaite, Kathleen Daly, David Miers, Paul McCold, Lynette Parker, George Pavlich, Daniel Van Ness, Lode Walgrave, Brian Williams, and Howard Zehr.

Thanks are also due to the authors and publishers whose work is reproduced here, for their prompt and helpful responses to my requests, and for allowing their work to be used in edited form. Finally, thanks are again due to my wife, Brigid, and our children Eleanor and Pierce, for their constant support and encouragement.

Sources and acknowledgements

The editor and publisher would like to thank the following for their kind permission to reproduce copyright material.

Part A

The extract from 'A new paradigm arises' by Ross London is reproduced with permission from FirstForumPress. The full text was published in *Crime, Punishment and Restorative Justice* (Boulder, CO: FirstForumPress, 2011).

The extract from ''The meaning of restorative justice', Gerry Johnstone and Daniel W. Van Ness is reproduced with permission from Routledge and the author. It was originally published in Johnstone, G. and Van Ness, D. (eds) *Handbook of Restorative Justice*, (Willan/Routledge, 2007), pp. 5–23.

Retributive Justice, Restorative Justice by Howard Zehr is reproduced with permission from the Mennonite Central Committee, Office on Crime and Justice. It was originally published as an Occasional Paper (number 4 in the series *New Perspectives on Crime and Justice*) in September 1985 (MCC Canada Victim Offender Ministries Program and the MCC US Office on Crime and Justice).

The extract from 'Conflicts as Property' by Nils Christie is reproduced with the permission of Oxford University Press and the author. The full text was published in *The British Journal of Criminology*, Vol 17:1 (Jan. 1977) pp. 1–15.

The extract from 'Restitution: A New Paradigm of Criminal Justice' by Randy E. Barnett is reproduced with permission of the University of Chicago Press and the author. The full text was published in *Ethics*, Vol 87 (1977), pp. 279–301.

The extract from 'Restorative Justice and a Better Future' by John Braithwaite is reproduced with the permission of Dalhousie University and the author. It was originally published in the *Dalhousie Review*, Spring 1996, 76:1, pp. 9–32.

Part B

The extract from 'The Kitchener Experiment' by Dean E. Peachey is reproduced with the permission of Sage and the author. The full text is published in M. Wright and B. Galaway (eds) *Mediation and Criminal Justice* (London: Sage Publications, 1989), pp. 14–26.

The extract from 'Encounter' by Daniel W. Van Ness and Karen Heetderks Strong is reproduced with permission from Anderson Publishing. The original text was published in Daniel W. Van Ness and Karen Heetderks Strong (2006) *Restoring Justice* (Anderson publishing/LexisNexis).

The extract from 'The future of mediation' by Robert A. Baruch Bush and Joseph G. Folger is reproduced with permission from Wiley. The full text was originally published in Robert A. Baruch Bush and Joseph G. Folger (1994) *The Promise of Mediation* (San Francisco; Jossey-Bass).

The extract from 'Strategy for Community Conferences: Emotions and Social Bonds', by Suzanne M. Retzinger and Thomas J. Scheff is reproduced with permission from Lynne Rienner Publishers. The full version appears in in B. Galaway and J. Hudson (eds) (1996) *Restorative Justice: International Perspectives* (Monsey, NY: Criminal Justice Press), pp. 315–336. Copyright © 2010 by Lynne Rienner Publishers, Inc.

The extract from 'Peacemaking Circles' by K. Pranis is reproduced from Pranis, K (1997) 'Peacemaking Circles', *Corrections Today* (Dec.).

The extract from 'Navajo Restorative Justice: The Law of Equality and Justice' by Robert Yazzie and James W. Zion is reproduced with the permission of Lynne Rienner Publishers. The full text is published in Galaway, B. and Hudson J. (eds) (1996) *Restorative Justice: International Perspectives* (Monsey, NY: Criminal Justice Press), pp. 157–73. Copyright © 2010 by Lynne Rienner Publishers, Inc.

The extract from 'Restorative justice and prisons', by Kimmett Edgar and Tim Newell is reproduced with permission from Lynne Rienner Publishers. The full version appears in Edgar, K. and Newell, T. (2006) *Restorative Justice in Prisons* (Winchester: Waterside Press), pp. 22–26. Copyright © 2010 by Lynne Rienner Publishers, Inc.

The extract from 'Restorative justice and police-led cautioning practice' by David O'Mahony and Jonathan Doak is reproduced from O'Mahony, D. and Doak, J. (2009) 'Restorative justice and police-led cautioning practice', *Journal of Police Studies*, volume 2009–2, 11: pp. 139–158 (Maklu Publishers).

The extract from 'Restorative justice, gendered violence, and indigenous women' by Julie Stubbs is reproduced with permission from Oxford University Press. The full text was originally published in Ptacek, J. (ed) (2010) *Restorative Justice and Violence against Women* (Oxford: Oxford University Press), pp. 103–122.

The extract from 'Responding to hate crimes through restorative justice dialogue' by Robert B. Coates, Mark S. Umbreit and Betty Vos is reproduced with permission from Routledge. The full text was originally published in *Contemporary Justice Review*, 9(1) (2006), pp. 7–21.

The extract from 'Restorative justice and reparations' by Margaret Urban Walker is reproduced with permission from Wiley Blackwell. The full text was originally published in Walker, M. (2006) *Journal of Social Philosophy*, 37:3, pp. 377–395.

Part C

The extract from *Returning to the Teachings: Exploring Aboriginal Justice* (copyright © University of Saskatchewan) by Rupert Ross is reproduced with permission from the Penguin Group (Canada) a Division of Pearson Penguin Canada Inc.

The extract from 'Needs-based justice as restorative', by Dennis Sullivan and Larry Tifft is reproduced with kind permission from Lynne Rienner Publishers. The full version appears in Sullivan, D. and Tifft, l. (2001) *Restorative justice: healing the foundations of our everyday lives* (Monsey NY: Willow Tree Press), pp. 99–120. Copyright © 2010 by Lynne Rienner Publishers, Inc.

The extract from 'Seeking socio-ethical grounds for restorative justice' by Lode Walgrave is reproduced with permission from Willan/Routledge. The full text appears in Walgrave, L. (2008) *Restorative Justice, Self-interest and Responsible Citizenship* (Willan/Routledge), pp. 68–100.

The extract from 'Restorative justice and the philosophical theories of criminal punishment' by Conrad G. Brunk is reproduced with permission from SUNY press. The full text appears in Hadley, M. (ed.) *The Spiritual Roots of Restorative Justice* (Albany, NY: SUNY Press), pp. 31–56.

Part D

'Evaluation and restorative justice principles' by Howard Zehr is reproduced with permission from Willan/Routledge. The full text appears in principles' in Elliot, E. and Gordon, R. (eds.) (2005) *New Directions in Restorative Justice* (Willan Publishing), pp. 296–303.

'Does Restorative Justice Work?' by John Braithwaite is a slightly abridged version of Chapter 3 of his book, *Restorative Justice and Response Regulation* (Oxford: Oxford University Press, 2002). It is reproduced with permission from the publisher.

The extract from 'Restorative justice: the evidence' by Lawrence W. Sherman and Heather Strang is reproduced from Sherman, Lawrence W. and Strang, Heather (2007) *Restorative Justice: the Evidence* (London: The Smith Institute), pp. 8–9 and 12–24.

'Reducing recidivism: A task for restorative justice', Gwen Robinson and Joanna Shapland is reproduced with permission from Oxford University Press. This was originally published in Robinson, G. and Shapland, J. (2008) 'Reducing recidivism: A task for restorative justice', *British Journal of Criminology*, 48: pp. 337–358.

The extract from 'Repair or revenge?' by Heather Strang is reproduced with permission from Oxford University Press. The full text appears in Strang, Heather (2002) *Repair or revenge: victims and restorative justice* (Oxford: Oxford University Press).

Part E

The extract from 'Restorative Justice: The Real Story' by Kathleen Daly is reproduced with permission from Sage Publications. The full article is published in *Punishment and Society*, 4:1 (2002), pp. 5–79.

The extract from 'Responsibilities, Rights and Restorative Justice' by Andrew Ashworth is reproduced with permission of the author and Oxford University Press. The full version appears in a special edition of the *British Journal of Criminology* (42:3, 2002), on Practice, Performance and Prospects for Restorative Justice', edited by Kieran McEvoy, Harry Mika and Barbara Hudson. Ashworth's paper is at pp. 578–95.

The extract from 'The virtues of restorative processes, the vices of 'restorative justice' by Paul H. Robinson is reproduced with permission from the University of Utah. The full text was originally published in the *Utah Law Review*, 2003:1, pp. 375–88.

'Some sociological reflections on restorative justice' by Anthony Bottoms is reproduced with permission from the author and Hart Publishing. It was originally published in von Hirsch, A., Roberts, J., Bottoms, A., Roach, K. and Schiff, M. (eds.) (2003) *Restorative Justice and Criminal Justice: Competing or Reconcilable Paradigms* (Oxford: Hart Publishing), pp. 79–113.

The extract from 'Justice anew' by George Pavlich is reproduced with permission from Willan/Routledge. The full text appears in Pavlich, George (2005) *Governing paradoxes of restorative justice* (London: Glasshouse press).

The extract from 'The seductive vision of restorative justice' by Annalise Acorn is reproduced with permission from the University of British Columbia Press. The full text appears in Acorn, Annalise (2004) *Compulsory Compassion: A Critique of Restorative Justice* (Vancouver, University of British Columbia Press).

Every effort has been made to contact copyright holders for their permission to reprint selections in this book. The publishers would be grateful to hear from any copyright holder who is not here acknowledged and will undertake to rectify any errors or omissions in future editions of this book.

Part A

Overviews and early inspirations

Introduction

The pieces in Part A are intended to provide the reader with an overview of how the idea of restorative justice arose, the sorts of practices with which it is associated, and the theories and discourses which have attempted to make sense of it and which have provided the restorative justice movement with inspiration and a sense of direction. The section opens with an excerpt from Ross London's recent book *Crime, Punishment and Restorative Justice.* Although directed at a USA readership, the excerpt (with some specifically American references edited out) was selected on the basis that it provides an excellent general introduction to what restorative justice is, how it arose, and some of the issues and tensions that have arisen as the campaign for restorative justice has developed from espousing a Utopian ideal to proposing ideas for the reformation or transformation of criminal justice which have sufficiently broad appeal to win political and public acceptability. Initially developed as an alternative paradigm to 'traditional punitive justice' – emphasising the healing of the harm caused by crime over the punishment of its perpetrators – proponents of restorative justice are increasingly seeking to demonstrate that it cannot only exist alongside but can actually help further more conventional purposes of criminal justice such as retribution, deterrence and the rule of law. London, a firm advocate of restorative justice, seeks to ensure that the original focus of restorative justice is maintained, whilst at the same time it is developed into a feasible alternative to existing criminal justice theory and practice. Accordingly, he aims to persuade his fellow advocates of the need to develop a comprehensive jurisprudence of restorative justice as an approach to crime that can be applied to all offenders.

One thing London points to in his essay is the lack of a unified vision amongst those promoting restorative justice. In the second reading, Daniel Van Ness and I approach this issue *via* an exploration of a number of different and to some extent competing conceptions of 'restorative justice'. Writing against the tendency to attempt to encapsulate the essence of restorative justice in a short and neat definition, we suggest that disagreement over the meaning of restorative justice is, to some extent, inevitable and indeed valuable. Crucially, the essay from which this excerpt is drawn is an effort to ensure that some meanings of restorative justice are not simply forgotten or ignored as discussion of its virtues and limitations proceeds.

Howard Zehr's pamphlet 'Retributive Justice, Restorative Justice' (Chapter 3) can be seen as one of the first attempts to propose a new approach to crime and justice explicitly called 'restorative justice'. Published in 1986, the pamphlet was an attempt to think through the wider significance of a new practical experiment in criminal justice – the Victim Offender Reconciliation Programs (VORPs) – which sprang up in North America and elsewhere in the late 1970s and 1980s. Zehr suggests that the VORPs pointed towards a new model of crime and justice, one with roots in ordinary people's needs and experiences. In order to further develop this model, Zehr looked to the principles underlying ancient forms of community justice and 'covenant justice'. He suggests that a proper reading of history and the Bible reveals a radical notion of 'relational justice', informed by an ethic of love and forgiveness and focusing on restoration and the healing of relationships damaged by 'crime'. VORPs, he contends, are a practical demonstration that such an approach to crime and justice can work in contemporary Western societies. However, he concludes with a theme which occurs repeatedly in his subsequent writings. Throughout the history of criminal justice, efforts to bring about radical changes have been co-opted, and made to serve interests and goals quite different from those originally intended. Zehr warns that VORPS may share this fate. Hence, for Zehr, it is of crucial importance to ensure that restorative justice retains its integrity and remains true to its original vision.

Chapter 4 is a slightly abridged version of Nils Christie's renowned essay 'Conflicts as Property'. Christie's paper is about our attitude towards *conflicts* and the way we handle them. He challenges the tendency to think of conflicts as 'pathological' and as in need of speedy solution, best achieved by delegating the task of solving conflicts to professionals. Professionals can 'solve' conflicts quickly because they are trained to narrow down a dispute to a few 'relevant' issues, leaving out much that the parties to the conflict would want to discuss. As an alternative, Christie urges us to see conflicts as beneficial. In order to harvest their benefits, we need to cease searching for the most speedy and effective solutions. We have to be prepared to engage in lengthy and perhaps unending 'political' discussion of the issues in conflict, unconfined by 'legal' rules of relevance and other 'external' stipulations of what matters. To benefit from conflicts we must cease handing them over to professionals to solve. The parties directly involved must be at the centre of any search for solutions, surrounded by their families, friends and neighbours. Christie's paper has had enormous influence on proponents of restorative justice. Today, however, it tends to be more cited than read. Christie's dramatic statements about the state stealing conflicts and the need to return them to the people are repeated, but his more subtle and challenging ideas about conflict and its handling are forgotten. The essay is reproduced here in effort to encourage close reading and engagement with Christie's challenging ideas.

The next extract in this section is from a paper by American legal and political theorist, Randy E. Barnett, published in 1977. Barnett did not propose 'restorative' justice in the sense that the term is now understood. Nevertheless, there are very good reasons for including this piece amongst the key early inspirations of the restorative justice movement, and for recommending it as still relevant to anybody interested in restorative justice. Barnett introduced the idea, later taken up by Howard Zehr (see Chapter 3), that the failures of our criminal justice system could be analysed as a crisis of an old paradigm: punishment. This implied the need for a *radical* shift of perspective. Most other reforms of criminal justice could be understood as attempts to salvage the old paradigm; for Barnett, the system was beyond salvaging in such fashion. It needed to be discarded and replaced by an entirely new paradigm. Barnett's rigorous attempt to sketch the outlines of a new restitutive paradigm, and to show why many of the 'obvious' objections are either question–begging or easily met, can still be read with profit by anybody interested in seriously thinking through the pros and cons of restorative justice.

John Braithwaite entered the debate about restorative justice much later than Zehr, Christie and Barnett. His hugely influential book, *Crime, Shame and Reintegration* (1989, Cambridge University Press), made no explicit mention of restorative justice. In this book, the harmful disintegrative shaming (stigmatisation) typical of criminal justice interventions was contrasted with the constructive reintegrative shaming found in loving families and oriental societies such as Japan. Braithwaite's core thesis was that societies which engage in reintegrative shaming tend to have lower crime rates than others, and that a radical shift in crime policy – away from over-reliance on state punishment towards promoting and facilitating informal and moralising social control – was required. It was only later that Braithwaite began to depict restorative justice practices, such as family group conferences, as examples of reintegrative shaming at work and began to promote reintegrative shaming as a core aspect of restorative justice. In the essay reprinted here, Braithwaite attacks Western criminal justice systems as not only humiliating and stigmatising, but brutal, vengeful and hypocritical. Despite their harshness, these systems fail to prevent crime. The solution, for Braithwaite, is to replace stigmatic punishment with restorative justice, in which evil acts are condemned, but those who commit them are treated as essentially good people who, with love and social support, can be helped to turn away from crime and be restored to the community as responsible and valued citizens.

1   A new paradigm arises

Ross London

Restorative justice as both a philosophy and an implementation strategy developed from the convergence of several trends in criminal justice: the loss of confidence in rehabilitation and deterrence theory, the rediscovery of the victim as a necessary party, and the rise of interest in community-based justice.

In the 1970s and 1980s, […] faith in the criminal justice system was severely shaken. The optimistic beliefs of earlier decades that crime could eventually be eradicated by addressing the "underlying causes" of poverty, urban congestion, and discrimination had by now eroded. […] After nearly a century of attempts to reform and rehabilitate offenders, the inconsistent results of these efforts generated a pervasive sense that "nothing works."[1] The traditional concept of penance had long since been discarded, and even the efficacy of crime prevention by deterrence was questioned by criminologists who argued that a free society is unlikely to provide the inevitability of detection, apprehension, and swift punishment that is required for effective deterrence.[2] Crime theorists, no longer convinced that offenders could be induced to change by either threats or therapy, resurrected biological theories of criminality and stressed the need to identify and incarcerate the hard-core "incorrigibles" who were thought to be responsible for a disproportionate amount of crime. Even if the threat of incarceration docs not deter people from committing crimes, they argued, the walls and iron bars of prison effectively (if expensively) incapacitate offenders from further menacing the public as long as they are kept inside.[3] Other theorists argued for the merits of retributive justice, claiming that the state should impose punishment as a morally based response to blameworthiness of offenses rather than an attempt to change the character of offenders through rehabilitation.[4] During the 1980s, political leaders perceived a shift in public opinion away from rehabilitation and toward greater punitivity. Understanding full well that being labeled "soft on crime" was the kiss of death for their careers, politicians throughout the country withdrew their support for rehabilitation programs and began enacting ever-tougher sentencing laws with longer jail terms, mandatory sentences, elimination of parole, lifetime incarceration for repeat offenders, and juvenile "waivers" for treatment as adults. Then, to accommodate the flood of inmates that ensued, they appropriated millions for the construction of new prisons.

Yet despite creating the highest levels of incarceration in our nation's history and one of the highest rates of incarceration among developed nations, crime rates during the early 1980s continued to rise. Not only was the criminal justice system seen by many critics as ineffectual, unable to stem the epidemic of drug use, and, through its "get tough" tactics, the cause of further alienation and rebellion in the inner cities,[5] the system was increasingly deemed unresponsive to the needs of crime victims and their communities. The growing victims' rights movement sought to gain judicial acceptance of victims' entitlement to increased services, financial compensation and restitution, and intervention in the criminal justice process.[6] Some saw restitution not simply as a necessary component in sentencing, but as the basis of a new philosophy of justice in which accountability is achieved by offenders through actions to repair the damage they have caused rather than merely by accepting punishment.[7] Social critics from the Left renewed their attacks on the criminal justice system as a means of social control exercised by a repressive state,[8] and proposed decentralized, informal alternative means of resolving conflicts.[9] Prisoners' rights groups, with the support of a number of Christian groups, stressed the need to reintegrate, rather than permanently exclude, offenders.[10] The 1980s also saw a rise in interest in community-based problem solving and indigenous justice.[11] During this period, the "just deserts" theory, initially embraced by legislators as a principled solution to the problem of sentencing disparities that resulted from unbridled discretion, came under strenuous attack for being rigid, obsessed with punishment, retrospective, and more concerned with "uniformity rather than resolving genuine conflict and addressing underlying juvenile and interpersonal problems."[12]

Out of this amalgam of critiques of the existing criminal justice system grew an interest in a new conception of justice, one based on healing injuries rather than the assignment of blame and punishment for legal transgressions. This "restorative justice" alternative was envisioned to be essentially informal and nonpunitive. The adversarial nature of the prevailing criminal justice system, designed to protect the rights of the accused, was now seen as inherently non-restorative by discouraging candor and cooperation on the part of the accused and excluding the participation of the victim. These restorative justice theorists sought an alternative to a system that placed undue reliance on attorneys and judges, and in which many victims felt they were treated as little more than a "piece of evidence"[13] and who were "twice victimized, first by the offender and then by an uncaring criminal justice system that doesn't have time for them."[14] To some, this emphasis on victim restoration called for an end to criminal law, replacing it with the civil law protection of an individual's personal and property rights.[15]

This new vision of justice was understood to be an entirely new paradigm, not merely a means of reforming the system, but one in which retributive justice would be replaced by a justice that "grows out of love" and "seeks to make things right."[16] Under the "old paradigm," the system operated as an arena for the conflict between two adversaries having entirely different goals: (1) the state, which sought to control crime by obtaining a speedy conviction and a severe punishment; and (2) the defendant who sought protection against unfair and oppressive prosecution. In this adversarial system, the truth of accusations was to be determined by the clash of professional combatants who were well trained in complex rules and procedures designed to establish guilt or innocence without impairing the rights of the accused. Because a crime was prosecuted on behalf of the state, the victim of the crime had no separate standing in the courtroom and, consequently, was merely a witness rather than a party whose individual interests were to be protected. Under the "new paradigm" of restorative justice, however, the victim would become a central decision maker in a process of personal encounters and joint negotiation.

Ironically, restorative justice advocates contended that the new goal of repairing harm through informal encounters was not really a new innovation at all but, in fact, represented a return to ancient and tribal practices from which Western societies could learn a great deal. In ancient times, they claimed, an offense was not against the state, but against a person and a community.[17] The goal of conflict resolution therefore was not simply to assign blame for legal transgressions, but to restore wholeness to individuals and the community. Aboriginal justice, they maintained, involved more than just a resolution of a dispute or the proper assessment of legal liability; there also was an active effort to repair material, psychological, and relational damage. Beyond the harm suffered by the individual members of the group, crime represented a threat to the stability and peace of the community. Clan loyalty required collective retaliation for transgressions and, without a mechanism for negotiating conflicts, the danger of resort to a cycle of violent retaliation was very real. Thus, mediation was typically used to address transgressions within the clan and to establish peace between clans.

The basic features of this new but, in many ways, more traditional way of achieving justice began to coalesce during the 1990s. What was achieved was not so much a set of principles as a set of shared values and goals:

- Viewing crime as a source of harm, not simply as a transgression of law, and, consequently, specifying the mission of the criminal justice system as the repair of harm instead of only the determination of guilt and imposition of punishment;
- Involving the victim, the offender, and relevant community members to the fullest extent possible in voluntary negotiations;
- Providing compensation for the victim and achieving social reintegration of the offender; and
- Conducting personal encounters between the victim and offender to establish community peace, and not merely conformity to the law.

The original vision of restorative justice practice therefore consisted of informal, voluntary face-to-face encounters between the victim, the offender, and relevant community members. Through this dialogue, the parties come to greater understanding and empathy, the offenders express remorse, and all negotiate a plan for repairing the harm of crime, resulting in an agreement that emphasizes reparative solutions such as restitution, apology, and community service rather than only punishment.

Growing pains: searching for fundamentals and confronting challenges

As the restorative justice approach grew during the 1990s from an idealistic vision to implementation in actual practice—with more than 1,500 programs throughout the world and over 300 programs in the United States—certain strains developed between those who claimed to represent the "original, pure" vision of restorative justice and those who sought a larger role in determining the course of mainstream criminal practice. These tensions centered on two fundamental challenges to restorative justice theory and practice: (1) reconciling its advocacy of a nonpunitive response to crime with the public's insistence on deterrence and retribution; and (2) reconciling the value of private, informal justice with the needs of society and the rule of law.

Critics of the radically informal approach of restorative justice, both in academia and in the general public, questioned how such a system would be able to cope with the problems of protecting public safety, promoting offender rehabilitation, and ensuring the rights of the accused to a fair trial.[18] The resolution of cases by private negotiation, they contended, would contribute to greater lawlessness by substituting the interests of individual crime victims for the rule of law and by ignoring the interests of the general public not privy to that agreement.[19] Private grievants might be satisfied by the payment of compensation or the entry of consensual restraining order, for example, but the public at large might still be faced with the presence of a dangerous offender in their midst. Even in cases where a victim genuinely comes to forgive his or her assailant, the interests of the general public not privy to their agreement are not necessarily considered. Just as the state under the old paradigm was blind to the needs of victims, under this new system of private justice, the victim may be blind to the needs of society. Worse yet, if economically powerful offenders and criminal organizations are able to buy their way out of trouble, they can continue their criminal enterprises as before, writing off the occasional payment of restitution as the "cost of doing business."

As in the case of conventional prosecutions where the community representatives do not necessarily reflect the concerns of the victim, so too the victim does not necessarily concern himself or herself with the welfare of the community. Recognizing the greater ability of the formal criminal justice system to protect the interests of the general public—its insistence on public safety and its concern for "consistency, fairness, and efficiency"[20] in criminal procedure and sentencing—many restorative justice theorists have sought a balance between formal and informal justice. The danger of arbitrary and disparate sentences stemming from victim-offender settlements was intended to be controlled by judicial review, and the concern for community safety was meant to be protected by community participation. To some, however, the inclusion of the community as an interested party to the proceedings threatened a return to the retributive model[21] and a source of "net widening."[22] More fundamentally, the incorporation of the traditional legal system into restorative justice for the purpose of ensuring procedural safeguards and maintaining standards became viewed as a potential degradation to the core value of personal, informal encounters between the victim and offender.[23]

In addition to the problems raised by the new paradigm of informal, personal encounters, restorative justice had to address the issues raised by its rejection of punishment. Eliminating punishment would mean removing a sanction that many, if not most, citizens view as a necessary component of justice. Although there is universal agreement among restorative justice theorists that the singular fixation of traditional criminal justice with assigning blame and imposing punishment is incompatible with restoration, the legitimate use of punishment within a restorative context has been the subject of considerable debate. While the view of the "penal abolitionists" has been the abandonment of punishment altogether[24] or its replacement with a restitution model,[25] others concede a limited role in enforcing settlements or as a last resort for those incorrigibles who have proven to be unreceptive to restorative programs.[26] As against these views, some new voices have entered the debate in recent years: a small, but growing, minority of restorative justice theorists who have argued for a restorative function of punishment.[27]

[...]

Searching for fundamentals

Through its simultaneous emphasis on reparation to the victim, accountability to the community, and responsiveness to the rehabilitation needs of offenses, the concept of "restorative justice" has become increasingly inclusive but also increasingly amorphous. Furthermore, attempts that have been made to accommodate due process protections demonstrate the difficulty of creating a full-scale alternative to the existing system. Bazemore and Walgrave argued that the problems associated with privatization could be solved by recommending that legal institutions oversee individual encounters to ensure that minimal protections of the rights of the accused are respected.[28] Yet it is in defining the nature and extent of these minimal protections that difficulties arise. The United States Constitution grants to the accused such rights as the right to counsel, the presumption of innocence, the right to remain silent, and the right to trial. Restorative justice programs cannot compromise these rights by calling for "minimal" adherence: The Constitution has already defined what those minimal rights must be for all criminal cases.

As a result of these and other considerations, the growth of restorative justice has resulted in a constellation of values rather than a unified vision. After reviewing various formulations of restorative justice core principles, Bazemore and Walgrave concluded that "a full-fledged restorative justice alternative should offer as many legal safeguards as the traditional justice system, but it should be socially more responsible, provide more standing and support for crime victims and offer at a minimum no fewer opportunities for offender rehabilitation and reintegration than systems grounded in individual treatment assumptions."[29] In other words, at the same time as it accomplishes the goal of reintegrating the offender into the community, restorative justice ought to include all of the protections of the due process model and the offender benefits of the rehabilitation model as well as satisfying the need of the crime victim for reparation and the need of the community for safety.

The danger, of course, is that, in fashioning a program from such an all-inclusive wish list, not only will the original focus of restorative justice be lost, but individual components of the program also will suffer. On the other hand, the cost of maintaining allegiance to a vision of restorative justice as a *radical alternative* to existing criminal justice theory and practice is the continual marginalization of restorative justice to juvenile offenders and petty offenses.

If restorative justice is to play a role in reformation or transformation of the criminal justice system, it cannot proceed by a withdrawal into an arcane orthodoxy applicable only to petty juvenile offenses. Neither can it progress by simply acquiring more and more "tools," more vectors of interest, and more principles. What is thereby gained in comprehensiveness is lost in increasing incoherence. Thus, restorative justice theorists must propose a persuasive concept of restoration that can be applied to all offenders—juvenile and adult offenders, first-timers and repeat offenders. Furthermore, as restorative justice grows from a vision to an implementation strategy in the real world, it must develop a reasonable jurisprudence—one that provides a rational basis for the rule of law, procedural fairness, and just enforcement. The wholesale rejection of a positive role of the state in establishing and enforcing law in favor of private justice, which is advanced by some theorists, not only is a political barrier to greater acceptance of restorative justice, but it also neglects the vital role of government in ensuring the due process rights, equality of treatment, and protection of minorities.

The ability of restorative justice to help victims and communities recover from their losses and offenders gain reintegration cannot be based on a yearning for an idealized past or a homogeneous, communitarian society. Instead, it must be relevant to the inner cities as well as suburbs, small towns, and Native American reservations. It must apply to the hard cases as well as the easy cases, to violent crime as well as property crime, and to repeat offenders as well as first-timers. It must be appropriate for the cases that now fill the prisons as well as the cases that are routinely diverted away from the criminal justice system. The future of restorative justice therefore involves a critical choice: Should it remain as an exotic alternative to the conventional system, applicable to only a limited category of offenses and offenders? Or should it enter the criminal justice "mainstream" by offering a *comprehensive* model applicable to the widest variety of cases?

Finally, restorative justice must be embraced by the victims' rights community as a better way of doing justice. Remarkably, despite the streams of rhetoric extolling restorative justice as a means of victim empowerment and healing, little support has been forthcoming from victims rights' and victims' advocacy groups. Indeed, an extensive survey of victims' advocacy groups noted widespread dissatisfaction with restorative justice policy and practices involving feelings of "injustice, disrespect, exclusion, lack of empathy and irrelevance."[30] Some of this concern centered on the ambiguity of restorative justice goals and values, which derived from a "fractious collection of interests and personalities."[31] A criminal justice alternative dedicated to the interests of crime victims cannot afford to be regarded as "tone deaf to their aspirations."[32]

And so, as restorative justice continues into its third decade, with programs throughout the world and an ever-growing literature by its advocates, practitioners, and critics, it still can be aptly described as a "work in progress."[33] Devised by criminal justice visionaries in the 1980s as a new paradigm to replace what was viewed as a structurally flawed and misdirected system, criticized as a naïve rejection of hard-won constitutional rights, and fragmented into factions with different outlooks and strategies, restorative justice remains a promising but marginal development in criminal justice, still "in search of fundamentals."[34]

Notes

1 Lipton, Martinson & Wilks, "The Effectiveness of Correctional Treatment."
2 Sherman, *et al.,* "Preventing Crime;" Blumstein et al., *Deterrence and Incapacitation.*
3 Wilson & Herrnstein, *Crime and Human Nature.*
4 von Hirsch, *Doing Justice: The Choice of Punishments.*
5 Wright, *Justice for Victims and Offender.*
6 Elias, *The Politics of Victimization.*
7 Barnett & Hagel, "Assessing the Criminal," p. 15.
8 Pepinsky, *The Geometry of Violence and Democracy.*
9 Christie, "Conflicts as Property," pp. 1–15.
10 Colson & Benson, "Restitution as an Alternative to Imprisonment."
11 Wright & Galaway, *Mediation and Criminal Justice.*
12 Bazemore & Walgrave, "Restorative Juvenile Justice: In Search of Fundamentals," p. 46.
13 Cardenas, Juan, "The Crime Victim and the Prosecutorial Process," p. 371.
14 Umbreit, Coates & Kalanj, *Victim Meets Offender,* p. 196.
15 Barnett, "Assessing the Criminal: Restitution, Retribution and the Legal Process."
16 Zehr, *Changing Lenses,* p. 139.
17 Van Ness & Strong, *Restoring Justice* (3rd Ed.), p. 7.
18 Feld, "Rehabilitation, Retribution and Restorative Justice," pp. 17–44.
19 Ashworth, "Some Doubts About Restorative Justice," pp. 277–299.
20 Van Ness, "New Wine and Old Wineskins," p. 264.
21 McCold, "Paradigm Muddle," 2004.
22 Van Ness, *supra,* p. 272.
23 McCold, "Toward a Holistic Vision of Restorative Justice," pp. 357–358.
24 Bianchi & Van Swaaningen, *Abolitionism: Toward a Non-Repressive Approach to Crime;* Christie, *Limits to Pain.*
25 Barnett, "Restitution: A New Paradigm," pp. 279–301.
26 Braithwaite, "Restorative Justice and De-Professionalization," p. 29.
27 Daly, "Restorative Justice: The Real Story," pp. 58–60; Barton, "Empowerment and Retribution in Criminal Justice," p. 67; Miller & Blackler, "Restorative Justice: Retribution Confession and Shame," p. 88.
28 Bazemore & Walgrave, "Restorative Juvenile Justice: In Search of Fundamentals."
29 Bazemore & Walgrave, "Reflections on the Future of Restorative Justice," pp. 363–364.
30 Mika, *et al.,* "Listening to Victims," p. 35.
31 *Id.*
32 *Id.* p. 40.
33 Bazemore & Walgrave, "Reflections on the Future of Restorative Justice," p. 359.
34 Bazemore & Walgrave, "Restorative Juvenile Justice: In Search of Fundamentals," p. 45.

References

Barnett, Randy. "Restitution: A New Paradigm of Criminal Justice." *Ethics* 87 (1977): 279–301.

Barnett, Randy. "Assessing the Criminal: Restitution, Retribution and the Legal Process." In R. Barnett and J. Hagel, (eds.) *Assessing the Criminal.* Cambridge, MA: Ballinger, 1977.

Barton, Charles. "Empowerment and Retribution in Criminal Justice." In H. Strang and J. Braithwaite, (eds.). *Restorative Justice: Philosophy to Practice.* Hants, England: Dartmouth, 2000.

Bazemore, Gordon and Walgrave, Lode. "Restorative Juvenile Justice: in Search of Fundamentals and An Outline for Systemic Reform." In G. Bazemore and L. Walgrave, (eds.), *Restorative Juvenile Justice: Repairing the Harm of Youth Crime.* Monsey, NY: Criminal Justice Press, 1999.

Bazemore, Gordon and Walgrave, Lode. "Reflections on the Future of Restorative Justice for Juveniles." In G. Bazemore and L. Walgrave, (eds.), *Restorative Juvenile Justice: Repairing the Harm of Youth Crime.* Monsey, NY: Criminal Justice Press, 1999.

Blumstein, Alfred, Cohen, Jacqueline and Nagin, Daniel (eds.), *Deterrence and incapacitation: Estimating the Effects of Criminal Sanctions on Crime Rates, Report of the Panel of Deterrence and Incapacitation.* Washington, D.C.: National Academy of Sciences, 1978.

Braithwaite, John. "Restorative Justice and De-Professionalization." *The Good Society* 13, no. 1 (2004): 28–31.

Cardenas, Juan. "The Crime Victim and the Prosecutorial Process." *Harvard Journal of Law and Public Policy* 9 (1986): 357–98.

Christie, Nils. "Conflicts as Property." *British Journal of Criminology* 17 (1977): 1–15.

Colson, Charles and Benson, Daniel. "Restitution as An Alternative to Imprisonment." *Detroit College of Law Review* 2 (1980): 523–598.

Daly, Kathleen. "Restorative Justice: the Real Story." *Punishment and Society* 4 (2002): 55–79.

Elias, Robert. *The Politics of Victimization: Victims, Victimology and Human Rights.* New York, NY: Oxford University Press, 1986.

Lipton, Douglas, Martinson, Robert and Wilks, Judith. *The Effectiveness of Correctional Treatment: A Survey of Treatment Evaluation Studies.* New York, NY: Praeger, 1974.

McCold, Paul. "Toward a Holistic Vision of Restorative Juvenile Justice: A Reply to the Maximalist Model." *Contemporary Justice Review* 3 (2000): 357–414.

McCold, Paul. "Paradigm Muddle: The Threat to Restorative Justice Posed by its Merger with Community Justice." *Contemporary Justice Review* 7 (2004): 15–35.

Mika, Harry, Achilles, Mary, Halbert, Ellen, Amstutz, Lorraine, and Zehr, Howard. "Listening to Victims: A Critique of Restorative Justice Policy and Practice in the United States." *Federal Probation* 68 (2004): 32–38.

Miller, Seumas and Blackler, John. "Restorative Justice: Retribution Confession and Shame." In H. Strang and J. Braithwaite, (eds.), *Restorative Justice, from Philosophy to Practice.* Hants, England: Dartmouth, 2000.

Pepinsky, Hal. *The Geometry of Violence and Democracy.* Bloomington: Indiana University Press, 1991.

Sherman, Lawrence, Gottfredson, Denise, Mackenzie, Doris, Eck, John Reuter, Peter and Bushwan, Shawn. *Preventing Crime: What Works What Doesn't, What's Promising: A Report to the United States Congress.* Washington, D.C.: National Institute of Justice, 1997.

Umbreit, Marc, Coates, Robert and Kalanj, Boris. *Victim Meets Offender: The Impact of Restorative Justice and Mediation.* Monsey, NY: Criminal Justice Press, 1994.

Van Ness, Daniel and Strong, Karen. *Restoring Justice* (1st and 3rd editions). Cincinnati, OH: Anderson, 1997, 2006.

Von Hirsch, Andrew. *Doing Justice: The Choice of Punishments.* New York, NY: Hill and Wang, 1976.

Wilson, James and Herrnstein, Richard. *Crime and Human Nature.* New York: Simon and Schuster, 1985.

Wright, Martin. *Justice for Victims and Offenders.* Philadelphia, PA: Open University Press, 1991.

Wright, Martin and Galaway, Burt. (eds.) *Mediation and Criminal Justice: Victims Offenders and Community.* Newbury Park, CA: Sage, 1989.

Zehr, Howard. *Changing Lenses: A New Focus for Crime and Justice.* Scottsdale, PA: Herald Press, 1990.

2 The meaning of restorative justice

Gerry Johnstone and Daniel W. Van Ness

[…]

What sort of a concept is 'restorative justice'?

In what follows, in order to explain why 'restorative justice' is so profoundly contested, we will undertake a brief examination of the *type* of concept which restorative justice is.[1]

An appraisive concept

Most of those who use the term restorative justice consider it to be a constructive and progressive alternative to more traditional ways of responding to crime and wrongdoing. Hence, for its proponents, the judgement about whether a particular practice or situation is properly characterized as 'restorative justice' is not simply a matter of taxonomy, it is a matter of evaluation. The question is whether a particular practice or agenda meets the *standards* of restorative justice. The appraisive nature of the quest for a definition is brought out explicitly by Declan Roche:

> In the same way that counterfeit goods may tarnish the good reputation of a manu-facturers' brand label, programs that are called restorative when they are not can tarnish the concept… restorative justice should seek to prevent counterfeiters from benefiting from the good name of restorative justice. One way to do this is to continually clarify the meaning of restorative justice so that judgments can be made about how restorative a program or practice really is (2001: 343).

An internally complex concept

Not every constructive and progressive alternative to traditional interventions into crime and wrongdoing can be described as restorative justice. For such an alternative to be credibly described as restorative justice, it will usually have one or more of the following ingredients, which are presented in no particular order of importance:

1   There will be some relatively informal process which aims to involve victims, offenders and others closely connected to them or to the crime in discussion of matters such as what happened, what harm has resulted and what should be done to repair that harm and, perhaps, to prevent further wrongdoing or conflict.

2   There will be an emphasis on empowering (in a number of senses) ordinary people whose lives are affected by a crime or other wrongful act.

3   Some effort will be made by decision-makers or those facilitating decision-making processes to promote a response which is geared less towards stigmatizing and punishing the wrongdoer and more towards ensuring that wrongdoers recognize and meet a responsibility to make amends for the harm they have caused in a manner which directly benefits those harmed, as a first step towards their reintegration into the community of law-abiding citizens.

4   Decision-makers or those facilitating decision-making will be concerned to ensure that the decision-making process and its outcome will be guided by certain principles or values which, in contemporary society, are widely regarded as desirable in any inter-action between people, such as: respect should be shown for others; violence and coercion are to be avoided if possible and minimized if not; and inclusion is to be preferred to exclusion.

5   Decision-makers or those facilitating decision-making will devote significant attention to the injury done to the victims and to the needs that result from that, and to tangible ways in which those needs can be addressed.

6   There will be some emphasis on strengthening or repairing relationships between people, and using the power of healthy relationships to resolve difficult situations.

Few would deny the applicability of the concept of restorative justice to an intervention which clearly has all these ingredients. Quite often, however, interventions will possess some of these ingredients, but not others.[2] Whether or not a person defines such an intervention as 'restorative justice' will then depend on how important he or she regards any particular ingredient as being. For example, those who regard the first two ingredients as essential to restorative justice will be reluctant to apply the concept to an intervention which lacks them, even if it clearly possesses the other four. Moreover, they may be willing to apply the concept to an intervention which clearly has the first two ingredients even if some of the others are barely present.

An open concept

New and unforeseen developments can affect the way we use the concept of restorative justice. For instance, in the 1970s and 1980s, the concept was most commonly used in the context of North American experiments with victim–offender mediation and reconciliation (Peachey 2003). These programmes rarely included more participants than the victim, the offender and the facilitator. The facilitator was typically a trained community volunteer. Then, in the early 1990s, new 'conferencing' approaches to crime emerged from New Zealand and Australia, and were subsequently identified as a form of restorative justice (Zehr 1990: 256–62). In these, much larger groups of people, including the friends and family of the victim and offender, are brought together to discuss and decide a much wider range of issues. Furthermore, criminal justice officials, such as police, may participate in the conferences and even serve as facilitators. Several years later, peace-making circles of the First Nations peoples in North America began to be recognized by some criminal courts as a way to resolve criminal matters. Circles include not only victims, offenders and their 'communities of care', but interested members of the surrounding community as well. The involvement of criminal justice officials also expanded, with prosecutors and judges participating. These develop-ments, unforeseen in the late 1980s, had a profound impact upon the usage of the concept of restorative justice. It came to be understood by some as an approach that places high value on bringing together as many stakeholders affected by a crime as possible. Furthermore, the initial assumption that only community volunteers have sufficient neutrality to facilitate restorative processes has given way in some jurisdictions to an assumption that following best practice standards is sufficient to assure that criminal justice officials can provide the neutral setting necessary for authentic participation by offenders.

These are just two examples of how the generally accepted understanding of restorative justice in the 1970s and 1980s shifted because of developments that few would have anticipated in advance. In fact, those shifts have been resisted by some as departures from restorative justice principles and values (Umbreit and Zehr 1996: 24–9; Pranis 1997; McCold 2004b).

In sum, we suggest that restorative justice is an appraisive, internally complex and open concept that continues to develop with experience, and that this helps explain why it is so deeply contested.

Conceptions of 'restorative justice'

One of the significant implications of viewing restorative justice as a deeply contested concept is that there is not likely ever to be (indeed perhaps should not be) a single accepted conception of restorative justice. Instead, we must acknowledge the differing and indeed competing ideas about its nature. To ignore or gloss over these differences misrepresents the character of the restorative justice movement, presenting it as more unified and coherent than it actually is. Just as importantly, doing this presents it as a more limited and more impoverished movement than it truly is. In an effort to avoid such shortcomings, we will review three conceptions of restorative justice.[3]

The encounter conception of restorative justice

In recent years a set of new processes has been devised, developed and employed in social responses to incidents of criminal behaviour, processes such as victim–offender mediation, conferencing and circles (Johnstone 2003: part C; Van Ness and Strong 2006: ch. 4). What is most distinctive about these processes is that, rather than remaining passive while professionals discuss their problem and decide what to do about it, victims, offenders and others affected by some crime or misconduct meet face to face in a safe and supportive environment and play an active role in discussion and in decision-making. For instance, with the assistance of a facilitator, they speak openly but respectfully to each other about what happened, express their feelings and have a say in what is to be done about the matter. Such meetings are intended to be democratic experiences in which the people most affected by a problem decide among themselves how it should be dealt with (O'Connell *et al.* 1999: 17). Rather than being the chief decision-makers, professionals and state officials remain more in the background, making it possible for the stakeholders themselves to make the decisions (Christie 2003).

Many people refer to such processes as 'restorative justice' (Robinson 2003: 375). Indeed, this is probably the most common way of using the term. That is to say, 'restorative justice' is most commonly used as if it were interchangeable with mediation, conferencing, etc.[4] We will refer to this way of defining restorative justice as the *encounter* conception, a term which captures one of the central ideas of the movement: that victims, offenders and other 'stakeholders' in a criminal case should be allowed to encounter one another outside highly formal, professional-dominated settings such as the courtroom.

In order to understand this encounter conception what we need to ask, of course, is *why* encounters are thought to be better than 'courtroom' responses to crime. One possible answer could be that people who are most directly affected by a discussion and decision have a *right* to be meaningfully involved in the discussion and decision-making process. Adherents to this position might argue that this right must be respected even if doing so disturbs the efficient running of the justice machinery, and even if it results in 'solutions' to problems which strike professionals as unenlightened, wrong, absurd and not even in the best interests of the parties involved.[5]

There are some traces of the above rationale for encounter processes in the discourse of restorative justice. Significantly, however, this is not the main way in which proponents of restorative justice tend to argue for encounters. Rather, the more common argument is that such processes are useful for achieving a whole range of beneficial outcomes. This raises the question of how to characterize encounter processes which clearly fail to achieve such beneficial results: are these examples of restorative justice that have failed, or are they not examples of restorative justice? In order to explore this issue, it will be helpful if we provide a brief account of the beneficial effects typically attributed to encounter processes.

Proponents of encounter processes tend to argue that, when they are used in appropriate cases and properly conducted, a number of beneficial results can emerge. Some of these are familiar within the criminal justice system: rehabilitation (changing offenders' attitudes makes them less likely to commit new crimes), deterrence (it is difficult for offenders to meet with their victims, and to do so in the presence of family and friends) and reinforcement of norms (the process and the people involved underscore the importance of the norm that the offender has violated). Other benefits are new in the context of criminal justice: it offers victims avenues for receiving restitution, gives them the opportunity to be involved in decisions in the aftermath of the crime, can contribute to reduced fear and an increased sense of safety, and may help them understand offenders' circumstances that led to commission of the crimes (Robinson 2003: 375–6).

This transformative potential has led some to use encounters to allow the parties to achieve personal growth even if they do not settle claims that victims have against offenders. Umbreit (2001; see also Johnstone 2002: 140–50) contrasts settlement-driven mediation with what he calls humanistic mediation. In humanistic mediation the presenting conflict will receive some attention, but the focus is on helping the parties reach inner resolution through mediated dialogue. This begins with empowerment of the parties and a process of mutual recognition of the other's humanity:

> Through recognition, 'the parties voluntarily choose to become more open, attentive, [and] responsive to the situation of another, thereby expanding their perspective to include an appreciation for another's situation.' Whether an actual settlement occurs is quite secondary to the process of transformation and healing that occurs in their relationship …
>
> One of the most powerful and perhaps most controversial expressions of the transformative qualities of empowerment and recognition has been consistently observed in the small but growing application of mediation and dialogue between parents of murdered children and the offender. After lengthy preparation by the mediator, involving multiple individual meetings, the parties frequently, through a genuine dialogue about what happened and its impact on all involved, get beyond the evil, trauma, and inconsistencies surrounding the event to achieve an acknowledgement of each other's humanity and a greater sense of closure.
>
> (Umbreit 2001: 8–9, citations omitted)

Crucially, however, meetings of stakeholders may not turn out to be transformative or even restorative. They can be conducted in non-restorative ways and arrive at non-restorative results (see Young 2003) such as a now infamous conference which ended with the decision that the young offender should publicly wear a T-shirt emblazoned with 'I am a thief' (Braithwaite 2000). The encounter process alone is not enough to assure the desired results. The question then arises: does such an encounter that does not yield the desired results fall within the definition of restorative justice? Roche raises this issue starkly when he suggests that if we adhere to a strict encounter conception of restorative justice, it is difficult to explain why an encounter which resulted in such a decision should not count as an example of restorative justice. Indeed, he suggests: 'Viewed simply in process terms, any punishment meted out by a victim on an offender, such as lynching and stoning, may potentially satisfy the definition of restorative justice' (2001: 344).

It is important to be clear about what is going on here. Ambiguity over whether encounter processes are important in their own right (because they enable those affected by crime to meet and be involved in the process of deciding what is to be done about it) or are valued mainly because of the desirable outcomes that they can achieve (but will also fail to achieve) manifests itself in uncertainty over whether encounters which are conducted in 'non-restorative' ways and fail to deliver restorative outcomes fall within or outside the *definition* of restorative justice.

Recently, efforts have been made to resolve this issue by focusing as much upon the distinctive *values* of restorative justice as upon its distinctive *processes*. In these efforts, restorative justice becomes redefined, or perhaps we should say more sharply defined, as an encounter process which is guided and constrained by certain values. For instance, Braithwaite (2003: 9–13) suggests that there are three sorts of values to attend to: values that *constrain the process* to prevent it from becoming oppressive (he mentions the values of non-domination, empowerment, respectful listening and equal concern for all stakeholders, among others); values that *guide the process* and that can be used to measure the success of the process (values such as restoration of property, emotional restoration, restoration of dignity, compassion, social support and so forth); and values that *describe certain outcomes of the process* that may, but also may not, emerge from a successful restorative process (values such as remorse, apology, censure of the act, forgiveness and mercy).

Others have proposed alternative sets of values, and it will be necessary for adherents to the values-based encounter conception to continue refining and defining the values that must be present in a restorative process (see, for example, Braithwaite and Strang 2001: 12; Roche 2001: 347; Boyack *et al.* 2004: 1–12 Supp.). It will also be necessary for them to address the question of where these values come from and what their status is. For instance, what needs to be explained is the precise relationship, if any, between the values being proposed by leading advocates of restorative justice (who tend, after all, to be professionals) and the values adhered to by typical lay participants in encounters. And, to the extent that there are tensions between these two different sets of values, it needs to be made clear how these tensions are to be resolved. Important initial efforts to do just that are discussed in more detail by Kay Pranis [...].[6]

The reparative goal conception of restorative justice

There are many, however, who use the concept of restorative justice in a markedly different way; it is a distinctive state of affairs that we should attempt to bring about in the aftermath of criminal wrongdoing, and which might be said to constitute 'justice'. Those who use the concept in this way share, with adherents to an encounter conception, the goal of revolutionizing our response to offending and wrongdoing (cf. Wachtel 1997). However, their ideas about what this project entails are considerably different. For them, it involves a radical break with certain widely accepted 'wisdoms' about what needs to be done to re-establish just relationships when somebody commits a crime against another person (or persons).

Conventionally, we assume that if a person commits a serious wrong against another, a state of injustice arises which needs to be corrected. It tends to be further assumed that, in order to correct this state of injustice, the perpetrator of the wrong must undergo pain or suffering in proportion to the seriousness of the offence. Once the offender has suffered, according to his or her just deserts, the equilibrium has been restored and justice prevails.

Proponents of what we will call a reparative conception of restorative justice reject this way of thinking almost entirely. To be precise, they do agree that if a person commits a serious wrong against another an injustice arises which needs to be put right. However, they insist that simply imposing pain upon offenders is neither necessary nor sufficient to make things right. They argue that the imposition of pain upon offenders, while it occasionally provides us with a slight and short-lived sense that justice has been done, generally fails to deliver a rich and enduring experience of justice.[7] In order to create such an experience, other things need to happen. In particular, the harm which the crime has caused to people and relationships needs to be repaired. This is a very complex process, involving a wide range of things an offender might do to repair the material and symbolic harm he or she has caused to his or her victim(s) (see [...] also Zehr 1990). Some adherents to this reparative conception of restorative justice suggest further that reparation of harm is a *sufficient* ingredient of justice – i.e. in order to achieve justice it is not necessary that the offender undergoes pain or suffering.

What we want to explore briefly now is how this reparative conception of restorative justice relates to the encounter conception outlined earlier. At first sight, the two seem barely distinguishable, since it tends to be argued that in order to achieve the goal of repair of harm, encounter processes are almost indispensable. This argument is based upon a number of ideas. In particular, it is suggested that one of the chief ways in which victims are harmed by crime is that they lose their sense of personal power (Zehr 1990: 27). According to Zehr, one of the reasons why crime is so traumatic for its victims is that it upsets their belief in personal autonomy (1990: 24).

Hence, for the harm of crime to be repaired, this sense of personal power needs to be returned to them. However, when the case is then dealt with by conventional criminal justice processes, in which victims are largely neglected and expected to play a passive role while professionals make all the key decisions, the victim's sense of personal power is further damaged rather than repaired. For repair to take place, victims 'need a sense of control or involvement in the resolution of their own cases' (1990: 28). Other things that victims need in order to recover from the trauma of crime, according to Zehr and others, are answers to questions that only 'their' offenders can answer (and perhaps can only answer convincingly in face-to-face meetings) and the opportunity to express the way they feel about what happened to them and to have their feelings (such as anger, pain and fear) validated by others (1990: ch. 2). For these things to happen, an encounter process is virtually essential.

Turning to offenders, one of the key contributions of the restorative justice movement (broadly conceived) is to argue that, quite apart from any harm they may have suffered in the past (offenders often being the victims of past injustices), they too are harmed by their criminal wrongdoing, since this often has the affect of alienating them – or further alienating them – from their own community.[8] If this harm is to be repaired (i.e. if offenders are to be reintegrated into the community), things need to happen to repair this breach (Burnside and Baker 1994). One thing that can contribute to repair, indeed that may be necessary if repair is to take place, is for the offender to demonstrate genuine repentance and a willingness to make amends for his or her wrongdoing […]. One significant way in which offenders can do this is to meet with those harmed, listen respectfully to them, answer any questions they may have, apologize and agree to reasonable reparative actions which they suggest. Again, this all points to encounter processes.

An important question, however, is: what happens if such a process is not possible? What if the parties are unwilling or unable to meet? Those who adhere to the reparative conception of restorative justice argue that even then the justice system should respond in a way that repairs, rather than adds to, the harm resulting from crime. A simple example is a sentence of restitution rather than a fine or imprisonment (unless there are over-riding considerations of public safety, for example). Under this conception, restorative principles would become a profound reform dynamic affecting all levels of the criminal justice system, whether or not the parties to particular crimes eventually choose to meet. This would revolutionize the justice system, yielding a range of new, restorative responses to all kinds of crimes and circumstances:

> While these responses might differ greatly in the case of, say, a minor property crime by a first-time offender and a serious violent crime (based in part on the level of restrictive-ness imposed on an offender according to the threat imposed to public safety or to individual victims), restorative interventions would be carried out according to what must become widely understood basic principles and familiar processes.
>
> (Bazemore and Walgrave 1999: 45–74, 64)

The important point here is that adherents to a reparative conception of restorative justice, while they express a strong preference for encounter processes, also envisage the possibility of *partially* restorative solutions to problems of crime emerging outside such processes, including through reparative *sanctions* ordered and administered by professionals employed by the formal criminal justice system (Van Ness and Strong 2006). Those strongly committed to an encounter conception of restorative justice, on the other hand, have difficulty in seeing how interventions such as these can be properly included within the definition of restorative justice. They lack what, for adherents to an encounter conception, are the most crucial elements of restorative justice – i.e. meetings of key stakeholders to discuss what happened and to agree on what should be done about it (McCold 2004a). Even if they have repair of harm as one of their official goals, such reparative sanctions appear to strong adherents of the an encounter conception as professionally imposed measures masquerading as restorative justice in order to benefit from its good name (see the quotation from Roche, earlier in this chapter).

We saw earlier that adherents to an encounter conception of restorative justice have turned to 'restorative values' to provide guidance in order to counter certain problems with a pure encounter conception. In a similar vein, adherents to a reparative conception have turned to 'restorative principles' in order to ensure that the wide range of reparative interventions that they would include within the definition of restorative justice do not veer into becoming punitive and purely offender oriented. Principles are general guidelines that point from normative theory to specific application […]. They offer policy guidance to those designing systems or programmes that increases the likelihood that the result will be restorative.

These principles have been expressed in different ways. One useful collection, prepared by Zehr and Mika (Zehr 2002: 40), is called 'restorative justice signposts' and takes the form of ten indicators that work being done is actually restorative. Two examples of these indicators are 'show equal concern and commitment to victims and offenders, involving both in the process of justice', and 'encourage collaboration and reintegration rather than coercion and isolation'.

Bazemore and Walgrave (1999: 65) offer three principles to inform the government's role in restorative justice.[9] First, it would seek to ensure that all parties are treated with *equity,* meaning that they and others in similar circumstances will feel that they are treated similarly. Secondly, it would seek the *satisfaction* of the victim, offender and community. Thirdly, it would offer *legal protection* of individuals against unwarranted state action.

Van Ness and Strong (2006) identify three alternative principles on which a restorative system might be constructed:

> First, justice requires that we work to heal victims, offenders and communities that have been injured by crime. Second, victims, offenders and communities should have the opportunity for active involvement in the justice process as early and as fully as possible. Third, we must rethink the relative roles and responsibilities of government and community: in promoting justice, government is responsible for preserving a just order, and community for establishing a just peace.

Just as the values espoused in the encounter conception need continuing refinement and definition, so too do principles proposed to guide the reparative conception. Nevertheless, both serve a similar function within their respective conception: to increase the likelihood that what actually takes place in the new processes and justice structures is actually restorative.

The transformative conception of restorative justice

The restorative justice movement has tended to focus its efforts upon changing social responses to crime and wrongdoing. Its initial energies were focused upon revolutionizing societal responses to behaviour which we classify as crime and which is regarded as serious enough to warrant intervention by criminal justice agencies such as the police and correctional institutions. For the most part, this remains the main focus of the restorative justice movement, although it has also been applied to forms of misconduct which, although defined as rule-breaking, are usually not classified or handled as criminal offences, such as misconduct in schools [...] or in workplaces.

Others, however, go further still and suggest that both the initial and ultimate goal of the restorative justice movement should be to transform the way in which we understand ourselves and relate to others in our everyday lives (Sullivan and Tifft 2001; cf. Ross 1996 and some of the essays in Strang and Braithwaite 2001). The argument appears to be: 1) that, in the absence such transformations, any efforts to change specific practices, such as our social responses to crime, are unlikely to succeed and can even have effects quite different from those intended; and 2) that even if such changes do succeed, they can make only a peripheral contribution to the goal of achieving a just society – achieving that goal requires much deeper and more far-reaching transformations.

Such goals entail a conception of restorative justice significantly different from those we have described so far. Under this *transformative* conception, restorative justice is conceived as a way of life we should lead. For its proponents, among the key elements of this way of life is a rejection of the assumption that we exist in some sort of hierarchical order with other people (or even with other elements of our environment). Indeed, it rejects the very idea that we are ontologically separate from other people or even from our physical environment. Rather, to live a lifestyle of restorative justice, we must abolish the self (as it is conventionally understood in contemporary society) and instead understand ourselves as inextricably connected to and identifiable with other beings and the 'external' world.

This has implications in the way we use language (Ross 1996: ch. 5), the way we regard and treat other people and the environment, and the way in which we allocate resources – which should be on the basis of need rather than right or desert and with the recognition that the needs of all are equally important (Sullivan and Tifft 2001). In such a context, we would probably not make sharp distinctions between crime and other forms of harmful conduct, but simply respond to all harmful conduct (from crime, to economic exploitation, to the use of power in everyday life) in much the same way – by identifying who has been hurt, what their needs are and how things can be put right (cf. Zehr 2002: 38).

It is vision that animates and guides this conception. Restorative justice seems to evoke a passion and commitment among its adherents that cannot be explained by rational cost/benefit calculations. Stories are repeated of dramatic changes in attitude in which the victim and offender recognize within the other a common humanity, empathy develops and inner resolution takes place. But what animate proponents are not simply the transformations taking place in others; they are also, and equally importantly, the transformations they begin to experience inside themselves. Sullivan and Tifft (2005: 154–60) describe this as a transformation of the 'power-based self' to the true self, a 'being, a consciousness, of peace and gentleness' (p. 155). This does not happen automatically, but instead takes place through a discipline of self-criticism that leads eventually to self-transformation.

For those who come to see restorative justice as a way of life, this recognition that the most profound changes 'out there' require (and may generate) inner transformation has political implications. Quinney observes:

> All of this is to say, to us as criminologists, that crime is suffering and that the ending of crime is possible only with the ending of suffering. And the ending both of suffering and of crime, which is the establishing of justice, can come only out of peace, out of a peace that is spiritually grounded in our very being. To eliminate crime – to end the construction and perpetuation of an existence that makes crime possible – requires a transformation of our human being... When our hearts are filled with love and our minds with willingness to serve, we will know what has to be done and how it is to be done.
>
> (1991: 11–12)

[...]

Notes

1 This analysis is influenced by an important essay published in the 1950s by the philosopher W.B. Gallie on 'essentially contested concepts' and the work of the political theorist William Connolly, who has developed Gallie's ideas and applied them in the domain of political discourse (Gallie 1962; Connolly 1993). We believe that these classic works have very important lessons for the restorative justice movement, although in the space available here it is not possible to discuss these theoretical sources or to indicate how we have utilized them.
2 Given the nature of these characteristics, the question is usually to what extent are they present, rather than a simple are they or are they not present. See Van Ness (2003) on the need to think in terms of *degrees* of restorativeness.

3 We wish to emphasize that, while distinguishing these three conceptions is (in our view) useful for analysing debates about the meaning of restorative justice, we are not suggesting that any actual use of the concept of restorative justice can be neatly matched to a particular conception. Also, we are by no means suggesting that these three conceptions are *totally* distinct from each other; to the contrary we will point to numerous points of overlap.

4 Although there are some disputes over whether all these processes are properly called restorative justice, or over which of them is the purest form of restorative justice.

5 Analogously, one of the key arguments for democratic governance is that people have the right to govern themselves, even if they do so in what a minority (or outsiders) consider to be an unenlightened manner.

6 While our goal in this chapter is to introduce various ways of conceiving restorative justice, rather than to discuss particular issues in any detail, we do think it necessary to make one suggestion: that efforts to articulate a set of distinctive restorative justice values and to think through their status would be significantly advanced by a prior effort to describe with more sophistication than usual the range of values which underlie conventional criminal justice processes. To describe these processes – as is often done – as being underpinned simply by a desire to get even with those who hurt us or to respond to the hurt of crime with the hurt of punishment is too crude. A more fruitful starting point might be to recognize that conventional criminal justice practices tend to embody a wide range of values, and can be better understood as shaped by passionate struggles over which values should predominate in the penal realm, rather than being shaped by one particular set of values (see Garland 1990 for an account of the competition to shape the field of penal practices, in line with particular values and commitments, and of how this results in a highly complex institution which embodies and gives expression to a wide range of values, many of them contradictory). Also, we would go so far as to suggest that, rather than engage in wholesale rejection of traditional criminal justice values in favour of restorative justice values, the restorative justice movement might commit itself to devising responses to crime which incorporate the best of both. For instance, we might conceive of restorative justice as a process which enables people affected by crime to devise responses which meet *their* local needs and which are closely in keeping with *their* ethical ideals. We could then recognize that such a response needs to be bounded by broad values more often associated with the idea of the rule of law than with restorative justice. As Braithwaite elegantly puts it, restorative justice (the 'justice of the people') needs to be constrained by the 'justice of the law' (2003: 14–16).

7 See Zehr (1990) for a rich and sophisticated account of this position. We have relied heavily upon Howard Zehr's work in this section because we regard it as one of the most cogent expositions of, and arguments for, restorative justice available, and because of its influence on the restorative justice movement (Zehr is often referred to as 'the grandfather' of restorative justice – see Zehr 2002: 76). Just a few of the other works worth consulting in this context are Braithwaite (2002), Cayley (1998), Consedine (1999), Graef (2000), Johnstone (2002), Marshall (2001), Ross (1996), Sullivan and Tifft (2001), Wright (1996) and Van Ness and Strong (2006).

8 These ideas are explored in more depth in Johnstone (2002) and Van Ness and Strong (2006).

9 They call these 'values'.

References

Bazemore, G. and Walgrave, L. (1999) 'Restorative juvenile justice: in search of fundamentals and an outline for systemic reform', in G. Bazemore and L. Walgrave (eds) *Restorative Juvenile Justice: Repairing the Harm of Youth Crime.* Monsey, NY: Criminal Justice Press, 45–74.

Boyack, J., Bowen, H. and Marshall, C. (2004) 'How does restorative justice ensure good practice?', in H. Zehr and B. Toews (eds) *Critical Issues in Restorative Justice.* Monsey, NY: Criminal Justice Press and Cullompton: Willan Publishing.

Braithwaite, J. (2000) 'Standards for restorative justice.' Paper presented at the ancillary meetings of the Tenth United Nations Congress on the Prevention of Crime and Treatment of Offenders, Vienna, Austria, 10–17 April.

Braithwaite, J. (2003) 'Principles of restorative justice', in A. von Hirsch *et al.* (eds) *Restorative Justice and Criminal Justice: Competing or Reconcilable Paradigms.* Oxford:Hart Publishing.

Braithwaite, J. and Strang, H. (2001) 'Introduction: restorative justice and civil society', in H. Strang and J. Braithwaite (eds) *Restorative Justice and Civil Society.* Cambridge: Cambridge University Press.

Burnside, J. and Baker, N. (eds) (1994) *Relational Justice: Repairing the Breach.* Winchester: Waterside Press.

Christie, N. (2003) 'Conflicts as property', in G. Johnstone (ed.) *A Restorative Justice Reader: Texts, Sources, Context.* Cullompton: Willan Publishing (originally published in *British Journal of Criminology*, (1977) 17: 1–15.

Johnstone, G. (2002) *Restorative Justice: Ideas, Values, Debates.* Cullompton: Willan Publishing.

McCold, P. (2004a) 'Paradigm muddle: the threat to restorative justice posed by its merger with community justice', *Contemporary Justice Review*, 7: 13–35.

McCold, P. (2004b) 'What is the role of community in restorative justice theory and practice?', in H. Zehr and B. Toews (eds) *Critical Issues in Restorative Justice.* Monsey, NY and Cullompton: Criminal Justice Press and Willan Publishing.

O'Connell, T., Wachtel, B. and Wachtel, T. (1999) *Conferencing Handbook: The New Real Justice Training Manual.* Pipersville, PA: Piper's Press.

Peachey, D.E. (2003) 'The Kitchener experiment', in G. Johnstone (ed.) A *Restorative Justice Reader: Texts, Sources, Context.* Cullompton: Willan Publishing (originally published in M. Wright and B. Galaway (eds) (1989) *Mediation and Criminal Justice.* London: Sage).

Pranis, K. (1997) 'Restoring community: the process of circle sentencing.' Paper presented at the conference *Justice without Violence: Views from Peacemaking, Criminology, and Restorative Justice*, 6 June 6.

Quinney, R. (1991) 'The way of peace: on crime, suffering and service', in H.E. Pepinsky and R. Quinney (eds) *Criminology as Peacemaking.* Bloomington: Indiana University Press.

Robinson, P.H. (2003) 'The virtues of restorative processes, the vices of "restorative justice"', *Utah Law Review*, 1: 375–88.

Roche, D. (2001) 'The evolving definition of restorative justice', *Contemporary Justice Review*, 4: 341–53.

Ross, R. (1996) *Returning to the Teachings: Exploring Aboriginal Justice.* Toronto: Penguin.

Strang, H. and Braithwaite, J. (eds) (2001) *Restorative Justice and Civil Society.* Cambridge: Cambridge University Press.

Sullivan, D. and Tifft, L. (2001) *Restorative Justice: Healing the Foundations of Our Everyday Lives.* Monsey, NY: Willow Tree Press.

Umbreit, M. (2001) *The Handbook of Victim Offender Mediation: An Essential Guide to Practice and Research.* San Francisco, CA: Jossey-Bass.

Umbreit, M.S. and Zehr, H. (1996) 'Restorative family group conferences: differing models and guidelines for practice', *Federal Probation*, 60: 24–9.

Van Ness, D.W. and Strong, K.H. (2006) *Restoring Justice* (3rd edn). Cincinnati, OH: Anderson.

Wachtel, T. (1997) *Real Justice: How we can Revolutionize our Response to Wrongdoing.* Pipersville, PA: Piper's Press.

Young, R. (2003) 'Just cops doing "shameful" business? Police-led restorative justice and the lessons of research', in G. Johnstone (ed.) *A Restorative Justice Reader: Texts, Sources, Context.* Cullompton: Willan Publishing (originally published in Morris, A. and Maxwell, G. (eds) (2001) *Restorative Justice for Juveniles.* Oxford: Hart Publishing).

Zehr, H. (1990) *Changing Lenses: A New Focus for Crime and Justice.* Scottdale, PA: Herald Press.

Zehr, H. (2002) *The Little Book of Restorative Justice.* Intercourse, PA: Good Books.

3   Retributive justice, restorative justice

Howard Zehr

Let's start with what we know.

We know that the system we call 'criminal justice' does not work. Certainly, at least, it does not work for victims.

Victims experience crime as deeply traumatic, as a violation of the self. They experience it as an assault on their sense of themselves as autonomous individuals in a predictable world. Crime raises fundamental questions of trust, of order, of faith. And this is true for many crimes we consider 'minor' as well as for serious violent crimes.

Victims have many needs. They need chances to speak their feelings. They need to receive restitution. They need to experience justice: victims need some kind of moral statement of their blamelessness, of who is at fault, that this thing should not have happened to them. They need answers to the questions that plague them. They need a restoration of power because the offender has taken power away from them.

Above all, perhaps, victims need an experience of forgiveness. I do not have time here to explore this fully, and certainly I am not suggesting that forgiveness comes easily. I want to suggest, though, that forgiveness is a process of letting go. Victims need to be able to let go of the crime experience so that, while it will always – must always be – part of them, it will no longer dominate their lives. Without that, closure is difficult and the wound may fester for many years.

Much more needs to be said about what victims feel and need than is possible here – this has been only the briefest summary. My point, though, is this: Victims have serious important needs, yet few, if any, of them will be met in the criminal justice process.

In fact, the injury may very well be compounded. Victims find that they are mere footnotes in the process we call justice. If they are involved in their case at all, it will likely be as witnesses; if the state does not need them as witnesses, they will not be part of their own case. The offender has taken power from them and now, instead of returning power to them, the criminal law system also denies them power.

For victims, then, the system just is not working.

But it is not working for offenders either.

It is not preventing offenders from committing crimes, as we know well from recidivism figures. And it is not healing them. On the contrary, the experience of punishment and of imprisonment is deeply damaging, often encouraging rather than discouraging criminal behavior.

Nor is the justice system holding offenders accountable. Judges often talk about accountability but what they usually mean is that when you do something wrong you must take your punishment. I want to suggest that real accountability means something quite different.

Genuine accountability means, first of all, that when you offend, you need to understand and take responsibility for what you did. Offenders need to be encouraged to understand the real human consequences of their actions. But accountability has a second component as well: offenders need to be encouraged to take responsibility for making things right, for righting the wrong. Understanding one's actions and taking responsibility for making things right – that is the real meaning of accountability.

Unfortunately, though, our legal process does not encourage such accountability on the part of offenders. Nowhere in the process are offenders given the opportunity to understand the implications of what they have done. Nowhere are they encouraged to question the stereotypes and rationalizations ('It's no big deal; they deserved it; insurance will cover it') that made it possible for them to commit their offences. In fact, by focusing on purely legal issues, the criminal process will tend to sidetrack their attention, causing them to focus on legal, technical definitions of guilt, on the possibilities for avoiding punishment, on the injustices they perceive themselves to undergo.

The criminal process, then, not only fails to encourage a real understanding of what they have done: it actively discourages such a realization. And it does nothing to encourage offenders to take responsibility to right the wrong they have committed.

I am increasingly impressed at the parallels between what victims and offenders go through.

I have suggested that for victims, crime involves a question of power. Part of what is so dehumanizing about being a victim is that power has been taken away. What is needed for healing is an experience of empowerment.

But offenders also need an experience of empowerment. For many offenders, crime is a way of asserting power, of asserting self-identity, in a world which defines worth in terms of access to power. Crime, for many, is a way of saying 'I am somebody'. My friend, an armed robber, who grew up Black and poor, then spent 17 years in prison for his robberies, said it more clearly than most: 'At least when I had a shotgun in my hand I was somebody.'

Crime is often a way for offenders to assert power and worth, but in doing so they deny power to others. The unfortunate thing is that the criminal justice process compounds the problem by making pawns of both, by denying power to both victim and offender. The victim is left out of his or her own case; the offender's fate is decided by others, without encouragement to take responsibility for righting the wrong.

I have suggested that victims need to experience forgiveness. Offenders, too, need such an experience – how else are they to put their pasts behind them? But they also need opportunities for repentance and conversion. Confess, repent, turn around; admit responsibility, take responsibility for making things right, change directions – this is what needs to happen. But the criminal process has little room, provides little encouragement, for such events.

For offenders, the justice process will encourage anger, rationalization, denial of guilt and responsibility, feelings of powerlessness and dehumanization. As with victims, the wound will fester and grow.

So the system is not working for victims, and neither is it working for offenders.

We have known that for many years and have tried many reforms, and they have not worked either.

This is not to say that 'nothing works', that no 'reform' programs have been without good results for the persons involved. What does seem to be true is that most criminal justice reforms of the past century have not done what was intended. All too often they have been perverted, coopted, coming to serve ends different than those intended. They have not brought about substantial improvements in the process of justice. The system of justice seems to be so impregnated with self-interest, so adaptive, that it takes in any new idea, molds it, changes it until it suits the system's own purposes.

Why? Why are victims so ignored? Why are offenders dealt with so ineffectively? Why do so many reforms fail? Why is crime so mystified, so mythologized, so susceptible to the machinations of politics and the press?

It seems to me that the reasons are fundamental, that they have to do with our very definitions of crime and of justice. Consequently, the situation cannot be changed by simply providing compensation or assistance to victims, by providing the possibility of alternative sanctions for offenders, or by other sorts of 'tinkering'. We have to go to root understandings and assumptions.

Let's look at some of those assumptions and definitions.

When a crime is committed, we assume that the most important thing that can happen is to establish guilt. That is the focal point of our entire criminal process: to establish who did it. What to do with the person once guilt is established is almost an afterthought. The focus is on the past, not the future.

Another assumption we make is that of just deserts: everyone must get what is coming to them. The metaphysical order of the universe has been upset and the balance must be righted.

Everyone must get what is due, and what is due is pain. Nils Christie has been very helpful in teaching us to call a spade a spade: What we are doing is inflicting pain. Penal law would be more honestly called 'pain law' because in essence it is a system for inflicting graduated measures of pain.

Our legal system tends to define justice not by the outcome but by the process itself and by the intention behind it.

As Herman Bianchi has pointed out, it is the intention that matters. The intention of the law is to treat everyone fairly and equally, but whether that is actually achieved is less important than the design, the intention.

Moreover, the test of justice is whether or not the process was carried out correctly. We see justice as a system of right rules. Were the rules followed? If so, justice has been done. I could point to a variety of cases – including death penalty cases – where substantial questions of guilt or innocence remain unanswered but because the rules were followed, appeals have been exhausted and justice is considered to have been done.

So we define justice as the establishment of blame and the imposition of pain all administered according to right rules. But there is something even more basic: Our legal system defines crime as an offence against the state, the government. Legally it is the state which has been violated, and it is up to the state to respond. So it is a professional proxy for the state – the prosecutor who files charges, who pursues the case, who represents the victimized state. And it is a judge, another representative of the state, who decides the outcome.

It is no accident, then that the crime victim, the person who has been victimized is so left out of this process. He or she is not even part of the equation, not part of the definition of the offence. Victims are left out because they have no legal standing, because they are not part of the legal definition of the offence.

No wonder that in spite of our reforms, we have not been able to incorporate victims into the justice process in any integral way. While I think victim compensation and victim assistance are important programs, I am pessimistic about the possibilities for a substantial impact because they do not attack the fundamental issue – the definition of crime which excludes crime victims.

We define crime as an offence against the state. We define justice as the establishment of blame and the imposition of pain under the guidance of right rules.

I think it is essential to remember that this definition of crime and justice, as common-sensical as it may seem, is only one paradigm, only one possible way of looking at crime and at justice. We have been so dominated by our assumptions that we often assume it is the only way, or at least the only right way, to approach the issue.

It is not. It is not the only possible model or paradigm of justice – not logically, not historically.

Some of you may be aware of Thomas Kuhn's *The Structure of Scientific Revolutions*. Using the 17th-century scientific revolution as a model, Kuhn advances a theory of scientific revolutions which may have some bearing here.

Kuhn notes that the way we understand and explain the world at any time is governed by a particular model. A scientific revolution, and by implication an intellectual revolution, occurs when that model comes to be seen as inadequate and is replaced by a different model, a different way of understanding and explaining phenomenon [sic]. Scientific and intellectual 'revolutions' represent shifts in paradigms.

The classic scientific revolution of the 17th century is a case in point. Before Copernicus, human understanding of the universe was governed by the Ptolemaic paradigm or model. In this understanding the earth was central with planets and heavenly bodies whirling around in orbits which consisted of some sort of crystalline spheres. While this may seem ludicrous to us today, it seemed to fit what people saw and it meshed with important philosophical, scientific and theological assumptions. It was common-sensical. It was a paradigm which governed understandings and was used to explain phenomena.

For many years this paradigm seemed to fit, adequately explaining what was seen and experienced. But aberrations and dysfunctions cropped up – in fact, some were observed right from the start. At first, these aberrations seemed to offer no real threat to the paradigm. Adjustments could be made. For example, the phenomenon of retrograde motion – the fact that planets seemed to move backward briefly during rotation – was explained by adding 'epicycles' to the model. Apparently planets rotated in smaller orbits or spheres as they moved along in their larger orbits.

In the 16th century, Copernicus suggested a different model, one which put the sun at the center. Few, however, took his suggestion seriously. It flew in the face of too many assumptions, threatened too many theological and philosophical ideas. It seemed non-sensical. But by the early 17th century more accurate observations of the skies (made possible by telescopes and careful observations) began to create increasing problems in the old model. The number of 'epicycles' necessary to make the model work became ridiculous, for example.

Numerous efforts were made to shore up the model. Finally, though, a series of discoveries, synthesized by Isaac Newton in a new paradigm, brought about a revolution in our understanding of the universe. In this model, the sun is central to our galaxy. The 'laws' which govern the movement of planets are one with those which govern forces on the earth.

This understanding made modern science possible, became today's common sense, but is understood now by scientists to also be just one model, and an imperfect model at that. Newtonian physics is useful in everyday life, but it is inaccurate for much scientific work: The Einsteinian paradigm must be used to incorporate the complexity, the plasticity of time and space.

Kuhn's point, in short, is that the way we explain and make sense out of phenomena is governed by paradigms. Our paradigms, however, are often rather incomplete reflections of reality and do not adequately fit every situation. So we make adjustments, build in 'epicycles' to try to make them work. Gradually the number of aberrations grows. At the same time, we make attempts to salvage the model, adding more 'epicycles' until, hopefully, a new paradigm emerges, a new way of putting the pieces together that fits experience better. That is the structure, the pattern, of scientific and intellectual revolutions.

Why this long excursion into the history of science? First, it may help us to be more humble about our understandings, to see our definitions and assumptions as models rather than as absolutes. And second, it may suggest the possibility of a paradigm change in justice.

Randy Barnett has suggested that state-centered and punishment-centered assumptions constitute just such a paradigm and that this paradigm is in the process of breaking down. We may, he suggests, be on the verge of a revolution in our understanding of crime and justice.

As with the Ptolemaic paradigm, problems have been seen right from the start and they have multiplied with time. Thus we had to invent 'epicycles'.

The concept of proportionate punishment, an Enlightenment concept, was an attempt to limit the imposition of pain, to inflict it in measured, 'scientific' doses. It did not question the fact of imposing pain, but attempted to grade it to fit the offence. Prison caught on because it was a way of grading pain. Similarly, the Enlightenment did not question the centrality of the state's role, but concerned itself with limiting the arbitrary power of the state.

But that 'epicycle' did not work very well. Prisons also turned out to be brutal, needing reform right from the start. Even proportionate punishment failed to deter effectively. Proportionate punishment seemed to have its problems.

So the concept of rehabilitation was born, but that too led to problems. It didn't work and it was terribly susceptible to abuse. This reform, like the concept of proportionate punishment, attempted to rescue the paradigm without questioning fundamentals. When it did not work, the pendulum swung back to punishment. The underlying assumption that pain must be inflicted remains unquestioned.

Victim compensation, Barnett notes, can be seen as another such 'epicycle'. It, too, tries to tinker with the model, to correct a problem, but without asking basic questions.

But the dysfunctions are so great and so widely recognized that an intellectual revolution just might be possible. Disenchantment with the state/punishment paradigm, with what might be called the 'retributive paradigm', is so great that we may be on the verge of a paradigm change.

There are certain problems in applying Kuhn's pattern of paradigm change. It does not, for example take into account the politics of paradigm change. However, I want to make two points here. First, there are glimmers of hope that change may be coming. And second, it is important for us to step back and realize that our model is only that – one model, one paradigm. Other models can be conceived.

In fact, other models have predominated throughout most of western history. It is difficult to realize sometimes that the paradigm which we consider so natural, so logical, has in fact governed our understanding of crime and justice for only a few centuries. We have not always done it like this.

Let me interject a warning here. What I am going to suggest will be a bit scattered. I am going to jump through centuries, generalizing rather freely. While I have been working on this for some time, I have not yet had time to assimilate all my reading. So my suggestions also must be considered somewhat tentative.

My thesis is that western (and possibly early near-eastern) history has been dominated by a dialectic between what Bruce Lenman and Geoffrey Parker have called 'community justice' and 'state justice'.

State justice reared its head early – you can see it already in the Code of Hammurabi – but it has only come to be predominate in the past several centuries. Instead, community justice, has governed understandings throughout most of our history.

Several themes are important in an attempt to develop an historical perspective.

One theme has to do with the modern division between criminal and civil law. Criminal law is characterized by the centrality given to the state: The state is victim, and the state prosecutes. It is dominated by a coercive, punishment motif. Civil law, on the other hand, assumes that two private parties are in conflict, with the state being asked to arbitrate between them, and the outcome focuses largely on making things right, on compensation. The division of law into these two types is quite recent, an important historical development.

A second theme is included in the preceding theme. This is the idea that it is the state's responsibility, even monopoly, to prosecute. That too is new, although its roots go back to perhaps the 12th and 13th centuries.

A third theme is the assumption that punishment is normative. The idea of punishment is old, of course, but some scholars suggest that it is relatively recent that punitiveness became normal and dominant. This is contrary to common images of primitive, vigilante vengeance.

For most of our history in the West, nonjudicial, nonlegal dispute resolution techniques have dominated. People traditionally have been very reluctant to call in the state, even when the state claimed a role. In fact, a great deal of stigma was attached to going to the state and asking it to prosecute. For centuries the state's role in prosecution was quite minimal.

Instead, it was considered the business of the community to solve its own disputes. Even when state-operated courts became available, they were often places of last resort, and it was common to settle out of court after court proceedings had been initiated. Out-of-court settlements were so normal, in fact, that a new French legal code as late as 1670 prohibited the state from getting involved if the parties came to a settlement, even after proceedings had begun.

Most of our history has been dominated by informal dispute resolution processes for conflicts, including many of the conflicts today defined as crimes, and these processes highlighted negotiation/arbitration models. Agreements were negotiated, sometimes using community leaders or neighbors in key roles. Agreements were validated by local notables, by government notaries, by priests. Often parties would go before such a person, once an agreement was made, and make it binding. But it was negotiated rather than imposed.

To what extent these methods were used for the most serious crimes is still uncertain. Herman Bianchi, however, has argued that sanctuaries were a key part of western civilization for just this purpose: a place for those who committed the most serious crimes to run to, to be safe, while they negotiated an agreement with the victim and/or family.

The process emphasized negotiation, therefore, and the expected outcome was compensation. Restitution to victims was common, perhaps even normative, even though violent retribution is our usual picture.

Even an 'eye for an eye' justice focused on compensation. In some cases, it was a way of establishing restitution – the value of an eye for the value of an eye. Limit the response, in other words, and convert it to restitution.

When 'eye for an eye' justice was taken literally, however, it still was seen as compensation. When someone in a collectivist, tribal, clan society is killed or hurt, the balance of power between groups is upset. Balance is restored by repayment in kind. An eye for an eye, taken literally, is both a means of limiting violence and of compensating groups for the loss of, or damage to, one of its members.

Such justice is also a way of vindicating the victim. Both restitution and vengeance may often have been intended less to punish than to vindicate the moral rightness of the victim. In a small, tightly organized community, the victim needed a moral statement to the community that they were right and that the other person was wrong. They needed moral compensation.

So restitution was common. Violent revenge did occur, but it may not have happened as frequently as we often assume. And both restitution and vengeance may have been intended less as punishment than as moral vindication and as a means of balancing power.

Much more work needs to be done, but my point is this: We have had a long history of community justice in our culture. Until recently, it was not assumed that the state had a duty to prosecute most crimes, and certainly not assumed that the state had a monopoly on prosecution.

Through most of our history, two systems of justice have coexisted – state justice and community justice – which both complemented and conflicted with each other. Community justice tended to focus on restitution through a somewhat informal process of mediation and arbitration. State justice tended to be more punitive, more formal, and put the state at the center, although until recently it did not claim a monopoly.

Traditionally, at least on the Continent, when individuals wished to use state courts, individuals had to bring the complaint. The victim had to initiate proceedings and could decide when to terminate them. The state functioned as a kind of regulatory system. It was an accusatorial system: if you were a victim, you came forward and accused someone, and the state could not do anything unless you did this. If you did, the state would locate the accused person, bring them before you, and regulate the dispute. But the victim had to trigger the process and could terminate it as well.

During the 12th century, however, the state began to take a larger role and began to initiate some prosecutions. This process seems to have been tied, at least in part, to the revival of Roman law. It was during this time that Roman law was rediscovered; law schools began to teach it, and the Church picked it up and made it the basis of canon law.

The Inquisition was one outcome of this transformation of Roman law into canon law. In the Inquisition, the Church initiated prosecution, sought evidence and carried the prosecution through. Canon law, therefore, provided a model for state-initiated prosecution.

Evidently the state began to adopt this model which provided for a more aggressive, powerful role for the central authority. This takeover by the state was gradual and much resisted but eventually was victorious.

So this enlarged responsibility and power for the state in the prosecution of crime seems to have been based on the revival of Roman law, which was introduced through canon law, then adopted and secularized by the state.

Many reasons for this trend can be suggested. They may have to do with the breakdown of community or the needs of an emerging capitalist order. They seem to have something to do with Christian theology. They certainly have something to do with the dynamics of emerging nation states: I view the modern state as an exceedingly greedy institution which will keep growing unless we can keep it in check, and criminal law is one of its primary means of expressing power. But I do not pretend to understand how to sort out the roots of this process.

Although this is an oversimplification of reality, I am arguing that history has been a dialectic between two rival systems. Community justice was basically extra-legal, often negotiated, often restitutive. State justice was legal, expressing formal rationalism and rules, the rigidification of custom and principles derived from the Roman tradition into law. It was imposed justice, punitive justice, hierarchical justice.

During the past two centuries this latter model has won, but not without a fight, and not completely. In American history, for example, there has been a long and persistent history of alternative dispute resolution processes. Jerold Auerbach, in *Justice Without Law?*, outlines an amazing variety of examples. The state tried to co-opt them, and often eventually did, but they have been very persistent.

In fact, even in the United States the idea that the state ought to prosecute crimes is relatively new. Until a hundred years ago, it was not assumed that it was up to prosecutors to initiate all prosecutions; many were left to individuals to initiate.

We are beginning to recognize that a legal revolution has taken place in western history, a revolution with tremendous implications but until recently much neglected by historians. Its dimensions have included a separation of law into criminal and civil, an assumption of state centrality and monopoly in conflicts which are legally defined as criminal, a movement from private to public justice, an assumption that punishment is normative, a movement from custom to formal legal structures.

Parallel with the rise of the state as the central actor and the increase in punitiveness was the rise of the modern prison. Many would argue that it is no accident that these developments coincide chronologically.

I have suggested two historical models: state justice and community justice. There is, however, a third way: covenant justice. In some ways it has links with both community and state justice but in covenant justice the patterns are transformed. Millard Lind has outlined this well when he traces 'the transformation of justice from Moses to Jesus'.

Many assume that the primary theme of Old Testament justice is retribution, that an 'eye for an eye' is the central paradigm. This view is inadequate for a number of reasons.

Some have argued, for example, that the words we translate into English as retribution really do not mean that. Also, the phrase 'an eye for an eye' does not occur as often as most of us assume; the phrase is used, I believe, only three or four times. And we often misunderstand its function. An 'eye for an eye' was intended as a limit, not a command. If someone takes your eye, respond in proportion. Limit your response. Do this much, and only this much. An 'eye for an eye' was intended to introduce limits in a society unused to the rule of law.

Some have also argued that the concept was designed as a way of converting wrongs to compensation. As I suggested earlier, it may have been intended as 'the value of an eye for an eye'. And it was designed as way of maintaining a balance of power between groups.

Our understanding of an eye for an eye has often been off base, oversimplified, and has overemphasized its importance. An eye for an eye is NOT the central paradigm of Old Testament justice. Restitution, forgiveness, reconciliation are just as important, perhaps more important. In fact, in many ways the central theme of the Old Testament is a theology of restoration.

I have recently been rereading Leviticus, Exodus and Deuteronomy. I have been struck with how often forgiveness and restoration appear there. We have been so dominated by retributive language that we often overlooked these other themes.

So my first point about covenant law is this: Retribution is not as central to Old Testament justice as is often assumed, and we have often misunderstood the functions of this theme.

My second point is that we must understand that the meaning of law in the Old Testament is much different than ours today. Law certainly does not mean the legal formalism that is integral to today's understanding of law. Bianchi has helped us to understand that in the Old Testament, law is conversation, 'palaver'. Law is a 'wise indication' of the way we ought to go, and we ought to talk about that. Old Testament law does not have the sense of rigidity and formalism that our law does. Law points a direction, and it must be discussed.

We tend to see the Ten Commandments as purely prohibition: 'Do not do these things.' Bianchi suggests, however, that they should be read as promise. God is saying, 'If you walk in my ways, if you are true to my covenant, this is how you shall live. You will not kill. You will not commit adultery.' It's a promise.

The differences in our concepts of law are much more profound than I have outlined here. What is important is that we realize that we cannot simply transfer Old Testament laws to the [21st] century legal milieu.

Furthermore, justice in the Old Testament is not based on a state law model. In fact, a consistent theme is the warning against becoming like other nations with a coercive kingship structure. Israel's kings were to be different, subject to God and God's commandments. They were not to be above the law, not to be the source of law, as was the case in other nations.

Consequently, even when Israel adopted laws with parallels to those of other surrounding nations (for example, the Code of Hammurabi), they were transformed. They were set in a covenant context and did not assume the centrality of the state as others did.

Our information about the structure and administration of Old Testament law is quite fragmentary. However, it seems clear that the law was not administered by police and public prosecution. There was no police force which ran around, arresting people for wrongdoing. There were no state prosecutors to bring charges in formal courts. Instead, as Hans Boecker has described it for us, justice seems to have been done at the gate, at the open place in the city where people met, where things were happening, where the market took place, where people talked. If you had a complaint against someone, you brought it to this place. Here justice was done in a structured but democratic and fairly unbureaucratic way. It involved much negotiation, much discussion, and the focus was on a solution rather than some abstract concept of justice. The idea that justice is an abstract balancing was a Roman, not a Hebrew concept. Covenant justice was making things right, finding a settlement, restoring Shalom.

The key to Old Testament justice was the concept of Shalom – of making things right, of living in peace and harmony with one another in right relationship. Restitution and restoration overshadowed punishment as a theme because the goal was restoration to right relationships.

The test of justice, then, was not whether the right rules, the right procedures, were followed. Justice was to be tested by the outcome, by its fruits. As Bianchi has pointed out, if the tree bears good fruit, it is justice; if not, it is not justice. Justice is to be tested by the outcome, not the procedures, and it must come out with right relationships. Justice is a process of making things right.

Jesus continues and expands this theme of covenant justice. He focuses on the recovery of wholeness in community with one another and with God. In the New Testament as in the Old, justice has a relational focus.

And Jesus raises real questions about some of the central assumptions of today's retributive justice. He seems to suggest real caution about focusing on blame-fixing. He casts doubt on the idea of just deserts. And, his primary focus is on the ethic of love and forgiveness rather than punishment.

It seems to me that the central focus of covenant justice, in both its Old and New Testament forms, is on love, on restoration, on relationships. It is the kind of thing we talk about in VORP (Victim Offender Reconciliation Program). Crime is a wound in human relationships. The feelings that victim and offender have toward one another are not peripheral issues, as assumed by our justice system, but are the heart of the matter. Relationships are central.

Covenant justice also seems to focus more on problem-solving than on blame-fixing. As Bianchi has suggested, it focuses more on liabilities than on guilt. When you commit a crime, you create a certain debt, an obligation, a liability that must be met. Crime creates an obligation – to restore, to repair, to undo. Things must be made right. And the test, the focus, of justice is the outcome, not the process.

So the tension today is between three basic models. State justice is dominant but seriously flawed. Community justice has a long history and many possibilities, but it too has its pitfalls and has been largely co-opted by state justice. Then there is covenant justice. Our problem is to understand and find our way through these models.

But my goal today is quite limited: We must realize that many of the problems in the way we do justice today are rooted in our understanding of justice, and that this particular understanding is only one possible way, one paradigm. Others are possible, others have been lived out, others have actually dominated most of our history. In the long sweep of things, our present paradigm is really quite recent.

Now, if it is true that the problem lies in the way we understand crime and justice, how should we understand them? What would a new paradigm look like?

I would suggest that we define crime as it is experienced: as a violation of one person by another. Crime is a conflict between people, a violation against a person, not an offence against the state. The proper response ought to be one that restores. In place of a retributive paradigm, we need to be guided by a restorative paradigm.

I have tried to sketch out, in table form, the contrasting characteristics of the two paradigms (see Appendix). It is very sketchy and highly theoretical at this point, but might help to clarify the differences.

And the differences are significant.

The old paradigm makes the state into the victim, thus placing the state at the center, leaving out the individual victim, and denying the interpersonal character of the offence. The new paradigm defines crime as a conflict between persons, putting the individuals and their relationship at center stage.

The old paradigm is based on a conflictual, adversarial, model, but sees the essential conflict between individual and state, and utilizes a method that heightens conflict. The new paradigm recognizes that the essential conflict is between individuals and encourages dialogue and negotiation. It encourages victim and offender to see one another as persons, to establish or re-establish a relationship.

The central focus of the old paradigm is on the past, on blame-fixing. While the new paradigm would encourage responsibility for past behavior, its focus would be on the future, on problem-solving, on the obligations created by the offence.

Restoration, making things right, would replace the imposition of pain as the expected outcome in new paradigm justice. Restitution would be common, not exceptional. Instead of committing one social injury in response to another, a restorative paradigm would focus on healing.

Retributive justice defines justice the Roman way, as right rules, measuring justice by the intention and the process. Restorative justice would define justice the Hebrew way, as right relationships measured by the outcome.

As Auerbach has pointed out, modern justice grows out of and also encourages competitive individualism. A restorative, negotiated focus should encourage mutual aid, a sense of mutuality, of community, of fellowship.

In today's justice, all action is hierarchical, from the top down. The state acts on the offender, with the victim on the sidelines. Restorative justice would put victim and offender at the center, helping to decide what is to be done about what has happened. Thus the definition of accountability would change. Instead of 'paying a debt to society' by experiencing punishment, accountability would mean understanding and taking responsibility for what has been done and taking action to make things right. Instead of owing an abstract debt to society, paid in an abstract way by experiencing punishment, the offender would owe a debt to the victim, to be repaid in a concrete way.

Retributive justice as we know it views everything in purely legal terms. As Nils Christie has said, legal training is trained tunnel vision. In law schools, you are taught that only legally defined issues are relevant. Restorative justice will require us to look at behavior in its entire context – moral, social, economic and political.

All this is, of course, very fragmentary and very theoretical. However, as Kay Harris has pointed out, our problem in the past is that we have attempted to provide alternative programs without offering alternative values. We need an alternative vision, not simply alternative sentences.

What such a vision means in practice is still hard to say. Some have suggested that we abolish criminal law – a slightly radical but intriguing idea. Herman Bianchi is suggesting that, historically, it has been good to have competing systems – they provide a useful corrective to one another, and pose a choice for participants. So perhaps we need to work at setting up a separate but parallel justice system without abolishing the old. Perhaps, as Martin Wright suggests, we need to make more use of what we already have by 'civilizing' our legal process – that is, by drawing on and expanding the civil process that already exists.

All this raises many questions, of course, and suggests many dangers. Good intentions can, and often do, go awry; just look, for example, at the history of prisons, which were advocated by Christians with the best of intentions.

Should something like this be attempted on a societal level, or is it something that belongs primarily within the church? And what about the politics of paradigm change? Make no mistake: The criminal justice industry is big business, shot through with all kinds of self-interest and will not be changed.

Can such a model actually work? We know from VORP that it can work, that it does work in many cases, with certain kinds of crime. But are there limits? Where are they? It is our responsibility to find out.

That is our challenge. Will VORP be just another alternative program, an alternative that becomes institutionalized, ossified, co-opted until it is just another program, and perhaps not an alternative at all? Or will VORP be a means of exploring, communicating, embodying an alternative vision? Will it demonstrate that there is another way? Could it even be the beginning of a quiet revolution?

That is, at least in part, up to us. For me that is an exciting dream. But it is also an awesome responsibility.

Appendix: paradigms of justice – old and new

Old Paradigm: Retributive Justice	New Paradigm: Restorative Justice
1. Crime defined as violation of the state	1. Crime defined as violation of one person by another
2. Focus on establishing blame, on guilt, on past (did he/she do it?)	2. Focus on problem-solving, on liabilities and obligations, on future (what should be done?)

Old Paradigm: Retributive Justice	New Paradigm: Restorative Justice
3. Adversarial relationships and process normative	3. Dialogue and negotiation normative
4. Imposition of pain to punish and deter/prevent	4. Restitution as a means of restoring *both* parties; reconciliation/restoration as goal
5. Justice defined by intent and by process: right rules	5. Justice defined as right relationships: judged by the outcome
6. Interpersonal, conflictual nature of crime obscured, repressed: conflict seen as individual vs. state	6. Crime recognized as interpersonal conflict: value of conflict recognized
7. One social injury replaced by another	7. Focus on repair of social injury
8. Community on sideline, represented abstractly by state	8. Community as facilitator in restorative process
9. Encouragement of competitive, individualistic values	9. Encouragement of mutuality
10. Action directed from state to offender: • victim ignored • offender passive	10. Victim's and offender's roles recognized in both problem and solution: • victim rights/needs recognized • offender encouraged to take responsibility
11. Offender accountability defined as taking punishment	11. Offender accountability defined as understanding impact of action and helping decide how to make things right
12. Offence defined in purely legal terms, devoid of moral, social, economic, political dimensions	12. Offence understood in whole context – moral, social, economic, political
13. 'Debt' owed to state and society in the abstract	13. Debt/liability to victim recognized
14. Response focused on offender's past behavior	14. Response focused on harmful consequences of offender's behavior
15. Stigma of crime unremovable	15. Stigma of crime removable through restorative action
16. No encouragement for repentance and forgiveness	16. Possibilities for repentance and forgiveness
17. Dependence upon proxy professionals	17. Direct involvement by participants

References

Auerbach, J.S. (1983) *Justice Without Law?* (Oxford University Press).

Barnett, R. (1981) 'Restitution: A New Paradigm of Criminal Justice', in Galaway, B. and Hudson, J. (eds) *Perspectives on Crime Victims* (C.V. Mosby).

Bianchi, H. (1984) 'A Biblical Vision of Justice', *New Perspectives on Crime and Justice* (Mennonite Central Committee).

Berman, H.J. (1975) 'The Religious Foundations of Western Law', *The Catholic University of America Law Review,* Spring, pp. 490–508.

Boecker, H.J. (1980) *Law and the Administration of Justice in the Old Testament and Ancient East* (Augsburg Publishing House).

Christie, N. (1981) *Limits to Pain* (Columbia University Press).

Christie, N. (1984) 'Crime, Pain and Death', *New Perspectives on Crime and Justice* (Mennonite Central Committee).

Harris, K. (1987) 'Strategies, Values, and the Emerging Generation of Alternatives to Incarceration', *New York University Review of Law and Social Change,* 1, pp. 141–70.

Kuhn, T. (1970) *The Structure of Scientific Revolutions* (2nd edn) (University of Chicago Press).

Lenman, B. and Parker, G. (1980) 'The State, the Community and the Criminal Law in Early Modern Europe', in Gatrell, V.A.C. *et al.* (eds) *Crime and the Law: The Social History of Crime in Western Europe Since 1500* (Europa Publications).

Lind, M. (1982) 'Law in the Old Testament', in Swartley, W.M. (ed.) *Occasional Papers* (Council of Mennonite Seminaries).

Lind, M. (undated) 'The Transformation of Justice: From Moses to Jesus' (Mennonite Central Committee).

Wright, M. (1982) *Making Good: Prisons, Punishment and Beyond* (Burnett Books).

4 Conflicts as property

Nils Christie

Introduction

Maybe we should not have any criminology. Maybe we should rather abolish institutes, not open them. Maybe the social consequences of criminology are more dubious than we like to think.

I think they are. And I think this relates to my topic – conflicts as property. My suspicion is that criminology to some extent has amplified a process where conflicts have been taken away from the parties directly involved and thereby have either disappeared or become other people's property. In both cases a deplorable outcome. Conflicts ought to be used, not only left in erosion. And they ought to be used, and become useful, for those originally involved in the conflict. Conflicts *might* hurt individuals as well as social systems. That is what we learn in school. That is why we have officials. Without them, private vengeance and vendettas will blossom. We have learned this so solidly that we have lost track of the other side of the coin: our industrialised large-scale society is not one with too many internal conflicts. It is one with too little. Conflicts might kill, but too little of them might paralyse. I will use this occasion to give a sketch of this situation. It cannot be more than a sketch. This paper represents the beginning of the development of some ideas, not the polished end-product.

On happenings and non-happenings

Let us take our point of departure far away. Let us move to Tanzania. Let us approach our problem from the sunny hillside of the Arusha province. Here, inside a relatively large house in a very small village, a sort of happening took place. The house was overcrowded. Most grown-ups from the village and several from adjoining ones were there. It was a happy happening, fast talking, jokes, smiles, eager attention, not a sentence was to be lost. It was circus, it was drama. It was a court case.

The conflict this time was between a man and a woman. They had been engaged. He had invested a lot in the relationship through a long period, until she broke it off. Now he wanted it back. Gold and silver and money were easily decided on, but what about utilities already worn, and what about general expenses?

The outcome is of no interest in our context. But the framework for conflict solution is. Five elements ought to be particularly mentioned:

1. The parties, the former lovers, were in *the centre* of the room and in the centre of everyone's attention. They talked often and were eagerly listened to.
2. Close to them were relatives and friends who also took part. But they did not *take over*.

3. There was also participation from the general audience with short questions, information, or jokes.
4. The judges, three local party secretaries, were extremely inactive. They were obviously ignorant with regard to village matters. All the other people in the room were experts. They were experts on norms as well as actions. And they crystallised norms and clarified what had happened through participation in the procedure.
5. No reporters attended. They were all there.

My personal knowledge when it comes to British courts is limited indeed. I have some vague memories of juvenile courts where I counted some 15 or 20 persons present, mostly social workers using the room for preparatory work or small conferences. A child or a young person must have attended, but except for the judge, or maybe it was the clerk, nobody seemed to pay any particular attention. The child or young person was most probably utterly confused as to who was who and for what, a fact confirmed in a small study by Peter Scott (1959). In the United States of America, Martha Baum (1968) has made similar observations. Recently, Bottoms and McClean (1976) have added another important observation: 'There is one truth which is seldom revealed in the literature of the law or in studies of the administration of criminal justice. It is a truth which was made evident to all those involved in this research project as they sat through the cases which made up our sample. The truth is that, for the most part, the business of the criminal courts is dull, commonplace, ordinary and after a while downright tedious.'

But let me keep quiet about your system, and instead concentrate on my own. And let me assure you: what goes on is no happening. It is all a negation of the Tanzanian case. What is striking in nearly all the Scandinavian cases is the greyness, the dullness, and the lack of any important audience. Courts are not central elements in the daily life of our citizens, but peripheral in four major ways:

1. They are situated in the administrative centres of the towns, outside the territories of ordinary people.
2. Within these centres they are often centralised within one or two large buildings of considerable complexity. Lawyers often complain that they need months to find their way within these buildings. It does not demand much fantasy to imagine the situation of parties or public when they are trapped within these structures. A comparative study of court architecture might become equally relevant for the sociology of law as Oscar Newman's (1972) study of defensible space is for criminology. But even without any study, I feel it safe to say that both physical situation and architectural design are strong indicators that courts in Scandinavia belong to the administrators of law.
3. This impression is strengthened when you enter the courtroom itself – if you are lucky enough to find your way to it. Here again, the periphery of the parties is the striking observation. The parties are represented, and it is these representatives and the judge or judges who express the little activity that is activated within these rooms. Honoré Daumier's famous drawings from the courts are as representative for Scandinavia as they are for France.

    There are variations. In the small cities, or in the countryside, the courts are more easily reached than in the larger towns. And at the very lowest end of the court system – the so-called arbitration boards – the parties are sometimes less heavily represented through experts in law. But the symbol of the whole system is the Supreme Court where the directly involved parties do not even attend their own court cases.

4.   I have not yet made any distinction between civil and criminal conflicts. But it was not
     by chance that the Tanzania case was a civil one. Full participation in your own conflict
     presupposes elements of civil law. The key element in a criminal proceeding is that the
     proceeding is converted from something between the concrete parties into a conflict
     between one of the parties and the state. So, in a modern criminal trial, two important
     things have happened. First, the parties are being *represented*. Secondly, the one party
     that is represented by the state, namely the victim, is so thoroughly represented that she
     or he for most of the proceedings is pushed completely out of the arena, reduced to
     the triggerer-off of the whole thing. She or he is a sort of double loser; first, *vis-à-vis* the
     offender, but secondly and often in a more crippling manner by being denied rights to
     full participation in what might have been one of the more important ritual encounters in
     life. The victim has lost the case to the state.

Professional thieves

As we all know, there are many honourable as well as dishonourable reasons behind this
development. The honourable ones have to do with the state's need for conflict reduction
and certainly also its wishes for the protection of the victim. It is rather obvious. So is also
the less honourable temptation for the state, or Emperor, or whoever is in power, to use the
criminal case for personal gain. Offenders might pay for their sins. Authorities have in
time past shown considerable willingness, in representing the victim, to act as receivers of
the money or other property from the offender. Those days are gone; the crime control
system is not run for profit. And yet they are not gone. There are, in all banality, many interests at stake here, most of them related to professionalisation.

Lawyers are particularly good at stealing conflicts. They are trained for it. They
are trained to prevent and solve conflicts. They are socialised into a sub-culture with a
surprisingly high agreement concerning interpretation of norms, and regarding what sort of
information can be accepted as relevant in each case. Many among us have, as laymen,
experienced the sad moments of truth when our lawyers tell us that our best arguments in our
fight against our neighbour are without any legal relevance whatsoever and that we for God's
sake ought to keep quiet about them in court. Instead they pick out arguments we might find
irrelevant or even wrong to use. My favourite example took place just after the war. One of
my country's absolutely top defenders told with pride how he had just rescued a poor client.
The client had collaborated with the Germans. The prosecutor claimed that the client had
been one of the key people in the organisation of the Nazi movement. He had been one of
the master-minds behind it all. The defender, however, saved his client. He saved him by
pointing out to the jury how weak, how lacking in ability, how obviously deficient his client
was, socially as well as organisationally. His client could simply not have been one of the
organisers among the collaborators; he was without talents. And he won his case. His client
got a very minor sentence as a very minor figure. The defender ended his story by telling
me – with some indignation – that neither the accused, nor his wife, had ever thanked him,
they had not even talked to him afterwards.

Conflicts become the property of lawyers. But lawyers don't hide that it is conflicts they
handle. And the organisational framework of the courts underlines this point. The opposing
parties, the judge, the ban against privileged communication within the court system, the
lack of encouragement for specialisation – specialists cannot be internally controlled – it all
underlines that this is an organisation for the handling of conflicts. *Treatment personnel* are

in another position. They are more interested in *converting the image of the case from one of conflict into one of non-conflict.* The basic model of healers is not one of opposing parties, but one where one party has to be helped in the direction of one generally accepted goal – the preservation or restoration of health. They are not trained into a system where it is important that parties can control each other. There is, in the ideal case, nothing to control, because there is only one goal. Specialisation is encouraged. It increases the amount of available knowledge, and the loss of internal control is of no relevance. A conflict perspective creates unpleasant doubts with regard to the healer's suitability for the job. A non-conflict perspective is a precondition for defining crime as a legitimate target for treatment.

One way of reducing attention to the conflict is reduced attention given to the victim. Another is concentrated attention given to those attributes in the criminal's background which the healer is particularly trained to handle. Biological defects are perfect. So also are personality defects when they are established far back in time – far away from the recent conflict. And so are also the whole row of explanatory variables that criminology might offer. We have, in criminology, to a large extent functioned as an auxiliary science for the professionals within the crime control system. We have focused on the offender, made her or him into an object for study, manipulation and control. We have added to all those forces that have reduced the victim to a nonentity and the offender to a thing. And this critique is perhaps not only relevant for the old criminology, but also for the new criminology. While the old one explained crime from personal defects or social handicaps, the new criminology explains crime as the result of broad economic conflicts. The old criminology loses the conflicts, the new one converts them from interpersonal conflicts to class conflicts. And they are. They are class conflicts – also. But, by stressing this, the conflicts are again taken away from the directly involved parties. So, as a preliminary statement: Criminal conflicts have either become *other people's property* – primarily the property of lawyers – or it has been in other people's interests to *define conflicts away.*

[...]

Conflicts as property

Conflicts are taken away, given away, melt away, or are made invisible. Does it matter, does it really matter?

Most of us would probably agree that we ought to protect the invisible victims just mentioned. Many would also nod approvingly to ideas saying that states, or Governments, or other authorities ought to stop stealing fines, and instead let the poor victim receive this money. I at least would approve such an arrangement. But I will not go into that problem area here and now. Material compensation is not what I have in mind with the formulation 'conflicts as property'. It is the *conflict itself* that represents the most interesting property taken away, not the goods originally taken away from the victim or given back to him. In our types of society, conflicts are more scarce than property. And they are immensely more valuable.

They are valuable in several ways. Let me start at the societal level [...]. Highly industrialised societies face major problems in organising their members in ways such that a decent quota take part in any activity at all. Segmentation according to age and sex can be seen as shrewd methods for segregation. Participation is such a scarcity that insiders create monopolies against outsiders, particularly with regard to work. In this perspective, it will easily be seen that conflicts represent a *potential for activity, for participation.* Modern criminal control systems represent one of the many cases of lost opportunities for involving citizens in tasks that are of immediate importance to them. Ours is a society of task-monopolists.

The victim is a particularly heavy loser in this situation. Not only has he suffered, lost materially or become hurt, physically or otherwise. And not only does the state take the compensation. But above all he has lost participation in his own case. It is the Crown that comes into the spotlight, not the victim. It is the Crown that describes the losses, not the victim. It is the Crown that appears in the newspaper, very seldom the victim. It is the Crown that gets a chance to talk to the offender, and neither the Crown nor the offender are particularly interested in carrying on that conversation. The prosecutor is fed-up long since. The victim would not have been. He might have been scared to death, panic-stricken, or furious. But he would not have been uninvolved. It would have been one of the important days in his life. Something that belonged to him has been taken away from that victim.[1]

But the big loser is us – to the extent that society is us. This loss is first and foremost a loss in *opportunities for norm-clarification*. It is a loss of pedagogical possibilities. It is a loss of opportunities for a continuous discussion of what represents the law of the land. How wrong was the thief, how right was the victim? Lawyers are, as we saw, trained into agreement on what is relevant in a case. But that means a trained incapacity in letting the parties decide what *they* think is relevant. It means that it is difficult to stage what we might call a political debate in the court. When the victim is small and the offender big – in size or power – how blameworthy then is the crime? And what about the opposite case, the small thief and the big house-owner? If the offender is well educated, ought he then to suffer more, or maybe less, for his sins? Or if he is black, or if he is young, or if the other party is an insurance company, or if his wife has just left him, or if his factory will break down if he has to go to jail, or if his daughter will lose her fiancé, or if he was drunk, or if he was sad, or if he was mad? There is no end to it. And maybe there ought to be none. Maybe Barotse law as described by Max Gluckman (1967) is a better instrument for norm-clarification, allowing the conflicting parties to bring in the whole chain of old complaints and arguments each time. Maybe decisions on relevance and on the weight of what is found relevant ought to be taken away from legal scholars, the chief ideologists of crime control systems, and brought back for free decisions in the court-rooms.

A further general loss – both for the victim and for society in general – has to do with anxiety-level and misconceptions. It is again the possibilities for personalised encounters I have in mind. The victim is so totally out of the case that he has no chance, ever, to come to know the offender. We leave him outside, angry, maybe humiliated through a cross-examination in court, without any human contact with the offender. He has no alternative. He will need all the classical stereotypes around 'the criminal' to get a grasp on the whole thing. He has a need for understanding, but is instead a non-person in a Kafka play. Of course, he will go away more frightened than ever, more in need than ever of an explanation of criminals as non-human.

The offender represents a more complicated case. Not much introspection is needed to see that direct victim-participation might be experienced as painful indeed. Most of us would shy away from a confrontation of this character. That is the first reaction. But the second one is slightly more positive. Human beings have reasons for their actions. If the situation is staged so that reasons can be given (reasons as the parties see them, not only the selection lawyers have decided to classify as relevant), in such a case maybe the situation would not be all that humiliating. And, particularly, if the situation was staged in such a manner that the central question was not meting out guilt, but a thorough discussion of what could be done to undo the deed, then the situation might change. And this is exactly what ought to happen when the victim is re-introduced in the case. Serious attention will centre on the victim's losses. That leads to a natural attention as to how they can be softened. It leads into a discussion of restitution. The offender gets a possibility to change his position from being a listener to a discussion – often a highly unintelligible one – of how much pain he ought to receive, into a participant in a discussion of how he could make it good again. The offender has lost the opportunity to explain himself to a person whose evaluation of him might have mattered. He has thereby also lost one of the most important possibilities for being forgiven. Compared to the humiliations in an ordinary court – vividly described by Pat Carlen (1976) in [...] the *British Journal of Criminology* this is not obviously any bad deal for the criminal.

But let me add that I think we should do it quite independently of his wishes. It is not health-control we are discussing. It is crime control. If criminals are shocked by the initial thought of close confrontation with the victim, preferably a confrontation in the very local neighbourhood of one of the parties, what then? I know from recent conversations on these matters that most people sentenced are shocked. After all, they prefer distance from the victim, from neighbours, from listeners and maybe also from their own court case through the vocabulary and the behavioural science experts who might happen to be present. They are perfectly willing to give away their property right to the conflict. So the question is more: are *we* willing to let them give it away? Are we willing to give them this easy way out?[2]

Let me be quite explicit on one point: I am not suggesting these ideas out of any particular interest in the treatment or improvement of criminals. I am not basing my reasoning on a belief that a more personalised meeting between offender and victim would lead to reduced recidivism. Maybe it would. I think it would. As it is now, the offender has lost the opportunity for participation in a personal confrontation of a very serious nature. He has lost the opportunity to receive a type of blame that it would be very difficult to neutralise. However, I would have suggested these arrangements even if it was absolutely certain they had no effects on recidivism, maybe even if they had a negative effect. I would have done that because of the other, more general gains. And let me also add – it is not much to lose. As we all know today, at least nearly all, we have not been able to invent any cure for crime. Except for execution, castration or incarceration for life, no measure has a proven minimum of efficiency compared to any other measure. We might as well react to crime according to what closely involved parties find is just and in accordance with general values in society.

With this last statement, as with most of the others I have made, I raise many more problems than I answer. Statements on criminal politics, particularly from those with the burden of responsibility, are usually filled with answers. It is questions we need. The gravity of our topic makes us much too pedantic and thereby useless as paradigm-changers.

A victim-oriented court

There is clearly a model of neighbourhood courts behind my reasoning. But it is one with some peculiar features, and it is only these I will discuss in what follows.

First and foremost; it is a *victim-oriented* organisation. Not in its initial stage, though. The first stage will be a traditional one where it is established whether it is true that the law has been broken, and whether it was this particular person who broke it.

Then comes the second stage, which in these courts would be of the utmost importance. That would be the stage where the victim's situation was considered, where every detail regarding what had happened – legally relevant or not – was brought to the court's attention. Particularly important here would be detailed consideration regarding what could be done for him, first and foremost by the offender, secondly by the local neighbourhood, thirdly by the state. Could the harm be compensated, the window repaired, the lock replaced, the wall painted, the loss of time because the car was stolen given back through garden work or washing of the car ten Sundays in a row? Or maybe, when this discussion started, the damage was not so important as it looked in documents written to impress insurance companies? Could physical suffering become slightly less painful by any action from the offender, during days, months or years? But, in addition, had the community exhausted all resources that might have offered help? Was it absolutely certain that the local hospital could not do anything? What about a helping hand from the janitor twice a day if the offender took over the cleaning of the basement every Saturday? None of these ideas is unknown or untried, particularly not in England. But we need an organisation for the systematic application of them.

Only after this stage was passed, and it ought to take hours, maybe days, to pass it, only then would come the time for an eventual decision on punishment. Punishment, then, becomes that suffering which the judge found necessary to apply *in addition to* those unintended constructive sufferings the offender would go through in his restitutive actions *vis-à-vis* the victim. Maybe nothing could be done or nothing would be done. But neighbourhoods might find it intolerable that nothing happened. Local courts out of tune with local values are not local courts. That is just the trouble with them, seen from the liberal reformer's point of view.

A fourth stage has to be added. That is the stage for service to the offender. His general social and personal situation is by now well-known to the court. The discussion of his possibilities for restoring the victim's situation cannot be carried out without at the same time giving information about the offender's situation. This might have exposed needs for social, educational, medical or religious action – not to prevent further crime, but because needs ought to be met. Courts are public arenas, needs are made visible. But it is important that this stage comes *after* sentencing. Otherwise we get a re-emergence of the whole array of so-called 'special measures' – compulsory treatments – very often only euphemisms for indeterminate imprisonment.

Through these four stages, these courts would represent a blend of elements from civil and criminal courts, but with a strong emphasis on the civil side.

A lay-oriented court

The second major peculiarity with the court model I have in mind is that it will be one with an extreme degree of lay-orientation. This is essential when conflicts are seen as property that ought to be shared. It is with conflicts as with so many good things; they are in no unlimited supply. Conflicts can be cared for, protected, nurtured. But there are limits. If some are given more access in the disposal of conflicts, others are getting less. It is as simple as that.

Specialisation in conflict solution is the major enemy; specialisation that in due – or undue – time leads to professionalisation. That is when the specialists get sufficient power to claim that they have acquired special gifts, mostly through education, gifts so powerful that it is obvious that they can only be handled by the certified craftsman.

With a clarification of the enemy, we are also able to specify the goal; let us reduce specialisation and particularly our dependence on the professionals within the crime control system to the utmost.

The ideal is clear; it ought to be a court of equals representing themselves. When they are able to find a solution between themselves, no judges are needed. When they are not, the judges ought also to be their equals.

Maybe the judge would be the easiest to replace, if we made a serious attempt to bring our present courts nearer to this model of lay orientation. We have lay judges already, in principle. But that is a far cry from realities. What we have, both in England and in my own country, is a sort of specialised non-specialist. First, they are used *again and again.* Secondly, some are even *trained,* given special courses or sent on excursions to foreign countries to learn about how to behave as a lay judge. Thirdly, most of them do also represent an extremely *biased sample* of the population with regard to sex, age, education, income, class[3] and personal experience as criminals. With real lay judges, I conceive of a system where nobody was given the right to take part in conflict solution more than a few times, and then had to wait until all other community members had had the same experience.

Should lawyers be admitted to court? We had an old law in Norway that forbids them to enter the rural districts. Maybe they should be admitted in stage one where it is decided if the man is guilty. I am not sure. Experts are as cancer to any lay body. It is exactly as Ivan Illich describes for the educational system in general. Each time you increase the length of compulsory education in a society, each time you also decrease the same population's trust in what they have learned and understood quite by themselves.

Behaviour experts represent the same dilemma. Is there a place for them in this model? Ought there to be any place? In stage 1, decisions on facts, certainly not. In stage 3, decisions on eventual punishment, certainly not. It is too obvious to waste words on. We have the painful row of mistakes from Lombroso, through the movement for social defence and up to recent attempts to dispose of supposedly dangerous people through predictions of who they are and when they are not dangerous any more. Let these ideas die, without further comments.

The real problem has to do with the service function of behaviour experts. Social scientists can be perceived as functional answers to a segmented society. Most of us have lost the physical possibility to experience the totality, both on the social system level and on the personality level. Psychologists can be seen as historians for the individual; sociologists have much the same function for the social system. Social workers are oil in the machinery, a sort of security counsel. Can we function without them, would the victim and the offender be worse off?

Maybe. But it would be immensely difficult to get such a court to function if they were all there. Our theme is social conflict. Who is not at least made slightly uneasy in the handling of her or his own social conflicts if we get to know that there is an expert on this very matter at the same table? I have no clear answer, only strong feelings behind a vague conclusion: let us have as few behaviour experts as we dare to. And if we have any, let us for God's sake not have any that specialise in crime and conflict resolution. Let us have generalised experts with a solid base outside the crime control system. And a last point with relevance for both behaviour experts and lawyers: if we find them unavoidable in certain cases or at certain stages, let us try to get across to them the problems they create for broad social participation. Let us try to get them to perceive themselves as resource-persons, answering when asked, but not domineering, not in the centre. They might help to stage conflicts, not take them over.

Rolling stones

There are hundreds of blocks against getting such a system to operate within our western culture. Let me only mention three major ones. They are:

1. There is a lack of neighbourhoods.
2. There are too few victims.
3. There are too many professionals around.

With lack of neighbourhoods I have in mind the very same phenomenon I described as a consequence of industrialised living; segmentation according to space and age. Much of our trouble stems from killed neighbourhoods or killed local communities. How can we then thrust towards neighbourhoods a task that presupposes they are highly alive? I have no really good arguments, only two weak ones. First, it is not quite that bad. The death is not complete. Secondly, one of the major ideas behind the formulation 'Conflicts as Property' is that it is neighbourhood-property. It is not private. It belongs to the system. It is intended as a vitaliser for neighbourhoods. The more fainting the neighbourhood is, the more we need neighbourhood courts as one of the many functions any social system needs for not dying through lack of challenge.

Equally bad is the lack of victims. Here I have particularly in mind the lack of personal victims. The problem behind this is again the large units in industrialised society. Woolworth or British Rail are not good victims. But again I will say: there is not a complete lack of personal victims, and their needs ought to get priority. But we should not forget the large organisations. They, or their boards, would certainly prefer not to have to appear as victims in 5,000 neighbourhood courts all over the country. But maybe they ought to be compelled to appear. If the complaint is serious enough to bring the offender into the ranks of the criminal, then the victim ought to appear. A related problem has to do with insurance companies – the industrialised alternative to friendship or kinship. Again we have a case where the crutches deteriorate the condition. Insurance takes the conseqences of crime away. We will therefore have to take insurance away. Or rather: we will have to keep the possibilities for compensation through the insurance companies back until in the procedure I have described it has been proved beyond all possible doubt that there are no other alternatives left – particularly that the offender has no possibilities whatsoever. Such a solution will create more paper-work, less predictability, more aggression from customers. And the solution will not necessarily be seen as good from the perspective of the policy-holder. But it will help to protect conflicts as social fuel.

None of these troubles can, however, compete with the third and last I will comment on: the abundance of professionals. We know it all from our own personal biographies or personal observations. And in addition we get it confirmed from all sorts of social science research: the educational system of any society is not necessarily synchronised with any needs for the product of this system. Once upon a time we thought there was a direct causal relation from the number of highly educated persons in a country to the Gross National Product. Today we suspect the relationship to go the other way, if we are at all willing to use GNP as a meaningful indicator. We also know that most educational systems are extremely class-biased. We know that most academic people have had profitable investments in our education, that we fight for the same for our children, and that we also often have vested interests in making our part of the educational system even bigger. More schools for more lawyers, social workers, sociologists, criminologists. While I am *talking* deprofessionalisation, we are increasing the capacity to be able to fill up the whole world with them.

There is no solid base for optimism. On the other hand insights about the situation, and goal formulation, is a pre-condition for action. Of course, the crime control system is not the domineering one in our type of society. But it has some importance. And occurrences here are unusually well suited as pedagogical illustrations of general trends in society. There is also some room for manoeuvre. And when we hit the limits, or are hit by them, this collision represents in itself a renewed argument for more broadly conceived changes.

Another source for hope: ideas formulated here are not quite so isolated or in dissonance with the mainstream of thinking when we leave our crime control area and enter other institutions.

I have already mentioned Ivan Illich with his attempts to get learning away from the teachers and back to active human beings. Compulsory learning, compulsory medication and compulsory consummation of conflict solutions have interesting similarities. When Ivan Illich and Paulo Freire are listened to, and my impression is that they increasingly are, the crime control system will also become more easily influenced.

Another, but related, major shift in paradigm is about to happen within the whole field of technology. Partly, it is the lessons from the third world that now are more easily seen, partly it is the experience from the ecology debate. The globe is obviously suffering from what we, through our technique, are doing to her. Social systems in the third world are equally obviously suffering. So the suspicion starts. Maybe the first world can't take all this technology either. Maybe some of the old social thinkers were not so dumb after all. Maybe social systems can be perceived as biological ones. And maybe there are certain types of large-scale technology that kill social systems, as they kill globes. Schumacher (1973) with his book *Small is Beautiful* and the related Institute for Intermediate Technology come in here. So do also the numerous attempts, particularly by several outstanding Institutes for Peace Research, to show the dangers in the concept of Gross National Product, and replace it with indicators that take care of dignity, equity and justice. The perspective developed in Johan Galtung's research group on World Indicators might prove extremely useful also within our own field of crime control.

There is also a political phenomenon opening vistas. At least in Scandinavia social democrats and related groupings have considerable power, but are without an explicated ideology regarding the goals for a reconstructed society. This vacuum is being felt by many, and creates a willingness to accept and even expect considerable institutional experimentation.

Then to my very last point: what about the universities in this picture? What about the new Centre in Sheffield? The answer has probably to be the old one: universities have to re-emphasise the old tasks of understanding and of criticising. But the task of training professionals ought to be looked into with renewed scepticism. Let us re-establish the credibility of encounters between critical human beings: low-paid, highly regarded, but with no extra power – outside the weight of their good ideas. That is as it ought to be.

Notes

1 For a preliminary report on victim dissatisfaction, see Vennard (1976).
2 I tend to take the same position with regard to a criminal's property right to his own conflict as John Locke on property rights to one's own life – one has no right to give it away (*cf.* C.B. MacPherson (1962)).
3 [...] see Baldwin (1976).

References

Baldwin, J. (1976) 'The Social Composition of the Magistracy', *British Journal of Criminology*, 16, pp. 171–4.

Baum, M. and Wheeler, S. (1968) 'Becoming an Inmate', in Wheeler, S. (ed.) *Controlling Delinquents* (New York: Wiley), pp. 153–87.

Bottoms, A.E. and McClean, J.D. (1976) *Defendants in the Criminal Process* (London: Routledge & Kegan Paul).

Carlen, P. (1976) 'The Staging of Magistrates' Justice', *British Journal of Criminology*, 16, pp. 48–55.

Gluckman, M. (1967) *The Judicial Process among the Barotse of Northern Rhodesia* (Manchester: Manchester University Press).

Kinberg, O., Inghe, G. and Riemer, S. (1943) *Incest-Problemet i Sverige.* Sth.

MacPherson, C.B. (1962) *The Political Theory of Possessive Individualism: Hobbes to Locke* (London: Oxford University Press).

Newman, O. (1972) *Defensible Space: People and Design in the Violent City* (London: Architectural Press).

Schumacher, E.F. (1973) *Small is Beautiful: A Study of Economics as if People Mattered* (London: Blond & Briggs).

Scott, P.D. (1959) 'Juvenile Courts: The Juvenile's Point of View', *British Journal of Delinquency,* 9, pp. 200–10.

Vennard, J. (1976) 'Justice and Recompense for Victims of Crime', *New.Society,* 36, pp. 378–80.

5   Restitution

A new paradigm of criminal justice

Randy E. Barnett

[...]

In the criminal justice system we are witnessing the death throes of an old and cumbersome paradigm, one that has dominated Western thought for more than 900 years. While this paper presents what is hoped to be a viable, though radical alternative, much would be accomplished by simply prompting the reader to reexamine the assumptions underlying the present system. Only if we are willing to look at our old problems in a new light do we stand a chance of solving them. This is our only hope, and our greatest challenge.

The crisis in the paradigm of punishment

'Political revolutions are inaugurated by a growing sense, often restricted to a segment of the political community, that existing institutions have ceased adequately to meet the problems posed by an environment they have in part created... In both political and scientific development the sense of malfunction that can lead to crisis is prerequisite to revolution.'[1] Kuhn's description of the preconditions for scientific and political revolutions could accurately describe the current state of the criminal law. However, simply to recognize the existence of a crisis is not enough. We must look for its causes. The Kuhnian methodology suggests that we critically examine the paradigm of punishment itself.

The problems which the paradigm of punishment is supposed to solve are many and varied. A whole literature on the philosophy of punishment has arisen in an effort to justify or reject the institution of punishment. For our purposes the following definition from the *Encyclopedia of Philosophy* should suffice: 'Characteristically punishment is unpleasant. It is inflicted on an offender because of an offence he has committed; it is deliberately imposed, not just the natural consequence of a person's action (like a hangover), and the unpleasantness is *essential* to it, not an accompaniment to some other treatment (like the pain of the dentist's drill).'[2]

Two types of arguments are commonly made in defense of punishment. The first is that punishment is an appropriate means to some justifiable end such as, for example, deterrence of crime. The second type of argument is that punishment is justified as an end in itself. On this view, whatever ill effects it might engender, punishment for its own sake is good.

The first type of argument might be called the *political* justification of punishment, for the end which justifies its use is one which a political order is presumably dedicated to serve: the maintenance of peaceful interactions between individuals and groups in a society. There are at least three ways that deliberate infliction of harm on an offender is said to be politically justified.

1. One motive for punishment, especially capital punishment and imprisonment, is the 'intention to deprive offenders of the power of doing future mischief'.[3] Although it is true that an offender cannot continue to harm society while incarcerated, a strategy of punishment based on disablement has several drawbacks.

Imprisonment is enormously expensive. This means that a double burden is placed on the innocent who must suffer the crime and, in addition, pay through taxation for the support of the offender and his family if they are forced on to welfare. Also, any benefit of imprisonment is temporary; eventually, most offenders will be released. If their outlook has not improved – and especially if it has worsened – the benefits of incarceration are obviously limited. Finally, when disablement is permanent, as with capital punishment or psychosurgery, it is this very permanence, in light of the possibility of error, which is frightening. For these reasons, 'where disablement enters as an element into penal theories, it occupies, as a rule, a subordinate place and is looked upon as an object subsidiary to some other end which is regarded as paramount....'[4]

2. Rehabilitation of a criminal means a change in his mental *habitus* so that he will not offend again. It is unclear whether the so-called treatment model which views criminals as a doctor would view a patient is truly a 'retributive' concept. Certainly it does not conform to the above definition characterizing punishment as deliberately and essentially unpleasant. It is an open question whether any end justifies the intentional, forceful manipulation of an individual's thought processes by anyone, much less the state. To say that an otherwise just system has incidentally rehabilitative effects which may be desirable is one thing, but it is quite another to argue that these effects themselves justify the system. The horrors to which such reasoning can lead are obvious from abundant examples in history and contemporary society.[5]

[...]

3. The final justification to be treated here – deterrence – actually has two aspects. The first is the deterrent effect that past demonstrations of punishment have on the future of others; the second is the effect that threats of future punishment have on the conduct of others. The distinction assumes importance when some advocates argue that future threats lose their deterrent effect when there is a lack of past demonstrations. Past punishment, then, serves as an educational tool. It is a substitute for or reinforcement of threats of future punishment.

As with the goals mentioned above, the empirical question of whether punishment has this effect is a disputed one.[6] I shall not attempt to resolve this question here, but will assume *arguendo* that punishment even as presently administered has some deterrent effect. It is the moral question which is disturbing. Can an argument from deterrence alone 'justify' in any sense the infliction of pain on a criminal? It is particularly disquieting that the actual levying of punishment is done not for the criminal himself, but for the educational impact it will have on the community. The criminal act becomes the occasion of, but not the reason for, the punishment. In this way, the actual crime becomes little more than an excuse for punishing.

Surely this distorts the proper functioning of the judicial process. For if deterrence is the end it is unimportant whether the individual actually committed the crime. Since the public's perception of guilt is the prerequisite of the deterrent effect, all that is required for deterrence is that the individual is 'proved' to have committed the crime. The actual occurrence would have no relevance except insofar as a truly guilty person is easier to prove guilty. The judicial process becomes, not a truth-seeking device, but solely a means to legitimate the use of force. To treat criminals as means to the ends of others in this way raises serious moral problems. This is not to argue that men may never use others as means but rather to question the use of force against the individual because of the effect such use will have on others.

It was this that concerned del Vecchio when he stated that 'the human person always bears in himself something sacred, and it is therefore not permissible to treat him merely as a means towards an end outside of himself.[7]

[...]

It is not my thesis that deterrence, reformation, and disablement are undesirable goals. On the contrary, any criminal justice system should be critically examined to see if it is having these and other beneficial effects. The view advanced here is simply that these utilitarian benefits must be incidental to a just system; they cannot, alone or in combination, justify a criminal justice system. Something more is needed. There is another more antiquated strain of punishment theory which seeks to address this problem. The *moral* justifications of punishment view punishment as an end in itself. This approach has taken many forms.[8] On this view, whatever ill or beneficial results it might have, punishment of lawbreakers is good for its own sake. This proposition can be analyzed on several levels.

The most basic question is the truth of the claim itself. Some have argued that 'the alleged absolute justice of repaying evil with evil (maintained by Kant and many other writers) is really an empty sophism. If we go back to the Christian moralists, we find that an evil is to be put right only by doing good.'[9] This question is beyond the scope of this treatment. The subject has been extensively dealt with by those more knowledgeable than I.[10] The more relevant question is what such a view of punishment as a good can be said to imply for a system of criminal justice. Even assuming that it would be good if, in the nature of things, the wicked got their 'come-uppance', what behavior does this moral fact justify? Does it justify the victim authoring the punishment of his offender? Does it justify the same action by the victim's family, his friends, his neighbors, the state? If so what punishment should be imposed and who should decide?

It might be argued that the natural punishment for the violation of natural rights is the deserved hatred and scorn of the community, the resultant ostracism, and the existential hell of *being* an evil person. The question then is not whether we have the right to inflict some 'harm' or unpleasantness on a morally contemptible person – surely, we do; the question is not whether such a punishment is 'good' – arguably, it is. The issue is whether the 'virtue of some punishment' justifies the *forceful* imposition of unpleasantness on a *rights violator* as distinguished from the morally imperfect. Any *moral* theory of punishment must recognize and deal with this distinction. Finally, it must be established that the state is the legitimate author of punishment, a proposition which further assumes the moral and legal legitimacy of the state. To raise these issues is not to resolve them, but it would seem that the burden of proof is on those seeking to justify the use of force against the individual. Suffice it to say that I am skeptical of finding any theory which justifies the deliberate, forceful imposition of punishment within or without a system of criminal justice.

[...]

Punishment, particularly state punishment is the descendant of the tradition which imparts religious and moral authority to the sovereign and through him, the community. Such an authority is increasingly less credible in a secular world such as ours. Today there is an increasing desire to allow each individual to govern his own life as he sees fit provided he does not violate the rights of others. This desire is exemplified by current attitudes toward drug use, abortion, and pornography. Few argue that these things are good. It is only said that where there is no victim the state or community has no business meddling in the peaceful behavior of its citizens, however morally suspect it may be.[11]

Furthermore, if the paradigm of punishment is in a 'crisis period' it is as much because of its practical drawbacks as the uncertainty of its moral status. The infliction of suffering on a criminal tends to cause a general feeling of sympathy for him. There is no rational connection between a term of imprisonment and the harm caused the victim. Since the prison term is supposed to be unpleasant, at least a part of the public comes to see the criminal as a victim, and the lack of rationality also causes the offender to feel victimized. This reaction is magnified by the knowledge that most crimes go unpunished and that even if the offender is caught the judicial process is long, arduous, and far removed from the criminal act. While this is obvious to most, it is perhaps less obvious that the punishment paradigm is largely at fault. The slow, ponderous nature of our system of justice is largely due to a fear of an unjust infliction of punishment on the innocent (or even the guilty). The more awful the sanction, the more elaborate need be the safeguards. The more the system is perceived as arbitrary and unfair, the more incentive there is for defendants and their counsel to thwart the truth-finding process. Acquittal becomes desirable at all costs. As the punitive aspect of a sanction is diminished, so too would be the perceived need for procedural protections.

A system of punishment, furthermore, offers no incentive for the victim to involve himself in the criminal justice process other than to satisfy his feelings of duty or revenge. The victim stands to gain little if at all by the conviction and punishment of the person who caused his loss. This is true even of those systems discussed below which dispense state compensation based on the victim's need. The system of justice itself imposes uncompensated costs by requiring a further loss of time and money by the victim and witnesses and by increasing the perceived risk of retaliation.

[...]

Outline of a new paradigm

The idea of restitution is actually quite simple. It views crime as an offence by one individual against the rights of another. The victim has suffered a loss. Justice consists of the culpable offender making good the loss he has caused. It calls for a complete refocusing of our image of crime. Kuhn would call it a 'shift of world-view'. Where we once saw an offence against society, we now see an offence against an individual victim. In a way, it is a common sense view of crime. *The armed robber did not rob society; he robbed the victim.* His debt, therefore, is not to society; it is to the victim. There are really two types of restitution proposals: a system of 'punitive' restitution and a 'pure' restitutional system.

1. Punitive restitution. 'Since rehabilitation was admitted to the aims of penal law two centuries ago, the number of penological aims has remained virtually constant. Restitution is waiting to come in.'[12] Given this view, restitution should merely be added to the paradigm of punishment. Stephen Schafer outlines the proposal: '[Punitive] restitution, like punishment, must always be the subject of judicial consideration. Without exception it must be carried out by personal performance by the wrong-doer, and should even then be equally burdensome and just for all criminals, irrespective of their means, whether they be millionaires or labourers.'[13]

There are many ways by which such a goal might be reached. The offender might be forced to compensate the victim by his own work, either in prison or out. If it came out of his pocket or from the sale of his property this would compensate the victim, but it would not be sufficiently proportionate for the offender. Another proposal would be that the fines be proportionate to the earning power of the criminal. Thus, 'A poor man would pay in days of work, a rich man by an equal number of days' income or salary.'[14] Herbert Spencer made a proposal along similar lines in his excellent 'Prison Ethics', which is well worth examining.[15] Murray N. Rothbard and others have proposed a system of 'double payments' in cases of criminal behavior.[16] While closer to pure restitution than other proposals, the 'double damages' concept preserves a punitive aspect.

Punitive restitution is an attempt to gain the benefits of pure restitution, which will be considered shortly, while retaining the perceived advantages of the paradigm of punishment. Thus, the prisoner is still 'sentenced' to some unpleasantness – prison labor or loss of X number of days' income. That the intention is to preserve the 'hurt' is indicated by the hesitation to accept an out-of-pocket payment or sale of assets. This is considered too 'easy' for the criminal and takes none of his time. The amount of payment is determined not by the *actual harm* but by the *ability of the offender to pay*. Of course, by retaining the paradigm of punishment this proposal involves many of the problems we raised earlier. In this sense it can be considered another attempt to salvage the old paradigm.

2. Pure restitution. 'Recompense or restitution is scarcely a punishment as long as it is merely a matter of returning stolen goods or money... The point is not that the offender deserves to suffer; it is rather that the offended party desires compensation.'[17] This represents the complete overthrow of the paradigm of punishment. No longer would the deterrence, reformation, disablement, or rehabilitation of the criminal be the guiding principle of the judicial system. The attainment of these goals would be incidental to, and as a result of, reparations paid to the victim. No longer would the criminal deliberately be made to suffer for his mistake. Making good that mistake is all that would be required. What follows is a possible scenario of such a system.

When a crime occurred and a suspect was apprehended, a trial court would attempt to determine his guilt or innocence. If found guilty, the criminal would be sentenced to make restitution to the victim.[18] If a criminal is able to make restitution immediately, he may do so. This would discharge his liability. If he were unable to make restitution, but were found by the court to be trustworthy, he would be permitted to remain at his job (or find a new one) while paying restitution out of his future wages. This would entail a legal claim against future wages. Failure to pay could result in garnishment or a new type of confinement.

If it is found that the criminal is not trustworthy, or that he is unable to gain employment, he would be confined to an employment project.[19] This would be an industrial enterprise, preferably run by a private concern, which would produce actual goods or services. The level of security at each employment project would vary according to the behavior of the offenders. Since the costs would be lower, inmates at a lower-security project would receive higher wages. There is no reason why many workers could not be permitted to live with their families inside or outside the facility, depending again, on the trustworthiness of the offender. Room and board would be deducted from the wages first, then a certain amount for restitution. Anything over that amount the worker could keep or apply toward further restitution, thus hastening his release. If a worker refused to work, he would be unable to pay for his maintenance, and therefore would not in principle be entitled to it. If he did not make restitution he could not be released. The exact arrangement which would best provide for high productivity, minimal security, and maximum incentive to work and repay the victim cannot be determined in advance. Experience is bound to yield some plans superior to others. In fact, the experimentation has already begun.[20]

While this might be the basic system, all sorts of refinements are conceivable, and certainly many more will be invented as needs arise. A few examples might be illuminating.

With such a system of repayment, victim *crime insurance* would be more economically feasible than at present and highly desirable. The cost of awards would be offset by the insurance company's right to restitution in place of the victim (right of subrogation). The insurance company would be better suited to supervise the offender and mark his progress than would the victim. To obtain an earlier recovery, it could be expected to innovate so as to enable the worker to repay more quickly (and, as a result, be released that much sooner). The insurance companies might even underwrite the employment projects themselves as well as related industries which would employ the skilled worker after his release. Any successful effort on their part to reduce crime and recidivism would result in fewer claims and lower premiums. The benefit of this insurance scheme for the victim is immediate compensation, conditional on the victim's continued cooperation with the authorities for the arrest and conviction of the suspect. In addition, the centralization of victim claims would, arguably, lead to efficiencies which would permit the pooling of small claims against a common offender.

Another highly useful refinement would be *direct arbitration* between victim and criminal. This would serve as a sort of healthy substitute for plea bargaining. By allowing the guilty criminal to negotiate a reduced payment in return for a guilty plea, the victim (or his insurance company) would be saved the risk of an adverse finding at trial and any possible additional expense that might result. This would also allow an indigent criminal to substitute personal services for monetary payments if all parties agreed.

Arbitration is argued for by John M. Greacen, deputy director of the National Institute for Law Enforcement and Criminal Justice. He sees the possible advantages of such reform as the '... development of more creative dispositions for most criminal cases; for criminal victims the increased use of restitution, the knowledge that their interests were considered in the criminal process; and an increased satisfaction with the outcome; increased awareness in the part of the offender that his crime was committed against another human being, and not against society in general; increased possibility that the criminal process will cause the offender to acknowledge responsibility for his acts.'[21] Greacen notes several places where such a system has been tried with great success, most notably Tucson, Arizona, and Columbus, Ohio.[22]

Something analogous to the medieval Irish system of *sureties* might be employed as well.[23] Such a system would allow a concerned person, group, or company to make restitution (provided the offender agrees to this). The worker might then be released in the custody of the surety. If the surety had made restitution, the offender would owe restitution to the surety who might enforce the whole claim or show mercy. Of course, the more violent and unreliable the offender, the more serious and costly the offence, the less likely it would be that anyone would take the risk. But for first offenders, good workers, or others that charitable interests found deserving (or perhaps unjustly convicted) this would provide an avenue of respite.

Restitution and rights

These three possible refinements clearly illustrate the flexibility of a restitutional system. It may be less apparent that this flexibility is *inherent* to the restitutional paradigm. Restitution recognizes rights in the victim, and this is a principal source of its strength. The nature and limit of the victim's right to restitution at the same time defines the nature and limit of the criminal liability. In this way, the aggressive action of the criminal creates a *debt* to the victim. The recognition of rights and obligations make possible many innovative arrangements. Subrogation, arbitration, and suretyship are three examples mentioned above.

They are possible because this right to compensation[24] is considered the property of the victim and can therefore be delegated, assigned, inherited, or bestowed. One could determine in advance who would acquire the right to any restitution which he himself might be unable to collect.

[...]

Advantages of a restitutional system

1. The first and most obvious advantage is the assistance provided to victims of crime. They may have suffered an emotional, physical, or financial loss. Restitution would not change the fact that a possibly traumatic crime has occurred (just as the award of damages does not undo tortious conduct). Restitution, however, would make the resulting loss easier to bear for both victims and their families. At the same time, restitution would avoid a major pitfall of victim compensation/welfare plans: Since it is the criminal who must pay, the possibility of collusion between victim and criminal to collect 'damages' from the state would be all but eliminated.

2. The possibility of receiving compensation would encourage victims to report crimes and to appear at trial. This is particularly true if there were a crime insurance scheme which contractually committed the policyholder to testify as a condition for payment, thus rendering unnecessary oppressive and potentially tyrannical subpoenas and contempt citations. Even the actual reporting of the crime to police is likely to be a prerequisite for compensation. Such a requirement in auto theft insurance policies has made car thefts the most fully reported crime in the United States. Furthermore, insurance companies which paid the claim would have a strong incentive to see that the criminal was apprehended and convicted. Their pressure and assistance would make the proper functioning of law enforcement officials all the more likely.

3. Psychologist Albert Eglash has long argued that restitution would aid in the rehabilitation of criminals. 'Restitution is something an inmate does, not something done for or to him... Being reparative, restitution can alleviate guilt and anxiety, which can otherwise precipitate further offences.'[25] Restitution, says Eglash, is an active effortful role on the part of the offender. It is socially constructive, thereby contributing to the offender's self-esteem. It is related to the offence and may thereby redirect the thoughts which motivated the offence. It is reparative, restorative, and may actually leave the situation better than it was before the crime, both for the criminal and victim.[26]

4. This is a genuinely 'self-determinative' sentence.[27] The worker would know that the length of his confinement was in his own hands. The harder he worked, the faster he would make restitution. He would be the master of his fate, and would have to face that responsibility. This would encourage useful, productive activity and instill a conception of reward for good behavior and hard work. Compare this with the current probationary system and 'indeterminate sentencing' where the decision for release is made by the prison bureaucracy, based only (if fairly administered) on 'good behavior'; that is, passive acquiescence to prison discipline. Also, the fact that the worker would be acquiring *marketable* skills rather than more skillful methods of crime should help to reduce the shocking rate of recidivism.

5. The savings to taxpayers would be enormous. No longer would the innocent taxpayers pay for the apprehension and internment of the guilty. The cost of arrest, trial, and internment would be borne by the criminal himself. In addition, since now-idle inmates would become productive workers (able, perhaps, to support their families), the entire economy would benefit from the increase in overall production.[28]

6. Crime would no longer pay. Criminals, particularly shrewd white-collar criminals, would know that they could not dispose of the proceeds of their crime and, if caught, simply serve time. They would have to make full restitution plus enforcement and legal costs, thereby greatly increasing the incentive to prosecute. While this would not eliminate such crime it would make it rougher on certain types of criminals, like bank and corporation officials, who harm many by their acts with a virtual assurance of lenient legal sanctions.[29] It might also encourage such criminals to keep the money around for a while so that, if caught, they could repay more easily. This would make a full recovery more likely.

A restitutional system of justice would benefit the victim, the criminal, and the taxpayer. The humanitarian goals of proportionate punishment, rehabilitation, and victim compensation are dealt with on a *fundamental* level making their achievement more likely. In short, the paradigm of restitution would benefit all but the entrenched penal bureaucracy and enhance justice at the same time. What then is there to stop us from overthrowing the paradigm of punishment and its penal system and putting in its place this more efficient, more humane, and more just system? The proponents of punishment and others have a few powerful counterarguments. It is to these we now turn.

Objections to restitution

1. Practical criticisms of restitution. It might be objected that 'crimes disturb and offend not only those who are directly their victim, but also the whole social order'.[30] Because of this, society, that is, individuals other than the victim, deserves some satisfaction from the offender. Restitution, it is argued, will not satisfy the lust for revenge felt by the victim or the 'community's sense of justice'. This criticism appears to be overdrawn. Today most members of the community are mere spectators of the criminal justice system, and this is largely true even of the victim.[31] One major reform being urged presently is more victim involvement in the criminal justice process.[32] The restitution proposal would necessitate this involvement. And while the public generally takes the view that officials should be tougher on criminals, with 'tougher' taken by nearly everyone to mean more severe in punishing, one must view this 'social fact' in light of the lack of a known alternative. The real test of public sympathies would be to see which sanction people would choose: incarceration of the criminal for a given number of years or the criminal's being compelled to make restitution to the victim: While the public's choice is not clearly predictable, neither can it be assumed that it would reject restitution. There is some evidence to the contrary [...].

This brings us to a second practical objection: that monetary sanctions are insufficient deterrents to crime. Again, this is something to be discovered, not something to be assumed. There are a number of reasons to believe that our *current* system of punishment does not adequately deter, and for the reasons discussed earlier an increase in the level of punishment is unlikely. In fact, many have argued that the deterrent value of sanctions has less to do with *severity* than with *certainty*,[33] and the preceding considerations indicate that law enforcement would be more certain under a restitutional system. In the final analysis, however, it is irrelevant to argue that more crimes may be committed if our proposal leaves the victim better off. It must be remembered: *Our goal is not the suppression of crime; it is doing justice to victims.*

[...]

Notes

1 Kuhn, T. (1970) *The Structure of Scientific Revolutions* (2nd edn) (Chicago, IL: University of Chicago Press), p. 92.

2 Benn, S.I. (1967) 'Punishment', in Edwards, P. (ed.) *The Encyclopedia of Philosophy* (New York, NY: Macmillan) p. 29 (emphasis added).

3 Oppenheimer, H. (1913) *The Rationale of Punishment* (London: University of London Press), p. 255.

4 Ibid.

5 See Szasz, T. (1963) *Law, Liberty, and Psychiatry* (New York, NY: Macmillan).

6 See, e.g. Yochelson, S. and Samenow, S.E. (1976) *The Criminal Personality. Vol. 1. A Profile for Change* (New York, NY: Jason Aronson) pp. 411–16.

7 Del Vecchio, G. (1969) 'The Struggle against Crime', in Acton, H.B. (ed.) *The Philosophy of Punishment* (London: Macmillan), p. 199.

8 For a concise summary, see Oppenheimer, p. 31.

9 Del Vecchio, p. 198.

10 See, e.g. Kaufman, W. (1973) *Without Guilt and Justice* (New York, NY: Peter H. Wyden), esp. Chap. 2.

11 This problem is examined, though not ultimately resolved, by Edwin M. Schur in his book *Crimes without Victims – Deviant Behavior and Public Policy, Abortion, Homosexuality, and Drug Addiction* (Englewood Cliffs, NJ: Prentice Hall, 1965).

12 Mueller, G.O.W. (1965) 'Compensation for Victims of Crime: Thought before Action', *Minnesota Law Review*, 50, p. 221.

13 Schafer, S. (1970) *Compensation and Restitution to Victims of Crime* (2nd edn) (Montclair, NJ: Patterson-Smith), p. 127.

14 Ibid.

15 Spencer, H. (1907) 'Prison-Ethics', in *Essays: Scientific, Political and Speculative* (New York, NY: Appleton & Co.), 3, pp. 152–91.

16 Rothbard, M.N. (1972) *Libertarian Forum*, 14:1, pp. 7–8.

17 Kaufmann, p. 55.

18 The nature of judicial procedure best designed to carry out this task must be determined. For a brief discussion of some relevant considerations, see Laster, R.E. (1970) 'Criminal Restitution: A Survey of its Past History and an Analysis of its Present Usefulness', *University of Richmond Law Review*, 5, pp. 80–98; Galaway, B. and Hudson, J. (1975) 'Issues in the Correctional Implementation of Restitution to Victims of Crime', in Galaway, B. and Hudson, J. (eds) *Considering the Victim: Readings in Restitution and Victim Compensation* (Springfield, IL: Charles C. Thomas), pp. 351–60. Also to be dealt with is the proper standard of compensation. At least initially, the problem of how much payment constitutes restitution would be no different than similar considerations in tort law. [...]

19 Such a plan (with some significant differences) has been suggested by Smith, K.J. in *A Cure for Crime: The Case for the Self-determinate Prison Sentence* (London: Duckworth, 1965), pp. 13–29; see also Tannehill, M. and Tannehill, L. (1970) *The Market for Liberty* (Lansing, MI, privately printed), pp. 44–108.

20 For a recent summary report, see Galaway, B. (1977) 'Restitution as an Integrative Punishment.' Paper prepared for the Symposium on Crime and Punishment: Restitution, Retribution, and Law, Harvard Law School, March.

21 Greacen, J.M. (1975) 'Arbitration: A Tool for Criminal Cases?', *Barrister*, Winter, p. 53; see also Galaway and Hudson, pp. 352–55; 'Conclusions and Recommendations, International Study Institute on *Victimology*, Bellagio, Italy, July 1–12', *Victimology*, 1 (1976), pp. 150–1; Goldfarb, R. (1976) *Jails: The Ultimate Ghetto* (Garden City, NY: Anchor Press/Doubleday) p. 480.

22 Greacen, p. 53.

23 For a description of the Irish system, see Peden, J.R. (1973) 'Property Rights in Medieval Ireland: Celtic Law versus Church and State.' Paper presented at the Symposium on the Origins and Development of Property Rights, University of San Francisco, January; for a theoretical discussion of a similar proposal, see Spencer, pp. 182–6.

24 Or, perhaps more accurately, the compensation itself.

25 Eglash, A. (1958) 'Creative Restitution: Some Suggestions for Prison Rehabilitation Programs', *American Journal of Correction*, 40: November–December, p. 20.

26 Ibid.; see also Eglash's 'Creative Restitution: A Broader Meaning for an Old Term', *Journal of Criminal Law and Criminology*, 48, 1958, pp. 619–22; Galaway, B. and Hudson, J. (1972) 'Restitution and Rehabilitation – Some Central Issues', *Crime and Delinquency*, 18, pp. 403–10.
27 Smith, pp. 13–29.
28 An economist who favors restitution on efficiency grounds is Gary S. Becker, although he does not break with the paradigm of punishment. Those interested in a mathematical 'cost-benefit' analysis should see his 'Crime and Punishment', *Journal of Political Economy*, 76, 1968, pp. 169–217.
29 This point is also made by Minocher Jehangirji Sethna in his paper, 'Treatment and Atonement for Crime', in Viano, E.C. (ed.) *Victims and Society* (Washington, DC: Visage Press, 1976), p. 538.
30 Del Vecchio, p. 198.
31 McDonald, W.F. (1976) 'Towards a Bicentennial Revolution in Criminal Justice: The Return of the Victim', *American Criminal Law Review*, 13, p. 659; see also his paper 'Notes on the Victim's Role in the Prosecutional and Dispositional Stages of the Criminal Justice Process' (presented at the Second International Symposium on Victimology, Boston, September, 1976); Kress, J.M. (1976) 'The Role of the Victim at Sentencing.' Paper presented at the Second International Symposium on Victimology, Boston, September.
32 McDonald, pp. 669–73; Kress, pp. 11–15. Kress specifically analyzes restitution as a means for achieving victim involvement.
33 Yochelson and Samenow, pp. 453–57.

6 Restorative justice and a better future

John Braithwaite

Imagine two robbers

A teenager is arrested in Halifax for a robbery. The police send him to court where he is sentenced to six months' incarceration. As a victim of child abuse, he is both angry with the world and alienated from it. During his period of confinement he acquires a heroin habit and suffers more violence. He comes out more desperate and alienated than when he went in, sustains his drug habit for the next 20 years by stealing cars, burgles dozens of houses and pushes drugs to others until he dies in a gutter, a death no one mourns. Probably someone rather like that was arrested in Halifax today, perhaps more than one.

Tomorrow another teenager, Sam, is arrested in Halifax for a robbery. He is a composite of several Sams I have seen. The police officer refers Sam to a facilitator who convenes a restorative justice conference. When the facilitator asks about his parents, Sam says he is homeless. His parents abused him and he hates them. Sam refuses to cooperate with a conference if they attend. After talking with his parents, the facilitator agrees that perhaps it is best not to involve the parents. What about grandparents? No, they are dead. Brothers and sisters? No, he hates his brothers too. Sam's older sister, who was always kind to him, has long since left home. He has no contact with her. Aunts and uncles? Not keen on them either, because they would always put him down as the black sheep of the family and stand by his parents. Uncle George was the only one he ever had any time for, but he has not seen him for years. Teachers from school? Hates them all. Sam has dropped out. They always treated him like dirt. The facilitator does not give up: 'No one ever treated you okay at school?' Well, the hockey coach is the only one Sam can ever think of being fair to him. So the hockey coach, Uncle George and older sister are tracked down by the facilitator and invited to the conference along with the robbery victim and her daughter, who comes along to support the victim through the ordeal.

These six participants sit on chairs in a circle. The facilitator starts by introducing everyone and reminding Sam that while he has admitted to the robbery, he can change his plea at any time during the conference and have the matter heard by a court. Sam is asked to explain what happened in his own words. He mumbles that he needed money to survive, saw the lady, knocked her over and ran off with her purse. Uncle George is asked what he thinks of this. He says that Sam used to be a good kid. But Sam had gone off the rails. He had let his parents down so badly that they would not even come today. 'And now you have done this to this poor lady. I never thought you would stoop to violence,' continues Uncle George, building into an angry tirade against the boy. The hockey coach also says he is surprised that Sam could do something as terrible as this. Sam was always a troublemaker at school. But he could see a kindly side in Sam that left him shocked about the violence. The sister is invited to speak, but the facilitator moves on to the victim when Sam's sister seems too emotional to speak.

The victim explains how much trouble she had to cancel the credit cards in the purse, how she had no money for the shopping she needed to do that day. Her daughter explains that the most important consequence of the crime was that her mother was now afraid to go out on her own. In particular, she is afraid that Sam is stalking her, waiting to rob her again. Sam sneers at this and seems callous throughout. His sister starts to sob. Concerned about how distressed she is, the facilitator calls a brief adjournment so she can comfort her, with help from Uncle George. During the break, the sister reveals that she understands what Sam has been through. She says she was abused by their parents as well. Uncle George has never heard of this, is shocked, and not sure that he believes it.

When the conference reconvenes, Sam's sister speaks to him with love and strength. Looking straight into his eyes, the first gaze he could not avoid in the conference, she says that she knows exactly what he has been through with their parents. No details are spoken. But the victim seems to understand what is spoken of by the knowing communication between sister and brother. Tears rush down the old woman's cheeks and over a trembling mouth.

It is his sister's love that penetrates Sam's callous exterior. From then on he is emotionally engaged with the conference. He says he is sorry about what the victim has lost. He would like to pay it back, but has no money or job. He assures the victim he is not stalking her. She readily accepts this now and when questioned by the facilitator says now she thinks she will feel safe walking out alone. She wants her money back but says it will help her if they can talk about what to do to help Sam find a home and a job. Sam's sister says he can come and live in her house for a while. The hockey coach says he has some casual work that needs to be done, enough to pay Sam's debt to the victim and a bit more. If Sam does a good job, he will write him a reference for applications for permanent jobs. When the conference breaks up, the victim hugs Sam and tearfully wishes him good luck. He apologises again. Uncle George quietly slips a hundred dollars to Sam's sister to defray the extra cost of having Sam in the house, says he will be there for both of them if they need him.

Sam has a rocky life punctuated by several periods of unemployment. A year later he has to go through another conference after he steals a bicycle. But he finds work when he can, mostly stays out of trouble and lives to mourn at the funerals of Uncle George and his sister. The victim gets her money back and enjoys taking long walks alone. Both she and her daughter say that they feel enriched as a result of the conference, have a little more grace in their lives.

I will return to the meanings of this story.

Institutional collapse

Few sets of institutional arrangements created in the West since the industrial revolution have been as large a failure as the criminal justice system. In theory it administers just, proportionate corrections that deter. In practice, it fails to correct or deter, just as often making things worse as better. It is a criminal *injustice* system that systematically turns a blind eye to crimes of the powerful, while imprisonment remains the best-funded labour market programme for the unemployed and indigenous peoples. It pretends to be equitable, yet one offender may be sentenced to a year in a prison where he will be beaten on reception and then systematically bashed thereafter, raped, even infected with AIDS, while others serve 12 months in comparatively decent premises, especially if they are whitecollar criminals.

While I do believe that Canada's criminal justice system is more decent than ours in Australia, all Western criminal justice systems are brutal, institutionally vengeful, and dishonest to their stated intentions. The interesting question is why are they such failures.

Given that prisons are vicious and degrading places, you would expect fear of ending up in them would deter crime.

There are many reasons for the failures of the criminal justice system to prevent crime. I will give you just one, articulated in the terms of my theory in *Crime, Shame and Reintegration.*[1] The claim of this theory is that the societies that have the lowest crime rates are the societies that shame criminal conduct most effectively. There is an important difference between reintegrative shaming and stigmatization. While reintegrative shaming prevents crime, stigmatization is a kind of shaming that makes crime problems worse. Stigmatization is the kind of shaming that creates outcasts; it is disrespectful, humiliating. Stigmatization means treating criminals as evil people who have done evil acts. Reintegrative shaming means disapproving of the evil of the deed while treating the person as essentially good. Reintegrative shaming means strong disapproval of the act but doing so in a way that is respecting of the person. Once we understand this distinction, we can see why putting more police on the street can actually increase crime. More police can increase crime if they are systematically stigmatizing in the way they deal with citizens. More police can reduce crime if they are systematically reintegrative in the way they deal with citizens.

We can also understand why building more prisons could make the crime problem worse. Having more people in prison does deter some and incapacitates others from committing certain crimes, like bank robberies, because there are no banks inside the prison for them to rob, though there certainly are plenty of vulnerable people to rape and pillage. But because prisons stigmatize, they also make things worse for those who have criminal identities affirmed by imprisonment, those whose stigmatization leads them to find solace in the society of the similarly outcast, those who are attracted into criminal subcultures, those who treat the prison as an educational institution for learning new skills for the illegitimate labour market. On this account, whether building more prisons reduces or increases the crime rate depends on whether the stigmatizing nature of a particular prison system does more to increase crime than its deterrent and incapacitative effects reduce it.

A lack of theoretical imagination among criminologists has been one underrated reason for the failure of the criminal justice system. Without theorizing why it fails, the debate has collapsed to a contest between those who want more of the same to make it work and those who advance the implausible position that it makes sense to stigmatize people first and later subject them to rehabilitation programmes inside institutions. With juvenile justice in particular, the debate [...] has see-sawed between the justice model and the welfare model. See-sawing between retribution and rehabilitation has got us nowhere. If we are serious about a better future, we need to hop off this see-saw and strike out in search of a third model.

For me, that third model is restorative justice. During the past decade a number of different labels – reconciliation (Dignan,[2] Marshall,[3] Umbreit[4]), peacemaking (Pepinsky and Quinney[5]), redress (de Haan[6]) – have described broadly similar intellectual currents. Philip Pettit and I have sought to argue for republican criminal justice (Braithwaite and Pettit,[7] Pettit with Braithwaite[8]). Yet the label that has secured by far the widest consent during the past few years has been that employed by Zehr,[9] Galaway and Hudson,[10] Cragg,[11] Walgrave,[12] Bazemore,[13] Umbreit,[14] Consedine,[15] Peters and Aertsen,[16] Messmer and Otto,[17] Marshall,[18] McElrea,[19] McCold,[20] Maxwell,[21] Carbonatto,[22] Crawford, Strong, Sargeant, Souryal and Van Ness,[23] Denison,[24] Knopp,[25] Mackey,[26] Morrell,[27] Van Ness[28] and Young[29] – restorative justice. It has become the slogan of a global social movement. For those of us who see constructive engagement with social movement politics as crucial for major change, labels that carry meaning for activists matter. In this spirit, I now wish that I had called reintegrative shaming restorative shaming.

What is restorative justice?

Restorative justice means restoring victims, a more victim-centred criminal justice system, as well as restoring offenders and restoring community. First, what does restoring victims mean? It means restoring the *property loss* or the *personal injury*, repairing the broken window or the broken teeth (see Table 6.1). It means restoring a *sense of security*. Even victims of property crimes such as burglary often suffer a loss of security when the private space of their home is violated. When the criminal justice system fails to leave women secure about walking alone at night, half the population is left unfree in a rather fundamental sense.

Victims suffer loss of dignity when someone violates their bodies or shows them the disrespect of taking things which are precious to them. Sometimes this disrespectful treatment engenders victim shame: 'He abused me rather than some other woman because I am trash', 'She stole my dad's car because I was irresponsible to park it in such a risky place'. Victim shame often triggers a shame–rage spiral wherein victims reciprocate indignity with indignity through vengeance or by their own criminal acts.

Disempowerment is part of the indignity of being a victim of crime. According to Pettit and Braithwaite's republican theory of criminal justice,[30] a wrong should not be defined as a crime unless it involves some domination of us that reduces our freedom to enjoy life as we choose. It follows that it is important to *restore any lost sense of empowerment* as a result of crime. This is particularly important where the victim suffers structurally systematic domination. For example, some of the most important restorative justice initiatives we have seen in Australia have involved some thousands of Aboriginal victims of consumer fraud by major insurance companies.[31] In these cases, victims from remote Aboriginal communities relished the power of being able to demand restoration and corporate reform from 'white men in white shirts'.

The way that Western legal systems handle crime compounds the disempowerment that victims feel, first at the hands of offenders and then at the hands of a professional, remote justice system that eschews their participation. The lawyers, in the words of Nils Christie 'steal our conflict'.[32] The western criminal justice system has, on balance, been corrosive of deliberative democracy, though the jury is one institution that has preserved a modicum of it. Restorative justice is deliberative justice; it is about people deliberating over the consequences of a crime, how to deal with them and prevent their recurrence. This contrasts with the professional justice of lawyers deciding which rules apply to a case and then constraining their deliberation within a technical discourse about that rule–application. So restorative justice restores the *deliberative control of justice by citizens.*

Table 6.1 What does restoring victims mean?

Restoring victims
- Restore property loss
- Restore injury
- Restore sense of security
- Restore dignity
- Restore sense of empowerment
- Restore deliberative democracy
- Restore harmony based on a feeling that justice has been done
- Restore social support

Restorative justice aims to *restore harmony based on a feeling that justice has been done.* Restorative harmony alone, while leaving an underlying injustice to fester unaddressed, is not enough. 'Restoring balance' is only acceptable as a restorative justice ideal if the 'balance' between offender and victim that prevailed before the crime was a morally decent balance. There is no virtue in restoring the balance by having a woman pay for a loaf of bread she has stolen from a rich man to feed her children. Restoring harmony between victim and offender is only likely to be possible in such a context on the basis of a discussion of why the children are hungry and what should be done about the underlying injustice of their hunger.

Restorative justice cannot resolve the deep structural injustices that cause problems like hunger. But we must demand two things of restorative justice here. First, it must not make structural injustice worse (in the way, for example, that the Australian criminal justice system does by being an important cause of the unemployability and oppression of Aboriginal people). Indeed, we should hope from restorative justice for micro-measures that ameliorate macro-injustice where this is possible. Second, restorative justice should restore harmony with a remedy grounded in dialogue which takes account of underlying injustices. Restorative justice does not resolve the age-old questions of what should count as unjust outcomes. It is a more modest philosophy than that. It settles for the procedural requirement that the parties talk until they feel that harmony has been restored on the basis of a discussion of all the injustices they see as relevant to the case.

Finally, restorative justice aims to *restore social support.* Victims of crime need support from their loved ones during the process of requesting restoration. They sometimes need encouragement and support to engage with deliberation toward restoring harmony. Friends sometimes do blame the victim, or more commonly are frightened off by a victim going through an emotional trauma. Restorative justice aims to institutionalize the gathering around of friends during a time of crisis.

Restoring offenders, restoring community

In most cases, a more limited range of types of restoration is relevant to offenders. Offenders have generally not suffered property loss or injury as a result of their own crime, though sometimes loss or injury is a cause of the crime. Dignity, however, is generally in need of repair after the shame associated with arrest. When there is a victim who has been hurt, there is no dignity in denying that there is something to be ashamed about. Dignity is generally best restored by confronting the shame, accepting responsibility for the bad consequences suffered by the victim and apologizing with sincerity.[33] A task of restorative justice is to institutionalize such *restoration of dignity* for offenders.

The sense of insecurity and disempowerment of offenders is often an issue in their offending and in discussion about what is to be done to prevent further offending. Violence by young men from racial minorities is sometimes connected to their feelings of being victims of racism. For offenders, *restoring a sense of security and empowerment* is often bound up with employment, the feeling of having a future, achieving some educational success, sporting success, indeed any kind of success.

Many patches are needed to sew the quilt of deliberative democracy. Criminal justice deliberation is not as important a patch as deliberation in the parliament, in trade unions, even in universities. But to the extent that restorative justice deliberation does lead ordinary citizens into serious democratic discussion about racism, unemployment, masculinist cultures in local schools and police accountability, it is not an unimportant element of a deliberatively rich democracy.

The mediation literature shows that satisfaction of complainants with the justice of the mediation is less important than the satisfaction of those who are complained against in achieving mutually beneficial outcomes.[34] Criminal subcultures are memory files that collect injustices.[35] Crime problems will continue to become deeply culturally embedded in western societies until we reinvent criminal justice as a process that restores a sense of procedural justice to offenders.[36]

Finally, Frank Cullen[37] has suggested that there could be no better organizing concept for criminology than *social support,* given the large volume of evidence about the importance of social support for preventing crime. The New Zealand Maori people see our justice system as barbaric because of the way it requires the defendant to stand alone in the dock without social support. In Maori thinking, civilized justice requires the offender's loved ones to stand beside him during justice rituals, sharing the shame for what has happened. Hence the shame the offender feels is more the shame of letting his loved ones down than a western sense of individual guilt that can eat away at a person. The shame of letting loved ones down can be readily transcended by simple acts of forgiveness from those loved ones.

Restoring community is advanced by a proliferation of restorative justice rituals in which social support around specific victims and offenders is restored. At this micro level, restorative justice is an utterly bottom-up approach to restoring community. At a meso level, important elements of a restorative justice package are initiatives to foster community organization in schools, neighbourhoods, ethnic communities, churches, [and] through professions... who can deploy restorative justice in their self-regulatory practices. At a macro level, we must better design institutions of deliberative democracy so that concern about issues like unemployment and the effectiveness of labour market programmes have a channel through which they can flow from discussions about local injustices up into national economic policy-making debate.

The universality of restorative traditions

I have yet to discover a culture which does not have some deep-seated restorative traditions. Nor is there a culture without retributive traditions. Retributive traditions once had survival value. Cultures which were timid in fighting back were often wiped out by more determinedly violent cultures. In the contemporary world, as opposed to the world of our biological creation, retributive emotions have less survival value. Because risk management is institutionalized in this modern world, retributive emotions are more likely to get us into trouble than out of it, as individuals, groups and nations.

The message we might communicate to all cultures is that in the world of the twenty-first century, you will find your restorative traditions a more valuable resource than your retributive traditions. Yet sadly, the hegemonic cultural forces in the contemporary world communicate just the opposite message. Hollywood hammers the message that the way to deal with bad guys is through violence. Political leaders frequently hammer the same message. Yet many of our spiritual leaders are helping us to retrieve our restorative traditions – the Dalai Lama, for example. Archbishop Desmond Tutu in his Forward [sic] to Jim Consedine's new edition of *Restorative Justice,* correctly sees a 'very ancient yet desperately needed truth' as underlying restorative justice processes 'rooted as they are in all indigenous cultures, including those of Africa'. He sees his Truth and Reconciliation Commission as an example of restorative justice.

All of the restorative values in Table 6.1 are cultural universals. All cultures value repair of damage to our persons and property, security, dignity, empowerment, deliberative democracy, harmony based on a sense of justice and social support. They are universals because they are all vital to our emotional survival as human beings and vital to the possibility of surviving without constant fear of violence. The world's great religions recognize that the desire to pursue these restorative justice values is universal, which is why some of our spiritual leaders are a hope against those political leaders who wish to rule through fear and by crushing deliberative democracy. Ultimately, those political leaders will find that they will have to reach an accommodation with the growing social movement for restorative justice, just as they must with the great religious movements they confront. Why? Because the evidence is now strong that ordinary citizens like restorative justice.[38] When the major political parties did their door-knocking during our last election in Canberra, they found that the thousands of citizens who had participated in a restorative justice conference mostly liked the justice they experienced.

It is true that the virtues restorative justice restores are viewed differently in different cultures and that opinion about the culturally appropriate ways of realizing them differ greatly. Hence, restorative justice must be a culturally diverse social movement that accommodates a rich plurality of strategies in pursuit of the truths it holds to be universal. It is about different cultures joining hands as they discover the profound commonalities of their experience of the human condition; it is about cultures learning from each other on the basis of that shared experience; it is about realising the value of diversity, of preserving restorative traditions that work because they are embedded in a cultural past. Scientific criminology will never discover any universally best way of doing restorative justice. The best path is the path of cultural plurality in pursuit of the culturally shared restorative values in Table 6.1.

A path to culturally plural justice

A restorative justice research agenda to pursue this path has two elements:

1. *Culturally specific investigation of how to save and revive the restorative justice practices that remain in all societies.*
2. *Culturally specific investigation of how to transform state criminal justice both by making it more restorative and by rendering its abuses of power more vulnerable to restorative justice.*

On the first point, I doubt that neighbourhoods in our cities are replete with restorative justice practices that can be retrieved, though there are some. Yet in the more micro context of the nuclear family, the evidence is overwhelming from the metropolitan US that restorative justice is alive and well and that families who are more restorative are likely to have less delinquent children than families who are punitive and stigmatizing.[39]

Because families so often slip into stigmatization and brutalization of their difficult members, we need restorative justice institutionalized in a wider context that can engage and restore such families. In most societies, the wider contexts where the ethos and rituals of restorative justice are alive and ready to be piped into the wider streams of the society are schools, churches and remote indigenous communities. If it is hard to find restorative justice in the disputing practices of our urban neighbourhoods, the experience of recent years has been that they are relatively easy to locate in urban schools.[40] This is because of the ethos of care and integration which is part of the western educational ideal (which, at its best, involves a total rejection of stigmatization) and because the interaction among the members of a school community tends to be more intense than the interaction among urban neighbours.

Schools, like families, have actually become more restorative and less retributive than the brutal institutions of the nineteenth century. This is why we have seen very successful restorative conferencing programmes in contemporary schools.[41] We have also seen anti-bullying programmes with what I would call a restorative ethos which have managed in some cases to halve bullying in schools.[42]

More of the momentum for the restorative justice movement has come from the world's churches than from any other quarter. Even in a nation like Indonesia where the state has such tyrannical power, the political imperative to allow some separation of church and state has left churches as enclaves where restorative traditions could survive. Religions like Islam and Christianity have strong retributive traditions as well, of course, though they have mostly been happy to leave it to the state to do the 'dirty work' of temporal retribution.

When I spoke at a conference on restorative justice in Indonesia last month, I was struck in a conversation with three Indonesians – one Muslim, one Hindu and one Christian – that in ways I could not understand as an agnostic, each was drawing on a spirituality grounded in their religious experience to make sense of restorative justice. Similarly, I was moved by the spirituality of Cree approaches to restorative justice when a number of native Canadians visited Canberra [...]. There is something important to learn about native American spirituality and how it enriches restorative justice. It seems clear to me that it does enrich it, but I do not understand how. [...]

[...] Canadian indigenous communities are a cultural resource for the whole world. Because they have not been totally swamped by the justice codes of the West, they are a cultural resource, just as the biodiversity of [the North American] continent supplies the entire world a genetic resource. The very people who by virtue of their remoteness have succumbed least to the Western justice model, who have been insulated from Hollywood a little more and for a little longer, the very people who are most backward in Western eyes, are precisely those with the richest cultural resources from which the restorative justice movement can learn.

Important scholarly work is being done to unlock the cultural codes of restorative justice in [Canadian] indigenous communities. 'Healing circles', what a profound cultural code that is to unlock for the rest of the world.[43] How much we all have to learn from the experience of the Hollow Water community in dealing with an epidemic of child abuse through healing circles. Therese Lajeunesse's report on Hollow Water is already a wonderful resource for the world.[44] Joan Pennell and Gale Burford[45] have done a splendid job in their reports which document the conferences for dealing with family violence in Newfoundland, which are quite distinctive from, and doubtless in some ways superior to, the conferencing models we have applied in the Southern Hemisphere. I have already remonstrated with them about the need to pull all this illuminating research together into a book that can also have a massive effect internationally, as could a book on Hollow Water. So point 1 of the reform agenda of restorative justice is a research programme to retrieve the restorative justice practices of not only native communities, but also of the schools and churches of dominant urban cultures. Scholars like Carol LaPrairie and Don Clairmont are among the Canadian scholars who are doing vital work in advancing point 1 of this agenda.

Point 2 of the agenda is to explore how to transform state criminal justice. In our multicultural cities I have said that we cannot rely on spontaneous ordering of justice in our neighbourhoods. There we must be more reliant on state reformers as catalysts of a new urban restorative justice. In our cities, where neighbourhood social support is least, where the loss from the statist takeover of disputing is more damaging, the gains that can be secured from restorative justice reform are greatest. When a police officer with a restorative justice ethos arrests a youth in a tightly knit rural community who lives in a loving family, who enjoys social support from a caring school and church, that police officer is not likely to do much better or worse by the child than a police officer who does not have a restorative justice ethos. Whatever the police do, the child's support network will probably sort the problem out so that serious reoffending does not occur. But when a police officer with a restorative justice ethos arrests a homeless child in the metropolis like Sam, who hates parents who abused him, who has dropped out of school and is seemingly alone in the world, it is there that the restorative police officer can make a difference that will render him more effective in preventing crime than the retributive police officer. At least that is my hypothesis, one we can test empirically and are testing empirically.

In the alienated urban context where community is not spontaneously emergent in a satisfactory way, a criminal justice system aimed at restoration can construct a community of care around a specific offender or a specific victim who is in trouble. That is what the story of Sam is about. With the restorative justice conferences being convened in multicultural metropolises like Auckland, Adelaide, Sydney and Singapore, the selection principle as to who is invited to the conference is the opposite to that with a criminal trial. We invite to a criminal trial those who can inflict most damage on the other side. With a conference we invite those who might offer most support to their own side – Sam's sister, uncle and hockey coach, the victim's daughter.

In terms of the theory of reintegrative shaming, the rationale for who is invited to the conference is that the presence of those on the victim side structures shame into the conference, the presence of supporters on the offender's side structures reintegration into the ritual. Conferences can be run in many different ways from the story of Sam's conference. Maori people in New Zealand tend to want to open and close their conferences with a prayer. The institutions of restorative justice we build in the city must be culturally plural, quite different from one community to another depending on the culture of the people involved. It is the empowerment principle of restorative justice that makes this possible – empowerment with process control.

From a restorative perspective, the important thing is that we have institutions in civil society which confront serious problems like violence rather than sweep them under the carpet, yet do so in a way that is neither retributive nor stigmatizing. Violence will not be effectively controlled by communities unless the shamefulness of violence is communicated. This does not mean that we need criminal justice institutions that set out to maximize shame. On the contrary, if we set out to do that we risk the creation of stigmatizing institutions.[46] All we need do is nurture micro-institutions of deliberative democracy that allow citizens to discuss the consequences of criminal acts, who is responsible, who should put them right and how. Such deliberative processes naturally enable those responsible to confront and deal with the shame arising from what has happened. And if we get the invitation list right by inviting along people who enjoy maximum respect and trust on both the offender and victim side, then we maximize the chances that shame will be dealt with in a reintegrative way.

[...]

Beyond communitarianism versus individualism

Some criminologists in the West are critical of countries like Singapore, Indonesia and Japan where crime in the streets is not a major problem because they think individualism in these societies is crushed by communitarianism or collective obligation. Their prescription is that

Asian societies need to shift the balance away from communitarianism and allow greater individualism. I don't find that a very attractive analysis.

Some Asian criminologists are critical of countries like the US and Australia because they think these societies are excessively individualistic, suffering much crime and incivility as a result. According to this analysis, the West needs to shift the balance away from individualism in favour of communitarianism, shift the balance away from rights and toward collective responsibilities. I don't find that a very attractive analysis either.

Both sides of this debate can do a better job of learning from each other. We can aspire to a society that is strong on rights and strong on responsibilities, that nurtures strong communities and strong individuals. Indeed, in the good society strong communities constitute strong individuals and vice versa. Our objective can be to keep the benefits of the statist revolution at the same time as we rediscover community-based justice. Community justice is often oppressive of rights, often subjects the vulnerable to the domination of local elites, subordinates women, can be procedurally unfair and tends to neglect structural solutions. Mindful of this, we might reframe the two challenges posed earlier [...]:

1. *Helping indigenous community justice to learn from the virtues of liberal statism – procedural fairness, rights, protecting the vulnerable from domination.*
2. *Helping liberal state justice to learn from indigenous community justice – learning the restorative community alternatives to individualism.*

This reframed agenda resonates with the writings of Canadians such as Donald Clairmont[47] and Marianne Nielsen, who writes that native communities 'will have the opportunity of taking the best of the old, the best of the new and learning from others' mistakes so that they can design a system that may well turn into a flagship of social change'.[48] Together these two questions ask how we save and revive traditional restorative justice practices in a way that helps them become procedurally fairer, in a way that respects fundamental human rights, that secures protection against domination? The liberal state can be a check on oppressive collectivism, just as bottom-up communitarianism can be a check on oppressive individualism. A healing circle can be a corrective to a justice system that can leave offenders and victims suicidally alone; a Charter of Rights and Freedoms a check on a tribal elder who imposes a violent tyranny on young people. The bringing together of these ideals is an old prescription – not just liberty, not just community, but liberté, egalité, fraternité. Competitive individualism has badly fractured this republican amalgam. The social movement for restorative justice does practical work to weld an amalgam that is relevant to the creation of contemporary urban multicultural republics. Day to day it is not sustained by romantic ideals in which I happen to believe like deliberative democracy. They want to do it for Sam and for an old woman who Sam pushed over one day. That is what enlists them to the social movement for restorative justice; in the process they are, I submit, enlisted into something of wider political significance.

Notes

1 Braithwaite, J. (1989) *Crime, Shame and Reintegration* (Cambridge: Cambridge University Press).
2 Dignan, J. (1992) 'Repairing the Damage: Can Reparation Work in the Service of Diversion?', *British Journal of Criminology,* 32, pp. 453–72.
3 Marshall, T.F. (1985) *Alternatives to Criminal Courts* (Aldershot: Gower).

4 Umbreit, M. (1985) *Crime and Reconciliation: Creative Options for Victims and Offenders* (Nashville, TN: Abington Press).

5 Pepinsky, H.E. and Quinney, R. (1991) *Criminology as Peacemaking* (Bloomington, IN: Indiana University Press).

6 de Haan, W. (1990) *The Politics of Redress: Crime, Punishment and Penal Abolition* (London: Unwin Hyman).

7 Braithwaite, J. and Pettit, P. (1990) *Not Just Deserts: A Republican Theory of Criminal Justice* (Oxford: Oxford University Press).

8 Pettit, P. with Braithwaite, J. (1993) 'Not Just Deserts Even in Sentencing', *Current Issues in Criminal Justice,* 4, pp. 225–39.

9 Zehr, H. (1990) *Changing Lenses: A New Focus for Criminal Justice* (Scottdale, PA: Herald Press); Zehr, H. (1985) 'Retributive Justice, Restorative Justice'. *New Perspectives on Crime and Justice. Occasional Papers of the MCC Canada Victim Offender Ministries Program and the MCC US Office of Criminal Justice,* 4, September.

10 Galaway, B. and Hudson, J. (1990) *Criminal Justice, Restitution and Reconciliation* (Monsey, NY: Criminal Justice Press); Galaway, B. and Hudson, J. (eds) *Restorative Justice: International Perspectives* (Monsey, NY: Criminal Justice Press).

11 Cragg, W. (1992) *The Practice of Punishment: Towards a Theory of Restorative Justice* (London: Routledge).

12 Walgrave, L. (1995) 'Restorative Justice for Juveniles: Just a Technique or a Fully Fledged Alternative?' *The Howard Journal,* 34:3, pp. 228–49; Walgrave, L. (1993) 'In Search of Limits to the Restorative Justice for Juveniles'. Unpublished paper presented to the International Congress on Criminology, Budapest, 23–27 August.

13 Bazemore, G. (1993) *Balanced and Restorative Justice for Juvenile Offenders: An Overview of a New OJJDP Initiative* (Washington, DC: Office of Juvenile Justice and Delinquency Prevention).

14 Umbreit, M. (1995) 'Holding Juvenile Offenders Accountable: A Restorative Justice Perspective', *Juvenile and Family Court Journal,* Spring, pp. 31–42; Umbreit, M. (1994) *Victim Meets Offender: The Impact of Restorative Justice and Mediation* (Monsey, NY: Willow Tree Press); Umbreit, M. (1989) 'Crime Victims Seeking Fairness, not Revenge: Towards Restorative Justice', *Federal Probation,* 53:3, pp. 52–7.

15 Consedine, J. (1995) *Restorative Justice: Healing the Effects of Crime* (Lyttleton, New Zealand: Ploughshares Publications).

16 Peters, T. and Aertsen, I. (1995) 'Restorative Justice: In Search of New Avenues in the Judicial Dealing with Crime: The Presentation of a Project of Mediation for Reparation', in Fijnaut, C. *et al.* (eds) *Changes in Society, Crime and Criminal Justice in Europe* (Antwerpen: Kluwer Law and Taxation Publishers).

17 Messmer, H. and Otto, H.U. (1992) 'Restorative Justice: Steps on the Way toward a Good Idea', in Messmer, H. and Otto, H.U. (eds) *Restorative Justice on Trial* (Dordrecht: Kluwer Academic).

18 Marshall, T. (1992) 'Grassroots Initiatives towards Restorative Justice: The New Paradigm?'. Unpublished paper for the Fulbright Colloquium, 'Penal Theory and Penal Practice', University of Stirling, September.

19 McElrea, F.W.M. (1994) 'Restorative Justice – the New Zealand Youth Court: A Model for Development in other Courts', *Journal of Judicial Administration,* 4:1, pp. 33–54.

20 McCold, P. (1995) 'Restorative Justice and the Role of Community.' Unpublished paper presented to the Academy of Criminal Justice Sciences annual conference, Boston, March.

21 Maxwell, G. (1995) 'Some Traditional Models of Restorative Justice from Canada, South Africa and Gaza', in McElrea, F.W.M. (ed.) *Rethinking Criminal Justice. Vol. 1. Justice in the Community* (Auckland: Legal Research Foundation).

22 Carbonatto, H. (1995) *Expanding Options for Spousal Abuse: The Use of Restorative Justice. Occasional Papers in Criminology: New Series* 4 (Wellington: Institute of Criminology).

23 Crawford, T., Strong, K., Sargeant, K., Souryal, C. and Van Ness, D. (1990) *Restorative Justice: Principles* (Washington, DC: Justice Fellowship).

24 Denison, K. (1991) *Restorative Justice in Ourselves: New Perspectives on Crime and Justice* (Issue 11) (Akron, PA: Mennonite Central Committee Office of Criminal Justice).

25 Knopp, F.H. (1992) 'Restorative Justice for Juvenile Sex Offenders.' Paper presented to the National Council of Juvenile and Family Court Judges, Lake Tahoe/Reno, 16 November.

26 Mackey, V. (1990) *Restorative Justice: Towards Nonviolence* (Louisville, KY: Presbyterian Criminal Justice Program, Presbyterian Church (USA)).

27 Morrell, V. (1993) 'Restorative Justice: An Overview', *Criminal Justice Quarterly*, 5, pp. 3–7.

28 Van Ness, D. (1993) 'New Wine and Old Wineskins: Four Challenges of Restorative Justice', *Criminal Law Forum*, 4, pp. 251–76.

29 Young, M. (1995) *Restorative Community Justice: A Call to Action* (Washington, DC: National Organization for Victim Assistance).

30 Pettit, P. and Braithwaite, J. (1990) *Not Just Deserts: A Republican Theory of Criminal Justice* (Oxford: Oxford University Press).

31 See Fisse, B. and Braithwaite, J. (1993) *Corporations, Crime and Accountability* (Cambridge: Cambridge University Press), pp. 218–23.

32 Christie, N. (1978) 'Conflicts as Property', *British Journal of Criminology*, 17, pp. 1–15.

33 On this issue, I find the work of Tom Scheff and Suzanne Retzinger on by-passed shame illuminating. Scheff, T. and Retzinger, S. (1991) *Emotions and Violence: Shame and Rage in Destructive Conflicts* (Lexington, MA: Lexington Books).

34 Pruitt, D.G. (1995) 'Research Report: Process and Outcome in Community Mediation', *Negotiation Journal*, October, pp. 365–77, at p. 374.

35 Matza, D. (1964) *Delinquency and Drift* (New York, NY: Wiley), p. 102.

36 Tyler, T. (1990) *Why People Obey the Law* (New Haven, CT: Yale University Press).

37 Cullen, F.T. (1994) 'Social Support as an Organizing Concept for Criminology: Presidential Address to the Academy of Criminal Justice Sciences', *Justice (Quarterly*, 11:4, pp. 527–59.

38 See, for example, Morris, A. and Maxwell, G. (1992) 'Juvenile Justice in New Zealand: A New Paradigm', *Australian and New Zealand Journal of Criminology*, 26, pp. 72–90; Hyndman, M., Thorsborne, M. and Wood, S. (1996) *Community Accountability Conferencing: Trial Report* (Department of Education, Queensland); Goodes, T. (1995) 'Victims and Family Conferences: Juvenile Justice in South Australia.' Unpublished paper; Moore, D. with Forsythe, L. (1995) *A New Approach to Juvenile Justice: An Evaluation of Family Conferencing in Wagga Wagga: A Report to the Criminology Research Council* (Wagga Wagga: The Centre for Rural Social Research); Clairmont, C. (1994) *Alternative Justice Issues for Aboriginal Justice* (Atlantic Institute of Criminology, November).

39 See the discussion of the evidence on this in Braithwaite, *Crime, Shame and Reintegration*, pp. 54–83.

40 Hyndman *et al., Community Accountability Conferencing*.

41 Ibid.

42 Olweus, D. (1994) 'Annotation: Bullying at School: Basic Facts and Effects of a School Based Intervention Program', *Journal of Child Psychology and Psychiatry*, 35, pp. 1171–90; Farrington, D.P. (1993) 'Understanding and Preventing Bullying', in Tonry, M. (ed.) *Crime and Justice: Annual Review of Research. Vol. 17* (Chicago: University of Chicago Press); Pitts, J. and Smith, P. (1995) *Preventing School Bullying. Police Research Group: Crime Detection and Prevention Series Paper* 63 (London: Home Office); Pepier, D.J., Craig, W., Ziegler, S. and Charach, A. (1993) 'A School-based Antibullying Intervention', in Tattum, D. (ed.) *Understanding and Managing Bullying* (London: Heinemann).

43 Melton, A.P. (1995) 'Indigenous Justice Systems and Tribal Society', *Judicature*, 79:3, pp. 12 and 33; Four Worlds Development Project (1984) *The Sacred Tree* (Alberta: Four Worlds Development Press).

44 Lajeunesse, T. (1993) *Community Holistic Circle Healing: Hollow Water First Nation* (Solicitor General Canada, Ministry Secretariat).

45 Burford, G. and Pennell, J. (1995) *Family Group Decision Making: New Roles for 'Old' Partners in Resolving Family Violence* (St Johns, Newfoundland: Memorial University of Newfoundland); Pennell, J. and Burford, G. (1994) 'Attending to Context: Family Group Decision Making in Canada', in Hudson, J. *et al.* (eds) *Family Group Conferences: Perspectives on Policy and Practice* (Monsey, NY: Criminal Justice Press); Pennell, J. and Burford, G. (1994) 'Widening the Circle: Family Group Decision Making', *Journal of Child and Youth Care*, 9:1, pp. 1–11; Burford, G. and Pennell, J. (forthcoming) 'Family Group Decision Making: An Innovation in Child and Family Welfare', in Galaway, B. and Hudson, J. (eds) *Child Welfare Systems: Canadian Research and Policy Implications*.

46 Retzinger, S. and Scheff, T. (1996) 'Strategy for Community Conferences: Emotions and Social Bonds', in Galaway, B. and Hudson, J. (eds) *Restorative Justice: International Perspectives* (Monsey, NY: Criminal Justice Press).

47 Clanmont, D. (1994) 'Alternative Justice Issues for Aboriginal Justice.' Unpublished Manuscript, Atlantic Institute of Criminology, November.

48 Nielsen, M. (1992) 'Criminal Justice and Native Self-Government', in Silverman, R. and Nielsen, M. (eds) *Aboriginal Peoples and Canadian Criminal Justice* (Toronto: Butterworths), p. 255.

Part B

Practices, applications and their rationales

Introduction

Part B contains a number of readings describing the core forms of restorative justice practice, contexts in which these practices have been applied, and problems to which they have been applied. The section starts with Dean E. Peachey's account of the now famous 'Kitchener Experiment' which began in 1974 and is regarded by many as the start of restorative justice. Peachey shows how a Mennonite probation officer, applying the pacifist ideas of that faith to responses to crime, initiated an experiment in which offenders met their victims and offered them restitution. In the early part of the experiment, the goal of reconciling victims and offenders emerged as the central purpose of this process. Later, however, other goals emerged: encouraging offenders to take responsibility for their behaviour; challenging the victims' stereotypes of offenders; empowering lay people (victims, offenders and community volunteers) in the criminal justice process. Such goals have since become core features of restorative justice discourse and practice, although somewhat ironically the notion that reconciliation should be the core goal of restorative processes was subsequently put in question.

Chapter 8 is an excerpt from Daniel Van Ness and Karen Strong's leading textbook on restorative justice. In this chapter they explain the idea of encounter, which they regard as one of the four cornerposts of a restorative approach to crime (the others being amends, reintegration and inclusion). Here, the major processes of restorative justice – viz. mediation, conferencing and circles – are introduced. Van Ness and Strong identify the key elements of all of these encounters: meeting, narrative, emotion, understanding and agreement. They point to the potential of these processes to move the relationship between victims and offenders from one of hostility towards one of reconciliation, whilst also acknowledging that complete reconciliation will be rare. Importantly, they then go on to discuss three strategic issues that need to be considered by those seeking to create schemes that enable victims and offenders to encounter each other outside the courtroom, and in particular the issue of accountability for the conduct and outcomes of such encounters.

In the following three excerpts the core restorative processes of mediation, conferencing and circles are analysed and discussed in depth. In Chapter 9, mediation scholars Robert Bush and Joseph Folger explore the promise of mediation. They challenge the most common way of viewing mediation, viz. as a process for producing voluntary settlement of disputes, and argue that it has much greater potential: to engender moral growth by generating two important effects which they call empowerment and recognition. For Bush and Folger, mediation practitioners need to recognise that its key benefit lies in the transformative power of the intervention itself and indeed that mediation has the potential to express a new and higher vision of life. In a similar vein, Suzanne Retzinger and Thomas Scheff argue, in Chapter 10, that conferencing should be thought of, not so much as a process for achieving agreements about material reparation, but as a process that can produce symbolic reparation. As sociologists who had previously undertaken pathbreaking microsociological research into the sociology of emotions, they observed a number of restorative conferences in Australia when this was still a relatively novel process. Their analysis of the play of emotions and social relationships during conferencing is still one of the most powerful explanatory accounts of the power of conferencing available and their related set of 'tactics' for removing impediments to symbolic reparation has had a significant impact on the development of the process itself. Kay Pranis describes a different set of restorative practices, viz. peacemaking circles, in Chapter 11. As with the processes described in the previous two chapters, Pranis suggests that peacemaking circles are not simply alternative means of deciding 'sentences' in criminal justice cases. Rather, their function is to enable members of the community to gather around a particular problem and create positive solutions and, in the very process of doing this, to build stronger communities. Hence, a common theme in accounts of the three core types of restorative justice encounter – mediation, conferencing and circles – is that we will fail to grasp their full potential if we think of them merely as vehicles for making decisions that are conventionally made by professionals in courts. Rather, their real value lies in their transformative power upon the lives of those who participate in them.

The peacemaking circles described by Pranis are particularly associated with the justice traditions of indigenous peoples of North America. To understand them, it is useful to look more broadly at these traditions. Hence, the next reading is about the Navajo peacemaker courts that were established as part of a broader struggle by Navajos to run their affairs in accordance with their own cultural traditions rather than in accordance with concepts, values and institutions imposed by the surrounding 'Anglo–European' culture. The ideas on which the peacemaker courts are based are described by two practitioners and advocates of Navajo peacemaking: Robert Yazzie and James W. Zion. One of the most distinctive features of the Navajo court, according to this account, is that there are no judges. Rather, Navajo justice is an 'egalitarian' process in which the parties to a dispute, with their relatives, assisted by a peacemaker, resolve things themselves. The aim is conciliation rather than to divide disputants into winners and losers. One of the main values of this account of Navajo peacemaking is that it demonstrates how far-reaching the implications of restorative justice are. A *radical* shift towards restorative justice would mean more than a shift in our forms of sanctioning criminal misconduct and more than a shift towards a more participatory justice procedure. Taken to its logical conclusion, it would mean a shift in our conception of law itself. As Yazzie and Zion's piece shows, examples of restorative justice from 'other cultures' are really examples of radically different notions of law.

The following readings explore the use of restorative processes within two institutional settings: prisons (Chapter 13) and the police (Chapter 14) and their applications to a range of specific problems such as gendered and racial violence (Chapter 15), hate crimes (Chapter 16) and historical injustice and mass political violence (Chapter 17). In Chapter 13, Kimmett Edgar and Tim Newell note the tensions between restorative justice and imprisonment, yet argue that the two need not be seen as incompatible opposites. If restorative justice is to be applicable to serious crimes, advocates and practitioners need to recognise and explore the potential for restorative justice in prisons, especially its potential for empowering prisoners to take responsibility for their actions and to make amends to their victims. However, one of the key ways in which restorative justice has proliferated has been through the growth of restorative cautioning schemes, whereby traditional police cautions are replaced by restorative cautions whereby the police seek to reintegrate offenders (in most schemes young offenders).

In Chapter 14, David O'Mahony and Jonathan Doak trace the emergence and growth of restorative cautioning in a number of countries, consider what the research evidence tells us about its effectiveness and the implications of that evidence, and look at the role of the victim in the process.

In Chapter 15, Julie Stubbs considers the controversy over what, if anything, restorative justice has to offer to victims of domestic violence and sexual assault. Offences of gendered violence are often excluded from restorative justice schemes. Stubbs explores both the reasons for this and the case for using restorative justice to promote victims' interests in cases of gendered violence. Importantly, she highlights developments that are needed – in the conception, theory and practice of restorative justice – if the case for restorative justice is to gain support. Interestingly, Stubbs explores the issues at stake in this debate through an exploration of responses to violence against women and children in indigenous communities. Another difficult area for restorative justice is hate crime or – as Coates, Umbreit and Vos put it in Chapter 16 – 'bias-motivated crimes and hate charged situations'. They report on a two-year study of the use of restorative justice dialogue to confront the presence and impact of hate within organisations and communities. The work of these authors represents their attempts to explore the full social potential of restorative justice – in this case focusing on its potential for replacing the hate that fuels violence within our societies with understanding and respect.

Exploration of the potential applications of restorative justice is taken further still in the final chapter of this section, in which Margaret Urban Walker explores the role restorative justice might play in repairing the harm caused by large-scale historical injustices and mass political violence. Walker starts by introducing existing ways of thinking about the issue of reparations for mass violence. Efforts to encourage reparation often run into an impasse as a result of conceptual, practical and political difficulties. Restorative justice, she suggests, may offer a more adequate and feasible way of imagining the task of reparation. Walker's essay is reproduced here partly as a challenge to those promoting restorative justice to think more deeply about the concept of moral repair – a concept which arguably lies at the very heart of restorative justice.

7   The Kitchener experiment

Dean E. Peachey

The Victim/Offender Reconciliation Program in Kitchener, Ontario, is frequently recognized as the forerunner of programmes that bring convicted offenders into face-to-face meetings with their victims to explore interpersonal reconciliation and build a plan for reparation (Alper and Nichols, 1981: 69–70; Umbreit [1989]).

Ideas and innovations sometimes have humble, and even unplanned beginnings. A Saturday night vandalism spree by a couple of intoxicated teenagers resentful of the local police in a small town called Elmira was hardly the making of headlines or criminal justice history. And when the two young men were subsequently apprehended and pleaded guilty on 28 May 1974 to twenty-two counts of wilful damage, they had no idea that their experiences would be told and retold as the 'Elmira Case' in countless articles, speeches, and conference presentations. They were simply instructed to return to court in July to receive their sentences, and they spent the next couple of months in their homes in Elmira, a few miles north of Kitchener, Ontario.

The probation officer who was assigned to prepare their pre-sentence reports was hardly a crusading reformer. But he was prone to dreaming about new ways of doing things. Mark Yantzi had worked in the probation office in Kitchener for five years, after being a full-time volunteer under a programme sponsored by the Mennonite Central Committee (MCC). To be so directly tied to a part of the criminal justice system was itself an experiment for him as a Mennonite: the church had traditionally maintained a separation from government affairs, and particularly from the legal system with its reliance on coercive power.

At a meeting of a committee that MCC had just convened to explore other forms of involvement with the criminal justice system, the recent vandalism case from Elmira was discussed. 'Wouldn't it be neat for these offenders to meet the victims?', Yantzi said to the group (Bender, 1985). As a member of the Mennonite church, which has maintained a strong pacifist tradition since its beginnings in the Protestant Reformation in the sixteenth century, Yantzi liked the practical peace-making implications of offenders and victims meeting each other. He then dismissed the idea, assuming that the judge would not even entertain such a notion.

Dave Worth, another participant in the meeting who worked for MCC, challenged Yantzi to give it a try. After struggling over whether to risk his reputation as a probation officer by suggesting something that had no basis in law, Yantzi accepted Worth's challenge. When he submitted his pre-sentence report to the judge, Yantzi enclosed a letter suggesting that 'there could be some therapeutic value in these two young men having to personally face up to the victims of their numerous offences'.

On the day the case was scheduled for sentencing, Worth and Yantzi met in chambers with Judge Gordon McConnell of Provincial Court to present their plan to him. The judge replied that he did not think it was possible for him to ask the offenders to meet the victims. Worth and Yantzi resigned themselves to the inevitable, and went into the courtroom to await the case. When the case was called, the judge ordered a one-month remand to allow time for the convicted pair to meet the victims and assess their losses, 'with the assistance of Dave Worth and Mark Yantzi'. As Worth recounts the scene:

> I don't know who was more surprised. I remember that Bill Morrison, the Crown Attorney, turned to look at us with a quizzical expression on his face (as if to say, what is this all about?). The two offenders certainly looked confused. The judge had a smile on his face. Mark and I looked at each other. Now what were we going to do? (Worth, 1986)

Accompanied by Worth and Yantzi, the two offenders (aged 18 and 19) retraced their steps from the night of vandalism. They visited each of the places where they had damaged property, slashed tyres, or broken windows. The circuit took them to private homes, two churches, and a beer store. The probation officer and the MCC representative simply stood by with their notepads while the two youths knocked on doors, explained who they were, and why they were there. In all they spoke to twenty-one victims (an additional victim had moved and could not be contacted) whose damages totalled $2189.04. Approximately half of that amount had already been covered by the victims' insurance policies, leaving $1065.12 in actual losses to the victims.

On 26 August the youths appeared in court and Yantzi reported to the judge what had happened. The judge ordered a $200 fine for each, and placed them on probation for eighteen months. Drawing on the information that was presented to him, the judge included as a term of the probation order that each youth should make restitution in an amount up to $550 to be paid to the victims as the probation officer arranged. Both the fine and the restitution were to be paid within three months.

Three months later the youths had visited all the victims and handed each a certified cheque for the amount of his or her loss. The experience of personally confronting the victims had been a difficult one for the two teenagers, but one that also had its rewards. One of them commented afterwards, 'I didn't quit because of my self-respect, and I didn't want to have to look over my shoulder all the time' (Yantzi and Worth, 1977).

On receiving the restitution payments, the victims expressed a wide variety of reactions, as reflected by the following comments:

> Thanks, I never expected to see that money. I think I'll spend it in a very special way to help somebody else.

> Thanks a lot. I was young, too, only some of us didn't get caught.

> Aren't you ashamed of yourself? You know this really isn't going to cover it all. Who is going to pay for all those trips to Guelph for parts? Who is going to pay when they raise my insurance premiums? I don't want anybody to go to jail, but you know I hope we don't ever have this problem with you again, or anybody else.
>
> (Yantzi and Worth, 1977)

This first experimental case identified issues that were to continue to haunt the concept throughout succeeding years: multiple victims with a range of personal responses, the involvement of insurance companies in restitution,[1] and the considerable time lapse between the occurrence of an offence and the completion of the restitution process. But the experiment was also successful beyond everyone's expectations.

Buoyed by their results, Worth, Yantzi, and the MCC committee continued to brainstorm ideas and refine the process upon which they had stumbled. Although they were unaware of anyone else who was conducting victim/offender meetings of this type, they were operating in a milieu that encouraged experimentation. The Elmira case occurred at a time when the Canadian Law Reform Commission was issuing a series of working papers on alternative ways of dealing with offenders, and the Ontario probation service was just beginning to promote community involvement in corrections.[2] Elsewhere a few groups were starting to promote restitution as a primary response to crime (e.g. Hudson and Galaway, 1977). Only a few years earlier the Columbus (Ohio) Night Prosecutor Program began operating as the widely publicized forerunner of numerous programmes in the United States to mediate minor disputes out of court.

The intuitive and experiential orientation of the Kitchener group distinguished them from some of these other initiatives. Yantzi and his colleagues did not work toward a defined set of objectives. Instead, they continued to experiment with a handful of cases, while they tried to understand what it was that they were attempting to do. When they eventually formulated a programme proposal in the summer of 1975, they used the name Victim/Offender Reconciliation Project. The name was awkward, but it deliberately reflected their emerging perspective on the work. *Reconciliation* between victims and offenders was becoming an important goal. The use of the term 'project' as compared to 'programme' also indicated a deliberate effort to remain fluid and avoid becoming settled into any particular mode of operation:

> We see ourselves as being continually involved in a process of refining our purpose and function. The project was not begun with a definitive plan, and it is still exploring new avenues of application. We are learning by our mistakes and successes and are moving slowly but steadily, making every effort to consult with and keep informed those persons affected directly or indirectly by our project.
>
> (Yantzi and Worth, 1977: 1)

The evolutionary nature of the project complicates the current task of chronicling its development. The Kitchener VORP has operated under three distinctly different organizational structures. Office forms and statistics kept by the project have moved through successive transformations, and the earliest information categories do not necessarily match current ones. For example, the probation base of the initiative in its early years meant that despite the avowed emphasis on meeting the needs of both victims and offenders, early records pertained almost entirely to offenders. Aside from some short-term research efforts, little is known about the victims in the first few years of the programme.

In late 1975 two people were hired as 'researchers' for seven months through a government employment programme. They worked under Yantzi's supervision, their principal methodology being participant observation, as they conducted and reflected on victim/offender meetings. During this phase VORP dealt with 61 offenders and 128 victims, mostly involving property-related offences. Forty-eight offenders met their victims and 46 of these reached an agreement and followed through on it.

Eventually some structures developed for the project. By 1977 one-half of Yantzi's workload as a probation officer was devoted to VORP. He was supervised in this work by a steering committee composed of representatives from probation, the MCC, and community volunteers. Although the project name highlighted reconciliation, the organizers increasingly saw VORP as a testing ground for several ideas. Meeting the victim face to face and repaying the losses were viewed as ways of encouraging offenders to take greater responsibility for their actions. Although victims received the concrete benefits of restitution, the VORP process was also a way of challenging victims' stereotypes about 'offenders' through personal contact.

Beyond these readily apparent notions, however, the organizers developed a distinctive emphasis on empowering lay participation in the justice-making process. The goals of restitution and personal encounter could have been met through court-ordered restitution or apologies. But as it evolved, the programme developed a stronger view that the victim and the offender should be the ones to decide how much would be paid, and according to what timetable. Influenced by Christie (1977), Yantzi and Worth began to talk about how the state had 'stolen' conflicts away from individuals and developed a monopoly on the criminal justice process. The innovators became reformers as they began to envision a fundamentally different approach to justice – one that placed the disputing parties at centre stage and defined justice primarily as psychological and material restoration rather than as retribution.

This concern for deprofessionalizing the criminal justice process and enhancing citizen participation was extended to the project's staffing. Volunteers played an increasingly important role as case workers who visited victims, explained the project, and then set up and facilitated the victim/offender meetings. Yantzi's role became one of coordinating and supervising the volunteers. Initially volunteers received only a half-day of orientation to VORP. By 1980 this had grown to a twenty-hour curriculum including information about the criminal justice process and training in mediation skills.

Undoubtedly because of its probation base, the project functioned as a post-conviction sentencing alternative. The usual procedure was for a judge to place the offender on probation, with participation in VORP being a term of the probation order. Judges began to exercise this option in an increasing variety of cases, sometimes with less than satisfactory results. In November 1975, a memorandum to judges and prosecutors indicated that VORP had been most successful when the victims were individuals or small businesses. The same report attempted to suggest some uniform wording for the probation order that would instruct the person being sentenced to 'come to mutual agreement with the victim regarding restitution, with the assistance of the Probation Officer or a person designated by the Probation Officer. If no agreement can be reached, the matter will be referred back to court.' The brief report concluded on a visionary note: 'It is our hope that the process of bringing victims and offenders together to reach a mutual agreement regarding restitution will become the norm.'

Yantzi interviewed each offender referred by the judge to explain the reconciliation process. Although VORP was prescribed in the probation order, Yantzi stressed to offenders that they could choose not to meet the victim and allow the court to determine the amount of restitution. Not surprisingly, about 90 per cent of the offenders opted to deal with the victim rather than take their chances with the judge.

No longer did the mediator simply follow an offender to the victim's door and observe as the anxious individual explained the purpose of the visit. After the offender agreed to participate in the project, a volunteer visited the victim to explain VORP and respond to the victim's questions about the process. Approximately 80 per cent of the victims opted to participate subsequently in victim/offender meetings that were arranged at the convenience of both parties.

The most common place for the reconciliation meeting was the home or business where the crime had occurred. Sometimes, however, the probation office was used, and the mediators even experimented with a park bench and a hamburger restaurant as meeting places.

The project dealt primarily with breaking and entering, theft, vandalism, and other property offences. Although most situations involved fairly small amounts of money, it was not uncommon to handle cases involving several thousands of dollars. If an offender failed to live up to the terms of the agreement, the project would attempt to renegotiate a more workable payment schedule, or otherwise salvage the case. Rarely did offenders default entirely on the agreement. When this happened, however, they were charged with a breach of probation, and returned to court.

The project's novel, yet common-sense approach of 'making right the wrong', soon began to attract considerable attention beyond Kitchener. Presentations by Yantzi and Worth at criminal justice conferences led to requests for training and consultation in a number of Ontario communities. VORP was cited in books and articles on criminal justice innovations (e.g. PREAP, 1976). The interest spilled over into the popular media as well, and the project received coverage in periodicals such as *Reader's Digest* as well as news and feature programmes on national television.

Despite its widespread publicity, the Kitchener programme was never subjected to a formal evaluation. Although numerous undergraduate and graduate students at local universities have studied the programme as a part of course projects,[3] a more rigorous evaluation has not been attempted. In part, the programme's sponsors have discouraged an evaluation, fearing that attempts to measure programme outcomes would focus too heavily on restitution or monetary results. 'How do you measure reconciliation?' has been an oft-repeated question whenever the possibility of an evaluation has been discussed. The difficulty and expense of developing measures that would assess the reconciliation process were generally deemed prohibitive for so small a programme. The lack of a readily available control group also contributed to the low interest in rigorous research.

Despite this lack of empirical documentation, the Ontario probation service actively promoted the development of similar programmes throughout the province. Although approximately twenty VORPs were initiated in Ontario by the early 1980s, the province never undertook a comprehensive research programme on VORP.[4]

Through all this activity, the Kitchener VORP remained relatively small. By 1980, the annual case-load had grown to 144 offenders and 149 victims, and Yantzi was relieved of his remaining probation case-load to work full time for VORP and other innovations.

The Kitchener group remained true to their innovative intentions. They began to think that in some cases – most notably those where the victim and offender already knew each other – it would be best if mediation could take place *before* the case went to court or even entered the criminal justice system. The adversary nature of the legal system with its emphasis on determining guilt or innocence seemed particularly unsuited for handling cases between acquaintances, where both may have contributed to a disagreement leading to an assault or property damage. By handling such conflicts through mediation it might be possible to resolve the dispute to the satisfaction of both parties, and prevent it from escalating to the point where a more serious offence might take place.

Thus, in 1980, they created the Community Mediation Service to deal with neighbourhood and interpersonal disputes outside the legal system.[5] Since it worked with cases before they went to court, or even before charges were laid, it was deemed to be outside the mandate of probation. Community Mediation Service came to be sponsored by the MCC, and within a few months VORP moved from being a joint Probation—MCC project to exclusive MCC sponsorship. However, Probation continued to fund VORP through a contract with MCC, as a part of their increasing emphasis on privatizing services in the community.

Within a year, Yantzi and others involved in VORP also began formulating ideas for providing additional services to victims of crime. For a while the programme became known as

Victim/Offender Services, as they conducted a victims' needs assessment. This led to the creation of a separate Victim Services programme under MCC in 1982.[6] After seven years of involvement with VORP, Yantzi left the project to work full-time with the new victims' programme.

Victim Services gradually developed an extensive programme of self-help groups for victims of rape and incest. Once again, concern for dealing with both parties to a crime and a readiness to experiment took the victims' programme in new directions. In December 1982, Yantzi and his associates also began to work with sexual offenders, and especially with families where incest had occurred. Self-help groups were set up not only for victims, but also for offenders, and the mothers and siblings in the families.

The quest for new understandings of reconciliation has also been applied to this area. Although in some cases incest spells the dissolution of the family unit, there are other times when the family decided to stay together or to re-integrate upon the offender's release from prison. In such situations the programme has provided an on-going peer support group for couples who are dealing with similar situations. The programme has also sponsored week-end retreats on sexuality that bring together sexual offenders and victims of sexual abuse.

A further organizational metamorphosis occurred in 1982 as the growing cluster of programmes formed their own structure independent of MCC. This move was in accord with an MCC objective of establishing new programmes, and then allowing them to develop an independent status in the community. The new 'umbrella' organization was called 'Community Justice Initiatives', to demonstrate a concern for working toward the goal of justice in the community, through an evolving pattern of methods.

VORP continued to operate as a distinct service, but around this time the letterhead was changed to read 'Victim Offender Reconciliation *Program*'. Perhaps some forms of institutionalization were inevitable. In any event, the individuals operating VORP were responding to concerns that VORP should be seen as an enduring operation rather than of a limited duration, as implied by the term 'project'.

[...]

If measured by the current case volume, the Kitchener VORP appears to be in a frustrated decline. If, however, the experiment that began in 1974 is viewed not as an attempt to build a fixed programme model, but rather as a continuing effort to apply principles of reconciliation and interpersonal healing to the criminal justice system through a growing number of ways, then indeed the innovations have borne fruit. The principles underlying victim/offender meetings have been applied in the Kitchener community to situations ranging from minor neighbourhood disputes to more serious cases of sexual abuse. The concern for helping victims deal with the psychological consequences of crime has given rise to a broadened range of services to victims. Efforts to deprofessionalize some of the process have given rise to volunteer involvement in a variety of programmes and a continuing emphasis on self-help responses to problems.

In a larger context, the Kitchener experiment provided the inspiration that led to further innovation in dozens of communities in Canada, the United States, and Europe [...].

Finally, it must be recognized that unlike a 'demonstration project', which attempts to demonstrate a known process, a true experiment is a risky venture into uncharted waters. Demonstrations may fail, but experiments in themselves do not succeed or fail. They only yield information that can be used to revise or further refine the process under investigation. To quote again from Yantzi and Worth: 'We are learning by our mistakes and successes and moving slowly but steadily, making every effort to consult with and keep informed those persons affected directly and indirectly by our project' (1977: 1). So the factors identified in this chapter that may have contributed to the reduced VORP case-load may also present suggestions for addressing some of the problems encountered in Kitchener and elsewhere. By comparison, they also highlight the significant successes that victim/offender reconciliation programmes have achieved in numerous other communities.

Notes

1 The Crown Prosecutor suggested in this case that restitution should be paid to the insurance companies that had reimbursed some of the victims for a portion of the losses. The judge rejected this proposal, but in subsequent cases the judges did at times require restitution to be paid to insurance companies.
2 The Kitchener programme would likely never have developed were it not for the receptive attitude of the area probation manager, John Gaskell. A native of England who was familiar with contemporary British probation innovations, he had already championed Yantzi's efforts to develop a volunteer probation programme. Although he was initially dubious about the legality of victim/offender meetings, he released an increasing portion of Yantzi's time for the VORP, and became a staunch proponent of the project who encouraged experimentation while requiring minimal demonstrations of immediate benefits.
3 One of these studies (Dittenhoffer and Ericson, 1983) was published and raised some critical questions about the programme, but its appearance in a law journal did not attract much attention from individuals working in corrections.
4 A small evaluation was conducted of the Ajax–Pickering programme in 1982–3 by the Ministry of Correctional Services, but because of methodological problems, it has not been released to the public.
5 Community Mediation Service was a pioneer project in Ontario, and is [at the time of writing] the longest continuously operated programme of its type in Canada. It has been instrumental in facilitating the development of similar programmes through publications, training courses, and convening two national workshops on mediation.
6 The Victim Services programme has two components. For the first part MCC persuaded the local police to operate a service to victims, using civilian employees of the police department to provide information and emotional support to victims. MCC sponsored a second 'community' component, housed in the same office with VORP and the Community Mediation Service. The purpose of the community component was initially open-ended. It was intended to serve victims who might not fall within the mandate of the police programme, as well as to fulfil an advocacy function for victims. Its primary work gradually developed in self-help responses to sexual abuse. The programme now sponsors over fifteen self-help groups for victims and offenders in sexual abuse.

References

Alper, B.S. and Nichols, L.T. (1981) *Beyond the Courtroom: Programs in Community Justice and Conflict Resolution* (Lexington, MA: Lexington Books).

Bender, J. (1985) 'Reconciliation Begins in Canada', *Christian Living,* 32:12, pp. 6–8.

Christie, N. (1977) 'Conflict as Property', *British Journal of Criminology,* 17:4, pp. 1–15.

Dittenhoffer, T. and Ericson, R. (1983) 'The Victim Offender Reconciliation Program: A Message to Correctional Reformers', *University of Toronto Law Journal,* 33, pp. 315–47.

Hudson, J. and Galaway, B. (1977) *Restitution in Criminal Justice* (Lexington, MA: D.C. Heath).

Peachey, D. and Skeen, C. (1986) *Directory of Canadian Dispute Resolution Programs* (Kitchener, Ontario: Network for Community Justice and Conflict Resolution).

PREAP (1976) *Instead of Prisons: A Handbook for Abolitionists* (Syracuse, NY: Prison Research Education and Action Project).

Umbreit, M. (1989) 'Violent Offenders and their Victims', in Wright, M. and Galaway, B. (eds) *Mediation and Criminal Justice: Victims, Offenders and Community* (London: Sage).

Worth, D. (1986) 'VORP: A Look at the Past and Future', *Community Justice Report,* 5:1, Supplement.

Yantzi, M. and Worth, D. (1977) 'The Developmental Steps of the Victim/Offender Reconciliation Project.' Unpublished paper.

8 Encounter

Daniel W. Van Ness and Karen Heetderks Strong

At the end of his epic poem *The Iliad,* Homer recounts an extraordinary midnight meeting between Achilles, the greatest of Greek warriors, and Priam, king of Troy. For 10 years, the Greeks have besieged Troy, and many warriors on both sides have died. Two recent deaths have particular importance to these two men. Achilles is mourning the death of his companion Patroclus, killed by Hector, Priam's son and the leader of the Trojan forces. Priam in turn grieves for Hector, killed by Achilles in battle as retaliation for the death of Patroclus. Achilles has denied burial to Hector's body, choosing instead to disgrace it by dragging it around the city of Troy at the back of his chariot and leaving it exposed to the sun and vulnerable to dogs and scavenger birds. The gods have protected Hector's body from decay and from being torn apart by animals, waiting for Achilles's anger to subside and for him to return the body to Troy for proper burial. However, Achilles's grief and anger do not dissipate, even after Patroclus's funeral and the daily humiliations of Hector's body. Finally, the gods order him to return the body and they bring Priam to Achilles's tent under cover of darkness and their protection to negotiate the release of the body.

The two bitter enemies meet for the first time. Each considers himself to be the victim of a great loss, and they weep as they remember their dead loved ones. Priam appeals to Achilles by reminding him of his own father, who would long to have Achilles' body returned were he the one who had been killed. Stirred by pity, Achilles agrees to return the body, and further agrees to a cease-fire for 12 days while Troy mourns the death of its hero.

In his description of this remarkable meeting, Homer paints a complete picture that depicts sharp emotions (grief, pity, anger, fear, admiration, and guilt), carefully chosen words, an awareness of non-verbal communication, and symbols of hospitality and respect. Achilles washes and covers Hector's battered body, afraid that Priam's natural resentment at its degrading treatment would provoke his own explosive anger. They eat together and as they talk with and observe one another, each comes to a reluctant admiration for the other's strength and wisdom. Achilles prepares a bed for Priam and promises protection on his return trip to Troy.

This meeting offers only an interlude; war resumes at the conclusion of Hector's funeral. Within days, both Achilles and Priam are dead; Achilles is killed in battle before the walls of Troy, and Priam in the following days when Troy is finally defeated. Interestingly, though, Homer did not include those events in *The Iliad.* Instead, he concludes with this dramatic meeting and a brief account of Hector's funeral. His theme, the dreadful consequences of Achilles's anger to both Greeks and Trojans, is completed as he describes the two men's encounter.[1]

Encounter is one of the corner posts of a restorative approach to crime. It is greatly restricted in conventional criminal justice proceedings by rules of evidence, practical considerations, and the dominance of professional attorneys who speak on behalf of their clients.

It is further restricted by the exclusion of key parties: primary and secondary victims. But even defendants are silent pawns in the courtroom, often failing to even comprehend what is taking place because of the arcane language and procedures used.[2]

The guarantee that accused offenders may confront their accusers in court is a well-established international human right. In recent years, some jurisdictions have increased the possibilities for victims of crime to express themselves in, or at least to listen to, court proceedings. Some jurisdictions allow victims to remain in the courtroom to hear testimony about their cases, even though they may themselves be witnesses. Others have given victims the right to address the sentencer (usually the judge) about the impact of the crime on their lives. These innovations are beneficial for victims, and they may have some indirect impact on the attitudes of offenders, but they—like the defendant's right of confrontation—are limited by the adversarial and judicial dimensions of courtroom proceedings, and by the definition of crime as an offense against government.

In this chapter we will consider several approaches that permit parties to crime to encounter one another outside of the courtroom. We will describe several such programs, including victim–offender mediation, conferencing, circles, and impact panels. We will discuss both common and distinguishing elements among these approaches and will consider strategic and programmatic issues to be explored as their use is expanded.

Mediation

Victim–offender mediation programs (VOMs) first appeared in the 1970s, and were a direct contributor to the restorative justice movement. VOMs offer victims and offenders the opportunity to meet together with the assistance of a trained mediator to talk about the crime and to agree on steps toward justice. Unlike a court process, these programs seek to empower the participants to resolve their conflict on their own in a conducive environment. Unlike arbitration, in which a third party hears both sides and makes a judgment, the VOM process relies on the victim and offender to resolve the dispute together. The mediator imposes no specific outcome; the goal is to empower participants, promote dialogue, and encourage mutual problem-solving.[3]

The first programs used the name "victim–offender reconciliation program" to emphasize that movement toward reconciliation was an optimal outcome, whether or not the parties actually achieved it. However, some objected to the word "reconciliation" as unnecessarily (and unhelpfully) value-laden. Victim support advocates were concerned that the term implied a duty on the part of victims to reconcile with their offenders. They preferred "mediation" or even better, "dialogue," because those terms described the process rather than a possible outcome. Mark Umbreit has suggested that the "primary goal of victim offender mediation and reconciliation programs is to provide a conflict resolution process which is perceived as fair by both the victim and the offender."[4] For this reason, most programs now are referred to as victim–offender mediation programs. We will follow this convention for several reasons. Many crimes involve victims and offenders who were strangers to one another before the offense and, hence, "reconciliation" is not applicable. Furthermore, many victims and offenders who complete the VOM process do not become friends. Apology and forgiveness after a relatively brief meeting can be offered in only a limited way. However, it is important not to lose sight of the fact that reconciliation—however incipient—is a possible result of the process of dialogue.

There is a basic structure to the VOM process, although, like other encounter approaches, its operation should "... be dynamic, taking into account the participants and empowering them to work in their own ways."[5] The meeting allows the victim and offender to pursue three basic objectives: to identify the injustice, to make things right, and to consider future intentions.[6] Identifying the injustice begins as both parties talk about the crime and its impact from their own perspective and as they hear the other party's version of the events. Some practitioners have called this "telling their stories." It is during this stage that the parties put together a common understanding of what happened and talk about how it affected them. Both are given the opportunity to ask questions of the other, the victim can speak about the personal dimensions of the victimization and loss, and the offender has a chance to express remorse. Discussion of how to make things right comes through identifying the nature and extent of the victim's loss and exploring how the offender might begin to repair the harm caused by the criminal act. This agreement is typically reduced to writing and specifies the amount of financial restitution, in-kind services, or other reparation to which both parties agree. Then the parties consider the future by, for example, setting restitution schedules, follow-up meetings, and monitoring procedures, furthermore, meetings frequently include discussions about the offender's plans to make a better future by such actions as addressing alcohol or other drug problems, resisting negative family or peer pressures, and devoting time to productive activities such as work, hobbies, or community assistance.

Restorative justice program research to date underscores the often remarkable power of well-run victim–offender mediation. Such encounters help victims achieve a sense of satisfaction that justice is being done and cause offenders to recognize their responsibility in ways that the usual court process does not. Victims confront the offender, express their feelings, ask questions, and have a direct role in determining the sentence. Offenders take responsibility for their actions and agree to make amends to the victim. Offenders often have not understood the effect their actions had on their victims, and this process gives them greater insight into the harm they caused as well as an opportunity to repair the damage. Both victim and offender are confronted with the other as a person rather than a faceless, antagonistic force, permitting them to gain a greater understanding of the crime, of the other person's circumstances, and of what it will take to make things right.

Conferencing

Family group conferencing (FGC), initiated by legislation in 1989 in New Zealand, was subsequently adapted in Australia and is now being used in one of its various forms around the world. This program actually has traditional roots—the New Zealand model was adapted from the "whanau conference" practiced by the Maori people. The conference process has been most extensively used in cases involving juveniles, although conferences involving adult offenders (sometimes referred to as community group conferences) are increasingly being used as well.

Conferences differ from VOMs in several ways. First, the process is facilitated, not mediated. The facilitator (or "coordinator," in the New Zealand model) assists the group, making sure the process remains safe for all involved and that it does not wander into irrelevant side issues. (While this is also true of the mediation programs just described, it is not true of some programs that are far more directive and also use the VOM name.) Second, conference participants include not only the victim and offender but also their families or supporters, sometimes referred to as their community of care. The arresting police officer and other criminal justice representatives may also be present. A typical conference might have a dozen or more people in attendance, although conferences have been conducted with substantially more participants. Third, while many VOM programs emphasize the importance of pre-encounter preparation of the parties in individual meetings, conferences are usually conducted with minimal if any preparation of the parties.

Conferences open with the facilitator explaining the procedure. Then the offenders begin telling what happened in response to open-ended questions from the facilitator. The victims follow in a similar fashion, and describe their experiences, express how this has affected them, and direct questions (if they have them) to the offenders. The victims' families and friends, and then the offenders' families and friends add their thoughts and feelings. Following this phase, the group discusses what should be done to repair the injuries caused by the crime. The victims and their families and friends have an opportunity to state their expectations, and the offenders and their supporters respond. Discussion continues until conference participants agree to a plan, which is then reduced to writing.

Evaluation studies of conferencing indicate that victim satisfaction with conferences is very high. Restitution agreements are reached in virtually all cases, and these agreements are typically completed without police follow-up. Repeat criminal behavior is less than what would normally be expected. Offenders develop empathy for their victims; families of offenders report that their child's behavior has changed; support networks are strengthened; and the relationships between parents and police officers improve.

Circles

Circles are a community-based decision-making approach that is increasingly used in restorative programs. The basic model used for circles was derived from aboriginal peace-making practices in North America. Circles are facilitated community meetings attended by offenders, victims, their friends and families, interested members of the community, and (usually) representatives of the justice system. The facilitator is a community member (called a "keeper") whose role is primarily to keep the process orderly and periodically to summarize for the benefit of the group. Participants speak one at a time, and may discuss and address a wide range of issues regarding the crime, including community conditions or other concerns that are important for understanding what happened and what should be done. The focus is on finding an approach that leads to a constructive outcome, in which the needs of the victim and community are understood and addressed along with the needs and obliga-tions of the offender. The process moves toward consensus on a plan to be followed and how it will be monitored. Circles do not focus exclusively on sentencing, and the process itself often leads participants to discover and address issues beyond the immediate issue of a particular crime. When sentencing is involved, the circle plan outlines the commitments required of the offender and may also include commitments by others such as family and community members. Noncompliance with the circle plan results in the case being returned to the circle or to the formal court process.

The imprint of traditional rituals is visible on circle sentencing processes and structures, to

> ...listen to conflicts to discover the potentials for positive change that they may hold for us. Conflicts are openings, doorways to new ways of being together. Because they occur within the whole, they bear a meaning that in some way relates to the whole. Perhaps the way things were wasn't entirely working; conflicts invite us to explore how to change them. Perhaps we've accepted norms that conflicts call us to reevaluate.[7]

Because they do not have to focus solely on the crime, the victim, and the offender, participation in circles is not restricted to the immediate parties to the crime and those closest to them. Circles can include any community members who choose to participate. Every participant is heard—both in expressing their perspectives and feelings about the crime or other issues, and in proposing and committing to solutions. The circle process allows for expression of its members' norms and expectations, leading to a shared affirmation by the circle—not just for the offender, but for the community at large. This context offers renewed community identity and strengthens community life for its members through their participation.

A circle process is initiated when an offender or victim makes application. Support groups may be formed for the victim and the offender. Multiple circles may be held with the support groups before the larger circle occurs. After the circle process has produced a plan by consensus of the whole circle, follow-up circles typically monitor it.

To date, relatively little research on sentencing circles is available, although stories abound to support the general benefits of these processes. Gordon Bazemore and Mark Umbreit report that a study by Judge Barry Stuart in Canada "indicated that fewer offenders who had gone through the circle recidivated than offenders who were processed by standard criminal justice practices."[8] However, it will be of considerable interest when research is available on a more comprehensive set of outcomes reflecting the circle process' objective to bring a measure of healing to the community, the victim, the offender, and their families.

Impact panels

Not all offenders are caught. Moreover, even when a crime is "solved" by the conviction of the offender, the victim or offender may not wish to meet with the other, or there may be logistical problems that prevent such a meeting from taking place. In each of these instances, victim–offender panels may provide willing parties an opportunity for a kind of surrogate encounter.

A victim–offender panel (VOP) is made up of a group of victims and a group of offenders who are linked by a common kind of crime, although they are not "each other's" victims or offenders. In other words, where VOM and conferencing involve crime victims and their offenders, VOPs bring together groups of unrelated victims and offenders. The purpose of these meetings is to help victims find resolution and to expose offenders to the damage caused to others by their crime, thereby producing a change in the offender's attitudes and behaviors.

VOPs are much more varied in form and content than VOMs and conferencing. A program in England, for example, brings together victims of burglary with youthful offenders who have been convicted of unrelated burglaries. The two groups of four to six persons each meet for three weekly sessions of 90 minutes each. During the meetings, there is discussion and role-play involving all of the participants.

In the United States, Mothers Against Drunk Driving (MADD) organizes Victim Impact Panels (or Drunk Driving Impact Panels, if offenders or other nonvictims are included) to expose convicted drunk driving offenders to the harm caused to victims and their survivors. The offenders are typically ordered to attend by a judge or probation officer. The victims are selected by MADD or other victim support groups based on two criteria: whether the experience of telling their story is likely to be more helpful than harmful for the victim, and whether they are able to speak without blaming or accusing offenders. There is a single meeting, lasting 60 to 90 minutes, during which the victims speak. Carefully screened offenders may participate as panel members if they have shown remorse, have completed all aspects of their sentence, or have agreed that participation will not result in a reduction of their sentence, and if a screening committee has determined that the remorse expressed seems genuine and that the offender will be an effective speaker. There is no interaction between the victims on the panel and the offenders in the audience, although if the victims agree, there may be a brief question-and-answer period or informal conversation at the conclusion of their presentations.

The Sycamore Tree Project, a program run by Prison Fellowship organizations in New Zealand, England and Wales, Colombia, and a dozen other countries, brings groups of five to six victims into prison to meet with similar numbers of prisoners.[9] Using a prepared curriculum, they discuss issues including responsibility, confession, repentance, forgiveness, restitution, and reconciliation. At the end of the six- to 12-week project, they draw from their experiences in the program to draft letters addressed (but not delivered) to their own victims or offenders. The program is a prelude to more direct encounters when possible and is an alternative when none is available.

Studies suggest that VOPs can be beneficial to victims and offenders who participate. Victims in the burglary panels reported that they were less angry and anxious as a result of the meetings. Offenders demonstrated a better understanding of the impact of their crime on victims: the number of offenders who believed that burglary victims were more upset about having a stranger come into their house than they were about losing property increased significantly. Research on drunk driving panels has shown a dramatic change in the attitudes of offenders and in the likelihood of recidivism, and it has also shown a significant benefit to the victim participants: 82 percent reported that it had helped in their healing. These results were even more dramatic when the participants were compared with a control group of non participants after controlling for other variables (such as counseling and elapsed time since the crash); participants manifested a higher sense of well-being, lower anxiety, and less anger than nonparticipants. Studies of offender attitudes before and after participating in Sycamore Tree Project have found that offenders' thinking had become significantly less criminogenic.

Elements of encounter

We should note that the previous descriptions are of prototypes or models. In practice, the apparent differences may very well disappear, depending on the circumstances. A "mediation" program may include family members and supporters, for example. Furthermore, some programs calling themselves "victim–offender mediation" or "conferences" may not include key elements of these models. For example, in some programs the "mediation" consists of shuttle diplomacy by a mediator who meets with each party, but does not bring them together. In some "conferences" the victim does not participate. While there can be benefit to the participants in these practices, they cannot be considered fully restorative.

The illustration of encounter in Homer's *The Iliad* helps identify several elements that contribute to a process of restoration. The first, of course, was that Achilles and Priam actually met. This was not the story of shuttle diplomacy, or of negotiation by proxies. Priam came to Achilles's tent for the meeting, and the two men talked and ate together. The second is that they spoke personally; each told the story from his own perspective. This personalized approach has been called narrative. They did not attempt to generalize or universalize, but instead spoke with feeling about the particulars of the decade-long conflict that concerned them most. The third is related; they exhibited emotion in their communication. They wept as they considered their own losses. They wept as they identified with those of the other. They experienced not only sorrow but also anger and fear. Emotion played a significant role in their interaction. A fourth element is understanding. They listened as well as spoke, and they listened with understanding, which helped them acquire a degree of empathy for the other. Fifth, they came to an agreement that was particular to Priam's grievance and was achievable. Achilles agreed to turn over Hector's body for burial and in addition gave the Trojans time to conduct Hector's funeral.

These elements are also found in the encounter programs described above. All involve meetings between victims and offenders. In mediation, conferencing, and circles, the victims meet with their own offenders; with VOP, the meetings are between representative victims and offenders. This means that what takes place during the encounter directly engages the other party. This is in contrast to court proceedings, in which the best that will happen is that each party will be able to observe the other's statements to the judge or jury.

At the meeting, the parties talk to one another; they tell their stories. In their narratives, they describe what happened to them, how it has affected them, and how they see the crime and its consequences. This is a subjective rather than objective account; consequently, it has integrity both to the speaker and to the listener. MADD suggests to victim panelists in drunk driving panels:

> Simply tell your story…After you've given the facts about the crash, talk about how you feel NOW—not yesterday or a week ago or when the crash happened. This will keep your story relevant and poignant and protect you from giving the same presentation over and over again. Speak what is true for you, and you can trust that it will be "right."[10]

Narrative permits the participants to express and address emotion. Crime can produce powerful emotional responses that obstruct the more dispassionate pursuit of justice to which courts aspire. Encounter programs allow those emotions to be expressed. This can foster healing for both victims and offenders. All of the encounter programs described above recognize the importance of emotion in training facilitators, preparing participants, and establishing ground rules. As a result, crime and its consequences are addressed not only rationally but from the heart as well.

The use of meeting, narrative, and emotion leads to understanding. As David Moore has observed about conferencing, "in this context of shared emotions, victim and offender achieve a sort of empathy. This may not make the victim feel particularly positive about the offender but it does make the offender seem more normal, less malevolent."[11] Likewise, for offenders, hearing the victims' story not only humanizes their victims but also can change the offenders' attitude about their criminal behavior.

Reaching this understanding establishes a productive foundation for agreeing on what happens next. Encounter programs seek a resolution that fits the immediate parties rather than focusing on the precedential importance of the decision for future legal proceedings. Encounter, therefore, opens up the possibility of designing a uniquely crafted resolution reflecting the circumstances of the parties. Further, they do this through a cooperative process rather than an adversarial one—through negotiation that searches for a convergence of the interests of victim and offender by giving them the ability to guide the outcome.

Do these elements—meeting, narrative, emotion, understanding, and agreement—yield reconciliation when combined? Not necessarily. Achilles and Priam's meeting did not result in the two men becoming friends, nor did it end the surrounding hostilities. However, it did increase their ability to see each other as persons, to respect each other, and to identify with the experiences of the other, and it made it possible for them to arrive at an agreement. In other words, some reconciliation had occurred. As Claassen and Zehr have noted:

Hostility and reconciliation need to be viewed as opposite poles on a continuum. Crime usually involves hostile feelings on the part of both victim and offender. If the needs of victim and offender are not met and if the victim-offender relationship is not addressed, the hostility is likely to remain or worsen... If however, victim and offender needs are addressed, the relationship may be moved toward the reconciliation pole, which in itself is worthwhile.[12]

Strategic issues

Encounters between victims and offenders have a number of advantages, as we have seen, but they also raise some important issues that should be considered carefully before implementing or using such programs. This chapter will conclude with a review of three strategic issues of particular importance to policymakers and practitioners:

1. How to minimize coercion of participants.
2. Whom to include in the encounter.
3. Accountability for conduct and outcomes of encounters.

Minimizing coercion

One of the central attributes of contemporary criminal justice is that it is coercive: government has the authority to punish offenders and to compel others (including victims) to participate in the process. Encounter programs, on the other hand, are committed to voluntary participation. There is an obvious difficulty in maintaining a truly voluntary process in the context of the highly coercive criminal justice system. Offenders may agree to participate in hopes of a more lenient sentence. This does not necessarily render the offender's participation involuntary or coerced. The existence of sentencing alternatives that produce results more onerous than those achieved by an encounter does not constitute coercion unless the alternatives are either nonexistent or unjust.

A poorly trained facilitator could exert pressure on the victim in an attempt to overcome early and natural resistance to meeting with the offender. While pressure is wrong, it is appropriate and important that victims as well as offenders receive complete and accurate information about the alternatives they have for resolving the dispute. Eric Gilman suggests that mediation be only one of several options that are offered to victims. He describes the approach used by the Victim Offender Meeting Program of the Clark County Juvenile Court in Vancouver, Washington:

Through a thoughtfully worded letter and/or phone contact, this initial connection with the victim seeks to:

- acknowledge the harm done to the victim and express the community's concern about the harm, and express the community's commitment to hold the offender accountable in ways that are meaningful to the victim (acknowledgement)
- provide the victim with general information about the justice system and specific information about what is happening in their case (information)
- offer victims the opportunity to talk about the impacts of the crime on them (a voice)
- provide choices for participation in the justice process (a choice to participate).[13]

Those who choose to participate—victims as well as offenders—should do so because they believe that there is an advantage to taking this approach. The key, however, is to offer the option of an encounter process as honestly, objectively, and nonjudgmentally as possible so that those who choose otherwise can simply allow the criminal justice system to take its usual course.

Parties involved

As we have seen, the various encounter approaches differ regarding the number of parties involved and the roles they play in the process. The VOM process typically includes a mediator, the crime victim, and the offender—those parties who are most directly involved. Sometimes the victim or offender asks to have parents or friends present, or even (on rare occasions) to be represented by a surrogate. In some programs, the community may be formally represented through designated participants. When there are multiple victims, each victim has the opportunity to participate, and if it is decided that they should meet separately, there could be as many VOM processes as there are victims. Conferences, on the other hand, include family and friends of the parties as well as criminal justice representatives, along with the facilitator. When there are multiple victims and offenders, they and their families may be included in a single conference. Circles involve the offender, victim, support persons for each, criminal justice representatives, and community members—all facilitated by a community member.

Facilitators. In mediation, conferencing, and circles, facilitators are responsible for approaching the victims and offenders, helping prepare them for the meeting, and then guiding the actual meeting. Although many programs rely on trained volunteer facilitators, in the case of serious or violent crimes in which a greater level of therapeutic expertise is needed, professional facilitators may be used instead. In the meetings, facilitators help guide the interaction as needed, ideally following whatever process enhances communication between the victims and offenders and allows the parties to develop their own plan together. Facilitators will take corrective action if the process becomes physically or emotionally dangerous for anyone.

Facilitators do not decide what will happen, as judges or arbitrators do. Nor are they advocates for either the victim or offender in achieving their goals for the reconciliation process. They do not press an offender to show remorse or a victim to speak words of forgiveness. Their function is to regulate and facilitate communication within the encounter setting to create a safe environment in which the parties can make their own decisions. This means that facilitators must remain alert to the potential for new harm to victims, either through the way the process proceeds or because the victims are not ready for the encounter. The victims' needs and the timing of the victims' recovery—particularly when the crime was serious or violent—are critical considerations in deciding when or whether cases should be brought to an encounter.

This description refers to the way that facilitators are expected to work when programs are well-run. Training and selection of facilitators is an extremely important function of an effective program, as is in-service training and evaluation according to standards that reflect best practices and restorative values.

Victims. Victims who choose to participate in encounter processes have the opportunity to ask questions of the offender, express their feelings about what occurred, and suggest ways the offender can begin to make things right. According to one study, victims' three most important goals in entering an encounter process were to: (1) recover some losses,

(2) help offenders stay out of trouble, and (3) have a real part in the criminal justice process. However, once they had participated in the encounter these goals changed.

> [Victims] were most satisfied with (a) the opportunity to meet the offender and thereby obtain a better understanding of the crime and the offender's situation; (b) the opportunity to receive restitution for loss; (c) the expression of remorse on the part of the offender; and (d) the care and concern of the mediator. Even though the primary motivation for participation was restitution, the most satisfying aspect of the experience was meeting the offender.[14]

A subsequent study found that 80 percent of victims who had participated in a mediation meeting reported that they had "experienced fairness," compared with fewer than 40 percent of victims who had chosen not to enter the program. These victims defined "fairness" as the right to participate directly in the process, as rehabilitation for the offender, as compensation for the victim, as punishment of the offender, and as the offender's expression of remorse. As noted above, studies of family group conferences and circles indicate a similar degree of victim satisfaction.

Although facilitators are trained not to side with either victims or offenders, the process recognizes that victims generally stand in a different moral position than the offender, having been wronged as opposed to causing the harm.[15] There are several ways this happens. First, offenders participate only if they have accepted responsibility for what they have done. Second, the process itself focuses on the wrongdoing by engaging the parties directly in conversation about it. Third, the parties examine the moral implications of the offender's actions.

Offenders. The encounter process puts offenders "in the uncomfortable position of having to face the person they violated. They are given the… opportunity to display a more human dimension to their character and to even express remorse in a very personal fashion."[16] Genuine acceptance of responsibility can indicate the beginning of a change of heart in the offender, but such acceptance may take some time.

Encounter processes, however, do change offenders' attitudes. According to one study, offenders' reasons for agreeing to participate in encounters included avoiding harsher punishment, getting beyond the crime and its consequences, and making things right. After completing the process, however, they reported that their criteria for satisfaction had changed.

> (O)ffenders were most satisfied with: (a) meeting the victim and discovering the victim was willing to listen to him or her; (b) staying out of jail and in some instances not getting a record; (c) the opportunity to work out a realistic schedule for paying back the victim to "make things right." Strikingly, what offenders disliked most was, also, meeting the victim. This reflects the tension between, on the one hand, the stress experienced in preparation for meeting the victim, and, on the other hand, the relief of having taken steps "to make things right."[17]

It is not surprising that offenders experience this tension because of what they have done. Allowing the offender and victim to address what happened in a nonjudicial context gives the offender freedom to repair some of the damage he or she caused by the crime, and thus gain a better moral footing in the situation.

Support persons and community members. The presence or absence of support persons and community members is a significant difference between the prototypical models of VOMs, conferences, and circles. In VOMs, the principal parties are the victim and offender. In conferences, the family, support group members (the "community of care"), and criminal justice professionals are full participants and play an active role in the process up to and including agreement on a plan of action. In circles, this involvement is expanded to include anyone interested in attending for whatever reason, including community members who have no relationship with the victim or offenders (the "community of interest").

Government representatives. In both the conferencing and circle models, government representatives may participate. These may include the arresting police officer, a social worker, the prosecutor, or the judge—although typically not all of those individuals. In some instances these people serve as facilitators, and in others they are merely participants. Declan Roche recommends that justice system personnel not serve as facilitators because their decision-making roles within the coercive criminal justice system make it difficult for them to be perceived as neutral conveners.[18]

One might ask whether the state should have a participatory role in a restorative process, and if so, why. [...] the government and community make different contributions to establishing safety. The government's responsibility is to provide a just order, while the community's is to build a just peace. Order is established in several ways: first, through the use of coercive power when necessary to bring about order in a chaotic environment, such as after a natural disaster or civil disturbances; second, by creating orderly processes for dealing with crimes and their aftermath; and third, by providing in legislation a clear statement about the conduct that society deems to be criminal. It is in this latter role that government representatives may participate; they bring the perspective of society at large, which means, as Roche suggests, that victims are free to be forgiving if they wish, without sacrificing the principle that criminal behavior is harmful and wrong.[19]

Accountability for conduct and outcomes of encounters

In criminal cases, accountability is generated in several ways. First, the parties are allowed representation by attorneys, who may make motions concerning the process and outcome in court, may object if they feel the judge or other party is taking inappropriate action, and may appeal to a higher court if the judge rules against them. In addition, adult court proceedings are typically open to the public and media, which means that all participants are vulnerable to public exposure. Encounters, on the other hand, typically take place in private, and usually without lawyers present. Although a well-trained facilitator can help ensure effective practice, the question arises about the accountability of the facilitator and parties to participate in good faith and in keeping with restorative principles and values.

Roche[20] has explored this issue in a research project involving 25 programs in six countries. He found that several forms of accountability are present during encounters. One is what he calls deliberative accountability, which stems from the nature of the encounter process itself. Each party becomes accountable to the others to explain their positions because decisions are made on the basis of consensus. Consequently, it is necessary for participants to explain their point of view in order to persuade the others. This creates a kind of balance of power in which no party is able to dominate the others. This informal accountability was supplemented in most programs by the availability of an alternative forum if a party was unhappy with the deliberative process. For example, offenders could choose to leave the restorative encounter and demand a hearing in open court.

This is not the only check against domination by parties over others in the encounter. Another is to include friends and supporters of the parties to offer them encouragement and assistance. This might be particularly useful when parties feel intimidated by other parties, or when one of the parties has difficulty expressing opinions and perspectives. Some programs allow professional advocates to participate, such as in Australia, where offenders may bring lawyers and victims a victim advocate. In Belgium, attorneys routinely attend encounters in order to advise their clients during the proceedings. A third approach identified by Roche is to carefully prepare the parties before the encounter and screen out those who would not be able to participate without dominating or being dominated. This preparation can include provision of legal information.

In addition, the meeting can be structured to reduce domination. One example Roche offers is of a conferencing scheme that provides for a short break in the middle of the meeting so that young offenders may talk with their families. This allows them to express any concerns privately to their families that they may be reluctant to bring to the attention of the whole group.

More traditional forms of accountability are useful as well, according to Roche.[21] He reports that some of the programs he researched allow observers, although they differ over who may observe. Others permit some form of external review. *The United Nations Basic Principles on the Use of Restorative Justice Programmes in Criminal Matters* states that after an encounter the agreement should be reviewed by the law enforcement or judicial officials who referred them in the first place. Roche proposes, however, that this review be only procedural and not substantive so that the officials do not substitute their opinions about the outcomes, but merely ensure that the process itself is protected.

Notes

1 Annalise Acorn (*Compulsory Compassion: A Critique of Restorative Justice*. Vancouver: UBC Press, 2004) has criticized our use of this story, accusing us of both misunderstanding and misappropriating the account in an attempt to present Homer as "a fellow booster of their agenda. There is a quackery here—a kind of false advertising—that we ought not to overlook." (p. 92). Her assertion is that we suggest that Achilles and Priam achieved reconciliation to right relationship, although she inconsistently concedes that we place the story in context as an interlude in a decades-long war that concludes shortly thereafter with the death in battle of both men. She complains that we fail to present all of Achilles's motives in returning the body: pity might have been part of his motivation, but so were gifts brought by Priam and especially the insistence of the gods that he return the body (although we had mentioned the gods' order in previous editions, we have underscored it in this edition so there can be no mistake).

The premise of Acorn's book is that "[t]he seductive vision of restorative justice seems, therefore, to lie in a skilful deployment—through theory and story—of cheerful fantasies of happy endings in the victim-offender relation, emotional healing, closure, right-relation and respectful community. Yet, as with all seductions, the fantasies that lure us in tend to be very different from the realities that unfold. And the grandness of the idealism in these restorative fantasies, in and of itself, ought to give us pause." (p. 16) Having adopted this view of restorative justice and its advocates, she assumes that this is what we had in mind; that this story is an attempt to weave "cheerful fantasies of happy endings." Based on that assumption, she complains that we haven't gotten the story right and that our failure to do so was intentional.

But we do not believe that restorative justice promises or even is primarily about happy endings. We make this explicit in the last two paragraphs on page 72 (paragraphs that appeared in the previous two editions as well). Happy endings may emerge for some participants in restorative processes, but certainly not for all, as we have stated in this chapter and elsewhere in all three editions of this book. And as Acorn grudgingly acknowledges, we have emphasized that this late-night meeting was a brief non-violent encounter in the midst of a savage war. So why do we use this story to begin the chapter on encounter? Because it offers remarkable insights on what can happen when adversaries meet and communicate authentically. The tension, barely-contained anger, pragmatic negotiations, grudging admiration and nonverbal communication so powerfully presented by Homer ring true. This was a *true* encounter of adversaries and neither a formalized negotiation by proxies nor a judicial proceeding before the gods in which neither party speaks to the other. It includes features that are often found in restorative encounters.

But, asks Acorn, in what way is this *justice*? The answer is that it is not. Neither Priam nor Achilles has admitted guilt, a prerequisite of virtually all restorative encounters. Although Acorn believes that Achilles is at fault (as, presumably, do most who read this story), Achilles himself does not. He views this as simply a meeting between adversaries with comparable moral standing. That is not the case in restorative encounters. It is the admission of one of the parties to wrongdoing that makes an encounter *justice*.

2 One of this book's authors (Van Ness) is an attorney who practiced criminal law for a time. On one occasion, the family of an indigent client awaiting trial in the county jail contacted Van Ness; he agreed to represent the accused. The next court date, which was simply a status hearing in which the judge would determine whether the case was ready to go to trial, was the following day. During that hearing, Van Ness informed the judge that he would be representing the client, and that he had not yet received a transcript of the preliminary hearing from the prosecutor, but that the other discovery had been made available that morning. The prosecutor indicated that the transcript would be available in two weeks. Following local custom, Van Ness stated that, notwithstanding that delay, the defense was answering ready for trial and demanding trial under the Speedy Trial Act. The judge continued the case for another 30 days, but (again following local custom) did not mark the case ready for trial. The next hearing would be another status hearing.

When Van Ness spoke with his client after the hearing, it became clear that he had no idea what had taken place. He had heard his previous lawyer, a public defender, demand trial at the last court appearance, and had therefore assumed that the trial would commence that day. Van Ness explained that the demand for a trial simply triggered the Speedy Trial Act, which provided that if he were not tried within 120 days he would be released. The demand for trial was made solely to protect his right to a speedy trial and not because either side was in fact prepared to go to trial. That was not the only point of confusion; the defendant (understandably, as no one had ever explained it) had no idea what discovery was or why it was important. He remembered the preliminary hearing as a court appearance in which something more than usual happened, but at the time he had thought it was the trial and had been surprised that the public defender representing him had not permitted him to testify. He was shocked to learn that the case would not be going to trial even on the next court date, and was dismayed to learn that it would probably not be tried until the 120-day period was nearly over.

3 We should note that there are differences between mediation conducted by community-based nonprofit organizations and those conducted by judicial authorities. We will not discuss the differences here, because the role of the judicial authorities is very different in civil law and common law countries. For discussion of this issue, see Martin Wright, "Restorative Justice: For Whose Benefit?" and Jacques Faget, "Mediation, Criminal Justice and Community Involvement: A European Perspective" in The European Forum for Victim-Offender Mediation and Restorative Justice, ed., *Victim-Offender Mediation In Europe: Making Restorative Justice Work* (Leuven, Belgium: Leuven University Press, 2000). The process we describe here will be more familiar to those in common law countries. Furthermore, some programs call themselves "victim-offender mediation" but use a process of "shuttle diplomacy" between the victim and offender. In these programs the mediator acts as an intermediary in negotiating a restitution settlement, and the victim and offender are unlikely to meet. These programs are undoubtedly an effective way to determine how amends will be made, and they provide limited opportunities for indirect communication. They may be very useful when one or both of the parties do not want more contact. However, because the contact is only indirect, we do not include these programs as encounters. We suggest that they should instead be considered as processes leading to amends.

4 Mark Umbreit, "Mediation of Victim Offender Conflict," *Missouri Journal of Dispute Resolution* (Fall 1988): 85, 87.

5 Howard Zehr, "VORP Dangers," *Accord.* A Mennonite Central Committee Canada Publication for Victim Offender Ministries 8(3) (1989): 13.

6 While directing the VORP of the Central Valley program in California, Ron Claassen developed mediator training that presents the basic components as they are discussed here. We are indebted to Claassen for a number of the following insights concerning mediation.

7 Kay Pranis, Barry Stuart, and Mark Wedge (2003). *Peacemaking Circles: From Crime to Community.* St. Paul, MN: Living Justice Press. 77.

8 Gordon Bazemore and Mark Umbreit, *Conferences, Circles, Boards, and Mediations: Restorative Justice and Citizen Involvement in the Response to Youth Crime* (Office of Juvenile Justice and Delinquency Prevention, U.S. Department of Justice, September 1, 1999), 28.

9 The England and Wales version has been modified due to prison regulations. In that version one victim participates and the offender group can be as high as 20.

10 Janice Harris Lord, *Victim Impact Panels: A Creative Sentencing Opportunity* (MADD, 1990), 23.

11 David Moore, "Evaluating Family Group Conferences," in David Biles and Sandra McKillop. eds., *Criminal Justice Planning and Coordination: Proceedings of a Conference Held 19–21* April 1993, Canberra (1994). 213.

12 Ron Claassen and Howard Zehr, *VORP Organizing: A Foundation in the Church* (Elkhart, IN: Mennonite Central Committee, U.S. Office of Criminal Justice, 1989), 5.

13 Eric Gilman, *Victim Offender Meetings: A Restorative Focus tor Victims.* RJ Online (online journal), December 2004. Available at http://www.restorativejustice.org/editions/2004/December (downloaded 2 December 2005).

14 Mark S, Umbreit, "The Meaning of Fairness to Burglary Victims," in Burt Galaway and Joe Hudson, eds., *Criminal Justice, Restitution, and Reconciliation* (Monsey, NY: Criminal Justice Press, 1990), 50.

15 This is not always true, of course, and what can emerge from a restorative encounter is a more complete picture of the dynamics and interaction between the victim and offender than may emerge during a trial.

16 Mark S. Umbreit, "Mediation of Victim Offender Conflict," *Missouri Journal of Dispute Resolution* (Fall 1988): 9–10.

17 Robert Coates and John Gehm, "An Empirical Assessment," in Martin Wright and Burt Galaway, eds., *Mediation and Criminal Justice* (Newbury Park, CA: Sage, 1989), 254.

18 Declan Roche, *Accountability in Restorative Justice,* (Oxford: Oxford University Press, 2003). 105–106.

19 Ibid., p. 105.

20 Ibid., p. 81–103.

21 Ibid., p. 188–225.

9   The future of mediation

Robert A. Baruch Bush and Joseph G. Folger

Roughly twenty-five years ago, in a variety of places around the United States, many groups and individuals became interested in a process of dispute resolution called *mediation*. While mediation had long been used in labor disputes, the new surge of interest extended to many other contexts, including community, family, and interpersonal conflict. The development of mediation in these new areas is referred to in this book as the *contemporary mediation movement* or, simply, the *mediation movement*.

Mediation has grown remarkably over the past two and a half decades. Prior to 1965, the use of mediation outside the labor relations arena was practically unheard of. Then, in the late 1960s, attention was focused on mediation from two very different directions: civic leaders and justice system officials saw in mediation a potential for responding to urban conflict and its flash points; and community organizations and legal reformers saw in mediation a potential for building community resources alongside the formal justice system. Though the motives and approaches were quite different, the combined effect was to make the idea of mediation of "neighborhood" or community disputes, if not a household word, a widely accepted and legitimate concept.

In practical terms, this meant the expansion of the community mediation field from a few isolated programs in 1970 to nearly two hundred by the early 1980s and to more than double that number today (Johnson, 1993*).* Moreover, as a result *of its acceptance* in this field, mediation was tried (and usually accepted) in an increasingly broad range of nonlabor disputes: divorce, environmental, housing, institutional (including prisons, schools, and hospitals), small-claims, personal injury and insurance, and general business disputes; and claims involving government agencies (Singer, 1990). In the last five years or so, this trend has accelerated. Private businesses and even lawyers are finding mediation more and more attractive, spurring the start-up and expansion of for-profit mediation services.

Across the mediation movement, mediation is generally understood (based on its previous use in the labor field) as an informal process in which a neutral third party with no power to impose a resolution helps the disputing parties try to reach a mutually acceptable settlement. This common formulation captures some of the major features of the process, especially its informality and consensuality. It also reflects the view that the most significant effect of the process is the production of a voluntary settlement of the dispute.

Beyond the level described by such conventional definitions, however, the mediation process contains within it a unique potential for transforming people—engendering moral growth—by helping them wrestle with difficult circumstances and bridge human differences, in the very midst of conflict. This transformative potential stems from mediation's capacity to generate two important effects, empowerment and recognition. In simplest terms, *empowerment* means the restoration to individuals of a sense of their own value and strength and their own capacity to handle life's problems. *Recognition* means the evocation in individuals of acknowledgment and empathy for the situation and problems of others. When both of these processes are held central in the practice of mediation, parties are helped to use conflicts as opportunities for moral growth, and the transformative potential of mediation is realized.

At the outset of the contemporary mediation movement, few fully grasped either the special capacity of mediation for fostering empowerment and recognition or the immense importance of these two transformative phenomena. Nevertheless, many had strong intuitions on both counts. Therefore, even though the emphasis was on mediation's capacity to help resolve disputes and effectuate settlements, there was an awareness that mediation had other important though less tangible impacts. It was as though a researcher had discovered a substance, very useful for one purpose, that she realized was capable of other valuable effects; but she had not yet determined what those other effects were or how they could be generated.

Gradually, practitioners and scholars have gained a clearer picture of the effects of mediation apart from settlement per se. Increasingly, attention is being paid to the special capacities of the process to generate empowerment and recognition. Some have even come to realize that working for empowerment and recognition usually results in reaching settlement as well, while focusing on settlement usually results in ignoring empowerment and recognition. So, while these different dimensions of mediation are not necessarily mutually exclusive or inconsistent, the relative emphasis given to them makes a crucial difference.

Slowly, many in the mediation movement have begun to grasp how important empowerment and recognition are, and why. The broader significance of these phenomena is becoming clearer as dispute resolution scholars see that mediation's transformative dimensions are connected to an emerging, higher vision of self and society, one based on moral development and interpersonal relations rather than on satisfaction and individual autonomy. Scholars and thinkers in many fields have begun to articulate and advocate a major shift in moral and political vision—a paradigm shift—from an individualistic to a relational conception. They argue that, although the individualist ethic of modern Western culture was a great advance over the preceding caste-oriented feudal order, it is now possible and necessary to go still further and to achieve a full integration of individual freedom and social conscience, in a relational social order enacted through new forms of social processes and institutions.

Mediation, with its capacity for engendering moral growth through empowerment and recognition, represents an opportunity to express this new relational vision in concrete form. Indeed, this potential is what drew many to it in the first place. Mediation was appealing not because resolution or settlement was good in itself and conflict evil, but because of the way in which mediation allowed disputing parties to understand themselves and relate to one another *through and within conflict.* In short, many have come to feel that empowerment and recognition—the transformative dimensions of mediation—matter as much or more than settlement, and they matter not only in themselves but as expressions of a much broader shift to a new moral and social vision. As such, their importance is primary and immense.

So, like the researcher who finally grasped the fuller workings and importance of her mysterious discovery, some in the mediation field have, after two decades, begun to gain a fuller appreciation for the workings and importance of mediation as a transformative process. At the same time, however, the practice of mediation has moved steadily away from placing these transformative dimensions at the heart of the process. Although mediation has a unique *potential* for achieving empowerment and recognition, mediation practice has not realized that potential. Substantial evidence today suggests that mediation practice still focuses largely on settlement, perhaps even more so than in the early years of the movement. It rarely generates empowerment and recognition, and even then it generally does so serendipitously rather than as a result of mediators' conscious efforts. The transformative potential of mediation, and how to realize it through empowerment and recognition, receives far too little attention today in mediation theory, policy, and practice. Precisely how and why this situation exists, and what can be done about it, are the main subjects of this book.

But in a larger sense, this is not simply a book about mediation. This is a book about a process that has the potential to express concretely a new and higher vision of human life, and therefore it is also about the difficulties of pursuing that vision in practical reality. The future of mediation is a matter of general and serious concern, because it implicates the future of an emerging relational vision of society as a whole. If the vision cannot be expressed in a concrete context such as mediation, it remains mere theory. Just as that vision contemplates an integration of individual freedom and social conscience, mediation offers a potential means to integrate the concern for right and justice and the concern for caring and interconnection. In short, mediation presents a powerful opportunity to express and realize a higher vision of human life. To help capture this opportunity and to bring that vision into reality are the larger purposes of this book.

Those in the mediation movement who believe that this higher vision of human interaction can be realized in mediation have seen powerful glimpses of it in practice. From time to time, cases unfold in ways that seem to go beyond what typically happens in mediation. What is often most striking about such cases is how insignificant the final settlement seems in view of the transformative accomplishments of the intervention itself. The ground the parties create for interacting with each other makes the itemized terms of an agreement seem insignificant, almost superfluous. Indeed, by the end of these cases, asking the parties to commit to specific points in an agreement seems almost unnecessary, because the parties themselves are changed in ways that eclipse any particular problem or dispute.

One of the cases recently mediated at a court-annexed community mediation program in Queens, New York, illustrates in a general way what transformative mediation looks like. The case, a dispute involving an assault charge, shows in concrete terms what gets accomplished in mediation when at least some transformative opportunities for empowerment and recognition are realized.

The sensitive bully

Regis, a large, stern-looking middle-aged black man, had filed an assault charge against Charles, a young black man of medium height and slight build. Regis came to the mediation with his thirteen-year-old son, Jerome; Charles came alone. After the mediator provided an opening statement about the purpose and ground rules of mediation, he asked Regis to explain why he was there. In a loud, agitated voice and rambling style, Regis said he was fed up with what had been dished out to his son. He said that this guy (pointing across the table to Charles) chased and attacked Jerome and Jerome's friends several times over the past few months. The last time he attacked Jerome, Regis said he had enough. He went after this guy and "pinned him to the street." He said he didn't want to punch him out, just let him know that this would not happen again. As Regis said this, he pulled a silver badge out of his shirt pocket, raised his voice, and said threateningly that he was a correctional officer at Rykers Island Penitentiary and that he "wanted this guy locked up."

The mediator intervened at this point and asked Regis how well he knew Charles. Regis said he did not know him at all. All he knew was that this guy didn't live in the neighborhood.

He thought he walked through the area on his way to work and that was when he would harass Jerome and his friends. The mediator then asked whether he knew why Charles might have come after his son. Regis said that Jerome was a minor so any reason would be out of the question. If Charles had an issue with Regis's son, he should have brought it to Regis, not attack a thirteen-year-old. The mediator raised a few other questions to clarify what happened since the altercations, then asked whether Regis wanted to say anything else. Regis said he wanted this guy locked up so he would leave his son alone.

The mediator then asked Regis's son to describe how he saw the dispute. Jerome seemed somewhat withdrawn and reluctant to speak. He said that his "father told everything there was to say." He was asked whether he wanted to add anything to his father's statements. He said no.

Then the mediator turned to Charles and asked him to describe how he saw things. Answering with an undefensive, lump-in-the-throat tone, he started by saying, "Maybe I made a mistake, maybe it wasn't right. I'm not even sure it was always him [looking at Jerome]. But he was always in the group. That I do know." He said that all he wanted to do was to be able to walk through the area as he always had to catch the bus on his way to work or to visit his girlfriend, Claudia. The mediator asked whether Claudia lived in the neighborhood. He said she did. He said that nearly every time he walked through the block or approached his friend's house, Jerome and his friends were there "saying words" to him. He used this expression several times, without being more specific. He said he tried to ignore the kids but finally went up to them and said, "Look, I don't know you—I don't even know your names. Why are you bugging me? I'm not starting with any of you. I just want to walk though the neighborhood." Charles then said Regis attacked him and warned him to leave his son alone. Still speaking somewhat pensively, Charles said he did not want to have anything to do with this guy's family and that he would be willing to walk a different way to get to the bus stop or Claudia's.

At this point Regis interrupted Charles. He started to say that Charles could continue to walk through the neighborhood. He didn't have to walk a different way. The mediator interrupted Regis and asked him to write down what he wanted to say and save it until after Charles finished.

Charles repeated that he didn't need to walk close to Jerome's house anymore but he was worried that if "something else came up, something I didn't have anything to do with, I don't want to be blamed for it." The mediator asked for several clarifications about whether any other factors contributed to the incidents with Jerome and his father. Charles indicated that there was nothing else between them—he did not know Jerome or his father at all. Finally, the mediator asked whether Charles wanted to say anything else at this point. He asked specifically whether Charles wanted to say more about the "words" from Jerome and his friends that had bothered him so much. Charles said no. It was obviously a sensitive subject.

After offering a brief summary of both men's accounts, the mediator turned back to Regis and asked him what he had wanted to say while Charles was speaking. Regis looked toward his son and said, somewhat sternly, "I know kids can be cruel. I told Jerome and his friends not to be cruel, not to throw rocks when we all live in glass houses. I told him that little things like that can lead to larger things like this." He then changed the focus of his comments, turned directly toward the mediator, and said, "You know, he [pointing across the table to Charles] has a bad limp. And I told Jerome not to be cruel."

During the silence that followed Regis's revealing comments, the mediator noticed that Charles had an elevated heel on one of the boots he was wearing; clearly, this condition was the subject of the "words" he had referred to. The mediator asked Charles if he knew that

Regis had talked to Jerome and his friends about not being cruel. Charles said he didn't know what Regis had said to them. But he was clearly affected by what Regis had just said.

The mediator then focused on what both parties wanted to see happen. Both men offered their sense of what might prevent future problems. There was a discussion of ways in which Charles could get to Claudia's house and catch the bus without walking near Jerome's block. This was followed by a discussion of ways to deal with Jerome's friends and their attitudes and actions toward Charles. Various options were raised and considered. When the parties had focused on certain steps as the ones they felt would resolve the situation, the mediator asked them to help draw up what they wanted to include in a final settlement. In the end, the agreement included (1) a statement that Charles would not attack Jerome and his friends, (2) a statement that Jerome would not name-call and would ask his friends not to name-call, (3) a description of the route Charles would walk through the neighborhood when he caught the bus and visited Claudia, and (4) a commitment that the parties would exchange addresses so that if any issues came up or if Charles was thought to be involved in any incidents with Jerome or his friends, the two men could contact each other directly to discuss the matter.

* * *

The terms the parties agreed to in this case alleviated a serious and potentially volatile dispute between two relative strangers. The agreement addressed Regis's concerns about protecting his son's safety, and it met Charles's need to walk, unharassed, through the neighborhood. In this sense, the case is a classic instance of successful mediation: it produced a settlement that reflected workable solutions to a problem that had escalated severely.

But in another sense, the agreement reached was a very minor part of what this mediation accomplished. In fact, when the parties agreed on a settlement at the end of the session, it was almost an anticlimax. And the subsequent agreement-writing endeavor seemed somewhat contrived. It was as if these men were being asked to demonstrate that the subtle exchange that had just occurred between them could fit into a settlement framework. It felt as if the terms they were being encouraged to articulate—where Charles would and would not walk, what Jerome would not say to Charles and what he would say to his friends—did not greatly matter, because something had taken place that made any specific agreement unnecessary. It seemed clear that Charles would not attack Jerome, even if he walked through Jerome's neighborhood and was taunted about the limp the way he had been in the past. Given this sense, drafting an agreement about Charles's route through the neighborhood appealed almost superfluous, as if fulfilling some preordained ritual of agreement writing rather than documenting what the parties had actually accomplished.

What happened during the session was much more powerful than the terms of the agreement the parties ultimately signed. These two men came to see each other differently, by recognizing that they were alike—that they both wanted and deserved each other's acknowledgment as fellow human beings. In stating that he may have made a mistake in attacking the abusive teens, Charles acknowledged the father's outrage at the threat to his son's well-being. Even Charles's undefensive demeanor suggested that he was in touch with the father's concern about his son. In stating that Jerome and his friends were cruel, Regis acknowledged the emotional pain someone with a severe limp could feel at such ridicule. When Regis revealed that he had told his son "we all live in glass houses," Regis acknowledged that he, too, may have wounds that could easily be opened by careless words or teenage pranks. He acknowledged that he shared, with Charles, in the vulnerabilities of being human.

It was this exchange of acknowledgments that made it very unlikely that Charles would attack, even if insults were hurled in the future. Being in earshot of such ridicule simply didn't matter half as much now that Charles knew, firsthand, that someone understood the pain such insults could inflict. He had something to draw from—a source of strength—that would mute the hurt, even if Regis could not change his son or his son could not change his friends. The connection Charles made with another human being, in this mediation, would help buffer him from thoughtless cruelties.

Both men also found, through their interactions with each other during the mediation session, capacities within themselves to address a problem in ways they may never have learned in the streets of Queens, or in the court in which the original assault charge was filed. 'They had examined their own feelings, considered the consequences of moving toward or against each other, and relied on their own (sometimes intuitive) insights about human strengths and frailties in deciding what to say to each other and in making commitments to each other. They both knew, at some level, that during the hour and a half session *they* had made choices—about revealing parts of themselves, about acknowledging concerns for each other—that had powerful, reparative effects. They were aware, at some level, that they themselves had made decisions and commitments that redirected an escalation that easily might have ended up in Queens' homicide files. As a result of this experience of their own power to redirect events, they left the session with a greater awareness of their own potential resources—resources they could draw from when confronted with other escalating circumstances.

Seeing the crossroads

From time to time, mediators experience sessions much like this one. Not surprisingly, they tend to chalk these cases up to luck, to view them as instances of mediation's elusive potential. They usually conclude that the parties had a good day or were just "ready to settle." Although many disputes do take serendipitous turns, especially under the watchful eyes of a third party, these turns may only be serendipitous because we have come to expect (and emphasize) something quite different. Practitioners may be chalking potentially instructive cases up to luck because they do not have the frameworks to do otherwise—to think of and understand these cases on their own terms and to intervene consciously in ways that foster such outcomes.

What the Sensitive Bully case (and others like it) suggests is that an approach to practice is possible that realizes the transformative potential of the mediation process. But taking this approach means turning off a road that the mediation movement has been following for some time. It means seeing that a crossroads lies ahead and that staying on mediation's current course may mean missing a promising route. Our goal is to offer a clear road map of the choices, a map that describes where mediation is and where it might (or might not) head.

The crossroads we see facing the mediation movement is reflected in the difference between two approaches to mediation that are described and contrasted in this book. Each has roots reaching back to the beginnings of the mediation movement; each is connected to a different dimension that has always been seen as one of the potentials of the mediation process. The first approach, a *problem-solving approach,* emphasizes mediation's capacity for finding solutions and generating mutually acceptable settlements. Mediators make moves that influence and direct parties—toward settlements in general, and even toward specific terms of settlement. As the mediation movement has developed, the problem-solving potential of mediation has been emphasized more and more, so that this kind of directive, settlement-oriented mediation has become the dominant form of practice today.

The second approach, a *transformative approach* to mediation, emphasizes mediation's capacity for fostering empowerment and recognition, as illustrated in the most general way by the Sensitive Bully dispute. Transformative mediators concentrate on empowering parties to define issues and decide settlement terms for themselves and on helping parties to better understand one another's perspectives. The effect of this approach is to avoid the directive-ness associated with problem-solving mediation. Equally important, transformative media-tion helps parties recognize and exploit the opportunities for moral growth inherently presented by conflict. It aims at changing the parties themselves for the better, as human beings. In the course of doing so, it often results in parties finding genuine solutions to their real problems. However, as the movement has grown and developed, the transformative potential of mediation has received less and less emphasis in practice.

We believe that the transformative approach should become the primary approach to practice in all the contexts in which mediation is used, reversing the direction in which the mediation movement has been heading. Our goal is to explain why this shift in practice should occur, showing both the limitations of the problem-solving approach and the strengths of the transformative approach. We delineate the transformative approach to mediation, contrasting it with other approaches, giving concrete case illustrations, and suggesting how it can be implemented in the present institutional context of the mediation movement.

References

Johnson, J.M. *Dispute Resolution Directory*. Washington, D.C.: American Bar Association, 1993.
Singer, L.R. *Settling Disputes: Conflict Resolution in Business, Families, and the Legal System*. San Francisco: Westview Press, 1990.

10 Strategy for community conferences

Emotions and social bonds

Suzanne M. Retzinger and Thomas J. Scheff

These remarks are based primarily on the observation of nine community conferences in Canberra, Adelaide, and Campbelltown, AUS, in December 1994, but are also influenced by the published work of Braithwaite and his associates (1989, Brathwaite and Mugford, 1994; Moore, 1993), and conversations with Braithwaite, Terry O'Connell, John McDonald and Larry Sherman. We were strongly impressed by the power of the conference format. We consider it to be a justice machine. A movement, partially independent of what actually occurs during the formal conference, seems to be set in motion that lends toward justice and reconciliation.

Material and symbolic reparation processes occur side by side during community conferences. The process involving material reparation leads to the actual settlement: the undertakings agreed upon by the participants to compensate the victims and society for the offender's crimes. The settlement usually involves restitution or compensation for damage done, and some form of community service. The process of arriving at a settlement is entirely verbal, highly visible, and largely unambiguous: it provides the ostensible purpose for the meeting. Underlying the process of reaching a settlement is another, much less visible process of symbolic reparation. This process involves the social rituals of respect, courtesy, apology, and forgiveness, which seem to operate independently of the verbal agreements that are reached. Symbolic reparation depends on the emotional dynamics of the meeting and the state of the bonds between the participants. This chapter seeks to clarify the emotion process and the stale of the bonds in community conferences, since they are much more ambiguous than the process of reaching verbal agreement. Awareness and negotiation of shame dynamics, in particular, are the keys to effective conferences.

The ideal outcome, from the point of view of symbolic reparation, is constituted by two steps: the offender first clearly expresses genuine shame and remorse over his or her actions. In response, the victim takes at least a first step towards forgiving the offender for the trespass. These two steps are the *core sequence*. The core sequence generates repair and restoration of the bond between victim and offender, after this bond had been severed by the offender's crime. The repair of this bond symbolizes a more extensive restoration that is to take place between the offender and the other participants, the police and the community. Even though the emotional exchange that constitutes the core sequence may be brief, perhaps only a few seconds, it is the key to reconciliation, victim satisfaction, and decreasing recidivism.

The core sequence also effects the material settlement. Emotional conciliation typically leads directly to a settlement that satisfies the participants, one that is neither too punitive nor too lenient, but seems more or less inevitable. Without the core sequence, the path towards settlement is strewn with impediments: whatever settlement is reached does not decrease the tension level in the room, and leaves the participants with a feeling of arbitrariness and dissatisfaction. Thus, it is crucially important to give symbolic reparation at least parity with material settlement. Unless this is done, conferences may turn out, in the long-run, to be only marginally better than traditional court practices. Symbolic reparation is the vital element that differentiates conferences from all other forms of crime control.

The vital component of symbolic reparation, the core sequence, did not occur, however, during the formal part of the nine conferences we observed. Difficulty, tension, and arbitrariness were observed in reaching an agreement in all nine cases. However, in three of the nine cases, the vital movement from shame and remorse to forgiveness may have occurred immediately after the formal end of the conference. In two of the cases, the victims had conversations with the offenders, as they were awaiting forms to sign. In the third case, the facilitator, who saw the participants out of the building, reported that the victim had patted one of the offenders on the shoulder after he had made a tearful apology to her. These three instances suggest that it might be advantageous to build in delay after the formal end of the conference, such as the signing of a written agreement, which would allow the participants to finish their unfinished business of symbolic reparation. Built-in delay to the completion of the conference may turn out to be a significant part of the process of reparation, allowing oversight to the actions of the formal conference. The extraordinary complexity of the conference and the high levels of emotional tension make it likely that some such oversight will be necessary in a large number of cases, perhaps in the majority. In many cases, even a highly trained and skilful facilitator might find it difficult to overcome the impediments to symbolic reparation.

Symbolic reparation, unlike material settlement, depends entirely upon the play of emotions and social relationships during the conference. These dynamics are governed by two types of events. First, the management of shame, the master emotion, not only in the offender and supporters, but also in all the other participants, including the facilitator. Second, the degree of mutual identification and understanding which prevails: the slate of the bond between the participants. The dynamics of social bonds are as important as shame, but the focus here is on shame dynamics. Since we treat bonds and emotions as equivalent, parallel phenomena, our proposals with regard to shame can easily be translated into bond language. The symbolic outcome of conferences depends upon the management of shame; symbolic reparation will occur to the extent that shame and related emotions are evoked and acknowledged by the participants. On the other hand, symbolic reparation will not occur to the extent that shame and related emotions are denied.

Shame as the master emotion

Discussion of shame dynamics is difficult, because of limitations of the concept of shame in Western societies, where it is subject to extensive repression (Scheff, 1990: Retzinger, 1991; Scheff and Retzinger, 1991; Scheff, 1994). This repression is both caused by, and gives rise to, rampant individualism. These ideas are documented in Elias's magisterial study (1983) of the historical development of modern civilization. Elias used excerpts from European advice manuals over the last five hundred years to show the gradual but implacable repression of shame. The idea that one can be ashamed of being ashamed leads to the concept of continuous loops of shame, which is an explanation of the mechanism of repression.

One indicator of repression is the difference between the treatment of shame in the languages of modern and traditional societies. In European languages, and especially in English, the concept of shame is extremely narrow and negative. In the English language, shame has the meaning of disgrace and profound emotional pain. But in other European languages, there is both a shame of disgrace (as in the French *honte)* and a positive, everyday shame (as in the French *pudeur),* which refers to modesty, shyness, and (at least in classic Greek) awe. The possibility that there was once a positive shame in English is suggested by the word humility (because of its relation to humiliation), but humility has lost its relationship to shame in modern English.

The narrowness and negativeness of the concept of shame in modern societies is still more strongly suggested by comparison with the shame lexicon in the languages of traditional societies. The shame lexicon in Mandarin Chinese is much larger than those or modern societies (Shaver *et al.,* 1992). The Mandarin emotion lexicon also contains a large number of shame-anger combinations unknown in English. The shame lexicon is rich in traditional societies because its members are sensitive to social relationships, requiring awareness of shame and embarrassment, in contrast to the individualism of modern societies. The small and narrow lexicon of shame in Western languages, especially English, suggests that most forms of shame are being overlooked or avoided.

Recovering the positive facets of shame and the breadth of the shame concept from the maws of repression and silence is necessary if we are to understand shame dynamics. The positive aspects of shame have been explored by Lynd (1958), Tompkins (1963) and Schneider (1977). Lynd offers a representative statement. "The very fact that shame is an isolating experience also means that if one can find ways of sharing and communicating it, this communication can bring about particular closeness with others..." (1958, p.66). The idea expressed in this passage is crucially significant for community conferences; if the offender can come to the point of "sharing and communicating" shame, instead of hiding or denying it, the damage to the bond between the offender and the other participants may be repaired.

Recovering the actual breadth of the shame concept is also important for the conference process because shame is a Protean presence among all the participants. The offender stands publicly accused of wrongdoing and will be ashamed. The offender's supporters will be ashamed because of their relationship to him or her. The victim will be ashamed in the sense of feeling betrayed, violated, and/or impotent. The victim's supporters, in so far as they identify with him or her, will share this kind of shame. Disguised and denied shame inhibits the participants from repairing the bonds between them: it therefore blocks symbolic reparation. Retzinger (1991) has developed a systematic procedure for identifying shame, no matter how hidden or disguised, by reference to visual, verbal, and nonverbal cues. Members of modern societies require retraining in shame language, especially the language of gesture and innuendo, in order to become aware of shame in themselves and others.

We have drawn from the work of Lynd (1958), Tomkins (1963), Goffman (1967), Lewis (1971) and others to treat shame as a large family of emotions and affects (Scheff, 1990; Retzinger, 1991; Scheff and Retzinger, 1991; Scheff, 1994). Our definition includes the positive aspects of shame, what Schneider called "sense of shame", as well as embarrassment, humiliation, shyness, modesty, and feelings of discomfort, awkwardness, inadequacy, rejection, insecurity and lack of confidence. We give particular emphasis to loops or chains of shame and anger, as in Mandarin Chinese. The concept is much broader than the way shame is used in vernacular English, and recovers the broadness of the concept that is in use in traditional societies.

The most detailed treatment of shame in traditional societies can be found in a discussion of *whakamaa,* the conception of shame in Maori society (Metge, 1986). *Whakamaa* means shy, embarrassed, uncertain, inadequate, incapable, afraid, hurt, depressed, or ashamed (Metge, 1986). Only the inclusion of afraid (fear) differs from our usage. But the examples that Metge uses for afraid suggest not the emotion of fear (danger to life or limb), but social fear, that is, anticipation of shame. As in our usage, *whakamaa* concerns not only feelings, but also relationships. Maori usage also stresses the importance of acknowledging shame, and the disruptive consequences when shame is not acknowledged.

Because of repression of shame, community conferences conducted in modern societies may be more problematic in terms of emotions and relationships than those conducted in Maori and other tribal societies. Most traditional societies, like the Maoris, have a subtle and wide-ranging language of emotions and relationships which we in the West have lost. The understanding of shame in its positive, broad, and relational sense might be a crucial issue in the training of conference facilitators. How can a brief training significantly change the repression of shame and the individualism that has been inculcated by modern societies? The discussion of shame dynamics seeks to bring this issue into the open.

A theoretical issue of great importance for the operation of conferences is the difference between pathological and normal shame. Effective crime control requires normal (reintegrative) rather than pathological shame (Braithwaite, 1989). By paying close attention to the particular way shame is manifested, it is possible to distinguish, moment by moment, between the two forms of shame as they occur in social interaction. According to our theory, manifestations of normal shame, although unpleasant, are brief, as little as a few seconds. Shame, anger, and other related emotions which persist for many minutes are pathological. Shame is a highly reflexive emotion, which can give rise to long-lasting feedback loops of shame; one can be ashamed of being ashamed, and so on, around the loop, resulting in withdrawal or depression. Another loop is being angry that one is ashamed, and ashamed that one is angry, and so on around the loop. Furthermore, shame-anger loops can occur between, as well as within, participants. Indignation can be contagious, resulting in mutual and counter-indignation. Both individual and social emotional loops can last indefinitely. Persistent, relentless emotions, such as continuing embarrassment, indignation, resentment and hatred, are always pathological.

Shame plays a crucial role in normal cooperative relationships, as well as in conflict. Shame signals a threat to the social bond, and is therefore vital in establishing where one stands in a relationship. Similarly, pride signals a secure bond. Shame is the emotional cognate of a threatened or damage bond, just as threatened bonds are the source of shame. This equation allows shame language to be translated into relationship language, and *vice versa*. Goffman (1967) has argued that normal shame and embarrassment are an almost continuous part of all human contact: this is why the visible expression of shame by the offender looms so large in symbolic reparation. When we see signs of shame and embarrassment in others, we are able to recognize them as human beings like ourselves, no matter what the language, cultural setting, or context. Overcoming the public's narrow view of shame is the principal impediment to success for the conferences, and not far behind is training facilitators to be aware of and to manage shame.

Paths to symbolic reparation: reframing indignation and eliciting painful emotions

The offender needs to be in a state of perfect defencelessness, to use Moore's (1993) suggestive terminology, to clearly express genuine shame and remorse. Tavuchis (1991) makes a similar statement in his discussion of the effective apology. The offender needs to lay him or herself completely at the mercy of the victim, uncovering repressed emotions. This is a task of some magnitude since, in modern societies, states of perfect defencelessness are unusual even in private, much less at a public gathering. How is the offender to overcome the effects of repression in the presence of the participants whose own emotions are highly repressed? The principal paths may be reframing displays of moral indignation against the offender and eliciting a vivid expression of the painful emotions caused by the offender's crime, by at least one of the participants, usually a victim or a supporter of the victim (O'Connell, personal communication). These two paths are related; reframing aggressive emotions can lead to vivid expressions of painful emotions.

Moral indignation is a particular manifestation of shame and anger. The victim, especially, is likely to feel the shame or helplessness, impotence, betrayal, and/or violation caused by of the offence. However, this shame is not usually acknowledged, but masked by anger. Repetitive and relentless anger at the offender is an effective defence against feeling shame. It is unacknowledged shame that drives repetitive episodes of moral indignation. If this shame can be acknowledged (along with other hidden emotions such as grief and fear), anger and moral indignation directed towards the offender will be relatively short lived and manageable.

Although other emotions are also important, moral indignation is emphasized, since this was the emotion we saw displayed most frequently and most intensely. There were two conferences which were exceptions. One was a drink-driving case. The overwhelming emotional movement in this conference was massive denial by the offender and his supporters. Rather than being too far from the other participants (isolated), this offender was too close (engulfed). The other exception was a case involving illegal use of an automobile. The crime was a technicality, since the offender had not known that the auto was stolen when she entered it. The predominate emotion at this conference was embarrassment, not by the offender and her mother, but by the facilitator, the arresting officer, and by us, the observers. Moral indignation against the offender(s) was the predominate emotion at the other seven conferences. It requires skill and sensitivity on the facilitator's part to recognize and rechannel this. Moral indignation is composed of shame and anger. The anger component is usually visible; in repetitive moral indignation, it is a mask for the underlying shame. Shame is carefully hidden, not only from others but also from oneself. The feelings of anger, violation, helplessness, and impotence that haunt victims are indications of hidden shame.

The shame component, the main emotional freight carried by indignation, is even hidden in dictionary definitions, which emphasize only anger. To find the shame component, we have to go to the root word, indignity, which means a humiliating insult to someone's self-respect. Labov and Fanshel (1977) hint at the key indicators of self-righteous indignation when they describe what they call "helpless anger" (shame-anger) in one of their subjects. Rhoda, directed towards her aunt, Editha: "...she [Rhoda] is so choked with emotion at the unreasonableness of Editha's behavior that she cannot begin to describe it accurately" (p. 191). Labov and Fanshel continue in the same passage, attempting to describe the indicators of helpless anger, using terminology such as helpless exasperation and sarcastic exasperation. Rhoda's language, they say, implies that Editha's "violation of normal standards is so gross to the point of straining (her) verbal resources".

This description of "helpless anger" comes close to what we saw as self-righteous indignation at the conferences, particularly the term exasperation, and the idea that the helplessly angry person feels unable to describe the enormity of the other's trespass. The point is not that the subject feels unable, but that the trespass feels so overwhelming that it would defy description by anyone. The feeling that an emotion seems so unmanageable is a clue to the repression of the occluded emotions which drive the conscious ones. Use of the term sarcasm points towards a second dimension of indignation: the subject seems to feel that the enormity of the trespass is so obvious that the audience should (but does not) feel as strongly about it as he or she does. The sarcasm is directed not only at the offender, but also at the audience, who are not as angry about the offence as they should be. Repetitive indignation interferes both with the mutual identification (a secure bond) between victim and offender and between the victim and the rest of the participants. The participants are isolated from one another to the extent that indignation, a shame-anger loop, pervades a conference.

This analysis suggests a central point about the management of indignation. The expression or anger should be refrained so that the underlying emotions (shame, grief, fear) can surface and be discharged. Unless shame is acknowledged, expressions or indignation are likely to continue without relief (Scheff, 1990; Retzinger, 1991; Scheff and Retzinger, 1991; Scheff, 1994). The detection and refraining of moral indignation is a crucial component of effective conferences.

When moral indignation is repetitive and out of control, it is a defensive movement in two steps: denial or one's own shame, followed by projection or blame onto the offender. I am not dishonorable in any way, whereas the offender is entirely dishonorable. The participants must see themselves as being like the offender rather than unlike him or her, in order to identify with the offender (there but for the grace of God go I). Moral indignation interferes with the identification between participants. Uncontrolled repetitive moral indignation is the most important impediment to symbolic reparation and reintegration. To the extent that it is rechannelled, it can be instrumental in triggering the core sequence of reparation.

Shame/rage spirals can take a form other than moral indignation. Forms such as self-righteous rage (Horowitz, 1981) or narcissistic rage (Kohut, 1971) are not often seen at conferences. These other forms are likely to be more intense than indignation, and more likely to lead to verbal or physical assault. Unacknowledged shame in moral indignation is closer to the surface, and is more easily accessed by skillful questioning.

Two types of moral indignation

Moral indignation appeared in two forms, self-righteous indignation, the more flagrant form, and moral superiority, the more covert form. Self-righteous indignation was expressed most frequently and relentlessly by the victims, but also, in some cases, by the victims' supporters and even by the offenders' supporters, especially the offenders' parents. This emotion is expressed by what is said, but much more strongly, by how it is said, and in what context. For example, the victims in a fraud case in Canberra bombarded the offender with demands for the return of the money by one victim, and demands that the offender help protect the other victim's reputation. Not only the words, but also the manner of both victims conveyed their own self righteousness and their feelings of betrayal by the offender, their distrust of him, and their feelings of helplessness and anger. The repetition of their demands, despite the responses of the offender, the crying of the offender's wife, and the attempts by the facilitator and the investigating officer to intervene, clearly signalled the victims' intense indignation. Labov and Fanshel (1977) have suggested that repetition of a request, especially if it disregards the other's responses, is at least challenging and, in many cases, actually insulting. Repetition implies disrespect in several ways: that the indignant person is not listening to the offender, or that the offender is not listening to the indignant person, or more potently, that the offender is lying.

Self-righteous indignation was also expressed frequently and intensely in a break-in and theft case in Campbelltown. In this case, not only the victim, but also the parents of the offenders expressed indignation. The victim's flagrant indignation took the form of incredulity, not so much that the crime could have been perpetrated against her, but that the offenders were capable of such a deed. In the case of the parents, the incredulity was more that their children could be involved, that is, that the conference involved the parents. The parents in a Canberra shoplifting case also indirectly expressed incredulity that their son could be a thief. Most of their comments seemed to distance them from the offender, their son; they were hardly the kind of people to be spending time in a police station. Incredulity, hardly being able to believe what has happened, seems to be the chief visible cue to self-righteous indignation.

A second, more covert form of moral indignation occurs frequently, particularly by the police, in the form of lecturing the offender. The arresting officer in the cases we saw in Adelaide always gave some form of moral instruction to the offender. This tactic signals the moral superiority of the instructor to the offender, and therefore threatens the bond of mutual identification between them. In one case, even the facilitator joined the chorus: he gave the offenders a lengthy lecture on the nature of conscience. The lecture usually contains a threat as well, which also disrupts rather than builds the social bond. Threat implies that the offender is not responsible, but needs an external goad to make him or her behave. If mutual identification occurs, threat is unnecessary.

In Adelaide, the arresting officer always threatened the offenders with court. At first, the arresting officer in the break-in and theft case we observed in Adelaide was highly respectful towards the offender, and solicitous of his rights, both in the content and manner of what was said when she reported the nature of the offence. But later in the conference, perhaps because from her point of view the offender had not expressed shame and remorse clearly enough, she became very emotional, lecturing the offender on how stupid and silly it was to break the law, and on the certainty of strong punishment. At this point, her outburst showed self-righteous indignation, as well as moral superiority.

At the same conference, the victim of the break-in expressed moral indignation, and perhaps a sense of violation, by her repetitive discussion of the keys and locks of her house and the material goods that were stolen. The discussion of finding the stolen key, the problem of changing the locks, and the costs, went on for some time. It absorbed a significant proportion of the conference time, together with her discussion of the material losses. In this instance, and perhaps in several others, a skilled facilitator might have been able to interrupt the display of indignation, by interpreting it in terms of a sense of betrayal, helplessness, loss, and violation. In the fraud case, and in several others, it would have taken a great deal of skill and self-confidence on the part of the facilitator to be able to stem the torrent. It may be necessary to allow a preliminary outburst of indignation against the offender, but it is important that the facilitator be trained to detect repetitive waves of indignation, and be able to reframe them.

The hidden shame component in indignation

Moral indignation of one of the victims in a case of school vandalism was so indirect as to be difficult to manage, even for a skillful facilitator. This instance illustrates the way in which shame that underlies indignation can be hidden from others and from oneself. The victim, "Fred Johnson", was a middle-aged teacher at the school that was vandalized. The vandalism was defamatory statements about the teachers spray-painted on the walls of the school. He was the principal victim: unlike the other teachers, each having only one defamation. Johnson had three:

Johnson is an old fogey.
Mr. Johnson sucks dick with Mr. Smith (another teacher).

Mr. Johnson is a bald-headed cocksucker.

The author of these defamations was unknown. The offender admitted to spray-painting only one statement, one which intimated a homosexual relationship between two students. Under repeated questioning, the offender indicated that he had no knowledge of the authors of the defamations against the teachers. The facilitator seemed somewhat puzzled by Mr. Johnson's presence at the conference, since she had understood he was to attend only if the principal could not be there to represent the school. Mr. Johnson explained that he decided to attend together with the principal because he also had some comments to make. Mr. Johnson first denied injury to himself. He explained that teaching as long as he had, "this kind of slander was water off a duck's back". He further denied injury by explaining, somewhat defiantly, that contrary to what students think, teachers stick together; one of his fellow teachers had phoned him about the defamations so that he would not be surprised by them.

Like his presence, there was a gratuitous element to these comments. They seemed somewhat unnecessary, and were carefully addressed to the air rather than to a particular person. Having denied injury, he then launched into an indirect verbal assault of the offender. He stated that when he counsels students, he tells them that such slander is cowardly. Johnson was insulting the offender, but only indirectly since he was calling him a coward only by implication. He repeated three more times this insinuation that students who resort to such actions are cowards, underhanded, have no guts. The offender's mother felt called upon to refute the charge of cowardice when it was her turn. She said that her son could not be a coward, because he plays rugby union!

Mr. Johnson's words and manner suggest a shame/rage spiral. He seems to have been humiliated by the defamations, but did not acknowledge this feeling to himself or others. For example, a statement such as "I was upset and offended by the graffiti" would be a step towards acknowledgment of shame. Instead, he denied injury, but made an indirect verbal assault on the offender. Rather than express his shame and anger, he attacked his putative attacker. His cycle of insult and counter-insult is counterproductive; it is the basis for all destructive and unending conflicts (Relzinger, 1991; Scheff, 1994).

The basic problem with indignation, a kind of impotent anger (shame/anger loop), is that, if it is repeated enough, it can damage the potential bond between the indignant participant and the offender. The torrent of criticism and disrespect gives rise to defensiveness on the part of the offender, the very opposite of the goal of symbolic reparation. This problem can be insidious, because the offender often displays cool from the beginning. This display, although it is a mask for shame, unfortunately triggers defensive anger in the participants, creating a vicious circle. The basic job of the facilitator is to ask questions which cut through the defensive stance of the participants. In this way, the conferences maintain a balance between the participants' anger at the offender and their respect for him or her, between shaming and reintegration. One way of contributing to this end would be to enlarge upon the formula used when separating the offense from the offender. Perhaps it is not enough to make this distinction abstractly. It might sometimes be necessary, if the air is thick with indignation, after condemning the offence, to ask the offender's supporters to name some of the offender's good traits. The facilitator could then summarize their positive comments, to bring the distinction between the bad offence and the good offender into high relief. This tactic would need to be handled with some skill and discretion to avoid antagonizing the victim's camp. Such initial support might make it possible for the offender to remain emotionally open in the face of moral indignation. Perhaps, if a space of this kind were created initially for the offender, he or she would become less defensive, whatever the participants' emotional responses.

Encouraging the expression of painful emotions

Complementing the refraining of moral indignation is another tactic (O'Connell, personal communication, 1994). The offender may express genuine shame and remorse, even if he or she has defended him or herself against moral indignation. If one or more of the victims, or supporters of the victim, clearly express painful emotions (such as grief) that was caused by the offender's crime, the offender may be caught off guard and identify with that pain, even to the point that his or her defences are breached. Under these conditions, he or she will then show the shame and remorse that are necessary to generate the beginnings of forgiveness in the victim. An example was the victim who was highly indignant during the whole formal conference. However, when the offender offered her a tearful apology, she patted him on the shoulder, indicating identification and a step towards forgiveness. It is for this reason that O'Connell (personal communication, 1994) gives emotionality pride of place in the convening and facilitation of conferences. The chief focus of the facilitator in organizing and presiding should be setting the conditions that will allow painful emotions (such as grief and shame) to be felt, expressed, and shared by the victim, the offender, and other participants. However, O'Connell is referring to an emotionality that is primarily the painful emotions and not the aggressive ones, such as rage and anger. The goal of the facilitator is to encourage the former and to rechannel the latter. If aggressive emotions are interrupted and reframed, they may give rise to the expression of the painful emotions that are needed to trigger the core sequence. O'Connell's focus on emotionality and ours on shame gives rise to the following set of tactics that can be used to remove impediments to symbolic reparation.

1. *Have the facilitator convene his or her own conference.* He or she should personally telephone each of the participants beforehand, even if they have been invited by the victim or the offender. The facilitator needs to establish a preliminary bond with each of the participants prior to the conference. The personable facilitator can begin to connect with each participant, even by telephone. He or she can gather pertinent information that might not be included in the written documents, help to remove impediments to actually coming to the conference and maximally participating in it, or exclude those who might sabotage reparation. The initial telephone call may also give the facilitator preliminary information about the emotional openness of each of the participants. The most important reason for the telephone call is to begin the process of bond formation that is necessary to ensure the success of a conference. Secure bonds are needed between at least some of the participants if the conference is to support the expression of painful emotions.

2. *Maximize the number of participants.* The reason for this tactic is directly related to emotionality. The larger the number of persons, the more likely that at least one of them will be emotionally open and able to express painful emotions, even in a tense situation. A large number also allows more possibilities for mutual identification, and for compensating for facilitator error. The expression of painful emotions caused by the offender's crime is usually the trigger for the core sequence of remorse and forgiveness. Large numbers of participants and telephone calls to each put a strain on the facilitator's time and patience. Unless the reasons are well understood, these two tactics will get short shrift.

3. *Question victims and their supporters on the very first feeling they had when they learned of the crime.* The first and other early feelings are likely to be painful emotions, such as grief, fear, and shame (in the form of helplessness and impotence). Usually, these first feelings are quickly covered up by anger and indignation. However, a skillful facilitator can help the victims find and acknowledge these early feelings, which will give them relief. Expression of these painful feelings can also have a profound effect on the offender, since

they reveal the inner person of the victims: wounded, suffering beings like the offender. The importance of eliciting the victims' first feelings cannot be overstressed.

4. *Hold the conference as soon as possible after the offence.* Any substantial amount of delay will probably diminish the emotionality of the conference, or cause other problems. After a long delay, the conference will be an anticlimax, since the emotions involved will either have subsided or have been resolved. A delay of three months before one of the Adelaide conferences had destructive consequences. The case involved three offenders who had committed destructive acts against their school on two different occasions; on a subsequent occasion, one of the offenders had assaulted another of the offenders. The delay served to separate one of the offenders, the one who had committed the assault, from the other two. In the three-month interval before the conference, two of the offenders had made their peace with the school authorities; their families had worked out restitution with the school. This development only served to further isolate the offender who had not made restitution. The accolades which were given the two rehabilitated offenders served as denunciations of the third offender. In re-integrating the two boys, the participants, except the facilitator, took on some of the characteristics of a lynch mob towards the third boy. Had the facilitator known of these developments, he would not have held a single conference, but had one conference for the two boys (or even cancelled it), and another one for the third boy. Unless the conferences are held in a timely fashion, they may be subverted by developments during the waiting period

5. *Recognize that no intentional shaming is necessary.* The format of the community conference leads automatically to intense shame in the offender. At several of the conferences, when the offenders were asked why they did not bring their friends to the conference to support them, they answered that they did not want them to know. That is to say, they were already ashamed even before the conference began. Most people find the focusing of public attention on them embarrassing, even if caused by a good deed. Everyone will find the situation laden with shame when public attention arises out of a misdeed. Intentional shaming in the form of sustained moral indignation, or in any other guise, brings a gratuitous element into the conference, the piling of shame on top of the automatic shaming that is built into the format. This format is an automatic shaming machine. Since the automatic part is only implicit it is less likely to arouse the offenders' defences. Shame can arise spontaneously from within the offender. But, in a formal already heavy with shame, even small amounts of overt shaming are very likely to push the offender into a defensive stance, to the point that he or she will be unable to even feel, much less express, genuine shame and remorse.

6. *Ensure the specicity of consequences.* Attempts by participants to shame the offender by referring to conceivable, but indirect, consequences of the offence may be counter-productive. Examples are the use of videos of the results of car crashes, and members of the public as victims in a drink-driving case, evoking by the investigating officer of the losses to the public at large, from white collar crime in a fraud case, and calling of large-scale graffiti as copycat crimes by the principal in connection with the single graffiti of the offender in the graffiti case. These generalized consequences are apt to be shrugged off by the offender as completely unrelated to him, and in so doing, he mobilizes his defences. The consequences likely to have emotional effects on the offender are only those that are clearly and directly related to his own actions. This is the reason why victims are recruited from among the offender's supporters in drink driving cases. The poor judgment that causes driving after excessive drinking usually has other damaging consequences among those close to the offender. With encouragement from the facilitator, the offender's supporters are likely to air their emotions in a way that will bring home to the offender the destructiveness of his behavior. Poor judgment is a tactical concept, not a label to be used publicly. If the facilitator is to

recruit victims from among the offender's supporters, he or she can use it in his or her own thinking to locate injuries caused by the offender's behavior to his own supporters. This idea is somewhat tricky, since it points to some kinds of offender behavior which may not be strictly illegal. For example, wife-beating is illegal, but verbal abuse is not, no matter how relentless and emotionally damaging.

7. *Drink-driving cases.* There is a large volume of these cases, and they are likely to be quite different from most other offences. A further difficulty is that most of the cases are a result of the detection of an illegal level of alcohol, so that there are no real victims due to the offence itself, and no direct possibility of restitution. The offender is usually an adult, rather than a juvenile, an adult who is adroit at denying responsibility for trespasses. Particularly important in these cases is knowledge of prior offences. Whether or not the offender has a drinking problem may be unclear from the first offence, but will become increasingly clear with each subsequent offence. People with drinking problems usually work out persuasive means of denial. They not only are able to persuade others of their inno-cence, but themselves as well. They are skilled at diverting blame from themselves to others, circumstances, the environment, anything that comes to hand.

A closely related problem is that the offender's supporters and, at times, even the victim's supporters and/or the facilitator, may collude with the offender's denial. In one case, the offender readily acknowledged that he had drunk a six pack of beer, but insinuated that he or any other normal man could handle that amount of drink without interfering with his ability to drive. The implication being that drinking such a large amount was the norm, and there-fore should not be illegal. As long as the offender is in denial, the likelihood of feeling shame and remorse is small. This is the reason for recruiting victims from among the offender's ostensible supporters. Anyone with a drinking problem is likely to insult and injure at least some of those close to him. By carefully questioning the supporters, a facilitator may often find at least one victim among them. The offender will be duly asked if he has a drinking problem. But the most powerful question is the one that is directed towards the offender's supporters, "Has his drinking ever been a problem for you?" This question may uncover a real victim at a conference for a victimless crime. The encounter with this victim may yield a moment of authentic shame and remorse from the offender.

8. *Multiple offenders* and *offences.* Conferences with more than one offender and/or date of offence suggest the need for flexibility in following the question protocol that the facilita-tors have learned. This protocol, which involves some four questions, is not intrusive when there is only one offender and one offence. But at conferences with three offenders, and in one case, three separate dates of offences, the procedure took on a mechanical quality. Asking each offender four questions for each offence resulted in the facilitator monopolizing the floor, rather than spontaneous give-and-take among the participants. One way of avoid-ing this dilemma would have been to ask the first offender each question only once. Then, instead of repeating the question, the facilitator could have asked each of the other offenders if they had anything to add. A second issue concerning multiple offences involves the order in which the offences are taken up. The order was chronological at the conference involving multiple offences that we attended. But this ordering violated the principle of emotionality, because the most emotionally laden offence was not the first in time but the last (it involved an assault by one of the offenders on the other). Allowing airing of this offence to occur last distorted the discussion of the two prior offences, since the room was heavy with tension between the assaulted boy and his assaulter. The discussion of this offence and the agree-ment reached partially resolved the emotional tension between the two boys, but by this time it was too late to have any effect on the discussions of the two earlier offences. A skilled

facilitator needs to foresee some of the emotional dynamics of each conference in order to ensure maximum effectiveness.

9. *Match silence with silence.* Many offenders, especially juveniles, will offer minimal responses, rather than being full-fledged participants. They manage a stance of cool, if not hostile, detachment. At an Adelaide conference on theft, the offender, a large 16-year-old boy, gave minimal responses throughout the conference. His posture was what is described by the Maori as *whakamaa* response to public embarrassment, showing the facilitator the top of his head by staring at his toes. However, near the end of the conference, when it was time for him to apologize, he surprised us. Looking the victim right in the eye, he said the obligatory "I'm sorry that I took your money". But he added, on his own, the additional apology, "I shouldn't have taken advantage of you". His second apology was meaningful to all of us, because it was obvious that the victim was somewhat retarded. How can such additional responses be elicited when they are not forthcoming?

At times, skillful follow-up questions may elicit an additional response. But such questions will often be met with silence. Attentive silence on the part of the facilitator may work better than follow-up questions. Such silences require some self-confidence, and also, at times, quieting of other participants who want to rush in to fill the silence. Facilitator silence allows space for the offender, and may be less intrusive than probing questions.

10. *Build in an automatic delay after the completion of the conference.* If the participants only (no facilitators, police officers, or observers) are confined in a small space, conversation among them may lead to symbolic reparation, even if none occurred during the conference itself.

11. *Perform emotion exercises.* Another step may also be helpful in training facilitators. The present training sessions are oriented towards newcomers without experience of conferences. A second three-day training session for those who have had at least several months' experience as facilitators might now be in order. This second session could help the trainees make sense of the sessions they facilitated, their successes and failures. Unlike the initial session, it could be focused directly on emotions and relationships, since experiences at conferences would have prepared trainees to appreciate this approach. The second session could also be to lead directly into the arrangement of ongoing supervision; it might even be called a supervisory session.

One component of each of these advanced training sessions should be an exploration of the domain of emotions. Entering the realms of emotions can be problematic, because they are seldom discussed and little understood. Since most of us are embarrassed about emotions, one way to make the traverse is to begin with shared laughter, the kind that discharges embarrassment. Jokes work for some, but a more reliable method is to share with the class some humorous (that is, embarrassing) incidents from one's own life. This approach also allows the members of the class to identify with the teacher as a person like themselves. Without mutual identification in the class, learning is apt to be slow and tedious.

Conclusion

The basic ideas and practices of community conferences radically contradict police culture and, indeed, the general culture of our societies in innumerable ways. Three days of training, or even a month, are not going to enable a trainee to throw off the beliefs and practices that have brought him or her to adulthood, and to a professional career, and enable him or her to interact in harmony with his or her colleagues. Some kind of continuing education will be necessary if the knowledge and attitudes fostered in training are not to be jettisoned later. The flow of events in conferences is rapid, complex, and often ambiguous. They tax the ingenuity and resourcefulness of even the most effective group worker. Thought needs to be given to the training and supervision of facilitators, and to provision for oversight.

Who should operate conferences? We have no recommendation as to whether police, social workers or mediators should fill the role of conference facilitators. However, whoever is chosen, it is important that the police be included in the early stages of planning the transition from court to conference, and that they are treated as an integral part of the new program. Since the police are the first to contact offenders, they have the power to help or hinder conferencing by their degree of cooperation. We also recommend that, whoever are chosen as facilitators, they be given specific training in recognizing and managing emotions, as indicated in # 11 above. Conferences will begin to transform the dominant police and welfare culture, to the extent that police officers and other facilitators develop the understanding and skill needed for effective conferences. This transformation, together with community-building and empowerment in the control of crime, are the three great goals of the conferencing movement. For this reason, the development of training, supervision and oversight for facilitators contains a powerful force for changing our society in fundamental ways.

This chapter has outlined a strategy for maximizing the effectiveness of community conferences in the control of crime, and for training facilitators. These conferences are state-of-the-art among all current innovations for crime control. It is possible that the use of emotionality in generating mutual identification and secure social bonds may also have application to areas other than crime control. At the low end of the range of applications would be individual and family psychotherapy, and marriage counselling. The idea of the core sequence may be applied, not only in repairing the bonds between clients but also those between client and practitioner. This same idea may also be important in education for generating secure bonds between teacher and student and, therefore, more rapid and deeper learning. Finally, at the high end, the use of the conference format might be applied in mediation between groups, such as international disputes. The inclusion of techniques for encouraging the expression of vulnerable emotions and rechannelling aggressive ones might produce welcome innovations in conflict resolution.

References

Braithwaite. J. (1989). *Crime, Shame and Reintegration.* Cambridge, UK: Cambridge University Press.

—— and S. Mugford (1994). "Conditions of Successful Reintegration Ceremonies." *British Journal of Criminology* 34:139–171.

Elias. N. (1983). *The Civilizing Process* (3rd edn). New York. NY: Vintage.

Goffman, E. (1967). *Interaction Ritual.* New York. NY: Anchor.

Horowitz, M. (1981). "Self-Righteous Rage and Attribution of Blame." *Archives of General Psychiatry* 38:1233–1238.

Kohut, H. (1971). *Thoughts on Narcissism and Narcissistic Rage. The Search for Self.* New York, NY: International University Press.

Labov, W. and D. Fanshel (1977). *Therapeutic Discourse.* New York, NY: Academic Press.

Lewis, H.B. (1971). *Shame and Guilt in Neurosis.* New York, NY: International Universities Press.

Lynd. H. (1958). *On Shame and the Search for Identity.* New York, NY: Harcourt.

Metge, J. (1986). *In and Out of Touch: Whakamaa in Cross Cultural Perspective.* Wellington, NZ: Victoria University Press.

Moore, D. (1993). "Shame, Forgiveness, and Juvenile Justice." *Criminal Justice Ethics.* Winter/
    Spring:3–25.
O'Connell, T. (1994). Personal communication. December.
Retzinger, S. (1991). *Violent Emotions.* Newbury Park, CA: Sage.
Scheff, T. (1990). *Microsociology.* Chicago, IL: University of Chicago Press.
—— (1994). *Bloody Revenge.* Boulder, CO: Westview Press,
—— and S. Retzinger (1991). *Emotions and Violence.* Lexington, MA: Lexington Books.
Schneider. C. (1977). *Shame, Exposure, and Privacy.* Boston, MA: Beacon Press.
Shaver, P.R., S. Wu and J.C. Schwartz (1992). "Cross cultural Similarities and Differences in
    Emotions and Their Representation." In M.S. Clark (ed.). *Review of Personality and Social
    Psyhcology.* Vol 13, Newbury Park, CA: Sage.
Tavuchis, N. (1991). *Mea Culpa: The Sociology of Apology and Reconciliation.* Stanford, CA:
    Stanford University Press.
Tomkins, S. (1963). *Affect, Imagery, Consciousness*, Vol. 2. New York, NY: Springer.

11 Peacemaking circles

Kay Pranis

A young man in his early 20s sits, his head hanging down, in a circle of chairs. Around the circle sit community members, elders, the young man's sister, a judge and a probation officer. Notably missing are his mother and friends, many of whom had agreed to attend this Sentencing Circle. The Keeper, a respected community member skilled in peacemaking and consensus-building, opens the session with a prayer and a reminder that the circle has been convened to address the behavior of this young man, who killed his sister's cat in a drunken outburst. An eagle feather is passed around the circle. As the feather is passed, each member of the circle expresses his or her feelings about the crime and raises questions or concerns. The young man expresses regret about his actions and a desire to change his harmful behavior. His sister, the victim of this crime, talks about her anger and sadness, but also about her love for her brother. An elder mentions that the young man owes something to the animal kingdom and suggests building a bird feeder and feeding the birds. Another community member comments on the inability of the young man to cry and suggests grief and anger counseling. Attendance at Alcoholics Anonymous and community service also are suggested. One community member volunteers to help the young man with the bird feeder and several others offer to accompany him on his first visit to the counselor when he acknowledges that it may be difficult for him to go alone.

Community members also speak about the young man's strengths and potential. As the evening progresses, the young man holds his head higher and higher. Toward the end of the discussion, he tells the group that he had no idea he had so much support in the community. The suggestions of the group are incorporated into a sentencing agreement. The circle ends with a prayer honoring participants for their wisdom and support. The group then adjourns for a potluck supper and chatter.

Peacemaking origins

A peacemaking circle is a community-directed process, developed in partnership with the criminal justice system for involving all those affected by an offense in deciding an appropriate sentencing plan which addresses the concerns of all participants. According to Barry Stuart, author of *Building Community Justice Partnerships: Community Peacemaking Circles,* the principles of negotiation, mediation, consensus-building and peacemaking that shape the peacemaking or sentencing circle process have been part of the dispute resolution process in European and Asian communities for centuries. The process as it has evolved today, most recently within the Yukon Territory in Canada, however, is most similar to one still used to resolve conflicts in Canada's aboriginal communities. "The partnerships formed within Yukon community peacemaking and sentencing circles draw heavily upon aboriginal

Figure 11.1 Peacemaking circle.

concepts of peacemaking and the practices typically found in mediation and consensus-building processes," Stuart writes. "Community circles are neither wholly western, nor aboriginal, but combine principles and practices from both in creating a community-based process to respond to conflict in a manner that advances the well-being of individuals, families and the community."

After six years of experience in the Yukon, peacemaking circles are now spreading across Canada. A pilot project in central Minnesota involving the Mille Lacs Band of Chippewa Indians, the Mille Lacs County District Court, the Minnesota Department of Corrections and Midstate Probation has been in place for one year. Several urban, suburban and rural communities in Minnesota also are developing the process to fit local needs. Each of these projects is a collaborative effort among community members, nonprofit community organizations, judges, local corrections officials, police, victim services, defense attorneys and prosecuting attorneys.

The process

Peacemaking circles use traditional circle ritual and structure to create a respectful space in which the victim, victim supporters, offender, offender supporters, judge, prosecutor, defense counsel, police, court workers and all interested community members can speak from the heart in a shared search for understanding of the event. The participants also identify the steps necessary to address the harm caused by the offense and to prevent future occurrences.

The peacemaking circle process typically involves several steps leading to the actual sentencing:

- an application by the offender to the circle process;
- the creation of a support system for the offender;
- the creation of a support system for the victim;
- a healing circle for the victim;
- a healing circle for the offender; and
- the sentencing circle.

After the sentencing circle, there may be follow-up circles at appropriate intervals to review progress on the sentencing agreement.

Healing circles

While a sentencing circle is open to anyone who wishes to attend, healing circles are private. The victim or offender for whom the healing circle is being held may choose who attends the healing circle. The healing circle normally includes the support system of that person and several other community members who are active in the circle process.

The healing circle is based on several important principles: respect for each individual, confidentiality, commitment to positive outcomes, openness to hearing the pain of others and an understanding that the pain of one affects all.

The healing circle for the victim involves the community directly in validating that the victim did not deserve what happened and demonstrates that the community cares about the victim and is willing to share the pain the victim is experiencing. Participation in a healing circle is a choice for a victim. Information from the healing circle about the harm of the offense to the victim and the wishes of the victim regarding what the offender should do to make amends are shared with the offender support group to assist them in developing an appropriate plan for the offender to present to the sentencing circle.

The healing circle for the offender involves the community in naming the harm created by the offense and in exploring the issues faced by the offender which may have contributed to the behavior. It also demonstrates the willingness of the community to work with the offender to make the changes necessary for him or her to become a contributing member of the community. Typically, the offender healing circle will begin to identify elements which should be part of the sentencing plan.

Healing circles begin with a prayer or reflection, followed by a welcome and explanation of the process by the Keeper. An eagle feather, or other object symbolizing respect and wisdom, is passed clockwise around the circle for everyone to introduce themselves. The feather then is passed again, allowing each participant to speak from the heart to the person for whom the healing circle is being held. Participants may speak only when holding the feather. The feather may go around the circle many times to exhaust all the things that need to be said. Participants may pass the feather without speaking if they wish. Spirituality and expression of emotion are critical aspects of the healing circle process. The circle is closed, as it began, with a prayer or reflection. Many healing circles are followed by a potluck meal for all participants.

Additional applications

Healing circles have been used in circumstances other than the sentencing process. They can be used to provide support and share the pain of victims whose offenders are never caught. Victims whose cases never reach court often feel neglected or isolated in facing the pain of their loss. Through a healing circle, the community can reach out and surround that victim with care and affirm that what happened was wrong and that the victim was not responsible for the crime.

The Mille Lacs project has twice held healing circles for juveniles who were nearing release from state juvenile correctional facilities. The healing circles provided an opportunity to hear the fears of the juveniles regarding their return to the community and the fears of the community about the return of the juveniles. The outcome of such healing circles may be particular conditions of release which address community concerns and commitments by the community for support to address the offenders' concerns.

Healing circles also can be conducted with adult offenders returning to the community after a prison sentence. Successful community reintegration upon release is one of the most difficult challenges faced by offenders and communities. Healing circles create a process for working through intense emotions and constructing solutions to perceived problems. The healing circle provides an opportunity for the community to clearly communicate its expectations and to make commitments for support if those expectations are met.

Community building

The sentencing circle described in the opening paragraph provided an opportunity for all those impacted by the crime to talk about their concerns. But this circle did more than determine a sentence for the perpetrator. The young man later joined the Community Justice Committee and today participates in healing and sentencing circles for others. When asked what turned his life around, he always replies, "Support from the community."

The circle process is not simply a process for finding more appropriate justice; it is an exercise in building community, because it brings community members together in a forum which allows exploration of underlying causes of crime and encourages each community member to offer his or her gifts or capacities to the process of finding solutions and implementing them.

Participation in circles builds the skills of community members in talking about difficult issues. Crime and victimization are among the most emotional issues in communities. The circle process allows full expression of emotions and channels the energy of those emotions toward positive solutions. Feeling respected and being heard allow participants to move beyond anger and fear to listening and caring about one another.

Each time the community gathers around a difficult problem and finds a way to make the situation better, the community builds its capacity to solve problems.

Democracy at work

Circles operate in a very democratic way; decisions are based on consensus and everyone involved – victim, offender, judge, prosecutor, community members – must agree that the decision is one with which they can live. Consensus-based decision-making provides protection for powerless voices which are not protected by the usual conceptualization of democracy as majority rule. In the case of crime, the powerless voices might be those of either the victim or the offender. Consensus-building models require the group to pay attention to the interests of all participants. Participation in decision-making circles is open to anyone who wishes to have a voice in the outcome. This openness is essential to avoid domination by any particular subgroup of the community and to maintain trust by the community in the process.

The physical format of circles carries a message of equality and respect for all. In a circle, all are connected. Titles are dropped in circles, as are other symbols of authority, such as the judge's robe. Every participant in the circle is assumed to have a positive contribution to make.

Community involvement

The criminal justice system can exercise enormous power over the bodies of offenders, but it is relatively powerless in affecting the minds and hearts of offenders. The behavior change we want from offenders comes primarily from the heart and mind. On the other hand, communities do have significant power to change hearts and minds. Again and again, chronic, long-term offenders who have gone through the circle process say that community support made the difference for them.

Community members have another enormous advantage over criminal justice professionals. They are present in the offenders' lives all day, every day. The community is in a much better position to know what is going on in an offender's life. It can monitor the offender's progress and identify where there is a need for more limits or more support.

Similarly, community members often are in a better position to provide support and protection to victims. They can be available at all times and they may be able to monitor the victim's safety much more closely than the system can.

The community also has resources which are not available to the system. A family member or a neighbor of an offender can offer to help the person get to Alcoholics Anonymous every week or a businessman can offer a job. Those are resources not available to the criminal justice system. Circles draw on the life experiences of all the participants to understand the problem at hand and to devise workable solutions. The more diverse the circle membership, the greater the variety of life experiences which may offer wisdom and hope for the future of the community.

12 Navajo restorative justice

The law of equality and justice

Robert Yazzie and James W. Zion

[...]

Egalitarian conceptions of decision-making process

The process of law flows from conflict to judgment or a final decision. It is important to understand who makes the decision to resolve a conflict and how that decision is made. The very process of decision-making points to the healing component of Navajo justice. State systems use judges to make the decisions. The judges are selected on the basis of their education to hear the facts, apply the law and make wise decisions for others. This is alien to the Navajo concept of freedom and individuality, where one person cannot impose a decision on another. Instead, Navajos are their own judges in an egalitarian process.

What happens when there is a dispute? First, a person who claims to be injured or wronged by another will make a demand upon the perpetrator to put things right. The term for this is *nalyeeh,* which is a demand for compensation; it is also a demand to readjust the relationship so that the proper thing is done. In a simple situation such as theft, confrontation of the thief with a threat of public disclosure is usually sufficient. Women who are wronged by a sexual impropriety have the right to confront the offender in a public place to disclose the insult and demand compensation for it. In situations where individuals are unable to make a direct demand, or do not wish to do so, they will seek the help of relatives. There have been situations where young women herding sheep are sexually wronged; a relative of the woman will approach the man's relatives to talk out the situation and demand some sort of compensation or arrangement to mend it [...].

There are more formal dispute resolution methods to talk out disputes. A victim or a victim's relative will approach a *naat'aanii* to request his or her assistance in talking out a particular problem. A *naat'aanii* is a respected community leader, and often a basis for that respect is the very fact that a civil leader is also a clan leader. The *naat'aanii*-peacemaker will summon the interested parties for a group discussion of what to do. An important difference between state system adjudication and peacemaking is the identity of the participants and their role. Peacemaking is not a confrontation between two particular individuals who are immediately involved in the dispute, but a process that involves the family and clan relations of victims and perpetrators as active participants. They are involved because they have an interest in the matter; what affects their relative affects them. Relatives have an opinion about the nature of the dispute or what should be done to resolve it.

A *naat'aanii* will give notice to everyone affected and designate a place to talk out the problem. The process always begins with prayer, which is essential to the healing nature of peacemaking. Prayer is a process that summons supernatural help; the Holy People are called to participate directly. They are not summoned to be a witness, a custom that is reflected in the giving of the oath in courts. *Naat'aaniis* are called in to help the parties and to answer their demands for justice. The prayer is also an opportunity for the *naat'aanii* to focus the minds of the parties on a process that is conciliatory and healing, not confrontational and winner-take-all. Following prayer, the parties have an opportunity to lay out their grievances. There is venting, as in other mediation processes, where the victim has an opportunity to disclose not only the facts, but their impact. People have an opportunity to say how they feel about the event and make a strong demand that something be done about it. Relatives also have an opportunity to express their feelings and opinions about the dispute.

The person accused of a wrongful act also has an opportunity to speak. Human behavior is such that we often put forward excuses or justifications for our conduct. Many Navajo peacemaking cases involve alcohol abuse. A common psychological barrier where an individual is alcohol-dependent is denial. The person will say, 'I don't have a drinking problem'. In adjudication, a defendant accused of an alcohol-related crime will challenge the court to prove that he or she has an alcohol problem to be addressed in some sort of treatment program. Often, defendants referred to such programs do not wholeheartedly participate, using denial to fool themselves. Another barrier is minimalization, where someone excuses conduct by saying, 'It's no big deal'. We see this in domestic violence cases, where a batterer says, 'It's no big deal for an Indian man to beat his wife'. In some child sex abuse cases, perpetrators (falsely) claim that it is traditional to have sex with a stepchild or a young woman who has barely reached puberty. A third barrier is externalization, the excuse that the offence is someone else's fault. 'It's her fault!' a batterer will say. 'If she didn't nag me all the time I wouldn't have to beat her.' Or, 'It's her fault – if she would do what she is supposed to do, I wouldn't be forced to push her around.' Another facet of externalization is excuses. 'It's not my fault; I'm just a dependent alcoholic and I can't help myself.' Many criminal defendants attempt to excuse their conduct by saying, 'I was drunk'. There is also a systemic excuse that is related to anomie (Greek for without law).

The police model inherited by the Navajo Nation has severe limitations. There are not enough police to patrol a rural nation that is larger than nine states. Limited police officers, who must prepare cases in a system where there is proof beyond a reasonable doubt and a defendant cannot be compelled to testify, limits the effectiveness of adjudication. The Navajo Nation also has an imposed social work model for child welfare which is overburdened. Accordingly, when the police or social work system is overburdened we sometimes hear the institutional excuse, 'we can't do anything'.

How does peacemaking address these excuses; these barriers to solving problems? It confronts them directly. In peacemaking, the person who is the focus of the discussion gets to explain his or her excuses in full, without appearing before a judge to determine whether or not they are true. Instead, judges are the people who know the wrongdoer best – his or her spouse, parents, siblings, other relatives and neighbors. They are the reality check for excuses. In a case involving family violence, a young man related his excuses, exhibiting denial, minimalization and externalization. One of the people who listened was the young man's sister. She listened to his story and confronted him by saying, 'you know very well you have a drinking problem'. She then related the times she had seen him drunk and abusive. Having broken the barrier, she told her brother she loved him very much and was willing to help him if only he would admit his problems. He did. In another case, a young woman went to court to establish paternity for her child. The young man she said was the father denied it. The judge sent the case into peacemaking, where the parents and relatives of both were present. They immediately announced that the purpose of the meeting was to decide what to do with *their* grandchild. The families knew about the couple's relationship and the fact of paternity, so the case was quickly settled. The young man was not employed, so the families developed a plan whereby he would cut and haul firewood for the mother until he got a job. In peace-making, the people who know the facts directly or know the people in the process very well are the ones who develop the facts of the situation. They are not laid out for a judge to decide, but for the participants to discuss and know. The talking-out process of peacemaking is designed to clarify the situation and, where necessary, get to the root of the problem. Excuses do not prevail in a process that fosters full discussion to solve problems.

Peacemaking is a remedy for the 'we can't do anything' excuse. Most cases in Navajo peacemaking are those brought directly by the people. For example, there was a situation where a couple broke up when their son reached adulthood. The man ran off with another woman, leaving his wife to make the mobile home payment. She had little education and no job. She got a low-paying job in a laundromat, but that was not sufficient to make the monthly payment. She went to the local legal aid program for a divorce to assure the payment, but was told that the program was overburdened and did not take divorce cases. The woman began going to her husband's place of work to demand money. Very soon, the receptionists and fellow employees made it known she was not welcome. One day, the woman confronted her husband in the parking lot and demanded the money for the mobile home payment. When he refused, she hit him. He got a domestic violence restraining order from the court, and the woman sought advice about what it meant and what she should do. She was advised to seek peacemaking. Within a few days, a peacemaking session was scheduled and the husband agreed to make the mobile home payment. The peacemaker set up a follow-up meeting to assure the agreement was carried out. In the meantime, the domestic violence case was dismissed.

The Navajo Nation child welfare program is overburdened with abuse and neglect cases. Accordingly, we see many applications for guardianships of children brought by grand-mothers, aunts and other relatives of children. A guardianship is a form of private child welfare action in Navajo practice, and relatives seek court confirmation of arrangements to care for children. Often, relatives seek temporary guardianships to allow parents an opportunity to deal with personal problems or seek employment to create a stable house-hold. In most state systems, child welfare cases are confrontational and challenge adults to explain why they are bad parents. Navajos use peacemaking for guardianship cases, and that forum allows relatives to discuss what is best for their children. Parents assert their excuses for the way they deal with their children, but the focus is genuinely upon the best interests of the child. There is no judge or social worker to make the determination of what is best for a child – the people most closely connected with the child make that decision. Direct access to swift justice within the community addresses the 'we can't do anything' excuse, and the process utilizes readily available resources for problem solving. There is no need for a confirming medical statement in domestic violence cases, or for a home study in child welfare cases. The people who have a dispute treat it as a problem to be resolved within families, and take direct action on their own.

In peacemaking, a *naat'aanii* has persuasive authority. Peacemakers are chosen by local units of Navajo Nation government on the basis of their standing in the community and respect for their abilities. Peacemakers can be removed at any time should they lose respect. A peacemaker does not have the authority to make a decision for others or to impose a decision, but his or her power is not merely advisory. A *naat'aanii* has an opinion, and the process prompts him or her to express it. Given that peacemakers are chosen because of their wisdom and planning abilities, the process encourages them to act as guides and teachers.

Their opinion will most likely have a strong impact on the decision of the group. The opinion is expressed in something called the lecture – an unfortunate rendering in English because the process is not an abstract exhortation about morality; it is a very practical and concrete process. The peacemaker knows all about the situation given that the parties and their relatives have an opportunity to vent, accuse, exhibit psychological barriers and engage in discussions to clarify things. He or she will then provide reality therapy and perform values clarification in a talk designed to guide the parties. The talk focuses on the nature of the problem and uses traditional precedent to guide a decision.

Navajos have a great deal of respect for tradition, and they recognize both a form of traditional case law and a corpus of legal principles. The case law can be in the form of what happened in the time of creation, e.g. what First Man and First Woman, the Hero Twins or the Holy People did to address a similar problem. The case may involve Coyote or Horned Toad, and the foolishness of what Coyote did or the wisdom of Horned Toad to resolve a similar conflict. There are principles to be derived from ceremonial practice, songs, prayers, or other expressions of Navajo doctrine. The *naat'aanii* draws upon traditional teachings to propose a plan of action for the parties in order to resolve their dispute. Many peacemaking sessions are short, lasting only a few hours, but where emotions are particularly strong or it is difficult to break down the psychological barriers, peacemaking can last longer. The peacemaker may call a halt to the discussions to allow time for reflection and prepare for a resumption of talks on another day.

When the lecture is done, the parties return to a discussion of the nature of the problem and what needs to be done to resolve it. Planning is a major Navajo justice value that is sometimes ignored in state practice. *Nahat'a,* or planning process, is very practical. Non-Navajos sometimes mock traditional practice. For example, there are Navajos who look into the future using a crystal. A non-Navajo might ridicule that, but Navajos explain how it is done. When you hold a crystal in your hand, you see that it has many facets. You examine each closely, and upon a full examination of each side of the crystal you can see it as a whole. That describes *nahat'a,* where the parties closely examine each facet of the dispute to see it as a whole. The talking-out phase fully develops the facts so the parties can fully understand the nature of the problem that lies beneath the dispute. The lecture phase draws upon traditional wisdom for precedent and guidance. The prayer commits the parties to the process. Following full discussion, the parties themselves serve as the judges and make a decision about what to do. It is most often a practical plan whereby people commit themselves to a course of action.

Often, the action is in the form of *nalyeeh,* which also translates as restitution or reparation. Payments can be in the form of money to compensate for actual out-of-pocket loss. There are also payments in the form of horses, jewelry or other goods. The payment can be symbolic only and not compensate for actual loss. The focus is not upon adequate compensation, as in state tort or contracts doctrines, but upon a make-whole kind of remedy. The feelings and relationships of the parties are what is most important. For example, there are cases involving sexual misconduct where the victim demands symbolic compensation, often in the form of horses, cows or sheep. Can a price tag be placed on a rape? The act of delivering cattle as compensation is visible in a rural community. Members of that community will most likely know about the event, and the public act of delivering cattle or horses shows the woman's innocence. It reinforces her dignity and tells the community she was wronged.

Non-Navajo corporate parties have also participated in peacemaking, such as in a wrongful death-products liability case brought before the Navajo Nation courts in 1994. A child got scorched to death in a clothes dryer, and the child's parents brought a standard wrongful death manufacturer negligence suit. The corporate defendants were very nervous about the possible outcome before a Navajo jury. The child's parents were not so much concerned about getting money as they were with dealing with the emotional impact of their child's death. The parties went into peacemaking without their lawyers present, and they fully discussed the problem of what to do about the loss of the child. They addressed the parents' feelings about their loss and what the corporate defendants could and should do about it. The result was a monetary settlement that was within the range of usual rural Arizona state court verdicts. More importantly, the parties discussed what symbolic act the manufacturer and laundromat operator could take to assume responsibility for the death. Negotiated compensation can address the costs of actual loss, but it can also be an agreed resolution with only a symbolic payment. It addresses relationships.

Peacemaking also involves personal commitments to deal with underlying behavior. It can involve agreements to attend a ceremony. For example, the Honorable Irene Toledo of the Ramah District Court recognized that many violent assaults brought before her involved Vietnam veterans and other Navajos who returned from war. Upon examining the cases more closely, she recognized the presence of post-traumatic stress disorder from war. She also recognized that veteran parents were teaching their children violent behaviors. Navajos are familiar with war from many centuries of conflict with Spanish, Mexican and American invaders. There is a Navajo ceremony that addresses post-traumatic stress disorder, and it is quite effective in dealing with the memories of war. Judge Toledo urged some of the defendants to have the ceremony done, as well as to seek treatment through a Veterans Department hospital. Some replied, 'I'm modern and I don't really believe in that tradition'. The judge used peacemaking as a form of counseling for the defendants to urge them to have the ceremony performed. One veteran reported that while he 'did not believe in it', he had the ceremony done and it worked.

Peacemaking is used to overcome psychological barriers and self-imposed impediments to personal responsibility. Parties in peacemaking will often agree to seek traditional ceremonies or modern counseling as part of the resolution of the dispute. When they do, they are fully committed to the process and they cooperate with traditional or modern treatment programs. One pilot project of the Navajo courts was the Minority Male Program. It was designed to offer diversion alternatives for persons charged with driving while intoxicated. Peacemaking proved successful in getting beneath the problem of drunk driving by motivating people to recognize that they indeed did have a drinking problem and should do something about it. Recidivism rates dropped for those who went through peacemaking.

Relationships and relatives are an important distinction that makes peace-making unique. A person who agrees to pay *nalyeeh* may not have the personal wealth or means to do so. It is traditional for family and clan members to make the payment on their relative's behalf. The tradition is not simply that relatives assume obligations for others, although that is fundamental to Navajo society. When an individual commits a wrong against another, it shames the person's relatives – 'He acts as if he had no relatives'. The family will keep an eye on the offender to assure there will be no future transgressions. Where there is a particularly malicious or heinous act, community members will 'kill with the eyes'. That describes a practice where people keep a watch for an offender, and use social pressure to keep him in line with the community's expectations of proper behavior. We recognize this dynamic of Navajo custom for modern adjudication as well. Both the Rules for Domestic Violence Proceedings and the Navajo Nation Sentencing Policy include provisions to require offenders to get family member sureties for bonds to assure future good conduct. We call this the 'traditional probation officer', where we recruit family members to assume supervisory obligations.

What makes peacemaking work? Peacemaking is based on relationships. It uses the deep emotions of respect, solidarity, self-examination, problem-solving and ties to the community. Navajo common law recognizes the individual and individual rights, but it differs from Western individualism in that the individual is put in his or her proper place within community relationships. Western legal thought speaks to 'me' and 'I', but the individual is viewed in the isolated context of individual rights. In Navajo legal thinking, an individual is a person within a community, it is impossible to function alone. They say that Navajos always go home: Navajos who have better potentials to earn a high income in a big city return home to a lesser-paying job because they cannot live outside Navajo society. Navajos responded to recent disclosures that the Navajo Nation has the lowest family and per capita incomes of all Indian nations of the US, and the highest poverty rate, by pointing out that their rural economies and lifestyles are a matter of choice. Yes, there is a great deal of poverty in the Navajo Nation and limited economic opportunities, but Navajos live as Navajos.

An important Navajo legal term is *k'e,* for which there is no corresponding word in English. *K'e* is the cement of Navajo law; it describes proper relationships, and underlies and fuels consensual justice. It is what allows a traditional justice system to operate without force or coercion. It allows people to be their own judges and to enforce binding judgments without jails or sheriffs.

Peacemaking agreements can be reduced to judgment and enforced as any other court judgment. In practice, the people prefer informal agreements and often do not seek court ratification of it in a formal judgment. Relationships and methods designed to build or reinforce them, supported by the strong emotional force of *k'e,* are the underpinnings of peacemaking. It is not a system of law that relies upon authority, force and coercion, but one that utilizes the strengths of people in communities.

Corrective, restorative and distributive justice

Most state law methods are based on corrective justice. That is, the hierarchy of power attempts to maintain social control using state authority. The difficulty lies in abuses of authority, and people tend to resist being told what to do. They respond better when they buy into or accept a decision that they help make. Navajo justice methods are corrective in the sense that they attempt to get at causes that underlie disputes or wrongdoing. They address excuses such as denial, minimalization and externalization in practical ways in order to adjust the attitudes of wrongdoers. The methods educate offenders about the nature of their behaviors and how they impact others, and help people identify their place and role in society in order to reintegrate them into specific community roles. Navajo justice methods recognize the need to implement justice in a community context, because ultimately the community must solve its own problems. Navajo families, clans and communities were stripped of their long-standing responsibility for justice in adjudication and in the police and social work models. There are now more than 250 peacemakers in the Navajo Nation's 110 communities, and they accept that responsibility with a great deal of enthusiasm and energy. Navajo corrective justice can be immediate because it is carried out in communities. People expect an immediate resolution of their problems, and they do not want to wait on the schedules of judges and police officers.

Navajo corrective justice is actually restorative justice. It is not so much concerned about correction of the person as it is about restoring that person to good relations with others. This is an integrative process whereby the group as a whole examines relationships and mends a relationship gone wrong. Navajo justice uses practical methods to restore an offender to good standing within the group. Where the relationship does not exist in the first place (e.g. as with dysfunctional families), peacemaking builds new relationships that hopefully will function in a healthy manner. Another way to describe the result of peacemaking is *hozho nahasdlii*. The phrase describes the result of 'talking things out' and reaching a consensual conclusion. It says, 'now that we have done these things and gone through this process, we are now returned to a state of *hozho*'. The process determines the outcome, and is one of restored mutual and reciprocal relationships with a group functioning as a whole.

Another function of Navajo justice is known as distributive justice. Where there is an injury, the group identifies resources to address it. For example, when a Navajo is arrested and charged for an offence, relatives will collect money to post a money bond or buy a bail bond. When a family member is injured in an accident, others give financial support. It is a form of insurance, also known as *nalyeeh*. In peacemaking, there are practical discussions of the injured person's needs and who has the resources to address it. Need is served with monetary, material and even emotional support. Distributive justice asks, 'what do we have and how can we help?' It is based on reciprocal obligations founded in *k'e* for *hozho*.

Does peacemaking actually work? Is it romantic or practical? Does peacemaking speak to universals of human behavior or is it culture-specific to Navajos? The *Hozhooji Naat'aanii* (Peacemaker Division of the courts) staff report that recidivism rates among wrongdoers are only about 20%. There are reports of people telling of their personal satisfaction with peacemaking and how it has made a difference to their lives. Peacemaking does deal with homicides or murders (without using those classifications), and there are instances of deaths within family groups (and sometimes among strangers) where peacemaking is used to resolve the emotions and hardships that come in the wake of the killing of one person by another. The question of the kinds of cases handled is not as relevant as the result, restorative justice. Navajo cultural perspectives are unique. They are a product of the Navajo language and of the concepts it expresses. Navajo ceremonial practice and the norms, values and moral principles it maintains are perhaps unique to Navajos. However, we believe that we have identified human behavior that is universal and grounded in the norms of many cultures. We use psychological discourse and approaches to explain peacemaking so we can show the outside world what Navajos are doing. They are very practical, pragmatic and concrete in what they do.

13 Restorative justice and prisons

Kimmett Edgar and Tim Newell

[…]

Our basic purpose in writing this book is to contribute to the growth of restorative processes in prison. We believe that restorative justice has great potential to humanise prisons, improve safety, enhance social order, and make the experience less hostile and damaging for all concerned. We believe that a completely transformed prison, centred on restorative values, would:

- begin to address society's obligations to victims of crime;
- serve as a place of safety in mediating between people who have been deeply harmed and those who have caused the harm; and
- occupy a crucial position in the reintegration of offenders into society.

The main obstacle to this goal of the restorative prison is a deep tension that needs to be acknowledged from the start. On one hand, there is the view that restorative justice is a soft option. From this perspective, prisons are meant to be punitive, and any notion of making them less damaging would detract from their roles of retribution and deterrence. On the other hand, there are restorative justice advocates (and others) who believe that imprisonment is so damaging that the only way forward is to abolish prisons. From the first perspective, introducing restorative justice into prisons is viewed with suspicion, as a way of making custody too easy for criminals. From the second perspective, restorative justice totally contradicts the use of punishment and prisons.

Russ Immarigeon described the distance between restorative justice and prisons in these terms:

> Incarceration is the institutional manifestation of the punitive impulse that restorative justice is designed and intended to challenge.
>
> (Immarigeon, 2004: 150)

If he is right, then the whole point of prisons is to punish; the whole point of restorative justice is to heal; and the two cannot be reconciled. From this perspective, there is only one criterion by which restorative projects should be judged: their effectiveness at steering offenders away from the inevitably damaging experience of prison. Restorative projects must, by this test, be diversions from custody.

When restorative justice and prisons are defined as opposites, every move by a prison system to treat prisoners with greater respect can be viewed with suspicion. Immarigeon quoted two apologists for restorative justice who feared that prisons would exploit the reputation restorative justice has built up.

We must avoid the danger that imprisonment, with all its known disadvantages, is 'packaged as restorative justice.' The hijacking of restorative justice initiatives is a real threat, certainly when it concerns a possible new legitimation of imprisonment.

(cited in Immarigeon, 2004: 143)

If restorative justice can be linked to prisons, this might make imprisonment more attractive to the courts, and, through 'net-widening' increase the problems of overcrowding. For example, if courts decide to use restorative justice agreements as conditions for community sentences, and sanction any breaches with prison, then restorative justice processes could result in more people being sent to prison.

The fact that we are writing this book shows that we do not accept the terms of this interpretation: we do not see restorative justice and prisons as opposites by definition. Nonetheless, we respect the tension between the two. In one sense, our answer to the tension is a consistent thread throughout the remainder of this book.

Carolyn Boyes-Wilson described the distance between restorative philosophy and the criminal justice system in stark terms:

The state operates through impersonal and rationalized procedures administered by disinterested professionals with specialized legal, administrative and penal expertise. The goal is to punish, manage or rehabilitate people who violate the law in order to maintain control over its jurisdiction. Restorative justice, by contrast, seeks to delegate decision making and control to those individuals directly involved in the incident. The goal is to harness the power of relationships to heal that which has been harmed and to empower the community to engage in processes of repair, reconciliation and redemption in order to restore balance in the wake of harm.

(Boyes-Wilson, 2004: 215)

But unlike restorative theorists who argue that restorative justice should pursue a totally separate path, Boyes-Wilson embraced the creative tension between the two:

The incompatibility between the institutions of the justice system and restorative justice may generate a kind of creative tension that opens space for the transformation of those institutions.

(Boyes-Wilson, 2004: 216)

In a similar vein, Barb Toews works promoting restorative philosophy to prisoners near Philadelphia. She defends her work in prisons by raising tough questions about the impact of restorative justice on prisons, and the effects of prisons on restorative justice. With Jackie Katounis, she wrote:

We are challenged to explore what restorative justice, as a philosophy, has to say about the prison environment itself...

Is restorative justice possible in prison without challenging the violent and punitive prison values and practices?

Without challenging the prison environment, are we condoning violence and saying that harming offenders is OK?

... Is restorative justice about transforming people's lives to the fullest extent possible or only to the degree we allow while punishing them?

Does punishment and prison even have a role in restorative justice?

(Toews and Katounis, 2004: 112–113)

Here are some of the main limitations of the prison that we believe impede its capacity for restorative work:

- *coercion*—running an institution by giving orders and backing them up with punitive sanctions limits empowerment;
- *separation*—a structure designed to maintain physical separation between the victim and the perpetrator cannot facilitate dialogue to the same degree as a more open setting;
- *controlled regime*—these limit the offender's opportunities to make amends. An offender in prison could not offer to compensate the victim directly by, for example, painting his or her fence or digging the garden; and
- *punishment*—the punishment at the heart of imprisonment is the deprivation of liberty. Thus every encounter between a victim and his or her offender would take place in a setting that fundamentally restricted the options available to the offender.

Recently in England and Wales, restorative approaches as a diversion procedure for young and minor offenders have expanded. The public perception of restorative justice is possibly only a partial image, due to the publicity given to work with youth. But when restorative justice is thought to be limited to its practice with young offenders in the community, the wider relevance of the philosophy can be neglected.

While restorative justice and prisons continue to be seen as opposite points of the spectrum, the potential of restorative justice to work with serious offending will be severely restricted. The victims of serious crimes are let down when prisons are not used as places of restoration for offenders, victims and their communities. Prisons are full of people in desperate need of restoration – those most damaged and damaging in our society. Unresolved conflicts about their relationships with their victims and their community often remain within the person no matter how many personal development opportunities for change and learning they have taken in prison.

So, how can a prison provide restorative opportunities? Marian Liebmann and Stephanie Braithwaite produced a summary of restorative work being undertaken in prisons in 1999. We refer the reader to that work, acknowledging that in this field things change very quickly. We will not attempt to provide an up-to-date report on all the restorative work in prisons at present. Rather, we can take a broader view by listing some of the developments that show how restorative justice can be used to good effect within prisons. Some of this is based on the restorative justice in prisons project that Tim championed just before leaving HM Prison Service.

To set the scene for the areas we discuss in this book, some of the obvious areas for restorative approaches in prison are:

- meeting the needs of crime victims, including (but not limited to) developing victim empathy in prisoners, facilitating victim-offender mediation or conferences and prison outreach to victims' groups;
- making amends—opportunities that enable the offender to repay the victim (e.g., via a trained probation officer's facilitation); also indirect reparation (for example, through Inside Out Trust workshops or through charity jog-a-thons);

- offender restoration and rehabilitation, by taking full advantage of offending behaviour courses, and/or drug and alcohol treatment;
- staff industrial relations, including the provision of mediation for disputes arising between members of staff; and
- operational functions, such as discipline, complaints, sentence planning, maintaining family ties, and pre-release work.

The capacity of a prison to benefit from restorative justice depends primarily on making the environment safe. Unless prisoners can be free of victimisation while they are in prison, they are unlikely to be able to focus their attention on those they have damaged by their offending behaviour. Thus the need to create and sustain safe, healthy prisons is vital for the future development of restorative justice in prisons. Restorative practice can help this process through a change in the typical methods of managing conflicts inside — and this is why there is such potential for restorative justice to influence operational functions in prisons. We have made the point that restorative justice restores relationships and brings a problem-solving focus to incidents of harm.

An underlying theme throughout this book is the impact of restorative justice on the traditional responses to trouble. The questions at the heart of the restorative justice response are simple, but when asked in settings that are safe and respectful, they can lead to remarkable results:

- Describe in your own words what happened.
- What were you thinking at the time?
- Who do you think has been affected by what happened?
- In what ways were they affected?
- What should happen to put things right?

Consider how these questions could influence the ways officers conduct induction, sentence planning, or in dealing with disputes between prisoners. Consider how senior management could use these questions in facilitating adjudications (disciplinary hearings), responding to prisoner complaints or dealing with officers' concerns.

Conclusion

The potential for restorative justice in prisons is considerable. It should not be seen primarily as a tool towards reducing recidivism (although there is evidence that this will happen) but as a means towards empowering offenders to take responsibility for their actions and to make amends to their victims and their communities. Nor should the work be entered into without much preparation and careful development, based on experience. The Prison Service[1] lacks experience in restorative justice work and should consult with practitioners in the community where there is established expertise.

To build a consensus that prisons can become more restorative cannot be done without this partnership. To sustain this work in prisons the offering of support must come from the community. Guided by restorative justice, prisons can become true places of healing and transformation for the community as well as for those directly affected by crime: victims and offenders.

References

Boyes-Wilson, Carolyn (2004) 'What Are the Implications of the Growing State Involvement in Restorative Justice?' in Zehr and Toews, 215–226.

Immarigeon, Russ (2004) 'What is the Place of Punishment and Imprisonment in Restorative Justice?' in Zehr and Toews (2004), 143–154.

Toews, Barbara and Jackie Katounis (2004) 'Have Offender Needs and Perspectives been Adequately Incorporated into Restorative Justice?' in Zehr and Toews, 2004.

Zehr, Howard and Barbara Toews (eds) (2004) *Critical Issues in Restorative Justice*, Devon: Willan Publishing.

14 Restorative justice and police-led cautioning

David O'Mahony and Jonathan Doak

Police-led restorative cautioning schemes have their roots in Australia where they were developed in the early 1990s, mostly as an alternative approach to traditional cautioning practices (Wemmers and Canutó, 2002; Dignan, 2005). The approach spread and was taken up and used in various forms in New Zealand and America, particularly in Minnesota and Pennsylvania in the mid-1990s (McCold, 2000). It then spread considerably and North American facilitators have promoted the approach and trained many facilitators worldwide (McCold and Wachtel, 1998).

In the United Kingdom restorative cautioning (now replaced by 'final warnings' and 'reprimands' under the Crime and Disorder Act 1998) programmes have been used in a number of police forces, particularly by the Thames Valley police and more recently by the police in Northern Ireland. The approach is largely based around Braithwaite's ideas of 'reintegrative shaming' (Braithwaite, 1989). In essence these schemes seek to deal with crime and its aftermath by attempting to make offenders ashamed of their behaviour, but in a way which promotes their reintegration into the community (Young and Gould, 1999). In this sense, it is different to the traditional police caution, which has been described by Lee (1998) as a 'degrading ceremony' in which the young person, most often a first-time and minor offender, is given a stern 'dressing-down' by a senior police officer.

The restorative caution, on the other hand, attempts to reintegrate the young person, after they have admitted what they did was wrong. It focuses on how they can put the incident behind them, for example by repairing the harm through such things as reparation and apology (O'Mahony and Doak, 2004). It thereby allows the young person to move forward and reintegrate back into their community and family. The whole process is usually facilitated by a trained police officer and often involves the use of a script or agenda that is followed in the conferencing process. The victim is encouraged to play a part in the process, particularly to reinforce upon the young person the impact of the offence on them, but as Dignan (2005) notes, restorative cautioning schemes have (at least initially) placed a greater emphasis on the offender and issues of crime control, than on their ability to meet the needs of victims.

An important aspect of police-led restorative cautioning is that is often used as a diversionary method for cases where an offence has been committed and guilt established, but it is not deemed necessary to resort to prosecution through the courts. Such diversionary practices are often used very effectively for young people who have committed relatively minor offences, or have not have offended before. In Northern Ireland, for example, the police operate a Youth Diversion Scheme, which is made up of a group of specialist youth police officers who consider all juvenile cases that come to the attention of the police. The police officers in the Youth Diversion Scheme have four broad options available. Firstly, they can decide to take 'no further action', in which case the young person is not processed any further than being referred to the police Youth Diversion Scheme. This is most commonly used when there is insufficient evidence to establish that a crime was committed, or the offence and circumstances were so trivial it is not considered worth pursuing. Secondly, the police may give an 'informed warning' which is an informal action and occurs where there is evidence that a crime has been committed, but a warning is considered sufficient to deal with the matter. Such warnings are usually given to the young person and their parent(s) but they do not result in any formal criminal record for the young person – although a note of these warnings is kept for one year. Alternatively, the police may decide to give a 'restorative caution' to the young person. This can only take place if the young person admits to the offence, there is sufficient evidence to prosecute and the young person and their parent(s) give informed consent to the caution. Police restorative cautions are recorded as part of a criminal record and kept for two and a half years and should the young person re-offend, may be cited in court. The last option is for the police to refer the case to the Public Prosecution Service for prosecution through the courts. This is usually reserved for more serious offences, or where the young person has had previous warnings or prosecutions.

One of the major achievements of the Youth Diversion Scheme in Northern Ireland is that it only resorts to prosecuting a relatively small proportion of young people referred to it. Typically, only about 5–10% of cases dealt with through the Youth Diversion Scheme are referred for prosecution and only about 10–15% are given restorative cautions. The majority (about 75–80%) are dealt with informally, through 'informed warnings' or no further police action is taken. So, normally, only 5–10% of cases dealt with by the Youth Diversion Scheme are prosecuted through the courts, about 15% are given formal cautions and about 80%, are usually dealt with informally.

It should also be underlined that the concept of 'diversion' in Northern Ireland usually refers to diverting individuals out of the criminal justice system, rather than diverting them into some other programme or activity (which is often the case in other jurisdictions). Indeed, diverting young people away from the courts is generally seen as a more progressive response than formally prosecuting them. The police have been operating such a policy of promoting the diversion young people away from formal criminal processing for a number of years and they have encouraging reconviction data to support their policy, which shows that only about 20% of juveniles cautioned in Northern Ireland went on to re-offend within a one to three year follow-up period (Mathewson, Willis and Boyle, 1998) whereas about 75% of those convicted in the juvenile courts were reconvicted over a similar period (Wilson, Kerr and Boyle, 1998).

Restorative justice in practice: restorative cautioning

The following sections consider research evidence on how restorative cautioning has operated in a number of jurisdictions before going on to consider the implications of such findings on the development of policy and practice.

Police-led restorative cautioning has been practised widely across Australia, New Zealand, the USA and the United Kingdom. It is mostly used as a diversionary mechanism to avoid prosecution. As noted above, it provides a forum for the police to bring together young offenders and their victims, with their respective families and supporters, which can explore the effects of the harm on the victim, as well as the potential ways of providing redress. The conferences are generally organised, managed and facilitated by a police officer and examine ways of providing redress to the victim and reintegrating the offender. However, as with all restorative interventions, the management role of the facilitator is not that of a sentencer who imposes solutions on the parties (O'Mahony and Doak, 2004). The goals of police-led conferencing are to encourage young offenders to achieve empathy towards their victim and assume responsibility for their actions; to allow victims to move towards forgiveness and healing; and to empower citizens to address their own problems (McCold, 1996; Moore and O'Connell, 1994; Young and Goold, 1999). The following sections consider research evidence on how such schemes have operated in a number of jurisdictions before moving on to consider the implications of such findings on the development of policy and practice in relation to restorative cautioning.

Australia

The police-led conferencing developed in Wagga Wagga, New South Wales involved the adaptation of the New Zealand model of family group conferencing for the purposes of community-orientated policing (Moore and McDonald, 1995). In the first instance, offenders were brought together with their family and friends to decide how to respond to the offence, as in the New Zealand model, but the scheme was then extended to include victims and their supporters. Although the local Australian programme itself has since been superseded by a statutory youth conferencing regime, the non-statutory basis of the original project has been replicated by police forces in other parts of Australia, as well as further afield.

Of the various different types of restorative processes, it has been the police-based schemes which have been subjected to the most intense appraisals. One of the most significant evaluations to date has been the Re-integrative Shaming Experiments (RISE) project, which was instigated in 1995 under the auspices of the Australian National University in partnership with the Australian Federal Police. The project, based in Canberra, randomly assigned cases to a police-led conference or a court hearing, and sought to compare the effectiveness of each procedure. The project sought to test a number of hypotheses including: whether offenders and victims found conferences to be fairer than court; whether there was less repeat offending after a conference than after court; and whether the public costs of providing a conference were no greater than the cost of processing offenders in court.

In addition, the project also aimed to examine the use of 'shaming' in conferences, theorising that conferences would produce more positive 'reintegrative' shaming (Braithwaite, 1989) than court. In order to make such a comparison, a randomised controlled trial was implemented in which offenders were randomly allocated to either court or conferencing (Strang, 2002: 70–72). The RISE project was not confined to juvenile offenders and focused on four distinct offence groups: drink driving offences of any age; shoplifting by under 18 year olds; property crime with victims and offenders under 18 years of age; and violent crime by offenders under 30 years of age. To be eligible to participate in the programme, the offender had to admit to the offence and be resident in the area covered by the project. In addition, he or she had to be informed that the case was diverted to conferencing randomly and they had the choice to be dealt with by a court if preferred (Strang, 2002).

In terms of its evaluation, the researchers arrived at the 'inescapable' conclusion that "both victims and offenders can name many ways in which they prefer conferences to court" (Sherman et al, 1998: 165). Perceptions of fairness amongst victims and offenders were higher and observations reported greater participation, emotional intensity, procedural justice, apologies, forgiveness and time and effort given to justice in conferences than in court (Sherman et al, 1998). Furthermore, conferences were said to increase offenders' respect for the law and the police, and over 70% of contractual obligations were fulfilled by offenders (Sherman and Strang, 2007). In terms of testing Braithwaite's theory of

reintegrative shaming the research interestingly reported more stigmatic shaming in conferences than in court. This, however, was attributed to the fact shaming rarely occurs in court
in any form.

Victim analyses were carried out only on juvenile property crime and youth violence.
High levels of victim participation were reported with 82% of property victims and 91% of
violence victims in attendance. By contrast, victims whose cases were assigned to court
attended very infrequently, except where they had been called to give evidence. By contrast,
conferencing enabled many victims to receive an apology, whereas apologies were never
made in court. In terms of satisfaction, victims found conferencing fairer than court.
Interestingly, there was also some difference in degrees of satisfaction between victims of
property crime and those of violence, but there was nevertheless a "moderately high level of
satisfaction regarding procedural justice" amongst both (Sherman et al, 1998: 151). This
discrepancy in satisfaction levels may be explained by the nature of the crime. Some victims
of violence were said to have suffered substantial harm, illustrated by the fact that 62% of
these victims required medical treatment.

By and large, the research reflects positively on the RISE experiment and concludes that
"as long as there is at least no difference in both costs/and recidivism, the advantages of
increased respect for police and greater victim involvement suggest that police-led conferencing is a desirable addition to the criminal justice system" (Sherman et al, 1998: 160).

A similar scheme of youth conferencing was introduced in South Australia under the
Young Offenders Act 1993. Under the Act, the police may refer a juvenile offender (aged
10–17 years) to a conference, providing the offence in question is 'minor' in nature. Although
the legislation itself does not define which offences are considered 'minor', the South
Australian Police Department has issued protocols offering guidance. In practice, these
basically stipulate that cases suitable for a conference include those involving any offence
for which the youth has already been formally cautioned, any offence which the police
considers desirable for the victim's participation and any offence resulting in a loss of
property between AU$5000 and $25000 (Strang, 2001)[1]. However, the extent of police
discretion, coupled with the fact that magistrates can also refer court matters to a conference,
has meant that quite serious cases may be also be subjected to conferencing, including some
sexual assaults and robberies (Strang, 2001)[2].

In terms of the operation of the conference itself, one of the key differences from the
Wagga Wagga model is that the conferencing was located under the umbrella of the Youth
Court, rather than the police. Thus, whilst the police make the vast majority of referrals, and
possess a power of veto over the outcome, the conference process itself is overseen by Youth
Justice Coordinators employed by the Courts Administration Authority Family Conference
Team. In order for a conference to proceed, a specialist Police Youth Officer and the Youth
Justice Coordinator must be present. The role of the police officer is to describe the offence,
to provide information about any absent victims, and contribute to the discussion and the
outcome (Daly et al, 1998).

At least two people must agree with the outcome reached in the conference, namely the
police and the offender (SAPOL General Order number 8980, cited by Strang, 2001). If no
agreement is reached, the matter is referred to the Youth Court where a magistrate determines the appropriate way to proceed. The agreement itself may require the offender to pay
compensation not exceeding AU$25,000[3]; to undertake community service of up to 300
hours; and to apologise to the victim. In 2003, approximately 1 in 5 juveniles was dealt with
by way of a youth conference, and agreement was reached in 83% of all referred cases. The
most popular disposal was some form of undertaking, such as entering into a commitment to

attend school, counselling, or abide by a curfew. In two-thirds of cases the offender agreed to apologise to the victim; agreed to pay compensation in one quarter of cases; and agreed to undertake some form of community work in 19% of cases (Wundersitz and Hunter, 2005).

An earlier evaluation undertaken by Wundersitz (1996) found that the successful operation of conferences often varied according to the characteristics of the offender. Conferences were less likely to be completed if the young person was female or if they were Aboriginal. Victims were present only in around half of all conferences, which the author attributes to a lack of resources on the part of the organiser. In terms of implementing the agreement, the overall success rate was around 80% with regard to all forms of offences.

Further research has examined how conferences have been used in South Australia, particularly for more serious offences (Daly, 2001) and this has shown the process to be successful in producing high levels of satisfaction for victims, offenders, police and coordinators, in terms of being treated fairly, with respect and having a voice in the process. This research found the conferences were less restorative than expected, in that there were less positive exchanges between the offender, supporters and victim. However, the conferences reduced victims' fear and anger, and one year after the conference the majority of victims said the conference was worthwhile and they were satisfied with the outcome (Daly, 2001).

The United States and the United Kingdom

The use of police-based conferencing outside of Australasia was developed in the mid-1990s, following a series of training sessions in Minnesota and Pennsylvania conducted by police officers from the Australian Capital Territory. In Bethlehem, Pennsylvania, for example, conferencing began in November 1995, and by the end of 1997, police had conducted some 64 conferences involving 80 juvenile offenders (McCold and Wachtel, 1998). The scheme was confined to misdemeanours, with strict controls on the types of offence which could be referred: only minor assaults were eligible, no sex offences, or crimes related to drink or drugs were eligible, and it only applied to first-time offenders arrested locally. When a case arose which met the criteria, a liaison officer would approach an offender, who then had the choice whether to admit the offence and undergo a conference, or he could, if he so chose, contest his case at court.

Findings were broadly similar to those of RISE project. Of those who had undergone a restorative conference, over 90% of both victims and offenders expressed satisfaction, felt they were treated fairly, and would recommend conferencing to others. Victim satisfaction seemed particularly high, with 96% of victims expressing satisfaction, compared with 79% whose cases were assigned to court and 73% among those victims who had declined to participate in a restorative conference and whose cases subsequently were heard at court. Victims also stated that they felt their opinion was taken into account (94%), and almost all offenders (94%) said that they had acquired a better understanding of how the offence had affected the victim (McCold and Wachtel, 1998). Significantly, the study also reported that the vast majority of police officers were able to conduct conferences in conformity with restorative justice and due process principles, providing they were given adequate training and supervision. The Bethlehem Project has been replicated by numerous other police departments across North America, with broadly positive evaluations in Indianapolis (McGarrel et al, 2000), and in Regina, Canada (Wemmers and Canuto, 2002).

Police-led conferencing has also been fairly widespread in the United Kingdom. In 1994, Thames Valley Chief Constable Charles Pollard committed himself to introducing the Wagga Wagga model in Thames Valley. A programme was established to train police officers and implement a variety of restorative-based processes, including a complaints system and a comprehensive monitoring/evaluation package. From 1998, conferencing was to be integrated across all aspects of policing in the area, with all cautions being carried out using the restorative philosophy (Young, 2001). Police officers administering cautions were thus told to organise a restorative cautioning session for all offences that would have been formerly dealt with by way of traditional caution. All those affected by the offence, including the offender, victim and any relevant supporter/family member would be invited to attend the session. Police officers would then receive training and use a prepared script to facilitate a structured discussion about the harm caused by the offence and how it might be repaired.

The Thames Valley scheme was subject to an intense evaluation from 1998–2001 (Hoyle et al, 2002). During this period, 1,915 restorative conferences took place at which victims were present. In a further 12,065 restorative cautions, victims were not present, but the cautioning officer attempted to input some form of victim perspective. In a somewhat mixed evaluation, the researchers reported that offenders, victims and their supporters were generally satisfied and felt they had been treated fairly. However, a significant minority of victims and offenders felt they had not been adequately prepared for the process, or felt they had been pressured into it. Nonetheless, overall both victims and offenders believed that the encounter helped offenders to understand the effects of the offence and induced a sense of shame in them, which is a particularly important goal of a restorative intervention. Over half of the participants reported gaining a sense of closure and felt better because of the restorative session, and four-fifths saw holding the meeting as a good idea. Indeed, almost a third of offenders entered into a formal written reparation agreement at the restorative caution. Within a year, the majority of these had been completely fulfilled and only three remained completely unfulfilled.

The researchers found that the implementation of the restorative cautioning model in individual cautions was sometimes deficient, with facilitators occasionally excluding certain participants or asking inappropriate questions (eg, relating to prior offending or attempts to gather criminal intelligence). Some two-fifths of offenders reported feeling stigmatised as a 'bad person' and some officers appeared to pressurise offenders into apologising or making reparation. More generally it was found that some officers tended to dominate discussions and did not allow other participants to freely express themselves. However, the researchers noted that practice had improved considerably towards the end of the research period. Overall, their impression was that restorative cautioning represented a significant improvement over traditional cautioning, and was more effective in terms of reducing recidivism (Hoyle et al, 2002).

As regards adult offenders, restorative principles are also contained in the new scheme of 'conditional cautions' introduced in England and Wales by the Criminal Justice Act 2003. Conditional Cautioning enables the Crown Prosecution Service (CPS) to issue a caution to a first-time or minor offender as an alternative to prosecution. A number of conditions are attached to the caution, which must be aimed at either rehabilitating the offender and/or ensuring that he or she makes reparation to the victim or the wider community, and it is envisaged that restorative justice processes will form a part of, or will contribute towards these conditions. Offenders who fail to comply with the conditions will usually be prosecuted for the original offence. Participation in a scheme may form part of an offender's caution in and of itself, or the conditions themselves may represent the outcome of such a process (Home Office, 2005). Under section 23 of the 2003 Act, the CPS may only offer such a caution if the officer has evidence that the person has committed an offence; the relevant prosecutor decides that there is sufficient evidence to charge the person with the offence and grounds for giving a conditional caution; the offender admits the offence to the authorised person; an explanation of the effect of a caution and the warnings about the consequences of failure to observe the conditions has been given; and, finally, the offender signs a document that sets out details of the offence, an admission, consent to the caution and consent to the attached conditions.

It has been suggested, however, that this scheme pays only very limited lip-service to the idea of restorative justice for two main reasons. First, conditional cautions are not intended to replace traditional non-statutory police cautions, and are only used in a small minority of cases[4]. They were introduced as an alternative option where the imposition of conditions are seen as being a more effective way of addressing the offender's behaviour or making reparation to the victim or the community (Doak, 2008). Secondly, like many of the other measures listed above, it can be said to be only partly restorative, in so far as victims are not actively involved in the process and, as Dignan (2006: 273) observes, 'no attempt is made to "privilege" or "prioritise" restorative over rehabilitative interventions, even in cases involving direct victims.'

Northern Ireland

As noted above the Thames Valley model was replicated in slightly different guises by a number of police forces across the United Kingdom, and was subject to further evaluation following the implementation of a similar model for juvenile offenders in Northern Ireland from March 2003. However, unlike most other jurisdictions, Northern Ireland has placed restorative principles at the core of its youth justice system following the recommendations of the Criminal Justice Review in March 2000. Indeed, Northern Ireland is currently the only part of the United Kingdom to adopt a mainstreamed statutory based restorative conferencing system for young offenders facing prosecution through the courts (O'Mahony and Campbell, 2006).

The new statutory based youth conferencing system was introduced on a pilot basis in late 2003 and the youth conferencing arrangements have footing in the Justice (Northern Ireland) Act 2002 (O'Mahony and Campbell, 2006). The statutory measures provide for two types of disposal, diversionary and court-ordered conferences. Both types of conference take place with a view to a youth conference co-ordinator providing a plan to the prosecutor or court on how the young person should be dealt with for their offence. Diversionary conferences are referred by the Public Prosecution Service and are not intended for minor first time offenders – who are normally dealt with by the police by way of a warning or police caution. Court ordered conferences, on the other hand, are a mandatory requirement for all but the most serious young offenders appearing before the youth courts. For the prosecutor or courts to make use of the restorative conference the young person must admit to the offence and consent to the process (O'Mahony and Campbell, 2006).

Outside the new youth conferencing scheme in Northern Ireland the police still operate their system of cautions and informed warnings (short of referral to prosecution). The police now use a restorative approach in the delivery of such cautions. This police-led practice was subjected to an evaluation in two pilot areas: one based in Ballymena, County Antrim and the other in Mountpottinger, Belfast. Both schemes adopted a restorative approach for juveniles under 17 years of age. All the young people had admitted involvement in the offence, but were diverted away from prosecution by way of a formal caution, delivered using a restorative framework.

The research examined a total of 1,861 juvenile liaison referrals made between May 1999 and September 2000, including 969 cases from Mountpottinger and 892 from Ballymena (O'Mahony et al, 2002). The team also collected more detailed information about the backgrounds of individuals and any previous contacts they had with the police from a random sample of 265 case files, including all cases dealt with by way of restorative caution or conference (n=70).

On examination of the cases that were dealt with using a restorative model, it was found that there were clear differences in practice between the two pilot areas. In Mountpottinger, where the restorative scheme evolved from traditional cautioning practice, the sessions appeared to be used as an alternative to the traditional caution. Here, the vast majority of restorative cases were dealt with by way of a restorative caution without the presence of the victim, and only a small number were dealt with by a restorative conference including a victim. In Ballymena, however, the scheme had been developed from a local 'retail theft initiative', and generally only dealt with shoplifting cases. Here, 25 of the 28 cases resulted in a restorative conference, though these mostly used a surrogate victim who was drawn from a volunteer panel of local retailers and only three cases were dealt with by way of a restorative caution.

The restorative sessions were usually facilitated by a trained police officer. While the majority of the restorative cautions took place in a police station, most of the conferences (primarily in Ballymena) took place elsewhere. Levels of victim participation were generally low, with the actual victim attending only 20% of the conferences and in the Ballymena area (where most conferences took place), a surrogate victim was invariably used (usually a member of the local retail management group). The young person and their parent(s) normally attended, and occasionally a social worker or a teacher was also in attendance. The majority (over 90%) of the restorative sessions resulted in a written or verbal apology to the victim and in only 8% of the cases did the young person refuse to apologise. Though few of the sessions resulted in any compensation or reparation, this appeared to be due to the fact that the majority of cases in both locations involved retail thefts, where goods were normally recovered immediately.

The evaluation found that the police were strongly committed to restorative ideals and had applied considerable effort in attempting to make the new scheme a success. There was clear evidence that the practice of delivering the conferences was a significant improvement in police practice and offenders and victims were generally pleased with the way their cases were dealt with. However, a number of pertinent concerns were identified by the researchers including the lack of meaningful involvement of victims in many of the conferences. Some of the venues used for conferences were not ideal, and sometimes they were held in the local police station rather than a 'neutral' location. The restorative sessions were also found to be resource-intensive, as they took a considerable amount of police time to organise, set-up and administer – often for relatively minor offences. Furthermore, there was some evidence that they were unnecessarily drawing some petty first-time offenders into what was a demanding and intense process.

In relation to this latter point, the researchers expressed concern that the majority of conferences were not being used as an alternative to prosecution. Instead, they were used mostly for less serious cases involving young juveniles (12 to 14 years) that previously may not have resulted in formal action (O'Mahony and Doak, 2004). For instance, over 90% of the restorative conference cases were for minor thefts, and 80% involved goods with a value of under £15.00[5]. Indeed, in over half the cases, goods were worth less than £5[6]. It was not uncommon to come across cases where a considerable amount of police time had been invested in arranging a full conference for the theft of a chocolate bar or a can of soft drink. Indeed, the profile of those given restorative cautions and conferences was more similar to those given 'advice and warning' under the pre-existing regime than those cautioned previously and was not at all similar to those referred for prosecution. Some of the people dealt with under the scheme were very young, had no previous police contact or had only committed relatively trivial offences.

These findings highlight the danger that when informal alternatives are introduced into the criminal justice system they may serve to supplement rather than supplant existing procedures (Dignan and Lowey, 2000; O'Mahony and Deazley, 2000). The question is thus raised as to whether it is appropriate to use restorative conferences which directly involve victims, which are obviously costly and time-consuming, for mainly first-time offenders involved in petty offences. It could be argued that a better course of action might be to deal with such cases by way of a caution using a restorative framework, rather than attempting to provide a full conference with the victim present.

The role of victim

Before concluding, it is worth briefly highlighting some general points concerning the role of victims in restorative cautioning. Overall, research suggests that victims are usually glad that they chose to participate in the process and report feeling less anger following the encounter (Daly, 2001; Sherman et al, 1998; Strang et al, 2006; Doak and O'Mahony, 2006). In their evaluation of the Thames Valley initiative, Hoyle et al (2002) reported that two thirds of victims found the restorative encounter had positively influenced their perceptions of offenders and the vast majority found it helpful in coming to terms with the offence. Similarly, victims participating in restorative programmes have reported being less fearful of being re-victimized by the offender when compared with court-based samples (Umbreit, 1994). These findings tend to support an emerging body of literature in the field of therapeutic jurisprudence which provides some indications of a range of psychological benefits for victims that may flow from a restorative encounter (Sherman and Strang, 2007).

Notwithstanding the potential benefits of participation outlined above, the success of some police-led schemes has been partly blighted by the relatively low levels of victim participation (eg Hoyle et al, 2002; O'Mahony et al, 2002). Inevitably, in certain circumstances some victims will be unwilling to be involved in any restorative process, notwithstanding the best efforts of the organisers. For example, victims of trivial offences may simply feel that there is little point in the process for them and that their time and energy could be better spent elsewhere.

In cases where victims do not wish to participate organisers have developed innovative ways of sidestepping some of the barriers so a further degree of restorativeness can be injected into the procedure. For instance, the facilitator may offer the victim an opportunity to communicate indirectly either through a letter, written statement, audio recording, or through some form of 'shuttle' mediation. Alternatively, he or she may attempt to 'feed in' a victim's perspective by informing the offender of the typical reaction and impact of the type of offence upon a victim of that particular type of offence. To this end, police in Northern Ireland have relied heavily on so-called 'surrogate' victims, who were mostly individuals who had experienced similar types of offending in the past (O'Mahony and Doak, 2004). The idea had evolved from an earlier retail theft initiative which used a panel of volunteer shopkeepers to impress upon young shoplifters the impact of their actions on local businesses, the livelihoods of shopkeepers and their staff. The panel was incorporated into the new restorative conferencing scheme, and panel members were used to represent the views of the victim, if an actual shopkeeper declined to participate. Since many of the cases that were dealt with by conferencing involved shoplifting, the scheme appeared to work well. It addressed a problem whereby it was difficult to get shopkeepers to attend conferences, especially when the value of the goods was generally low and these had usually been recovered immediately when the young person was apprehended. In that sense, the surrogates brought a strong victim's perspective into the process and appeared to have had more of an impact on the young people than the facilitator simply reading a letter from a victim or recounting something the victim had said about the offence.

Yet the use of surrogate victims also had a number of distinct disadvantages over using the direct victim. For instance, it may well have been the case that the impact of the restorative process on the offender, and the potential for reintegrative shaming to occur, was diminished by the fact that offenders did not have to explain their actions to the real victim at the conference. Using a surrogate also obviously detracted from the restorative goals of conferencing, where there should be a process of empowerment, dialogue, negotiation and agreement between *all* the parties. From the victim's perspective there were obvious disadvantages as the victim does not get the opportunity to confront the offender, to have the offender explain their actions, and importantly to understand circumstances and reasons behind the offence (as well as negotiate compensation or restitution) – all of which are theoretically central to the conferencing process.

Conclusions

The evidence relating to the use of restorative principles in police-led cautioning is on the whole positive. Such practice, which emphasises trying to get the offender to appreciate the consequences of their actions, particularly on the victim, their own family and broader community, appears to be beneficial, not least to young people. There are many examples in the research of young offenders being moved by the realisation of the impact of their actions, brought about by such conferences. The research also consistently shows that levels of participant satisfaction were generally high, and both offenders and victims were usually happy with the process and outcome. Indeed, most police officers themselves report the process as significantly better than the traditionally delivered caution, which usually only involved a stern telling off or reprimand, without any 'restorative' element.

However, it is important to acknowledge a number of potential caveats, particularly when restorative practices are used as a diversionary method, short of prosecution. Restorative cautions are generally more resource-intensive, and thus more costly to administer, than traditional practices, especially when efforts to facilitate victim participation are factored in. They can also be onerous and challenging for young first-time offenders, to be brought face to face with their victim. Best practice requires that considerable effort needs to be invested in preparing both victims and offenders for such encounters. If an agreement is reached, it will require monitoring and victims should be kept informed as to whether or not the offender has complied with the terms of the agreement. Bearing this in mind, restorative cautions which directly involve victims might be more appropriately targeted to more serious circumstances and offences. Otherwise, it may be more realistic to focus the delivery of restorative cautions, as a diversionary method, based in a restorative framework. This would emphasise the impact of the offence on the victim and community, within a restorative model, but would not necessarily require having to bring every victim to a conference. Such a model could exploit other valuable means of victim input noted above and while recognising that they may fall short of achieving the ideals restorative justice, they may be a more realistic response to low level offending, for victims, offenders and the police. Certainly, they represent a fundamental improvement in the delivery of the traditional caution.

On a broader policy level, there are also more fundamental benefits in placing restorative principles at the centre of police cautioning. It has, for example, been suggested that the process of normalising policing in Northern Ireland could be bolstered by the additional transparency that the presence of the police officer may bring (O'Mahony and Doak, 2006). Here, the presence of at least one police officer is mandatory[7], which may encourage offenders, who have traditionally felt alienated and antagonistic towards the police, to put a 'human face' to individuals officers. In their evaluation of the RISE project in Australia, Sherman et al (1998) noted that police-led conferencing helped to foster a great sense of respect for the law and the police. In this sense, restorative practices may be used to complement other community-based policing practices and policies, and assist in the longer-term project of developing a dynamic and lasting partnership between the police and all sections of the community.

Notes

1 Approximately €2,600–€13,100.
2 The scheme is purely diversionary in nature, but for a brief period in the early 1990s, the Port Adelaide Youth Court interpreted the Act as providing for the use of conferencing as a sentencing option.
3 Approximately €13,100.
4 So-called 'simple' police cautions remain on a non-statutory footing and remain within the discretion of the police rather than the CPS.
5 Approximately €20.00.
6 Approximately €6.50.
7 Justice (NI) Act, s57, inserting Article 3A in the Criminal Justice (Children) (Northern Ireland) Order 1998.

Bibliography

Braithwaite, J. *Crime, Shame and Reintegration,* Cambridge, Cambridge University Press, 1989.
Daly, K. 'Conferencing in Australia and New Zealand: Variations, Research Findings, and Prospects' in A. Morris and G. Maxwell (eds) *Restoring Justice for Juveniles: Conferencing, Mediations and Circles,* Oxford, Hart Publishing, 2001.
Daly K., Venables, M., McKenna, M., Mumford, L, and Christie-Johnston, J. *South Australia Juvenile Justice (SAJJ) Research on Conferencing, Technical Report No. 1: Project Overview and Research Instruments,* Brisbane, Griffith University, 1998.
Dignan, J. *Understanding Victims and Restorative Justice,* Maidenhead: Open University Press, 2005.
Dignan, J. 'Restorative Justice in Criminal Justice and Criminal Court Settings' in G. Johnstone and D. Van Ness (eds) *Handbook of Restorative Justice,* Cullompton, Willan Publishing, 2006.
Dignan, J. and Lowey, K. *Restorative Justice Options for Northern Ireland: A Comparative Review,* Criminal Justice Review Research Report No 10, Belfast, HMSO, 2000.
Doak, J. *Victims Rights, Human Rights and Criminal Justice: Reconceiving the Role of Third Parties,* Oxford, Hart, 2008.
Doak, J, and O'Mahony, D. 'The vengeful victim? Assessing the attitudes of victims participating in restorative youth conferencing', *International Review of Victimology* 13: 157, 2006.
Home Office, *Cautioning of Adult Offenders,* London: Home Office Circular 30/2005, 2005.
Hoyle, C, Young, R. and Hill, R. *Proceed with Caution: An Evaluation of the Thames Valley Police Initiative in Restorative Cautioning,* York, Joseph Rowntree Foundation, 2002.
Lee, M. 1998 *Youth Crime and Police Work,* London, MacMillan Press, 1998.

McCold, P. 'The Role of the Community in Restorative Justice' in B. Galaway and J. Hudson (eds) *Restorative Justice: International Perspectives*, Monsey, NY, Criminal Justice Press, 1996.

McCold, P. 'Towards a Mid-range Theory of Restorative Criminal Justice: A Reply to the Maximalist Model', *Contemporary Justice Review*, 3: 357, 2000.

McCold, P. and Wachtel, B. *Restorative Policing Experiment: The Bethlehem Pennsylvania Police Family Group Conferencing Project*, Pipersville, PA, Community Service Foundation, 1998.

McGarrel, E., Olivares, K., Crawford, K., and Kroovand, N. *Returning Justice to the Community. The Indianapolis Juvenile Restorative Justice Experiment*, Indianapolis, IN, Hudson Institute, 2000.

Moore, D.B. and McDonald, J.M. 'Achieving the Good Community: A local police initiative and its wider ramifications' in K.M. Hazelhurst, *Perceptions of Justice Issues in Indigenous and Community Empowerment*, Brookfield, Ashgate, 1995.

Moore, D.B. and O'Connell, T. 'Family conferencing in Wagga Wagga: a communitarian model of justice' in C. Alder and J. Wundersitz (eds) *Family Conferencing and Juvenile Justice: The Way Forward or Misplaced Optimism?* Canberra, Australian Institute of Criminology, 1994.

O'Mahony, D. and Campbell, C. 'Mainstreaming Restorative Justice for Young Offenders through Youth Conferencing: The Experience of Northern Ireland' In Junger-Tas and Decker (eds) *International Handbook of Juvenile Justice*, The Netherlands, Springer, 2005.

O'Mahony, D., Chapman, T., and Doak, J. *Restorative Cautioning: A Study of Police Based Restorative Cautioning Pilots in Northern Ireland*, Belfast, Northern Ireland Office, 2002.

O'Mahony, D. and Deazley, R. *Juvenile Crime and Justice*, Criminal Justice Review Group Research Report 17, London, HMSO, 2000.

O'Mahony, D. and Doak, J. 'Restorative Justice: Is more better?' *Howard Journal*, 43: 484, 2004.

O'Mahony, D. and Doak, J. 'The Enigma of Community and the Exigency of Engagement: Restorative Youth Conferencing in Northern Ireland', *British Journal of Community Justice*, 4: 9, 2006.

Sherman, L. and Strang, H. *Restorative Justice: The Evidence*, London, Smith Institute, 2007.

Sherman, L., Strang, H., Barnes, J., Braithwaite, J., Inkpen, N. and Teh, M. *Experiments in Restorative Policing: a progress report on the Canberra Reintegrative Shaming Experiments*, Canberra, Australian Institute of Criminology, 1998.

Strang, H. *Repair or Revenge: Victims and Restorative Justice*, Oxford, Clarendon Press, 2002.

Strang, H., Sherman, L., Angel, C.M., Woods, D.J., Bennett, S., Newbury-Birch, D. and Inkpen, N. 'Victim Evaluations of Face-to-Face Restorative Justice Conferences: A Quasi-Experimental Analysis', *Journal of Social Sciences*, 62: 281, 2006.

Umbreit, M. *Victim Meets Offender: The impact of restorative justice and mediation*, New York, Criminal Justice Press, 1994.

Wemmers, J-A. and Canuto, M. *Victims' Experiences with, Expectations and Perceptions of Restorative Justice: A Critical Review of The Literature*, Ottawa, Statistics Canada, 2002.

Wunderstitz, J. and Hunter, N. *Juvenile Justice in South Australia: Where are we now?* Information Bulletin No 40, Adelaide, Office of Crime Statistics and Research, 2005.

Wilson, D., Kerr, H. and Boyle, M. *Juvenile Offenders and Reconviction in Northern Ireland*, Northern Ireland Office, Research Findings 3/98, Belfast, Northern Ireland Office, 1998.

Young, R. 'Just Cops Doing 'Shameful' Business? Police-led Restorative Justice and the Lessons of the Research' in A. Morris and G. Maxwell (eds) *Restorative Justice for Juveniles: Conferencing, Mediation and Circles,* Oxford, Hart, 2001.

Young, R. and Goold, B. 'Restorative police cautioning in Aylesbury – from degrading to reintegrative shaming ceremonies?', *Criminal Law Review* 126,1999.

15 Restorative justice, gendered violence, and indigenous women

Julie Stubbs

The application of restorative justice (RJ) for offences such as domestic violence and sexual assault continues to be highly contested, but the debate has become more complex and nuanced. I begin this chapter with a consideration of theoretical constraints on the capacity of RJ to promote victim interests, and then provide an overview of the debate with respect to offences of gendered violence. I use the term "gendered violence" to reflect the range of behaviors referred to in the relevant literature. Much of this research is specific to domestic violence or sexual assault, but I also draw from research concerning Indigenous communities that commonly refers to a wider range of violent practices and includes a more expansive notion of family than is common in the domestic violence literature. In the second part of the chapter, I examine literature concerning RJ responses to gendered violence in Indigenous communities. Research and commentary on Indigenous communities often fails to engage with the intersection of gender and race (or other social relations), and thus Indigenous women's needs and interests within RJ processes are still commonly obscured. The discursive character of RJ requires that participants tell their stories and that reasoned discussion will occur, resulting in an agreed upon outcome.[1] The capacity of parties to participate effectively is rarely questioned, yet victims in particular may face real obstacles to full participation. I argue that the opportunities and risks afforded by the discursiveness of RJ can be magnified by the impact of colonization on Indigenous women. I conclude by urging the consideration of hybrid developments that move beyond the oppositional contrast between RJ and criminal justice and adopt antisubordination as a principle in working toward safe and just outcomes.

The benefits of restorative justice for victims of crime

The benefits of RJ claimed for victims of crime include a wide range of symbolic, material, therapeutic, and moral outcomes (Stubbs 2007). International reviews have highlighted wide diversity between and within jurisdictions and some uncertainty about the prevailing RJ models, practices, and policies in use (Miers 2007). This diversity may be celebrated by some RJ proponents who emphasize restorative values rather than any one model (Pranis 2007), but the details of given schemes matter profoundly when assessing the merits and safety of RJ for victims, offenders, and the community. Much of the extant evidence has been derived from evaluations of programs for juvenile offenders, with less detail available regarding adult schemes.

Studies have found wide variations in victim participation rates in different schemes (from 7% to 85%, Dignan 2003:137). A growing body of evidence suggests that victims and other participants report high levels of satisfaction with RJ (Strang 2002; Sherman and

Strang 2007) although satisfaction has been conceptualized and measured inconsistently (Van Ness and Schiff 2001; Wemmers and Canuto 2002). Daly found high levels of satisfaction and perceived procedural fairness among participants, but less evidence for "restorativeness"; "these findings suggest that although it is possible to have a process perceived as fair, it can be harder for victims and offenders to resolve their conflict completely or to find common ground" (2001:76). Victims have reported reduced levels of fear, anxiety, and anger and show less interest in seeking vengeance (Strang 2002), and emerging research suggests a reduction in symptoms of posttraumatic stress after participating in RJ (Strang et al. 2006; but see Cheon and Regehr 2006). However, Daly has found that RJ "may do little to assist victims who have been deeply affected by crime" (2005:164); she noted "the variable nature of restorative processes, which can be contingent on the offence, the... victim and the subjective impact of victimisation" (2005:167). Many other claims have not been tested empirically, and few studies have specifically examined gender relations within RJ (but see Cook 2006; Daly 2002b). Claims of benefits for the community also may have a positive impact for victims and offenders, but Kurki's observation that "community level outcomes are yet to be defined and measured" (2003:294) continues to be apt.

The aspirations of the RJ movement to deliver such a range of benefits to victims of crime are laudable. However, the capacity of RJ to advance victims' interests remains limited by several factors. First, it does not have "its own concept of either victim or victimization" and thus lacks a foundation for challenging opposing claims (Green 2007:184–5). Second, a theoretical basis for how and why RJ might benefit victims is rarely articulated (Acorn 2004; Strang et al. 2006). Third, despite emerging evidence that experiences of RJ might vary according to victim, offender, and offence characteristics and to the subjective experience of victimization, little theoretical or empirical work guides practice in responding to these issues. Fourth, the tendency of much RJ literature to theorize crime as a discrete incident is at odds with research demonstrating that domestic violence is commonly recurrent and escalating and that the threat of violence may be ongoing and not reducible to discrete incidents (Coker 2002; Stubbs 2002). These are very salient concerns when dealing with offences such as domestic violence or sexual assault, which are not universally denounced nor well understood and where victim blaming is common (Coker 2002).

Debating the merits of restorative justice for gendered violence

The use of RJ for cases of domestic violence, or other gendered violence, continues to be controversial. The debate has been summarized by Daly and Stubbs (2006; see also Curtis-Fawley and Daly 2005; Edwards and Sharpe 2004). Proponents typically point to the opportunity for victims to participate and have a voice and receive validation, and for offenders to take responsibility, for a communicative and flexible environment and relationship repair (if that is a goal; Daly and Stubbs 2006). Those who oppose the use of RJ or urge caution point to risks such as victim safety being compromised in the process, possible manipulation of the process by offenders, pressure on victims to participate and/or agree to an outcome, communities that are under-resourced to support the parties, the lack of a community consensus condemning the violence, mixed loyalties among possible supporters, poor prospects for changing the offender's behavior, and the possibility that RJ may be seen to symbolize a lenient approach (Daly and Stubbs 2006). A more nuanced debate has begun to emerge as commentators recognize the diversity of victims' experiences and engage with empirical findings that suggest that outcomes may be more contingent than indicated by earlier accounts. Achilles and Zehr acknowledge that some RJ programs have been naïve in "attempting to apply restorative approaches in highly problematic areas (such as domestic violence) without adequate attention to complexities and safeguards" (2001:93). Commentary is beginning to differentiate between types of gendered violence and their prospects for the safe use of RJ or similar processes (Curtis-Fawley and Daly 2005). For instance, Hopkins, Koss and Bachar (2004; Hopkins and Koss 2005) see merit in adapting RJ for responding to date rape, but urge caution with respect to using RJ for ongoing intimate violence without further evidence that it can be pursued safely.

The literature commonly emphasizes the opportunities afforded to participants by the discursive character of RJ, such as the ability to tell their stories and participate in determining an agreement about how to redress the harm. Pranis says that "personal narratives are the primary source of information and wisdom [in RJ] but... the critical element is to use [them] to understand the harms, the needs, the pains and the capacities of all participants so that *an appropriate new story* can be constructed" (emphasis added, 2002:31). Barbara Hudson summarizes what is appealing about RJ as "the openness of story telling and exploration of possibilities for constructive and creative responses to offences" (2003:192). RJ offers the victim of domestic violence "the opportunity to choose how to present herself... [to express] *her* feelings, her understanding of events, her wishes and demands for the future..." (Hudson 2003:183, emphasis in the original). However, Hudson recognizes that the discursiveness of RJ is not without problems, such as the risk of domination and the reproduction of power relations (2006), and she emphasizes the need for "strong procedural safeguards" (2003:183). As Daly (2002a) has pointed out, RJ offers both opportunities and risks in freeform discussion. We know little about how meaning is constructed in RJ processes and whose stories might prevail (Stubbs 2007). Few empirical studies have examined how social relations such as gender, race, class, or age are expressed in RJ (Daly and Stubbs 2007; but see Cook 2006). There is no reason for confidence that a "new story" derived in the RJ process will necessary reflect a progressive understanding of victimization or gendered violence (Coker 2002; Stubbs 2007). As Roche has argued, the informality of a restorative process may permit a range of possible outcomes, including tyranny (2003). Without an explicit commitment to challenging subordination, older, limited understandings of gendered violence may prevail (Busch 2002). Questions remain about the extent to which the values orientation of RJ is adequate to ensure victim's interests are met in the absence of an explicit normative commitment to challenging subordination (Coker 2006; Hudson 2006).

Although it is common for RJ guidelines to indicate that victim safety is a key principle, Wemmers notes that no study in her review had asked "whether restorative measures respond to victims' need for security and to their fear of crime" (2002:53). A related concern is the finding by Presser and Lowencamp that offender-screening criteria on RJ encounters were not "victim oriented, research-driven, nor consistently applied" (1999:335).

Consultations with victims and victim advocates

Advocacy groups in several jurisdictions, particularly Canada, have undertaken consultations relating to RJ responses to gendered violence. Somewhat belatedly, governments or other key agencies have begun to consult communities concerning the future development of RJ. The findings have varied in detail but the prevailing view urges caution; consultation reports commonly emphasize concerns about victim safety, offender accountability, fears about the possible re-privatization of gendered violence, and questions about whether women's organizations and communities have the resources to take on the demands that might arise from RJ.

Stephanie Coward found that professionals and practitioners in the women's movement in Canada did not oppose RJ per se, but were concerned about its use for domestic violence. They pointed to a lack of consultation with women's and victims' groups, the likely effects of power imbalances between the parties, a lack of training and evaluation standards, and questions such as: would domestic and sexual violence be denounced sufficiently in such processes?; would women's groups' attempts to have the criminal justice system take the offences seriously be undermined?; would victims be given an informed choice about participating?; and would resources be made available to the community to deal with such issues? (Coward 2000). Similar findings have been reported across Canada (Lund and Devon Dodd 2002; Provincial Association of Transition Houses Saskatchewan 2000; Rubin 2003; [...]).

The Canadian Aboriginal Women's Action Network (AWAN) is "strongly opposed to the application of restorative justice measures in cases of violence against Aboriginal women and children" and has urged a moratorium on new developments, in part because "there has been no emphasis in case law or in current restorative justice models on the legacy of colonialism for Aboriginal women and children: racism, sexism, poverty, and violence" (AWAN 2001: para 2; Cameron 2006). That position was reached after extensive research and consultations with Aboriginal women and communities (Stewart, Huntley, and Blaney 2001). Participants identified potential in RJ but "women expressed fear that restorative justice reforms would fail to address the underlying power inequity rife in communities from years of oppression" (Stewart et al. 2001:39). They noted that alternative justice approaches operate on a "premise that presupposes a healed community," existing models had "a lack of accountability and structure," and "a failure to do follow-up with offenders and enforce sentences would further add to their victimization" (Stewart et al. 2001:40). They were also concerned about the use of diversion, resources predominantly going to offenders, victim-blaming, and risks to the safety of women and children in communities and in restorative processes. McGillivray and Comaskey reached similar findings in their study with Aboriginal women in Manitoba. The women saw community-based dispute resolution for dealing with intimate violence "as partisan and subject to political manipulation" (1999:143) and worried that offenders might stack the process with their supporters and avoid responsibility for their actions, and that diversion may meet offenders' needs but not victims' needs for safety. Respondents expressed dissatisfaction with aspects of conventional criminal justice but did not reject the Anglo-Canadian criminal justice system on cultural grounds. In a somewhat similar vein, The Native Women's Association of Canada has offered conditional support to RJ, recommending that funding be provided for 'restorative, "alternative" and Indigenous justice initiatives' but 'only when it is clear that Aboriginal women and their needs have been fully included' (2008:11).

Outcomes in Canada have been uneven. A federal/provincial/territorial working party on spousal abuse recommended *against* the use alternative justice processes such as RJ in spousal violence cases *except* where nine specified conditions were met, supported by training and resources (Ministry of Justice [Canada] 2003). In Prince Edward Island, the Justice Options for Women project considered RJ in limited circumstances in which RJ was victim-initiated and post-charge only (Lund and Devon Dodd 2002), but ultimately RJ was not adopted (Justice Options for Women 2006). The province of Nova Scotia has a moratorium on RJ for spousal/partner violence and sexual assaults (Rubin 2003). However, RJ is used for offences including violence against women in British Columbia (Cameron 2006) and Alberta (Edwards and Haslett 2003), and circle sentencing and other community-based programs used for Indigenous offenders in several jurisdictions include gendered violence.

150   *Julie Stubbs*

In Australia, Curtis-Fawley and Daly (2005) sought the views of advocates from sexual assault, child sexual assault, and domestic violence services in two states. Respondents saw possible benefits in RJ for gendered violence, such as giving victims a chance to speak in a way that courts did not provide, redressing power imbalances by giving emphasis to the victim, and the possibility of avoiding criminal justice altogether. However, they feared that victims could be revictimized, that RJ might be seen as a "soft" option, or that RJ practice may fall short of its ideals. Some rejected the idea that RJ should be a complete alternative to criminal justice [...].

A New Zealand study of adult victims of child sexual assault found some support for a RJ-like process but some diffidence on the part of respondents about what that might mean in practice; the respondents worried about the power of the offender to manipulate the process and whether the process would be victim-centered (Jülich 2006; [...]). The majority of submissions to a New Zealand government inquiry on the use of RJ for family violence supported RJ, but the strongest support was from RJ practitioners. Those opposed thought that RJ was inappropriate or dangerous due to power imbalances, a lack of specialist training and expertise among RJ practitioners, and the need for "strong state sanction" (Parker 2004). However, proponents also urged caution and emphasized the need for "careful assessment and screening of cases and the paramount importance of victim safety" (Parker 2004:5) and the need for extra time and resources for such matters. A model of best practice developed subsequently by the New Zealand Ministry of Justice recommends that RJ is used only in "appropriate cases" and states that "[t]he use of restorative justice processes in cases of family violence and sexual violence must be very carefully considered... and will not always be appropriate" (2004: Principle 8, no page numbers).

Consultations by the U.K. government attracted opposition from some women's advocacy organizations: Refuge (2003) and Women's Aid (2003) were open to the use of RJ for other offences but voiced strong opposition to RJ being used for sexual offences and domestic violence. In South Africa, the Commission on Gender Equality also has recommended against the use of RJ for sex offences or domestic violence due to concerns about victim safety (Commission on Gender Equality 2004).

Experience with restorative justice programs

Offences of gendered violence are often excluded from contemporary RJ programs, but historically, models now labeled restorative often included such offences within generic schemes. For instance, gendered violence has been included by victim–offender reconciliation programs (Umbreit 1990) and victim–offender dialogue meetings from the 1980s (Genesee County n.d.). Umbreit and colleagues reported that a "surprising number" (2000:7) of victim–offender mediation programs in the United States include domestic violence (1%), familial sexual assault (9%), and stranger sexual assault (7%) (2000:8). However, no evaluations of responses by these programs to gendered violence have been identified. Prisons departments in several countries operate RJ programs post-conviction; these are typically not limited by offence type and in some cases may involve direct encounters between the victim and offender, in which all parties consent (Van Ness 2007). From 1991 to 1994, nearly half of the victim–offender mediations undertaken in a Langley, British Columbia project with inmates were for sexual assault matters (Roberts 1995:39). An evaluation reported few differences by offence type, but noted that adult survivors of child sex offences judged offenders to "lack authenticity" (Roberts 1995:111) and recommended longer-term follow-up with all victims.

The youth justice conferencing models in South Australia (SAJJ) and New Zealand are atypical in that they are state-funded programs that respond to the full range of offending by young people and thus routinely include sexual offences and family violence (Parker 2004). Daly has reported findings of several studies of sexual offences by young people in SAJJ; she finds that conferences were a better option for victims than courts, because offenders admit responsibility and an outcome is achieved, whereas a large proportion of court cases are dismissed or withdrawn (Daly 2005). New Zealand also uses Family Group Conferences (FGC) for child protection matters, in which sexual and/or physical abuse issues may be raised (Parker 2004). In addition to funding pre-sentence, court-referred RJ schemes that exclude domestic or family violence, the New Zealand Government also funds community-based schemes. The latter schemes vary—some are diversionary and others are post-conviction schemes—and some include domestic violence, family violence, and sexual offences. Community schemes are also funded by other sources. A review of five government-funded community schemes that include family violence is underway,[2] but little is currently known about the processes, safeguards, or outcomes used in those schemes (Parker 2004).

Recently the Australian Capital Territory has taken a distinctive approach by legislating for RJ to be used for both young offenders and adults across a wide range of offences. Domestic violence offences, which may include some sexual offences, are to be included in a future stage II once a policy platform for managing those matters has been developed,[3] but will be referred to the scheme only after a guilty plea or conviction. The *Crimes (Restorative Justice) Act (2004)* requires that a chief executive determine the suitability of a matter for RJ after considering factors such as any power imbalance between the parties and the physical and psychological safety of parties (s.33); it remains unclear how that assessment will be undertaken.

In addition to generic programs that include some offences of gendered violence, a small number of adult RJ programs deal specifically with domestic violence, sexual violence, and/or other forms of gendered violence; some of those were reviewed by Stubbs (2004). Few programs have been subject to evaluation and most available documentation is purely descriptive, thus there is little available evidence on which to assess the claims made.

The work of Joan Pennell and colleagues is particularly influential in debates over the potential for RJ to respond effectively to gendered violence. The Family Group Decision Making Project in Newfoundland and Labrador focused on child welfare but commonly involved various forms of family violence (Pennell and Burford 2002). It is widely seen as a very promising model based in feminist praxis, planned in conjunction with government and nongovernment agencies, women's advocates and Indigenous organizations, and with the capacity to generate resources to assist the parties in redressing the harm caused. Evaluations were positive, but the project was discontinued contrary to the wishes of the local Inuit community because the federal funding was time-limited.[4] The North Carolina Family Group Conferencing Project is a similar project focused on child welfare also undertaken by Pennell and others. Building on this experience with child welfare, Pennell and Francis (2005) document the process they used to engage battered women, advocates, and other stake-holders in planning a coordinated approach to safety planning for women and children under the auspices of a domestic violence program, drawing on formal and informal services and supports. It seems that offenders may be included in the process in some circumstances […].

The DOVE program in the U.K. traces its roots to FGC in Newfoundland, Labrador, and New Zealand; victims/survivors of domestic violence, their children, and supporters attend a FGC with the objective of preparing a plan to enhance their safety. Perpetrators sometimes attend. A formative evaluation of the program (Social Services Research and Information Unit 2003) documents 30 referrals; nine cases proceeded to a FGC but parties agreed to participate in the research in only six cases. Outcomes were mixed: fewer children were on the child protection register, and only one family had further incidents recorded by police in the immediate follow-up period, but several stakeholders offered less support for the program at the 1-year point than they had initially. Four victims rated FGC as very good as a tool for dealing with domestic violence, but two had mixed feelings (Social Services Research and Information Unit 2003).

RESTORE was an innovative RJ program developed by Mary Koss and colleagues at the University of Arizona together with criminal justice personnel and community advocates. It responded to early feminist criticisms of RJ by careful design: cases of "ongoing intimate violence" were excluded, consistent with their preference for a cautious approach centered on victim safety (Hopkins et al. 2004 [...]). It was limited to first-time offenders who pleaded guilty to misdemeanor sex offenses, where victims and offenders were aged at least 18 years, relied on consent by victim and offender, and was court-ordered. A similar program is being established in New Zealand, which seems to contemplate the inclusion of a wider range of sexual offences, including adult survivors of child sexual assault (Jülich 2006 [...]).

Restorative justice and indigenous peoples

RJ may offer opportunities for community engagement in new justice forms that benefit Indigenous communities. However, the aspirations of Indigenous groups often embrace wider visions of justice, including self-determination (Cunneen 2003; Nancarrow 2006; Smith 2005), and the alternative justice initiatives pursued in Indigenous communities are not confined to RJ (Cameron 2006; Cunneen 2007; Marchetti and Daly 2004; Memmott et al. 2006). There are problems in conflating Indigenous justice with RJ, but no agreement on how to differentiate between the two. Circle sentencing is commonly designated as an example of RJ but Marchetti and Daly (2004) disagree and classify it as an Indigenous justice practice; the Hollow Water Community Holistic Circle healing program (Couture et al. 2001) is often claimed as RJ but is more expansive and multilayered than typical models of RJ. Research needs to analyze the specific features of different models and to consider the level of control or ownership Indigenous people have in any scheme. Few Indigenous schemes have been evaluated, and Dickson-Gilmore and LaPrairie lament that continued assertions of success in the absence of evaluative data actually hinder future developments (2005). The fact that some Indigenous people are participants in mainstream models of RJ also is often overlooked.

It is commonly assumed that RJ will be beneficial for Indigenous people (and peoples) in contrast to conventional criminal justice, which has been so damaging. However, debates that pit RJ against criminal justice obscure the fact that many extant RJ practices are not alternatives but are grafted onto criminal justice and may deflect attention from other possibilities more aligned with Indigenous aspirations. Claims that RJ is derived from Indigenous modes of dispute resolution are overgeneralized and have attracted strong criticism because they ignore important differences between Indigenous peoples and their practices and because the claims have sometimes substituted for consultation with Indigenous peoples about the development or imposition of RJ programs (Cunneen 2003; Daly 2002a; Dickson-Gilmore and LaPrairie 2005; Tauri 1999).

One key dimension on which programs differ is the legal and political framework in which they operate. For instance, the Navajo Nation has the authority "to exercise jurisdiction over tribal matters" (Cunneen 2007:124; see also Coker 2006); by contrast, Indigenous Australians have no recognized basis to "develop their own jurisdiction over legal matters... except... where the state permits them to do so as a matter of policy or practice" (Cunneen 2007:124). In Canada, sentencing circles developed from judicial sentencing discretion (McNamara 2000). So, whereas Navajo peacemaking functions within Navajo law, developments in Australia and Canada typically "fit within the broader criminal justice framework" (Cunneen 2007:124). However, some Indigenous commentators object strongly to RJ or Indigenous justice practices that rely on the state. For instance, Smith decries developments that add to the power of the criminal justice system, and she promotes political organizing to "challenge state violence and build communities" (2005:729; Incite! 2003[...]). She notes that gendered violence is not separable from state violence, as the former has been an integral tactic of colonization.

Dickson-Gilmore and LaPrairie argue that claims that sentencing circles[5] in Canada offer self-governance or empowerment are overstated since, although participants may have a role in shaping the sentence, the power typically remains with the judge (Dickson-Gilmore and LaPrairie 2005). However, the politics of such developments are complex and vary by jurisdiction (Daly and Stubbs 2007). Circle sentencing has begun to be introduced in some parts of Australia. These developments have adapted Canadian practices, often with support by Australian Indigenous organizations such as the Aboriginal Justice Advisory Council in New South Wales or by Indigenous communities (Marchetti and Daly 2004). Cunneen provides both optimistic and pessimistic readings of RJ and its relationship to Indigenous justice ideals. His pessimistic account sees RJ as coinciding with criminal justice practices emphasizing individual responsibility and more punitive measures, in a bifurcated system in which Indigenous people are denied the benefits associated with RJ ideals and are "channelled into more punitive processes" (2007:119). His more optimistic reading sees hybrid developments of RJ with criminal justice, such as in sentencing circles and Indigenous courts, as offering opportunities for the pursuit of social justice and for Indigenous communities to develop "organically connected restorative justice processes that resonate with Indigenous cultures" to replace "state-imposed forms of restorative justice" (2007:120).

RJ is often promoted as community-based and as a mechanism for transforming communities, but insufficient attention has been paid to the capacity of communities to develop and sustain RJ processes (Blagg 2002; Crawford and Clear 2001). Dickson-Gilmore and La Prairie (2005) have drawn renewed attention to questions about the resources available to Indigenous communities to take on responsibilities arising from RJ. For instance, they stress the costs of circle sentencing on under-resourced communities that may be held responsible for monitoring and supporting offenders without additional resources to fund that work. AWAN's (2001) statement opposing RJ for violence against Indigenous women and children in Canada demonstrates the significance of this concern; they emphasize the lack of necessary services to support victims on reserves and the contraction of state funding for off-reserve services.

Restorative justice, gendered violence, and indigenous women[6]

Indigenous women's responses to RJ have emphasized concerns about violence to women and children. As noted in the consultations described earlier, respondents were typically open to the principles of RJ, often in conjunction with self-determination, but they differed in their assessment of whether RJ ideals could be realized in their community or context. There is strong agreement in the literature that responses to violence against women and children in Indigenous communities need to be community-driven, crafted with the full involvement of Indigenous people and these responses must reflect the needs and capacities of particular communities (Behrendt 2002; Blagg 2002; Kelly 2002; Memmott et al. 2006). However, they also must recognize that "women are part of that community too" (Stewart et al. 2001:57). Nonetheless, significant debates continue among Indigenous women about the way forward. Cameron has described the different approaches adopted by Indigenous women in Canada: some have a focus on culture, with self-determination as their primary goal, whereas others focus on both culture and gender and see "the gendered nature of intimate violence in their communities and the failures of both conventional and Aboriginal justice systems to address it" (2006:55). Similarly, within Australia, some Indigenous women stress the need for inclusive community-wide healing (Atkinson 2002; Lawrie and Matthews 2002), while others see an urgent task in pursuing safety for women and children (Greer 1994).

Some Indigenous women's advocates and scholars are concerned that the community focus of RJ may obscure or trump the interests of women and children. The risks and opportunities afforded by the discursive character of RJ described earlier may be magnified by the impact of colonization. As Cunneen has observed, "gendered patterns of knowledge and culture" have been distorted by colonization; it cannot be assumed that RJ "will privilege or indeed give a voice to minority women" (2003:187). Some accounts of Indigenous programs commonly cited by RJ scholars as successful have been challenged, especially by Indigenous women, as failing to address women's interests (LaRoque 1997; Nahance 1992; Nightingale 1994). Critical accounts of circle sentencing in some Canadian Indigenous communities demonstrate how well-intended attempts to respond to cultural differences may have silenced some women and put their safety at risk (Crnkovich 1996; Goel 2000). This problem is not confined to RJ but may occur in other justice practices when attempts to accommodate culture fail to recognize the different interests within communities; intersecting social relations including but not limited to sexism and racism, may subject women to multiple disadvantage (Crenshaw 1991; Razack 1994 [...]).

Circle sentencing was recently piloted in one New South Wales Indigenous community and has been extended to other communities. The preliminary evaluation report is based on the first 13 cases; eight of these are documented as case studies. It is very positive, citing a high level of satisfaction among participants and finds that participants were able to discuss the effect of the offence on the victim(s) openly. The Aboriginal elders were seen as the greatest strength of the program, instilling morals and values, and lending authority and legitimacy to the process (Potas et al. 2003). However, the findings also suggest a need for closer attention to the interests of victims of gendered violence. At least two case studies included domestic violence but with no mention of any safety planning or follow-up with victims. Most victims reported that they had been unclear about what to expect and were unprepared for the "emotional intensity" of the process (2003:40). Some participants wanted more women involved "to ensure that participants are particularly sensitive to the feelings of victims and offenders, and that they have an adequate awareness of the dynamics of domestic violence" (2003:41). A separate women's panel for domestic violence was also suggested.

Coker (1999, 2006) has offered qualified support for the use of Navajo peacemaking in response to domestic violence. She distinguishes peacemaking from typical RJ on three dimensions: Peacemaking was designed and is run by the Navajo Nation, whereas most RJ used for Indigenous persons is controlled by non-Indigenous agencies; peacemaking uses "concepts of gender harmony," which provide "a powerful cultural resource for addressing domestic violence"; and individuals may choose to initiate the process independently of any legal process (2006:69). However, she remains concerned that participation may be coerced, that too little attention is focused on victim safety, and that there is little engagement between peacemaking and battered women's advocates [...].

Conclusion

The literature reviewed in this chapter indicates that some openness to RJ principles exists, but that a prevailing skepticism remains about what that might mean in practice. This skepticism is well-founded for both theoretical and empirical reasons. Without a strong normative commitment to antisubordination and a clear theoretical framework for understanding victimization, *generic* models of RJ cannot be relied on to promote victim interests in cases of gendered violence, nor to challenge racism or other forms of prejudice. New responses to gendered violence are more likely to be effective, safe, and responsive to difference when the design and practice is guided by the principle of antisubordination and draws on the expertise of women's advocates in the communities that they serve. Commentators have long urged RJ practitioners and women's advocates to learn from each other (Coker 2002 [...]). The oppositional contrast of RJ to conventional criminal justice so common in the literature is not helpful in advancing future developments. New approaches arc likely to require state and non-state resources and coercive back-up to ensure safety and compliance, and thus are apt to be hybrid models that draw from both RJ and conventional criminal justice (Hudson 2002). For instance, RESTORE could be characterized in this way. Although there is strong resistance to the diversion of offenders who commit gendered violence (Curtis-Fawley and Daly 2005; Hudson 2002; McGillivray and Comaskey 1999), RESTORE seemed to meet such concerns in the use of diversion *from* court *into* therapeutic programs with regular monitoring and follow-up of offenders [...].

Future developments would be aided by a greater recognition of the distinctions between Indigenous justice and RJ. Indigenous women often desire community control of justice initiatives but also recognize obstacles to safe and just outcomes in their communities, especially when proposals fail to recognize the impact of colonization and of violence on women and children. Not all communities are well-placed to take this on, and debates would do well to avoid the presumption of "a healed community" (Stewart et al. 2001:30) or the idealization of community. The preconditions for sustainable and effective new justice models must be identified. These are likely to include mechanisms to facilitate women's engagement in the planning and delivery of new initiatives and the provision of resources to allow women to be genuine participants in any justice process, to support victims of gendered violence within the community, and to develop and sustain the community infrastructure that underpins community-based justice initiatives where they are appropriate.

Acknowledgments

I wish to acknowledge the research assistance of Dr. Kelly Richards.

Notes

1 In addition to its reliance on oral discourse, RJ is also discursive in another sense; it invokes a set of underlying concerns and themes about what it means to be restorative and what processes and outcomes are expected.
2 Crime Research Centre, University of Victoria Wellington. Retrieved March 30, 2007 (http://www.vuw.ac.nz/cjrc/rescarch-projects/current-projects/FiveSites.aspx).
3 J. Hinchey, personal communication, November 10, 2006.
4 J. Pennell, personal communication, June 28, 2007.
5 They distinguish sentencing circles from healing circles and see the latter as being more community-based (Dickson-Gilmore and LaPrairie 2005).
6 Some Indigenous women within Australia prefer the term "family violence" rather than "domestic violence" (or other alternatives) to reflect the wider range of relationships and contexts within which violence occurs in Indigenous communities. However, it is acknowledged that patterns of family violence within Indigenous communities are highly gendered (Memmott et al. 2006). This chapter draws on a range of international sources that use different terminology to refer to violence against women and children within Indigenous communities. The various terms used in this section reflect those used in the literature from which it was derived and, unless otherwise stated, are used interchangeably.

References

Aboriginal Women's Action Network (AWAN). 2001. *Aboriginal Women's Action Newark (AWAN Policy): The Implications of Restorative Justice in Cases of Violence Against Aboriginal Women and Children.* Retrieved March 30, 2007 (http://www.casac.ca/english/awan.htm).

Achilles, Mary and Howard Zehr. 2001. "Restorative Justice for Crime Victims: The Promise and the Challenge." pp. 87—99 in *Restorative Community Justice: Repairing Harm and Transforming Communities,* edited by Gordon Bazemore and Mara Schiff. Cincinnati, OH: Anderson Publishing.

Acorn, Annalise. 2004. *Compulsory Compassion: A Critique of Restorative Justice.* Vancouver: University of British Columbia Press.

Atkinson, Judy. 2002. "Voices in the Wilderness: Restoring Justice to Traumatised Peoples." *The University of New South Wales Law Journal* 25:233–41.

Behrendt, Larissa. 2002. "Lessons from the Mediation Obsession: Ensuring That Sentencing Alternatives Focus on Indigenous Self-Determination." pp. 178– 190 in *Restorative Justice and Family Violence,* edited by Heather Strang and John Braithwaite. Melbourne: Cambridge University Press.

Blagg, Harry. 2002. "Restorative Justice and Aboriginal Family Violence: Opening a Space for Healing," pp. 191–205 in *Restorative Justice and Family Violence*, edited by Heather Strang and John Braithwaite. Melbourne: Cambridge University Press.

Busch, Ruth. 2002. "Domestic Violence and Restorative Justice Initiatives: Who Pays If We Get It Wrong?" pp. 223–248 in *Restorative Justice and Family Violence*, edited by Heather Strang and John Braithwaite. Melbourne: Cambridge University Press.

Cameron, Angela. 2006. "Stopping the Violence: Canadian Feminist Debates on Restorative Justice." *Theoretical Criminology* 10:49–66.

Cheon, Aileen and Cheryl Regehr. 2006. "Restorative Justice Models in Cases of Intimate Partner Violence: Reviewing the Evidence." *Victims and Offenders* 1:369–394.

Coker, Donna. 2002. "Transformative Justice: Anti-Subordination Processes in Cases of Domestic Violence." pp. 128–152 in *Restorative Justice and Family Violence,* edited by Heather Strang and John Braithwaite. Melbourne: Cambridge University Press.

——2006. "Restorative Justice, Navajo Peacemaking and Domestic Violence." *Theoretical Criminology* 10:67–86.

Commission on Gender Equality (South Africa). 2004. *Submission to the Portfolio Committee on Correctional Services Draft White Paper on Corrections in South Africa.* Retrieved March 30, 2007 (http://www.cge.org.za/userfiles/documents/submission4feb04final.doc).

Cook, Kimberly. 2006. "Doing Difference and Accountability in Restorative Justice Conferences." *Theoretical Criminology* 10:107–124.

Couture, Joe Ted Parker, Ruth Couture, and Patti Laboucane. 2001. *A Cost-Benefit of Hollow Water's Community Holistic Circle Healing Process.* Ottawa: Solicitor General.

Coward, Stephanie. 2000. "Restorative Justice in Cases of Domestic and Sexual Violence: Healing Justice?" *AiR: Abuse Information & Resources for Survivors.* Retrieved March 30, 2007 (http://www.hotpeachpages.net/canada/air/rj_domestic_violence.html).

Crawford, Adam and Todd Clear. 2001. "Community Justice: Transforming Communities Through Restorative Justice? pp. 127–49 in *Restorative Community Justice,* edited by Gordon Bazemore and Mara Schiff. Cincinnati, OH: Anderson Publishing.

Crenshaw, Kimberle. 1991, "Mapping the Margins: Intersectionality, Identity Politics and Violence Against Women of Color." *Stanford Law Review* 43:1241–1300.

Crnkovich, Mary. 1996. "A Sentencing Circle." *Journal of Legal Pluralism* 36:159–181.

Cunneen, Chris. 2003. "Thinking Critically About Restorative Justice." pp. 182–194 in *Restorative Justice: Critical Issues,* edited Eugene McLaughlin, Ross Fergusson, Gordon Hughes, and Louise Westmarland. London: Sage, in association with The Open University.

—— 2007. "Reviving Restorative Justice Traditions?" pp. 113–131 in *Handbook of Restorative Justice,* edited by Gerry Johnstone and Daniel W. Van Ness. Cullompton, Devon, UK: Willan.

Curtis-Fawley, Sarah, and Kathleen Daly. 2005. "Gendered Violence and Restorative Justice: The Views of Victim Advocates." *Violence Against Women* 11:603–638.

Daly, Kathleen. 2001. "Conferencing in Australia and New Zealand: Variations, Research Findings and Prospects." pp. 59–84 in *Restorative Justice for Juveniles: Conferencing, Mediation and Circles,* edited by Allison Morris and Gabrielle Maxwell. Oxford, UK: Hart Publishing.

—— 2002a. "Restorative Justice: The Real Story." *Punishment & Society* 4:55–79.

—— 2002b. "Sexual Assault and Restorative Justice." pp. 62–88 in *Restorative Justice and Family Violence,* edited by Heather Strang and John Braithwaite. Melbourne: Cambridge University Press.

—— 2005. "A Tale of Two Studies: Restorative Justice from a Victim's Perspective." pp. 153–174 in *New Directions in Restorative Justice: Issues, Practice and Evaluation,* edited by Elizabeth Elliott and Robert Gordon. Cullompton, Devon, UK: Willan.

Daly, Kathleen and Julie Stubbs. 2006. "Feminist Engagement with Restorative Justice." *Theoretical Criminology* 10:9–28.

——2007. "Feminist Theory, Feminist and Anti-Racist Politics, and Restorative Justice." pp. 149–170 in *Handbook of Restorative Justice,* edited by Gerry Johnstone and Daniel W. Van Ness. Cullompton, Devon, UK: Willan.

Dickson-Gilmore, Jane and Carol LaPrairie. 2005. *Will the Circle Be Unbroken: Aboriginal Communities, Restorative Justice and the Challenges of Conflict and Change.* Toronto: University of Toronto Press.

Dignan, Jim. 2003. "Towards a Systematic Model of Restorative Justice," pp. 135–156 in *Restorative Justice and Criminal Justice: Competing or Reconcilable Paradigms?* edited by Andrew von Hirsch, Julian Roberts, and Anthony Bottoms. Oxford, UK: Hart Publishing.

Edwards, Alan and Jennifer Haslett. 2003. *Domestic Violence and Restorative Justice: Advancing the Dialogue.* Paper presented to 6th International Conference on Restorative Justice, June 1–4, Vancouver, British Columbia, Canada. Retrieved March 30, 2007 (http://ww.sfu.ca/cfrj/fulltext/haslett.pdf).

Edwards, Alan and Susan Sharpe. 2004. *Restorative Justice in the Context of Domestic Violence: A Literature Review.* Edmonton, Canada: Mediation and Restorative Justice Centre. Retrieved March 30, 2007 (http://www.mrjc.ca/forms/CM%20Documents/RJ-DV%20Lit%20Review%20PDF.pdf).

Genesee County. n.d. *Victim-Offender Dialogue Meetings and Community Conciliation Cases.* Retrieved March 30, 2007 (www.co.genesee.ny.us/dpt/communityservices/conccases.html).

Goel, Rashmi. 2000. "No Women at the Center: The Use of the Canadian Sentencing Circle in Domestic Violence Cases." *Wisconsin Women's Law Journal* 15:293–334.

Green, Simon. 2007. "The Victims' Movement and Restorative Justice." pp. 171–191 in *Handbook of Restorative Justice,* edited by Gerry Johnstone and Daniel W. Van Ness. Cullompton, Devon, UK: Willan.

Greer, Pam. 1994. "Aboriginal Women and Domestic Violence in NSW." pp. 64–78 in *Women, Male Violence and the Law,* edited by Julie Stubbs. Sydney: Institute of Criminology.

Hopkins, C. Quince and Mary P. Koss. 2005. "Incorporating Feminist Theory and Insights into a Restorative Justice Response to Sex Offenses." *Violence Against Women* 11:693–723.

Hopkins, C. Quince, Mary P. Koss, and Karen J. Bachar. 2004. "Applying Restorative Justice to Ongoing Intimate Violence: Problems and Possibilities." *St. Louis University Public Law Review* 23:289–311.

Hudson, Barbara. 2003. "Victims and Offenders." pp. 177–194 in *Restorative Justice and Criminal Justice: Competing or Reconcilable Paradigms?* edited by Andrew von Hirsch, Julian Roberts, and Anthony Bottoms. Oxford, UK: Hart Publishing.

—— 2006. "Beyond White Man's Justice: Race, Gender and Justice in Late Modernity." *Theoretical Criminology* 10:29–48.

Incite!. 2003. *Incite! Women of Color Against Violence Community Accountability Principles/Concerns/Strategies/Models Working Document.* March 5. Retrieved February 26, 2009 (http://www.incite-national.org/index.php? s=93).

Jülich, Shirley. 2006. "Views of Justice Among Survivors of Historical Child Sexual Abuse: Implications for Restorative Justice in New Zealand." *Theoretical Criminology* 10:125–138.

Justice Options for Women (Who Are Victims of Violence). 2006. *Justice Options for Women: Phase 4. Designing a PEI Domestic Violence Treatment Option Court Process.* Charlottetown, PEI, Canada. Retrieved March 30, 2007 (http://www.isn.net/~tha/justiceoptions/Feb_2006_project_update.pdf).

Kelly, Loretta. 2002. "Using Restorative Justice Principles to Address Family Violence in Aboriginal Communities." pp. 206–222 in *Restorative Justice and Family Violence*, edited by Heather Strang and John Braithwaite. Cambridge, UK: Cambridge University Press.

Kurki, Leena. 2003. "Evaluating Restorative Justice Practices." pp. 291–314 in *Restorative Justice and Criminal Justice: Competing or Reconcilable Paradigms?* edited by Andrew von Hirsch, Julian Roberts, and Anthony Bottoms, Oxford, UK: Hart Publishing.

LaRoque, Emma. 1997. "Re-examining Culturally Appropriate Models in Criminal Justice Applications." pp. 75–96 in *Aboriginal and Treaty Rights in Canada: Essays on Law, Equity and Respect for Difference,* edited by Michael Asch. Vancouver: University of British Columbia Press.

Lawrie, Rowena and Winsome Matthews. 2002. "Holistic Community Justice: A Proposed Response to Family Violence in Aboriginal Communities." *The University of New South Wales Law Journal* 25: 228–232.

Lund, Kirsten and Julie Devon Dodd. 2002. *Justice Options for Women Who Are Victims of Violence Final Report.* Retrieved March 30, 2007 (http://www.isn.net/~tha/justiceoptions/finalreport.pdf).

Marchetti, Elena and Kathleen Daly. 2004. "Indigenous Courts and Justice Practices in Australia." *Trends and Issues in Crime and Criminal Justice* No.277. Canberra: Australian Institute of Criminology.

McGillivray, Anne and Brenda Comaskey. 1999. *Black Eyes All of the Time: Intimate Violence, Aboriginal Women and the Justice System.* Toronto: University of Toronto Press.

McNamara, Luke. 2000. "The Locus of Decision-Making Authority in Circle Sentencing: The Significance of Criteria and Guidelines." *Windsor Yearbook of Access to Justice* 18:60–114.

Memmott, Paul, Catherine Chambers, Carroll Go-Sam, and Linda Thomson. 2006. "Good Practice in Indigenous Family Violence Prevention—Designing and Evaluating Successful Programs." Issues Paper: 11 Australian Domestic & Family Violence Clearinghouse. Retrieved March 30, 2007 (http://www.austdvclearinghouse.unsw.edu.au/Word%20Files/Issues_Paper_11.doc).

Miers, David. 2007. "The International Development of Restorative Justice." pp.447–467 in *Handbook of Restorative Justice*, edited by Gerry Johnstone and Daniel W. Van Ness. Cullompton, Devon, UK: Willan.

Ministry of Justice (Canada). 2003. *Final Report of the Ad Hoc Federal-Provincial-Territorial Working Group Reviewing Spousal Abuse Policies and Legislation.* Prepared for Federal-Provincial-Territorial Ministers Responsible for Justice. Retrieved March 30, 2007 (http://www.justice.gc.ca/en/ps/fm/reports/spousal. html#15ii).

Ministry of Justice (NZ). 2004. *Principles of Best Practice for Restorative Justice Processes in Criminal Cases.* Retrieved March 11, 2007 (http://www.justice.govt.nz/restorative-justice/partb.html).

Nahanee, Teressa. 1992. "Dancing with a Gorilla: Aboriginal Women, Justice and the Charter." Paper prepared for the Royal Commission on Aboriginal Peoples, Canada. On file with the author.

Nancarrow, Heather. 2006. "In Search of Justice for Domestic and Family Violence: Indigenous and Non-Indigenous Australian Women's Perspectives." *Theoretical Criminology* 10:87–106.

Native Women's Association of Canada. 2008. *Aboriginal Women in the Canadian Criminal Justice System: A Policy Paper.* Retrieved 1 October 2008 (http://www.nwac-hq.org/en/documents/Aboriginal-WomenintheCanadianJusticeSystem.pdf).

Nightingale, Marg. 1994. *Just-Us and Aboriginal Women.* Report prepared for the Aboriginal Justice Directorate, Department of Justice, Canada.

Parker, Wendy. 2004. *Restorative Justice and Family Violence: An Overview of the Literature.* Wellington, NZ: Ministry of Justice.

Pennell, Joan and Gale Burford. 2002. "Feminist Praxis: Making Family Group Conferencing Work." pp. 108–127 in *Restorative Justice and Family Violence*, edited by Heather Strang and John Braithwaite. Melbourne: Cambridge University Press.

Pennell, Joan and Stephanie Francis. 2005. "Safety Conferencing: Toward a Coordinated and Inclusive Response to Safeguard Women and Children." *Violence Against Women* 11:666–692.

Potas, Ivan, Jane Smart, Georgia Brignell, Brendan Thomas, and Rowena Lawrie. 2003. *Circle Sentencing in New South Wales: A Review and Evaluation.* Sydney: Judicial Commission of New South Wales. Retrieved March 30, 2007 (http://www.lawlink.nsw.gov.au/ajac.nsf/pages/reports).

Pranis, Kay. 2002. "Restorative Values and Family Violence." pp. 23–41 in *Restorative Justice and Family Violence,* edited by Heather Strang and John Braithwaite. Cambridge, UK: Cambridge University Press.

—— 2007. "Restorative Values." pp. 59–74 in *Handbook of Restorative Justice*, edited by Gerry Johnstone and Daniel W. Van Ness. Cullompton, Devon, UK: Willan.

Provincial Association of Transition Houses Saskatchewan (Canada). 2000. *Restorative Justice: Is it Justice for Battered Women? Report on the April 2000 Conference.* Retrieved March 30, 2007 (http://www.abusehelplines.org/restorative_justice_l21006.pdf).

Presser, Lois and Christopher Lowenkamp. 1999. "Restorative Justice and Offender Screening." *Journal of Criminal Justice* 27:333–343.

Razack, Sherene. 1994. "What Is To Be Gained by Looking White People in the Eye? Culture, Race, and Gender in Cases of Sexual Violence." *Signs* 19:894–923.

Refuge (UK). 2003. *Refuge Response to Restorative Justice—Government Consultation.* Retrieved March 30, 2007 (http://www.refuge.org.uk/cms_content_refuge/attachments/policyAndResearch/RestorativeJustice.pdf).

Roberts, Tim. 1995. *Evaluation of the Victim Offender Mediation Project, Langley B.C. Final Report.* Ottawa: Solicitor General Canada. Copy on file with the author.

Roche, Declan. 2003. *Accountability in Restorative Justice.* Oxford UK: Oxford University Press.

Rubin, Pamela. 2003. *Restorative Justice in Nova Scotia: Women's Experience and Recommendations for Positive Policy Development and Implementation, Report and Recommendations.* Retrieved March 30, 2007 (http://www.nawl.ca/ns/en/documents/Pub_Brief_NSRestorativeJustice03_en.pdf).

Sherman, Lawrence W. and Heather Strang. 2007. "Restorative Justice: The Evidence." Retrieved March 30, 2007 (http://www.smith-institute.org.uk/pdfs/RJ_full_report.pdf).

Smith, Andrea. 2005. "Book Review: Restorative Justice and Family Violence." *Violence Against Women* 11:724–730.

Social Services Research and Information Unit. 2003. *The Dove Project: The Basingstoke Domestic Violence Family Group Conference Project. Phase I (Pilot): January 2001 to December 2002.* Portsmouth, UK: University of Portsmouth. Retrieved March 30, 2007 (http://www.hants.gov.uk/daybreakfgc/Main_ReportPortsmouth.pdf).

Stewart, Wendy, Audrey Huntley, and Fay Blaney. 2001. *The Implications of Restorative Justice for Aboriginal Women and Children Survivors of Violence: A Comparative Overview of Five*

Communities in British Columbia. Vancouver, British Columbia: Aboriginal Women's Action Network. Retrieved March 30, 2007 (http://epc.lac-bac.gc.ca/100/206/301/law_commission_of_canada-cf/2006-1206/www.lcc.gc.ca/research_project/01_aboriginal_l-en.asp).

Strang, Heather. 2002. *Repair or Revenge: Victims and Restorative Justice.* Oxford, UK: Clarendon Press.

Strang, Heather, Lawrence Sherman, Caroline Angel, Daniel Woods, Sarah Bennett, Dorothy Newbury-Birch, and Nova Inkpen. 2006. "Victim Evaluations of Face-to-Face Restorative Justice Conferences: A Quasi-Experimental Analysis." *Journal of Social Issues* 62:281–302.

Stubbs, Julie. 2002. "Domestic Violence and Women's Safety: Feminist Challenges to Restorative Justice." pp. 42–61 in *Restorative Justice and Family Violence,* edited by Heather Strang and John Braithwaite. Cambridge, UK: Cambridge University Press.

——. 2004. "Restorative Justice, Domestic Violence and Family Violence." *Australian Domestic & Family Violence Clearinghouse, Issues Paper* No. 9. Retrieved March 30, 2007 (http://www.austdvclearinghouse. unsw.edu.au/PDF%20files/Issues_Paper_9.pdf).

——. 2007. "Beyond Apology? Domestic Violence and Critical Questions for Restorative Justice." *Criminology and Criminal Justice* 7:169–187.

Tauri, Juan. 1999. "Explaining Recent Innovations in New Zealand's Criminal Justice System: Empowering Maori or Biculturalising the State." *Australian and New Zealand Journal of Criminology* 32:153–167.

Umbreit, Mark. 1990. "Victim-Offender Mediation with Violent Offenders: Implications for Modification of the VORP Model." pp. 337–351 in *The Victimology Handbook: Research Findings, Treatment, and Public Policy,* edited by Emilio Viano. New York: Garland Publishing.

Umbriet, Mark, Jean Greenwood, Claudia Fercello, and Jenni Umbreit. 2000. *National Survey of Victim-Offender Mediation Programs in the United States.* St. Paul, MN: Center for Restorative Justice & Peacemaking, School of Social Work, University of Minnesota.

Van Ness, Daniel W. 2007. "Prisons and Restorative Justice," pp. 312–324 in *Handbook of Restorative Justice,* edited by Gerry Johnstone and Daniel W. Van Ness. Cullompton, Devon, UK: Willan Publishing.

Van Ness, Daniel and Mara Schiff. 2001. "Satisfaction Guaranteed? The Meaning of Satisfaction in Restorative Justice." pp. 47–62 in *Restorative Community Justice: Repairing Harm and Transforming Communities,* edited by Gordon Bazemore and Mara Schiff. Cincinnati, OH: Anderson Publishing.

Wemmers, Jo-Anne. 2002. "Restorative Justice for Victims of Crime: A Victim Oriented Approach to Restorative Justice." *International Review of Victimology* 9:43–59.

Wemmers, Jo-Anne and Marisa Canute. 2002. *Victims' Experiences with, Expectations and Perceptions of Restorative Justice: A Critical Review of the Literature.* Ottawa: Department of Justice Canada, Policy Centre for Victim Issues. Retrieved March 30, 2007 (http://Canada.justice.gc.ca/en/ps/rs/rep/rr01–9.pdf).

Women's Aid (UK). 2003. *Women's Aid Consultation Response to Restorative Justice—The Government's Strategy.* Retrieved March 30, 2007 (http://www.womensaid.org.uk/page.asp?section=00010001000900030004005).

16 Responding to hate crimes through restorative justice dialogue

Robert B. Coates, Mark S. Umbreit and Betty Vos

Introduction

Hate fuels violence. This is a strongly held belief among those who work diligently to respond to crimes of hate and to prevent such acts. Hate is seen as an underlying factor, whether the acts being carried out against individuals and groups arise from biases based upon race, ethnicity, gender, sexual orientation, religion, disability, or age.

While quick and unfettered reaction from law enforcement and the courts is viewed as critical in response to crimes of hate, many, including members of law enforcement and the judiciary, believe that the battle against hate and its consequences must be won by breaking down the stereotypes, attitudes, and world views that foster hate in the first place. That battle is fought within churches, schools, other community organizations, the media, families, and person-to-person relationships.

One means for combating hate is dialogue. Obviously, this is not a new idea. Dialogue has been used across the centuries as a means for reducing conflict, enhancing relationships, and negating hate. On occasion, dialogue has been successful; at other times, the call for dialogue has not been heard, or invitations to dialogue have been rejected.

Today, a multitude of groups and organizations promote various forms of dialogue between hostile individuals and groups. Some of those organizations and groups are entirely locally based and largely carry out their work informally. Others are part of national and international organizations that provide numerous resources and guidance for promoting and carrying out dialogue.[1]

There seems to be no clear best way of "doing dialogue" to prevent acts of hate. Concerned community groups and individuals often sort through a range of dialogue approaches trying to agree upon what is a best fit for their own circumstances and resources. Often, these groups do not rely upon a single dialogue approach but rather (sometimes to the consternation of dialogue advocates) co-mingle and merge various approaches. Just as there is a great need for dialogue in our communities, schools, and churches, there are many voices of dialogue.

Here, we describe one such voice: restorative justice dialogue. This form of dialogue has emerged and been refined over the past several decades largely in the juvenile and criminal justice arena. More recently, restorative justice dialogue has been applied, nationally and internationally, to situations fueled by hate and entrenched political violence. Examples of former enemies, including parents of murdered children, engaging in restorative dialogue can be found in Northern Ireland, Israel/Palestine, and South Africa.

In 2001, the Center for Restorative Justice and Peacemaking at the University of Minnesota received funding from the Andrus Family Foundation to seek out, document, and support ongoing efforts in the United States where local communities either responded to acts of hate through dialogue or used dialogue to help prevent such acts. Over a two-and-a-half-year period, seven such communities were identified. The situations being addressed included a cross burning at a residence, interracial conflicts in a school, post 9-11 threats against a mosque and its leaders, the murder of a transgendered youth, promoting understanding between Somalis and non-Somalis in an urban setting in the US, racism across reservation boundaries, and building relationships between Arabs and Jews in an urban area addressing, among other issues, the conflicts in Israel and the occupied territories (Umbreit, Coates, and Vos, 2003).

During that same period, funding available to the Center from other sources supported ongoing efforts to explore a restorative justice dialogue approach to conflict in two international arenas: the conflict in Northern Ireland, and the Israeli-Palestinian conflict. Representatives of national and international projects gathered in St. Paul, Minnesota, to participate in a two-day forum in 2002 to share their own stories of fostering dialogue in the face of hate and to listen to those of others.

The present article draws upon the seven case studies, the forum, and the international work to describe how restorative justice dialogue is used to respond to acts of hate and to prevent acts of hate.

Restorative justice dialogue defined

Before proceeding to a presentation of selected cases, we offer a brief definition of restorative justice dialogue. In the fields of juvenile and criminal justice, restorative justice dialogue generally refers to a number of approaches under the restorative justice rubric. Restorative justice is seen as "a process to involve, to the extent possible, those who have a stake in a specific offense and to collectively identify and address harms, needs, and obligations, in order to heal and put things as right as possible" (Zehr, 2002, p. 37). While there are any number of approaches within this process designed to impact victims, offenders, communities, and systems, some of those approaches typically involve dialogue—bringing together victims, offenders, and community members in face-to-face dialogue to work through ways of holding offenders accountable and repairing harm done while offering opportunities for offender change. The dialogue-based approaches include victim–offender mediation, family group conferencing, and peacemaking circles (Umbreit, Coates, and Vos, 2002).

While each dialogue has a unique cast of characters and conflicts to address, a typical pattern often emerges (Umbreit, 2001). Most often the victim, particularly in victim–offender mediation, is invited to begin and will explain what it felt like to be harmed, whether it be by loss of property or by physical or verbal assault. The offender will follow with his or her story of what happened and what led to the offense. The victim will then have the opportunity to pose any number of questions: Why me? Was the violation planned? Why did the offender take a child's teddy bear that had no monetary value? What did it feel like to be caught? How does the offender feel about it all now? The offender responds as he or she is able.

The next phase of a typical dialogue will focus on how the offender may repair the harm done. Depending upon the particular agreement forged by participants, such repair may include an apology, service to the community, or restitution to the victim. Sometimes victims ask an offender to make a commitment to stay out of trouble, or perhaps to hold down a job or complete an educational program. Participants are often quite creative in shaping a set of actions for the offender to carry out that fits the nature of the crime. For example, two juveniles apprehended for bicycle theft entered into a dialogue with the victim family through a peacekeeping circle. It was agreed upon by family members, community representatives, and offenders that the youths would take responsibility for repairing and painting some old broken-down bicycles which they then delivered to a community organization that served families who could not afford to purchase bikes (Coates, Umbreit, and Vos, 2003).

Depending on the nature of the conflict and complexity of the case, dialogue is likely to involve preparatory meetings with participants, a face-to-face meeting among participants, and some form of follow-up. More serious and complex cases may require any number of preparatory meetings, face-to-face dialogues, and follow-up.

Case illustrations

Of the seven community responses we studied, four explicitly worked with restorative justice dialogue approaches. At least some participants in each of the other three communities had received some training in restorative justice or victim–offender mediation. Participants in each community expressed a desire to learn more about how restorative justice dialogue might best be integrated into their overall response to hate. We have selected three of the communities for the more detailed case studies presented below. In cases A and C, a restorative justice dialogue approach was explicitly drawn upon; in case B, several key organizers had received restorative justice training. The subsequent discussion will draw upon all seven communities, as well as upon the international experience.

Case A: Response to racial conflict in a school

Central High School was fractured across racial lines, reflecting the fear and tension within the larger community of Fairmont.[2] A Minnesota town of some 30,000 was being encroached upon by a larger metropolitan center. Condos and apartment complexes were replacing open farmland and stands of tall pine. Increasingly, local residents had to commute to the city for work. And, although small in number, minorities exiting from the inner city sought new opportunities in what appeared to be a pleasant tranquil community.

Resentment, fear, and hate bubbled to the surface in the high school environment. Minority youth were called names and spat upon. Pictures of blacks hanging from tree limbs were cut out of books and taped to the lockers of African-American students. The letters "KKK" were scratched on lockers. At a community celebration a young African-American youth was assaulted by five white boys wielding a baseball bat. Although not seriously injured, he was terrified. His enraged adoptive white parents complained to the school authorities about the ongoing harassment.

School personnel mounted an awareness campaign. African-American studies were offered and included a focus on the civil rights and peace activities of the 1960s. Outside speakers led exercises on discrimination. These efforts had little impact.

Conflict within the school spilled over into the community and vice versa. A local businessman was visited by a group of adults from the community and told that his business would be boycotted if he continued to allow his daughter to date a black youth.

As the cauldron of hatred continued to simmer and occasionally boil over, school officials, law enforcement, and a local youth service agency were determined to resolve the conflict. They invited the assistance of a county-based mediation team.

Given the volatility of the school environment, it was decided to hold a meeting as quickly as possible. A large meeting, at the school, was set for three weeks later. Within very tight time constraints, letters went out to families of high school students that school personnel had identified, inviting them to participate in a pre-conference to explain the larger meeting and the guidelines to be followed there, and to give them an opportunity to share their concerns about and experiences with the racial conflicts that threatened the fabric of their school and community. Seven pairs of mediators facilitated the pre-conferences. Each pair worked with four families. These families were asked to invite to the pre-conference aunts, uncles, grandparents, and even neighbors. Invitations to the large meeting snowballed.

By the end of the three weeks, over 150 people, each having been prepared in a preconference, gathered at the high school. While the meeting was open to anyone who wanted to attend, mediators were confident that because of the large number of persons who had gone through a pre-conference, the group would hold itself accountable to the guidelines of the process such as being respectful and not interrupting.

On the stage of the high school auditorium two mediators facilitated a group of 10 students, encouraging them to talk about their fears and experiences. A tiny young black girl spoke of the intimidation she felt when she was accosted in a darkened school hallway by three "jocks." They responded by telling her they had no intention of really harming her; they were only trying to scare her. The girl's tears spoke clearly of their success. A black youth who blamed the jocks for his banishment and personal abuse learned that his troubles actually began when hate-filled words had been hurled at him from a passing car by a white youth who had been his best friend. The black youth had not seen his friend duck out of view: thus, the jocks in the car were subjected to the charge of racism. Another white youth, who had been expelled by the school administration, was vindicated by the dialogue among students on the stage. It became clear to many participants that racial conflict was fueled by both whites and blacks. Everyone in the school was a victim.

The next day student representatives met with school personnel to take steps to reduce harassment. A major outcome was administrators agreeing that the first line of response to student conflict would be referral to peer mediators rather than investigation and expulsion.

Case B: Responding to the murder of a transgendered youth

On June 16, 2001, Fred Martinez, an openly transgendered 16-year-old Navajo, was brutally murdered near Cortez, Colorado. The community's response to his murder was intense. Some citizens refused to believe his death was the result of hate. Others were horrified that a youth might have been killed because of his sexual identity and for being Navajo. Many wanted a thorough investigation. Concern for the safety of other gay, lesbian, bisexual, and transgendered (GLBT) youth and adults living in the Four Corners region was heightened. While the police department was reluctant to label the crime a hate crime, they pursued its investigation as if it were.

The regional Four Corners Gay and Lesbian Alliance for Diversity (4cGLAD) played a pivotal role in responding to the Martinez family and assisting the community in its efforts to come to grips with the effects of the crime rippling across the Cortez community and region. Because the Alliance is spread across such a broad geographic region, much of the work in the Cortez community depended upon individual contacts and personal relationships with leaders in the police department and the school system.

Local newspapers became a focal point for expressing public outrage and concern. These papers were attacked in numerous letters to the editor for writing about Martinez's sexual orientation instead of treating the murder as just another tragic crime. Members of the 4cGLAD and the local chapter of Parents and Friends of Lesbians and Gays (PFLAG) also used letters to the editor to convey their concern for the Martinez family, to encourage thorough investigation and prosecution, and to counter misinformation about gays and the gay community.

The 4cGLAD received crucial logistical support from state and national organizations including the Colorado Anti-Violence Program, National PFLAG, and the National Gay and Lesbian Alliance Against Defamation (GLAAD). Assistance was especially sought with handling the press, particularly the national press, and how best to relate to national organizations. Outside help was handled cautiously because it was believed that, particularly given the rural border town nature of Cortez, local matters could best be managed by local people.

Two key community gatherings were organized in response to Fred Martinez's slaying. More than 100 persons attended a candlelight vigil about a month after his death. Individuals from the Cortez region spoke of Fred Martinez's death, his life, and his legacy. Support was offered to Fred's mother and family. Local speakers were joined by nationally known figures who had been personally impacted by sexually-oriented hate crimes including Judy Shepherd and Carolyn Wagner. Participants described the vigil as "poignant," "moving," "powerful," and "hopeful." One woman's T-shirt summed up much of what was said and felt: "Hate is not a family value."

A community forum entitled "Hurt, Hope and Healing: Our Community Responds to Fred Martinez's Murder" was held. Part of the 4cGLAD mission and experience base had been sponsoring and planning community forums "encouraging dialogue with the lesbian, gay transgender community and the community at large" (Umbreit, Coates & Vos, 2003, pp. A-18). The two-hour forum attracted a diverse group of about 150 persons. Considerable effort was made to create a safe environment for exchange. There was a "covenant" of sorts whereby participants agreed not to "rant and rave." Speakers included a gay/lesbian activist, a state representative who had co-sponsored hate crime legislation, and a member of the Martinez family.

During one segment of the forum, the floor was open to anyone who identified him or herself to speak for two minutes. Comments ranged from possible motives behind the Martinez murder to attitudes toward gay, lesbian, bisexual, and transgendered persons, sexual discrimination in the schools, and the right of individuals to hold their own beliefs. Biblical passages were cited supposedly supporting anti-gay positions. A local pastor declared that "homosexuality was a matter of choice." A gay man responded that he "couldn't recall ever choosing to be gay." Many argued that whatever one's understanding of homosexuality might be, it should not be used to justify hate and murder.

"People didn't march out with their minds completely changed," one organizer said. "But what they did do is exist in a room where there were other gay people. And I'm sure for some that was a first." Still, participants were reminded as they left of just how much work was left to be done. A poster on a truck parked across the street read: "No Gays in the Four Corners."

One participant claimed long after that gathering occurred that the forum "created a tone for the dialogue that, I think, is ongoing." And the Four Corners story does continue. Several participants credit the forum with sparking their commitment to work towards assuring safety in the community schools. The result was the creation of a new entity, the Four Corners Safe Schools Coalition, in which many who were involved in helping organize the response to the Martinez murder continue to work to create an environment in which the seeds of hate do not flourish but rather are replaced by those of tolerance and mutual respect.

Case C: Response to a Post 9-11 hate crime

On September 11, 2001, within hours of the attack on the New York City Twin Towers, Tammam Adi, director of the Islamic Cultural Center in Eugene, Oregon, received a phone call. A screaming voice swore death on the Muslim community in retaliation for the

"NYC slaughter." Later that afternoon, the same man left a similar message on the mosque's answering machine. Mrs. Adi initially retrieved that message. Police traced the call and made an arrest.

Did the man act alone? The Adis, like many in the Muslim community, feared for their safety. A police officer was assigned to protect them; his duties included opening their mail and routinely checking their car. Mrs. Adi gave up wearing the traditional head scarf. A boy approached the Adis' daughter and said, "We should round up all the Muslims and shoot them."

Yet in the midst of hate there was an outpouring of support from the broader community including church leaders, interfaith organizations, and university groups. Media coverage was extensive. Although that coverage was generally regarded favorably within the Muslim community, concern remained that the press might promote stereotypical images of Muslims.

The offender indicated a desire to apologize for his actions and make amends. The prosecuting attorney, who had previous experience with the Community Accountability Board that operated in the offender's neighborhood, initiated efforts to seek a mediated dialogue.

Three mediators first met with the offender. He acknowledged that he had been enraged by the pictures and stories of the Twin Towers attack and had made the threatening phone calls to scare the Muslim leader. Later, he claimed, he was mortified by his actions. Now, he wanted to do something to help make things right.

A week later the mediators met with the Adis who, early on, expressed interest in meeting the man who had so upset their lives. They, too, desired to find some way of mending the harm. In addition to wanting to know "why he did it to us," they voiced concern for the pain caused to the entire Muslim community. Therefore, the Adis wanted the dialogue to take place in a public way in order to educate and to promote healing across the broader community.

On October 10, the Adis met the offender face-to-face. In addition to the mediators, over 20 persons were present representing the community and the justice system. The tense two-and-a-half-hour meeting began with the anxious offender making an apology followed by an attempt to explain his emotions and his ongoing anger issues. The Adis asked questions about why the offender had made the calls. Mr. Adi also told of how death threats in Middle Eastern culture are very serious. Throughout, Mr. Adi was keenly aware that the man who had threatened his life and that of his family never made eye contact with him. Community participants expressed sympathy for the Adis and made clear their willingness to help hold the offender accountable while supporting his efforts to change. Tension prevailed at the meeting's conclusion. Although the Adis remained unsatisfied with the offender's level of candor, they agreed to carry out the initial plan of meeting a second time. Mrs. Adi believed there was still potential for healing.

During a debriefing, a mediator learned that the offender had felt "overwhelmed" by the DA's presence and "under pressure to provide the right response." Also, the offender said that he'd been deeply offended by a community member's comment that he wasn't fit to raise children. Six years previously in mid-September, the man had lost a baby son. His grief remained turbulent and he had experienced bouts of depression each September since. The mediator encouraged him to share his story at the next dialogue session.

The Adis used the time between the two meetings to sharpen their questions and to specify their requests for restitution.

The second meeting began with the Adis asking their questions. They received clear assurance that the man would not do something like that again. Community members detailed the ongoing impact of the crime on the larger community. The offender informed the group of his counseling progress and of his new job. And he spoke directly about his own loss of his baby son. Sharing that grief developed a connection with the victims. The man became "more human and genuine." After a series of additional questions, Mr. Adi said, "I am satisfied with what I've heard. I think we can move forward."

At the Adis' request, the offender agreed to make a public apology. If that action jeopardized the man's job, Mr. Adi was prepared to speak to the man's employer. The Adis also wanted the offender to attend two upcoming lectures on Islam. He was also encouraged to cooperate with news coverage of the case, continue his counseling, and speak about his experience to teens at a juvenile detention center. As the meeting ended, Mr. Adi reached across the table and shook the man's hand.

The offender's apology letter to the Adis and the Muslim community appeared on the editorial page of the *Register-Guardian* on November 18. A front page story also appeared covering the Adis' story. After attending the first two lectures on Islam, the offender decided to attend more.

Restorative justice dialogue process

The process of restorative justice dialogue is similar whether it is used to work with victims of burglary and their offenders or with persons impacted by hate-motivated crime. That process can be influenced greatly by contextual conditions such as involvement of outside interest groups and the media; some of these contextual factors will be discussed in the next section. Even given the shifting influences of context, the restorative justice dialogue process follows certain patterns.

Participation in restorative justice dialogue is invitational

No-one is required to participate in dialogue—not direct victims of hate, not indirect victims of hate, not even perpetrators of hate. Each individual is invited and his or her participation is voluntary. This does not mean that there won't be pressures to participate or not participate. Those pressures may come from family members, friends, and various groups with whom the potential participant identifies. But the group or organization offering restorative justice dialogue cannot require persons to meet.

Who is invited is a matter of strategy and may depend upon the nature of the harm and availability of participants. Traditionally, restorative justice dialogue begins with inviting victims and offenders, significant support persons that they may identify, and possibly representatives of the larger community or neighborhood. This process was followed closely in Eugene, Oregon post 9-11 case.

In the case involving racial conflict in a Minnesota school, several incidents over time were identified but no single incident or group of combatants was the focus. Instead, the school environment and the broader community were regarded as the victims. Therefore, while potential dialogue participants may have been initially selected based on particular incidents, the pool of potential participants snowballed as those who agreed to participate suggested still others. The resulting dialogue involved individuals from the school and the community. Organizers were then in a position to facilitate follow-up dialogues if necessary with smaller groups, perhaps focused on a particular incident of abuse.

In the Colorado case responding to the murder of Fred Martinez, invitations were made community-wide and regionally to bring together persons concerned about the Martinez family and about possible continuing threats to members of the GLBT community.

While resources were devoted to providing support to the Martinez family, there was no attempt to bring that family and the murder suspect/family together. The focus of dialogue was on the community and groups. We want to note that while restorative justice dialogue is increasingly being used with survivors of violent crime, including relatives of murder victims who desire answers to lingering questions, such dialogues typically take place years after the precipitating event (Umbreit, Vos, Coates, and Brown, 2003).

So while participants in restorative justice dialogue are invited and participate voluntarily, who is invited will depend upon a strategic decision about a beginning point. In some situations, the specifics of the case make it more reasonable to begin with a small number of persons most directly impacted by the crime and then move to a broader community dialogue. In other situations it will make more sense to begin with a community-wide dialogue or forum and narrow down to smaller meetings afterwards.

Preparation of participants

In order to provide a safe context for face-to-face dialogue, participants need adequate preparation regarding ground rules for their own behavior as well as what to expect from the mediator/facilitator and from others in the room. Many participants benefit from this pre-meeting opportunity to tell their stories and identify the questions for which they seek answers with an unbiased listener. Others, both victims and offenders, want to be assured that they won't be abused by the process.

The depth of preparation will be determined by the nature of the case and the resources available to the organizing group. In the Minnesota racial conflict case, teams of two mediators met with everyone who was directly invited to the dialogue. Since it was an open forum, some individuals may have come without preparation but it was believed that the norms of respectful dialogue were established by the considerable effort devoted to preparing participants. Preparation for the Colorado forums may have been less formal but no less intense. Again, there was considerable thought and planning devoted to preparing those who might participate. These were also events open to the public, so efforts were taken to assure the security of the participants without creating an atmosphere of fear. Organizers believed that establishing a two-minute time limit on comments, setting the tone of initial speakers, requiring all who spoke to identify themselves, and encouraging respectful interaction proved more helpful than the single security officer who was nearby.

Although acceptance of ground rules generally means that they will be followed, there are exceptions. In another community, ground rules for a peaceful march between a synagogue and a mosque specified that marchers were not to carry or display political symbols. One key organizer drove a car along the march with car horn blaring while waving Palestinian flags. That action caused considerable rift within the organizing group and the interest groups represented by it.

The dialogue

Whether the dialogue takes place among a small number of persons including victims, offenders, and community representatives or a large number of persons in a community-wide forum, with or without offenders present, the flow of the dialogue usually involves the following: (1) individuals share how the threat or actual acts of hate impacted them; (2) questions are raised about why the crimes happened (were they random events, had the victim/s been singled out, what had the offenders hoped to gain, how did those crimes impact others in the neighborhood or community); (3) participants examine what can be done to prevent such acts of hate happening again; and (4) sometimes, agreement is reached on how offenders can begin to repair the harm they have caused.

A frequent threat to the dialogue process is the tension between those individuals who see inherent merit in the process of persons in conflict sharing their experiences and those who want to move immediately to action. Those who value the process of dialogue point out that dialogue itself is action because it brings together persons who seldom interact constructively with one another. Such dialogue can be a critical step in tearing down barriers and building relationships. And, at least within the restorative justice dialogue framework, it is often a springboard for actions that repair harm done. Others see dialogue as primarily more talk and often claim there is no time for "just talk." Dialogue proponents counter that it takes time to build bridges. Bridge-building requires persons threatened by conflict to get to know one another which in turn requires face-to-face sharing of personal experiences.

This tension between and among individuals and organizations coalescing to deal with the threat of hate looms large and can undermine well-intended efforts. If a group is perceived as moving too slowly, there is the risk of losing the support of individuals who want to see more immediate action. On the other hand, if a group is perceived as moving too quickly without gathering information through building relationships, then there is the risk of losing support from persons who favor a more grounded base for action (Coates, 1989). If there are enough groups and organizations involved in the community, individuals will likely find the best fit for their own level of desire for action. Still, in those situations, there will remain a need for organizations with differing orientations toward dialogue and action to co-ordinate and find a working balance.

Cumulative dialogues

In classic restorative justice dialogue cases, the dialogue meeting where plans for repairing harm are made may also be followed up with another dialogue session to discuss how well those plans are being carried out and how participants are feeling about that. Even though the impact of crime—be it burglary, rape, or identity theft—may continue to affect individuals throughout a lifetime, there is a fairly clear beginning and ending, at least from the perspective of the formal justice system. With hate crimes and the threat of hate within a community there is a sense that no such ending exists and even the beginning may be blurred. Thus, cumulative dialogues may be more likely where the potential for acts of hate is perceived. In the Rapid City/Pine Ridge area of South Dakota, an ongoing series of small dialogue forms are crafted to deal with racism and fears lingering from unsolved murders of previous years. In Albuquerque, continuous efforts are made to bring together Jews, Palestinians, and Christians to find common ground amongst differences and to consider how strife in the Middle East impacts life in New Mexico. In Colorado, the focus of dialogue broadened from the immediate response to the murder of Fred Martinez to how to prevent such acts of hate from happening again. A primary focus of continuous dialogue became stopping bullying in the schools.

Restorative dialogue depends to a large part on building, at least for a brief period of time, a relationship among persons in conflict. Once established, these relationships frequently develop more fully. Again, with the more standard criminal justice cases, observers and participants are often surprised by the personal connections made between all parties involved. Victims and offenders may share a lot in common or very little. At a minimum, they share an event that altered or even shattered their lives. Likewise in communities impacted by crimes of hate, there has been a coalescing of sorts around a tragic event. Relationships established in the heat of the response may be built upon to create more targeted dialogues with the intent of changing policies and attitudes and reducing the threat of hate.

Changing context for restorative justice dialogue

Intensity of impact

Crime of any kind can impact individual victims and offenders intensely. Crimes of hate often generate heightened intensity across larger numbers of individuals. This heightened intensity may be, in part, the result of individuals identifying with the group that is a target of hate. It may be, in part, a matter of community pride—that "those kinds of things don't or shouldn't happen here." Or it may be a response to an ongoing issue of community policy, such as community policing or safe schools. For example, in Colorado many persons got involved not only because they were repulsed by the murder of Fred Martinez and feared for the safety of members of the GLBT community, but also because they shared a passion about creating school environments that are safe for all students and staff. Similarly, the Minnesota school racial conflict case focused on conflicts between the races but also broadened to consider issues of safety within the school and community no matter what the initial trigger might be.

Individuals and organizations attempting to respond to crimes and intimidation based on hate will often be faced with strongly held beliefs and depths of emotion. Strong intensity will probably generate more response and interest, and the process of creating safe places in which dialogue may occur will require even more attention to detail and focused preparation than may be the case in more general crimes.

Media

Dealing with the media was a concern at each of the sites documented here. In Minnesota there was fear that the local press would deny that racial conflicts existed in the community. Also there was concern that larger regional and statewide media outlets might overstate and thereby exacerbate the problem. In Colorado, Oregon, and South Dakota, participants expressed concern that the media might describe the target groups—GLBTs, Muslims, and Native Americans, respectively—in only stereotypical ways. Efforts were made by most groups dealing with the impact of hate to develop relationships with members of the press. These were frequently tenuous relationships with little trust. Often, participants believed that journalists had the power to sensationalize or polarize a story and thereby make the work of conflict resolution between disparate groups at the local level even more difficult.

Organizers in Colorado were particularly wary of national press coverage and how even the presence of such journalists might overwhelm the local community. In that particular case, worst fears were not realized. Local press coverage was regarded as quite fair and even insistent on having a thorough law enforcement investigation; national attention was relatively brief. In Colorado, as in other communities, the press provided a forum through its letters to the editor for concerned as well as irate citizens to voice their opinions, fears, and hopes. Organizers learned quickly that they too must have citizens ready to come forward and write letters providing contrasting viewpoints if necessary. Negative letters may or may not provide an accurate view of what a particular community is thinking but there is the fear on the part of organizers that such letters may in fact shape opinion.

Outside interest groups

The power of hate draws the attention of persons and groups who are miles away from the precipitating events. Regional, national, and international interest groups can provide useful resources and positive support for local community groups who find themselves thrown helter-skelter into an intense battleground. PFLAG and GLAAD provided useful advice and "media packages" that helped persons in the Cortez/Durango area respond to media interest. Groups based in Israel and Palestine were drawn upon by participants in the Albuquerque organization devoted to reducing tension between Palestinians and Jews. Somalians in Minnesota remain members of clans based in their native land; Minnesota Somalians support their fellow clansmen abroad and the wisdom of those clansmen is drawn upon to help solve conflict within the local Somali community.

While such outside interest groups can provide useful resources, they can also jeopardize local efforts. A major concern for some organizers in Colorado was that Fred Martinez not become a *cause célebré,* thereby overshadowing the actual pain and needs of his family. Local organizers made sure that representatives of regional and national GLBT groups had to go through local contacts before having any access to family members. Organizers within the Minneapolis Somali community value deeply the connection they maintain with the homeland clans but also worry that conflicts between clans in Somalia could generate conflict between local clan members, and that these ties to the homeland and any resulting conflicts would be misunderstood by persons outside their culture.

Managing outside interest groups required considerable co-ordination in several sites. Local groups after an incident of hate must quickly determine how they want to draw upon the experience and resources of outside groups while maintaining control over how the local response is co-ordinated. Much local support can be lost if ideas and planned actions are perceived as coming "from the outside." Local citizens want a stake in solutions to their own problems.

These outside interests group can potentially provide another function which was not seen in any of the sites documented here. That is, in communities where citizens do not acknowledge what has happened in their midst or are unable to organize to respond to hate targeted at specific groups, outside interest group intervention can publicize what has occurred, identify local citizens/groups who may have a stake in change, and even invite persons to engage in dialogue.

After the crisis recedes

Restorative justice dialogue mediators/facilitators working with traditional criminal justice cases often struggle with when and how to close a case (Umbreit, Vos, et al., 2003). Victims and offenders involved in serious and violent crimes continue to have needs long after participating in dialogue. Emotional wounds linger and anniversaries of precipitating events often re-open those wounds. In some programs, mediators/facilitators close cases a month after dialogue unless there is expressed desire on the part of both parties to meet again. Individuals are referred to appropriate victim or offender services if needed. In other programs, mediators/facilitators remain available for phone calls for a year or so. And in other programs cases are never "closed."

Persons using dialogue to confront the presence and impact of hate within organizations and communities also have to contend with the question "When are we finished?" Some will take the position that once a specific conflict has been dealt with and defused, then it is time to move on to other cases, situations, or even communities. For example, in Oregon the mediators involved in the post 9-11 case went back to the important work of offering restorative justice dialogue to victims and offenders going through the criminal justice system. They stand ready, of course, to be part of their community's response to any new act of hate.

Others respond to the question "When are we finished?" with a resounding "Never." These individuals and groups typically view specific acts or threats of hate as being symptomatic of broader issues and problems. Thus once a crisis recedes, they tend to move into a prevention mode. They will try to sort out underlying factors and conditions that breed and tolerate hate. This shift in emphasis may even mean that new organizations are created or joined to achieve better the enlarged goal of preventing hate. In the Rapid City/Pine Ridge South Dakota region, many persons have worked for years to increase understanding and respect between Native Americans and whites. And various organizations and associations have evolved during that time period in an effort better to match resources with desired outcomes.

In the Four Corners region of Colorado, many persons who were active through 4cGLAD and PFLAG in responding to the murder of Fred Martinez are now participating in the Four Corners Safe Schools Coalition based in Durango. The link is clear for these individuals: hate is learned in families, schools, and communities. The extent to which a respectful understanding of gays and lesbians and sexual orientation in general is fostered, the extent to which bullying of students by students for whatever reason is curtailed, the extent to which straights and non-straights recognize a common ground through creating a safe environment for schools—to that extent, the chances of the murder of another Fred Martinez are greatly reduced and the quality of community life enhanced for all.

Just as the use of restorative justice dialogue approaches to conflict resolution will vary given the nature of the precipitating incident and the resources available, so will the question of closure vary from one community to another, from one organization to another, and from one individual to another.

Conclusion

"At the heart of this [restorative justice dialogue] approach is the sharing of personal story in a safe context by persons who might otherwise never meet or listen to one another respectfully, with an eye toward not only healing the conflict between those persons present but also healing the larger community from which they come" (Vos, Coates, and Umbreit, 2002, p. 16). These concluding words were gleaned from a two-day dialogue among participants who expend much energy and time doing battle with hate by inviting persons caught in hatred to gather and engage each other in some form of dialogue.

Depending on the context and situation, dialogue may involve sharing only a bit of one's personal story or sharing much more. Participants will probably tap strongly held emotions and may have firmly held beliefs challenged—not necessarily in an "in your face" manner but rather through hearing the genuine pain and joys of others. Through the process of respectful exchange participants may learn about things that matter not only to others but also to themselves. They may even be surprised by discovering common ground.

If hate fuels violence, then restorative justice dialogue offers at the very least an opportunity for replacing hate with understanding and respect.

Notes

1 A sampling of such groups includes: the International Institute for Sustained Dialogue; Public Conversations; the National Coalition for Dialogue and Collaboration; the National Peace Foundation; Search for Common Ground; and the Anti-Defamation League.
2 Location and names in this first case study have been disguised to protect the identity of those who were involved. Names and locations of the remaining two case studies are a matter of public record.

References

Coates, R. B. (1989). Social work advocacy in juvenile justice: Conceptual underpinnings and practice. In A. Roberts (Ed.), *Juvenile justice: Policies, programs, and services* (pp. 245–278). Chicago: Dorsey Press.

Coates, R. B., Umbreit, M. S., and Vos, B. (2003). Restorative justice circles: An exploratory study. *Contemporary Justice Review, 6,* 265–278.

Umbreit, M. S. (2001). *The handbook of victim offender mediation.* San Francisco: Jossey-Bass.

Umbreit, M. S., Coates, R. B., and Vos, B. (2002). The impact of restorative justice conferencing: A multi-national perspective. *British Journal of Community Justice,* 1(2), 21–48.

Umbreit, M. S., Coates, R. B., and Vos, B. (2003). *Final report: Community peacemaking project: Responding to hate crimes, hate incidents, intolerance and violence through restorative justice dialogue.* St. Paul, MN: Center for Restorative Justice and Peacemaking, University of Minnesota.

Umbreit, M. S., Vos, B., Coates, R. B., and Brown, C. A. (2003). *Facing violence: The path of restorative justice and dialogue.* Monsey, NY: Criminal Justice Press.

Vos, B., Coates, R. B., and Umbreit, M. S. (2002). *Community peacemaking project roundtable report.* St. Paul, MN: Center for Restorative Justice and Peacemaking, University of Minnesota.

Zehr, H. (2002). *The little book of restorative justice.* Intercourse, PA: Good Books.

17 Restorative justice and reparations

Margaret Urban Walker

In her book *Between Vengeance and Forgiveness,* Martha Minow begins a chapter on reparations with a brief discussion of restorative justice. She characterizes restorative justice as
seeking "repair of social connections and peace rather than retribution against offenders;"
she describes it as "building connections and enhancing communication between perpetrators and those they victimized, and forging ties across the community...."[1] Later in the same
chapter, however, when talking about monetary reparations, Minow says the "core idea"
behind reparations is *compensatory* justice, the view that "wrongdoers should pay victims
for losses" to wipe the slate clean.[2]

Several recent discussions of reparations for historical injustice and mass political violence
reject the idea that compensatory or, as I will call it, corrective justice is the relevant or
primary category for reparations involving groups or large numbers of individual victims of
injustice.[3] Roy Brooks considers the "tort model" of pursuing compensation from institutions
and private parties through legal action, a secondary, morally deficient and relatively unpromising avenue. He advances an "atonement model" of reparations premised on "the post-
Holocaust vision of heightened morality, victim-perpetrator identity, egalitarianism, and
restorative justice."[4] Although Brooks does not define restorative justice, his account of
atonement makes apology central and sees monetary and other reparations as necessary to
make apologies believable. Janna Thompson situates her argument for historical obligations
to repair past wrongs, such as the theft of lands from indigenous people or the injustice
of slavery, in a conception of "reparation as reconciliation" in contrast to a "legalistic" one of
"reparation as restoration." The aim of reparations on this view is "to repair relations damaged
by injustice—not to return to a state of affairs that existed before the injustice was done."[5]

Ruti Teitel, in her extensive study of transitional justice practice, finds that "reparatory
practices have become the leading response in the contemporary wave of political transformation," but that reparatory practices in political transition "defy categorization as either
criminal or corrective justice" by both redressing individual rights violations and signifying
responsibility for criminal wrongdoing.[6] Naomi Roht-Arriaza appeals to "a basic maxim of
law that harms should be remedied" in a discussion of reparations for mass violence, but
argues that individual court-ordered reparations are both impractical in cases where there are
many victims and inadequate to address collective elements of harm in situations of mass
conflict or repression where communities are targeted for violence and are sometimes made
complicit in atrocities.[7] She advocates collective reparations, like community development,
community participatory adjudication or preferential access to services, while recognizing
that such collective measures may fail to adequately address or protect victims of political
violence. Discussing cases of mass violence and repression, Pablo de Greiff makes the most
extensive and pointed argument against a "juridical" approach to reparations that aims to

re-establish the status quo ante by proportionate compensation for harms. Compensating for harms on this legalistic conception entails problems of quantification and generalization of harms, as well as interpersonal comparisons of suffering, creating divisive hierarchies of victims and clouding the relationship of reparations programs to other justice measures. He proposes an expressly "political" conception of reparations programs that measures their effectiveness in terms of social justice; reparations programs should express and create conditions for recognition, civic trust, and social solidarity between victims and others in societies undergoing political transition.[8]

The field of application for reparations is broad, comprising cases where wrongs are discretely episodic and the concrete means of repair (for example, monetary compensation) are fairly straightforward, cases of gross and murderous violation of massive numbers of human beings during a specific period of political repression or persecution, and group histories of destruction, dispossession, subjugation, and degradation of status that span centuries. The nature and background of particular cases of injury, as well as the foreground of current social relationships and practical political possibilities, matter decisively for how injury and responsibility are apt to be understood, and what measures of repair are apt to be available and meaningful. I do not wish to deny that what many writers call a "legalistic" or "juridical" understanding of reparations—basically, reparation as an exercise of corrective justice—might be usefully applied in some cases. Nor do I attempt to draw a single line of demarcation between cases where corrective justice will serve adequately as a model for reparation and those to which it is wholly inapt. I propose to explore an alternative to corrective justice as a framework for reparations in certain kinds of cases.

Although there is no consensus on even a formal characterization of corrective justice, conceptions of corrective justice as a moral ideal suppose a *moral baseline* of acceptable conduct or due care and regard for the security, dignity, or well-being of others. Corrective justice demands "correction" of what are presumed to be discrete lapses from that prior or standing moral baseline in particular interpersonal or institutional transactions with individuals, or unacceptable impacts of the action or omission of some individuals upon others.[9] For this reason, corrective justice may be at least artificial and perhaps incoherent in addressing histories, acts, or forms of injustice that consist in radical *denial* of moral standing or in relentless enforcement of *degraded* moral status of individuals, especially when these are systemic conditions and persist over extended periods of time. Conditions of moral exclusion and degradation, typically embodied either in legal exclusion from certain standings, the absence of political rights or the enforcement of diminished political and civil status, are invariably based on group membership defined either by putatively natural or elective attributes (race, gender, ethnicity, religious creed, disability, sexuality) or by proscribed political activity or membership. These conditions may endure for centuries (histories of dispossession and cultural and physical destruction visited on indigenous people by European colonization) or be relatively transient (political persecutions under particular regimes).

The "problem of the baseline" is not adequately comprehended by corrective justice. Rather, I will argue, it is the construction of morally adequate relations in and through the establishment of defensible and shared moral baselines that is a requirement of justice in certain cases, along with reparation for the manifold effects of the absence or unacceptability of such baselines and the usually repetitive failure to recognize, admit, or correct this. Restorative justice, I will argue, is a more adequate framing ideal for reparative practice where there is a need to *establish* a governing understanding of "right relationship" and to approach its realization, rather than to intervene episodically to correct deviations from an existing standard. I will explore some ways that restorative justice is more *instructive* concerning what injuries of denial and degradation involve, and so what it means to address and redress them, as well as whose responsibility it might be to do so. I will argue that restorative justice accommodates and perhaps requires bottom-up and incremental attempts at repair as a social and political process, a process that may be signified but is not exhausted by a particular reparations program or reparative gesture like a public apology. I identify six core values of restorative justice and explain its guiding aim of "restoring relationships." I examine a distinctive orientation within restorative justice to compensation as one among many means to repair, to articulating wrongs and harms fully, to processes that "leverage" responsibility, and to the active role of communities of varying types in doing justice. The case I address briefly in conclusion is that of African-American reparations.

Corrective justice and the moral baseline

Critics of a corrective justice model of reparations—whether they call it "legalistic," "compensatory," "juridical," or "reparatory"—find conceptual, practical, political, and moral grounds for criticism. Conceptually, it is fair to say, as de Greiff does, that corrective justice tends to focus on mechanisms of restitution or compensation and to emphasize some representative relationship, usually "pro-portionality," between compensation and injury. It is not easy to pry corrective justice thinking away from legal paradigms of compensating for undue loss and injury, although often compensation in political or historical cases is apt to be, and perhaps in the interests of political feasibility and social solidarity must be, symbolic. Practically, dealing with compensation for very large numbers of victims of political violence or oppression poses financial burdens and political snares in many transitional contexts where reparations compete for limited resources. Administrative arrangements for implementing reparations mechanisms can become costly, divisive, and demoralizing if they are too fine-grained in vetting eligibility. In some cases, like histories of chattel slavery, sexual enslavement, or genocide, the meaning of compensation is powerfully shaped by the larger frame: other gestures of recognition, acknowledgment, atonement, memorializing, social support and guarantees of prevention determine whether financial compensation sends an acceptable and dignifying message to victims and perpetrators, as well as to society generally. It may often be these other nonmonetary measures that are possible, valuable, and necessary, whether or not monetary compensation is likely or wise. Reparations policies must be politically feasible, but neither can they appear as cheap buyouts or fail to address victims directly and to validate their experience of suffering and specific experience of injustice, lest they add further moral insult to moral and material injury. The balance of individual and collective reparative measures, and delicate matters of fit among monetary, service, and rehabilitation packages and more symbolic gestures, can seem to outstrip the rather basic idea of a "give back" that has dominated corrective justice thinking since Aristotle. These problems are real and pressing, but they might be understood as symptoms of a deeper issue. The framework of corrective justice strains, because it has never been meant to deal with either a massive scale of serious mayhem or a protracted and brutal subjugation and mutually ramifying indignities and atrocities that characterize oppressive and violently repressive systems. But what is the "framework of corrective justice"?

There is no canonical formal characterization of the kind of justice that sets right wrongful or undue losses and injuries any more than there is a single accepted terminology. Some writers emphasize a right to reasonable security from undue losses imposed even by others' nonculpable acts while others delimit the occasions for corrective justice to cases of wrong-doing or the violation of rights.[10] Some see corrective justice as a remedial mechanism to restore just distributions, while others see corrective justice as more autonomous and directed to maintaining a basis for stable expectations that facilitate social cooperation in various interactions, at least to some extent independently of the justice of underlying distributions.[11] A common function of corrective justice in numerous accounts, however, is that there is a standard of moral acceptability for the impact we have on each other through our actions and interactions, and that corrective justice responds to correct those impacts of action and interaction that fall outside of that standard of moral acceptability, however it is characterized. This is the standard I call the *moral baseline,* and it may be set in terms of just distribution, a kind of right or rights, a norm of fairness, standards of due care and attentiveness, or the dignity and respect-worthiness of persons.

Unsurprisingly, contemporary authors are inclined to characterize the moral baseline of corrective justice in the language of moral equality. Gerald Gaus describes compensatory justice as aiming at restoration of "moral equality."[12] Bernard Boxill's early piece on black reparations sees justice as requiring equal consideration between equals, and so an acknowledgment of the error of treatment that fails to respect equality and a reaffirmation of belief in equality of the injured party.[13] It seems possible, however, for corrective justice to function as a principle in societies with differentiated and even hierarchically organized statuses with reciprocal but not symmetrical obligations and responsibilities; there, too, will be due and undue treatment and recognition, and so a need for redressing interactions and impacts that deprive some parties of what they rightfully claim. Hammurabi's laws, for example, include many specific rules not only for punishing prohibited acts but also for correcting transactions involving slaves and masters, husbands and wives, parents and children, who are not supposed to enjoy equality of status in the modern sense.

There is, then, a duality within corrective justice. Its moral function might be described as defining and preserving reciprocity and responsibility between individuals (or groups) for their actions and impacts on each other in certain respects (identified by particular norms) in a social order defining proper places and allowing stable interpersonal expectations.[14] Yet the norms that set the baselines for acceptable treatment and due care and attention that give corrective justice its specific content—what actions or impacts it is a requirement of justice to correct, and what reparative actions will constitute correction—may themselves be morally indefensible; at the extreme, an assumption of reciprocity may be absent. When norms define unequal statuses based on bogus forms of innate superiority, fabricated natural hierarchies of authority or natural divisions of talent and interest, or when they opportunistically deny rights or effective protection and remedies to powerless, despised or stigmatized groups, then indefensible moral baselines of corrective justice, or the absence of moral baselines with respect to members of some despised group, become part of that for which justice requires a remedy. Corrective justice is only as morally legitimate as the baselines it treats as morally compelling. The legitimacy of baselines becomes an issue in cases of gross or systemic mistreatment or deprivation of rights characteristic of oppressive social structures and, in somewhat different ways, in political episodes where states, often with some legal basis ("emergency powers"), terrorize or mistreat segments of their own population. Societies over time may come to adopt more justifiable baselines that move toward more uniform recognition of equal worth and dignity of all members. This recognition of equal dignity sets the stage for addressing the problem of faulty baselines that both license unjust treatment and are a cause of it. It does not, however, solve this problem, although measures that acknowledge precisely that situation we might expect to be part of what corrective justice demands.

Corrective justice uses its moral baseline to identify and attach obligations of repair to faulty performance under the standards, *not* to faulty standards. Further more, corrective justice, if it is to be a basis for reparations, requires principles that can span cultural and national communities. While international and humanitarian law and evolving best practices purport to set a universal standard of moral equality, it is an aspirational standard that does not and in many instances cannot define stable expectations for those whose more local communities and cultures, legal and social, play by very different rules. Thus, the framework of corrective justice seems to predicate the normal operation of legitimate standards of conduct and impact in order to secure performance or repair for failure in, or untoward outcomes due to, the performance of actors. It is not accidental that one analysis that clearly identifies the problem of the baseline is Andrew Sharp's study of the search for justice between Maori and Pakeha people of New Zealand. Sharp adopts a legalistic conception of restitution and compensation, but incorporates not only the idea of "reciprocal exchange between two equal parties" in his definition of reparative justice, but also the proviso that the parties recognize "the same standards of right."[15] Sharp's focus on justice claims in an intercultural, historical, and post-colonization context brings the problem of a shared baseline to the fore. It is also one reason for Sharp's sobering conclusion that "in conditions of biculturalism, strict justice is actually impossible."[16]

Strict justice may well be impossible in any case of gross violence or systemic degradation, yet the question of how best to conceive the measure of justice remains. Discussions of reparation continue to invoke the ideal of corrective (or compensatory or reparative) justice, which in turn is pulled inevitably toward legal models of responsibility to compensate for wrongful harm. The basic idea of "compensating" for harm is stretched in various practical, symbolic, or moral directions, or is assimilated to the compensatory framework by referring to the "remedies" and "satisfaction" due to victims of serious wrong, staying with the fundamental idea of "giving back" in order to set right.[17] Given the limitations of the framework of corrective justice, I explore the potential of another less philosophically familiar picture of justice.

Restorative justice: a conception and its values

Restorative justice is not yet part of the shared philosophical language of justice theory. Nor does restorative justice sit easily with the priority of "ideal theory" that has controlled much thinking about justice in the late twentieth century. Ideal theory was identified by Rawls as the necessary starting point of justice theory. Ideal theory assumes a "well-ordered society" in which "everyone is presumed to act justly and to do his part in upholding just institutions."[18] Within the Rawlsian framework, compensatory justice is essentially part of "partial compliance theory" that deals with injustice. Restorative justice begins from and defines itself in terms of the reality of violation, alienation, and disregard among human beings. Its central concept of "restoring relationships" supposes that it is disregard or violation of acceptable human relationships that stands at the core of its agenda, practically and philosophically.

Restorative justice was introduced to many for the first time when it was invoked as the guiding conception of South Africa's Truth and Reconciliation Commission.[19] The theory and practice of restorative justice, however, began two decades earlier in criminal justice applications with experiments such as victim-offender mediation programs and forms of family or community conferences. I suggest that six central restorative justice values repeat throughout an extensive and growing literature.[20]

1. Restorative justice aims above all to repair the harm caused by wrong, crime, and violence.
2. Restorative justice makes central the experiences and needs (material, emotional, and moral) of victims.
3. Restorative justice insists on genuine accountability and responsibility taking from those who are responsible for harm, ideally directly to those who have suffered the harm.
4. Restorative justice seeks to return ownership of the resolution of wrong, crime, and harm to those primarily affected and those who can in turn effect meaningful repair: to those who have done wrong or are responsible for harm, to victims, to immediate communities of care of victims and offenders, and to larger affected or interested communities.
5. Restorative justice aims at offering those responsible for wrong and harm the opportunity through accountability and repair to earn self-respect and to be reintegrated without stigma into their communities.
6. Restorative justice seeks to build and strengthen individuals' and communities' capacities to do justice actively, and not to surrender the role of doing justice to experts, professionals, or "the state," which should play facilitating roles.

These core values serve the ultimate aim and guiding norm of restorative justice, "restoring relationships." In restorative justice, what demands repair is a state of relationship between the victim and the wrongdoer, and among each and his or her community, that has been distorted, damaged, or destroyed. Serious harm to individuals creates a relationship charged with powerful negative feelings and burdened with losses that can continue to mar a victim's life. Restorative justice targets a situation of negative connection or disconnection that might be an ongoing source of threat, insult, anger, fear, and grief.[21] It is not always possible, nor is it always desirable, to restore relationship between those who have done or allowed harm and those who have suffered at their hands or by their indifference or carelessness. In some cases where restoration between victims and offending persons is possible, it can nevertheless mean only a wary coexistence. In any case, however, it is necessary to attempt to restore morally habitable conditions for those wronged within their supporting network of relationships and in their communities. At a minimum, others must acknowledge the wrong and harm done to victims and accept the legitimacy of victims' demands for recognition and redress. Where some bear responsibility (in any of several ways) for the wrong done to others, apology, combining acknowledgment of wrong, responsibility for wrong, and repudiation of wrong, is in order.[22] Resentment of victims' claims to repair, victim-blaming or indifference to a victim's violation and suffering is the antithesis of restoration: it tells the victim that the wrong is denied or that he or she does not matter.

The terminology of "restoration" is sometimes criticized because it implies *return* to a condition of relationship that either did not exist or was unacceptable.[23] I propose that we understand "restoration" in all contexts as normative: "restoration" refers to repairs that move relationships in the direction of *becoming morally adequate,* without assuming a morally adequate status quo ante. Morally adequate relations are ones in which three conditions obtain. In them, people are *confident* that they share some basic standards for the treatment of each other. People are able to *trust* each other to abide by those standards or at least to acknowledge fault if they (or others) do not abide by them. And so, finally, people are entitled to be *hopeful* that unacceptable treatment will not prevail, that unacceptable behavior will not be defended or ignored where it occurs, and that victims will not be abandoned in their reliance on our shared commitment to our standards and to each other.[24]

The ideal of restorative justice is that its values should be expressed both in the structure of processes of dealing with violence and injustice and in the outcomes of doing so.

Paradigmatic restorative justice practices, such as victim-offender dialogue, group conferences, truth commissions, or apologies (personal or public), not only aim at adequate forms of relationship as an outcome but require participants to *act out* the morally adequate relationships at which they aim. The practices involve responsive and respectful forms of encounter, interaction, and expression, such as offenders directly facing and hearing victims; victims being able to confront offenders and to seek information directly from offenders about what happened and why they were targeted, information that is often critical to victims' own understanding, peace of mind, and sense of blamelessness. Offenders, too, are able to represent themselves, and in doing so may be able to represent their own human vulnerabilities and their regret or shame as well as their willingness to apologize and make amends, affirming their competence and self-respect as moral agents. In some formats, other participants encourage more honest, responsive, and responsible interaction between victim and offender, and they can exert pressure as well as provide support for plans of restitution, compensation, or service that aim at repair.

A corrective justice framework tends to make compensation—making good a victim's loss—central, with pressures toward defining a metric of loss and, ideally, compensation in some proportion to loss. There are familiar challenges for this approach, including the obscurity of counterfactual claims about what victims "would have" had, and puzzles about how much of what they might have had they now deserve to receive.[25] Many serious harms and injustices, such as the murder of a loved one or the expropriation of a people's land and destruction of their language and culture due to genocidal practices of colonization, create losses that are not literally compensable at all. Restorative justice, too, emphasizes material and practical amends that address victims' losses and needs, but restitution and compensation in a restorative framework play instrumental and symbolic roles in repairing relationships, including the role of adding weight to expressive interpersonal gestures such as apology and expressions of sorrow, shame, guilt, or desire to relieve the victims' pain and anger. The direct concern of restorative justice is the moral quality of future relations between those who have done, allowed, or benefited from wrong and those harmed, deprived, or insulted by it. In some cases, compensation or restitution will be indispensable to signify full recognition, respect, and concern to victims. In other contexts, material reparation might be unnecessary, and in no cases is it, by itself, sufficient for signaling appropriate moral regard. Compensation by itself need not signal responsibility for injury, much less regret or atonement by those responsible. Without a surrounding framework of respectful acknowledgment, responsibility, and concern, compensation can take on insulting, condescending, or dismissive meanings. The nature and meaning of restitution or compensation in restorative justice should emerge from a practice of communication centered on the needs and understandings of victims as well as wrongdoers' deepened understanding of the nature and meaning of the victims' loss and of the nature and extent of their own responsibility.

A second difference between restorative justice and corrective justice approaches concerns the common phenomenon of denial, evasion, or minimizing of responsibility by those implicated in wrongdoing. Corrective justice, like retributive justice, requires that responsibility of particular parties be established in order to determine who must or should "pay" for wrong, through punishment or compensation. Ironically, this almost guarantees that the "bigger" the injustice the more contested will be the antecedent premises of responsibility. The more massive, collectively supported or tolerated, or historically extended an injustice is, the easier it will be to argue that assignments of responsibility are unclear, incoherent, or unfair, and so that arguments for large-scale redress cannot get started, or measures of redress are narrowly targeted to a few parties. Restorative justice practices by contrast *typically* create the conditions to *leverage* responsibility, that is, to move people from a minimal or peripheral sense of connection and responsibility to a richer and more demanding perception of what harms the wrong does and how they might be related to it.

In restorative justice practices that address ordinary crime, such as victim-offender mediation, conferences, or peacemaking circles, once offenders and other responsible or concerned parties are willing to engage in restorative justice practice, it is common for this movement toward greater and broader acceptance of responsibility to occur. Those who have already assumed some responsibility come to a deepened sense of the reality, extent, and consequences of what they have done to another human being. It is also common for others concerned, such as families or communities, to begin to see themselves as implicated, either by connections they have not before examined or admitted, or by a realization that they can make a difference by contributing to or assisting with some form of repair. Victims along with others may want to take an active role in the restorative outcome or in a continuing process of repair. Restorative practice is thus *dynamic with respect to responsibility.* It may not be necessary to establish responsibility extensively, exclusively, or certainly in order to engage in restorative justice; restorative justice practice may be the way to discover, induce, deepen, extend, and clarify responsibilities that are unnoticed, resisted, or denied at the outset of a process, or have been reassuringly assigned to some small number of target individuals. Institutional, governmental, and community exercises in restorative justice, including projects of finding and telling truths, create the opportunity and the medium for apparent responsibilities to be acknowledged, but also for additional responsibilities, both backward- and forward-looking, to be discerned and accepted.[26]

A third feature of restorative justice lies in its fostering a full exploration of the nature and impact of the wrong and of the rupture in relationship that explains it or results from it. Communicative interaction and voice for victims, whether in the form of a face-to-face conference or in the form of an official truth process after political violence, aim to create an adequate description of the wrong, which is essential to assessing the requirements of repair. Trudy Govier points to research that shows a substantial "magnitude gap" between victims and perpetrators (and sometimes, we might note, between either and third parties) in evaluating the seriousness of harms.[27] As injustices grow in magnitude, violence, and historical duration, the reality, nature, intent, and seriousness of violations become predictably contested, and the need for a careful and detailed articulation of the full story of violence, oppression, terror, or subjugation becomes both a reparative activity and a measure of the adequacy of other measures of repair.

Finally, restorative justice makes communities of varying sizes and descriptions central in several ways. Communities may be harmed, materially and morally, by wrongs to their members and to their resources, including their moral resources of trust and hopefulness. Communities can also serve as actors or as guarantors of repair and restoration of relationships. When individuals primarily responsible for wrongs and harms are unavailable or are unwilling to accept responsibility and to seek to redress their wrongs, restoration may devolve to communities or networks within communities. Indeed, the emphasis in restorative justice on catalyzing and strengthening the capacity of individuals and communities to do justice in the wake of wrongdoing suggests that official actors in the legal system or government are by no means the only actors and should not always be the principal actors in attempting to bring justice to bear. Restorative justice encourages "bottom-up" efforts at justice, while not excluding official roles or responsibilities. Restorative justice supports not a zero-sum but a "both-and" approach to responsibility for restoration of relations.

The idea of "community" is used very flexibly in restorative justice, but there is a practical basis for allowing the identification of the relevant community in context. The harmed community and the community that can effectively respond to support repair need not be the same collectivity. It might be that neither community possesses an organizational structure and executive function to undertake actions corporately and representatively; the relevant collectivities might be relatively unstructured or informal, like a locality or neighborhood. The community that can effectively respond need not do so, or even be able to do so, corporately; it might be that its members or some groups of members act out of it, or on its behalf, or in its name. And there might also be multiple responsible communities, some institutionally embodied and represented, and others not, that can and should play roles in addressing and redressing injustice. In some restorative justice practices in the criminal context, like forms of conferencing or peacemaking circles, the community or communities can encompass individuals and groups that see themselves as harmed by the crime, others that have reason for concern, and others still who are potential sources of support and guarantee of plans for repair in which they themselves might or might not participate. In a restorative justice perspective, communities that matter can be multiple and differently situated with respect to a crime or injustice. Relevant communities might not be *given* in advance, but rather formed in response to the demands of doing justice in the wake of specific wrongs.[28]

Black redress and a restorative justice perspective

I want to illustrate very briefly the productive nature of a restorative justice perspective for one kind of case where a shared moral baseline has never been firmly and reliably in effect. The case is the failure of "black redress," to use Roy Brooks's succinct phrase for the need in the United States to address and redress several hundred years of enslavement, legal subjugation and exclusion and legally tolerated exposure to violence extending from the seventeenth to the mid-twentieth century. This history of injustice arguably continues today in society's acquiescence in persisting and repeatedly documented inequalities of wealth, health, freedom, civic respect, and life prospects for African Americans, and in widespread resistance to and resentment of the topic of reparations for slavery and its sequels in the general—majority white—public. I do not undertake here to repeat the history of cruel and profound injustice punctuated by opportunities and failures to repair that others have ably provided.[29] What I add here is that restorative justice identifies the problem and the path to reparation in a way better suited to this kind of case than does the corrective model.

Restorative justice targets the damage or distortion in relationship that is both a cause and an effect of wrongs. A problem that lies at the heart of the continuous and continuing sequence of enslavement, legal subjugation, and persisting exposure to violence, discrimination, and neglect of enslaved Africans in American and African-American citizens is the profound distortion of relationship, socially and emotionally, between the still rigid and polarized raced groups, "black" and "white," that are constituted by this very distortion. A deep and unexamined contempt of whites for blacks is the most salient and disturbing symptom of the distortion. The attitude of contempt ranges from the benign contempt of indifference to the history, current condition, and future of African Americans to the angry contempt of defensive hostility and overt racism of many whites toward blacks, especially when asked to pay attention to the history or present conditions of injustice. Focusing on whites' attitudes toward blacks, however, is both incomplete and deceptive; the legacy of race and white supremacist racism also decisively shapes the self-understanding of whites. The contempt or indifference allows whites not to feel that they are part of an urgent present problem and allows them to be ill-informed and uncurious, or complacently but often mistakenly confident, in what they know about the history and legacies of racial oppression. It allows whites to think of the history of race in America as something that happened to African Americans and not what happened to whites. Part of the self-understanding of whites, as decades of critical race theory reveals, is not to know what whiteness means; to think that race and racial oppression have to do with blacks and other non-white people; and to feel right-minded in condemning unconscionable things that were done to African Americans "long ago," even though legally enforced segregation is within the memory of many living individuals who have never received reparation.[30] For African Americans, the basis for earned trust in whites is lacking; worse, its emergence is undermined by continuing evidence of racism and the persistence of the denial or minimization of the reality of racism still common in white America, as well as indifference or hostility to appeals for reparation that reappear punctually throughout American history from slavery times.[31] Deeper lies the assault on the hopefulness of many African Americans who face reduced life chances and the reality that their children may for another generation contend with the insults and obstacles of racism, and the results of poverty, poor education, crime, and incarceration, that others blithely ignore or deny.[32]

A telling symptom of a disconnected, evasive, or hostile attitude of white Americans to the unredressed history of injustice to African Americans is reported opposition among white Americans toward a U.S. government apology for slavery or that larger history. Polls continue to show heavy white opposition to—and black support for—an official national apology for slavery.[33] Apology is the most minimal but unambiguous and foundational gesture of repair. Not to apologize is to fail to accept, and refusal to apologize is to deny, the fact of the wrong, the seriousness of the wrong, responsibility for the wrong, repudiation of the wrong, or all of these.[34] Official apologies, furthermore, not only acknowledge and accept responsibility for a past wrong, but typically serve to signal a recognized need to re-establish institutional moral credibility, an intent to establish a certain version of events as the official story, and a public resolve to accept a correct moral standard for future conduct.[35] To resist an official apology reveals opposition to this definitive public correction of course. Another dimension of apology, often crucial to its effect but not always adequately noted, is the empathetic function of apology. Apologies are often inadequate or disappointing to the one harmed if they do not manage to convey appreciation of the suffering, anger, mistrust, or grief the victim experiences as a result of the wrong.[36] To refuse apology can mean refusing to acknowledge that these universal human responses to injury and disrespect are fitting.

There are compelling arguments for the U.S. government as a continuing institution that bears responsibility for its roles in accepting and protecting slavery and then in legitimating the degraded Jim Crow citizenship that currently living individuals and communities have endured.[37] I agree that the federal government is an appropriate and important locus of responsibility for apology and further reparative measures. Yet restorative justice, while not rejecting the importance of moral responsibilities of government, offers a distinctive perspective: justice is done both in and by restoring moral relationship and so affirming, perhaps for the first time, a truly shared moral baseline of reciprocal responsibility and equal dignity. Governmental actions alone are not adequate to that task, and government action on more local—state and municipal—levels might represent in a more immediate way communities with which people identify, especially if those communities address their own local histories of racial violence, exploitation, or exclusion. Institutions like corporations, churches, and universities are other localities for the identification and exploration of unre- dressed racial wrongs.

At the same time, the "restoration of relationship" sought within restorative justice terms, pursued on local levels by governmental, institutional, and civic initiatives, could create better conditions for the pursuit of national reparations, material and symbolic, for African Americans. Putting a priority on historical inquiry, dialogue, and voice of those concerned or affected, and inviting active engagement in the present with the past, open opportunities that restorative justice distinctively seeks. There can be fuller articulation of wrongs, discovery of their consequences and space for acknowledgment of responsibilities of various kinds, including past involvement or acquiescence in unacceptable practices, recognition of benefits from racial inequality, irresponsible or defensive ignorance of facts, or the ability to contribute to changing the future. Legacies of racial violence and oppression will predictably have affected African Americans in immediate ways (including incidents of violence and victimization that may have remained unknown in families and communities), but may also have affected whites and other racial minorities negatively. Past cooperative efforts across racial lines might also come into focus alongside practices that used race to stigmatize and humiliate citizens. Local initiatives can explore forms of reparation—memorials, celebrations, history projects, museums, educational programs, genealogy projects, public art, dramatic performance, and others—that meaningfully address the nature of wrongs and moments of constructive change in particular communities whose identities and boundaries might be reconfigured by such initiatives.

Conclusion: untangling relations and incubating reparations

I have described restorative justice as an approach to reparations that *could* be adopted, but I was prompted to think about the restorative justice and reparations by reflecting on an actual surge in local initiatives to deal with unredressed racial injustice and violence against African Americans in the past ten to fifteen years.

The Greensboro Truth and Reconciliation Commission, America's first self-named truth commission, is a privately financed project to examine the 1979 shootings of five anti-racist community activists by Klansmen and neo-Nazis that will release its final report in May, 2006. A 500-page report released in 2005 was commissioned by the General Assembly of North Carolina to explore the overthrow by whites of the government of the town of Wilmington in 1898, ending black participation in local government until the civil rights era. The state of Florida passed a compensation program in 1994 for survivors of a white race riot that destroyed the town of Rosewood in 1923. An investigation of the Tulsa Race Riot of 1921 in which whites destroyed the prosperous black community of Greenwood published its report in 2002, recommending reparations for survivors and descendants; reparations have so far not been enacted. The state of Virginia recently matched private funds to provide scholarships for state residents who were unable to continue their education when Prince Edward County and other locales shut down public schools in the 1950s rather than desegregate them. Several cities, including Chicago, Philadelphia, and Los Angeles, have passed ordinances requiring disclosure of links to slavery by corporations receiving municipal business. Charleston, South Carolina, is preparing to open the Old Slave Mart Museum in an original building where slave auctions were held until 1863. In 2001, on the occasion of the university's 300th anniversary, three doctoral candidates at Yale University researched Yale's use of slave-trade money and choices to honor slave-traders and defenders of slavery in the naming of its colleges. Ruth Simmons, Brown University's first African-American president, formed a University Steering Committee on Slavery and Justice in 2003 to research Brown's historical ties to slavery. Prosecutors have reopened notorious civil rights era murder cases in which indictments or convictions were impossible to secure at the time, in what are appropriately named "atonement trials," while states have begun to consider mass or individual pardons for thousands of people who violated segregation laws or were convicted due to racial bias.

These developments might be seen as fragmentary justice or alternative remedies where justice has failed. I suggest we see them instead as multiple, local initiatives that might be better understood under the rubric of restorative justice. These initiatives arise from or address communities and institutions, in some cases through government and law and in others through the effort or the leadership of individuals. They aim to address victims or descendants, to acknowledge buried or unredressed injustices, to create accountability, to offer gestures or repair, to respond to the needs of living victims, and to memorialize victims who are beyond the reach of justice. Placed within the framework of restorative justice, these efforts are parts of a decentralized and incremental work of restoration and reparation that seems fitted to the historical length, breadth, and complexity of the injustice in question. These actions might also build momentum toward the passage of Representative John Conyers's H.R. 40 proposal for a national commission to examine the history and effects of slavery and its sequels to the present day, to explore ways to educate the American public and to study the question of reparations, itself a measure in the spirit of restorative justice, inviting public dialogue and seeking a fuller accounting of wrongs.

Whether or not a national apology or reparations are achieved in the near or the longer term, diverse and dispersed initiatives at different levels are particularly fitting in a case of deeply distorted relations, mystifying and incomplete histories, and transgenerationally entrenched alienation within and between groups. A striking model for what is needed in such a case is provided in Manu Meyer's discussion of *ho'oponopono,* a traditional Hawaiian peacemaking practice that addresses troubled family relations. The practice aims at "examining one layer at a time, of inching toward the source of trouble to untangle emotion, actions, and motivations, which will, in turn, uncover yet another, deeper layer of the same."[38] It requires a clear view of the problem and a disciplined and guided work of "untangling" thoughts and emotions that stand between people and in the way of understanding and addressing the wrong or conflict. Could there really be a shortcut through a process like this, given centuries of distorted and violent racialized relations in the United States?

I have argued that restorative justice provides a more adequate way to conceptualize injustice and its compounding causes and effects over generations in a case such as the relationship between white Americans and African Americans. Restorative justice outlines a more varied menu of mutually supporting ways of addressing such injustice than does corrective justice as usually understood. My brief for the superiority of restorative justice as an approach to reparations in certain cases, however, need not be seen as completely excluding the relevance of corrective justice. Conceptually, corrective justice might be seen as a limit case of restorative justice where there has been a local violation of a standing norm in the context of mutually authoritative standards; in fact, the theory of restorative justice has been developed largely within a criminal justice context as a way to address victims' rights to a direct and constructive response of accountability and repair from offenders who have harmed them in a particular criminal act. Practically, corrective justice and its idea of compensation as an expression of responsibility may well be one effective and familiar (and effective because familiar) concrete format for signifying and sealing between parties an understanding of right relationship, or a decisive step in the direction of such an understanding, that had been lacking previously. Symbolically, corrective justice may convey counterfactually the "restoration" of what should have existed but in reality did not previously obtain.

This symbolism—of equal parties settling a debt required by their reciprocal recognition under shared norms—might be particularly apt at a certain point in cases where reparation, including acknowledgments of and apologies for a history of varied and gross mistreatment, comes very late: after a brutally oppressed, viciously stigmatized, and persistently disadvantaged group has survived and struggled its way to recent formal equality, as is true of African Americans. In order to perform this symbolic function, however, it will likely have to consolidate a more varied and complex process of historical accounting, acknowledgment, cultivating trust and making amends for which restorative justice provides the rationale.

Thanks to editors Kok-Chor Tan and Rahul Kumar for suggestions on the final draft of this essay.

Notes

1 Martha Minow, *Between Vengeance and Forgiveness* (Boston: Beacon Press, 1998), 92.
2 Ibid., 104.
3 The systematic treatment of reparations has only recently emerged as a philosophical topic and there is no uniform terminology for the species of justice that imposes obligations to repair wrongful losses; writers speak variously of compensatory justice, corrective justice, reparative justice, reparatory justice, and rectificatory justice. In contrast to the concept of "distributive justice," which is widely viewed as justice in the distribution of socially produced benefits and burdens, varied terminology surrounding justice in repair also reflects a lack of consensus about the moral function of corrective justice, whatever it may be called. I will use the terminology of "corrective" justice and return later to the question of how to characterize its basic moral function.
4 Roy L. Brooks, *Atonement and Forgiveness: A New Model for Black Reparations* (Berkeley and Los Angeles: University of California Press, 2004), xv, xvi, 11, 19, 141, 148, and 211.
5 Janna Thompson, *Taking Responsibility for the Past: Reparation and Historical Injustice* (Cambridge: Polity Press, 2002), xix.
6 Ruti Teitel, *Transitional Justice* (New York: Oxford University Press, 2000), 127–28.
7 Naomi Roht-Arriaza, "Reparations in the Aftermath of Repression and Mass Violence," in *My Neighbor, My Enemy: Justice and Community in the Aftermath of Mass Atrocity,* eds. Eric Stover and Harvey M. Weinstein (Cambridge: Cambridge University Press, 2004), 121–23.
8 Pablo de Greiff, "Justice and Reparations," in *The Handbook of Reparations,* ed. Pablo de Greiff (New York: Oxford University Press, 2006), 451–77.
9 No doubt contemporary discussions of corrective or compensatory justice in the Anglo-American literature are heavily influenced by Anglo-American legal practices concerning tort and contract. See the opening of Cass R. Sunstein, "The Limits of Compensatory Justice," in *Compensatory Justice,* ed. John W. Chapman (New York and London: New York University Press, 1991) on "five basic principles" of compensatory justice in this legal tradition.
10 On a right to security of person or possession from lapses of care, even if not culpable, as the moral basis of corrective justice, see D. N. MacCormick, "The Obligation of Reparation," *Proceedings of the Aristotelian Society* 78 (1977–78): 175–94; on corrective (or "rectificatory") justice as applying to violations of rights, see Rodney Roberts, "Justice and Rectification: A Taxonomy of Justice," in *Injustice and Rectification,* ed. Rodney Roberts (New York: Peter Lang, 2002), 7–28. Jules Coleman considers nonculpable infringement of rights as well as culpable rights violation and other wrongdoing as requiring recognition of the victims' loss and the worthiness of repair, in Jules Coleman, "Corrective Justice and Property Rights," in *Injustice and Rectification,* ed. Rodney Roberts (New York: Peter Lang, 2002), 53–65.
11 James W. Nickel, "Justice in Compensation," *William and Mary Law Review* 18, no. 2 (1976): 379–88, considers the purpose of compensatory justice the protection of just distribution by both preventing and undoing acts that disturb such distributions. It is fair to say that corrective justice is more typically not seen as reducible to, or essentially a means to, just distributions.
12 Gerald F. Gaus, "Does Compensation Restore Equality?" in *Injustice and Rectification,* ed. Rodney Roberts (New York: Peter Lang, 2002), 93–94.

13 Bernard Boxill, "The Morality of Reparation," in *Injustice and Rectification,* ed. Rodney Roberts (New York: Peter Lang, 2002), 128. Aristotle's original account of corrective justice in *Nichomachean Ethics,* 1132 "treats the parties as equal" in rectifying unjust gains and losses between parties even when, in Aristotle's hierarchical view of human worth, they clearly are *not* so.

14 See Coleman, "Corrective Justice and Property Rights," on the "local" character of corrective justice that "has to do with the baseline or background norms governing wrongdoing within a particular community, and with 'local understandings' of more general norms," p. 61.

15 Andrew Sharp, *Justice and the Maori* (Auckland: Oxford University Press, 1997), 34.

16 Ibid., 23.

17 Current standards for reparations are defined by the United Nations Commission on Human Rights, "Revised Set of Basic Principles and Guidelines on the Right to Reparation for Victims of Gross Violations of Human Rights and Humanitarian Law / prepared by Theo van Boven pursuant to sub-commission decision 1995/117," United Nations Document E/CN.4/Sub.2/1996/17.

18 John Rawls, *The Theory of Justice* (Cambridge, MA: The Belknap Press, 1971), 8.

19 South Africa's Truth and Reconciliation Commission said restorative justice: seeks to redefine crime from offense against the state to any injury to and violation of particular human beings; is based on reparation as the healing and restoration of victims, offenders, families, and the larger community; encourages all stakeholders to be directly involved in resolving conflict, with the state and legal profession in facilitating roles; and aims at offender accountability and full participation of victims and offenders in putting things right. See "Concepts and Principles," *Truth and Reconciliation Commission of South Africa Report* (London: Palgrave Macmillan, 1999), vol. 1, chap.5, par. 82. Essays in Robert I. Rotberg and Dennis Thompson, *Truth v. Justice: The Morality of Truth Commissions* (Princeton, NJ: Princeton University Press, 2000) discuss restorative justice in the TRC.

20 Sources include Howard Zehr, *Changing Lenses: A New Focus for Crime and Justice* (Scottsdale, PA: Herald Press, 1995); Dennis Sullivan and Larry Tifft, *Restorative Justice: Healing the Foundations of our Everyday Lives* (Monsey, NY: Willow Tree Press, 2001); Gordon Bazemore and Mara Schiff, eds., *Restorative Community Justice: Repairing Harm and Transforming Communities* (Cincinnati, OH: Anderson Publishing, 2001); Heather Strang and John Braithwaite, *Restorative Justice and Civil Society* (Cambridge: Cambridge University Press, 2001). John Braithwaite, *Restorative Justice and Responsive Regulation* is most comprehensive in its theoretical scope and review of empirical studies. Gerry Johnstone, ed., *A Restorative Justice Reader: Texts, Sources, Context* (Portland, OR: Willan Publishing, 2003) provides a full overview of the field. A usefully brief summary discussion of current restorative justice practices is provided by Gordon Bazemore and Mark Umbreit, "A Comparison of Four Restorative Conferencing Models," in *A Restorative Justice Reader: Texts, Sources, Context,* ed. Gerry Johnstone (Portland, OR: Willan Publishing, 2003), 225–43. A related literature on peacemaking with emphasis on traditional or adapted indigenous practices includes: Kay Pranis, Barry Stuart, and Mark Wedge, *Peacemaking Circles: From Crime to Community* (St. Paul, MN: Living Justice Press, 2003); Robert Yazzie, " 'Life Comes From It,': Navajo Justice Concepts," *New Mexico Law Review* 24, no. 2 (1994): 175–90; Barbara E. Wall, "Navajo Conceptions of Justice in the Peacemaker Court," *Journal of Social Philosophy* 32, no. 4 (2001): 532–46; and Manu Meyer, "To Set Right— Ho'oponopono: A Native Hawaiian Way of Peacemaking," *The Compleat Lawyer* 12, no. 4 (1995): 30–35.

21 On the complexity of victims' responses, and the predictable needs for voice, validation of the reality of their violation and suffering, and vindication in experiencing some form of proper redress, see Margaret Urban Walker, "The Cycle of Violence," *Journal of Human Rights* 5, no. 1 (2006): 81–105.

22 One recent account of varied forms of "accountability" for harms is Christopher Kutz, *Complicity: Ethics and Law for a Collective Age* (Cambridge: Cambridge University Press, 2000).

23 Harvey M. Weinstein and Eric Stover propose "reclamation" as a more fitting term for retrieving a social and moral situation from barbarity or disorder. See their "Introduction: conflict, justice, and reclamation," in *My Neighbor, My Enemy: Justice and Community in the Aftermath of Mass Atrocity,* eds. Eric Stover and Harvey M. Weinstein (Cambridge: Cambridge University Press, 2004), 15.

24 See Margaret Urban Walker, *Moral Repair: Reconstructing Moral Relations After Wrongdoing* (New York: Cambridge University Press, 2006) for a defense of these constitutive conditions of moral relationship.

25 Two discussions that explore these problems in cases of long-running and still continuing historical injustices are George Sher, "Ancient Wrongs and Modern Rights," *Philosophy and Public Affairs* 10, no. 1 (1980): 3–17, and Jeremy Waldron, "Superseding Historic Injustice," *Ethics* 103, no. 1 (1992): 4–28.

26 See Marc Forget, "Crime as Interpersonal Conflict: Reconciliation Between Victim and Offender," in *Dilemmas of Reconciliation: Cases and Concepts,* ed. Carol A. L. Prager and Trudy Govier, (Waterloo, ON: Wilfrid Laurier University Press, 2003) on the dynamic quality of restorative justice.

27 Trudy Govier, *Forgiveness and Revenge* (London: Routledge, 2002), 128.

28 Paul McCold and Benjamin Wachtel refer to "micro-communities created by the incident of a crime" as the "means through which healing and re-integration is possible," in Paul McCold and Benjamin Wachtel, "Community Is Not a Place: A New Look at Community Justice Initiatives," in *A Restorative Justice Reader: Texts, Sources, Context,* ed. Gerry Johnstone (Portland, OR: Willan Publishing, 2003), 300. See also Howard Zehr, *Changing Lenses: A New Focus for Crime and Justice* (Scottsdale, PA: Herald Press, 1995) on the relation between restorative and community justice.

29 See Brooks, *Atonement and Forgiveness* and Andrew Valls, "Racial Justice as Transitional Justice," *Polity* 36, no. 1 (2003): 53–71, on the continuity and failure to repair. Ronald P. Salzberger and Mary C. Turck, *Reparations for Slavery: A Reader* is a useful compendium of the repeated proposals for reparation and the issues raised. Robert Sparrow, "History and Collective Responsibility," *Australasian Journal of Philosophy* 78, no. 3 (2000): 346–59, presents a thoughtful and moving discussion of the historical continuity of injustice to Australia's Aboriginal people, with implications for historically continuous and continuing injustices to other groups.

30 Charles Mills, *The Racial Contract* (Ithaca, NY: Cornell University Press, 1997) characterizes white racial consciousness as an "epistemology of ignorance."

31 Brooks, *Atonement and Forgiveness,* 4–19, provides a summary of this history. See also David Lyons, "Corrective Justice, Equal Opportunity, and the Legacy of Slavery and Jim Crow," *Boston University Law Review* 84, no. 5 (2004): 1375–1404. Danielle Allen's *Talking to Strangers: Anxieties of Citizenship since Brown v. Board of Education* (Chicago: University of Chicago, 2004) sees race relations in the United States as exposing a more general problem of "trust-generating citizenship" that is acute in the case of relations between blacks and whites in America.

32 See Walker, *Moral Repair,* chap. 6, for a fuller discussion of the structure of contempt.

33 Joe R. Feagin and Eileen O'Brien, "The Growing Movement for Reparations," in *When Sorry Isn't Enough: The Controversy Over Apologies and Reparations for Human Injustice,* ed. Roy Brooks (New York: New York University Press, 1999), 341–44, cites a 1997 ABC News poll that reports two-thirds of white Americans resist the idea of an apology from the federal government for slavery, and 88 percent rejected reparations. Ellis Cose, *Bone to Pick: Of Forgiveness, Reconciliation, Reparation, and Revenge* (New York: Atria Books, 2004), 171, reports a more recent September, 2003 poll finding thirty percent of whites (compared with seventy-nine percent of blacks) believe blacks are due an apology for slavery, and four percent of whites were in favor of compensation for slavery, compared with sixty-seven percent of blacks. The United States Senate, however, recently passed by voice vote an apology for failing to enact federal legislation against lynching decades ago. See Sheryl Gay Stolberg, "Senate Issues Apology Over Failure on Lynching Law," *New York Times,* June 14, 2005.

34 A most helpful recent account of apology is Aaron Lazare, *On Apology* (New York: Oxford University Press, 2004). On official apology see also Trudy Govier and Wilhelm Verwoerd, "The Promise and Pitfalls of Apology," *Journal of Social Philosophy* 33, no. 1 (2002): 67–82.

35 Kathleen A. Gill, "The Moral Functions of an Apology," in *Injustice and Rectification,* ed. Rodney Roberts (New York: Peter Lang, 2002), 119–122.

36 Ibid., 114; Govier and Verwoerd, "The Promise and Pitfalls," 71; and Lazare, *On Apology,* 44.

37 Discussions include: Brooks, *Atonement and Forgiveness;* Robert Fullinwider, "The Case for Reparations," *Report of the Institute for Philosophy and Public Policy* 20, no. 2/3 (2000), in the University of Maryland Institute for Philosophy and Public Policy website, http://www.puaf. umd. edu/IPPP/reports/vol20sum00/case.html (accessed April 8, 2006), reprinted in Salzberger and Turck, *Reparations for Slavery,* 141–51; and Rahul Kumar and David Silver, "The Legacy of Injustice: Wronging the Future, Responsibility for the Past," in *Justice in Time: Responding to Historical Injustice,* ed. Lukas H. Meyer (Baden-Baden: Nomos Verlagsgesellschaft, 2004), 145–58.

38 Meyer, "To Set Right—Ho'oponopono," 33.

Part C

Philosophies and values

Introduction

Whilst the focus now shifts to the philosophies and values of restorative justice, it is important to stress that there is no sharp distinction between the discussions of practice in the previous section and the discussions of philosophies and values in this section. The practices described and analysed in Part B embody distinctive ideas and value commitments, whilst the 'philosophical' discussions in this section are simply attempts to bring these ideas and values more to the foreground.

The section opens with an excerpt from Rupert Ross's book *Returning to the Teachings*. As Assistant Crown Attorney in northwestern Ontario, Ross was responsible for criminal prosecutions in remote Cree and Ojibway First Nations. In September 1992 he embarked upon a three-year secondment with the Aboriginal Justice Directorate of Justice Canada, in which he examined Aboriginal approaches to justice in the context of the wider visions of life of which they form a part. The reading here is part of his fascinating report on his findings and personal struggle to understand the Aboriginal inclination for healing and peacemaking justice. Ross shows how the idea of punishing solitary offenders is quite alien to traditional Aboriginal life, in which the proper response to 'crime' is the teaching and healing of all the parties involved. He then illustrates how this healing strategy works with the most serious offences and offenders.

In Chapter 19, Dennis Sullivan and Larry Tifft suggest that restorative justice is difficult to understand because we tend to think of justice as being about either upholding people's rights and/or ensuring that benefits and burdens are distributed in accordance with what people deserve. In order to grasp the value and meaning of restorative justice, we need to abandon such perspectives and think of justice as essentially being about arranging our relationships and daily lives in such a way that the needs of all, as they are defined by each person, are met. Sullivan and Tifft point to the cultural barriers which prevent us from adopting a needs-based conception of justice, but also point to forms of collaboration within which we can begin to acquire such a sense of justice and hence become more morally developed.

Sullivan and Tifft's piece represents a different way of thinking about the potential value of restorative justice from that which is more common in debate about its merits. The case for restorative justice is more usually made by pointing to its instrumental benefits: the socially useful outcomes of its practices. Lode Walgrave, whilst keen to highlight those benefits, makes it clear that his preference for restorative justice is based less upon his perception of its 'effectiveness', more on the fact that it is in tune with his ethical intuitions. Hence, Chapter 20 is the result of his search for 'the socio-ethical foundations of restorative justice'. His concept of common self-interest is an ambitious attempt both to reconcile a concern for self interest with an ethic of care for others and to show how this ethical stance points towards restorative rather than punitive justice. It is reproduced here in the hope of stimulating a still very under-developed debate about something that is too often assumed rather than argued: the ethical superiority of restorative justice over retributive punishment.

Chapter 21 contains a more direct account, by Conrad Brunk, of the implications for restorative justice of more traditional normative theories of punishment. Brunk argues that philosophical theories of punishment raise important questions about justice that any approach to criminal justice must answer. Moreover, he suggests that by treating these questions as unimportant or even illicit, restorative justice advocates help to ensure that restorative justice is not taken seriously in jurisprudential circles. Yet, suggests Brunk, restorative justice has the potential to provide much more satisfying answers to the questions posed by theories of punishment than are provided by other traditions. Hence Brunk points not only the necessity, but also the value, for those interested in promoting restorative justice to engage seriously with the philosophy of punishment.

18 Returning to the teachings

Rupert Ross

The movement towards teaching and healing

> Probably one of the most serious gaps in the system is the different perception of wrong-doing and how to best treat it. In the non-Indian community, committing a crime seems to mean that the individual is a *bad person* and therefore must be punished [...] The Indian communities view a wrongdoing as *a misbehaviour which requires teaching or an illness which requires healing.*
>
> (Emphasis added)

That paragraph came from a justice proposal prepared in 1989 by the Sandy Lake First Nation, a remote Oji-Cree community in northwestern Ontario. I quoted it towards the end of my first book, *Dancing with a Ghost*. In the three and a half years since its publication, I have heard almost identical statements in Aboriginal communities from one coast to the other.

I remember, for instance, meeting with a chief, his young council and some elders at a remote Cree First Nation in northwestern Ontario. At one point I asked what the community used to do in traditional times, before the courts came, to those who misbehaved. An old lady (and I adopt that phrase as a term of respect common with Aboriginal people) answered immediately. Through the interpreter she said, 'We didn't do anything *to* them. We *counselled* them instead!' Her emphatic Cree suggested that she couldn't understand why I would ask such a question. At the same time, the hand-covered grins of the councillors told me that they had regularly felt the power of her certainty about the wisdom of the old ways.

For the longest time, I didn't fully believe pronouncements like that. I suspected that people were giving me romanticized versions of traditional justice, with all of the punishments removed to make things look rosier than they really were. The more I looked, however, the more I saw how widespread this preference towards teaching and healing – and away from punishment – really was.

It wasn't until a few years ago, however, in a remote, fly-in Cree community of five hundred people that I understood on an emotional level how deep the commitment to teaching and healing really was. It is a story that will take a while to tell, but it is important that the full setting be understood.

The three cree women

As the Crown Attorney, I had flown into the community several days before court for what we called our 'Advance Day.' With me was another lawyer, the Duty Counsel, whose job was to act as a public defender of sorts. Together, we were to prepare for the court day by interviewing witnesses and examining how accurate and necessary the charges were. In the majority of cases, such advance work weeds out improper charges, reduces the need for trials and helps all parties come up with sentencing proposals for the judge that seem most realistic in the circumstances.

The community's solitary policeman met us at the gravel airstrip, then drove us into the community over snow-packed roads. The temperature was about −30°C, it was still and sunny, and woodsmoke rose straight up from the hundred or so chimneys of the village. We dropped the Duty Counsel off at the Band Office and carried on to the policeman's office. It was a tiny, plywood-floored hut with a woodstove, a metal desk, a single filing cabinet, a one-bunk holding cell and an outhouse. He had put a fire in the woodstove some hours earlier, so I no longer had to wear my mitts. I unzipped my parka but kept it on.

As he filled me in on the dozen or so cases on the court list, I began to breathe a small sigh of relief. None of them looked serious enough that I would feel obliged to ask the court to impose a jail term. That meant that we were unlikely to have any contested trials, for nothing inspires please of 'Not Guilty' like the news that the Crown is looking for jail. We quickly settled into some small talk, chatting about things like problems in the community, the extent of the drinking, what kind of hockey team was being assembled for the upcoming tournament down in Sioux Lookout, whether the kids here were sniffing gasoline, and so forth. It was at that point, almost casually, that he mentioned that the community had formed a 'Police Committee' of six men and six women, and that they had been working with each of the people charged, as well as their families. In fact, he told me, they had prepared detailed recommendations for all the cases and would appear at court to ask the judge if they could speak. When I asked what kinds of recommendations to expect, he answered something like 'Oh, just probation and counselling, that kind of stuff.'

A few days later, we returned to the community for the actual court.

There is something about northern courts they neglected to tell us in law school: one of the more important jobs of the Crown Attorney involves getting to the local school, hall, gymnasium, church, office or other makeshift courthouse as early as possible, then locating and setting up just the right number of trestle tables and stacking chairs to accommodate the likely turnout. That was how I began that court day, for the police officer was out at the airstrip waiting for Judge Fraser's plane. Both of our local judges, Don Fraser and Judyth Little of the Ontario Court (Provincial Division), prefer putting those tables in a 'circle' shape, hoping that this will reduce the adversarial nature of the process. Instead of having the accused and his lawyer sit directly opposite the Crown and the police like boxers on opposite sides of the ring, they are spread around the circle together with probation officers, translators, alcohol workers and anyone else who might have a contribution to make. My own impression is that such an arrangement does make people feel more comfortable and also contributes to a fuller community participation. Perhaps people feel better joining as equals a group discussion aimed at finding solutions than they do making formal and solitary suggestions to an all-powerful judge.

As time passed that morning, people filed into the gymnasium and milled about, helping themselves to coffee provided by the band. The Duty Counsel was scurrying about doing last-minute checks with various people. When the police officer returned with Judge Fraser, his court clerk and reporter, they took their seats and the court was opened. I advised him of the existence of the Police Committee, and he invited them to come forward. Instead of twelve people, as I had expected, three women emerged from the group at the back of the room. Judge Fraser gave them seats just to his right, directly opposite me. One of them looked to be in her sixties or seventies, another in her forties and the third in her twenties.

I should have said that there were *four* of them, because they had brought an infant along, snugly wrapped in its *tikinagan*, or cradle board. They laid the *tikinagan* flat on the trestle table in front of them, where all three could watch, touch, feed, coo and tickle. The baby stayed there through the entire court, causing no commotion at all. I should mention that in northern courts Judges Fraser and Little not only tolerate but welcome such additions. While we've never really talked about it, I suspect that they too see it as a reminder of something Aboriginal communities always stress whenever we come into them: that we are all assembled to help make life better for the next generation. Having some of that generation actually present often proves to be a valuable reminder when we start to get caught up in our self-important roles!

One of the cases on the list, the one that makes me remember that day, concerned a man who had assaulted his wife. It was not, in strictly physical terms, a serious assault, for it involved 'only' a couple of slaps. There had been no bruising or other injury. The police officer expressed his concern, however, that violence might have been used before and might be escalating. The court shared his concern, for the accepted wisdom in urban Canada is that by the time a woman reports an assault by her partner, it's the thirty-fifth time, on average, that he's done it to her.

The charge of assault was read out. The husband, a man in his twenties, entered his guilty plea. Because of that, I was permitted to 'read in' a short summary of the events, instead of making witnesses give evidence themselves. It sounded like so many other summaries I had read in over the years: he had been drinking that evening, an argument had developed over some minor matter and he had slapped her twice. She had taken their two small children to her family's house overnight, returning in the morning after he had sobered up. End of story. In normal circumstances, this would have been followed by a short lecture on using violence, a sentence imposing a fine or community service work and a Probation Order requiring (I can hear the chant so clearly!) that for six months the accused must 'keep the peace and be of good behaviour and abstain absolutely from the consumption of alcohol or attending at premises where alcohol is sold or dispensed. That means no house parties either. If anyone starts drinking, you leave. Do you understand?'

Except that in this case the Police Committee had their own ideas. They were put before the judge by the Duty Counsel, and they were far more complex than I was expecting them to be.

As the first stage of their proposal, they suggested that the offender go out of the community to attend a thirty-day alcohol treatment program in the distant urban centre of Thunder Bay. It was their understanding, however, that the drinking was just a surface problem that could not be solved on its own. If the reasons for the drinking were not looked at and dealt with, it would continue – course or no course. We were told that certain things had happened to the man as a boy, things he had never talked about until now. They didn't give us any more details, except to say that the elders were once again coming forward to help the young people learn what they needed to know to 'live a good life' and that the young man was beginning to open up to them.

Next, they recognized that there was a serious lack of communication between husband and wife. They felt that both of them were carrying burdens alone, and that neither had really understood what was going on with the other. For that reason, they recommended that they both go the following week to a neighbouring community to attend a three-day series of workshops being held on family violence and family communication. Further, when those workshops were repeated a week later in their home community, they had to attend then as well. In that way, perhaps they could begin to break down the silences that had come between them.

At that point, I felt I was hearing one of the most thorough assessments possible. They were not, however, finished.

They told us that the children still had to be considered. Those children had seen the violence at home and were confused by it. The committee felt that if the children were not involved in understanding things, talking about them and helping to turn them around, they would grow up to repeat their father's behaviour themselves. The last recommendation therefore involved having the whole family attend a month-long family healing program available at another neighbouring community, once all the other steps had been carried through.

After the Duty Counsel finished summarizing the plan and explaining that the offender would be a willing participant, Judge Fraser turned to the three women. He asked them if they wished to speak to the court themselves, instead of through the Duty Counsel. As I recall, it was the woman in her forties who spoke to us, in Cree. The transcript records the interpreter as saying the following (with the real name of the offender removed by me):

> She stated that she feels [the offender] is very sincere in his desire to seek help and treatment, and after deliberations of the other committee members they set a plan for him. That the problems [the offender] has stem from his childhood and are finally surfacing. And also that [the offender] has indicated a desire to seek help. And also that it's a good sign that he included his wife and his whole family in that process. And she feels, you know, that healing will come, that all of them seek help.
>
> In the past this was not the case, but we're getting more organized at the community level. And trying to find ways of trying to help people in our community setting, rather than have the people that are charged be taken away. They come back with the same problems, too, so the band is trying to take a different approach.

Judge Fraser included all their recommendations in the Probation Order. He also reminded the offender that it wasn't just the promises in the Probation Order that were important, but the fact that he had made the promises to his own community and to the Police Committee, which was trying to help him. The offender nodded that he understood.

At the end of the day, when all the cases had been heard, something else happened. The three women turned to Judge Fraser and, through the interpreter, thanked him for giving them the chance to give their thoughts to the court. Judge Fraser seemed to be as moved as I was, not only by the depth of their concern and the thoroughness of their analysis throughout the day, but by the fact that they should be extending their thanks to him at the end of it. As best I recall, he replied that he should be thanking *them* instead. He also said something to the effect that, in his view, their approaches to problems in their community could help show the way to the rest of Canada.

A number of things struck me at the time.

One was the fact of that 'thank you.' I know that very formal expressions of appreciation before and after speaking are common, for respect must always be shown to other people, whether a consensus has been reached or substantial issues remain unresolved. In my view, however, there was something else at work that day, an extra emphasis in that 'thank you,' as if it had been a *special* privilege to be able to give the community's perspective to the court. That, in turn, made me wonder how excluded they must have felt from the court up to that day. When they thanked Judge Fraser for 'giving' them the opportunity to speak, I wondered once again what it must be like to suspect, from past dealings, that the outsiders who possess all the power don't really want to hear a single thing you have to say. For how many decades had they been hearing that kind of a message, and in how many ways?

In the face of that history, I once again marvelled at the immense respect they continued to show us as we kept flying in to do 'our' business with them, using only 'our' ways, then flying back out the very same day. There is one remote community in northwestern Ontario that prepares a feast for the court party each court day, with pots of wild rice, bannock, fish and game stew carried into the schoolhouse where we hold court. Those feasts take place despite the fact that, as I hope to demonstrate in the pages that follow, almost every aspect of our Western approach to justice breaks traditional Aboriginal law.

But it was not just their continuing respect for us that struck me that day. I was also inspired by the thoroughness and sophistication of their analysis. There were no Western Ph.D.'s in that group, but their knowledge of the ways in which dysfunctions – or 'disharmonies' – spread and multiply within families and from generation to generation could have stood up against the best material I have seen come out of Canadian universities. That day, when I compared the sophistication of their recommendations to our usual courtroom response of 'probation, abstention from alcohol, and fine or community service work,' I felt just the way Judge Fraser did – that we should be thanking them instead.

I was also struck by the fact that punishment did not even seem to be an *option* that day, even amongst the women on that Police Committee – despite the fact that the victim was a woman and family violence seemed to be a major concern in the community. Why were they not saying the kinds of angry things I was used to hearing from the victims of family violence elsewhere in Canada? Their position reminded me of the old Cree lady who was so perplexed when I asked what they'd 'done to' people who'd misbehaved in traditional times. The approach they seemed to take went beyond a belief that punishment wasn't necessary in that particular case, for punishment simply didn't seem to be an option in the first place.

Listening to how they approached the problem was a turning point of sorts for me. I had been hearing Aboriginal people talk about 'justice-as-healing' a great deal, but I still had some doubts about how deep-rooted that approach really was. It almost seemed as if everyone had attended the same lecture somewhere and had decided to dress themselves up in the same philosophical clothes, just to look superior to the Western system. What I saw from those three women in that tiny Cree community ended my doubts about such things. What they offered was not an imported response designed to support some romantic reinvention of traditional approaches. Instead, as I felt it then and know it now, it came from the hearts of all of them and from the accumulated understandings of centuries.

I acknowledge that I shared the scepticism of many observers about how 'traditional' such healing approaches really are. I have found, however, that my scepticism just couldn't survive the eyes and voices of so many old people, men and women alike, speaking only their own ancient languages, all looking dumbfounded (or outraged!) at my suggestion that punishment might be used to make things better. Nor could it withstand sitting in the sexual abuse healing circles at Hollow Water, an Ojibway community east of Lake Winnipeg, where the ancient teachings of the medicine wheel come to life to move victims and offenders forward out of their hurt and anger. As a result, my scepticism has gone into a complete meltdown. I now see teaching and healing as cornerstones of traditional Aboriginal thought.

In saying that, I want to be careful about a number of things.

First, what I have said does not mean that traditional responses to dangerous individuals were so generous in every case. Community welfare had to come first, and if a particular individual resisted (or was beyond) community efforts aimed at healing, then banishment to the wilderness was a viable, if regretted, option. I have never heard an Aboriginal community say that healing can work with everyone; what I have heard, however, is that it is shortsighted to offer healing to no one at all and to rely entirely on deterrence and jail instead.

Second, what I have said does not mean that traditional responses to dangerous individuals cannot contain elements of pain. As I will later explore, some teaching is indeed painful, and some healing is much more painful than simply hiding from the truth in a jail cell. I am saying instead that imposing pain for its own sake, strictly as punishment, unaccompanied by efforts to move people forward out of their problems, seldom seems to be an option. An eye-for-an-eye approach, I am told, leads only to the blindness of all (a phrase which suggests an alternate explanation for why the Statue of Justice is blindfolded as she holds up her scales!).

Third, I don't mean to suggest that healing is the central goal of every Aboriginal community – or even the numerical majority – at this particular point in history. A great many focus on punishment instead, and some propose punishments that are more severe than those of the Western courts. Many traditional people suggest, however, that such perspectives were simply the inevitable result of generations of imposed Western approaches, including the use of corporal punishment in residential schools. They point, for instance, to the fact that the Navajo are now moving away from their once-famous Western-based tribal courts and reinvigorating traditional peacemaking processes instead. Colonization strategies, they say, have touched everything, including dispute resolution, and are making it difficult for many communities to break free of punitive approaches and re-root themselves in restorative approaches instead.

Fourth, I don't mean to suggest that all Aboriginal leaders who now speak the language of healing are doing so out of an honest commitment to the betterment of their communities. Sadly, there are many dysfunctional communities where the groups in power promote 'traditional healing programs' for one reason only: to prevent their abusive friends from being truly called to account in *anyone's* justice system. Western or Aboriginal. It is not the teachings themselves that are responsible for such abuse; it is their misuse by desperate people in desperately ill communities.

After my experience of the last several years, I now hold the view that there is one best way for communities to deal with the problems that show up as charges in criminal courts: the traditional teachings need to be brought back to prominence once again, rather than being discounted as inadequate relics of a simpler past. In a number of communities, this has already been done: the teachings have been brought forward into fully twentieth-century flower by good people determined to replace silence and suffering with honesty, hope and health.

So I offer my own conclusion: the three Cree women were not a fluke or an oddity, or a special case. Instead, they spoke from an ancient conviction shared by a great many Aboriginal peoples, a conviction that the best way to respond to the inevitable ups and downs of life, whether defined as 'criminal' or not, is not by punishing solitary offenders. The focus might be shifted instead towards the teaching and healing of all the parties involved, with an eye on the past to understand how things have come to be, and an eye on the future to design measures that show the greater promise of making it healthier for all concerned.

[...]

Healing inside the whirlwind of sexual abuse

The community holistic circle healing program at hollow water

Hollow Water is a village of some six hundred people on the east shore of Lake Winnipeg, almost at the end of the physical road – but significantly out in front when it comes to building traditional values and teachings into effective, modern-day justice processes. In tackling the most taboo subject of all, sexual abuse within families, the Hollow Water healing team has had to immerse itself totally in relationships, and in all the illnesses that can pervert them through the generations. It has proven to be a painful, often tortuous, process for all concerned.

It began in 1984, when a group of people got together to discuss community problems, especially concerning youngsters. Many of them were 'social service providers' such as the child protection worker from the Manitoba Children's Aid Society, the community health representative, the nurse in charge and the NADAP (Native Alcohol and Drug Addiction Program) worker, together with people drawn from the RCMP, the Frontier School Division of the Manitoba Department of Education and community churches. The majority of the team members were Aboriginal women from the community, many of whom were volunteers, but the team included non-Aboriginal people as well.

Their concern at the time was the level of substance abuse, vandalism, truancy, suicide and violence involving community children. The more the team worked with them, however, the more their attention turned to the kinds of homes those children returned to each day. Over time, they came to face the reality that those homes were often plagued by high levels of alcohol and drug abuse, as well as family violence. The violence in those homes was seldom acknowledged in the community, much less dealt with.

When the focus shifted from the children to the behaviour of their parents, however, things took another turn, this one more disturbing still. In looking for the causes of the substance abuse and violence among the adults, the team came to confront a frightening possibility – the possibility that underneath everything else lay generations of sexual abuse, primarily within families and involving children, that no one wanted to admit, even to themselves.

One of the first decisions as a group was to break down the professional barriers between them. They found that they each operated in separate chains of command, reporting to separate agencies. Just as importantly, they were each controlled by confidentiality rules that kept them from sharing information with each other, even when they were dealing with the same 'clients' or families. They were all working in isolation, often dealing with separate aspects of each troubled person. As long as that continued, they predicted that the result would be a further splintering of those people – exactly the opposite of their shared goal of creating 'whole' people.

As a result of this discovery, one of their earliest accomplishments was the creation of a true team approach of sharing their information fully with each other. Outside professionals, highly regarded by the team for their knowledge and experience, were seen from the outset as important to the project's success, but they were required to 'sign on' to the team approach. They also had to permit a 'lay' member of the team to be with them at all times, so their skills could be learned by community members. This pairing was also a way for team members to help train the professionals to work within a holistic framework. Partnership was, and remains, the model. Having sat in some healing circles at Hollow Water, I can say that there are no colours or races or genders in those circles – only people committed to helping others.

Team training

They also embarked on a lengthy process of training themselves to work as a team. The more they came together, the more they were surprised to find they had been trained in different, sometimes contradictory, methods of intervening with troubled people. It all depended on whether the issue was defined as 'suicide prevention,' 'substance abuse,' 'mental health,' 'child protection' or whatever. Each 'problem' had its own separate 'solution' in the compartmentalized approach of outside agencies. The more they shared information with each other, the more they realized that the dysfunctional people they dealt with were very good at telling each worker just what they wanted to hear and manipulating all the systems at once to their own advantage!

The need for common training was apparent, and over the course of five years they created over twenty different training programs for themselves. Many of them were based on Western models for intervention and healing, but others included reaching out to Aboriginal communities outside Hollow Water to explore traditional ways and teachings. At every step, they took the best from everything they explored, creating a comprehensive program that reflects both traditional Aboriginal and contemporary Western approaches.

When their attention was inevitably drawn to the issue of sexual abuse, however, they hit a snag. This had to do with the fact that the majority of the team members were members of a severely 'ill' community. As such, they had not escaped the intergenerational chains of sexual abuse that were pulling everyone else down. Many of them were victims too, but they had never acknowledged that fact to anyone. As time went by, their commitment to helping their community forced them to confront their own secrets, first in their own hearts and minds, and then in the presence of other team members. It was a turning point for them, for their program and for their community. The healers came to the open acknowledgment that they too needed healing and that they would have to move some distance along their own healing paths, as individuals and as a group, before it would be safe for them to reach out to others.

I don't know how they accomplished what they did, both with and for each other. I have been with them in their healing circles as they reach out to other people, sharing their own stories of abuse, helping sketch the pathways that lead both victims and abusers out of self-hatred, alienation, anger and despair. I do know that their stories are still accompanied by vibrant pain and tears and that it is understood their healing path will require time and attention, likely for the rest of their lives. I also know that, thanks to many of the teachings they have sought out and restored, they now operate within complex and formal processes designed to take away as much of the pain as possible.

When they began to be honest with each other for the first time, however, they were largely on their own, separated from many of those teachings by generations of Western church workers intent on the complete disappearance of the sweat-lodge, the sacred fire, the shaking tent, the talking circle and all the other cleansing resources developed over the course of centuries. These traditions are coming back to Hollow Water now, for those who choose to use them, but they were not at hand when those first disclosures between team members were made. I marvel at the strength, commitment and determination of all of them in those early days. No army unit in any war has undergone a more daunting trial by fire nor built a greater sense of common spirit and dedication.

Healing strategy

The community strategy the team developed involves a detailed protocol leading all the participants through a number of steps or stages. They include the initial disclosure of abuse, protecting the child, confronting the victimizer, assisting the (non-offending) spouse, assisting the families of all concerned, co-ordinating the team approach, assisting the victimizer to admit and accept responsibility, preparing the victim, victimizer and families for the Special Gathering, guiding the Special Gathering through the creation of a Healing Contract, implementation of the Healing Contract and, finally, holding a Cleansing Ceremony designed, in their words, to mark 'the completion of the Healing Contract, the restoration of balance to the victimizer, and a new beginning for all involved.'

The Healing Contract is similar to the 'sentence' created by Family Group Conferences. Designed by all the parties involved in, or personally touched by, the offence, it requires that they each 'sign on' to bring certain changes or additions to their relationships with all the others. Such contracts are never expected to last for less than two years, given the challenges of bringing true healing in the context of sexual abuse. One of them is still being enforced six years after its creation.

This community healing takes place outside the normal criminal justice process – although links to the system are maintained. When someone alleges that they have been abused, the CHCH assessment team evaluates the complaint as quickly as possible. If it appears to be valid, the team swings into action. I was present at one such organizing session and found myself comparing it to a complex military operation. After selecting two team members to make the initial confrontation with the victimizer (instead of the police, but with full police backup if necessary), other team members 'fanned out' to be with all the others who would be affected by the disclosure. That meant that the non-offending spouse, brothers and sisters, grandmothers and grandfathers, aunts and uncles – everyone affected – would have a helper at their side to explain what had been alleged, the processes that were to be followed and the help that might be made available to everyone. No one would be left either in the dark or in their own painful isolation.

The victimizer is approached by two members of the team at a time and place most likely to permit the best atmosphere for honesty and progress. They communicate the allegations and listen to the response. They do not expect immediate acknowledgment, for their own experience with sexual abuse has taught them to expect denials, minimizations, victim blaming, hostile manipulations and the like. When they tell the victimizer that criminal charges are about to be laid, they also say that they are available to accompany him or her through the criminal justice process as long as sincere efforts are being made to accept responsibility and go through the healing process. If that is not agreeable, the victimizer is on his own. Out of forty-eight cases dealt with through to the spring of 1996, only five have failed to enter into – and stay with – the program.

The victimizer is then accompanied to the police station where he or she is formally charged and asked to provide a statement. While that statement would probably not be admissable in court, it is seen as a first step in the long process of accepting responsibility. The team then requires the victimizer to enter a guilty plea to the charges in court as quickly as possible.

The team then asks the court to delay sentencing for as long as possible. Experience has taught that they need a great deal of time to work with the victim, the offender, the families of each and the community as a whole before they can provide the court with a realistic assessment of the challenges and possibilities each case presents. Ideally, the team would like to see sentencing delayed until the Special Gathering has produced the Healing Contract. Unfortunately, that complex process often takes much more time than the courts permit, and sentencing often takes place before real commitments to sustained healing can be expected.

When the community healing process was first established, the team restricted its in-court activities to the preparation of a Pre-Sentence Report. This was a large document, analysing everything from the offender's state of mind, level of effort and chance of full rehabilitation, to the reactions, feelings, plans and suggestions of all people affected. Special attention was paid to the victim, the non-offending spouse and the families of each. The report also detailed a proposed plan of action, stated whether or not the parties themselves had achieved a Healing Contract and requested that any Probation Order require the offender to continue to co-operate fully with the team's healing efforts. If a jail sentence was imposed, they did what they could to arrange regular work with the offender while in custody and to prepare every-one for the day of release.

More recently, however, the team has moved its processes into the courtroom itself. In December 1993, after months of separate healing circles with all the people affected by the case, a man and his wife came before the Associate Chief Judge of Manitoba's Provincial Court, Judge Murray Sinclair, for sentencing. They had jointly been involved in the sexual abuse of their three daughters, had pleaded guilty and had worked with the team. This was the first time the team had organized its own process to complement that of the court.

Since then, an elaborate sentencing procotol has been established, using a circle format. There are actually two circles, one within the other. The inner circle is for those who wish to speak, the outer one for those who wish to observe and listen. About two hundred people attended that first in-court circle, and over ninety-five attended the second one, held in August 1994.

Before court opens in the morning, the community conducts a pipe ceremony, hangs the flags, smudges or purifies the court buildings with the smoke from smouldering sweetgrass, places the community drum and eagle staff in the courtroom, serves breakfast to people from outside the community and offers an elder tobacco as a request for a prayer to guide the sentencing circle.

The sentencing proceeds according to a number of steps agreed to with the presiding judge: personal smudging (usually with sage or sweetgrass); an opening prayer; court tech-nicalities like confirming the guilty plea; an outline of the ground rules by the presiding judge; a first 'go-round,' where the participants say why they came to be in the court that day; a second go-round, where all the participants are given the chance to speak directly to the victim; a third go-round, where all the participants are allowed to speak to the offender about how the victimization has affected them, the families and the community at large; a fourth go-round, where the participants outline their expectations to the offender and give their views about what needs to be done to restore balance; the passing of sentence by the judge; and a closing prayer. Following that, the participants may stay to use the circle for sharing or 'debriefing' purposes. I will speak later of the rules that govern how each person is required to participate in such circles, for they are integral parts of the healing strategy.

Out of forty-eight offenders in Hollow Water over the last nine years, only five have gone to jail, primarily because they failed to participate adequately in the healing program. Of the forty-three who did, only two have repeated their crimes, an enviable record by anyone's standards. Of those two, one reoffended at a very early stage, before the sentencing had actu-ally taken place. The second reoffended when the program was in its infancy. Since that reoffending, he has completed the formal healing program and is now a valuable member of the team, given his personal knowledge of the ways victimizers try to avoid responsibility.

More recently, after sentencing has taken place, the team requires that the process be repeated publicly at six-month intervals, without the court party, to reaffirm the promises of all, to honour whatever healing steps have been taken and to maintain community expecta-tions of offenders.

At all times, from the moment of disclosure through to the Cleansing Ceremony, team members have the responsibility to work with, protect, support, teach and encourage a wide range of people. It is their view that since a great many people are affected by each disclo-sure, all of them deserve assistance. Just as importantly, all must be involved in any process aimed at creating healthy dynamics and breaking the intergenerational chain of abuse.

I indicated that many of the team members from the community are themselves victims of long-standing sexual abuse. Even former victimizers who have completed the formal healing process successfully are being asked to join the team. The personal experience of team members in the emotional, mental, physical and spiritual complexities of sexual abuse gives them an extraordinary rapport with victims and victimizers alike. I sat with them in circles as they shared their own histories as a way to coax others out of the anger, denial, guilt, fear, self-loathing and hurt that must be dealt with if health is to be re-established. Their personal experience also gives them the patience needed to stay with long and painful processes, and to see signs of progress that might escape the notice of others. It also gives them the insight to recognize who is manipulating or hiding in denial, and the toughness to insist that they keep moving towards greater honesty. The word 'healing' seems such a soft word, but, as I will show later, Hollow Water's healing process is anything but soft. In fact, jail is a much easier alternative, because it does not require the victimizer to face the real truths about abuse.

Crimes too serious for jail?

While the Western justice system seems to have forged an unbreakable link between 'holding someone responsible for their crime' and sending them to jail, the Community Holistic Circle Healing Program (CHCH) at Hollow Water fiercely denies the wisdom of that connection. In 1993 they drafted a 'Position Paper on Incarceration,' in which they discuss their objections, as well as their reasons, for choosing the healing and teaching path instead. It stands as the most eloquent plea I have come across thus far.

They described, for instance, two realizations which caused them to abandon their initial support for using jail in cases which were felt to be 'too serious' for a strictly healing approach. To use their words, they realized:

(1) that as we both shared our own stories of victimization and learned from our experiences in assisting others in dealing with the pain of their victimization, it became very difficult to define 'too serious.' The quantity or quality of pain felt by the victim, the family/ies and the community did not seem to be directly connected to any specific acts of victimization. Attempts, for example, by the courts – and to a certain degree by ourselves – to define a particular victimization as 'too serious' and another as 'not too serious' (e.g. 'only' fondling vs. actual intercourse; victim is daughter vs. victim is nephew; one victim vs. four victims) were gross over-simplifications, and certainly not valid from an experiential point of view; and

(2) that promoting incarcertaion was based on, and motivated by, a mixture of feelings of anger, revenge, guilt and shame on our part, and around our personal victimization issues, rather than in the healthy resolution of the victimization we were trying to address.

Incarceration, they concluded, actually works against the healing process, because 'an already unbalanced person is moved further out of balance.' The team also came to believe that the threat of incarceration prevents people from 'coming forward and taking responsibility for the hurt they are causing.' It reinforces the silence, and therefore promotes rather than breaks, the cycle of violence that exists. 'In reality,' the team wrote, 'rather than making the community a safer place, the threat of jail places the community more at risk.'

The position paper goes on to speak of the need to break free of the adversarial nature of Western courts, the barrier to healing that arises when defence lawyers recommend complete silence and a plea of 'not guilty' and the second 'victimization' that occurs when victims are cross-examined on the witness stand. In their view, the 'courtroom and process simply is not a safe place for the victim to address the victimization – nor is it a safe place for the victimizer to come forward and take responsibility for what has happened.'

Noting that this acceptance of responsibility is more difficult yet more effective than a jail sentence, the team concluded:

> Our children and the community can no longer afford the price the legal system is extracting in its attempts to provide justice in our community.

The need to break the silence is great. The Hollow Water team presently estimates that 80 per cent of the population of their community, male and female alike, have been the victims of sexual abuse, most often at the hands of extended family members and usually for long periods of time. Just as shockingly, they now estimate that a full 50 per cent of the community's population, male and female, has at one time or another sexually abused someone else.

In fact, many knowledgable Aboriginal people tell me that there are hundreds of such communities across Canada, all of them stuck in the silence and denial that characterized Hollow Water only nine years ago. The program director of an Aboriginal treatment program for substance abuse told me that 100 per cent of the people coming to her centre have been the victims of sexual abuse. Another prominent Aboriginal woman told me that she does not have one close Aboriginal woman friend who has escaped sexual abuse.

In the next chapter, I will begin my exploration of where the healing perspective comes from, what sustains it and how it can penetrate even the most pain-filled relationships. First, however, I'd like to tell a story, one which gave me my first clues as to how abuse gets passed from generation to generation, multiplying as it goes, until entire communities become engulfed by it. Of all the stories I know, it gives the clearest picture of the incredible whirlwinds of anger, guilt and denial which communities like Hollow Water must ultimately confront. Until we gain some understanding of how this state of affairs came into being, mapping a way out of it remains almost impossible.

Carl and the cancer of abuse

This story is about a boy from another community, a boy I will call Carl, though that is not his real name. When he first came to the attention of the justice system at age fifteen, Carl stood charged with forcible confinement and with the sexual abuse, both anal and vaginal, of two girls. They were four and six years old.

Carl was one of five children growing up in a remote reserve of some four hundred people. His community had no airstrip, no sewer system, no running water, virtually no employment – and only one telephone

In his first five or six years, a number of events began to shape him. He saw his Dad repeatedly beat and rape his mother in drunken rages. He, in turn, was regularly beaten by his father, sometimes for trying to protect her. His mother also beat Carl, on orders from his father. She did it, he believed, only to keep from being beaten herself. His Dad also forced him into oral and anal sex with him, then forced his mother to join in or be beaten herself

While these acts were being repeated, Carl learned a number of things. He learned how his Dad blamed his Mom for his own rages, screaming that it was always her fault. He learned that his father justified his anger by pointing to her 'failures' as a wife, mother, housekeeper, cook and so on. Carl began to see things in the same way, to believe that the violence was all her fault, that she 'deserved' it.

More than that, he learned how to endure all the violence within his family in total silence. In the words of the probation officer, he 'lived in dread of what would happen if he ever told or shared the family secret.' At the same time, Carl began to develop a real anger towards his neighbours and his community because, as he phrased it, 'They didn't see, and thought Dad was so nice.'

Unable to reach outside the family for help, he came to rely on his brothers. On one occasion, they all joined together in attacking their father to rescue their mother from another brutal assault.

It should come as no surprise that they all began to sniff solvents, especially gas. It was the only way to escape.

When Carl was five or six, it became known to outsiders that his Dad was sexually abusing one of his older brothers. As a result, a child protection agency placed Carl with his grandparents in another reserve community. He stayed there until he was eight or nine, separated from his brothers and sisters, his only allies. Unfortunately, living with his grandparents did not result in an end to the abuse. A male cousin some six years older than Carl forced him into oral and anal sex on a regular basis, often bribing him with cigarettes and drugs. That abuse continued sporadically until his final arrest in 1992, at age fifteen.

When he was eight or nine, Carl's Dad remarried and quit drinking. He took Carl home, and for a while things were fine. The new wife was a good person, whom he trusted. Then, in the second year there, his Dad started drinking again, and the violence returned. On one occasion when his Dad struck him, the new wife came to protect him and his Dad turned on her. She was pregnant at the time and lost the baby as a result of that assault. Carl blamed himself for the loss of the baby. Not surprisingly, he began sniffing solvents more frequently.

Then, by his own admission, he started taking his anger out on people less powerful than himself. At age nine, he forced intercourse on a six-year-old girl who was his cousin. In his own words, he did so on 'countless' occasions. At age ten, he forced intercourse on an eight-year-old girl, and did so some four or five times. At age ten, he forced anal intercourse on a five-year-old boy.

Then, when Carl was about ten or eleven, his Dad's new wife arranged for him to return to his grandparents, apparently afraid for him, but unaware of what had happened there before. He stayed with his grandparents until he was nearly thirteen. During that period, the male cousin who had sexually assaulted him resumed his abuse, supplying him with marijuana and hashish as rewards this time. He grew to use them almost daily. Another boy, who was about five or six years older, forced him into acts of oral and anal sex on four or five occasions, pretending to others that he was there to teach him martial arts. At the same time, Carl began to threaten his grandparents and to steal from them to buy drugs. He also continued to abuse others. He forced intercourse on a nine-year-old girl after watching a porno movie. He also forced intercourse on a girl his own age, a girl whom he says he liked. He also began to think about suicide, later telling the probation officer: 'I remember feeling ashamed and wanting to kill myself. I'd tell myself that I was no good and that I should just kill myself.'

In fact, he attempted suicide several times, later saying: 'I was having bad memories of Dad slapping [the new wife] around, and being sexualy victimized as well.' Because of the suicide attempts and threats of violence to others, he was placed in a group home a couple of months before his thirteenth birthday. That, however, changed nothing. While there, he learned that his Dad's new wife had committed suicide. He had now lost the one person who had not abused him, the one person he trusted, and he blamed himself for her suicide.

Then, in the spring of 1991, at age thirteen, he went back to his Dad. He was using hash and marijuana on an almost daily basis, smoking with his brother, his uncles, his cousins – and even his Dad. He also resumed his own abusive behaviour. He again forced intercourse on his younger cousin, sometimes being assisted by one of his brothers. It was also at this time that he committed the offences that brought him to court – forcing anal and vaginal sex on the two girls aged four and six, keeping them imprisoned for several hours. In his words later, it was 'as my father had done to us.' He was charged with those offences.

In the words of the probation officer who prepared the evaluation report for court, Carl had learned a number of things growing up in such conditions: (1) ' He learned as a young child both to lie and pretend, to protect himself from his father's violence.' The primary lie was that his family life was good, while secondary lies involved such things as why he was staying away from home. (2) 'He... learned to become a sexual perpetrator. His victimization experiences [led] him to de-value himself and his very existence. It was only a matter of time before he started de-valuing the needs of others. In his own words: 'I told myself that I was no good. I'm a nobody. I'll only end up in jail anyway, so I'll do what I want... I victimized to regain the power I lost when I was being victimized.'

In summary, this fifteen-year-old boy was sexually victimized by at least *four* people: his father, his mother, an older cousin and another older boy. At the time of his sentencing, he acknowledged victimizing at least the following *seven* people: a six-year-old girl cousin, repeatedly; an eight-year-old girl some four or five times; a five-year-old boy, once; a nine-year-old girl, once; a same-age girlfriend, several times; and two little girls, aged four and six. Since his sentencing into custody and treatment, he has now acknowledged sexually abusing at least another six people. This boy is only fifteen.

As this one painful story illustrates, the cancer of sexual abuse, as long as it remains hidden, spreads from generation to generation, multiplying as it goes. In many communities, health-care workers estimate that such sexual abuse spans three or four generations. It is considered an illness because it is passed from one person to another as victims try to compensate for their own degradation by degrading others. This was the situation facing the people of Hollow Water, although they didn't know its full horror at the time.

As Hollow Water has learned, however, it is impossible to deal with the Carls of this world simply by prosecuting their abusive fathers. Instead, it is necessary to ask how those abusive fathers got that way, how the illness that erupts as sexual abuse got started. Until that is done, until the factors that first spawned such disharmonies are identified and dealt with, the illness will continue to afflict one generation after another.

The most basic question, then, is: Where did it all begin? At this early stage there is one thing I would like to make clear: all the evidence I have seen thus far sends me the unequivocal message that such widespread abuse was *not* a part of traditional life. In fact, it appears to have been a very rare occurrence, and the object of strong condemnation.

For instance, many early explorers, like David Thompson, were moved to comment on how much love and protection children were afforded and how much they were the healthy centre of a strong and caring society. At the same time, sophisticated measures designed to prevent such abuse were prominent in traditional society, and these are still used in communities where such traditions have been maintained. In the Medewewin Lodge of the Ojibway, for instance, a place in the circle remains reserved for the Deer Clan, despite the fact that no members of the Deer Clan have existed for centuries. The disappearance of this most gentle, song-filled and poetic clan is traced in Ojibway storytelling to their refusal to heed the Creator's warning against incest, even when their continued misbehaviour sent them afflicted children. As a result, the Creator was left with no choice but to see to the disappearance of the entire clan. The vacant place that still remains within the Midewewin Lodge thus stands as a reminder from those ancient times that incest is abhorrent in the Creator's eyes.

There are a great many other practices and traditions that were clearly established to prevent sexual abuse – including the prohibition of direct communication in some groups between fathers and daughters during adolescence. I leave it to others to present them more completely than my knowledge permits. I only wish to indicate my present view that the plague of sexual (and other) abuse that afflicts so many Aboriginal communities is not a 'natural' event within what the settler nations called a 'pagan' society. On the contrary, I see it as an almost inevitable consequence of historically labelling *everything* Aboriginal as pagan, of declaring at every step and in every way that every aspect of traditional life was either worth less than its European equivalent – or just plain worthless.

Losing the centre

One event in particular began to guide me towards this most uncomfortable conclusion. A few years ago, I heard an Ojibway woman tell her story at a workshop on sexual abuse. She told us that she had been born into a tiny community that survived on its trapping, hunting, fishing and rice harvesting. Then, at age six or seven, she was taken away to residential school, along with all the other school-age children. She stayed there until she was sixteen. Contrary to what I expected, her sexual abuse did not begin at that school. While there were unquestionably many schools where the physical abuse of children, sexual and otherwise, seems to have been commonplace, she was in one where 'only' the children's language, spirituality, culture and worldview were abused – as the priests and nuns tried to train the 'Indian' out of them. This woman was not sexually abused until, at the age of sixteen, she was released from school and went back to her tiny village. First it was an uncle, then older cousins – her own people.

She spoke to the workshop about how she handled the abuse of her 'Indianness' by the nuns and priests and the abuse of her body by her relatives. She first went into the predictable downspin of alcohol and drugs, winding up on the streets of a city, abusing herself in virtually every way. Then, to the surprise of many, she did what she calls a 'complete flip.' She got sober, went back to school, graduated from university, got married and had children. She thought everything was fine.

Then, she told us, a day came when one of her daughters returned from school with a straight-A report card. She asked her daughter why there were no A-plus marks on it. The daughter's tearful response was to ask why they had to be *better* than everyone else, and in everything they did. It was at that point that her mother understood that she was still hiding from her sexual abuse, that she had only traded alcohol and drugs for perfectionism. She began to understand that she still had not come to grips with the pain, the guilt and the 'dirtiness' of being a victim of sexual abuse. Needless to say, the fact that she had been abused by her own people did not help.

In the years that followed, she returned to her tiny community and began to speak openly about what had happened to her, about the sexual abuse that had caught so many people in its web. Despite hostility and fear, she persisted. She sought guidance from the elders about how to face up to realities, how to put the pain behind her, how to embark on healing both for herself and for the community. It was, she told us, the elders who helped her understand the reason why it was her own people, her own family, who had abused her that way. 'I began to learn,' she said, 'that the people I came back to at age sixteen were not the same people I had left at age six. The change began on the day we were taken from them.'

I will never forget how powerfully her simple declaration affected the room. I could almost feel everyone being jolted into sharing her realization: her abusers, Aboriginal people all, did not abuse because they were Aboriginal people, but because they were *changed* Aboriginal people. If that was so, then there was something they could do to reverse the downward spiral that had everyone so firmly in its grip: they could look back to see when the changes began, what they were, how they touched people – and how they might be *reversed.* In other words, there was a chance that they could rescue themselves.

As she spoke, it became clear that residential schools were not the solitary cause of social breakdown amongst Aboriginal people. Rather, they were the closing punctuation mark in a loud, long declaration saying that nothing Aboriginal could possibly be of value to anyone. That message had been delivered in almost every way imaginable, and it touched every aspect of traditional social organization. Nothing was exempt, whether it was spiritual belief and practices, child-raising techniques, pharmacology, psychology, dispute resolution, decision making, clan organization or community governance. In time, even economic independence was stripped away as governments built community schools, which made it impossible for families to tend traplines often a hundred kilometres back in the bush. Even the law added its voice to the degradation, making it illegal to possess medicine bundles, vote in Canadian elections, hold a potlach to honour the assistance of others or (difficult as this is to believe) hire a lawyer even to *ask* a court to force governments to honour their treaty obligations.

Taking the children away to residential school was, in a way, just an exclamation mark ending the sentence that declared: All things Aboriginal are inferior at best, and dangerous at worst. When the children were gone, however, so was the centre of life for everyone left behind. I find it impossible to imagine the feelings that must have swamped all those mothers and fathers, aunts and uncles, grandmothers and grandfathers. Some of them thought that such a drastic step was necessary for future generations to gain the skills needed to survive in the non-Native world. Some of them, however, still rage at the arrogance of such a move and lament the loss of social and personal health that followed for everyone concerned. No matter how much the outsider's education was desired, what was left behind for all the adults was a gargantuan hole, out of which many were unable to climb.

Those of us in the criminal justice field are familiar with studies of what happens in one-industry towns where the mine or mill closes. When those jobs suddenly vanish, the unemployed are robbed of one source of self-esteem: the ability to provide adequately for their families. Alcohol and drug use increase measurably, along with the rate of family violence. If the loss of that *one* source of self-esteem can have such a significant effect, what must have been the effect on all of Canada's Aboriginal people as our institutions attacked *every* aspect of their lives?

Try a short exercise in role reversal, imagining a non-Aboriginal mine worker whose job was taken away by all-powerful outsiders. Imagine that he knew he had no realistic chance of ever qualifying for another one. Imagine that he was unable to go for comfort and help to his own churches and his own psychiatrists and hospitals, because those same outsiders had made them illegal. Imagine that, whenever he went to their versions of such helping places, the professionals who staffed them could not speak his language, but demanded that he learn theirs. Imagine, as well, that all those powerful outsiders held him, his language and his culture in such low esteem that they forcibly removed his children, to raise them to be just like them. Imagine, at that point, waking up to silence throughout your entire community, where only the week before there had been the raucous voices of new generations. What reason would there be even to get out of bed?

And what happens when you are told, from every direction and in every way, that you and all your people have no value to anyone, no purpose to your lives, no positive impact on the world around you? No one can stand believing those things of themselves. No one can bear considering themselves worthless, essentially invisible. At some point people brought to this position stand up and demand to be noticed, to be recognized as being alive, as having influence and *power*. And the easiest way to assert power, to prove that you exist, is to demonstrate power over people who are weaker still, primarily by making them do things they don't want to do. The more those things shame and diminish that weaker person, the more the abuser feels, within the twisted logic of victimization, that they have been empowered and restored themselves. Further, nothing is more attractive to those who need to feed off the denigration of others than the road of sexual abuse, and the safest and easiest sexual abuse is of children.

19 Needs-based justice as restorative

Dennis Sullivan and Larry Tifft

Grasping the value of a restorative, needs-based approach to justice is extremely difficult for many people today because the reward/punishment ideas and structures of our hierarchical and globalizing political economy that influence how we relate with one another and live our lives are not based on meeting people's needs. Rather than need, our relationships and daily lives are predominately organized on one or the other of two different justice ideas and arrangements – rights and deserts. In rights-based social arrangements or hierarchies, it is believed that one should receive benefits, privileges, and burdens, hold rights, and have access to resources solely on the basis of his or her rank or place. In deserts-based social arrangements or hierarchies, it is believed that a person should receive benefits, privileges, and burdens and have access to resources on the basis of merit or desert, according to the efforts he or she has put forth. Deserts-based arrangements embody the widely-held cultural belief that we should receive benefits on the basis of what we have done, according to our contributions (Kleinig, 1971; Lamont, 1994).

Most people in our society believe that if a person works hard and puts forth great effort, he or she will be rewarded and live well (Feinberg, 1970). And when it comes to burdens and punishments, most believe that a person should bear burdens and receive punishments based solely on his or her actions. One should not be burdened, that is, it is unjust to be burdened on the basis of, for example, heritage, birth-order, or sex–all ascriptive criteria. Those who critique rights-based distributive justice assert that such distributions are unjust because one does not choose to be born female/male, black/white, in a particular birth-order, or to a particular position or class privilege or deprivation. In response to the injustice and burden of being ascribed a social position and being denied the opportunity to receive benefits and burdens on the basis of one's actions, the familiar remedies such as equal opportunity and equal rights programs have been developed. Deserts-based ideas of justice are also clearly embodied in the notion that no one should be punished or incarcerated or executed if he or she has not committed a harmful act or crime. In retributive language, no one should be doing the time if he or she has not done the crime (Miller, 1999).

As a consequence of our great exposure to deserts- and rights-based ideas and arrangements, it is perhaps unreasonable to expect us to have much competence in bringing about reconciliation between someone who has been harmed and the person or persons responsible for that harm. Not having embraced needs-based living arrangements and restorative values in our daily lives – in our families, schools, and workplaces – we generally lack a reservoir of experiences to draw from to manage the complex of ideas, feelings, and decisions that arise when we seek to create and apply restorative values and meet needs in a harm situation. Doing this is, to a considerable degree, counter-cultural, counter-relational and, in the eyes of some, madness.

But, we need to keep in mind that a lack of understanding about how deserts- and rights-based political economies work in our lives does not exist simply because we are talking about a needs-based approach to justice. We see, and increasingly so, fewer and fewer people who are aware of the nature of the political economy that underlies even their own sense of themselves and how this self is created and proceeds in relationships with others. This is true even for those who profess a familiarity with religious principles and who tell us that they apply these principles in their everyday dealings with others. The problem is that, in far too many instances, many of us do treat matters of justice as if feelings, bodily needs, and ideas were not grounded in relationships and vice versa. Regardless, one of the primary reasons that anyone of us puts off making such an examination of self, our relationships, and what kind of justice prevails in these relationships is that it is a very painful process. By taking on such a task in earnest, we are making a commitment to examine the foundations of the social ethic by which we live and treat others which, in turn, requires us to scrutinize our desires and self-needs-satisfaction motives. What we find might contradict how we perceive ourselves and project ourselves into the world and what kinds of actions we believe we are responsible for (Klein, 1964).

At the most basic level, the political economy of relationship that each of us develops is a measure of the relative value or worth we assign to ourselves and to others. When we develop a rights- or deserts-based political economy, we create a classification or ranking system whereby we situate some people as more worthy and others as less worthy; some of more, and others of less, value. And personal worth here is defined in terms of the degree to which a person is considered worthy of our attention: that is, of having his or her needs met in everyday situations and especially in times of crisis (Herman and Chomsky, 1988). These political economies of relationship reflect the reasons or justifications we proffer to legitimate this classification system, our definitions of superior/inferior, as well as specify the actions we should take (what are most cost-effective) to produce the best payoff in support of these conceptual and social arrangements. Once our personal political economy is set in motion, we develop a working sense of what we expect of others, what we think they expect of us, and how much we think we should charge them for our efforts and talents relative to what they mean to us or what they have done for us. Of course, such decisions may be influenced by our feelings about what others have charged us in the past. So an important maxim when harms and felt injustices occur might be, "You made me suffer a loss and now, to you, I will do likewise," because you deserve this loss and because such action is necessary to preserve the (in this example) deserts-basis of our relative positions in the hierarchy.

Deserts-based justice

In accord with this deserts-based position, many people believe that personal and communal well-being are best served when personal ambition and personal gain are fostered. When it comes to income, for example, it is believed that whatever people earn through their talents and efforts, they deserve to keep. Justice is done when the size of a person's income reflects her or his abilities and efforts. This also means, however, that when someone fails at an endeavor, as we indicated at the outset, he or she deserves whatever pain, loss, burden or punishment derives from his or her misguided actions and efforts. Justice is done when available benefits and burdens are eventually distributed in proportion to what someone did to merit them (Lane, 1986; Miller, 1986).

When it comes to issues of power and control in personal relationships, a deserts-based political economy of life translates into a belief that the person who has achieved a higher status because of his or her achievements deserves to participate in daily affairs in proportion to that status. Let us imagine that we have a family composed of two parents and two young children that operates according to a deserts-based social ethic. Let us also assert that the mother makes $60,000 a year and the father $40,000, and that neither child contributes resources to the family's collective wealth. Deserts-based thinking would have it that each person deserves to participate in decisions about the family's use of its resources, and in other matters affecting the family, according to the level of each person's earnings or financial contribution. Personal worth, participation in family decision-making processes, and ultimately one's power is commensurate with each person's contribution.

In this illustration, since the children make no financial contribution to the family, they are allowed no participation in the family's economic decision-making processes, and are accorded little or no access to the family's wealth except that level of access determined by the family's deserving superiors. In effect, the person who has the most prevailing currency is likely to have the greatest say in how the family is organized and run, how needs will be defined, whose needs are defined as legitimate and satisfied, in what order, and with how much of the family's resources. In the family's collective narrative, the "deserving" power holder's story will count most, her or his account of life will prevail. With the degree of allowable participation of some defined from without, by others, participation (by those over whom power is exercised) will be limited to that of an observer, a spectator or voyeur of one's life. Those family members whose lives are lived through the experiences of those who exercise power over them, experience "mental alienation; a permanent reduction of the self to a condition of tutelage, as in minors or madmen" (Brown, 1966, p. 117). With one's voice constantly muted, a sense of one's true self is negated, and gradually, a person begins to believe that she or he is not merely a subordinate, but, in fact, an inferior who has limited needs or needs that are not worthy of serious consideration by others.

In such a political economy, in the family, the school, the workplace, and in the society generally, those with the greater contributions of wealth and resources in effect whittle down the human dimensions of others to a size that fits within their organization's profit or ideological margins. Some of us, therefore, are forced to pay a price in our daily life because of our lesser, imposed, deserts-based status, as we are forced to pick up the bill for others mutely. It is easy to say that those in power (those successful in the exercise of power) deserve to be rewarded for what they do for others or to them, but most of us pay this price out of fear that our well-being will be lessened further or, when we clamor for an equal voice, of having that voice or life taken away altogether (Chomsky, 2000).

When it comes to responding to a harm situation within this kind of economy, the intention of those who live according to such arrangements and values is to impose a counter-loss upon the person responsible for the harm because this person *deserves* that loss. His or her actions threatened existing deserts arrangements. Since deserts-based justice has to do with equalizing unequal situations, it is believed that this equalization can be best achieved through the equalization of loss, through the creation of equal ill-being. Only through the imposition of a counter-debt can the original debt be paid. Paradoxically, only through the imposition of a counter-debt will the "believed to be just" pattern of interaction that has been violated, be restored.

When a child steals money from his or her mother's purse, a counter-debt is extracted to restore the rights of the mother to deny access to her purse and the resources within it (her personal private property rights). The counter-debt lets the child know that property rights and distributions are to be upheld even if they disallow the child's needs from being met. When a child hits a sibling, a counter-debt is deserved, perhaps in kind (as most U.S. parents claim), to restore the right of the person hit to deny others access to his or her physical person, his or her autonomy. And even if the in-kind hitting perpetuates the cycle of harm or violence, it serves notice as to the legitimacy of a parent's right or deserved privilege to exercise a pattern of parental power and control, parental hierarchy. Whether or not the hit affects either child's behavior, it serves to let each child know who is in power and that power relationships are acceptable – to be restored, to be reestablished when parental rules are violated.

We should note here, as well, that a child hit by his or her sibling does not deserve to be hit (nor does anyone ever deserve to be hit) and so, according to deserts-based logic, this person does not deserve our attention. Meeting this hurt sibling's needs does not follow desert-based logic, because the child has not acted so as to deserve our attention. Only the person who has harmed has acted so. We can see why retributive attention has turned almost exclusively to the acting, and therefore deserving, *offender*. Acting to meet the needs of the *victim* is not a worthy enterprise for this person has not acted to deserve our attention. Moreover, attending to this person's needs does not necessarily preserve or restore the arrangements, deserved privileges, or rights that were violated by the harm.

When we examine the ramifications of this kind of political economy, it is not surprising that the possibility of achieving a justice that fosters personal healing and need-meeting is almost always thwarted because deserts-based actions destroy human presence. They shut people down. They are personally deconstructive (Denzin, 1984; Scarry, 1985; Tifft, 1993), and produce a kind of non-presence: those subjected to the violence of power are forced to sacrifice their true self, voice, energies, and talents to pay for the satisfaction of the power-wielder and the social arrangements for which the power-wielder acts as a representative. And, we have to keep in mind here that this power-wielder might be a parent, teacher, physician, boss or employer as well as an agent of the state or corporate decision-maker and that the deficit-creating acts can and do occur in all spheres of our lives (Tifft, 1993; Chomsky, 1994a).

As we have seen, sometimes these processes occur in very subtle ways, and even close familiarity with our fellows at home, school or work does not seem to diminish our ability to prefer our own status to theirs, even when these others are suffering considerably. For example, during the winter of 1997, a woman who worked in an office of a New York State agency had to leave work early one day because she was having great difficulty breathing. When she returned to work the following day, she told her supervisor and coworkers that her chronic asthmatic condition had become quite aggravated because others in the office were wearing to work each day heavy fragrances in the form of colognes and perfumes. Sensitive to her suffering and needs, her supervisor called a meeting of everyone in the office to discuss this issue. During the meeting it was discovered that four or five other workers had also experienced adverse physical reactions to fragrances, some even suffering migraine headaches on a fairly regular basis. To respond to the needs of these suffering persons, it was suggested that the office be declared "fragrance-free."

Some coworkers were immediately sympathetic to the needs of their colleagues and agreed to declare the office "fragrance-free." They said that the health needs of those who were suffering (needs-based) should take precedence over individual personal preferences for bodily enhancement. There were others at the meeting, however, who said that they did not wish to change the way things were, asserting that each person who worked in the office should have the free choice or the right to wear whatever fragrances they wanted (rights-based). In contrast to these persons' perspectives, there were still others who insisted that the issue was not a matter of individual freedoms or rights or individual health needs, but of deserts. They claimed that, while it was unfortunate that some who worked in the office were suffering from others' use of perfume – and agreed that those who were suffering had done nothing to deserve their headaches and aggravated asthma attacks – they had worked in the agency for a long period of time and had put forth a great amount of energy and skill to attain a certain grade level and, therefore, deserved to wear whatever they wanted in the office (deserts-based). These persons and those who asserted that they had a right to wear whatever they wanted at any time, in essence, believed that their feelings, freedoms, rights, and earned privileges – their political economies of relationship – should take precedence over those of their coworkers who claimed to be harmed and, therefore, in need. After some very intense discussions, and faced with the consciousness that exercising one's earned privileges, or one's personal rights would directly lead to significantly harming others whom one must work with and relate to each day, everyone in the office eventually agreed to declare their common workplace "fragrance-free." A needs-based, face-to-face political economy prevailed.

Even in the service industry, where the needs of the customer are said to be paramount, we see a similar initial insensitivity to the needs of those who are suffering. When several of us were returning from the annual meeting of the American Society of Criminology in Toronto by train, we were seated in a car designated for Albany passengers traveling coach class. But, while waiting for the train to depart, we moved to the next car because all of us had begun to smell sickening diesel fumes. We felt nauseous. Having told the conductor who was passing through about the reason for our move, he said he too smelled the fumes and that our move was fine with him.

However, shortly after we were situated in our new digs, a second conductor came through and asked why we were not sitting in the Albany car. We told her about the fumes. She said such fumes sometimes appear at the beginning of a trip but usually go away, and requested that we return to our designated car. We told her we still did not feel well, and told her that we informed her colleague. She said in a somewhat unbelieving manner that she would ask him whether that was the case, that is, whether we had told him. She then made a further effort to get us to return to the first car, but we insisted that we were still not feeling well and that under no circumstances were we returning there. She said, well, if you are sick....

What is interesting about this encounter is that, when we look at the possible range of responses available to the conductor to handle the situation, she never asked how we felt. She never asked if she could do anything for us, in some way respond to our needs under the circumstances. She never inquired about the well-being of the other passengers who remained in the first car. Rather, her concern was how to reintegrate the "offenders" she encountered into the conditions they deserved via purchases regardless of how deleterious these conditions were for them.

Needs-based justice

From these illustrations we can see how difficult it is for someone to put a needs-based concept of justice into practice in her or his own life because doing so requires that we abandon the principal currency of our deserts-based and rights-based perspectives, namely, power – whether that power be derived from one's personal accreditation, through the authority of the state, or the mandates of a market corporation. When we examine what is required to embrace a restorative approach to justice, we see a political economy in which the needs of all are met, but met as they are defined by each person. Such an approach toward justice puts a great premium on the participation of everyone, and on the expression of the voice of each. In other words, the well-being of everyone involved in a given social situation is taken into account: that is, everyone involved is listened to, interacted with, or responded to on the basis of her or his present needs. In social arrangements structured for the satisfaction of the needs of all, the feelings, thoughts, sentiments, and needs of everyone involved are of paramount concern from the outset, structurally. Everyone feels that his or her present needs have been presented, acknowledged, respected, and met, and, therefore, feels justly "treated" (Kropotkin, 1924). When differences in need exist, for whatever reason, they are not dismissed, or homogenized, or sacrificed in the interest of a standardized format, but rather, are reconciled with each other so that all involved feel equally "treated" even if differentially treated. The aim of needs-based, restorative justice is to respond to the unique needs of each person, and thereby achieve "equal well-being" (Kropotkin, 1924; Piercy, 1976). Hence, the importance of voice to find out what those needs are.

Introducing needs-based justice into family life is sometimes very difficult because many parents (and many children agree) feel that they are not doing justice to each of their children unless they distribute equally to each child, even when what is distributed may be less or more than what each child needs. If Mary receives $10, so must Quinn and Harry and Erin. This is so because each child is equal in a rights-based sense of each holding the same position of being a child of the parents. Through this distribution they might have satisfied the requirements of equality of position but not those of equality of well-being.

Let us consider a situation in a family where there are three children and each needs a writing implement for school. One says she needs a fountain pen, the other a computer, and the third, a pencil. Clearly, there are great differential costs in the items requested and each reflects a different way of going about one's business in the world. The fountain pen might cost $30, the computer $900, and a box of pencils only a few dollars. If each of the children was given what she or he said each needed regardless of the cost, each of the children will feel that her or his needs have been met; each will feel that justice has been done, for each will feel a level of well-being that is equal to that of her or his siblings. Here, we see needs-based justice as achieving, not equal distribution, but an equality of well-being. Clearly, within families that operate according to a needs-based economy, parents can respond to, provide for, support, and show love for each of the children in quite different ways, with quite different resources, while still achieving justice and fostering the growth of each child, for each child feels that his or her uniqueness is being cherished. The same holds true for children who are interacted with this way in school, and for adults interacted with this way in their places of work.

We are suggesting that by attempting to achieve equal well-being, we are not vitiating the requirements of equality, because a needs-based conception of justice "does not demand that each person receive the same physical treatment, rather that each person should be treated in such a way that he [sic] achieves the same level of well-being as every other" (Miller, 1976, p. 149). As we have shown in the case of the writing implements for children, it means that "physical resources such as food, medicine, and education should not be assigned in equal quantities to each man [sic], but in different proportions to different people, according to their peculiar characteristics" (Miller, 1976, p. 149). Clearly, such a view of justice and the practices it requires to achieve personal well-being differ radically from those of deserts-based and rights-based justice. In the former, needs are responded to according to the efforts, talents, and achievements, or failures of the person, and in the latter according to one's social position in the family hierarchy or one's social location as established by state law (Tifft and Sullivan, 2000).

When we speak of the aim of justice as achieving equal well-being, then, we see the great potential that restorative justice demonstrates. Proponents of restorative justice know that justice cannot be *done by* someone or *administered to* someone. Rather, as in family group conferencing, circle sentencing, victim-offender reconciliation programs, and other forms of restorative justice at their best, it can be created or achieved only when all involved in the given situation are participants taking the opportunity to *collaborate* in the justice-making process. This means that each of the people involved in the situation be given an opportunity to tell their stories (Baumeister et al., 1990), which might include not only the specifics about the harm in question, but also the structural dimensions that lie at the root of the harm (Dyke, 2000; Mika, 1989). But this will not be possible unless the stories of each person involved in a harm situation are taken seriously and viewed as authentic, which means that efforts are made to meet the needs of all the persons who have told their stories. Only then can all the participants in the process feel that justice has been done.

And, it is important to reiterate that the restorative aspect of justice does not mean simply responding to harms and injustices that have already been done so as to meet the needs of all involved, but, as well, striving to create patterns of interaction among us all that take into account the needs of all from the very outset, structurally. As indicated, by stipulating the essential nature of this structural requirement for justice-done, proponents of restorative justice raise considerable issue not only with how interpersonal harms are responded to – that is, via vengeful, punishing means – but also with power-based social arrangements and hierarchically-ordered relationships that by definition deny the possibility of the satisfaction of the needs of all (Sullivan and Tifft, 1998).

And even when we see the value in and seek ways to implement a needs-based, restorative justice when a harm has been done, we find ourselves up against some grave cultural barriers. Within the context of the growing market economy, many seem to have become confused about what a need is and what process a person must engage in to determine what his or her needs are. One result of this is, for example, that we have come to accept as needs whatever professionals of all ilk have indicated we must have for our well-being, whether that well-being, be defined in terms of health, knowledge, salvation, or bodily enjoyment (Sullivan, 1980). Consequently, what we have come to define as a human or personal need "is the individual offprint of a professional pattern; it is a plastic-foam replica of the mold in which professionals cast their staples...The good citizen is one who imputes standardized needs to himself [sic] with such conviction that he [sic] drowns out any desire for alternatives, much less for the renunciation of needs" (Illich, 1977).

But this does not mean that we reject needs as the basis for restoring severed relationships and for preventing relationships from becoming severed in the first place. "Need is essential as the basis for human economics, for it is that dimension of self or being that gives a person his or her uniqueness or difference – bodily, emotionally, and intellectually. It is through our needs, their recognition, expression, and satisfaction or denial, that we come to create, to be who we are" (Sullivan, 1980, p. 147). It is through the understanding, expression, and satisfaction of what our true needs are that, "we are most fully a part of the human race. Need 'qualifies' us, not [rights], status, wealth, or certification ribbons" (Sullivan, 1980, p. 147).

When we speak of equality of well-being as a goal, we are not suggesting that some state of finality will be achieved, for justice defined according to these terms is a dialectical process. We are always engaged in responding to a continually changing state of unequal well-being (Tifft, 1978). It is a process of presenting and listening to the other, of understanding, respecting and reconciling divergent realities and truths. Hence, justice-done restoratively requires that participants continually remain open to each other's concerns, ideas, needs, feelings, desires, pain and suffering, so that each can see the other not as a resource to be used or exploited or as an object to be derided or scorned, but as he or she is, similar to oneself, a person engaged in an unending struggle to become human, with dignity (Tifft and Sullivan, 1980; Burnside and Baker, 1994). And just as a person expressing him or herself does not remain static but is modified by engaging in such a shared venture, so too is the community of listeners simultaneously modified because the concerns at hand are now mutual. When such collaboration takes place, we experience the beginnings of a restorative community, of a political economy of peace and democracy (Pepinsky, 1995). Some would argue, and we would agree, that such a sense of justice resides at the core of moral development (Coles, 1997; Brazelton, 1982, 1992; Kropotkin, 1968) and that this is the quality by which each of us reveals his or her essential being to the world (Pieper, 1966).

But, as we have seen, others assert that we show our essential being to the world and meet our needs best through the accumulation and exercise of power. To the contrary, we suggest that power is a form of violence and that, while it might enhance the well-being of those who rely on it, it does, in fact, destroy the well-being of others and the possibility that their needs will be met. It will serve us well, at this point therefore, to examine power as a form of violence and how it vitiates the possibility of doing justice restoratively.

References

Baumeister, R.F., Stillwell, A., and Wotman, S.R. (1990). Victim and perpetrator accounts of interpersonal conflict: Auto-biographical narratives about anger. *Journal of Personality and Social Psychology*, 59, 994–1005.

Brazelton, T.B. (1982). *Becoming a family*. New York: Dell Publishing.

—— (1992). *To listen to a child: Understanding the normal problems of growing up*. Redding, MA: Addison-Wesley.

Brown, N.O. (1966). *Love's body*. New York: Random House.

Burnside, J., and Baker, N. (Eds.). (1994). *Relational justice: Repairing the breach*. Winchester, UK: Waterside Press.

Chomsky, N. (1994a). *Keeping the rabble in line: Interviews with David Barsamian*. Monroe, ME: Common Courage Press.

—— (2000, May 12). U.S. Colombia Policy. Paper presented at Roxbury Community College.

Coles, R. (1997). *The moral intelligence of children*. New York: Random House.

Denzin, N.K. (1984). Toward a phenomenology of domestic, family violence. *American Journal of Sociology*, 90, 483–513.

Dyck, D. (2000). Reaching toward a structurally responsive training and practice of restorative justice. *Contemporary Justice Review*, 3(3), 239–265.

Feinberg, J. (1970). The nature and value of human rights. *Journal of Value Inquiry*, 4, 243–257.

Herman, E., and Chomsky, N. (1988). *Manufacturing consent: The political economy of the mass media*. New York: Pantheon.

Illich, I. (1977). *Toward a history of needs*. New York: Pantheon.

Klein, M. (1964). Love, guilt and reparation. In M. Klein & J. Riviere (Eds.), *Love, hate and reparation* (pp. 57–119). New York: W.W. Norton & Company.

Kleinig, J. (1971) The concept of desert. *American Philosophical Quarterly*, 8, 71–78.

Kropotkin, P. (1924). *Ethics: Origin and development*. New York: Mother Earth Publications.

—— (1968). *The conquest of bread*. New York: Benjamin Blom.

Lamont, J. (1994). The concept of desert in distributive justice. *Philosophical Quarterly*, 44, 45–64.

Lane, R.E. (1986). Market justice, political justice. *American Political Science Review*, 80, 383–402.

Mika, H. (1989). Cooling the mark out? mediating disputes in a structural context. Paper presented at the North American Conference on Peacemaking and Conflict Resolution. Montreal, Quebec.

Miller, D. (1976). *Social justice*. Oxford: Oxford University Press.

—— (1999). *Principles of social justice*. Cambridge, MA: Harvard University Press.

Pepinsky, H.E. (1995). Peacemaking primer. *Peace and Conflict Studies*, 2, 32–53.

Pieper, J. (1966). *The four cardinal virtues*. Notre Dame, University of Notre Dame Press.

Piercy, M. (1976). *Woman on the edge of time*. New York: Fawcett Crest.

Scarry, E. (1985). *The body in pain: The making and unmaking of the world.* New York: Oxford University Press.

Sullivan, D. (1980). *The mask of love: Corrections in America; toward a mutual aid alternative.* Port Washington, NY: Kennikat Press.

—— and Tifft, L. (1998a). Criminology as peacemaking: A peace-oriented perspective on crime, punishment, and justice that takes into account the needs of all. *The Justice Professional,* 11(1/2) 5–34.

Tifft, L. (1978, November). The Definition and Evolution of Social Justice. Paper presented at the annual meeting of the American Society of Criminology. Dallas, Texas.

—— (1993). *Battering of women: The failure of intervention and the case for prevention.* Boulder: Westview Press.

—— and Sullivan, D. (1980). *The struggle to be human: Crime, criminology, and anarchism.* Over-the-Water, Sanday, Orkney, Scotland: Cienfuegos Press.

20 Seeking socio-ethical grounds for restorative justice

Lode Walgrave

Let me begin with an exercise in introspection. […] the instrumental promises of restorative justice practices are not bad. But imagine that no benefits were found: the victims were not systematically better off, the offenders did not understand better why their behaviour is unacceptable and/or they continued to reoffend as before, and no advantages were observed for community life or public safety. If the effectiveness of restorative justice were exactly the same as the impact of punitive justice, would I then give up the option? I do not think so. Unless its outcomes were significantly worse for the victim, for the offender or for public safety, I would probably stick to the option for restorative justice.

My choice for restorative justice is based primarily on non-instrumental reasons, rooted in my ethical intuitions. In this chapter, I try to make these intuitions more explicit. The reader must be warned. Those who expect a fully fledged ethical tract will be disappointed. I am not a professional ethicist. However, that does not prevent me from being aware that my ethical beliefs and attitudes are crucial in my orientation towards restorative justice.

[…]

In search of socio-ethical foundations for restorative justice

Ethical foundations or everlasting critical discourse on concrete ethics?

In line with postmodern philosophy, Pavlich rejects general ethical foundations for restorative justice (Pavlich 2002, 2005, 2007). For him, the potential of restorative justice resides in refusing 'a blackmail that commands us to come up with well-founded universal principles or else be condemned as unethical, immoral or just plain irrational' (2002: 2). General ethical principles are expressions of totalitarianism, a form of imperialism over thinking and behaviour. Pavlich states that 'a pervasive – "ambient" – uncertainty has gripped our ethical lives to the extent that we no longer place any faith in reason's ability to formulate universal maxims' (2007: 620). Referring to Lyotard and Derrida, he writes 'there is no such thing as justice *per se*' (ibid.: 621).

Instead, Pavlich presents ethics as indeterminate thinking, based on Derrida's concept of hospitality, by analogy with 'a host welcoming a stranger at the threshold of what will be negotiated ways of being with each other in the immediate future' (ibid.: 622). Thinking and behaving ethically is by definition indeterminate, because it is about making personal choices, taking personal responsibility for being with others. Relying on general ethical rules is not functional and strips behavioural options from personal responsibility, thus from their potential to be ethical. Pavlich does not employ a nihilistic language of 'anything goes'.

On the contrary, he imposes 'an immense responsibility upon us for every one of our ethical decisions and actions' (ibid.: 623). The choices are permanently to be submitted to reflection and discourse, holding out the continuous possibility of critical scrutiny. 'Critique is central to the structure of ethical life, as the all-important night watch that must never doze', Pavlich poetically writes (ibid.: 624).

'A restorative ethics could be understood as the critical work performed when subjects gather to name injustice or harm, and address promises of just patterns of being with others that are yet to come' (Pavlich 2002: 5). In Pavlich's view, restorative justice is at risk of losing its critical potential if it abandons this open ethical approach and gives way to what he calls the 'imitator paradox', becoming simply another variant of the traditional justice model steered by the hegemony of the powerful (Pavlich 2005)[…].

It is quite a challenge. Holding indeterminate situational morals, oriented towards being ethically with others, is an attractive perspective. Taking full responsibility for ethical choices based on concrete hospitality for others, while being open for debate and criticism, is probably the highest moral quality one can imagine. However, such morals are probably found only in the most mature, autonomous and self-critical people. Such people seem to combine Kohlberg's ideal moral stage, based on personally integrated principles and ideals (Kohlberg 1976), with Gilligan's ethics of care, based on sensitivity to others' needs and interests (Gilligan 1982). The majority of adults do not reach such a level of perfection, to say the least. If, as Pavlich rightly recalls (Pavlich 2007: 622), advancing general ethical principles could not avoid catastrophes like the Holocaust and other genocides, relying on individuals' ethical maturity would certainly not do better. The ethical maturity promoted by Pavlich is an exceptional state of mind.

Moreover, the kind of open dialogue-based critique that Pavlich has in mind is inspired by Habermas' ethics of discourse, built around the concept of *herrschaftfreie Dialog,* a dialogue free of power and pressure. I do not think that such totally open dialogue is possible in reality. A dialogue about resolving an injustice starts from the observation that an act or a situation actually is unjust and that (some of) the participants will (have to) do something about it. This is not just an intellectual difference in meaning. It is an emotional debate about how a strongly felt injustice will be repaired. Such a meeting is imbued with pressure, either from official coercive institutions in the background, or from participants in the process (Hudson 2006a).

Hence, it may be wiser – in the current imperfect state of affairs – to provide some ethical principles. They are not meant as a system of rigid obligations. The ideal principled man, as promoted by Kohlberg, is probably an insensitive and boring person. Kant's cramped principled judgment, that even if the world would perish the last criminal should be hanged, has been called a 'talionic sophism of a senile genius' (Polak, quoted in Van Stokkom 2005: 165). Well thought out, well documented principles may serve as references to orient judgment in critical ethical situations. While they are never definitively fixed and are not suitable for implementation in all critical situations, they may be beacons for the person who has to take personal responsibility for difficult ethical options and actions.

My understanding of Pavlich's reasoning is that he actually offers such an ethical principle. Imposing upon ethical actors the responsibility to accept reflection and discourse in order to provide a better and more open hospitality to others is a serious burden. Being a good host is an ethical request, even if the concrete quality of hospitality is to be defined through deliberation with the guest. Pavlich's ethical principles may be minimalistic, but they are nevertheless ethical principles. Reflecting on ethics without projecting principles – which may be provisional, transitional, debatable, intuitive or rational – is impossible. It is like pedalling in the air.

It is difficult to conceive of reflection and discourse on ethical decisions without provisional principles as starting points. How can you bring participants together in a dialogue about undoing the consequences of an injustice if they do not share the idea that there is actually an injustice to be repaired? How can you find together a 'just' response if you cannot communicate about why you consider a response is just or not? In the dialogue, you will present your – intuitive – view and argue it. Others will answer by rejecting, nuancing or improving your view, or by proposing a different approach. Principles and interests will be exchanged, moulded, synthesised, interpreted and made concrete, to be applicable and acceptable to all in the specific situation being discussed. The process begins with the opening of ethical (pre-)conceptions for debate.

My quest to explain my ethical drive toward the restorative justice option is meant as a contribution to what Pavlich describes as the everlasting debate on the ethics of understanding concrete injustices and how to repair them.

'*Victimalisation*' of morals

'It says in the Penal Code what you are not supposed to do, but it does not say why not. In the past, this was a task largely left to the ideological agents', Boutellier writes (Boutellier 2000: 18). In recent years, criminology and criminal justice have increasingly been stripped of moral reflections. In line with cultural postmodernist developments, the concept of crime is 'de-moralised', and criminal policy has become 'actuarial' – managing the problems caused by crime rather than solving them. To avoid further degradation, there is a need for a 'normative minimum' (Boutellier 1996: 19) to underpin and govern social life: criminal law will have to constantly find new points of moral departure in a morally fragmented society' (Boutellier 2000: 15). Returning to the earlier religion- or community-based moral systems is neither possible nor desirable, because the progression of individualisation has enlarged the scope of individual freedom. In a pluralistic and increasingly heterogeneous society, solidarity can no longer be based on a common identity or a generally accepted higher order such as religion, nation or community.

Boutellier finds his normative minimum in Rorty's 'are you suffering?' (Rorty 1989): 'the only thing that counts in a secular, liberal society is that people are vulnerable to humiliation and cruelty, pain and suffering; the extent to which we show ourselves to be sensitive to other people's experiences of this kind determines the morality of our culture' (Boutellier 2000: 15). When universalism is rejected in favour of a liberal pluralistic culture, the basis for solidarity is not general, but local and concrete: the shared rejection of observed cruelty and suffering. 'The victim is the central moral denominator in our secularized, pluralistic society... Solidarity in present-day secularized and pluralistic society is no longer linked to either God or a collectivity of the kind Durkheim has in mind, but to the position of the victim. This is what I call the *victimalisation of morality*' (ibid.: 16). The minimalistic common morals are based on the desire we share to avoid being victimised, and on our spontaneously felt emotional solidarity with those who are suffering. Regarding criminal justice: 'It is not so much the violation of the ideologically embedded norm that needs to be undone, but the concrete individual suffering that justice should be done to' (ibid.: 17). The quotation could have been written by a restorative justice advocate.

But it was not. Concern for the victimised is, of course, central in restorative justice, but victimalised ethics is too narrow an ethical basis for restorative justice.

1. A system of morals based only on fear of being victimised is weakened or even negative. It is as if the common interest is limited to avoiding suffering, while mutual support and solidarity, with a view to achieving together positive growth, happiness, wealth and so forth, have no moral value. I shall argue, on the contrary, that individuals and collectivities are bound by positive values and objectives. The pursuit of more autonomy, more happiness, more wealth, more aesthetic beauty, more pleasure is both an individual and a collective undertaking. It orients the value of behaviour and attitudes, and hence the moral criteria.

2. Advancing victimisation as a pragmatic choice for articulating a moral basis is a weak basis, making victimalised morals extremely 'volatile' (Daems 2007). Human suffering is variable, both in kind and in intensity, and does not always prompt equal solidarity. The theory leaves undetermined the criteria for recognizing victimisation. They may change over time, and depend on power play to determine the recognition or rejection of victim status. Feminist criminology, for example had to deliver a long struggle for some typically female dimensions of victimisation to be recognised. There will be deep disagreement about whether one should include victimisation of entire population groups by social economic injustice (and what this 'injustice' means) or by systematic political discrimination. These are moral questions going far beyond the simple victimalisation thesis.

3. Finally, Boutellier's position that restoring a collective dimension in morals is not feasible, and even not desirable, is highly debatable. Whereas Rorty calls his position 'liberal irony', I would call it liberal cynicism. The approach of both Rorty and Boutellier rests on a traditional liberal concept of liberty suspecting collective interests and approaches as possible threats to individual freedom. I shall argue that, on the contrary, restorative justice ethics consider community life and individual freedom as mutually dependent.

Ethics of care

In a response to Kohlberg's theory on moral development (1976), Gilligan expressed a 'different voice' (1982), which she called feminine morals as opposed to masculine morals. Whereas Kohlberg considers autonomous justice, based on rational universal principles, as the highest moral principle, Gilligan advances caring, based on empathy and sensitivity to human relations, as the most worthwhile moral attitude. Ethics of care do not refer to universal laws and rights. They are inherently relational and contextual, based on proximity and openness to needs (Gilligan 1982).[1] Emotions and affection are revalorised as opposed or complementary to objectivity and rationality.

Heidensohn (1986, cited in Masters and Smith 1998) used both moral approaches to characterise two models of justice. The (masculine) 'Portia model' actualises Kohlberg's 'ethics of principles', being abstract, rational and rights-based, as represented in the current justice model. The (feminine) 'Persephone model' is inspired by Gilligan's 'ethics of care', and is concrete, contextual, relational and expressive. Masters and Smith (1998) draw on this typology to understand what they call the shift in the ways of responding to crime. In their view, the 'relational justice practices such as victim-offender mediation and FGC [family group conferencing] ... are best understood with reference to the feminist "ethic of care"' (ibid.: 8).

Daly (2002) rightly is sceptical of the idea that there would be something like typical female ethics opposed to typical male ethics. But besides that, much of the rhetoric related to the restorative 'encounter', 'meeting the needs of both victim and offender' or 'healing' can indeed be understood as caring interventions. One could even see the ethics of care as an extension of the just-mentioned 'victimalisation of morals': victims are in need of care more than of principled justice (Leest 2004).

But restorative justice is more. It is first of all about ensuring that responsibility is taken for the suffering and harm caused and for the reparation of these consequences. The responsibility in the ethics of care underlines the responsibility of the well-off for those in trouble, of the strong for the weak, of the mother for the child. It is one-sided responsibility. It may lead to a rehabilitative or support approach for the offender, to the detriment of the victim's needs, or to holding the victim as an irresponsible and weak being in need of nothing but care. Responsibility in restorative justice is double sided. Also those who are cared for have to take up responsibility actively. How this responsibility/care balance is made concrete is deliberated in the restorative meetings, which may be hard, include negative emotions such as indignation and anger, and end in serious demands. As we have seen, it may include coercion.

Moreover, restorative interventions deal not only with private conflicts, but also with crimes that have a public dimension. Also the 'generalised other' is addressed. Taking active responsibility, possibly applying coercion to make reparative gestures and addressing the public dimension of the crime are intrinsic parts of restorative justice and transcend the ethics of care. It is difficult to see how such an approach corresponds to the purely caring and particularistic approach of the Persephone model (Van Stokkom 2004). Finally, restorative justice has to be framed within general justice principles, which are difficult to combine with a purely caring approach. Masters and Smith also recognise this danger: 'an ethic of care cannot and should not wholly supplant an ethic of justice' (1998: 16).

Communitarianism

Restorative justice recalls the fundamental *raison d'être* of the criminal justice system. Why is it forbidden, for example, to steal or to commit private acts of violence? Because if it were not forbidden, severe victimisations would occur all the time, which would provoke counteractions 'to make things even', leading to an escalation in mutual victimisation. Constructive social life would be impossible; society would be dominated by abuse of power and fear. Hence, what is logically the first concern of the social response to crime? It is to repair – as much as possible and in an orderly way – the harm done to the victim and the damage to social life.

Instead of the abstract legal order, the quality of social relations and social life in general are (re)positioned as the fundamental reasons for criminalising certain behaviour. The aim is to restore this quality, and not primarily to enforce public order. To achieve this, restorative justice relies mainly on cooperative processes among citizens, and not primarily on coercive intervention by the state. The assumption is that, in appropriate conditions, opponents in a conflict are willing to meet each other in mutual understanding and respect and able to find a constructive solution.

Concern for the quality of social life and belief in the potential of ordinary people to find solutions are not the monopoly of restorative justice. They are central to a much wider political and socio-ethical agenda. Its expression is found, for example, in the earlier mentioned 'restorative extensions' in non-criminalisable matters. While these and other practices operate in different contexts, with (partly) different objectives and with other actors,[2] they are all based on the same fundamentals, considering conflict and injustices primarily as threats to the quality of social life, and responding to them by involving as much as possible the direct stakeholders in inclusive processes with a view to taking action to restore the quality of social life.

Three questions now arise.

1.   What is this 'quality of social life'?
2.   How can we derive from it a socio-ethical perspective?
3.   Is it not naive to rely on the direct stakeholders in conflicts to find constructive solutions?

The third question is, in fact, an empirical question [...]. Here, I set out to answer the first two questions on philosophical and ethical grounds.

From community to communitarianism

The idea of community as a social space 'in which people know and care for one another' (Etzioni 1995: 31), based on shared values, norms and interests, is central in restorative rhetorics (Bazemore and Schiff 2001; Sullivan and Tift 2006a). This is understandable. Focusing on harm inevitably draws attention to the loss of peace and the social unrest in a community with crime in its midst. A community is more directly victimised by an offence than is the state.

Restorative justice presents community as both a means and an end. It is a means in that community is advanced as the *niche* of shared understanding and interest, where victim and offender can meet and find together a constructive solution. Restorative processes indeed require at least a minimal understanding of a common interest in a constructive settlement after the crime. But community is also seen as an end, in that some locate restorative justice in a broader communitarian agenda, aimed at enhancing community life and avoiding further alienation by the formal criminal justice interventions.

The link between restorative justice and an intuition of community may be important in practice but it is difficult to encapsulate it in a coherent theory. Three problems appear. First, even if it is not a territorial space (McCold and Wachtel 1997) community is presented as a 'web of affect-laden relationships' (Etzioni 1996: 127), or a set of 'dense networks of individual relationships' (Braithwaite 1989: 85). Community suggests an area, delimited mentally, socially or territorially, distinguishing an inside community from an outside non-community. It expands as far as the vague limits conceived by individuals. It is based on 'a sense of community', a 'perception of connectedness' (McCold and Wachtel 1997: 2). But it cannot be delimited. Community appears to be a subjective psychological entity rather than a set of characteristics of given collectivities (Crawford and Clear 2001: 135).

Secondly, building on communities for developing restorative responses to crime presupposes that communities really exist, which is far from evident (Crawford and Clear 2001; Bottoms 2003). It is difficult to mobilise the community to resolve a street robbery in which victim and offender live many kilometres from each other and belong to totally different social networks. Christie admitted that he had only weak arguments against scepticism about community. Of course, local networks of shared values and mutual solidarity do exist and function ("The death is not complete", Christie 1977: 12), but it is not possible to generalise them. Many crimes occur in non-community-like social settings, and solutions have to be found in such settings.

Thirdly, leaving the notion of community as a loose concept exposes it to possible misuse and excesses. Communities are not good per se. 'Communities are not the heavens of reciprocity and mutuality nor are they the utopias of egalitarianism, that some might wish' (Crawford 2002a: 138). The supposed *niche* of community may appear to be a hotbed of suffocating social control within and exclusionism towards the outside world. In the name of community, people are subjected to unreasonable control and stigmatisation. Local communities support repressive police forces and judges and vote for exclusionist politicians. The sharing of values and other social goods is limited to those who are considered to belong to the community. Those who do not are excluded and are often considered a threat. To the outside world, communities based on territory, ethnicity or religion may develop exclusionary tendencies, provoking possibly violent conflicts. This may lead to excessive nationalism and racism. Community contains 'the seeds of parochialism which can lead ... to atrocious totalitarian exclusions' (Pavlich 2001: 58).

In restorative justice, community is an icon, covering the informal, interdependent, respectful social environment in which exchanges can take place in order to repair the victim's harm, reintegrate the offender and restore community relations. But '... there is no necessary reason for the privileged association which now exists between the new communitarian images of community and the spirit of spontaneous collective solidarity' (ibid.: 67). Communitarianism does not, in fact, promote areas, but socio-ethics and values, to orient social life: a form of harmonious living together, based on recognised social attachments, shared values and beliefs, and mutual commitment. It is easy to understand that this spirit or these socio-ethical attitudes are activated more spontaneously towards members of what we subjectively define as 'our community' but they are not the monopoly or privilege of a given area defined by 'community'.

Hence, while there may be doubts about the appropriateness of community to characterise part of social reality, communi*tarianism* as a movement promoting an ideal of community may be a useful label for a socio-ethical movement.

Communitarianism versus liberalism

For communitarians, the awareness of being members of a family, being neighbours, sharing citizenship, having the same culture, believing in the same God, upholding the same values and beliefs, and thus being more likely to understand and support one another makes us deeply rooted in our social context, part of a community that we cannot erase. Our minds think, strive, judge, create, suffer and enjoy on the basis of our experiences in relation to others, with a view to achieving socially situated and valued objectives. We are inevitably bearers of social meanings and live in relation to social values (MacIntyre 1983). Communitarians argue that it is unrealistic and counterproductive to deny this and to promote unrestricted freedom and autonomy in individual choices and actions as liberals do (Bell 1993).

Communitarianism can go too far when it creates the illusion of community consensus 'by the identification of individuals and their interests with a symbolic collectivity and its interests' (Barber 2003: 149). If the view on the individuality of persons is lost, if the self is merged with the collectivity, it is vulnerable to 'all the grave risks of monism, conformism, and coercive consensualism' (ibid.: 150) which I suggested a few paragraphs ago.

We are more than just a part of a group. We have our private lives, needs and goals which we want to satisfy with the largest possible autonomy, free from interference by any person or agency. That is the liberals' point. For liberals, the highest possible value is freedom. Individuals must be given the right to self-determination, to choose autonomously how they will live. The role of the state should be limited to setting the conditions for the maximum possible self-determination by the citizens. State laws are contracts among free rational citizens, guaranteeing each contractor a space of justly divided liberty. Justice as fairness is crucial in such a vision (Kohlberg 1976; Rawls 1972).

However, extreme liberalism keeps up the illusion of totally free and rational individuals, while denying the huge differences between individuals in social, economic, intellectual and other capacities. In fact, the so-called contracts are imposed by the most powerful and influential on the most vulnerable. Liberalism without any correction finally amounts to the right of the strongest to exploit the weakest in society. That is why Rorty (1989), for example, keeps compassion with the suffering of others as grounds for local solidarity, and why Rawls (1972) accepts some state intervention to correct the most severe inequalities in social and economic resources, and launches the idea of a 'veil of ignorance' to reduce the risk of ruthless exploitation by the powerful.

But the highest value of liberalism remains self-determination. Liberalism basically holds a view of an atomic society, composed of lonely individuals permanently competing with one another for more freedom, wealth, power or pleasure. Competition may, indeed, stimulate, provoke creativity and contribute to progress in society. But if the soil of commonality is too poor, self-determination turns into selfishness, competition becomes combat and competitors change into enemies. The corrections to liberalism are too weak to prevent the current fragmentation of societies towards more selfishness, less mutual commitment and less participatory democracy. 'It is concerned more to promote individual liberty than to secure public justice, to advance interests rather than to discover goods, and to keep men safely apart than to bring them fruitfully together' (Barber 2003: 4). We shall come back to this in the last chapter.

Common self-interest

I am a communitarian because of self-interest. Psychodynamics teach that we are all driven by self-interest. Rather than trying to repress this, we should accept it and include it in our social embedding. Each individual has the desire to shape his own life as he wants it – materially, relationally, religiously, culturally, esthetically and hedonistically. But this shaping is not absolutely free. Obstacles beyond our influence prevent us from achieving all we wish. Also socio-ethical considerations may keep us from going straightforwardly for satisfying our desires. Because we must live together, the options and behaviour of others affect our own opportunities. Inversely, my options and behaviour have an effect on the lives of others. That creates mutual entitlements and responsibilities.

On the one hand, I am entitled to demand an ethical account from others. The drunk driving of one driver is a risk for us all so that we are entitled to stop such driving. The misbehaviour of one professor towards the students reflects negatively on the whole university community, so that the misbehaviour is a matter for all professors and students. In a globalised world, the decision of one government to go to war draws everyone into a situation of increased fear and risk of terrorism and is thus subject to the moral judgment of the whole world.

On the other hand, my personal rights and liberties allow me to make my own choices, and thus I am confronted by my social responsibilities. I can opt for purely ruthless, selfish choices, or I can include the interests of others and of social life in the choices I make. Whereas extreme liberals would stress the right to go for selfish interests (while not always advising to actually do so), extreme communitarians would plead for social pressure or even obligation to opt for the socially oriented choices.

The debate between liberals and communitarians is a socio-ethical debate. Liberties are a crucial good to cherish, but the full use of all legal rights and freedoms is not always ethically advisable. The question how to combine individual freedom and rights with the promotion of high quality in social life cannot be resolved empirically or by new laws and rules. It is a matter of socio-ethical understanding.[3]

Opting for common self-interest

While we have no choice about living with others, we do have a choice about *how* we live with others. Liberals consider the others as competitors, with whom they make minimal agreements on the rules of competition and on guaranteeing one another sufficient space for self-determination. The option then is, in fact, to reduce mutual hindrance. Paradoxically, that will not serve the interests of the competitors. Defining and consolidating the negotiated space for self-determination would imply an everlasting combat for maximum space, yielding winners and losers. Yet the winners also lose, because they must defend themselves permanently against the non-resigned losers and against the losers who develop 'innovative' ways (Merton 1938) of achieving their goals. Consolidating their 'winning position' costs them part of their freedom, by hiding in so-called gated communities, through a reduction in mobility, through the need for security measures, through the price of the criminal justice complex, etc. As we shall see in Chapter 6, neo-liberal policy increases fear of crime and obsession with crime control, to the detriment of the quality of social life even of the rich and powerful. The winners become prisoners of the fear they created themselves.

Instead of considering the others as competitors, I can also bundle my self-interest with that of others. The others then become allies in a common project for more autonomy and my self-interest is integrated in what I call a common self-interest. We try to 'resolve the war of private interests through the creation of public interests' (Barber 2003: 19). Throughout history, human cooperation has made life longer, less dependent on natural elements, more self-determined, more comfortable and more pleasant. But other human achievements have caused new insecurities and threats. To minimise the risks of the latter and maximise the chances of the former, pure self-interest has to be channelled by the socio-ethical understanding that self-interest is best served by integrating it in a common self-interest, a project to achieve more autonomy by promoting a high quality of social life.

The idea of a common self-interest may sound like a *contradictio in terminis*. It merges in one notion the seeming contradiction we are all living in: we are individuals with particular needs, wishes and ambitions, but we also are living with others with whom we cannot but share opportunities and goods. Instead of suppressing one or both elements, the concept of common self-interest actively joins both in orienting self-interest to a project of common self-interest, which is seen in turn to serve individual self-interests.

Indeed, to gain more autonomy, we need each other. The rich need employees in their businesses and factories, construction workers to build their luxury houses, wine-makers for their wines, instrument builders and musicians to make the music they enjoy, police for their security. These workers also need one another, but they also need the rich to set up businesses and to pay taxes, so that the governments can provide the basics for all. At first sight, this may look like a kind of childish Legoland. But it is not.

The underlying idea is that the more smoothly these mutual dependencies operate, based on mutual respect and understanding, the more space there will be for each individual to enjoy liberty and live his life as he wishes. It is in my interest to live in peace, to be part of a community that gives me and the others maximum space, based on respect for plurality and solidarity. It is in my interest also that the other members of the community agree with one another, keeping peace and understanding in our communal life, allowing me to live in peace and to do my own thing. Living in such a community is the common self-interest.

It is self-interest because I invest in such a community for my own profit. I promote such a community life, not because I am an unworldly idealist, but because I hope to get the maximum possible benefits from being part of it. But it is more than self-interest, because I am not alone in going for these benefits. If we all invest in social life, we all profit from its high quality. We do not divide the benefits, together we increase them. The more we share a commitment to the community, the greater are my personal possibilities to enjoy freedom.

What is presented here is not just communitarianism, because without specification, community may lead to the excesses described above. The idea here advances a particular view on the quality of social life as a guiding utopia which recognises my self-interest and my pursuit of autonomy, but combines it with the particular pursuits of others into a project of common self-interest. I would therefore call it 'social life ethics' rather than communitarian ethics.

I am in good company in seeing a version of self-interest as the basic drive in a communitarian political agenda. Chapter 6 will elaborate more on this, but it should be mentioned here that Putnam, for example, writes that our good citizenship is not because we obey 'some impossibly idealistic rule of selflessness, but rather because we pursued "selfinterest rightly understood"' (Putnam 2000: 135). We invest in social life in general because we expect reciprocity from community and the society we are living in. Braithwaite and Pettit (1990) advance 'dominion' as a social conception of freedom. It is the mutual assurance that fellow citizens and the state will respect individual rights and freedoms that increases the individual enjoyment of those rights and freedoms. Barber's quest is 'how to resolve the war of private interests through the creation of public interests, or how to discern in man's social condition the potential for a civic and moral liberty that can transcend the natural and negative freedom of solitary beasts' (Barber 2003: 19). A glimpse of such an idea is even observed in some liberals. As we just saw, Rawls and Rorty, for example, 'season' their self-determination with some social concerns. It is in fact common self-interest, as Boutellier writes: 'Our solidarity is not a value in itself, but is based on the recognition and acknowledgement of each other's possible suffering' (Boutellier 2000: 15).

It is this intuition of having a common self-interest that motivates victims and offenders to meet and to try to understand one another with a view to reaching a constructive solution that can contribute to restoring peace between them and in the community.

Common self-interest as a norm

It is not given by nature that we invest our self-interest in the project of common self-interest. It is ethical advice, as is seen best if the common self-interest is apparently not respected. Obvious disrespect is easily observed. Selfish types straightforwardly pursue uncompromised self-interest in terms of wealth, power and hedonistic pleasure. They force through the self-interests we all have. We may have derogatory thoughts about it because they do not contribute their share to the common interest, but, as long as they do not hinder relations or social life, we do not act severely against it. Some people, however, behave ruthlessly – in business, politics, sports, or private life – to the detriment of others and of the quality of social life. When this occurs we actively reject it, because we consider it an intrusion into our common interest. If everyone behaved like that, social life would turn into a permanent war.

Some will say 'Well, that's life', but I do not want such a life. It is my ethical choice not to accept such a way of life, and I am entitled to do so because of my (our) fate to develop our lives together. In my assumption, inserting my self-interest in a project of common self-interest is both realistic and idealistic. It is a typical Sisyphean position. Giving in to cynicism would be a kind of self-fulfilling prophecy. Resigning oneself to leaving the rock of selfishness at the bottom of the hill is to give up the hope for a better life, to drag it down into an arena of heartless and ruthless struggle for the survival of the fittest. But rejecting cynicism is accepting active responsibility in the everlasting struggle for a better social life while knowing that we shall never reach the ideal. We must keep trying to lift up the perception of self-interest towards more commonality as an essential dimension in our self-interest. Continuously trying to do better is the only way of avoiding degradation into much worse.

At the opposite remove to the selfish actors in the extreme, some people seem to act against their own self-interest to serve others or social life in general. Self-sacrificing behaviour is shown by mothers for their children, by fire fighters for possible victims in a blaze, by soldiers for their country and even by suicide terrorists who offer their life for the religious or political cause they espouse (in the self-interested hope of being happy in heaven). Sometimes there may be some doubts as to whether such behaviour is truly disinterested, but that is not the point here. Such mothers, fire fighters and soldiers are often called heroes, as are the terrorists by their supporters. It expresses admiration for them as exceptional people, who far exceed our own modest capacities. In fact, we praise such behaviour out of fear of the opposite in ourselves: pure selfishness.

Erasing self-interest completely in favour of common interest is not the ideal. Not only is it unrealistic, it would also relegate us to a community with suffocating social pressure and soft control, or bring about a totalitarian regime without personal initiative, progress or pleasure. Examples of such communities and regimes exist, and they are not attractive. To put it bluntly: if everyone sacrificed himself totally for the common interest, nobody would be left to enjoy it.

Sympathy as a ground for developing common self-interest

Sceptics may claim that believing in common self-interest is naive. They will refer to the current hardening of social life and human relations, as is visible through the abuse of power in (international) politics, mercilessness in business, cynical exploitation of legal rights, loss of engagement in community and selfishness in daily life. [...] They seem to leave little hope for common self-interest. But that is not the case.

It is an old wisdom that humans are bound by a basic empathy (see, for example, David Hume and Adam Smith, as in Braithwaite 2006: 402). One of the most striking examples of inter-human empathy was seen recently in the worldwide solidarity after the tsunami in South-East Asia in December 2005. The victims had no obvious connection with our everyday world, and there was no apparent self-interest in helping these people. Still, massive donations and support actions were set up, not only by governments and international organisations, but also by individuals and private groups. The only motive driving this huge movement was compassion with the victims. We spontaneously feel compassion when mass media show the miserable situations of refugees and victims of war, crimes or natural disasters.

At first sight, this observation confirms Rorty's previously mentioned position that human solidarity rests on a common wish to avoid suffering (Rorty 1989). But compassion with a sufferer is possible only through empathy, and empathy encompasses more than just the negative avoidance of suffering. We are also positively moved by the happiness of others, as displayed in movies or in real life (unless jealousy prevents it), and we enjoy the conclusion of peaceful agreements in which we are not directly involved. With people touched by war, we share the hope for peace. Humans are aware of their common self-interest, which is felt emotionally through empathy. It is the basis of their potential for mutual understanding and solidarity, despite differences in opinions and immediate interests. Solidarity goes far beyond negatively avoiding suffering; it is also the ground for constructing together a peaceful and emancipating community.

For several reasons, the potential for mutual empathy is not always activated to the same degree. The intensity depends on the degree of identification: we are more likely to sympathise with family members or fellow citizens than with more distant people. We support the football team of our own country, even if they play badly and brutally. Empathy may be diminished or blocked as a result of experiences in childhood, for example, or because of opposing immediate interests. Sometimes, the luck or success of others is experienced as a threat to our own prestige or interests, so that envy may prevent us from enjoying other people's good fortune. Living conditions and the stress of daily life may cause indifference. War situations lead to dehumanising the enemy. Persons diagnosed as psychopaths are even supposed to be psychologically incapable of feeling empathy. But these are variations and exceptions which do not alter the basic supposition that average people do in general feel empathy with other people.

Such deep human relationships are the key, for example, in the work of the French philosopher Emmanuel Levinas. Duyndam and Poorthuis (2003) open their book *Levinas* with the story of a tragedy as an illustration of Levinas' approach. In April 2002, the German town Erfurt was in shock. A student had walked around his school with a gun, killing 16 students and teachers. He finally faced his seventeenth potential victim, a teacher, in an empty classroom. The teacher called out to him 'Seh mich an!' [Look at me!]. But the schoolboy continued to curse and swear, and aimed his gun at the teacher. The teacher repeated 'Seh mich an!' And then suddenly, the boy dropped the gun and surrendered. What happened? What intangible force was stronger than the gun in the hands of the boy? The answer, in Levinas' words, is 'the face of the Other'.

Levinas' philosophy is not about ethics; it does not prescribe *how* we must behave. Its ambitions are to dig out the source of morals, to find out *why* we are unavoidably confronted with ethical responsibility. The source lies in the relation of the I with the Other. Morals are not, as in Kant, an imposed set of categorical imperatives resulting in absolute rights and wrongs, but are relational and located in life. The relation between me and the other begins with me. I cannot avoid being the centre of my world. The world exists for me only if I experience it. I discover the world and give it meaning. This is what Levinas calls *totaliser* (to totalise): through my observation, actions and giving meaning, I make the world my world.

The relation to another person, the other, is more complicated. I can make him a part of my world and consider him only in so far as he has a meaning for me. If I try to understand what the other feels and thinks, I do this through my own experiences; I consider the other as myself, as an *alter ego* (another I). But I can also consider the other as a fully fledged notme, recognising the otherness *(altérité)* of the other. In the recognition of the other as an other, I transcend my own world and touch the infinite (*L'infini*). In my relation to the other, I am profoundly caught in a tension between totality and infinity[4] (Levinas 1966). It makes the other vulnerable: he can be totalised and reduced through my interests and meanings, or he can be recognised in his otherness.

Levinas finds a metaphor for this vulnerability in the image of the face. The other offers me his face and, in doing so, invites me to assume my primary responsibility towards him, to care for the other. This responsibility is the basis for all morality. All that can be said about the good life, in terms of norms and values, rights and duties, obligations and proscriptions, or ideals, is deduced from my relation with the other and the invitation it holds to take primary responsibility. This invitation does not follow from the other's intentional actions; it is an inherent consequence of the encounter. But it remains an invitation, not an obligation. I can freely accept the invitation or not. I can concretise the acceptance by assuming my responsibility in my own way. But I cannot escape being invited to take my primary responsibility to care for the other. The more the other is vulnerable and does not or cannot lay any claim, the greater is my responsibility.

Contrary to the social life ethics proposed in this chapter, Levinas does not rely on reciprocity. For him, it is not because of a self-interested hope for reciprocity that I assume my responsibility to care for the other. It is an intrinsic primary invitation with which I, and I alone, am confronted, and which I have to decide to take up or not. It may lead to self-sacrifice, causing some to call Levinas' work a philosophy of holiness (de Saint-Cheron 2006).

One does not, however, have to believe in holiness or in complete self-sacrifice to recognise that people are sensitive to others and to the commonality in their fate. The capacity for empathy and for sympathy is the intuitive ground on which common self-interest can be developed. Whereas the first is a social emotional intuition, the latter is a more cognitive, more socially constructed vision.

Promoting common self-interest

Common self-interest is not a natural condition. It is a social cognitive construction based on the social emotion of sympathy. It is an ethical standard, to be learned through enculturation in upbringing, education, social relations and experiences. It is to be cultivated and encouraged in the community and in state interventions.

According to Kohlberg moral development occurs throughout six stages, classified in three levels, from an 'obedience and punishment orientation' to a 'conscience or principle orientation' (Kohlberg 1976: 376). Children begin at the selfish moral level, avoiding trouble or seeking opportunities for satisfying one's own needs, and ideally end as adults with autonomous moral judgments based on universal and consistent principles. Not all individuals reach the end stage. Development depends on maturity and social learning. The point here is not to discuss Kohlberg's theory but to illustrate the idea that moral development begins with selfishness and that surpassing selfishness is a matter of education and learning.

Let me add another example. In his original version of the social control approach, Hirschi (1969) distinguished four bonds to society: attachment to persons, commitment in a line of activities, involvement in conventional activities and beliefs in social norms and values. In my view, we must understand the emergence of these bonds in a dynamic way. First, children attach to persons, to their caring parents and later possibly to their nursery school teacher. These attachments provide the starting motivation for the children to commit themselves in, for example, education and to become involved in activities which are promoted by the parents and the teachers as conventional. Later, when the commitment and the involvement provide gratifications on their own, the children will also comply more easily with the norms and the values which facilitate these activities and the extended attachment to the 'generalised other'. It is the original intimate and need-satisfying attachment which forms the basis for the development of a more comprehensive, socially embedded moral view.

Likewise, investing self-interested motivation into the project of common self-interest is to be learned and promoted. It begins with selfish children who, like all humans, may feel some empathetic intuitions with their carers. These intuitions are opportunities to make them experience satisfaction in being with others and doing things together with them. During their growing up, children can experience gratification if they contribute to a collaborative ambience in their family, the class room, in their neighbourhood, among their peers. Gradually they (and adults) can be made to understand that their self-interest is best served in a respectful and supportive social climate. The goal is to bring them to recognise that pursuing their own career, wealth and pleasure goes together with doing their share in the pursuit of high-quality social life, that this is not a limitation of self-interest, but a canalisation of it in a social approach to their own opportunities and welfare. The pedagogy of such understanding will focus on promoting primarily the ethical attitudes of respect, solidarity and taking active responsibility [...].

Obviously, the school is an ideal environment for such pedagogy. Seeing the commonality in the pursuit of self-interest can be favoured through school programmes, the school ethos and in the way school performances are sanctioned positively and negatively. The latter must not only address the individual learning achievements, but appreciate also the socially constructive attitudes and behaviour, such as, for example, a cooperative and supportive attitude towards class mates, the contribution to a constructive class climate, the willingness for deliberation. And of course, using restorative processes in the response to school disciplinary problems is a crucial practice in such pedagogy.

But the school is not alone. Perceiving self-interest in close dependency with common interest is a vision that should be expressed in all social institutions and agencies, and be visible in all politics. It should, above all, speak through the way democracy is practised [...].

Ethical guidelines serving common self-interest

The ideal form of living together is a Utopia in which each individual enjoys a large margin of self-determination, in harmony with and supported by others who enjoy an equal margin and who cooperate in the quest for enlarging it. The margins and the harmony are not based simply on a negotiated distribution of liberty, but rather on the trust in the common self-interest that reciprocal help and support, when needed, will increase liberty for all. Hence, social life is based on permanent dialogue and participation. The distinction between society and community is meaningless, because the collectivity is governed with a view to individual and collective emancipation, in which autonomy and solidarity are not seen as opposed principles, but as mutually reinforcing. Social life draws its strength not from threat, coercion and fear, but from persuasion and motivation, based on trust, participation and mutual support.

The quality of social life depends on the commitment of the individuals. A collectivity that aims at this Utopia promotes the socio-ethical attitudes that serve it. We could call them virtues. Ethicists list a number of welfare-oriented and duty-based virtues, such as hospitality, mercifulness, forgiveness, loyalty, honesty and the like. Each of these individual attitudes is indeed important in developing constructive and peaceful social relations. But they are in my view included in three attitudes which are fundamental in the furtherance of social life driven by the pursuit of common self-interest: respect, solidarity and active responsibility. I shall argue that values, such as justice or freedom, result from these three.

Respect

Respect is an attitude that recognises the intrinsic value of the other. The recognition may be broad, taking in not only humans, but also nature and objects. It is ethical to respect nature as much as possible or not to destroy objects purposelessly. Respect is more than tolerance, which is a kind of resignation. I endure the noise of a youth party nearby because it would make things worse if I tried to stop it. I tolerate the tabloid press, but I do not see its intrinsic value and I do not respect it. Respect for humans recognises and esteems the intrinsic value of human beings. It is made concrete through the Universal Declaration of Human Rights, for example. The international community recognises that a number of rights are due to all humans, for the simple reason that they are human. Respect is recognisable also in the corrected liberal programmes as presented by Rawls or Rorty.

Respect for human dignity is a bottom-line obligation for all social institutions. Respect is the minimum condition for making living together possible. Respect for persons and groups in the community leads to acceptance of pluralism and multi-culturalism. Agnostics, Christians, Jews and Muslims have different beliefs and ways of life, but these differences are not a reason for withdrawal of esteem. On the contrary, they result in deliberation on how plurality can be preserved and contribute to the quality of social life.

Disrespect is actively rejected. Racist political parties disrespect immigrants. Fundamentalist Muslims disrespect non-Muslims. Such groups threaten the quality of social life in our heterogeneous societies. They intrude upon our common self-interest. If persuasion is not effective, they must be confronted actively, and their behaviour may be criminalised and possibly referred to coercive justice interventions (which, as I argued in the previous chapter, are not based on a punitive apriorism). Not that hardened racists will become more respectful by the criminal justice intervention, but it is an important message to the public at large that disrespect is by no means tolerated.

Solidarity

Solidarity is more specific than respect. People do not naturally feel solidarity with objects or with nature. Solidarity presupposes more commitment than does respect, because it includes a form of companionship and reciprocity of support. It draws on the basic inter-human sympathy described earlier, and it is crucial in bundling our individual self-interests into the project of common self-interest. If combined with pluralism (a consequence of respect), solidarity yields more freedom. We depend on one another to preserve our liberties and we are companions in our pursuit to extend our freedom.

The solidarity I have in view is not selective. It is solidarity with all humans, not with peers only. It is easy to deploy solidarity with peers or with equal partners, because the expectation of reciprocity is at hand. But solidarity with the weak, with those who cannot demand or enforce anything, is more difficult to summon. But still, it is necessary. If there is no solidarity with the weak, the exclusive solidarity among the well-off would in fact increase the gap between them and the weak. It would boost the permanent competitive struggle in the pure liberal societies we described above. Solidarity is most easily activated within a particular community, but as common self-interest is not linked to an area, solidarity should also transcend, the community level: 'this spirit of solidarity may be regarded as a forever-elusive promise of unpremeditated collective togetherness' (Pavlich 2001: 67).

Solidarity holds crucial added value in comparison with liberalism. It is more than avoiding suffering, as Rorty and Boutellier would say. To respect, solidarity adds the commitment to reciprocity, which contributes to common self-interest.

Unlike disrespect, a lack of solidarity cannot be actively suppressed. We are entitled to *demand* from one another not to degrade social life (through disrespect); we only can (and should) *promote* acting so as to improve social life (through solidarity). A society can exert solidarity and oblige its citizens to contribute to it by taxes and imposed contributions to social funds. But the attitude of solidarity cannot be imposed. Its lack is regrettable, but you cannot oblige people to feel companionship. A respectful relation without solidarity is meagre, but it can be a modus vivendi, a way to survive. It will not preclude living together, but it will yield a poor community life. Hence, a good society exerts solidarity and promotes it among its citizens to contribute to a richer community life.

Responsibility

Responsibility links a person to his acts and their consequences. It confronts the self with its own actions. Two kinds of responsibility exist. In passive responsibility, the person is confronted with his actions by others; this is typical in a top-down situation. Passive responsibility is central in the current criminal justice, where the offender has to submit to his responsibility for his acts, imposed by the system. Active responsibility contains a willingness to act. It is an awareness of the link between the self and the actions, and the behaviour that reflects this (Braithwaite and Roche 2001; Braithwaite 2002b).

Active responsibility is typical in leadership but does not automatically lead to ethically positive actions. Many tyrants and gang leaders probably take active responsibility for their choices and actions. That is why active responsibility must be exerted with a view to ethically desirable objectives.

[...]

The active responsibility of citizens is indispensable to the quality of social life. Indeed, a good society depends on committed participation by its citizens or, in Putnam's terms, on social capital. Participants in social life, or citizens, must take their responsibility and respond actively and autonomously to the obligations of social life. In social-life ethics, active responsibility must be oriented towards solidarity with a view to building the common self-interest. In the ideal situation, members take active responsibility for combating disrespect and promoting solidarity.

Other social values

In a self-interested communitarian Utopia, citizens behave according to these three ethical guidelines. However, our societies do currently not function like that and citizens mostly do not behave like that. In the absence of the ideal, we have to do with the achievable. Realistically, we must fall back on less idealistic guidelines to provide a minimum basis for living together. If we do not always take active responsibility driven by solidarity for all, we should at least try to keep as just a balance as possible in our relations, and guarantee for one another space for individual freedom. As long as we cannot summon up enough solidarity to achieve more social freedom for all, we have to divide the available space. It is the lack of these virtues in our current societies that makes it necessary to underline justice and freedom as separate goods.

Justice   Justice is for Rawls, for example, the 'uncompromising ... first virtue of social institutions' (1973: 3). Justice suggests a balance of benefits and burdens, rights and obligations, equally spread. It is a situation, not an individual characteristic of a person, not a virtue. Persons can be more or less righteous, meaning that they are sensitive to justice, that they commit themselves to accomplishing justice where they can. The question is whether righteousness (or probity, or integrity) is a separate socio-ethical guideline, on the same level as respect, solidarity and active responsibility. I do not think so. In my view, taking active responsibility in view of expressing respect and achieving solidarity for all will automatically yield situations which are recognised as 'just' by the stakeholders. A community driven by solidarity and calculating less preconceived balances of justice will achieve more self-determination through common self-interest than one which would assure just balances but offer scarce solidarity only. A problem would occur if solidarity were selective and did not address equally all members of the community. We would then indeed have to fall back on an idea of balance called 'justice'.

But according to what principles do we calculate the balance? Is it just that one citizen lives in a villa in a Brussels suburb and possesses a yacht in Saint Tropez and a chalet in the Swiss Alps, while another citizen living a few kilometres away in a deprived neighbourhood can barely feed his children? Conversely, one might cynically observe that the university professor has to earn his living by getting up early every morning and working hard till late at night, while the unemployed can sleep as long as he wants and still receives his weekly allowance.

Religious, naturalistic, formalistic, utilitarian and care-oriented ethical systems propose different particular visions of how to consider the balance. Rawls' theory of justice (1973), for example, is based on a 'veil of ignorance', the assumption that all members of society are uncertain about their future social position, which keeps them from unjustly abusing their current position. However, research does not confirm the existence of this veil of ignorance. On the contrary, most people have the realistic awareness that their future social position depends largely on their current one.

Out there, 'there is no such thing as justice per se' (Derrida, quoted in Pavlich 2007: 621). The justice balance can take different shapes. Liberals advance justice as the crucial value, and then try to impose their view on how justice has to be understood. It prevents them from having to consider seriously the value of solidarity. Their distributive approach sees benefits and burdens to be divided through confrontation and negotiation of competing interests. It also yields conflicts and abuse of power. In societies based on a distributive concept of justice, conflict is endemic.

That is why I argued to frame the justice ideal in the concept of solidarity. The justice balance is then based on mutual care and partnership, not on formal rights. 'Where there is sufficient community peace, there will be relatively little need for order. Where there is little peace, more order will be needed' (Van Ness 2002: 142). In Duff, we read: 'If people are bound together by strong bonds of mutual affection or concern ... there may be less need and less proper room for contractual definitions of their respective rights and obligations' (Duff 2001: 37). It is the lack of active responsibility for maintaining respect and solidarity which forces collectivities to fall back on formal justice. It is in the interest of the powerful to keep it like that. Hence the current position of justice as a separate and crucial ethical rule.

In principle, it should not be like that. If citizens and institutions took their responsibilities for ensuring respect and solidarity for all, justice would follow automatically, but in a different shape.

Freedom   Liberal freedom is understood as a situation exempt from constraints. In such a conception, my freedom ends where the freedom of others begins. It is as if the amount of freedom is fixed, to be distributed among citizens. Others are rivals in my struggle for the maximum possible amount of freedom. If freedom is an individual good, it includes the freedom of the strongest to exploit the weakest and to bend the rules of justice to one's own interests. But unframed freedom leads to abuses. In Russia, for example, the collapse of the communist regime created space for a wild and uncontrolled capitalism. It resulted in a wide gap between, on the one hand, a few very rich 'plutocrats' who used the margins of deregulation to build their fortunes on fraud and corruption and, on the other hand, the rest of the population which remains poor and powerless. The commotion in April 2006 provoked by the Danish caricatures of Mohammed is illustrative of how unframed freedom of speech can breach the obligation to respect the sensitivity of others.

That is why absolute individual freedom cannot be a fundamental good. It has to be limited by norms that contribute to the quality of social life. Freedom is a social good which needs to be seen through more fundamental principles of respect and solidarity. By intrinsically respecting fellow citizens as they are, you grant them the possibility to be different and to behave accordingly. Furthermore, solidarity will lead to support for others to express their differences freely. Christians help Muslims to build their mosques. Adults help to create space for the young to express their youth culture. The rich help the poor to put their lives back on track. It will lead to more mutual respect and a larger margin for self-determination to live the differences.

Of course, being different and having different interests can raise conflicts. Conflict can be stopped by a powerful intervention, leading to frustration and continuous discontentment. A conflict can also be an opportunity for deliberation about how individual self-interests can be respected and related to the common self-interest. If it is embedded in a climate of mutual respect, there is a considerable chance that negotiation will lead to peaceful solutions. And expressions of solidarity will contribute to finding constructive outcomes. Freedom is not the result of a struggle for selfish interests; it is what we grant to one another.

Wrong against common self-interest

The quality of social life is advanced as the common self-interest. As a consequence, a wrong is what harms the quality of social life.

Are other wrongs imaginable? We have seen in the previous chapter that Duff, for example, distinguishes wrong from harm. In his view, criminal punishment sanctions not so much the causation of harm but the commitment of a wrong (Duff 2002). What could such wrongs be? The death penalty, killing in war, abuse of power to impose harsh living conditions on entire populations, torture of prisoners (suspected of terrorism) – all these actions could be called intrinsically immoral, but they are committed in and by self-declared 'model democracies'. In political and professional life, lying and cheating are common. In sports, committing so-called 'professional faults' is normal. Hence it seems that moral rules and attitudes to them are framed according to the interests they serve. Freud argued that our morality is basically a psychodynamic construct to keep our libido within socially acceptable channels. For Durkheim, the function of morality is to preserve cohesion in society.

Fundamentally, morality and social norms are pragmatic, to preserve self-interest and social life. Evil is not an abstract moral category, as opposed to another abstract category of good. Evil is what hurts or threatens my human dignity, my physical integrity, my social and material territory and comfort, and my common self-interest. Rejection of a wrong is less inspired by an intrinsic attachment to right than by a pragmatic aversion to what our community sees as a threat to our personal and social lives and comfort. 'Crime injures feelings only in a secondary and derived way. Basically, it is the interests which it hurts.'[5] Fortunately, self-interest is mostly well understood as common self-interest, in terms of living in a harmonious collectivity, in a good social life (Putnam 2000). It is difficult to imagine a moral wrong that would be beneficial to social life,[6] or a moral good that would be detrimental to social life. Socio-ethical wrongs and social harmfulness coincide almost entirely.

We are discussing here *socio*-ethics in a self-interested communitarian perspective. Our *individual* ethics may cover a wider realm than the social. Moral judgment is partially a personal affair based on personal criteria. But socially, the only touchstone is common self-interest. Some behaviour may be considered ethically reprehensible but be irrelevant for the quality of social life. We may find excessive gluttony or spending of money on senseless luxury decadent or even immoral, but it is difficult to forbid it. Men may wear a beard and women dress in a burka to please Allah. Others cover their head to express their attachment to Jahweh. Still others feel obliged to attend a religious service every week to pray to God. They do so because of personal religious beliefs. A good society must facilitate religious activities out of respect for plurality, but it cannot impose religious obligations on those who do not believe in Allah, Jahweh or God. That would degrade social life into an absolutist regime with no freedom of thought or speech. It is what happened in Afghanistan under the Taliban's rule. The achievements of the Enlightenment guaranteeing personal rights and freedoms would be lost. A Talibanised society is not what we want. The public rule is not pleasing God but participating constructively in social life. The quality of social life is the ultimate value in the quest for socio-ethics.

A society that serves the quality of social life will limit enforcement of public order and norms to what is needed to ensure this quality. Why, for example, is there a debate about whether criminal justice should intervene in some types of sexual behaviour among consenting adults or in the use of drugs? While there may be a large majority which considers such behaviours undesirable or even unethical, there is no agreement on whether they are so harmful to other people or to social life that they justify the authorities' intrusion into individual rights and freedoms. Authorities cannot interfere coercively in our lives unless it serves to prevent harm to fellow citizens or to public life.

This harm principle is found in many propositions (Feinberg 1991). Von Hirsch and Jareborg (1990) distinguish four types of 'damage to standards of living' to decide on the blameworthiness of a crime. Braithwaite and Pettit (1990) speak in terms of 'intrusion upon dominion'. Boutellier (2000) advances 'victimalisation' as the 'moral minimum' to underpin a commonly acceptable criminal justice system. They all consider harm or damage to others or to collective life as the reason to criminalise behaviour. Of course, behaviour may be harmful by accident whereas wrongfulness lies in the *intention* to cause harm. But still, wrongfulness depends on *the harm* intended, and the degree of wrongfulness on the degree of harm intended.

That brings us back to the core business of this book – responding to crime. If harmfulness is the reason for criminalisation, should the social reaction not aim primarily to repair the harm rather than to punish the wrong? [...] we now clearly see the logical inconsistency of defining crime in terms of harm, as the reason for prohibiting behaviour, and responding to it by punishing, making reparation of the harm more difficult.

Comparing ethics in restorative justice and in punitive justice

At the end of the previous chapter, the punitive aphorism in the current criminal justice system was rejected. We can now test this aphorism against the guidelines for an ethics oriented towards common self-interest. At first glance, advancing respect, solidarity and active responsibility as the basis of socio-ethical behaviour may seem to be mere rhetoric. Who would object to these virtues? Let us examine whether they also guide the current criminal procedures.

Is respect an ethical guideline in the punitive apriorism in criminal justice? Respect for the victim is absent, because he is not included in the punitive reflections. The victim can, of course, ask for compensation according to civil law, but this procedure is subordinated to the public criminal procedure. Punitive retributivism is focused on the offender. Considering the offender as a moral agent and treating him in a just way recognises him as a competent responsible human being who understands right and wrong and is able to make free choices and decisions, and as a citizen with guaranteed rights. Retributivists consider it an expression of respect when they state that offenders have the right to be punished. But the respect is not complete. The offender is not respected as a whole person with personal interests and interpretations, possibly including a willingness to make up for his misbehaviour. In the end, the offender has to submit to a proportionate punishment. Once a crime has been committed, respect for the person is withdrawn. The offender is judged as a moral agent to be considered guilty, but not as a morally and socially competent citizen who might be motivated to contribute to a constructive response to the problems caused by his crime.[7]

I do not see solidarity – companionship and mutual support – in the punitive apriorism. The response does not support the victim. The suffering and harm of the victim are registered only to assess the guilt of the offender, not as needs that are important per se. Support for victims is located at the margins of the criminal justice system and allowed only in so far as it does not impede the criminal justice investigation and procedure aimed at imposing a proportionate punishment on the offender. That does not help the victim. On the contrary, the punishment usually hampers possible reparation. In restorative justice, principled solidarity with the victim is evident, though we shall see that practice sometimes fails in this regard. Solidarity with the offender appears through the attempt to avoid social exclusion. On the contrary, the offender is encouraged to make up for his conduct in order to preserve his position as an integrated member in social life.

Responsibility is central to retributivism. Current penal justice holds the offender responsible by imposing on him the obligation to respond for his misconduct, but again the responsibility is incomplete. Responsibility only means being forced into criminal procedures and accepting the negative consequences. It is a passive, retrospective form of responsibility to which the offender is submitted by the criminal justice system. He is not supposed to take active responsibility in order to try to find a constructive solution to the problems he created. The victim, equally, is considered only as a passive object of the victimisation. His only responsibility is to contribute to the criminal procedure by reporting the crime and acting as witness. Current criminal justice in fact burdens its agents with a crucial form of active responsibility: they must censure criminal behaviour and impose proportionate punishments, and do so according to legal procedures and other standards. As we have seen, restorative justice largely relies on active responsibility. The offender's active responsibility includes the obligation to contribute actively to the reparation of the harm. The victim is encouraged, but not obliged, to assume the general citizen's responsibility for trying to find peace- promoting solutions. Restorative justice also stands for responsible collectivities, bound by obligations to search for socially constructive responses within the rules of law.

This brief comparison demonstrates that socio-ethical attitudes or virtues, such as respect, solidarity for all and active responsibility, are more clearly inherent to restorative justice than to the punitive apriorism. Hence restorative justice is more likely to contribute constructively to social life and relations. The priority for the quality of social life, as expressed in the communitarian Utopia, underlies the bottom-up approach in restorative justice. It appears through a priority for informal regulations, as opposed to imposed procedures and outcomes. The point of departure for restorative justice, as in social life ethics, is that solutions must primarily be sought through the human and social resources in social life itself. This is opposed to the top-down approach in traditional criminal justice, where decisions are imposed according to strict rules, leaving restricted room for the views and interests of those directly concerned.

Conclusion

This chapter is based on two observations: (1) we all are pursuing self-interest in a broad sense, directly or indirectly; and (2) we cannot but be influenced and channelled by our inescapable living with others. From these observations, it follows that we can demand from one another that we do not hamper one another, and socio-ethically advise that we at least partly merge the achievement of our self-interest in a project of common self-interest, which is investing in the quality of our social life. Common self-interest expresses the intrinsic permanent tension between a tendency to satisfy our self-interest uncompromised and the ethical norm of channeling the achievement of our self-interests through a common self-interest. It may be seen as a paradox,[8] but it is a fundamental condition of our human existence. As for Sisyphus in the Greek myth, there is a permanent tension between the ideals we are pursuing and what we actually can achieve. An ideal community, as an area of shared values and interests, of mutual understanding, and of an emancipating balance between support and control, does not exist; it would be counterproductive to believe that it does. But still, we understand intuitively, based on partial and temporary experience, that such a community is a valuable ideal. We need this tension as a source of hope that things can go better than they currently do, and as a motivation to keep trying.

The majority of victims are not captured by anger or a need for revenge. What they want is repair, an explanation and the possibility of going on with their life in peace (Strang 2002). Most offenders understand that they have committed an unlawful act and that they risk a sanction for it, which they hope to keep as low as possible. That is probably a realistic estimation of how the two most prominent protagonists begin a restorative process. They hope to get something from it for their own sake. During the process, both begin gradually to understand that there is more. The victim becomes aware of the benefits he gets from the reparative actions by the offender and appreciates the restorative value of a well reintegrated offender; the offender realises the harm he has caused and understands that his social prospects will be better if he assumes his responsibility by making up for the harm he has caused. Both recognise that they have interest in finding a constructive solution, so that they can live in peace in a supportive social climate. Their self-interest is integrated in the project of common self-interest.

Common self-interest is the glue of social life. Promoting common self-interest is its drive [...] it is observable in social movements and a multitude of social, political, educational and problem-solving practices focused on enhancing the quality of social life. The socio-ethical basis explored in this chapter encompasses more than responding constructively to crime. It is about how citizens participate decisively in the way society and community are governed through social, economic, welfare and cultural policies, and about how they are committed and interact in daily life. Restorative justice, in the restricted version presented in the first chapter, is part of this social movement, is largely inspired by it and aims to contribute to its development, but it does not encompass the whole of this view. Restorative justice does not aim to change the way we live, but the way we deal with crime.

[...]

Notes

1 In the same sense, Nussbaum (1993) contrasted the old Greek concepts 'dikê' (Plato), the strict retributive approach which 'knows neither equity nor grace, but only cares for strict and simple justice' (Nussbaum 1993: 219), with 'epieikeia' (Aristoteles), which recognises 'imperfect human efforts and complex obstacles to doing well' (ibid.: 219), and leads to equity, mercy and more constructive ways of responding to crime. Nussbaum also called this 'good feminist thought' (ibid.: 248).
2 So, for example, conferencing in welfare issues or in school contexts may, more than conferencing in criminal matters, be seen through the ethics of care.
3 The moral relationship between pursuing self-interest and acting for the good of others is the subject of Bloomfield (2008). As this appeared after this manuscript was sent to press, I could not give it the full attention it deserves.
4 *Totalité et infini: essai sur l'extériorité* (1961) is considered the first grand opus by Levinas.
5 'Le crime ne blesse les sentiments que d'une façon secondaire et dérivée. Primitivement, ce sont les intérêts qu'il lèse' (Maxwell 1914, cit. in Debuyst 1990: 357).
6 Some would not agree. They may suggest that, for example, torturing a prisoner in order to extract information about criminal or terrorist networks may be ethically reprehensible, but beneficial for preserving safety in social life. It is not my view. The ethical rejection of inhumane and cruel treatment is not an abstract rule but based on a fundamental human right which is meant to safeguard a minimal quality in the way people and states interact. Moreover, one can doubt whether authorising torture really is constructive for social life.
7 This objection applies less to Duff's approach to punishment (2001), but the problem remains the punitive apriorism.
8 As Dan Van Ness wrote in a comment on an earlier version of this chapter: 'It is as though a person has articulated all the reasons to disbelieve that there is a God but then proposes living according to Christian values.'

References

Barber, B. (2003) *Strong Democracy. Participatory Politics for a New Age*, 20th anniversary edn. Berkeley, CA: University of California Press.
Bazemore, G. and Schiff, M. (eds) (2001) *Restorative Community Justice. Repairing Harm and Transforming Communities*. Cincinnati, OH: Anderson.
Bell, D. (1993) *Communitarianism and Its Critics*. Oxford: Clarendon Press.
Bloomfield, P. (2008) *Morality and Self-interest*. Oxford: Oxford University Press.
Bottoms, A. (2003) 'Some sociological reflections on restorative justice', in A. von Hirsch, J. Roberts, A. Bottoms, K. Roach and M. Schiff (eds), *Restorative Justice and Criminal Justice: Competing or Reconcilable Paradigms*. Oxford: Hart, pp. 79–113.
Boutellier, H. (1996) 'Beyond the criminal justice paradox. Alternatives between law and morality', *European Journal on Criminal Policy and Research*, 4 (4): 7–20.

Boutellier, H. (2000) *Crime and Morality. The Significance of Criminal Justice in Post-Modern Culture.* Dordrecht: Kluwer Academic.

Braithwaite, J. (1989) *Crime, Shame and Reintegration.* Cambridge: Cambridge University Press.

Braithwaite, J. (2002b) 'In search of restorative jurisprudence', in L.Walgrave (ed.), *Restorative Justice and the Law.* Cullompton: Willan, pp. 150–67.

Braithwaite, J. (2006) 'Doing justice intelligently in civil society', *Journal of Social Issues,* 62 (2): 393–409.

Braithwaite, J. and Pettit, P. (1990) *Not Just Desert. A Republican Theory of Criminal Justice.* Oxford: Oxford University Press.

Braithwaite, J. and Roche, D. (2001) 'Responsibility and restorative justice', in G. Bazemore and M. Schiff (eds), *Restorative Community Justice. Repairing Harm and Transforming Communities.* Cincinnati, OH: Anderson, pp. 63–84.

Christie, N. (1977) 'Conflicts as property', *British Journal of Criminology,* 17 (1): 1–15.

Crawford, A. (2002a) 'The state, community and restorative justice: heresy, nostalgia and butterfly collecting', in L. Walgrave (ed.), *Restorative Justice and the Law.* Cullompton: Willan, pp. 101–29.

Crawford, A. and Clear, T. (2001) 'Community justice: transforming communities through restorative justice?', in G.Bazemore and M. Schiff (eds), *Restorative Community Justice. Repairing Harm and Transforming Communities.* Cincinnati, OH: Anderson, pp. 127–49.

Daems, T. (2007) *Making Sense of Penal Change: Punishment, Victimization and Society.* PhD thesis in Criminology. Leuven: K.U. Leuven.

Daly, K. (2002) 'Restorative justice: the real story', *Punishment and Society,* 4 (1): 55–79.

de Saint-Chéron, M. (2006) *Entretiens avec Emmanuel Levinas (1992–1994).* Paris: PUF, Livre de poche.

Debuyst, C. (1990) 'Pour introduire une histoire de la criminology: les problématiques du départ', *Déviance et Société,* 14 (4): 347–76.

Duff, A. (2001) *Punishment, Communication and Community.* Oxford: Oxford University Press.

Duff, A. (2002) 'Restorative punishment and punitive restoration', in L.Walgrave (ed.), *Restorative Justice and the Law.* Cullompton: Willan.

Duyndam, J. and Poorthuis, M. (2003) *Levinas.* Rotterdam: Lemniscaat.

Etzioni, A. (1995) *The Spirit of Community. Rights, Responsibilities and the Communitarian Agenda.* London: Fontana Press.

Etzioni, A. (1996) *The New Golden Rule. Community and Morality in a Democratic Society.* New York: Basic Books.

Gilligan, C. (1982) *In a Different Voice: Psychological Theory and Women's Development.* Cambridge, MA: Harvard University Press.

Hirschi, T. (1969) *Causes of Delinquency.* Berkeley, CA: University of California Press.

Hudson, B. (2006a) 'Beyond white man's justice: race, gender and justice in late modernity', *Theoretical Criminology,* 10 (1): 29–47.

Kohlberg, L. (1976) 'Moral stages and moralization', in T. Lickona (ed.), *Moral Development and Behavior: Theory, Research and Social Issues.* New York: Holt, Rinehart & Winston, pp. 31–53.

Leest, J. (2004) 'Gevoelige zaken. Een zorgethisch perspectief op herstelrecht' ('Sensitive matters. A care-ethical perspective on restorative justice'), *Tijdschrift voor Herstelrecht,* 4 (1): 38–47.

Levinas, E. (1966) *De totaliteit en het oneindige: essay over de exterioriteit (Totality and Infinity: An Essay on Exteriority)*, trans, from French: *Totalité et infini:essai sur l'extériorité* (1961). Rotterdam: Lemniscaat.

McCold, P. and Wachtel, T. (1997) *Community Is Not a Place.* Paper presented at the International Conference on Justice without Violence, Albany, NY, 5–6 June. Online at: http://www.realjustice.org/pages/albany.html.

MacIntyre, A. (1983) *After Virtue. A Study in Moral Theory*, 2nd edn. Notre Dame, IN: University of Notre Dame Press.

Masters, G. and Smith, D. (1998) 'Portia and Persephone revisited: thinking about feeling in criminal justice', *Theoretical Criminology,* 2 (1): 5–27.

Merton, R. (1938) 'Social structure and anomie', *American Sociological Review,* 3 (3): 672–82.

Nussbaum, M. (1993) 'Equity and mercy', *Philosophy and Public Affairs,* 22 (2): 83–125; reprinted in J. Murphy (ed.) (1995) *Punishment and Rehabilitation*, 3rd edn. Belmont, CA: Wadsworth, pp. 212–48.

Pavlich, G. (2001) 'The force of community', in H. Strang and J. Braithwaite (eds), *Restorative Justice and Civil Society.* Cambridge: Cambridge University Press, pp. 56–68.

Pavlich, G. (2002) 'Towards an ethics of restorative justice', in L. Walgrave (ed.), *Restorative Justice and the Law.* Cullompton: Willan, pp. 1–18.

Pavlich, G. (2005) *Governing Paradoxes of Restorative Justice.* London and Portland, OR: Glasshouse Press.

Pavlich, G. (2007) 'Ethics, universal principles and restorative justice', in G. Johnstone and D. Van Ness (eds), *Handbook of Restorative Justice.* Cullompton: Willan, pp. 615–30.

Putnam, R. (2000) *Bowling Alone.* New York: Simon & Schuster.

Rawls, J. (1972) *A Theory of Justice.* Oxford: Oxford University Press.

Rorty, R. (1989) *Contingency, Irony and Solidarity.* Cambridge: Cambridge University Press.

Strang, H. (2002) *Repair or Revenge: Victims and Restorative Justice.* Oxford: Clarendon.

Sullivan, D. and Tift, L. (2006a) 'Introduction: the healing dimension of restorative justice: a one-world body', in D. Sullivan and L. Tift (eds), *Handbook of Restorative Justice.* Oxford: Routledge, pp. 1–16.

Van Ness, D. (2002b) 'Creating restorative systems', in L. Walgrave (ed.), *Restorative Justice and the Law.* Cullompton: Willan, pp. 130–49.

Van Stokkom, B. (2004) 'Verantwoorden en pacifiëren' ('Explaining and pacifying'), *Tijdschrift voor Herstelrecht,* 4 (1): 52–6.

Van Stokkom, B. (2005) 'Does punishment need hard treatment?', in E. Claes, R. Foqué and T. Peters (eds), *Punishment, Restorative Justice and the Morality of Law.* Antwerp and Oxford: Intersentia, pp. 165–77.

von Hirsch, A. and Jareborg, N. (1991) 'Gauging criminal harm: a living-standard analysis', *Oxford Journal of Legal Studies,* 11: 1–38.

21 Restorative justice and the philosophical theories of criminal punishment

Conrad G. Brunk

[...]

For centuries legal theorists and philosophers of law have been debating the issue of how to justify the practice of criminal punishment. What defines 'punishment' as a practice differing from other practices, such as pure revenge, or therapeutic aid, or moral reform? Is punishment in a legal context something quite different from discipline of children in a family context, or is their moral basis very similar? How does criminal punishment relate to the aims and functions of law in a society? Under what conditions can it be justified? Who can legitimately be punished? What is the appropriate form of punishment? How much punishment is appropriate to the offense or the offender?

Until the twentieth century the answers to these philosophical questions, at least in the Western legal and philosophical tradition, have fallen into two very different schools of thought. One of these, the retributivist, is strongly rooted in various religious and theological cultures, even though it has developed modern secular interpretations, which makes it of special interest for those interested in the spiritual roots of criminal justice. This school of thought views punishment largely in terms of doing justice to the offender in order to 'make the wrong right.' The other major school, the utilitarian, has almost entirely secular roots, and its view of legal punishment is much more functional. It is concerned primarily with using punishment as a tool for protecting the legal order by *deterring* offenders and would-be offenders from breaking the law.

In the twentieth century, two additional schools of thought have emerged, both of which have seen themselves somewhat as *alternatives* to punishment. The one, which actually came to dominate penal theory in Europe and North America, was the rehabilitation view, which sought to 'cure' or reform offenders, so that they could become law-abiding citizens. The other, the restitution view, has been far less widely accepted, but has contributed significantly to renewed interest in the rights and interests of victims. Its primary concern, like retributivism, is with righting the wrong, not by inflicting pain upon the offender but by compensating the victim.

The philosophical and jurisprudential debates over the justification of criminal punishment reflect several enduring concerns about what purposes it should serve in society. These concerns need to be taken seriously in any theory of punishment—not only because they tend to drive the political agenda surrounding penal practice, but also because they raise legitimate issues about justice in a society. These concerns about what a system of criminal punishment should accomplish can be summarized as follows:

1. It should *protect,* as much as possible, innocent, law abiding citizens from the harms the law is designed to prevent. It should do this by encouraging citizens generally to obey

the law or 'deterring' them from breaking it. The underlying assumption here is that the fundamental aim of law is to maintain a morally acceptable community (a 'moral order') in which all can live in relative peace, security, and well-being. If law is not obeyed, this aim is not accomplished.

2.   Offenders should receive their *just desert.* The underlying moral idea in this concern is that the punishment should be appropriate for, or should 'fit,' the crime—it should be appropriate for the nature of the offense, and it should be neither more nor less than offenders *deserve.*

3.   It should somehow *redress* the injustice done by the criminal offense by requiring offenders to 'pay for' their wrong-doing. The underlying moral concern here is that when a wrong is done to someone, justice requires that it be made right. There is also the assumption that the wrong-doer is the one who should make it right.

These three are by far the most strongly articulated concerns about criminal punishment, both in the public debate and in the traditional philosophical theories of punishment. However, there is one additional concern that occasionally is expressed in the debate, although until recently it has had far less influence on theory and policy:

4.   Punishment should not make the offender a 'worse' person. Ideally, it should even make him or her a better person. This concern takes different forms in different theories of punishment—as moral reform, as therapeutic 'cure,' as conformity out-of fear, or as a social integration.

The discussion below of the different philosophical theories of punishment will illustrate how each of them makes one of these concerns the primary one, and interprets it in a par- ticular way. However, most of these theories take all of these concerns seriously, especially the first three. In my opinion, any approach to criminal justice *must* provide an adequate response to all four of these concerns. One of the major reasons why Restorative Justice is not taken seriously in jurisprudential circles is that it is viewed as ignoring these fundamen- tal concerns, especially the first three. Unfortunately, the advocates of Restorative Justice often reinforce this perception by themselves, talking and writing as if these concerns are not important, or are even illicit. My aim is to show that Restorative Justice approaches can, and do, take these concerns seriously and in fact respond to them in a more adequate way than do the traditional theories.

In the following sections I want to summarize how each of the traditional theories of punishment has tried to address these fundamental concerns about criminal justice. I will also summarize some of the major criticisms each of these theories receives from proponents of the others. However, after summarizing these problems in the traditional theories, I want to show how the restorative approach to criminal justice avoids many of these problems in addressing the fundamental concerns.

The retributive approach

The retributive theory is probably the oldest theory of criminal punishment. Its roots are deeply set in religious and theological ideas, and it has its strongest impact in traditional theocratic political structures. In deeply religious theocratic societies, there is little or no distinction between a moral wrong, or 'sin,' and a legal wrong, or 'crime.' Since according to this view the civil law itself is part of the divine law, a legal offense is therefore an offense against the deity. Thus, it is natural that criminal punishment in such societies is indistinguishable from divine retribution. In many religions, a fundamental conception of moral wrongdoing, or sin, holds that the only way it can be atoned for is through the suffering of the offender, or, as in the Judeo-Christian tradition, the suffering of a sacrificial substitute. Hence the principle that "Only through the shedding of blood is there remission of sin."

It is easy to see how the retributive approach to punishment developed its focus upon pain, suffering, or even death, as the only thing that could 'pay for' a criminal offense. Only an eye can atone for an eye, or a tooth for a tooth, because it is primarily the deity who has been wronged, and how else does one 'recompense' a deity? If the injustice of an offense is the injured relationship with God, how else can the injury to God be restored except through the exaction of a similar injury—or an act of forgiveness and grace?

There is no need to engage in a debate about the theological merits of this view. It need only be pointed out here that, independent of its power as a theological concept, there is a serious question to be asked about its translation into the realm of civil law and politics. It would be wrong to infer from its theological significance its relevance or usefulness as a theory of civil law and punishment, especially in secular, pluralistic societies.[1]

There is, however, a moral intuition underlying the concept of divine retribution which is relevant. This intuition has both a light and a dark side. The dark side is the desire for vengeance which all of us are capable of feeling when we believe we are seriously wronged. It seems almost a universal human impulse. In many ancient societies the impulse for vengeance was institutionalized in the practice of the blood feud—of which modern genocidal warfare is the analogue. I suspect that the idea of divine vengeance grew out of this deep-seated, very human, emotion. However, it is important to understand that the desire for vengeance is related to a much loftier moral intuition, also widely embraced in diverse human cultures. In Western culture it is known as the Golden Rule. If we ought to "do unto others as we wish them to do unto us," then when others violate us in a serious way, it is natural to feel that they should have no objection to our treating them in exactly the same way. In other words, the impulse for vengeance is the dark, flip side of a profound moral principle, even though acting on the impulse at the same time violates it (you, in fact, would *not* want to be punished in this way, even if you had committed an offense).

The traditional philosophical theories of retributive punishment have tried to give a coherent explanation of why it is justifiable to wreak pain, suffering, deprivation, or death upon an offender. Modern secular retributive philosophers and legal theorists cannot do this in the traditional theological terms, so they look elsewhere for a coherent moral answer. The usual answer is that the infliction of a similar harm on the offender is the only way *justice can be restored.* How is it that justice can be restored by inflicting back upon the offender a harm similar to that which he or she inflicted upon others? The answer is that the offender *deserves* this harm, and to fail to give the offender the punishment would be an injustice to the *offender,* as well as to society and the victims. Further, the victims of the offense (like the deity in the theological version) have a *right* to see the harm inflicted upon the offender. In this story, justice is restored by retributive infliction of harm on the offender because the offender has been required to *take full responsibility* for his or her action. As several modern retributivists have put it, the offender has freely chosen to violate his or her victim, and thus has in some sense chosen the punishment.[2]

The retributive theory takes the primary aim of criminal punishment to be that of responding to the second and third fundamental concerns identified above. The point of punishment is to *right the wrong* done in the criminal offense. This is accomplished by focusing on the offenders and giving them their 'just deserts.' It is talked about in terms of 'paying back the debt' that is owed to society. The offenders' suffering or loss is what constitutes the 'pay back' to society and the victims.[3]

Despite many attempts to explain how the infliction of harm on offenders actually makes things right again, or 'restores justice,' retributive theorists have not offered a persuasive account. In retributive theory, the 'righting of the wrong' remains an abstract, almost metaphysical, proposition. Somehow the moral balance of the universe is restored by the suffering of the offender. Because of retributivism's preoccupation with infliction of harm as the means by which wrongs are made right, it simply blinds itself to the fact that the real injustice of an offense is the loss and harm suffered by the *victims*. This injustice is not addressed by the suffering of the offender—the loss is not restored, the suffering is not compensated, the broken relationships with victims and society are not mended. The injustice remains.[4]

In my view, the retributive theory of criminal punishment is correct in its basic premise— *that punishment must be directed at redressing the injustice of the offense.* It is also correct in its insistence that justice can be restored only when offenders are made to take responsibility for righting the wrong. The strongest aspect of the retributivist theory lies in its insistence that offenders be treated as morally responsible members of the community. They are not to be used as instruments for deterring others, and they are not to be treated as if they are sick and irresponsible. This is why retributivism insists that the punishment should 'fit the crime' in several respects. It should be appropriate in the sense that it should be neither more nor less than what is justly 'deserved.' This is the truth in retributivism's *lex talionis* principle—'eye for eye' means no more than one eye for one eye (hence, no head for an eye). In this sense it is a limiting principle. It is a concern that punishment not constitute an injustice to the offender. Unfortunately the retributivist preoccupation with pain infliction works against its own concern for just treatment of the offender, because in practice the typical pain and deprivation sanctions demoralize and dehumanize offenders.

So, there is much in the retributivist theory that is very close to Restorative Justice. Restorative Justice is also concerned primarily with *making the wrong right* or *restoring the justice* of the situation. It is concerned with demanding that offenders *take responsibility* for their actions by actively making things right with the victims. It is also concerned that punishment not treat offenders unjustly. But, as we shall see, Restorative Justice gives a much more concrete and practical account of how the injustice done to victims can be redressed, and of how justice can be done to the offender as well.

The utilitarian deterrence approach

The predominant modern theory of punishment has been the utilitarian deterrence view. In this view, the first of the fundamental concerns about punishment—that it should protect society from offenders—is primary. The justification of punishment lies in its ability to deter people from breaking the law. It is called the 'utilitarian' view because its sole criterion for deciding what kind and amount of punishment is justified is an assessment of the overall social consequences of the punishment—will it maximize the general social good?

The modern utilitarian approach to punishment was given its first systematic defense by the Italian scholar Cesar Beccaria, with his classic treatise *On Crimes and Punishments* (1764), and it was popularised in the nineteenth century by the influential British utilitarian philosophers Jeremy Bentham and John Stuart Mill. The utilitarian approach to punishment was considered in its day to be radically 'humanitarian' because its advocates were the first to call for limitations on punishment, including opposition to torture, corporal punishment, and capital punishment, and were leaders in the prison reform movement.

The utilitarians rejected the theological and metaphysical assumptions of the retributive theory, considering the idea that suffering can atone for wrong to be simply a rationalization for primitive emotions of revenge. Nevertheless, the utilitarian deterrence theory retained a preoccupation with *pain and suffering* as the most effective means of deterring potential offenders. This is because the theory is profoundly rooted in the modern theory of the state and law, which defines the state as that entity in a society having a monopoly on the use of force, and law simply as the rules or commands of the state backed up by the threat of that force.[5] Thus, the modern move from theocratic to secular conceptions of the state did not change the preoccupation with *pain and suffering* as the primary instrument of punishment.

The utilitarian criticism of retributivism is that it neglects the primary function of criminal punishment, which is to maintain obedience to the legal and social order and thereby protect the welfare of the citizens. Deterrence theory claims its greatest strength to be the protection of society and innocent victims from crime. Thus, it claims to be victim oriented. But in fact, by focusing entirely upon the *potential* victims of crime, it ignores almost completely the *actual* victims. By relying upon the infliction of harm as the major tool of deterrence, sentencing does nothing for the immediate victims of offenses. If retributivism fails because of its concern for restoring some abstract or metaphysical balance of justice, deterrence theory fails in a similar way by formulating punishments to deter unspecified potential offenders from harming unspecified potential victims. In both cases the injustice of the situation created by the actual violation of the actual victims of an offense remains largely irrelevant and unresolved. Deterrence theory provides no mechanism for 'righting the wrong.'

Many social scientific studies have called into question the efficacy of threats of pain, suffering, or deprivation in deterring potential offenders. Without getting into the debate about how deterrence works, or the extent to which it works, one thing that can be said is that there is nothing close to agreement about what the relationship is between the *severity* of criminal sanctions and the *efficacy* of those sanctions. There is considerable evidence that there is little correlation. The best correlation is not between severity of sanction and deterrent effect, but between the *certainty* and *immediacy* of the sanction and deterrent effect. This suggests that the most important consideration in dealing with offenders is not how much pain, suffering, or deprivation of liberty is imposed on them, but rather, how swift and sure the system is able to bring persons to account.

This first point has to do with what is often called 'general deterrence'—which is the effectiveness of the system of sanctions in deterring criminal offenses among the general population. But there is an equally important issue of 'specific deterrence'—which is the deterrence of the specific offender from offending again in the future. The system of imprisonment is so dear to 'law and order' hardliners, because it is thought to be a guarantee of specific deterrence. According to this view, society will be protected from the offenders for as long as they are incarcerated.

But, while incarceration is an effective *short-term* guarantee of social protection, it is notoriously bad as a *long-term* strategy. This is because it so often produces the 'ex-con' who emerges from his punishment even more alienated from society, more psychologically and morally debilitated, and better educated in the art of law-breaking. This person may pose a greater threat to the security of the society than before his or her incarceration.

Deterrence theory claims to give a rational way of determining 'appropriate' punishment—the best punishment is the one that provides the greatest deterrent value with the least cost to society and the least pain and suffering to the offender. But one of the most telling criticisms of deterrence theory comes from the retributivists, who point out the inherent injustice involved in the decision to punish the offender in a certain way because of the effect it will have on *other* potential offenders. It violates the basic moral principle that persons should not be treated solely as the means to accomplishing other social ends—because it justifies types and levels of punishment beyond what may be fair to the offender—as a way of deterring others ('general deterrence').

The rehabilitation approach

The classical debate about the justification of punishment has been between the two theories we have just considered. However, in the twentieth century two additional approaches have emerged, both of which have claimed to offer *alternatives* to punishment because they reject the 'infliction of harm' formula of the traditional views. The first of these, the rehabilitation model, has probably had more influence in the design of penal policy in Europe and North America in this century than any other view. The second, the restitution view, is just beginning to be felt in sentencing policy and in scholarly discussions.

The rehabilitation approach is rooted in the rise of the social and behavioral sciences in the early part of the century and the emergence of what many writers have called the 'therapeutic state.' It is based upon the conceptualization of crime as a deviant behavior stemming from an illness suffered by the offender, the offender's family, or the offender's society. The offender tends to be viewed either as 'patient' or 'victim' (or both). If 'patient,' the offender is not viewed as morally responsible for his actions— the offense is the product of the illness, for which the person is not responsible. The patient role, especially for mental or behavioral illnesses, does not include the capacity to take control of one's situation, one's 'cure' or, certainly, one's social problems. If 'victim,' the offender is also not viewed as morally responsible for the offense—which is a product of the dysfunctions of the social environment. The offender's 'illness' is the product of a larger social 'illness.' The offender is not to blame, and the solution is 'cure' (of both offender and society) rather than 'punishment.'

The prevailing language of penal theory and practice in the mid-twentieth century drew heavily on the rehabilitation model. Prisons came to be known as 'reformatories,' 'rehabilitation centers,' 'correctional facilities,' and what little prison reform took place in this century was largely aimed at providing therapeutic rehabilitation services for inmates. However, the rehabilitation model has been subjected to severe criticism from many quarters. Many social scientists have concluded that the therapeutic rehabilitation project in modern penal institutions has not been effective. There are several reasons for this. One is the recognition that enforced behavioral therapy is rarely successful. Inmates learn quickly how to go through the motions of rehabilitation in order to earn early parole and other concessions. Another is that there is little agreement among clinical professionals about what approaches to offender rehabilitation are appropriate or successful. In addition, the conditions of life in the average prison are far more detrimental to the rehabilitation or reform of inmates than any good served by therapeutic programs.

The general public perceives rehabilitation and reform as failures as well. Not only do many people consider rehabilitation programs ineffective, but also as too 'soft' on the offenders. The public generally resists the 'liberal' view of offenders as victims or patients, because it takes away all blame and all responsibility. In this respect lay persons express a profound agreement with retributive theory. This criticism of therapeutic rehabilitation is shared by many contemporary jurisprudents and the philosophers of law. The criticism is based on the principle that to treat offenders as victims or as patients is to treat them as nonresponsible moral agents, and is thus to deny them their dignity as persons. It is insulting to offenders to impose 'therapy' on them as if they were mentally ill or were merely the deterministic result of unfortunate social conditioning, and then to 'cure' them of their pattern of behavior. This is the forceful message of Anthony Burgess's best-seller novel, *A Clockwork Orange* (1962).

Advocates of a restorative approach to criminal justice sometimes align their view with the rehabilitation theory. But restoration, as will be made clear below, is not the same thing as 'rehabilitation,' at least not in a therapeutic sense. The therapeutic approach to punishment denies the need, even the possibility, of taking personal responsibility for one's actions. Why should one be encouraged to compensate victims if one is not 'at fault' or 'to blame' or 'responsible' in any way? True Restorative Justice is not the same thing as therapeutic rehabilitation. It is not the 'treatment' or 'cure' of a 'sick' offender or a 'sick' society. The restoration of the relationship between offenders and their victims or their society is something far more profound and complex than rehabilitation in the traditional sense of this term.

The restitution approach

All three of the theories of punishment we have considered so far focus primarily upon what should be done to *offenders*. The retributivists want to give them their just deserts, the utilitarians want to deter them (and other potential offenders) from offending, and the rehabilitationists want to cure them. None of them have much, if anything, to say about how criminal justice should take into account the injustice done to the actual *victims* of an offense. Public concern in recent years has recently turned to these victims, as more and more people ask why criminal justice in developed legal systems has largely ignored those who suffer most from offenses. The last two approaches to criminal justice I wish to consider—restitution and restoration—are responses to this growing concern for the role of victims in the criminal justice process.

The restitution approach has its theoretical roots in two recent, closely related economic and political schools of thought. These are neoclassical economics on the one hand, and political libertarianism on the other. Both schools are committed to a strong ideology of the 'minimalist state'—governments should intervene as little as possible in society, and the free market should be allowed to resolve many of the human conflicts governments have traditionally managed. This includes conflicts in the legal arena, which libertarians believe can be resolved largely through private courts and even private enforcers. So, all legal offenses, including criminal offenses, should be treated like compensable torts in civil law, which can be adjudicated in the free marketplace. In essence it reduces the criminal law to civil law (the law of torts). If I commit a criminal assault against you resulting in your injury, why should this be treated any differently than if I, as your mechanic, happen to injure you through a negligent failure to fix the brakes on your car (a civil matter)? In the latter case I am liable for the damages my negligence caused you, and I am required to compensate you. Why should I not simply be held 'liable' for the damage I caused you in the criminal assault? If in the civil case I have 'made everything right' when I pay the damages, why should I not be able to 'make everything right' for the assault in the same way?

Randy E. Barnett, a Chicago law professor, is one of the leading advocates of this approach.[6] In Barnett's view, in a 'pure restitution' system of justice the concept of moral fault would be eliminated (just as it is eliminated in tort law). The only question would be the extent of the 'loss' or harm caused to the victim, and the market value of that loss. Criminal offenses, as Barnett defines them, are not really 'wrongs' against victims. Essentially they are, broadly speaking, simply the 'cost of doing business' in a society. In Barnett's system, the wealthier one is, the more one is able to purchase the right to harm others (and to compensate them for the loss or harm). Every harm or loss is compensable; if compensated adequately, the 'wrong' is removed.

This view has been very attractive to advocates of Restorative Justice for several reasons. First, it rejects the punitive aspects of criminal justice. Barnett, for example, rejects the idea that 'punitive damages' (above those actually needed to compensate the victim's losses) should be awarded so as to add a deterrent effect to the sentence. Secondly, it defines offenses completely in terms of harms to individual victims and not harms to 'society' or to the legal or moral order, and places all the emphasis upon the right of the victim to be compensated. And finally, it establishes a system for evaluating the harms or losses suffered by victims, so that they can be compensated adequately.

However, as we shall see, this is not an adequate account of criminal justice from the point of view of Restorative Justice. Restorative Justice is concerned with the 'injustice' of an offense in a sense that is much broader than what can be defined simply as a monetary loss. It is concerned about the 'wrong' that has been done to the victim and society in terms of the sense of violation and loss of security, as well as the 'wrong' involved in the alienation of the offender from victim and society. Thus, while Restorative Justice is certainly about the compensation of victims, it is concerned with compensation in a much broader sense than is the restitution theory. Mere monetary restitution does not itself fulfill all the requirements of compensation for a wrong committed against a victim (e.g., the sense of violation and the loss of security). Restitution itself does not achieve *restoration* of the relationship between the offender and the victim or the offender and the community It does not deal with all the social and psychological aspects of the 'breach' represented by an offense. Most troubling, from the point of view of social justice, is the fact that the restitution approach significantly advantages the well-off in society over the less-well-off. In reducing crime to 'costs of business' it simply gives to the former opportunities to 'buy' their way past offenses against others that the poor do not have. This is restitution theory's greatest flaw—a flaw recognized most clearly by a full conception of Restorative Justice.

Restorative justice

The four previous approaches to criminal justice and punishment have been the dominant ones within jurisprudence and the philosophy of law, although only the first three have had significant impact upon Western legal and penal systems. Legal theorists are only now beginning to look at the Restorative Justice approach seriously. Strangely enough, it is not because of a sense that the traditional theories have not provided an adequate moral justification for the practice of criminal punishment (which in my view would be an accurate assessment). But rather, it is because the grassroots movement for Restorative Justice initiatives has forced the theorists to start taking it seriously.

One of the few serious attempts to formulate a comprehensive philosophical case for a restorative approach to criminal justice is Wesley Cragg's *The Practice of Punishment: Towards a Theory of Restorative Justice* (1992). Cragg argues that the fundamental goal of legal punishment (and its only moral justification) should be to resolve the disputes that are reflected in criminal offenses in ways that maintain the confidence of victims and the public at large in the capacity of law to fulfill its legitimate functions, and to do this with *the minimum amount of force and violence.* He argues very persuasively that neither of the two dominant traditional theories of justification for legal punishment—the retributive or the utilitarian/deterrent—succeeds in justifying the practice of punishment, for many of the reasons specified above.

According to Cragg, the main function of law is to provide a way of resolving conflicts in the society in a manner involving the minimum use of force and violence. This is the only moral foundation that can be found in a pluralistic society for law as a coercive system. Thus punishment, or sentencing, should be the means by which the law accomplishes this kind of resolution process. The sanctions imposed by the law should not focus on pain or suffering, either as a deterrent or as a 'desert', but on the resolution of the conflict represented by the offense. This 'restorative' resolution needs to be consistent with three objectives. First, the law should *demonstrate* to the public that both the society and those who enforce the law are fulfilling their responsibilities toward the legal order in a way that supports the public good. Secondly, the law should seek to *persuade* people to obey the law voluntarily. And third, the law should *enable* persons to live in accordance with the legal order.

Cragg identifies the central concern of a restorative approach to criminal justice—the resolution of the conflict which is represented in the criminal offense. Criminal sentencing should aim to go as far as possible in this by seeking to repair the damage caused by the offense, but also by ameliorating the conflict situation that produced the offense. This means that sentencing should not only seek as much as possible to repair the damage done to the victim, but it should seek to involve the offender in actively taking responsibility for that repair and also *enabling* offenders to reintegrate into a normal life in the community as law-abiding citizens.

If the aim of criminal justice is the resolution of conflict in a way that restores the preexisting justice or builds a new justice, this means that sentencing alternatives need to be as flexible and diverse as conflict situations can be complex. Because Restorative Justice is freed from the idea that criminal punishment has to 'pay back' the offender with a harm of some kind, it is also freed from a definition of justice in terms of an appropriate amount of harm (either for 'just desert' or for 'sufficient deterrence'); it is free to explore all kinds of ways in which a sentence can bring satisfaction to the victim, the offender, and the community. There need be no fixed a priori definition of a just sentence. A response that solves the problem between victim, offender, and the community in a just way cannot be criticized as "too soft" or "too harsh."

Despite the fact that Restorative Justice approaches are making great inroads into the actual sentencing practices of courts and are daily convincing more and more of those persons involved in law and corrections of its value, it has yet to attract serious discussion among jurisprudents and philosophers of law. The fact that Cragg's groundbreaking book has received little notice in the community of scholars for which it was written is evidence of this. Several reasons could be cited why the Restorative Justice conception has not made significant inroads into secular philosophies of punishment. These reasons have to do with the stereotypes of the Restorative Justice viewpoint held by its critics, stereotypes that are sometimes reinforced by the language of its advocates.

The power of the restorative conception of justice for dealing with the enduring concerns about criminal punishment can be illuminated by showing how it can answer the criticisms of its detractors. The stereotype of Restorative Justice that lies behind these criticisms originates in the traditional philosophical theories. The retributivists claim that the restorative view fails to give offenders 'what they deserve.' The utilitarians fear that the restorative view allows sentencing options which are too lenient to deter either the offender or other potential offenders from breaking the law. They also fear that by abandoning the traditional reliance upon incarceration, it fails to protect the innocent public from dangerous individuals. Can the restorative view answer these criticisms?

Restorative justice and the retributive concern for 'just desert'

We have seen how deeply the retributivist idea of 'just desert' is embedded in our culture. It has roots in many traditional religions as well as in some very important moral principles. But we have also seen that the underlying issue in 'just desert' and 'paying one's debt to society' is that offenders be treated as *morally responsible* persons who can therefore be *held accountable* for their actions and thus made to *take responsibility* for them. But retributive theory has never been able to give a plausible account of how the infliction of harm or deprivation of liberty amounts to *taking responsibility.* Even less has it been able to explain how it *rights the wrong* or *restores justice,* which it claims to do.

The Restorative Justice approach, however, gives a very concrete, practical account of the retributivist concern for 'taking responsibility.' It assumes that the victims of an offense are not simply abstract entities like the 'state' or the 'sovereign,' but rather concrete individuals, institutions, and communities whose interests the law protects. And the way an offender 'rights the wrong' done to the victims is by taking responsibility for the actual, material harm done to them; this is done by 'restoring' through his or her own action as much as is possible what has been lost, not just in financial terms, but also in what are often the much more profound psychological and spiritual terms.

The restorative approach also recognizes another concrete sociological fact: that the broken relationship caused by an offense can only be fully restored if those who are wronged are willing to *allow* the offender to take responsibility. Restoration of the offender, in other words, is the precondition for full responsibility-taking. And reconciliation with victims is often the precondition of full restoration. It is a mistake to defend Restorative Justice on the grounds that it chooses the values of mercy and forgiveness over justice, as many of its critics (and some of its defenders) argue. It is much more accurate to say that forgiveness and reconciliation are critical aspects of restoration, and restoration is an important precondition, if not part of the very definition, of *justice.*

Restorative Justice has much in common with the retributive view of punishment. This statement comes as a shock to many advocates of Restorative Justice, But both are founded upon the supposition that punishment has to do fundamentally with the task of helping people to become responsible members of the moral community. Thus, it ought not be dehumanizing, debilitating, or morally corrupting. Unfortunately, the traditional retributive *mechanism* of punishment—the infliction of pain, suffering, or deprivation—leads precisely to these consequences. Retribution as vengeance does not achieve the ends which the retributive justice theory itself seeks, but defeats them. Restorative Justice, by contrast, does achieve these ends.

Restorative justice and the utilitarian concern for deterrence and social protection

Any approach to criminal justice has to address the strong concern for social protection and deterrence of crime. This is true, not only because it is what the public demands of the criminal justice system, but more importantly because one of the fundamental purposes of law itself is the maintenance of public order, including the protection of the rights and interests of the citizens. Enforcement might not be the defining characteristic of law, as many modern legal positivists claim it to be, but it is a necessary part of the effective functioning of law.

Thus, the enforcement of law requires *sanctions* in some sense of that word, which serve to discourage or *deter* those persons who may not otherwise have sufficient motivation not to offend against the interests of others. Sanctions can take many forms. But, for the reasons discussed earlier, the traditional Western theories of punishment have fixated on threat of pain or deprivation of liberty as the *only* reliable legal sanctions.

Restorative Justice need not reject the idea of sanctions and deterrence. Instead, it has a broader, and I think more realistic, view of what can count as an effective sanction. It recognizes that the requirement that an offender *take responsibility* for his or her actions serves in most cases as an effective deterrent sanction. It is often argued that the 'threat' of requiring restitution, compensation, or reconciliation is not a sufficient sanction to deter potential offenders. It is not severe or harsh enough, at least not unless there are also 'punitive damages' added to the compensation.

In the earlier discussion of deterrence theory, we noted the debate about the extent to which deterrence works and about what makes it work. The preferred deterrent sanction in our society, incarceration, may be an effective *short-term* guarantee of social protection. But it is notoriously bad as a *long-term* strategy. This is because of what it does to its graduates, who emerge from prison psychologically and morally debilitated, and better educated in the art of lawbreaking. In the *long term,* the Restorative Justice approach can plausibly claim to meet the objective of social protection and deterrence more effectively than the utilitarian approach. If it succeeds in its aim to provide the offender the way back into constructive involvement in the community, its *specific deterrent* value will be better than that of the demoralized ex-con. It is not at all clear that the sanctions of Restorative Justice, including the requirement of restitution, are any less effective as a *general deterrent* than the infliction of harm or deprivation. Deterrence is a legitimate aim of law and its enforcement. But Restorative Justice can accomplish this aim, and it can do so without simply using the offender's punishment as an occasion to teach a lesson to other potential offenders. On this count Restorative Justice is once again in agreement with retributivism in its criticism of deterrence theory.

A realistic understanding of human nature and human society has to account for the fact that not all offenders will take even minimal steps in the direction of taking responsibility for their offenses and of reintegration into society as a law-abiding citizen. Advocates of Restorative Justice need not be idealistic or naive about this reality. Where full restoration is not achievable, Restorative Justice may well require protection of the innocent from continued exploitation. However, imprisonment or other forms of punitive deprivation are the *last,* not the first, resort of Restorative Justice.

Restorative justice and rehabilitation

Little needs to be said about this issue, because this is where the greatest strengths of the Restorative Justice approach are most apparent. The rehabilitation view of criminal justice takes as a central aim the restoration of offenders to their role as law-abiding citizens. However, as we have seen, the approach has largely failed to achieve its aim, in great measure because it has been too dominated by a 'therapeutic' model of rehabilitation. As argued earlier, this therapeutic approach to offenders has received widespread criticism from both retributivists and utilitarians: the first on the grounds that it is immoral and unjust to offenders, and the second on the grounds that it has not succeeded in rehabilitating most offenders.

The restorative approach to criminal justice, however, does not depend upon the therapeutic model of rehabilitation. Indeed, precisely because of its emphasis upon the need for offenders to *take responsibility* for their action, it treats them as responsible moral agents, not as sick patients to be treated. Of course, in those cases where offenders really do not have the capacity for morally responsible action, the therapeutic model may be appropriate, and is entirely consistent with, the restorative view.

The term 'rehabilitation,' however, is far too weak to capture the profound changes that take place in those who participate in the typical Restorative Justice processes. Those who are involved in these programs can provide moving accounts of radical personal changes which occur, not only in the lives of offenders who are brought to account, but also to their victims, their families, and the surrounding community. Sometimes these are expressed in explicit religious terms, sometimes not. But offenders, victims, families, mediators, judges, and lawyers who participate all speak of the 'magic,' or 'deeply spiritual' aspects of the events that take place when offenders come to terms with the pain they have inflicted on victims or their families and express repentance, and when victims or their families experience personal healing from offenders' acts of repentance and from their own ability to forgive. The term 'rehabilitation' is also too weak to describe the more mundane, but vitally important, ways in which Restorative Justice processes help offenders out of the destructive patterns of behavior that commonly lead them into breaches of the law, by opening up new social spaces for them in the community. An offender who has taken responsibility for repairing the harms done, and who has restored the trust and confidence of the community is 'rehabilitated' in a far broader sense than can be said of individualized therapeutic measures.

Restorative justice and restitution

Just as the modern rehabilitation theory has taken the valid ideas of reformation and rehabilitation in an unfortunate therapeutic direction, so has the modern restitution theory taken it in an unfortunate libertarian, economic direction. In both cases what is essentially a sound idea is given too narrow an interpretation. In both cases the restorative approach gives a much broader, and much more intellectually satisfying, as well as practical, account of the fundamental idea.

The powerful appeal of the restitutionist approach to criminal justice lies in the fact that it has been the only other approach to put the interests of the real, immediate *victims* of offense at the center of the process. It recognizes that the primary injustice of a criminal offense is the harm or loss suffered by its victims, and that there can only be *justice* when this harm or loss has been concretely addressed. But the restitutionist theory is restricted in several important respects which the restorative view remedies.

First, we have seen that by adopting the economic model of conflict resolution, it reduces the idea of restitution or compensation of victims purely to that of financial payback for harms done. Without question, financial compensation is an important part of the redress owed to victims, victims' families, and even to the community. In many cases there are no other ways to compensate for harms done. But Restorative Justice practitioners have developed many other creative ways to involve offenders in compensatory activities to victims and families, from contributions of labor and time to victims or to activities supported by victims, to involvement in organizations dedicated to amelioration of the conditions that lead to the type of offense. For example, a spouse abuser might 'compensate' his victim by working for an organization working against spousal abuse or raising money for a women's shelter. This kind of compensation has far more psychological, sociological, and moral power in 'righting the wrong' or 'restoring justice' than does simple financial payment.

Part of the restoration that needs to take place in 'making things right' includes the restoration of the offender to the moral community that has been alienated by the offense. This is a second factor that restitution theory ignores almost completely. By reducing criminal offenses to the level of simply a tort harm, it minimizes the moral aspect of the wrong committed against the victim. One of the most important aspects of the restoration of justice is the amelioration of the victims' sense that they have been *wronged.* A central aspect of the reconciliation process that is essential to Restorative Justice is dealing with this sense of wrong. That is why it is so important for victims to hear expressions of remorse and apology from offenders, so that they can let go of the anger and fear that is part of victimization, and ultimately even forgive the offender. This is also a critical part of what it means for the offender to *take responsibility* for the wrong done to the victim. Here again, Restorative Justice is on the side of the retributivist theory in insisting that the offender acknowledge the *wrongness* of the offense and take responsibility for the *wrong.*

This is related closely to a third narrowness in restitution theory which Restorative Justice remedies. Because restitution theory ignores the wrongness of the offense, it has nothing to say about the restoration or reintegration of offenders into the community. Payment of damages does not by itself accomplish restoration of an alienated offender—it is no different from the punitive payment of a fine. Restorative Justice integrates restitution into a larger process of reconciliation which speaks to the needs of the offender as well as the victim.

We noted earlier that the libertarian-oriented restitution theory permits, and even encourages, a gross injustice in its reduction of criminal offenses to economic exchanges. It greatly favors the wealthy in society, in effect bestowing upon them a 'right' to offend which the less wealthy do not have. Restorative Justice is concerned with the equity of sentencing. Its flexibility and openness to alternative forms of compensation take the social and economic inequalities in society seriously and find ways of ameliorating them. There is good reason to require from wealthy offenders, who can easily 'afford' their crimes, other forms of restitution than financial ones. And, there may be reasons of a different sort for permitting the same kind of restitution from those who cannot 'afford' the harms they cause to victims.

Finally, because of its deep roots in economic individualism, restitution theory is narrowly individualistic in its definition of *victims* as well. Only individual persons can be victims, and only individual persons need to be compensated. Advocates of Restorative Justice sometimes speak in these individualistic terms as well, partly in reaction to the way in which the traditional theories of justice have ignored individual victims in favour of abstractions such as 'the sovereign' or 'the people.' But criminal offenses do not simply wrong individuals; they also often wrong the community. When a crime of violence or invasion of privacy is committed in a community, it threatens the security of all who live there. It affects the psychology and the morale of the community itself. Therefore, Restorative Justice can, and should, take seriously the fact that the community can be one of the victims of crime, and that the restoration of justice requires 'making things right' with the whole community. The community, too, may need restitution and reconciliation.

Restorative justice and discretion

Restorative Justice is the only one of the approaches that provides a formal basis for the use of wide discretion in sentencing alternatives. This is an aspect of the approach that is often not recognized, even by its advocates. This is because those theories of punishment that define justice in terms of the appropriate level of pain or deprivation ('just desert' for the retributivists and 'optimal deterrence' for the utilitarian) are constrained by their accompanying 'pain formulae': "An offense of this magnitude requires this level of severity as punishment." Also, when pain is the essential element of punishment, there are few sentencing options open to a judge. Any sanction other than the standard, accepted options of prison, fine, or even death, are by definition forms of leniency.

By taking the focus of criminal justice away from the preoccupation with pain and suffering, and defining sanction in a much broader way, Restorative Justice permits a much more creative approach to sentencing alternatives. That sanction is most 'just' that best accomplishes the full restoration of offender, victim, and the community to a more satisfying relationship. Given the complexity of social relationships and personalities, there are numerous ways in which this restoration can be accomplished. Restorative Justice allows wide flexibility and discretion in sentencing without its being perceived as a compromise of justice. This is one of the strongest points made by Wesley Cragg.

Further, Restorative Justice is the only one of the theories of criminal justice that formally recognizes the inherent ambiguity of criminal offenses themselves. Our system of justice is constructed in such a way that it permits a criminal court to find a defendant either guilty or not guilty of the violation of a particular law. As many writers have pointed out, this means that the process of a criminal conviction abstracts from the whole social context in which the 'offense' took place, focusing only on those aspects of the situation that are relevant to the question of whether a law was broken.

There are good reasons having to do with procedural justice why courts should function in this way. It is necessary in order to protect persons from being convicted and punished unfairly, and to limit the coercive power of the law in society. However, at the level of sentencing, it is possible for courts to take into account a much broader range of issues surrounding the 'offense.' It is here that a Restorative Justice approach to 'restoring the justice of the situation' can mitigate the injustices that frequently result from the abstracted conviction process. A process of victim-offender reconciliation, for example, can look at the whole conflict situation that led to the abstract offense against the law and tailor the conflict resolution to all the factors in that situation.

Conclusion

Clearly, the Restorative Justice approach provides a much more satisfying answer to the traditional philosophical and jurisprudential questions of criminal justice than any of the other major theories. Where each one of the traditional theories attempts to address but one of the central concerns about the aims of criminal punishment, the restorative approach addresses them all. Indeed, it does so more effectively than approaches advocated by the traditional theories. It provides a far more convincing account of how punishment can 'make things right' than does the retributive theory. It addresses the question of social protection and deterrence, which is the primary concern of the utilitarian theory. It has a far more morally acceptable view of rehabilitation than does the traditional therapeutically oriented rehabilitation theory. It has a socially much richer view of what is involved in compensation for victims of punishment than does the libertarian restitutionist view. Finally, the restorative view of justice provides more flexibility and discretion in the sentencing process than any of the other approaches, allowing sentencing to mitigate many aspects of the conflict that are ignored by the usual conviction process in the courts.

Notes

1 This, I believe, is the meaning of one of the well-known admonitions in the Bible, which is most grievously violated by theocratic, retributive societies: "Beloved, never avenge yourselves, but leave room for the wrath of God; for it is written, Vengeance is mine, I will repay, says the Lord." (Romans 12:19, see also Deuteronomy 32:35 and Hebrews 10:30.)

2 Herbert Morris, "Persons and Punishment," *The Monist* 52, No. 4 (October 1968). Immanuel Kant, "The Right of Punishing," in *Philosophy of Law* (1887).

3 Herbert Morris tries to explain this 'paying back' in the following terms: The offender takes unfair advantage of law-abiding citizens by his or her offense. By punishing the offender with prison or other deprivation, the society 'takes back' this unfair advantage. This is how justice is restored.

4 This abstract account of 'paying the debt to society' was reinforced by the modern theory of the state, in two ways:
   a. The king, sovereign, or 'the people' in the abstract were the primary victim of criminal offenses. (Just as the deity is the victim of moral offenses in traditional theology.) This is why the 'debt' is also paid in the abstract.
   b. Since the modern theory of the state holds that monopoly on the use of force and violence is the definitive feature of the state, the suffering of this violence then constitutes the payment of the debt.

5 The modern theory of the state is usually attributed to the seventeenth-century English writer Thomas Hobbes in his book *Leviathan*. Modern political and social science has largely accepted Hobbes's view that political and moral order is maintained through the threat of force by the sovereign. Most modern utilitarians accept the legal positivist theory of law which defines law as commands or rules enforced through force and violence. See John Austin, "The Province of Jurisprudence Determined" in *Lectures on Jurisprudence*, 5th ed., Vol. 1 (R. Cambell, 1885), and H. L. A. Hart, *The Concept of Law* (New York: Oxford University Press, 1961).

6 Randy E. Barnett, "Restitution: A New Paradigm of Criminal Justice," 279–301. See also Barnett and Hagel, eds., *Assessing the Criminal: Restitution and the Legal Process* (1977).

Part D

Evaluating restorative justice

Introduction

Part D opens with a reading from Howard Zehr in which he points to the importance of evaluation and also outlines his ideas about how evaluation should be approached. Crucially, Zehr argues for a multi-method and multi-focused approach, in order to ensure not only that the effectiveness of restorative justice is assessed, but that evaluations are used to ensure that restorative justice remains grounded in commitments to respect, humility and listening to other voices.

Yet, the question which most people ask when they hear about restorative justice is 'does it work?' The next reading (Chapter 23) remains one of the most thorough and sophisticated attempts to answer this question, through a review of the available empirical evidence. Based on his analysis of numerous research reports, from all over the world, John Braithwaite presents a careful defence of the thesis that restorative justice restores and satisfies victims, offenders and communities better than existing justice practices. However, there is an important and controversial element to Braithwaite's argument that needs to be flagged up. For Braithwaite, restorative justice works best *when it is backed up by punitive justice*. Here, Braithwaite parts company with some proponents of restorative justice for whom punitive justice is completely unjustifiable. What Braithwaite advocates is certainly not abolition of punishment and its replacement by restorative justice. For him, this would probably render restorative justice ineffective. The most effective way of regulating crime is weak law enforcement and strong 'conversational regulation'. But the effectiveness of the latter depends upon it taking place within a larger system in which there is always the possibility of resorting to punitive justice. For Braithwaite, then, punishment is to be marginalised, placed in the background and used only as a last resort. But it is essential to have it there as a last resort if restorative justice is going to work.

A more recent assessment of the evidence about the effectiveness of restorative justice is Lawrence Sherman and Heather Strang's study, from which Chapter 24 is drawn. Amongst the key findings of this review were that restorative justice seems to reduce crime more effectively with more serious crimes and violent crimes rather than with less serious and property offences and that victims benefit from face-to-face restorative encounters. From this review, Sherman and Strang sought to identify 'best practice' for restorative justice. Another recent evaluative study is that carried out by a team led by Joanna Shapland funded by the UK Home Office's Crime reduction programme. Chapter 25 is an article based on this research in which Gwen Robinson and Joanna Shapland reflect upon what for many observers is the key question about restorative justice processes: can they reduce reoffending amongst those offenders who take part in them? Their answer, as in the previous two studies, is a carefully optimistic one. The final reading in this section shifts the focus away from the potential of restorative justice to reduce reoffending and focuses squarely on the question of whether restorative justice interventions offer better outcomes for victims. Drawn from Heather Strang's book-length study of this issue, the answer is again cautiously optimistic.

22 Evaluation and restorative justice principles

Howard Zehr

Introduction

I am going to begin with a disclaimer. I am not an evaluator, but I am an advocate of evaluation. I see myself as having two goals in this chapter: to raise some issues that make evaluations essential, then to suggest approaches to these issues that have implications for both practice and evaluation. The context of my comments is a deepening concern for what I call 'critical issues' in the restorative justice field. Toews and I have published a book – *Critical Issues in Restorative Justice* – in which we define critical issues in the following way:

> Critical issues are questions, forces or directions that affect the integrity or overall direction of the field including gaps in theory or practice and ways that restorative justice is in danger of going astray or failing to live up to its promise. The term 'critical' suggests that these issues are crucial to the field, but also implies a critical stance toward the field.
>
> (Zehr and Toews, 2004: ix)

These critical issues have been a longstanding concern of mine, starting when I first began in this field of work in the late 1970s. Unfortunately, though, our field has not always been very comfortable with such issues. In the early 1980s, for example, I presented to a group of practitioners in what I think was the forerunner of the Victim Offender Mediation Association. After raising some critical issues I received a hostile reaction from the audience. 'Why are you raising these kinds of questions?' they asked. 'What a downer.'

More recently, during the fall of 2002, I took a kind of international road trip, helping to facilitate a series of palavers – or as they say in New Zealand, 'hui' – around critical issues. We brought together various sectors – academics, policy makers, and practitioners – to identify and discuss some key concerns. The trip took me to England, to South Africa and to New Zealand, as well as places in North America. The following is a discussion of a few of the issues that have arisen in these dialogues.[1]

Some general issues and concerns

One of the issues with which people have been wrestling is whether we have been too focused, in restorative justice, on conferences and on individuals. In London, practitioners were asking, 'are we in danger of seeing the conference as a whole thing, not realising that many of these individuals have many other needs, other things going on in their lives that needed to be addressed? What do we do when other issues get unearthed in a conference? How do we provide the resources we need?' On a related note, are we individualising forms of wrongdoing that have a wider scope or context? Much like the criminal justice system, are we taking harms that have larger social, economic, political dimensions and treating them as individual wrongs, thereby helping to ignore underlying structural problems? Mamdani has offered a similar critique of the South African Truth and Reconciliation Commission – which claimed a restorative framework – arguing that individualising wrongdoing tended to gloss over economic and social apartheid (Mamdani, 2000).

One of my chief concerns is whether we are being as victim-orientated as we claim. Are we really delivering justice for victims or are we using victims for our own purposes? Despite efforts to include victims over the past several decades, the criminal justice system remains predominately offender-oriented: cases are defined and tracked through the system by offenders' identities, the primary focus is on what happens to offenders and most job descriptions in the system are oriented toward offenders. Moreover, many of us come to the restorative justice field from offender-related backgrounds. All this means that it is difficult, in practice, for restorative justice to be truly balanced. In theory, restorative justice offers a more central place to victims than probably any previous effort to correct the system. On the other hand, this claim could turn out to be primarily rhetorical. Many victims and victim service providers are deeply sceptical, and with good reason.

On the flip side, are we adequately addressing offender needs? We talk a lot about offender accountability but what about their other needs? And what about needs language itself? In a recent conversation Don Evans, a rehabilitation specialist in Canada, raised serious concerns about the impact of risk assessment in Canada and the United States. In restorative justice we often talk in terms of needs. What happens, Evans asked, when those needs began to be seen as criminogenic needs and become part of risk assessment? Moreover, are we thinking enough about the dynamics of offender transformation? For example, how do we deal with their narratives of victimisation? I am convinced that much offending grows of a sense of victimisation. As Gilligan (1996) has argued, violence can be seen as an effort to do justice or undo an injustice. Are we addressing this in our practices and theories? Or what about the processes offenders must go through to re-narrate their lives? I have recently read Maruna's (2001) book *Making Good* and I am trying to fully comprehend the implications. He interviewed offenders who have ceased to be involved in crime and found that those who successfully stop may have different understandings of their responsibilities than restorative justice advocates might prefer. Offenders turn their lives around, in part, by 're-storying' their lives. In that process, they have to incorporate the bad things they have done while still preserving their sense of identity and self-worth. To do that, they may not take responsibility as fully as we might like. How do we incorporate that into our work?

What about prisoners' worldviews? How does that affect their understandings of restorative justice? While sitting with some lifer friends several years ago, I suddenly realised that although we have spent much time articulating restorative justice from the standpoint of victims and the community, we have done little to articulate it from an offender or prisoner perspective. What would that involve?

There are also a whole set of questions around whether we are adequately addressing the ethnic and cultural dimensions of restorative justice. Although much more research is needed, some attention is being given to cultural biases and assumptions in our models of practice; however, what about our understandings of victimisation and offending? To what extent are they culturally shaped, and what are the implications for practice? What about the way we conceptualise restorative justice itself? What does it say when so many of the spokes people for this field are old white guys like me?

There are significant issues associated with indigenous justice, particularly the ways in which mainstream society or governmental structures may be appropriating these traditions and even using them as a means to recolonise people. In our Conflict Transformation Programme at Eastern Mennonite University, where practitioners come from 50 countries to learn together, participants often find that restorative justice serves as a way to legitimate and activate their own traditions. But are we giving adequate attention to the retributive and restorative elements that are in all our traditions? Are we talking enough about the fact that when restorative justice builds upon indigenous values, it often cannot be a simple resurrection of traditional approaches but rather a mix of traditional and modern human rights values? Are we giving adequate concern to how those traditions can be appropriated by others, to how they are being distorted and misused?

There are large issues associated with the role of the community. For instance, to what extent is community taking the place of victims? Are communities healthy enough to be doing the job that we are asking them to do? What do we mean by community? As one woman in New Zealand recently asked, as we rely heavily on volunteers are we feminising justice since, in many societies, women are the people who typically volunteer? What are the implications of that?

The use of shame has raised serious concerns for many. I am intrigued with honour and humiliation as keys to understanding offending behaviour, understanding victim behaviour and understanding the way people are experiencing justice. There are many concerns about the way we may be misinterpreting and misusing shame, however. We may be trying to shame people rather than learning that the focus ought to be on processes for removing and transforming shame. One day I am going to make a bumper sticker that says, 'Shame Happens'. The question is not how do we shame people, but what do we do about the shame that is there already?

In New Zealand, someone asked, 'what are people going to say, 200 years from now, about restorative justice? Was it an opportunity lost, or was it an opportunity misused?' How this movement turns out will hinge in part, I believe, on how we handle the following four areas.

Four critical issues

We need evaluation, and we need to pay attention to the results. Those of us who are restorative justice advocates and practitioners naturally believe we are doing a beautiful thing. How could anyone question it? We tell the good stories and ignore the bad; we engage in butterfly collecting, as some critics have charged. As a result of this mentality, we tend not to want evaluation. When we are evaluated, we do not want to listen to the results.

We desperately need evaluation, and evaluation has to be multi-method and multi-focus. We need to evaluate processes and outcomes, and we also need to evaluate the goals and functioning of our organisations. We need to evaluate what we are doing and how it compares to what we think we are doing. It is very interesting to evaluate a restorative justice programme by asking all the stakeholders and actors what they think they are doing and why. If you do this, you may find everybody is playing a different game and that they are not at all on the same page. The implications can be quite serious.

We also need to think carefully about how we do evaluation, what yardsticks we use, and what values – implicit and explicit – underlie our approach to evaluation. In a recently published chapter – 'Ways of Knowing for a Restorative Worldview' – Toews and I have argued that too often our assumptions and approaches to evaluation mirror those of the 'retributive' worldview (Zehr and Toews, 2003). We have advocated, instead, for a set of 'transformative guidelines' that call for a more restorative stance toward knowledge, our subjects and our roles.

A second essential is conscious and structured accountability. We need to make ourselves deliberately accountable to various sectors in society including, and especially, those we claim to serve. For example, to help guard against the biases and distortions noted above, we need victims looking over our shoulders, auditing our programmes. We need to have them on our boards and on our start-up committees. That goes for other players as well. Restorative justice advocates for accountability for offenders but accountability applies to service providers as well.

Third, we need to encourage dialogue between the various sectors involved. A number of us recently completed a 'listening project' with victims and victim services. We sent listening teams out to seven US states where we knew there were tensions between victim services and restorative justice. The listening teams were made up of one victim advocate and one prominent restorative justice advocate. We asked the teams to sit down with groups of victims and victim service providers, ask a series of open-ended questions and to just listen to what they said. A lot of very difficult but important things were heard in this important dialogue. We have published the results and are hoping that a similar dialogue will now go on locally in various communities (Mika et al., 2002).

The fourth imperative is to be clear about our principles, values and philosophies and having accomplished that, to do what I have come to call 'principled practice'. When observing New Zealand practitioners who are really getting it right, I realised that they were doing principled practice. The law in New Zealand sets down seven principles and seven goals for restorative practice (MacRae and Zehr, 2004). These practitioners were virtually carrying those principles and goals in their back pocket and for every decision they made, they were referring to those principles. In our Conflict Transformation Programme at Eastern Mennonite University, we have a practice sector called the Institute for Justice and Peacebuilding. As we assess the requests and opportunities for practice that come to us from around the world, our decisions are guided by a series of ten principles that we have agreed should shape our practice. When a request comes in, we literally do a written analysis using those ten principles. That is, in part, what I mean by principled practice. It requires clarity about our principles and values, and a commitment to be guided by them on a daily basis.

I recently completed a book that involved interviews with victims who had been through very severe violence (Zehr, 2001). The conversations confirmed the importance of metaphors in trauma and trauma healing. In fact, some people say that the process to transcend the trauma of severe violence is a process of changing metaphors. Victims used metaphors of trauma such as bricks on their chests, 'trauma bubbles', and pots of grief being carried on one's head. The metaphors were diverse and often individual. However, one metaphor used by almost everyone is the metaphor of a journey. They are on a journey, and it is a journey that never quite ends.

We in the restorative justice field are on a journey as well. It is a journey that is circuitous. It is a journey whose destination is unclear. I think it is also important to remember we are at a very early stage in that journey and that we will encounter many forks in the road. We need to make sure we do not take the wrong road but, if we do, we need to get back on the right track. To stay on the right road, or to get back on it, we need to be deliberate about four things: we need to be evaluated and to take the results seriously; we need to make ourselves accountable in conscious ways; we need to encourage open dialogues among the various sectors that are impacted by our work; and we need to not only articulate our principles but also let our practices be guided by those principles.

Conclusion

Restorative justice claims to be responsive to the needs of various individuals and stakeholders, including victims, offenders and communities. At its best, it creates an arena in which people can sort out, within limits, what justice means in their situations. Restorative justice is post-modern in its realisation that our truths about justice are contextual and that justice needs to be shaped from the community up. I close, then, with what has become my mantra: that restorative justice is above all about respect for all, and that such respect requires humility. In the meaning of humility I include the common understanding of not taking undue credit but, more importantly, I also include a deep appreciation for the limits of what we know: a recognition that what I 'know' is at best only part of reality, that what I 'know' is inevitably shaped by my biography and identity, that what I 'know' might not be generalisable to others. Central to restorative justice is a commitment to listen to other voices, including the dissonant ones. Only if we are grounded in respect and humility can we prevent the restorative approach to justice that seems so liberating to us from becoming a burden or even a weapon to be used against others, as has happened so often with the reforms of the past.

Note

1 Proceedings of the New Zealand hui are available in Juelich (2003).

References

Gilligan, J. (1996) *Violence: Reflections on a National Epidemic.* New York: Random House.

Juelich, S. (ed.) (2003) *Critical Issues in Restorative Justice: Advancing the Agenda in Aotearoa, New Zealand.* Auckland: Massey University Centre for Justice and Peace Development.

MacRae, A. and Zehr, H. (2004) *The Little Book of Family Group Conferencing, New Zealand Style.* Intercourse, PA: Good Books.

Mamdani, M. (2002) 'The Truth According to the TRC', in I. Amadiume and A. An Na'Im (eds), *The Politics of Memory.* London: Zed Books.

Maruna, S. (2001) *Making Good: How Ex-Convicts Reform and Rebuild Their Lives.* Washington, DC: American Psychological Association.

Mika, H., Achilles, M., Halbert, E., Stutzman-Amstutz, L. and Zehr, H. (2002) *Taking Victims and Their Advocates Seriously: A Listening Project.* Akron, PA: Mennonite Central Committee.

Zehr, H. (2001) *Transcending: Reflections of Crime Victims.* Intercourse, PA: Good Books.

Zehr, H. and Toews, B. (2003) 'Ways of Knowing for a Restorative Worldview', in E. Weitekamp and H.-J. Kerner (eds), *Restorative Justice in Context: International Practice and Directions.* Portland, OR: Willan Publishing.

Zehr, H. and Toews, B. (eds) (2004) *Critical Issues in Restorative Justice.* Monsey, NY and Portland, OR: Criminal Justice Press and Willan Publishing.

23 Does restorative justice work?

John Braithwaite

This chapter summarizes the now considerable empirical evidence about the effectiveness of restorative justice. The literature review is organized around three broad and simple hypotheses:

1. Restorative justice restores and satisfies victims better than existing criminal justice practices
2. Restorative justice restores and satisfies offenders better than existing criminal justice practices
3. Restorative justice restores and satisfies communities better than existing criminal justice practices

[...]

Restorative justice practices restore and satisfy victims better than existing criminal justice practices

A consistent picture emerges from the welter of data reviewed in this section: it is one of comparatively high victim approval of their restorative justice experiences, though often lower levels of approval than one finds among other participants in the process. So long as the arrangements are convenient, it is only a small minority of victims who do not *want* to participate in restorative justice processes. Consistent with this picture, preliminary data from Lawrence Sherman and Heather Strang's Canberra experiments show only 3 per cent of offenders and 2 per cent of community representatives at conferences compared with 12 per cent of victims disagreeing with the statements: 'The government should use conferences as an alternative to court more often' (Strang, 2000). Most of the data to date are limited to a small range of outcomes; we are still awaiting the first systematic data on some of the dimensions of restoration [...]. On the limited range of outcomes explored to date, victims do seem to get more restoration out of restorative justice agreements than court orders, and restorative justice agreements seem to be more likely to be delivered than court orders even when the former are not legally enforceable.

Operationalizing victim restoration

There is a deep problem in evaluating how well restorative justice restores. Empowerment of victims to define the restoration that matters to them is a keystone of a restorative justice philosophy. Three paths can be taken. One is to posit a list of types of restoration that are important to most victims [...]. The problem with this is that even with as uncontroversial a dimension of restoration as restoring property loss, some victims will prefer mercy to insisting on getting their money back; indeed, it may be that act of grace which gives them a spiritual restoration that is critical for them.[1] The second path sidesteps a debate on what dimensions of restoration are universal enough to evaluate. Instead, it measures overall satisfaction of victims with restorative justice processes and outcomes, assuming (without evidence) that satisfaction is a proxy for victims getting restoration on the things that are most important for them. This is the path followed in the review of the next section, largely because this was the kind of information available when the earlier version of the review was published in 1999. The third path is the best one but also the most unmanageable in large quantitative evaluations. It is to ask victims to define the kinds of restoration they were seeking and then to report how much restoration they attained in these terms that matter most to them.

As this book goes to press, Heather Strang (forthcoming) has completed a manuscript that pulls off something close to this third approach. Strang reviewed the empirical literature on what victims said they wanted out of the criminal justice process and then confirmed the accuracy of that list of aspirations on Canberra crime victims whose cases were randomly assigned to court versus restorative justice conferences. The set of victim preferences she identified were:

- A less formal process where their views count
- More information about both the processing and the outcome of their case
- To participate in their case
- To be treated respectfully and fairly
- Material restoration
- Emotional restoration, including an apology

Strang then went on to show that indeed these victim aspirations were more consistently realized in cases randomly assigned to conferences as opposed to court:

> Feelings of anger, fear and anxiety towards their offenders fell markedly after their conference while feelings of security for themselves and sympathy for their offender increased. The conference usually had a beneficial effect on victims' feelings of dignity, self-respect and self-confidence and led to reduced levels of embarrassment and shame about the offence. Overall, victims most often said their conferences had been a helpful experience in allowing them to feel more settled about the offence, to feel forgiving towards their offender and to experience a sense of closure.
>
> (Strang, 2000, pp. iv–v)

Strang's most striking result concerns the capacity of conferences to deal with the feeling of revenge that so often eat away at victims. More than half of court-assigned violence victims said they would harm their offender if they had the chance, compared with only 7 per cent of those assigned to restorative justice.

Notwithstanding the strong affirmation overall that victims were more likely to have their needs, especially their emotional needs, met in conference than in court, Strang found a subset of victims who were worse off as a result of their case being assigned to conference. She concluded that these were not so much cases that refuted principles of restorative justice as cases that revealed bungled administration of justice (see Box 1). One group of victims

Box 1: Scapegoating: procedural injustice and the forgotten victim

Matthew, the 24-year-old victim in this assault matter, was drinking on licensed premises when a fight broke out involving one of his friends. He said that in the general melee he tried to pull his friend out of the fight, when a 'bouncer' hit him over the head and ejected him into the car park, where the fighting continued involving both patrons and security staff. Subsequently Charlie, aged 18 and employed on security at the pub, attended the police station and made full admissions about having punched Matthew in the face. In the view of the apprehending officer, other staff were directing blame at Charlie and it appeared that he had been offered as the sole offender because he was young with no prior convictions and likely not to be prosecuted.

The conference was attended by a large number of supporters of both Matthew and Charlie. As soon as it began, Matthew said that Charlie could not have been the person who assaulted him because he did not look anything like that person. Charlie's employer and workmates insisted that it was Charlie who was the assailant (though his family did not appear to believe that he had been involved). There were many claims and counter-claims in the course of the conference flowing from poor police investigation into the incident, including allegations that the victim and his friends had provoked the brawl. It was complicated by poor and untrusting relations between the licensee and the police, who frequently attended incidents at his premises. After about an hour of acrimonious discussion, the conference was abandoned as it was apparent that there was no agreement on what had happened and no likelihood of reaching an outcome acceptable to all the parties.

After further enquiries the police decided to take no further action with the case. Matthew was very angry and disappointed: his rage at the injustice of having effectively nothing happen following the assault led to his carrying a knife for several months, and in fact to pull it out when the same friend again got into a fight. He spontaneously said at interview that if he 'ran into' his assailants from the original incident he would probably attack them in revenge for what happened to him. He had been very upset at the way the conference unfolded, although he believed that the police had been fair and that he had had an opportunity to express his views. He wished the case had gone to court because he believed that way all the co-offenders would have been prosecuted and punished (in fact this could not have happened as only Charlie had been identified as being involved). Two years after the incident he remained extremely angry because he saw the licensee and his security staff as having 'got away' with assaulting him.

Source: From Strang, 2000, p. 168

who were more dissatisfied than victims whose case was sent straight to court were those whose case was assigned to a conference, but the conference fell through and actually ended up going to court. The lesson here is that badly administered programs that do not deliver on their restorative promises to victims can actually make things a lot worse for them. Overall, Strang's results are extremely encouraging, especially since no one today would suggest that the Canberra program is the best one in Australia. Canberra is a first-generation program, and the evidence reviewed here suggests higher levels of satisfaction of victims and others in the later Australian programs that learned from some of its mistakes.[2]

Victim participation and satisfaction

While traditional criminal justice practices are notoriously unsatisfying to victims, it is also true that victims emerge from many restorative justice programs less satisfied than other participants. Clairmont (1994, pp. 16–17) found little victim involvement in four restorative justice programs for First Nations offenders in Canada. There seems to be a wider pattern of greater satisfaction among First Nations leaders and offenders than among victims for restorative projects on Canadian Aboriginal communities (Obonsawin-Irwin Consulting Inc., 1992a, 1992b; Clairmont, 1994; LaPrairie, 1995).

Early British victim–offender mediation programs reported what Dignan (1992) called sham reparation, for example, Davis's (1992) reporting of offers rather than actual repair, tokenism, and even dictated letters of apology. In some of these programs victims were little more than a new kind of prop in welfare programs: the 'new deal for victims' came in Britain to be seen as a 'new deal for offenders' (Crawford, 1996, p. 7). However, Crawford's (1996) conclusion that the British restorative justice programs that survived into the 1990s after weathering this storm 'have done much to answer their critics' (p. 7) seems consistent with the evidence. Dignan (1992) reports 71 per cent satisfaction among English corporate victims and 61 per cent among individual victims in one of the early adult offender reparation programs.

In New Zealand, victims attended only half the conferences conducted during the early years of the program[3] and when they did attend were less in agreement (51 per cent satisfaction) with family group conference outcomes than were offenders (84 per cent), police (91 per cent), and other participants (85 per cent; Maxwell and Morris, 1993, pp. 115, 120). About a quarter of victims reported that they felt worse as a result of attending the family group conference. Australian studies by Daly (1996) and Strang and Sherman (1997) also found a significant minority of victims who felt worse after the conference, upset over something said, or victimized by disrespect, though they were greatly outnumbered by victims who felt healing as a result of the conference. Similarly, Birchall *et al.* (1992) report 27 per cent of victims feeling worse after meeting their offender and 70 per cent feeling better in Western Australia's Midland Pilot Reparation Scheme. The Ministry of Justice, Western Australia (1994), reports 95 per cent victim satisfaction with their restorative justice conference program (Juvenile Justice Teams). Chatterjee (2000, p. 3) reports that 94 per cent of victims in Royal Canadian Mounted Police convened family group conferences were satisfied with the fairness of the agreement. McCold and Wachtel (1998) found 96 per cent victim satisfaction with cases randomly assigned to conferences in Bethlehem, Pennsylvania, compared with 79 per cent satisfaction when cases were assigned to court and 73 per cent satisfaction when the case went to court after being assigned to conference and the conference was declined. Conferenced victims were also somewhat more likely to believe that they experienced fairness (96 per cent), that the offender was adequately held accountable for the offence (93 per cent), and that their opinion regarding the offence and circumstances was adequately considered in the case (94 per cent). Ninety-three per cent of victims found the conference helpful, 98 per cent found that it 'allowed me to express my feelings without being victimized', 96 per cent believed that the offender had apologized, and 75 per cent believed that the offender was sincere. Ninety-four per cent said they would choose a conference if they had to do it over again. The Bethlehem results are complicated by a 'decline' group as large as the control group, where either offenders or victims could cause the case to be declined. In the Canberra RISE experiment, victim participation is currently 80 per cent (Strang, 2000). Reports on the Wagga Wagga conferencing model in Australia are also more optimistic about victim participation and satisfaction, reporting 90 per cent victim satisfaction and victim participation exceeding 90 per cent (Moore and O'Connell, 1994). Trimboli's (2000, p. 28) evaluation of the NSW Youth Justice Conferencing Scheme finds even higher levels of victim satisfaction than with the Wagga Wagga model conferencing programs, though lower levels of victim participation of 74 per cent than in Wagga and Canberra.

Trimboli's NSW victims were much more satisfied than the Canberra victims over being kept informed about what was happening, and were more likely to feel that they were treated with respect, that they had the opportunity to express their views in the conference, and that these views actually affected the decision on what should be done about the case. The highest published satisfaction and fairness ratings (both 98 per cent) have been reported by the Queensland Department of Justice conferencing program (Palk *et al.,* 1998). Seventy-eight per cent of victims felt the conference and the agreement helped 'make up for the offence', and only 6 per cent said they would be 'concerned if you met the young person in the street today' (Hayes *et al.*, 1998, pp. 26, 27). A high 90 per cent of offenders made verbal apologies, and a further 12 per cent made written apologies in this program. One reason for the program's exceptionally positive results is that it excludes conferencing from cases where victims do not wish to participate, meaning that no data are collected from the least cooperative victims who just want to walk away.

McGarrell *et al.* (2000, p. 45) not only found markedly higher levels of satisfaction among victims in cases randomly assigned to a restorative justice conference but also found that 97 per cent of conference victims 'felt involved', compared with 38 per cent of control group victims, and that 95 per cent of conference victims felt they had the opportunity to express their views, compared with 56 per cent of control group victims.

Umbreit and Coates's (1992) survey found that 79 per cent of victims who cooperated in four US mediation programs were satisfied, compared with only 57 per cent of those who did not have mediation (for earlier similar findings, see Umbreit, 1990). In a subsequent study Umbreit (1998) found victim *procedural* satisfaction at 78 per cent at four combined Canadian sites and 62 per cent at two combined English mediation sites. Victim satisfaction with *outcomes* was higher still: 90 per cent (four US sites), 89 per cent (four Canadian sites), and 84 per cent (two English sites). However, victim satisfaction was still generally lower across the sites than offender satisfaction. Eighty-three per cent of US mediation victims perceived the outcome as 'fair' (as opposed to being 'satisfied'), compared with 62 per cent of those who went through the normal court process. Umbreit and Coates (1992) also report reduced fear and anxiety among victims following mediation, a finding Strang (2000) has replicated on Canberra conferences. Victims afraid of being victimized again dropped from 25 per cent prior to mediation to 10 per cent afterward in a study by Umbreit and Coates (1992), again results comparable to those obtained by Strang on conferences. A survey of German institutions involved in model mediation projects found that the rate of voluntary victim participation generally ranged from 81 to 92 per cent and never dropped below 70 per cent (Kerner *et al.,* 1992).

McCold and Wachtel (2000) compared systematically thirty-nine program samples (including most of those discussed here) according to whether they were 'fully restorative', 'mostly restorative', or 'not restorative', where restorativeness was operationalized in terms of stakeholder participation. On average, victim perception of both fairness and satisfaction was highest for fully restorative programs and lowest for nonrestorative programs.

In summary, while many programs accomplish very high levels of victim participation, programs vary considerably on this dimension. Consistently, however, across disparate programs victims are highly satisfied with the fairness of procedures and outcomes – more satisfied than victims whose cases go to court, though not as satisfied as offenders and other participants in restorative justice processes. In a meta-analysis of 13 evaluations with a control group, Latimer, Dowden and Muise (2001) found victim satisfaction to be significantly higher in the restorative justice group. Victims also experienced reduced fear and increased emotional restoration after the restorative justice process. Heather Strang's (2000) data suggest, however, that one group whose satisfaction and emotional well-being are adversely affected by the offer of a restorative justice conference is victims whose conference falls through. This points up a methodological deficiency in most of the studies reviewed here (that does not apply to Strang's work): they measure satisfaction levels among victims whose conferences actually come to pass, failing to correct for the reduced levels of satisfaction that would apply if cases were included where conferences were offered but not delivered. Trimboli (2000) actually compares NSW results from completed conferences with RISE results of cases randomly assigned to conference (many of which actually ended up in court).

Honoring of obligations to victims

Haley and Neugebauer's (1992) analysis of restorative justice programs in the United States, Canada, and Great Britain revealed between 64 and 100 per cent completion of reparation and compensation agreements. I assume here, of course, that completion of undertakings that victims have agreed to is important for victim restoration. Marshall's (1992) study of cases referred to mediation programs in Britain found that over 80 per cent of agreements were completed. Galaway (1992) reports that 58 per cent of agreements reached through mediation in New Zealand were fully complied with within one year. In a Finnish study, 85 per cent of agreements reached through mediation were fully completed (Iivari, 1987, 1992). From England, Dignan (1992) reports 86 per cent participant agreement with mediation outcomes, with 91 per cent of agreements honored in full. Trenczek (1990), in a study of pilot victim–offender reconciliation projects in Braunschweig, Cologne, and Reutlingen, West Germany (see also Kuhn, 1987), reports a full completion rate of 76 per cent and a partial completion rate of 5 per cent. Pate's (1990) study of victim–offender reconciliation projects found a rate of noncompletion of agreements of between 5 and 10 per cent in Alberta, Canada, and less than 1 per cent in the case of a Calgary program. Wundersitz and Hetzel (1996, p. 133) found 86 per cent full compliance with conference agreements in South Australia, with another 3 per cent waived for near compliance. Fry (1997, p. 5) reported 100 per cent completion of agreements in a pilot of twenty-six Northern Territory police-coordinated juvenile conferences, and Waters (1993, p. 9) reported 91 per cent payment of compensation agreed in Wagga Wagga conferences. In another Wagga-style program, McCold and Wachtel (1998, p. 4) report 94 per cent compliance with the terms of conference agreements. McGarrell *et al.* (2000, p. 47) found 83 per cent completion of conference agreements in Indianapolis, compared with 58 per cent completion of diversion programs in the control group.

Umbreit and Coates (1992) compared 81 per cent completion of restitution obligations settled through mediation to 58 per cent completion of court-ordered restitution in their multisite study. Ervin and Schneider (1990), in a random assignment evaluation of six US restitution programs, found 89 per cent completion of restitution, compared with 75 per cent completion of traditional programs. Most of Ervin and Schneider's restitution programs, however, were not restorative in the sense of involving meetings of victims and offenders. Latimer, Dowden and Muise (2001, p. 17) found in a meta-analysis of 8 studies with a control group that restitution compliance was 33 per cent higher in the restorative justice cases than among controls. In summary, the research suggests high levels of compliance with restorative justice agreements, substantially higher than with court orders.

Symbolic reparation

One reason that the level of satisfaction of victims is surprisingly high in processes that so often give them so little material reparation is that they get symbolic reparation, which is more important to them (Retzinger and Scheff, 1996). Apology is at the heart of this: preliminary results from the RISE experiment in Canberra show that 71 per cent of victims whose cases were randomly assigned to a conference got an apology, compared with 17 per cent in cases randomly assigned to court; while 77 per cent of the conference apologies were regarded as 'sincere' or 'somewhat sincere', this was true of only 36 per cent of apologies to victims whose cases went to court (Strang, 2000). Sixty-five per cent of victims felt 'quite' or 'very' angry before the Canberra conferences, and 27 per cent felt so afterward. Obversely, the proportion of victims feeling sympathetic to the offender almost tripled (from 18 to 50 per cent) by the end of the conference (Strang, 2000). We will see that there is a large body of research evidence showing that victims are not as punitive as the rather atypical victims whose bitter calls for brutal punishment get most media coverage. Studies by both Strang and Sherman (1997) and Umbreit (1992, p. 443) report victim fear of revictimization and victim upset about the crime as having declined following the restorative justice process.

In Goodes's (1995) study of juvenile family group conferences in South Australia, where victim attendance ranges from 75 to 80 per cent (Wundersitz and Hetzel, 1996), the most common reason victims gave for attending their conference was to try to help the offender, followed by the desire to express feelings, make statements to the offender, or ask questions like 'why me' (what Retzinger and Scheff [1996] call symbolic reparation), followed by 'curiosity and a desire to "have a look"', followed by 'responsibility as citizens to attend'. The desire to ensure that the penalty was appropriate and the desire for material reparation rated behind all of these motivations to attend. The response rate in the Goodes (1995) study was poor, and there may be a strong social desirability bias in these victim reports; yet that may be precisely because the context of conference attendance is one that nurtures responsible citizenship cognitions by victims. Eighty-eight per cent of Goodes's (1995) victims agreed with the conference outcome, 90 per cent found it helpful to them, and 90 per cent said they would attend again if they were a victim again (Goodes, 1995).

With all these quantitative findings, one can lose sight of what most moves restorative justice advocates who have seen restorative processes work well. I am not a spiritual enough person to capture it in words: it is about grace, shalom. Van Ness (1986, p. 125) characterizes shalom as 'peace as the result of doing justice'. Trish Stewart (1993, p. 49) gets near its evocation when she reports one victim who said in the closing round of a conference: 'Today I have observed and taken part in justice administered with love.' Psychologists are developing improved ways of measuring spirituality – self-transcendence, meaning in life beyond one's self. So in the future it will be possible to undertake systematic research on self-reported spirituality and conferences to see whether results are obtained analogous to Reed's (1986, 1987, 1992) findings that greater healing occurred among terminally ill individuals whose psychosocial response was imbued with a spiritual dimension.

For the moment, we must accept an East–West divide in the way participants think about spiritual leadership in conferences. Maori, North American, and Australian Aboriginal peoples tend to think it important to have elders with special gifts of spirituality, what Maori call *mana,* attend restorative justice processes (Tauri and Morris, 1997, pp. 149–50). This is the Confucian view as well. These traditions are critical of the ethos Western advocates such as myself have brought to conferences, which has not seen it as important to have elders with *mana* at conferences. Several years ago in Indonesia I was told of restorative justice rituals in western Sumatra that were jointly conducted by a religious leader and a scholar – the person in the community seen as having the greatest spiritual riches and the person seen as having the greatest riches of learning. My inclination then was to recoil from the elitism of this and insist that many (if not most) citizens have the resources (given a little help with training) to facilitate processes of healing. While I still believe this, I now think it might be a mistake to seek to persuade Asians to democratize their restorative justice practices. There may be merit in special efforts to recruit exemplars of virtue, grace, *mana,* to participate. Increasingly, I am tempted to so interpret our experience with RISE in recruiting community representatives with grace to participate in drunk driving conferences where there is no victim. However, as Power (2000) and Miller and Blackler (2000) correctly point out, the Canberra experience with community representatives has been far from universally positive. Many have been decidedly short of *mana* and long on punitive speech. Nevertheless, a research and development program for restorative justice that still appeals to me is how to do well at locating elders with grace to act as community representatives in restorative justice programs in Western cities.

Restorative justice practices restore and satisfy offenders better than existing criminal justice practices

This section concludes that offender satisfaction with both corporate and traditional individual restorative justice programs has been extremely high. The evidence of offenders being restored in the sense of desisting from criminal conduct is extremely encouraging with victim–offender mediation, conferencing, restorative business regulatory programs, and whole-school antibullying programs, though not with peer mediation programs for bullying.[4] However, only some of these studies adequately control for important variables, and only five randomly assigned cases to restorative versus punitive justice. The business regulatory studies are instructive in suggesting that (1) restorative justice works best when it is backed up by punitive justice in those (quite common) individual cases where restorative justice fails and (2) trying restorative justice first increases perceived justice.

Fairness and satisfaction for offenders

[… Offenders] are more likely to respond positively to criminal justice processing when they perceive it as just. Moore with Forsythe's (1995, p. 248) ethnographic work concludes that most offenders, like victims, experienced quite profound 'procedural, material and psychological justice' in restorative justice conferences. Umbreit (1992) reports from his cross-site study in the United States an 89 per cent perception of fairness on the part of offenders with victim–offender mediation programs, compared with 78 per cent perceived fairness in unmediated cases. Umbreit (1998) reports 80 per cent offender perception of fairness of victim–offender mediation across four Canadian studies and 89 per cent at two combined English sites. The Ministry of Justice, Western Australia (1994), reports 95 per cent offender satisfaction with its restorative justice conference program (Juvenile Justice Teams). McCold and Wachtel (1998, pp. 59–1) report 97 per cent satisfaction with 'the way your case was handled' and 97 per cent fairness in the Bethlehem police conferencing program, a better result than in the four comparisons with Bethlehem cases that went to court. McGarrell *et al.* (2000, p. 45) report that conference offenders in Indianapolis were more likely than control group offenders to have 'felt involved' (84 per cent versus 47 per cent) and to feel they have had an opportunity to express their views (86 per cent versus 55 per cent). Coates and Gehm (1985, 1989) found 83 per cent offender satisfaction with the victim–offender reconciliation experience based on a study of programs in Indiana and Ohio. Smith, Blagg and Derricourt (1985), in a limited survey of the initial years of a South Yorkshire mediation project, found that 10 out of 13 offenders were satisfied with the mediation experience and felt that the scheme had helped alter their behavior. Dignan (1990), on the basis of a random sample of offenders (N = 50) involved in victim–offender mediations in Kettering, Northamptonshire, found 96 per cent were either satisfied or very satisfied with the process. [...] Barnes (1999) found higher perceptions of a number of facets of procedural and outcome fairness in RISE conferences compared with Canberra courts. However, Trimboli (2000, pp. 34–54) has reported even higher levels of offender perceptions of fairness and outcome satisfaction in NSW compared with RISE conferences. The strongest published result was again on 113 juvenile offenders in the Queensland Department of Justice conferencing program, where 98 per cent thought their conference fair and 99 per cent were satisfied with the agreement (Palk *et al.*, 1998). Ninety-six per cent of young offenders reported that they 'would be more likely to go to your family now if you were in trouble or needed help' and that they had 'been able to put the whole experience behind you'.

McCold and Wachtel (2000) compared systematically thirty-four program samples (including most of those discussed here) according to whether they were 'fully restorative', 'mostly restorative', or 'not restorative', where restorativeness was operationalized in terms of stakeholder participation. As with victim perceptions, offender perception of both fairness and satisfaction was highest for fully restorative programs and lowest for nonrestorative programs. For 13 studies with a control group, Latimer, Dowden and Muise's (2001, p. 14) meta-analysis found restorative justice offenders to be more satisfied about how their case was handled compared with controls.

Reduced reoffending as offender restoration

Meta-analysis of restitution programs suggests that these have some (modest) effect in reducing reoffending (e.g. Gendreau *et al.,* 1996; Cullen and Gendreau, 2000; see also Butts and Snyder, 1991; Schneider, 1986; Geudens and Walgrave, 1998; Schiff, 1998; Bazemore, 1999). I do not consider this literature here because most of these programs do not involve a restorative *process* (i.e. the restitution is usually imposed by a traditional court, often as punishment rather than in pursuit of any restorative *values*).

Pate (1990), Nugent and Paddock (1995), and Wynne (1996) all report a decline in recidivism among mediation cases. Umbreit, with Coates and Kalanj (1994) found 18 per cent recidivism across four victim–offender mediation sites (N=160) and 27 per cent (N=160) for comparable nonmediation cases at those sites, a difference that was encouraging but fell short of statistical significance. However, a follow-up in 2000 on these and several other programs on a much expanded sample of 1,298 again found mediation recidivism to be one-third lower than court recidivism (19 per cent versus 28 per cent), this time a statistically significant result after entering appropriate controls (Nugent *et al.* forthcoming). Similarly, Marshall and Merry (1990, p. 196) report for an even smaller sample than Umbreit, with Coates and Kalanj (1994) that offending declined for victim–offender mediation cases, especially when there was an actual meeting (as opposed to indirect shuttle diplomacy by a mediation), while offending went up for controls. However, the differences were not statistically significant. A German study by Dolling and Hartman (2000) found reoffending to be one-third lower in cases where victim–offender mediation was completed compared with a control group. The effect was significant after entering controls. However, including cases where mediation was not successfully completed reduced the *p* value to .08, which would not normally be accepted as significant.

In an experimental evaluation of six US restitution programs, Schneider (1986, 1990) found a significant reduction in recidivism across the six programs. This result is widely cited by restorative justice advocates as evidence for the efficacy of restorative justice. However, all but one of these programs seem to involve mandated restitution to victims without any mediation or restorative justice deliberation by victims and offenders. The one program that seems to meet the process definition of restorative justice, the one in Washington, DC, did produce significantly lower rates of reoffending for cases randomly assigned to victim–offender mediation and restitution compared with cases assigned to regular probation.[5]

There is no satisfactory evidence on the impact of the New Zealand juvenile family group conferences on recidivism. The story is similar with Wagga Wagga. Forsythe (1995) shows a 20 per cent reoffending rate for cases going to conference, compared with a 48 per cent rate for juvenile court cases. This is a big effect; most of it is likely a social selection effect of tougher cases going to court, as there is no matching, no controls, though it is hard to account for the entire association in these terms given the pattern of the data (see Forsythe, 1995, pp. 245–46).

Another big effect with the same social selection worry was obtained with only the first sixty-three cases to go through family group conferences in Singapore. The conference reoffending rate was 2 per cent, compared with 30 per cent over the same period for offenders who went to court (Chan, 1996; Hsien, 1996).

McCold and Wachtel's (1998) experimental evaluation of Bethlehem, Pennsylvania's, Wagga-style police conferencing program involved a more determined attempt to tackle social selection problems through randomization. Unfortunately, however, this study fell victim to another kind of selection effect as a result of unacceptably high crossover rates on the treatments assigned in the experiment. For property cases, there was a tendency for conferenced cases to have higher recidivism than court cases, but the difference was not statistically significant. For violence cases, conferenced offenders had a significantly lower reoffending rate than offenders who went to court. However, this result was not statistically valid because the violent offenders with the highest reoffending rate were those who were randomly assigned to conference but who actually ended up going to court because either the offender or the victim refused to cooperate in the conference. In other words, the experiment failed to achieve an adequate test of the effect of conferences on recidivism both on grounds of statistical power and because of unsatisfactory assurance that the assigned treatment was delivered.

Clearer results were obtained from McGarrell *et al.*'s (2000) Indianapolis Restorative Justice Experiment, which involved random assignment of young first offenders to a Wagga-style conference convened by the police versus assignment to the normal range of diversion programs. Rearrest was 40 per cent lower in the conference group than in the control group after six months, an effect that decayed to a 25 per cent reduction after twelve months. At the Winchester conference in 2001 McGarrell reported that the analysis of further cases revealed a decay to higher than this 25 per cent reduction, but these results are not yet published.

Preliminary reoffending results have been put up on the Web (aic.gov.au) by Sherman, Strang and Woods (2000) from the RISE restorative justice experiment in Canberra. In this experiment 1,300 cases were randomly assigned either to court or to a restorative justice conference on the Wagga model. While the experiment showed a sharp decline in officially recorded repeat criminal offending for violent juvenile and young adult offenders randomly assigned to conference in comparison to those assigned to court, the results were not encouraging on adult drunk drivers and juvenile property offenders (though not all the latter results were discouraging). Sherman, Strang and Woods (2000, p. 20) conclude that compared with court, the effect of diversionary conferences is to cause the following:

- Big drop in offending rates by violent offenders (by 38 crimes per 100 per year)
- Very small increase in offending by drink drivers (by 6 crimes per 100 offenders per year)
- Lack of any difference in repeat offending by juvenile property offenders or shoplifters (though after-only analysis shows a drop in reoffending by shoplifters)

The drunk driving results are particularly disappointing. These are conferences without a victim, as all cases involve nonaccidents detected by random breath testing. Sherman, Strang and Woods (2000, p. 11) interpret the pattern of the results as suggesting that courts reduce reoffending through their power to suspend drivers' licenses, a power not available to conferences in the experiment. However, more detailed decomposition of results is yet to be done on this question.

One conferencing program that has dealt convincingly with the social selection problem without randomization is a Royal Canadian Mounted Police program in the Canadian coal mining town of Sparwood, British Columbia. For almost three years from the commencement of the program in 1995 until late 1997, *no* young offender from Sparwood went to court.[6] All were cautioned or conferenced. Three youths who had been conferenced on at least two previous occasions went to court in late 1997. No cases have been to court during 1998 up until the time the data could be checked (20 October 1998). In the year prior to the program (1994), sixty-four youths went to court. Over the ensuing three years and nine months, this net was narrowed to eighty-eight conferences and three court cases. This was probably not just a net-narrowing effect, however. It looks like a real reduction in offending. According to police records, compared with the 1994 youth offending rate, the 1995 rate was down 26 per cent, and the 1996 rate was down 67 per cent. Reoffending rates for conference cases were 8 per cent in 1995, 3 per cent in 1996, 10 per cent in 1997, and 0 per cent for the first nine months of 1998, compared with a national rate of 40 per cent per annum for court cases (which is similar to that in towns surrounding Sparwood). Reoffending rates for Sparwood court cases prior to 1995 have not been collected. While social selection bias is convincingly dealt with here by the universality of the switch to restorative justice for the first three years, eighty-eight conferences are only a modest basis for inference.

Burford and Pennell's (1998) study of a restorative conference-based approach to family violence in Newfoundland found a marked reduction in both child abuse/neglect and abuse of mothers/wives after the intervention. A halving of abuse/neglect incidents was found for thirty-two families in the year after the conference compared with the year before, while incidents increased markedly for thirty-one control families. Pennell and Burford's (1997) research is also a model of sophisticated process development and process evaluation and of methodological triangulation. While sixty-three families might seem modest for quantitative purposes, this is actually a statistically persuasive study in demonstrating that this intervention reduced family violence. There were actually 472 participants in the conferences for the thirty-two families, and 115 of these were interviewed to estimate levels of violence affecting different participants (Pennell and Burford, 2000). Moreover, within each case a before and after pattern was tested against thirty-one types of events (e.g. abuse of child, child abuses mother, attempted suicide, father keeps income from mother) where events can be relevant to more than one member of the family. Given this pattern matching of families by events by individual family members, it understates the statistical power of the design to say it is based on only sixty-three cases. Burford and Pennell (1998, p. 253) also report reduced drinking problems after conferences. The Newfoundland conferences were less successful in cases where young people were abusing their mothers, a matter worthy of further investigation.

While the universality of the New Zealand juvenile conferencing program has made it difficult to evaluate the impact on recidivism compared with a control group, Maxwell, Morris and Anderson (1999) have now published an important evaluation of two adult programs, which they describe as sharing enough of the core principles of restorative justice to serve as case studies of restorative justice. Te Whanau Awhina (a program only for Maori offenders) and Project Turnaround refer adult offenders to a panel (rather akin to the Vermont Reparation Boards). However, family and social service providers for the family, victims and victim supporters, and the police also frequently attend. For 100 offenders referred to each of these schemes, both reoffending and the seriousness of reoffending were significantly reduced under both schemes compared with 100 controls matched for criminal history, demographic factors, and offence characteristics who went to court. Twelve-month reconviction rates were 16 per cent for Project Turnaround compared with 30 per cent for controls. For Te Whanau Awhina, reconviction was 33 per cent, compared with 47 per cent for controls.

Another important recent adult evaluation is of the John Howard Society's Restorative Resolutions program in Winnipeg (Bonta *et al.*, 1998). The seriousness of the offending gives special importance to this evaluation: there was 90 per cent success in reserving entry to the program to serious adult offenders who were facing a prosecutorial recommendation of at least six months prison time (and preferably having histories of incarceration and probation violation). Like the New Zealand programs discussed in the previous paragraph, Restorative Resolutions secured enough of the principles of restorative justice to be accepted as a test of the approach without securing all of them: notwithstanding good-faith consultation with victims, most offenders did not actually meet their victim, and eighteen offenders had their restorative resolution accepted by the court but then with a judicially imposed sentence on top of it. Since this initial report was published, there has been follow-up over three years of a control group of seventy-two offenders, carefully matched on a variety of risk factors; the seventy-two Restorative Resolutions serious offenders had half the criminal reoffending of the control group.

[A] recent study by Michael Little (2001), is of particular importance in that it applies restorative justice to the most persistent offenders. Little's study was conducted in Kent, England. It applied to juvenile offenders who either had been previously sentenced to custody or had failed to complete a community sentence. A second condition for entry was being charged or cautioned on three or more occasions for offences that would permit a court to sentence to custody. Basically they were the most persistent young offenders in Kent. Twenty-four offenders were randomly assigned to a multisystemic approach that involved a family group conference, joint and heightened supervision by police and social services staff, and improved assessment combined with an individual treatment plan and mentoring by a young volunteer. This was called the Intensive Supervision and Support Program. Fifty-five young offenders were assigned to two control groups. The reduction in rearrest during two years of follow-up was substantial and statistically significant. Because the treatment was multisystematic, however, there was no way of assessing whether it was restorative justice, some other component of the program, or a general placebo effect that produced the success. [Elsewhere] we consider the theoretical reasons why a combination of restorative justice and intensive rehabilitation in hard cases may be more effective than restorative justice and intensive rehabilitation alone. The results of this randomized trial are compelling because part of the intervention was more intensive police surveillance. This should have produced an increase in the number of offences detected by the police in the restorative justice group.

Restorative antibullying programs in schools, generally referred to as *whole-school* approaches (Rigby, 1996), which combine community deliberation among students, teachers and parents about how to prevent bullying with mediation of specific cases, have been systematically evaluated with positive results (Farrington, 1993; Pitts and Smith, 1995; Pepler *et al.*, 1993; Rigby, 1996) the most impressive being a program in Norway where a 50 per cent reduction in bullying has been reported (Olweus, 1993). Gentry and Benenson's (1993) data further suggest that skills for mediating playground disputes learned and practiced by children in school may transfer to the home setting, resulting in reduced conflict, particularly with siblings. The restorative approaches to bullying in Japanese schools, which Master's (1997) qualitative work found to be a success, can also be read as even more radically 'whole-school' than the Norwegian innovations (see Box 2).

However, Gottfredson's (1997) and Brewer *et al.*'s (1995) reviews of school peer mediation programs that simply train children to resolve disputes when conflicts arise among students showed nonsignificant or weak effects on observable behavior such as fighting. Only one of four studies with quasi-experimental or true experimental designs found peer mediation to be associated with a decrease in aggressive behavior. Lam's (1989) review of fourteen evaluations of peer mediation programs with mostly weak methods found no programs that made violence worse. It appears a whole-school approach is needed that not just tackles individual incidents but also links incidents to a change program for the culture of the school, in particular to how seriously members of the school community take rules about bullying. Put another way, the school not only must resolve the bullying incident; but also must use it as a resource to affirm the disapproval of bullying in the culture of the school.

Statistical power, randomization, and control have been weak in much of the research reported here. Fairly consistently encouraging results from these weak designs, however,

---

Box 2: Pig, pig, pig!

The incident began during the morning roll call when the boy in charge called a girl by her (unappreciated) nickname of 'pig'. The girl was offended and refused to answer, so the boy raised his voice and yelled the word several times … Later that morning during the break several children gathered around the girl and chanted, 'Pig, pig, pig'. Deeply hurt … she ran away from the group. For the remainder of the school day she did not speak a word; that afternoon she went home and would refuse to return for a week. The teacher in charge of the class had not been present during the periods when the girl was insulted, so she did not appreciate what had happened.

Later that day the girl's mother called to ask what had gone on. Immediately the principal began a quiet investigation in co-operation with the teacher. By that evening, parts of the story were known, and the principal visited the child's home to apologise to her parents. The next day, and on each successive day until the problem was solved, special teachers' meetings were held with all present to seek a solution. On three occasions the principal or the girl's homeroom teacher went to the girl's home and talked with her. The final resolution involved a visit by the entire class to the girl's home, where apologies were offered along with a request that the insulted girl forgive her friends. Two days later she returned to school, and two weeks later the teacher read a final report to the regular teachers' meeting and then apologised for having caused the school so much trouble.

Source: Cummings, 1980, pp. 118–19, cited in Masters, 1997

should be combined with the reduced reoffending evident under stronger designs in the studies by Schneider (1986), Olweus (1993) and the other antibullying researchers, Burford and Pennell (1998), the Sparwood police, Maxwell, Morris and Anderson (1999), Bonta Rooney and Wallace-Capretta (1998), McGarrell *et al.* (2000), and Little (2001). However, the research with the strongest design, by Sherman, Strang and Woods (2000), is encouraging only with respect to violent offenders. My own reading of the three dozen studies of reoffending reviewed is that while restorative justice programs do not involve a consistent guarantee of reducing offending, even badly managed restorative justice programs are most unlikely to make reoffending worse. After all, restorative justice is based on principles of socializing children that have demonstrably reduced delinquency when parents have applied them in raising their children (in comparison to punitive/stigmatizing socialization) (Braithwaite, 1989; Sampson and Laub, 1993). If we invest in working out how to improve the quality of the delivery of restorative justice programs, they are likely to show us how to substantially reduce reoffending. That investment means looking below the surface to understand the theoretical conditions of success and failure [...].

Restorative justice advocates are frequently admonished not to make 'exaggerated claims' for the likely effects on recidivism of a one- or two-hour intervention. Yet when it is modest benefits on the order of 10 to 20 per cent lower levels of reoffending that are predicted, it can be equally irresponsible to cite a study with a sample size of 100 (which lacks the statistical power to detect an effect of this order as statistically significant) as demonstrating no effect. If we are modest in our expectations, we should expect reviewers like Braithwaite (1999) to report a study by Umbreit (1994) on a small sample finding a nonsignificant reduction in offending and then in this review to have Braithwaite report an expanded sample by Umbreit and his colleagues to now be strongly significant. [Recently] there has been a surge of positive recidivism results from the United States, Canada, Germany, the United Kingdom, Australia, and New Zealand. [Most] of these very recent positive results are not incorporated into the meta analysis of thirty-two studies with control groups conducted for the Canadian Department of Justice by Latimer, Dowden and Muise (2001). Equally, Latimer, Dowden and Muise have uncovered unpublished evaluations of a dozen recent restorative justice programs not covered by the review in this chapter. Across their thirty-two studies Latimer, Dowden and Muise found a modest but statistically significant effect of restorative justice in reducing recidivism (effect size 0.07). This means approximately seven per cent lower recidivism on average in the restorative justice programs compared to controls or comparison groups. This is indeed a modest accomplishment compared to effect sizes for the best rehabilitation programs. During R and D on first and second generation programs, however, our interest should not be on comparing average restorative justice effect sizes with those of the best rehabilitation programs. It should be on the effect sizes we might accomplish by integration of best restorative justice practice with best rehabilitative practice [...]. One important difference in the conclusion reached from the set of studies reviewed in this chapter is that Latimer, Dowden and Muise found a bigger tendency for victim satisfaction to be higher in cases that went to restorative justice (effect size 0.19) than the tendency for offender satisfaction to be higher in restorative justice cases (effect size 0.10).

So now we must remember that it is possible to make Type II as well as Type I errors; we can make the error of wrongly believing that 'nothing makes much difference'. In recent criminological history we have seen this Type II error institutionalized in the doctrine that 'nothing works' with respect to offender rehabilitation. Restorative justice clearly has the promise to justify a huge R and D effort now. Certainly there are some notable research failures. Here we might remember the often-quoted retrospective of medical texts that it was not until the advances in medicine during World War I that the average patient left an encounter with the average doctor better off. The question at the beginning of the twentieth century was whether there was enough promise in medicine to justify a huge research invest-ment in it. Clearly there was, notwithstanding a lot of mediocre results from mediocre prac-tice. The results in this section show that there are very strong reasons to think that funding restorative justice R and D will be a good investment for the twenty-first century, especially when [...] restorative justice is conceived as a superior vehicle for delivering other crime prevention strategies that work, and conceived holistically as a way of living rather than just an eighty-minute intervention.

It may be that the key to explaining why the Indianapolis Juvenile Restorative Justice Experiment had a major effect on reoffending while the RISE adult drunk driving experi-ment did not can be understood in terms of the potential for restorative justice to be a supe-rior vehicle for prevention to be realized in the former case but not the latter. Eighty-three per cent of those randomly assigned to conferences in Indianapolis completed their diversion program, whereas completion occurred for only 58 per cent of the control group assigned to the standard suite of diversion options (McGarrell et al., 2000, p. 47). [Restorative] justice is potentially a superior vehicle for getting offenders and their families to commit to reha-bilitative and other preventive measures. The RISE drunk driving conferences generally did not confront underlying drinking problems, with police encouraging the view that drunk driving, not drinking, is the offence. Court did not do any better in this regard, but at least the Canberra courts took away driver's licenses, a preventive measure that was not available to conferences and that probably worked.

Reduced reoffending in corporate restorative justice programs

[Elsewhere] I recounted how corporate crime researchers like myself began to wonder if the more restorative approach to corporate criminal law might actually be more effective than the punitive approach to street crime. What made us wonder this? When we observed inspec-tors moving around factories (as in Hawkins's [1984] study of British pollution inspectors), we noticed how talk often got the job done. The occupational health and safety inspector could talk with the workers and managers responsible for a safety problem, and they would fix it – with no punishment, not even threats of punishment. A restorative justice reading of regulatory inspection was also consistent with the quantitative picture. The probability that any given occupational health and safety violation will be detected has always been slight and the average penalty for Occupational Safety and Health Administration (OSHA) viola-tions in the post-Watergate United States was $37 (Kelman, 1984). So the economically rational firm did not have to worry about OSHA enforcement: when interviewed, its repre-sentatives would say it was a trivial cost of doing business. Yet there was quantitative evidence that workplace injuries fell after OSHA inspections or when inspection levels increased (Scholz and Gray, 1990).

There was even stronger evidence that Mine Safety and Health Administration inspec-tions in the United States saved lives and prevented injuries (Braithwaite, 1985, pp. 77–84; Lewis-Beck and Alford, 1980; Perry, 1981a, 1981b; Boden, 1983). Boden's data showed that a 25 per cent increase in inspections was associated with a 7 to 20 per cent reduction in fatalities on a pooled cross-sectional analysis of 535 mines with controls for geological, technological, and managerial factors; these inspections took place at a time when the aver-age penalty for a successful citation was $173 (Braithwaite, 1985, p. 3). They were inspections ending with an 'exit conference' that I observed to be often quite restorative. Boden (1983) and the Mine Enforcement and Safety Administration (1977) found no association between the level of penalties and safety improvement, however.

This was just the opposite of the picture we were getting from the literature on law enforcement and street crime. On the streets, the picture was of tough enforcement, more police, and more jails failing to make a difference. In coal mines we saw weak enforcement (no imprisonment) but convincing evidence that what Julia Black later came to call 'conventional regulation' (Black, 1997, 1998) can work – more inspectors reduced offending and saved lives (Braithwaite, 1985).

My book was called *To Punish or Persuade: Enforcement of Coal Mine Safety,* and it concluded that while persuasion works better than punishment, credible punishment is needed as well to back up persuasion when it fails. Writing the book was a somewhat emotional conversion to restorative justice for me, as I came to it as a kind of victims' supporter, a boy from a coal mining town who wanted to write an angry book for friends killed in the mines. My research also found strong empirical evidence that persuasion works better when workers and unions (representing the victims of the crime) are involved in deliberative regulatory processes.[7] Nearly all serious mine safety accidents can be prevented if only the law is obeyed (Braithwaite, 1985, pp. 20–4, 75–7); the great historical lesson of the coal industry is that the way to accomplish this is through a rich dialogue among victims and offenders on why the law is important, a dialogue given a deeper meaning after each fatality is investigated. The shift from punitive to restorative justice in that industry and the results of that shift have been considerable. During the first fifty years of mine safety enforcement in Britain (until World War I), in a number of years a thousand miners lost their lives in the pits. Fatalities decreased from 1,484 in 1866 to 44 in 1982–83, after which the British industry collapsed. In the years immediately prior to World War I, the average annual number of criminal prosecutions for coal mine safety offences in the United Kingdom was 1,309. In both 1980 and 1981 there were none (Braithwaite, 1985, p. 4).

The qualitative research doing ride-alongs with mine safety inspectors in several countries resolved the puzzle for me. Persuasion worked much of the time; workers' participation in a dialogue about their own security worked. However, the data also suggested that persuasion worked best in the contexts where it was backed by the possibility of punishment.

In the United Kingdom during the 1970s, fifty pits were selected each year for a special safety campaign; these pits showed a consistently greater improvement in accident rates than other British pits (Collinson, 1978, p. 77). I found the safety leaders in the industry were companies that not only thoroughly involved everyone concerned after a serious accident to reach consensual agreement on what must be done to prevent recurrence but also did this after 'near accidents' (Braithwaite, 1985, p. 67), as well as discussing safety audit results with workers even when there was no near accident. In a remarkable foreshadowing of what we now believe to be reasons for the effectiveness of whole-school approaches to bullying and family group conferences, Davis and Stahl's (1967, p. 26) study of twelve companies that had been winners of the industry's two safety awards found one recurring initiative was 'safety letter to families of workers enlisting family support in promoting safe work habits'. That is, safety leaders engaged a community of care beyond the workplace in building a safety culture. In *To Punish or Persuade* I shocked myself by concluding that after mine disasters, including the terrible one in my hometown that had motivated me to write the book, so long as there had been an open public dialogue among all those affected, the families of the miners cared for, and a credible plan to prevent recurrence put in place, criminal punishment served little purpose. The process of the public inquiry and helping the families of the miners for whom they were responsible seemed such a potent general deterrent that a criminal trial could be gratuitous and might corrupt the restorative justice process that I found in so many of the thirty-nine disaster investigations I studied.

Joseph Rees (1988, 1994) is the scholar who has done most to work through the promise of what he calls *communitarian regulation,* which we might read as restorative regulatory justice. First Rees (1988) studied the Cooperative Compliance Program of OSHA between 1979 and 1984. OSHA essentially empowered labor-management safety committees at seven Californian sites to take over the law enforcement role, to solve the underlying problems revealed by breaches of the law. Satisfaction of workers, management and government participants was high because they believed the program 'worked'. It seemed to. Accident rates ranged from one-third lower to five times as low as the Californian rate for comparable projects of the same companies, as the rate in the same project before the cooperative compliance program compared with after (Rees, 1988, pp. 2–3).

Rees' next study of communitarian regulation was of US nuclear regulation after the incident at Three Mile Island. The industry realized that it had to transform the nature of its regulation and self-regulation from a rule book, hardware orientation to one oriented to people, corporate cultures, and software. The industry's CEOs set up the Institute of Nuclear Power Operations (INPO) to achieve these ends. Peers from other nuclear power plants would take three weeks off from their own jobs to join an INPO review team that engaged representatives of the inspected facility in a dialogue about how they could improve. Safety performance ratings were also issued by the review team; comparative ratings of all the firms in the industry were displayed and discussed at meetings of all the CEOs in the industry and at separate meetings of safety officers. Rees (1994) sees these as reintegrative shaming sessions. The following is an excerpt from a videotape of a meeting of the safety officers:

> It's not particularly easy to come up here and talk about an event at a plant in which you have a lot of pride, a lot of pride in the performance, in the operators … It's also tough going through the agonizing thinking of what it is you want to say. How do you want to confess? How do you want to couch it in a way that, even though you did something wrong, you're still okay? You get a chance to talk to Ken Strahm and Terry Sullivan [INPO vice presidents] and you go over what your plans are, and they tell you, 'No, Fred, you've got to really bare your soul'…. It's a painful thing to do.
>
> (Rees, 1994, p. 107)

What was the effect of the shift in the center of gravity of the regulatory regime from a Nuclear Regulatory Commission driven by political sensitivities to be tough and prescriptive to INPO's communitarian regulation (focused on a dialogue about how to achieve outcomes rather than rule book enforcement)? Rees (1994, pp. 183–6) shows considerable improvement across a range of indicators of the safety performance of the US nuclear power industry since INPO was established. Improvement has continued since the completion of Rees' study. For example, more recent World Association of Nuclear Operators data show scrams (automatic emergency shutdowns) declined in the United States from over 7 per unit in 1980 to 0.1 by the late 1990s.

[Elsewhere] we saw that shifting nursing home regulation from rule book enforcement to restorative justice was associated with improved regulatory outcomes and that the inspectors who shifted most toward restorative justice improved compliance most (those who used praise and trust more than threat, those who used reintegrative shaming rather than tolerance or stimatization, those who restored self-efficacy). [While these results are discussed else where, for] the moment, I simply report that communitarian regulation has had considerable documented success in restoring coal mining firms, nuclear power plants, and nursing homes in a more responsible approach to compliance with the law. Equally, writers such as Gunningham (1995) and Haines (1997) have shown that there are serious limits to communitarian regulation – rapacious big firms and incompetent little ones that will not or cannot respond responsibly. Deterrence and incapacitation are needed, and needed in larger measure than these regimes currently provide, when restorative justice fails (see also Ayres and Braithwaite, 1992; Gunningham and Grabosky, 1998).

Carol Heimer pointed out in comments on a draft of this chapter, 'If high-level white collar workers are more likely to get restorative justice, it may be because their corporate colleagues and other members of the society believe that their contributions are not easily replaced, so that offenders must be salvaged' (see Heimer and Staffen, 1995). This is right, I suspect, and a reason that justice is most likely to be restorative in the hands of communities of care that can see the value of salvaging the offender and the victim.

Restorative justice practices restore and satisfy communities better than existing criminal justice practices

In every place where a reform debate has occurred about the introduction of family group conferences, two community concerns have been paramount: (1) while victims might be forgiving in New Zealand, giving free rein to victim anger 'here' will tear at our community; (2) while families may be strong elsewhere, 'here' our worst offenders are alienated and alone, their families are so dysfunctional and uncaring that they will not participate meaningfully. But as Morris *et al.* (1996, p. 223) conclude from perspectives on this question summarized from a number of jurisdictions: 'Concerns about not being able to locate extended family or family supporters, to engage families or to effectively involve so-called "dysfunctional" families, about families forming a coalition to conceal abuse and about families' failing to honour agreements do not prove to have been well-founded in any of the jurisdictions reported in this book.'

In his discussion of the Hollow Water experience of using healing circles to deal with rampant sexual abuse of children in a Canadian First Nations community, Ross (1996, p. 150) emphasizes the centrality of restoring communities for restoring individuals: 'If you are dealing with people whose relationships have been built on power and abuse, you must actually *show* them, then give them the experience of, relationships based on respect... [so]... the healing process must involve a healthy *group* of people, as opposed to single therapists. A single therapist cannot, by definition, do more than *talk* about healthy relationships.'

The most sophisticated implementation of this ideal that has been well evaluated is Burford and Pennell's (1998) Family Group Decision Making Project to confront violence and child neglect in families. Beyond the positive effects on the direct objective of reducing violence, the evaluation found a posttest increase in family support, concrete (e.g. babysitting) and emotional, and enhanced family unity, even in circumstances where some conference plans involved separation of parents from their children. The philosophy of this program was to look for strengths in families that were in very deep trouble and build on them. [Elsewhere,] building on the work of Mary Kaldor (1999), I argue that this is the restorative justice prescription to the nature of contemporary armed conflict – find the islands of civility in the war-torn nation and build out from the strength in those islands of civil society.

Members of the community beyond the offender and the victim who attend restorative justice processes tend, like offenders, victims, and the police, to come away with high levels of satisfaction. In Pennell and Burford's (1995) family group conferences for family violence, 94 per cent of family members were 'satisfied with the way it was run'; 92 per cent felt they were 'able to say what was important'; and 92 per cent 'agreed with the plan decided on'. Clairmont (1994, p. 28) also reports that among native peoples in Canada the restorative justice initiatives he reviewed have 'proven to be popular with offenders... and to have broad, general support within communities'. The Ministry of Justice, Western Australia (1994) reports 93 per cent parental satisfaction, 84 per cent police satisfaction, and 67 per cent judicial satisfaction, plus (and crucially) satisfaction of Aboriginal organizations with its restorative justice conference program (Juvenile Justice Teams). In Singapore, 95 per cent of family members who attended family group conferences said that they bene-fited personally from the experience (Hsien, 1996). For the Bethlehem police conferencing experiment, parents of offenders were more satisfied (97 per cent) and more likely to believe that justice had been fair (97 per cent) than in cases that went to court (McCold and Wachtel, 1998, pp. 65–72). Parental satisfaction and perceptions of justice were similarly high in the Indianapolis experiment (McGarrell *et al.*, 2000). Eighty per cent of the conference parents 'felt involved', compared with 40 per cent for the children who were randomly assigned to other diversion programs. Ninety per cent of the conference parents felt they had the opportunity to express their views, compared with 68 per cent in the control group.

A study by Schneider (1990) found that *completing* restitution and community service was associated with enhanced commitment to community and feelings of citizenship (and reduced recidivism). While the evidence is overwhelming that where communities show strong social support, criminality is less (Cullen, 1994; Chamlin and Cochran, 1997), it might be optimistic to expect that restorative justice could ever have sufficient impacts in restoring microcommunities to cause a shift in the macro impact of community on the crime rate (cf. Brown and Polk, 1996). On the other hand, Tom Tyler's most recent book with Yuen Huo (Tyler and Huo, 2001) finds that procedural fairness by authorities quite strongly increases trust in authorities, and trust in authorities in turn has considerable effects in increasing identification with one's community and society and ultimately participation in the community. [In Tyler's work we] see there is consistent evidence that restorative justice is perceived as more procedurally fair in a number of ways compared with courtroom justice. Tyler's work opens up exciting new lines of research on why restorative justice might contribute to community building.

Building the microcommunity of a school or restoring social bonds in a family can have important implications for crime in that school or that family. Moreover, the restoring of microcommunity has a value of its own, independent of the size of the impact on crime. The previous section described how whole-school approaches can halve bullying in schools. There is a more important point of deliberative programs to give all the citizens of the school community an opportunity to be involved in deciding how to make their school safer and more caring. It is that they make their schools more decent places to live while one is being educated. Evidence from Australia suggests that restorative sexual harassment programs in workplaces may reduce sexual harassment (Parker, 1998). Again, more important than the improved compliance with the law may be the more general improvements in the respect with which women are treated in workplaces as a result of the deliberation and social support integral to such programs when they are effective.

We have seen restorative justice conferences where supporters of a boy offender and a girl victim of a sexual assault agreed to work together to confront a culture of exploitative masculinity in an Australian school that unjustly characterized the girl as 'getting what she asked for' (Braithwaite and Daly, 1994). Conversely, we have seen conferences that have missed the opportunity to confront homophobic cultures in schools revealed by graffiti humiliating allegedly gay men and boys (Retzinger and Scheff, 1996). After one early New Zealand conference concerning breaking into and damaging the restaurant of a refugee Cambodian, the offender agreed to watch a video of *The Killing Fields* and 'pass the word on the street' that the Cambodian restaurateur was struggling to survive and should not be harassed. A small victory for civil community life, perhaps, but a large one for that Cambodian man.

One of the most stirring conferences I know of occurred in an outback town after four Aboriginal children manifested their antagonism toward the middle-class matriarchs of the town by ransacking the Country Women's Association Hall. The conference was so moving because it brought the Aboriginal and the white women together, shocked and upset by what the children had done, to talk to each other about why the women no longer spoke to one another across the racial divide in the way they had in earlier times. Did there have to be such an incivility as this to discover the loss of their shared communal life? Those black and white women and children rebuilt that communal life as they restored the devastated Country Women's Association Hall, working together, respectfully once more (for more details on this case, see the Real Justice Web site at http://www.realjustice.org/).

One might summarize that the evidence of restorative justice restoring communities points to very small accomplishments of microcommunity-building and of modest numbers of community members going away overwhelmingly satisfied with the justice in which they feel they have had a meaningful opportunity to participate. Maori critics of Pakeha restorative justice such as Moana Jackson (1987) and Juan Tauri (1998) point out that it falls far short of restoring Maori community control over justice. Neocolonial controls from Pakeha courts remain on top of restorative justice in Maori communities. This critique seems undeniable; nowhere in the world has restorative justice enabled major steps toward restoring precolonial forms of community among colonized peoples; nowhere have the courts of the colonial power given up their power to trump the decisions of the Indigenous justice forums.

At the same time, there is a feminist critique of this Indigenous critique of community restoration. […]

With all the attention we have given to the microcommunity-building of routine restorative justice conferences, we must not lose sight of historically rare moments of restorative justice that reframe macrocommunity. I refer, for example, to the release of IRA terrorists from prison so that they could participate in the IRA meetings of 1998 that voted for the renunciation of violent struggle. I refer to much more partially successful examples, such as the Camp David mediations of President Carter with the leaders of Egypt and Israel (more partially successful because they excluded the Palestinians themselves) and to more totally successful local peacemaking such as that of the Kulka Women's Club in the highlands of New Guinea (see Box 3).

Conclusion

There do seem to be empirical grounds for optimism that restorative justice can 'work' in restoring victims, offenders, and communities. When the restorative practice helps bring a war-torn nation to peace, as in the civil wars of the Solomons and Bougainville (see Box 3: Kulka Women's Club, Peacemaking […]), we might say restorative justice works with dramatic effect. As the endeavors of the Truth and Reconciliation Commission in South Africa and those of a number of other nations now demonstrate, 'working' in terms of healing a nation is more important than working simply conceived as reducing crime. At a more micro level, 'working' as healing a workplace after sexual harassment (Parker, 1998), a

---

Box 3: Kulka Women's Club peacemaking

Alan Rumsey (2000) has documented the extraordinary intervention of the Kulka Women's Club to end a New Guinea highlands tribal war. The context is that, after an initial period of colonial pacification, in many parts of the New Guinea highlands tribal fighting has become worse, and more deadly, in recent decades, with guns replacing spears and arrows. What the Kulka Women's Club did on 13 September 1982 was to march between two opposing armies under the national flag, exhorting both sides with gifts to put down their arms, which they did. Note that as in so many of the important non-Western forms of restorative justice, the victims move the offenders by giving them gifts rather than asking for compensation (see the Javanese case at note 1, and the Crow practice of buying the ways (Austin, 1984, p. 36)).[8] The distinctive peacemaking intervention of the Kulka Women's Club seems to have been unique, rather than a recurrent Melanesian cultural pattern. Its importance is that it had a long-lasting effect, the peace having held until the present, during two decades when hostilities among surrounding tribes escalated. Though the intervention seems unique, Maev O'Collins (2000) links it to peace and reconciliation meetings organized by women in war-torn Bougainville and women marching in Port Moresby to protest against male violence. In June 2000 a group of seventy women wearing scarfs in the colors of the national flag approached the two warring groups in the Solomon Islands civil war, asking them to talk peace, which they did (*The Dominion*, 17 June 2000). Rumsay's (2000, p. 9) work is important because it shows the need for highly contextualized analysis of the macrotransformative moments of restorative justice: 'The very factors that make one area relatively conducive to peacemaking are the same ones that make it more difficult in the neighbouring region.'

---

school after bullying (Rigby, 1996), and a family after violence (Burford and Pennell, 1998) are exceptionally important outcomes that have been considered in this chapter. [...] Finally, to conceive 'working' in the traditional criminological way of reducing crime forgets victims. We conclude, following Strang (2000), that restorative justice mostly works well in granting justice, closure, restoration of dignity, transcendence of shame, and healing for victims.

All that said, we have found that restorative justice shows great promise as a strategy of crime reduction. A mistake criminologists could make now is to do more and more research to compare the efficacy of restorative justice, statically conceived, with traditional Western justice. Rather, we must think more dynamically about developing the restorative justice process and the values that guide it. In my view, this chapter demonstrates that we already know that restorative justice has much promise. The research and development agenda now is to enlarge our understanding of the conditions under which that promise is realized. It will become clear that my own theoretical position inclines me to believe that restorative justice can work better if it is designed to enhance the efficacy of deterrence, incapacitation, and particularly rehabilitation and community prevention. Obversely, these strategies of crime reduction can work better if they are embedded in a responsive regulatory pyramid that enhances the efficacy of restorative justice. It follows that comparing the efficacy of a pure restorative justice strategy with that of a pure punishment strategy is not the best research path for the future.

[...]

Notes

1 I am reminded of a village in Java where I was told of a boy caught stealing. The outcome of a restorative village meeting was that the offender was given a bag of rice: 'We should be ashamed because one from our village should be so poor as to steal. We should be ashamed as a village.'

2 The evidence reviewed below also in fact suggests lower levels of victim satisfaction and participation than in its predecessor the Wagga Wagga program, a difference I attribute to the extraordinary gifts Terry O'Connell brought to that program and the extraordinary way the Wagga community got behind the program.

3 The evidence seems to be that this was due mainly to limitations in the program administration that made it difficult for victims to attend, not to the fact that most victims did not want to attend; only 6 per cent did not want to meet their offender (Maxwell and Morris, 1996).

4 The word *extremely* has been added to this sentence since my 1999 review of the evidence, indicating an accumulation of encouraging results.

5 This test is reported in Schneider, 1986, but for mysterious reasons Schneider, 1990 reports only the nonsignificant differences between before and after offending rates for the control and experimental groups separately, rather than the significant difference between the experimental and control group (which is the relevant comparison).

6 I am indebted to Glen Purdy, a Sparwood lawyer in private practice, for these data. The data until early 1997 are also available at www.titanlink.com.

7 For example, DeMichiei *et al.*'s (1982, p. i) comparison of mines with exceptionally high injury rates with matched mines with exceptionally low injury rates found that at the low injury mines: 'Open lines of communication permit management and labor to jointly reconcile problems affecting safety and health; Representatives of labor become actively involved in issues concerning safety, health and production; and Management and labor identify and accept their joint responsibility for correcting unsafe conditions and practices.'

8 Cree elder Roland Duneuette tells the story of the father and mother of a homicide victim taking in the offender as a son to teach him the Cree ways. Alan Rumsay tells me that in the highlands of New Guinea more widely, when one tribe is owed substantial compensation by another that has wronged them, the process that leads to the paying of that compensation starts with the wronged tribe offering a gift to the wrongdoer. In New Guinea, even when the offender acts first by offering compensation to a victim, the preserving of relationships will often also involve the expectation of a smaller but significant reciprocal gift back to the offender by the victim. Such a way of thinking is not unknown in the West. We see it in *Les Misérables*, part of the Western literary canon, and in Pope John Paul visiting and presenting a gift to the man who shot him.

References

Austin, W.T. (1984) 'Crow Indian Justice: Strategies of Informal Social Control, *Deviant Behavior*, 5, pp. 31–46.

Ayres, I. and Braithwaite, J. (1992) *Response Regulation: Transcending the Deregulation Debate* (New York, NY: Oxford University Press).

Barnes, G. (1999) 'Procedural Justice in Two Contexts: Testing the Fairness of Diversionary Conferencing for Intoxicated Drivers'. PhD dissertation, Institute of Criminal Justice and Criminology, University of Maryland.

Bazemore, G. (1999) 'Communities, Victims, and Offender Rehabilitation: Restorative Justice and Earned Redemption', in Etzioni, A. (ed.) *Civic Repentance* (Lanham, MD: Rowman & Littlefield).

Birchall, P., Namour, S. and Syme, H. (1992) 'Report on the Midland Pilot Reparation Scheme'. Unpublished paper, Western Australia.

Black, J. (1998) 'Talking about Regulation', *Public Law,* spring, pp. 77–105.

Boden, L.I. (1983) 'Government Regulation of Occupational Safety: Underground Coal Mine Accidents 1973–1975'. Unpublished manuscript, Harvard School of Public Health.

Bonta, J., Rooney, J. and Wallace-Capretta, S. (1998) *Restorative Justice: An Evaluation of the Restorative Resolution Project* (Ottawa: Solicitor General Canada).

Braithwaite, J. (1985) *To Punish or Persuade: Enforcement of Coal Mine Safety* (Albany, NY: State University of New York Press).

Braithwaite, J. (1989) *Crime, Shame and Reintegration* (Cambridge: Cambridge University Press).

Braithwaite, J. (1999) 'Restorative Justice: Assessing Optimistic and Pessimistic Accounts', in Tonry, M. (ed.) *Crime and Justice: A Review of Research Vol. 25* (Chicago, IL: University of Chicago Press).

Braithwaite, J. and Daly, K. (1994) 'Masculinities, Violence and Communitarian Control', in Newbury, T. and Stanka, E. (eds) *Just Boys Doing Business* (London: Routledge).

Brewer, D.D., Hawkins, J.D., Catalano, R.F. and Neckerman, H.J. (1995) 'Preventing Serious, Violent, and Chronic Juvenile Offending: A Review of Evaluations of Selected Strategies in Childhood, Adolescence, and the Community', in Howell, J.C. *et al.* (eds) *A Sourcebook: Serious, Violent, and Chronic Juvenile Offenders* (Thousand Oaks, CA: Sage).

Brown, M. and Polk, K. (1996) 'Taking Fear of Crime Seriously: The Tasmanian Approach to Community Crime Prevention', *Crime and Delinquency,* 42, pp. 398–420.

Burford, G. and Pennell, J. (1998) *Family Group Decision Making Project: Outcome Report Volume I* (St John's: Memorial University, Newfoundland).

Butts, J. and Snyder, H. (1991) *Restitution and Juvenile Recidivism* (Pittsburgh, PA: National Center for Juvenile Justice).

Chamlin, M.B. and Cochran, J.K. (1997) 'Social Altruism and Crime', *Criminology,* 35, pp. 203–28.

Chan, W.Y. (1996) 'Family Conferences in the Juvenile Justice Process: Survey on the Impact of Family Conferencing on Juvenile Offenders and their Families', in *Subordinate Courts Statistics and Planning Unit Research Bulletin* (Singapore).

Chatterjee, J. (2000) *RCMP's Restorative Justice Initiative* (Ottawa: Research and Evaluation Branch, Community Contract and Aboriginal Policing Services, Royal Canadian Mounted Police).

Clairmont, D. (1994) 'Alternative Justice Issues for Aboriginal Justice.' Paper prepared for the Aboriginal Justice Directorate, Ottawa: Department of Justice.

Coates, R. and Gehm, J. (1985) *Victim Meets Offender: An Evaluation of Victim Offender Reconciliation Programs* (Valparaiso, IN: PACT Institute of Justice).

Coates, R. and Gehm, J. (1989) 'An Empirical Assessment', in Wright, M. and Galaway, B. (eds) *Mediation and Criminal Justice* (London: Sage).

Collinson, J.L. (1978) 'Safety: Pleas and Prophylactics', *Mining Engineer,* July: pp. 73–83.

Crawford, A. (1996) 'Victim/Offender Mediation and Reparation in Comparative European Cultures: France, England and Wales.' Paper presented at the Australian and New Zealand Society of Criminology Conference, Wellington, January–February.

Cullen, F.T. (1994) 'Social Support as an Organizing Concept for Criminology: Presidential Address to the Academy of Criminal Justice Sciences', *Justice Quarterly,* 11, pp. 527–59.

Cullen, P.T. and Gendreau, P. (2000) 'Assessing Correctional Rehabilitation: Policy, Practice, and Prospects', in Horney, J. (ed.) *Policies, Processes, and Decisions of the Criminal Justice System Vol. 3* (Washington, DC: US Department of Justice).

Cummings, W.I. (1980) *Education and Equality in Japan* (Princeton: Princeton University Press).

Daly, K. (1996) 'Diversionary Conference in Australia: A Reply to the Optimists and Skeptics.' Paper presented at the annual meeting of the American Society of Criminology, 20–23 November.

Davis, G. (1992) *Making Amends: Mediation and Reparation in Criminal Justice* (London: Routledge).

Davis, R.T. and Stahl, R.W. (1967) 'Safety Organization and Activities of Award-winning Companies in the Coal Mining Industry', *in Bureau of Mines Information Circular 8224* (Washington, DC: Bureau of Mines).

DeMichiei, J.M., Langton, J.F., Bullock, K.A. and Wiles, T.C. (1982) *Factors Associated with Disabling Injuries in Underground Coal Mines* (Washington, DC: Mine Safety and Health Administration).

Dignan, J. (1990) *An Evaluation of an Experimental Adult Reparation Scheme in Kettering, Northamptonshire* (Sheffield: Centre for Criminological and Legal Research, University of Sheffield).

Dignan, J. (1992) 'Repairing the Damage: Can Reparation Work in the Service of Diversion?', *British Journal of Criminology,* 32, pp. 453–72.

Dolling, D. and Harman, A. (2000) 'Reoffending after Victim-Offender Mediation in Juvenile Court Proceedings.' Paper to Fourth International Conference on Restorative Justice for Juveniles, Tübingen, Germany.

Ervin, L. and Schneider, A. (1990) 'Explaining the Effects of Restitution on Offenders: Results from a National Experiment in Juvenile Courts', in Galaway, B. and Hudson, J. (eds) *Criminal Justice, Restitution and Reconciliation* (New York, NY: Willow Tree Press).

Farrington, D.P. (1993) 'Understanding and Preventing Bullying', in Tonry, M. (ed.) *Crime and Justice Annual Review of Research. Vol. 17* (Chicago, IL: University of Chicago Press).

Forsythe, L. (1995) 'An Analysis of Juvenile Apprehension Characteristics and Reapprehension Rates', in Moore, D. *et al.* (eds) *New Approach to Juvenile Justice: An Evaluation of Family Conferencing in Wagga Wagga. A Report to the Criminology Research Council* (Wagga Wagga, Australia: Charles Sturt University).

Fry, D. (1997) *A Report on Diversionary Conferencing* (Alice Springs, Australia: Northern Territory Police).

Galaway, B. (1992) 'The New Zealand Experience Implementing the Reparation Sentence', in Messmer, H. and Otto, H.U. (eds) *Restorative Justice on Trial: Pitfalls and Potentials of Victim–Offender Mediation International Research Perspectives* (Dordrecht and Boston, MA: Kluwer Academic).

Gendreau, P., Clark, K. and Gray, G.A. (1996) 'Intensive Surveillance Programs: They Don't Work', *Community Corrections Report,* 3:3, pp. 1–15.

Gentry, D.B. and Benenson, W.A. (1993) 'School-to-Home Transfer of Conflict Management Skills among School-age Children', *Families in Society,* February, pp. 67–73.

Geudens, H. (1998) 'The Recidivism Rate of Community Service as a Restitutive Judicial Sanction in Comparison with the Traditional Juvenile Justice Measure', in Walgrave, L. (ed.) *Restorative Justice for Juveniles: Potentialities, Risks and Problems for Research* (Leuven: Leuven University Press).

Goodes, T. (1995) *Victims and Family Conferences: Juvenile Justice in South Australia* (Adelaide: Family Conferencing Team).

Gottfredson, D. (1997) 'School-based Crime Prevention', in Sherman, L.*et al.* (eds) *Preventing Crime: What Works, What Doesn't, What's Promising. A Report to the United States Congress* (Washington, DC: National Institute of Justice).

Gunningham, N. (1995) 'Environment, Self-regulation and the Chemical Industry: Assessing Responsible Care', *Law and Policy,* 17, pp. 57–109.

Gunningham, N. and Grabosky, P. (1998) *Smart Regulation: Designing Environmental Policy* (Oxford: Clarendon Press).

Haines, F. (1997) *Corporate Regulation: Beyond 'Punish or Persuade'* (Oxford: Clarendon Press).

Haley, J. assisted by Neugebauer, A.M. (1992) 'Victim–Offender Mediations: Japanese and American Comparisons', in Messmer, H. and Otto, H.U. (eds) *Restorative Justice on Trial: Pitfalls and Potentials of Victim–Offender Mediation – International Research Perspective* (Dordrecht and Boston, MA: Kluwer Academic).

Hawkins, K. (1984) *Environment and Enforcement: Regulation and the Social Definition of Pollution* (Oxford: Clarendon Press).

Hayes, H., Prenzler, T. with Wortley, R. (1998) *Making Amends: Final Evaluation of the Queensland Community Conferencing Pilot* (School of Criminology and Criminal Justice, Griffith University).

Heimer, C.A. and Staffen, L.R. (1995) 'Interdependence and Reintegrative Social Control: Labelling and Reforming "Inappropriate" Parents in Neonatal Intensive Care Units', *American Sociological Review,* 60, pp. 635–54.

Hsien, L.I. (1996) 'Family Conferencing Good for Young Delinquents: Report' *Straits Times,* 6 March.

Iivari, J. (1987) 'Mediation as a Conflict Resolution: Some Topical Issues in Mediation Project in Vantaa.' Paper presented to the International Seminar on Mediation, Finland, September.

Iivari, J. (1992) 'The Process of Mediation in Finland: A Special Reference to the Question "How to Get Cases for Mediation"', in Messmer, H. and Otto, H.U. (eds) *Restorative Justice on Trial: Pitfalls and Potentials of Victim-Offender Mediation – International Research Perspectives* (Dordrecht and Boston, MA: Kluwer Academic).

Jackson, M. (1987) *The Maori and the Criminal Justice System: A New Perspective – He Whaipaanga Hou. Report for New Zealand Department of Justice* (Wellington: Policy and Research Division, Department of Justice).

Kaldor, M. (1999) *New and Old Wars: Organised Violence in a Global Era* (Cambridge: Polity Press).

Kelman, S. (1984) 'Enforcement of Occupational Safety and Health Regulations: A Comparison of Swedish and American Practices', in Hawkins, K. and Thomas, J.M. (eds) *Enforcing Regulations* (Boston, MA: Kluwer-Nijhoff).

Kerner, H., Marks, E. and Schreckling, J. (1992) 'Implementation and Acceptance of Victim–Offender Mediation Programs in the Federal Republic of Germany: A Survey of Criminal Justice Institutions', in Messmer, H. and Otto, H.U. (eds) *Restorative Justice on Trial: Pitfalls and Potentials of Victim-Offender Mediation – International Research Perspectives* (Dordrecht and Boston, MA: Kluwer Academic).

Kuhn, A. (1987) 'Koperverletzung als Konflikt, Zwischenbericht 1987 zum Project Handschlag.' Unpublished paper cited in T. Trenczak, 'A Review and Assessment of Victim–Offender Reconciliation Programming in West Germany', in Galaway, B. and Hudson, J. (eds) *Criminal Justice, Restitution and Reconciliation* (Monsey, NY: Willow Press).

Lam, J.A. (1989) *The Impact of Conflict Resolution Programs on Schools: A Review and Synthesis of the Evidence* (Amherst, MA: National Association for Mediation in Education).

Lam, J.A. (1995) 'Altering Course: New Directions in Criminal Justice and Corrections. Sentencing Circles and Family Group Conferences', *Australian and New Zealand Journal of Criminology,* December, pp. 78–99.

La, Prairie, C. (1995) 'Altering Course: New Directions in Criminal Justice and Corrections, Sentencing-Circles and Family Group Conferences'. *Australian and New Zealand Journal of Criminology,* December: 78–99.

Latimer, J., Dowden, C. and Muise, D. (2001) *The Effectiveness of Restorative Justice Practices: A Meta-analysis* (Ottawa: Department of Justice, Canada).

Lewis-Beck, M.S. and Alford, J.R. (1980) 'Can Government Regulate Safety: The Coal Mine Example', *American Political Science Review,* 74, pp. 745–56.

Little, M. (2001) 'ISSP: An Experience in Multi-Systemic Responses to Persistent Young Offenders Known to Children's Services.' Unpublished paper, University of Chicago.

Marshall, T.F. (1992) 'Restorative Justice on Trial in Britain', in Messmer, H. and Otto, H.U. (eds) *Restorative Justice on Trial: Pitfalls and Potentials of Victim–Offender Mediation – International Research Perspectives* (Dordrecht and Boston, MA: Kluwer Academic).

Marshall, T.F. and Merry, S. (1990) *Crime and Accountability: Victim Offender Mediation in Practice* (London: Home Office).

Masters, G. (1997) 'Reintegrative Shaming in Theory and Practice'. PhD dissertation, Lancaster University.

Maxwell, G.M. and Morris, A. (1993) *Family, Victims and Culture: Youth Justice in New Zealand* (Wellington: Special Policy Agency and Institute of Criminology, Victoria University of Wellington).

Maxwell, G.M. and Morris, A. (1996) 'Research on Family Group onferences with Young Offenders in New Zealand, in Hudson, J. *et al.* (eds) *Family Group Conferences: Perspectives on Policy and Practice* (Sydney: Federation Press and Criminal Justice Press).

Maxwell, G.M., Morris, A. and Anderson, T. (1999) *Community Panel Adult Pretrial Diversion: Supplementary Evaluation. Research Report* (Wellington: Crime Prevention Unit, Department of Prime Minister and Cabinet and Institute of Criminology, Victoria University of Wellington).

McCold, P. and Wachtel, B. (1998) 'Restorative Policing Experiment: The Bethlehem Pennsylvania Police Family Group Conferencing Project' (Pipersville, PA: Community Service Foundation).

McCold, I. and Wachtel, T. (2000) 'Restorative Justice Theory Validation'. Paper presented to the Fourth International Conference on Restorative Justice for Juveniles, Tubingen, Germany (www.restorativepractices.org).

McGarrell, E.F., Olivares, K., Crawford, K. and Kroovand, N. (2000) *Returning Justice to the Community: The Indianapolis Juvenile Restorative Justice Experiment* (Indianapolis, IN: Hudson Institute).

Miller, S. and Blackler, J. (2000) 'Restorative Justice Retribution, Confession and Shame', in Strang, H. and Braithwaite, J. (eds) *Restorative Justice: Philosophy to Practice* (Aldershot: Ashgate Dartmouth).

Mine Enforcement and Safety Administration (1977) *A Report on Civil Penalty Effectiveness* (Washington, DC: Mine Enforcement and Safety Administration).

Ministry of Justice, Western Australia (1994) *Juvenile Justice Teams: A Six-Month Evaluation* (Perth: Ministry of Justice).

Moore, D.B. with Forsythe, L. (1995) *A New Approach to Juvenile Justice: An Evaluation of Family Conferencing in Wagga Wagga* (Wagga Wagga: Charles Sturt University).

Moore, D.B. and O Connell, T. (1994) 'Family Conferencing in Wagga Wagga: A Communitarian Model of Justice', in Alder, C. and Wundersitz, J. (eds) *Family Conferencing and Juvenile Justice* (Canberra: Australian Studies in Law, Crime and Justice, Australian Institute of Criminology).

Morris, A., Maxwell, G., Hudson, J. and Galaway, B. (1996) 'Concluding Thoughts', in Hudson, J. *et al.* (eds) *Family Group Conferences: Perspectives on Policy and Practice* (Sydney: Federation Press and Criminal Justice Press).

Nugent, W.R. and Paddock, J.B. (1995) 'The Effect of Victim–Offender Mediation on Severity of Reoffense', *Mediation Quarterly,* 12, pp. 353–67.

Nugent, W.R., Umbreit, M.S., Wiinamaki, L. and Paddock, G. (forthcoming) 'Participation in Victim–Offender Mediation and Re-offense: Successful Replication?, *Journal of Research on Social Work Practice.*

Obonsawin-Irwin Consulting Inc. (1992a) *An Evaluation of the Attawapiskat First Nation Justice Project* (Ontario: Ministry of the Attorney General).

Obonsawin-Irwin Consulting Inc. (1992b) *An Evaluation of the Sandy Lake First Nation Justice Project* (Ontario: Ministry of the Attorney General).

O'Collins, M. (2000) 'Images of Violence in Papua New Guinea: Whose Images? Whose Reality?', in Dinnen, S. and Ley, A. (eds) *Reflection on Violence in Melanesia* (Annandale, NSW, and Canberra: Hawkins Press/Asia Pacific Press).

Olweus, I. (1993) 'Annotation: Bullying at School – Basic Facts and Effects of a School-based Intervention Program', *Journal of Child Psychology and Psychiatry,* 35, pp.1171–90.

Palk, G., Hayes, H. and Prenzler, T. (1998) 'Restorative Justice and Community Conferencing: Summary of Findings from a Pilot Study', *Current Issues in Criminal Justice,* 10, pp. 138–55.

Parker, C. (1998) 'Public Rights in Private Government: Corporate Compliance with Sexual Harassment Legislation', *Australian Journal of Human Rights,* 5, pp. 159–93.

Pate, K. (1990) 'Victim–Offender Restitution Programs in Canada', in Galaway, B. and Hudson, J. (eds) *Criminal Justice, Restitution and Reconciliation* (New York, NY: Willow Tree Press).

Pennell, J. and Burford, G. (1995) *Family Group Decision Making: New Rules for 'Old' Partners in Resolving Family Violence. Implementation Report. Vol. 1* (St John's: Family Group Decision Making Project, School of Social Work, University of Newfoundland).

Pennell, J. and Burford, G. (1997) *Family Group Decision Making: After the Conference – Progress in Resolving Violence and Promoting Well-Being* (St John's: Family Group Decision Making Project, School of Social Work, University of Newfoundland).

Pennell, J. and Burford, G. (2000) 'Family Group Decision Making: Protecting Children and Women', *Child Welfare,* 79, pp. 131 –58.

Pepler, D.J., Craig, W., Ziegler, S. and Charach, A. (1993) 'A School-based Antibullying Intervention', in Tatum, D. (ed.) *Understanding and Managing Bullying* (London: Heinemann).

Perry, C.S. (1981a) 'Dying to Dig Coal: Fatalities in Deep and Surface Coal Mining in Appalachian States, 1930–1978.' Unpublished manuscript. Department of Sociology, University of Kentucky.

Perry, C.S. (1981b) 'Safety Laws and Spending Saves Lives: An Analysis of Coal Mine Fatality Rates 1930–1979.' Unpublished manuscript, Department of Sociology, University of Kentucky.

Pitts, J. and Smith, P. (1995) *Preventing School Bullying. Police Research Group Crime Detection and Prevention Series Paper 63* (London: Home Office).

Power, P. (2000) 'Restorative Conferences in Australia and New Zealand.' PhD dissertation, Law School, University of Sydney.

290   *John Braithwaite*

Reed, P. (1986) 'Developmental Resources and Depression in the Elderly', *Nursing Research,* 36, pp. 368–74.

Reed, P. (1987) 'Spirituality and Well Being in Terminally Ill Hospitalized Adults', *Research in Nursing and Health,* 10, pp. 335–44.

Reed, P. (1992) 'An Emerging Paradigm for the Study of Spirituality in Nursing', *Research in Nursing and Health* 15, pp. 349–57.

Rees, J.V. (1988) *Reforming the Workplace* (Philadelphia, PA: University of Pennsylvania Press).

Rees, J.V. (1994) *Hostages of Each Other: The Transformation of Nuclear Safety since Three Mile Island* (Chicago: University of Chicago Press).

Retzinger, S. and Scheff, T.J. (1996) 'Strategy for Community Conferences: Emotions and Social Bonds', in Galaway, B. and Hudson, J. (eds) *Restorative Justice: International Perspectives* (Monsey, NY: Criminal Justice Press).

Rigby, K. (1996) *Bullying in Schools and What to Do about It* (Melbourne: Australian Council for Educational Research).

Ross, R. (1996) *Returning to the Teachings: Exploring Aboriginal Justice* (London: Penguin).

Rumsey, A. (2000) 'Women as Peacemakers in the New Guinea Highlands: A Case from the Nebilyer Valley, Western Highlands Province', in Dinnen, S. and Ley, A. (eds) *Reflection on Violence in Melanesia* (Leichhardt, NSW: Hawkins Press).

Sampson, R. and Laub, J.H. (1993) *Crime in the Making: Pathways and Turning Points through Life* (Cambridge, MA: Harvard University Press).

Schiff, M.F. (1998) 'The Impact of Restorative Interventions on Juvenile Offenders', in Walgrave, L. and Brazemore, G. (eds) *Restoring Juvenile Justice* (Monsey, NY: Criminal Justice Press).

Schneider, A. (1986) 'Restitution and Recidivism Rates of Juvenile Offenders: Results from Four Experimental Studies', *Criminology,* 24, pp. 533–52.

Schneider, A. (1990) *Deterrence and Juvenile Crime: Results from a National Policy Experiment* (New York, NY: Springer-Verlag).

Scholz, J.T. and Gray, W.B. (1990) 'OSHA Enforcement and Workplace Injuries: A Behavioral Approach to Risk Assessment', *Journal of Risk and Uncertainty,* 3, pp. 283–305.

Sherman, L.W., Strang, H. and Woods, D. (2000) *Recidivism Patterns in the Canberra Reintegrative Sharing Experiments (RISE)* (Canberra: Centre for Restorative Justice, Australian National University).

Smith, D., Blagg, H. and Derricourt, N. (1985) 'Victim–Offender Mediation Project. Report to the Chief Officers' Group, South Yorkshire Probation Service', cited in Marshall, T. and Merry, S. (eds) *Crime and Accountability: Victim-Offender Mediation in Practice* (London: Home Office, 1990).

Stewart, T. (1993) 'The Youth Justice Co-ordinator's Role: A Personal Perspective of the New Legislation in Action', in Brown, B.J. and McElrea, F.W.M. (eds) *The Youth Court in New Zealand: A New Model of Justice* (Auckland: Legal Research Foundation).

Strang, H. (2000) 'Victim Participation in a Restorative Justice Process: The Canberra Reintegrative Shaming Experiments.' PhD dissertation, Australian National University.

Strang, H. (2001) *Victim Participation in a Restorative Justice Process* (Oxford: Oxford University Press).

Strang, H. and Sherman, L.W. (1997) *The Victim's Perspective. RISE Working Paper* (Canberra: Law Program, RSSS, Australian National University).

Tauri, J. (1998) 'Family Group Conferencing: A Case Study of the Indigenisation of New Zealand's Justice System', *Current Issues in Criminal Justice,* 10, pp. 168–82.

Tauri, J. and Morris, A. (1997) 'Re-forming Justice: The Potential of Maori Processes', *Australian and New Zealand Journal of Criminology,* 30, pp. 149–67.

Trenczek, T. (1990) 'A Review and Assessment of Victim–Offender Reconciliation Programming in West Germany', in Galaway, B. and Hudson, J. (eds) *Criminal Justice, Restitution and Reconciliation* (Monsey, NY: Willow Press).

Trimboli, L. (2000) *An Evaluation of the NSW Youth Justice Conferencing Scheme* (Sydney: NSW Bureau of Crime Statistics and Research).

Tyler, T. and Huo, Y.J. (2001) *Trust and the Rule of Law: A Law-abidingness Model of Social Control* (New York: Russel Sage).

Umbreit, M. (1990) 'Mediation in the Nineties: Pushing Back the Boundaries', *Mediation,* 6, pp. 27–9.

Umbreit, M. (1992) 'Mediating Victim–Offender Conflict: From Single-site to Multi-site Analysis in the US', in Messmer, H. and Otto, H.U. (eds) *Restorative Justice on Trial: Pitfalls and Potentials of Victim–Offender Mediation – International Research Perspectives* (Dordrecht and Boston, MA: Kluwer Academic).

Umbreit, M. (1998) 'Restorative Justice through Juvenile Victim–Offender Mediation', in Walgrave, L. and Bazemore, G. (eds) *Restoring Juvenile Justice* (Monsey, NY: Criminal Justice Press).

Umbreit, M. and Coates, R. (1992) *Victim-Offender Mediation: An Analysis of Programs in Four States of the US* (Minneapolis, MN: Citizens Council Mediation Services).

Umbreit, M. with Coates, R. and Kalanj, B. (1994) *Victim Meets Offender: The Impact of Restorative Justice and Mediation* (Monsey, NY: Criminal Justice Press).

Van Ness, D. (1986) *Crime and its Victims: What We Can Do?* (Downers Grove, IL: Intervarsity Press).

Waters, A. (1993) 'The Wagga Wagga Effective Cautioning Program: Reintegrative or Degrading?' BA honors thesis, University of Melbourne.

Wundersitz, J. and Hetzel, S. (1996) 'Family Conferencing for Young Offenders: The South Australian Experience', in Hudson, J. *et al.* (eds) *Family Group Conferences: Perspectives on Policy and Practice* (Sydney: Federation Press and Criminal Justice Press).

Wynne, J. (1996) 'Leeds Mediation and Reparation Service: Ten Years Experience with Victim-Offender Mediation', in Galaway, B. and Hudson, J. (eds) *Restorative Justice: International Perspectives* (Monsey, NY: Criminal Justice Press).

24 Restorative justice

The evidence

Lawrence W. Sherman and Heather Strang

Executive summary

Purpose and scope

This is a non-governmental assessment of the evidence on restorative justice in the UK and internationally, carried out by the Jerry Lee Center of Criminology at the University of Pennsylvania for the Smith Institute in London, with funding from the Esmée Fairbairn Foundation. The purpose of this review is to examine what constitutes good-quality restorative justice practice, and to reach conclusions on its effectiveness, with particular reference to reoffending.[1]

Varieties of restorative justice

The review employs a broad definition of restorative justice (RJ), including victim-offender mediation, indirect communication through third parties, and restitution or reparation payments ordered by courts or referral panels. Much of the available and reasonably unbiased evidence of RJ effects on repeat offending comes from tests of face-to-face conferences of victims, offenders and others affected by a crime, most of them organised and led by a police officer; other tests cited involve court-ordered restitution and direct or indirect mediation.

What we found

Repeat offending

The most important conclusion is that *RJ works differently on different kinds of people*. It can work very well as a general policy, if a growing body of evidence on "what works for whom" can become the basis for specifying when and when not to use it. As Tables 1 to 3 show, rigorous tests of RJ in diverse samples have found substantial reductions in repeat offending for both violence and property crime. Other tests have failed to find such effects, but with different populations, interventions or comparisons. In one rare circumstance, a small sample of Aboriginals in Australia, an offer of face-to-face RJ (and its partial completion) appears to have caused higher rates of repeat offending than CJ. This very limited evidence of backfiring can be balanced against the potential RJ may have as a full or partial alternative to incarceration for young adult offenders, who had much lower two-year reconviction rates (11%) in one Canadian study (N =138) than a matched sample (37% reconviction) who served their sentence in prison.

In general, *RJ seems to reduce crime more effectively with more, rather than less, serious crimes.* The results below (Tables 1 to 3) suggest RJ works better with crimes involving personal victims than for crimes without them. They also suggest that it works with violent crimes more consistently than with property crimes, the latter having the only evidence of crime increases. These findings run counter to conventional wisdom, and could become the basis for substantial inroads in demarcating when it is "in the public interest" to seek RJ rather than CJ.

Victim effects

The evidence consistently suggests that victims benefit, on average, from face-to-face RJ conferences. The evidence is less clear about other forms of RJ, with no unbiased estimates of the effects of indirect forms of RJ on victims. But when victims willingly meet offenders face to face, they obtain short-term benefits for their mental health by reduced post-traumatic stress symptoms (PTSS). This may, in turn, reduce their lifetime risks of coronary disease (which PTSS causes in military veterans), as well as reducing health costs paid by taxpayers.

Offences brought to justice

When RJ has been offered to arrestees before charging in New York and Canberra, RJ has always brought at least twice as many offences to justice – and up to four times as many. Whether such effects could be even greater with widespread take-up of RJ across a community is a major question to be answered.

A way forward

There is far more evidence on RJ, with more positive results, than there has been for most innovations in criminal justice that have ever been rolled out across the country. The evidence now seems more than adequate to support such a roll-out for RJ, especially if that is done on a continue-to-learn-as-you-go basis. Such an approach could be well supported by a "Restorative Justice Board" (RJB), modelled on the Youth Justice Board but on a smaller scale. An RJB could prime the pump for RJ, proposing new statutes and funding new solutions to the obstacles that now limit victim access to RJ. An RJB could monitor RJ practices, design tests of new RJ strategies, and continue to recommend systemic changes needed to make RJ as effective as possible. It could, in effect, take RJ from the drawing board to its widespread construction, while also remaining at the drawing board for on-going improvements in design based on new evidence.

How we found it

Searching for evidence

The search process for this review built on the literature search protocol approved by the International Campbell Collaboration for the authors' registered and on-going review of the effects of face-to-face restorative justice for personal victim crimes.[2] The search has been expanded for this review to encompass other forms of restorative justice and other kinds of crimes.

The following search strategies were used to identify evaluations of the effectiveness of RJ at helping victims and reducing reoffending:

- searches of online databases;
- searches of online library catalogues;
- searches of existing reviews of the literature on the effectiveness of RJ;
- searches of bibliographies of publications;
- examination of publications already in our possession;
- referrals by experts in the field.

Both published and unpublished reports were considered in these searches. The searches were international in scope, but were limited to studies written in English.

Weighing the evidence

For all questions of the causal effect of RJ on such outcomes as victim mental health and repeat offending, we restricted our review to reasonably unbiased estimates of the difference that RJ made in comparison to some form of CJ. We followed the methods used by the National Institute of Health and Clinical Excellence (NICE) to assess evidence on the effectiveness of medical treatments. These methods (NICE, 2006) require us to use the "PICO" principle (population, intervention, comparison and outcome), asking, with every study examined, for exactly what *population* the RJ *intervention,* in contrast to what *comparison group,* produced what *outcomes.*

In assessing the strength of the evidence in each study that offered a reasonably unbiased PICO analysis, we were able to apply the Home Office (2004) standards for reconviction studies. These standards are based in part on the Maryland scientific methods scale (Sherman et al, 1997), which set a minimum threshold of level 3 for the Maryland report to the US Congress, *Preventing Crime.* Level 3 requires that the outcomes of at least two relatively similar P and C (population and comparison) groups are compared with (P) and without (C) the intervention. This review adopts that threshold, so that all statements about what works to reduce repeat offending or improve victim outcomes are based on a comparison between reasonably similar cases receiving RJ or not receiving RJ. For questions of implementation and description, the report incorporates both qualitative and before/after quantitative research designs.

Studies selected

The search process and eligibility criteria resulted in the identification of 36 tests eligible for inclusion in our quantitative review of the impact of RJ. These consisted of 25 reasonably unbiased estimates of the impact of RJ on repeat offending, six reasonably unbiased estimates of the effects of RJ on victims, and five estimates of the effects of diversion from prosecution to RJ on offences brought to justice. These studies and point estimates are listed in Tables 1 to 5.

Synthesising the evidence

As the NICE (2006) manual for developing guidelines for practice indicates, it is important to avoid over-mixing of results from substantially heterogeneous populations, interventions, comparisons or outcomes ("PICOs"). Equations that lump together studies into "meta-analyses" with great differences on these dimensions may yield an overall estimate of "effect", but remain unclear as to the effect of what variety of intervention on which outcome for which population. A more conservative approach is to limit combinations of studies into "average" effects only when they share similar "PICOs". Given the diverse nature of the studies identified for this review, it is usually necessary to treat each study as the only point estimate of its particular PICO characteristics.

The review makes cautious exceptions to that rule on a limited basis. We report the findings on repeat offending grouped separately by property and violent crime, so that the reader may look for patterns in relation to this basic distinction in the kind of harm (physical or non-violent) that offenders do to victims. What we do not do is "vote count" the studies, declaring a verdict about whether RJ "works" or does not "work", either in general or in relation to specific characteristics of populations or interventions. The reason for that rule is that the available tests are by no means a fair "vote" from all possible tests. We do total the numbers of findings in different directions within broad domains, but this is merely for the convenience of the reader, who will want to do it anyway. We provide it only to emphasise the caution that is needed in interpreting the numbers.

[...]

Introduction and overview

Fifteen years ago, Gordon Brown proposed that government should be "tough on crime, tough on the causes of crime".[3] That proposal succinctly captured the complexity of the crime problem, and thus the complexity of effective responses to crime. It implied that any financial investment in crime prevention strategy should be backed by good evidence of effectiveness, something distinctly lacking in a simple call for being "tough". By even raising the issue of the causes of crime, the proposal opened the door to inventing new ways to deal with those causes.

The search for causes of crime logically begins with criminal justice policy itself. Three of every four new criminal convictions in England and Wales are *reconvictions* of previously convicted offenders.[4] At the least, this fact suggests a missed opportunity for more effective and preventive sentencing practices when offenders are convicted. At the worst, it suggests that the criminal justice system itself is a cause of crime – a cause on which government should be tough.

Many aspects of criminal justice have been blamed for causing crime among convicted criminals. Inadequate or ineffective rehabilitation programmes, lack of drug treatment, insufficient funding for resettlement after prison, and other specific policies have all been nominated as causes. Others have suggested something far more fundamental: the way in which society and government thinks about the actual and potential connections between victims, criminals and society. A "war-on-crime" (or team sports) mentality of "us versus them" recalls a classic American cartoon that appeared on Earth Day 1970: "We have met the enemy and he is us."[5] This view blames our failure to see how interdependent all members of our society are, with many law-abiding people being criminals, victims or both at some point in our lives.

Restorative justice is a way of thinking about what is best for the many connections among crime victims, their offenders and the criminal justice process. Restorative justice advocates suggest that conventional assumptions about these connections may be wrong:

that victims should be at the centre rather than excluded from the process, that victims and offenders are not natural enemies, that victims are not primarily retributive in their view of justice, that prison is not necessarily the best way to prevent repeat crime. The erroneous assumptions of conventional justice, the advocates suggest, contribute to rising public dissatisfaction with justice across the common law countries. This report considers whether restorative justice can do better, starting with more realistic and factual premises.

Offenders and victims, for example, are often assumed to be fundamentally different kinds of people. That assumption is largely mistaken, and can have critical and potentially devastating consequences for the administration of justice. It may induce more desire to seek revenge against offenders, when victims might prefer to evoke a sense of remorse for the wrong. The mistaken premise obscures the reality that most criminals have themselves been victims, some from an early age. Thus criminals and victims often have much in common from which to build closer social bonds.

Another assumption of conventional justice is that the necessarily adversarial character of *lawyers in court* requires adversarial relations between victims and offenders as well. This adversarial assumption oversimplifies the roles played by citizen participants in the justice system, or the roles victims and their supporters would like to play. Restorative justice, at least in principle, seeks ways for victims and offenders to co-operate in preventing future crime and repairing past harms.

The classic mistaken assumption of conventional justice is to punish criminals as if they will never come back from prison to live among us. But with rare exceptions, they all come back. When they do, we depend on them not to cause more harm in the community. We are all interdependent in a shrinking world: criminals, victims, and the wider society. High rates of reconviction suggest that we are not doing what is needed to support that interdependence.

The doctrine that tougher punishment deters crime by making offenders fearful has been widely falsified for many kinds of offenders (Sherman, 1993). The restorative justice theory is that justice can prevent crime by making offenders feel more sympathy for their victims. This premise may be just as plausible as the deterrence doctrine, if just as unreliable. If restorative justice can work to prevent crime and repair harm, it seems likely to do so by fostering remorse, not fear. The emotions of anger, shame, guilt and regret form a complex cocktail of feelings associated with crime and justice. If we are to make progress in achieving the crime prevention goals of justice, it may happen from better understanding of how we can mobilise those emotions more effectively.

Restorative justice (RJ) is the prime but not only example of the recent trend towards a more "emotionally intelligent" approach to criminal justice (Sherman, 2003). This report reviews what we know, with some confidence, about the effects of different approaches to RJ. It is distinctively contemporary in its emphasis on feelings and bonds among people, both within offenders' families and in their connections to victims and their families. Whether RJ can serve the people emotionally connected to each criminal incident remains to be seen. What is clear is that in a large number of crimes, RJ facilitators can readily identify people who care about the victims and offenders enough to try to deal with the aftermath.

Two claims

Restorative justice is a strategy that many people have advocated for responding to crime and intentional harm. Like many such strategies, it embraces a variety of forms with a single list of hypothesised outcomes. This report examines the available (and reliable) evidence on those hypotheses that has been produced to date, at least in the English language and within the scope of our search. It begins by stating the hypotheses that the 36 tests we found set out to examine.

These hypotheses can be summed up as two major claims, one about procedures, and one about effectiveness. The procedural claim is that restorative justice (RJ) is seen by victims and offenders as a more humane and respectful way to process crimes than conventional justice (CJ). The effectiveness claim is that RJ is better than CJ in producing important results that we want from justice: less repeat offending, more repair of harm to victims, fewer crimes of vengeance by victims, more reconciliation and social bonding among families and friends affected by crime, and more offences brought to justice.

Promising evidence

A systematic review of tests of these hypotheses offers promising evidence in support of both claims, although with caveats. Victims and offenders who participate in RJ are generally quite pleased with its procedures, more so than with CJ. Some of that evidence may be due to self-selection bias, but other tests eliminated that bias by giving participants little or no choice. This preference is accompanied by strong evidence that RJ is at least as effective in producing the desired results of justice as CJ, often more so, and only rarely (if powerfully) counterproductive. There are also indications of possible cost savings. This evidence is highlighted in the following extract.

Few advocates claim that RJ should ever be used when an offender *denies* having committed a crime. Rather, the effectiveness claim suggests that RJ will foster more offenders agreeing to accept responsibility for having caused harm criminally. The hypothesis is that RJ would thus help to bring more offenders and offences to justice, since fewer offenders will deny responsibility if offered the prospect of RJ than they do with CJ. In fact, offenders in five controlled tests in New York City and Canberra readily took responsibility for serious crimes and "declined to deny" their guilt – choosing instead the prospect of participation in deciding what should be done about their crimes.

Varieties of restorative justice

Most of the evidence we highlight (Tables 1 to 5) is based on just *one* of the many varieties of restorative justice, one that is possibly most consistent with the broad definition referenced by the Home Office (2003) strategy document, as quoted from Marshall (1999: 5): a process "whereby parties with a stake in a specific offence collectively resolve how to deal with the aftermath of the offence and its implications for the future". That variety is face-to-face conferences of offenders, victims and their supporters.

This method can substantially reduce repeat offending for some (but not all) kinds of crimes and offenders (Tables 1 to 3). It can reduce victims' desire for violent revenge against the offender (Table 4). Victims also suffer less intense post-traumatic stress symptoms after face-to-face restorative justice (Angel, 2005), returning to work and normal life sooner than they do without it – which should, in turn, reduce the long-term severity and costs of such health problems as coronary heart disease (Kubzansky et al, 2007).

Another "direct" form of restorative justice is victim-offender mediation, at which both victim and offender are present, often without other people affected by the crime, and where a mediator negotiates between them.

"Indirect" restorative justice usually describes any process by which offenders and victims communicate only through third parties, but not face to face. These methods include "shuttle communication", in which a mediator or facilitator may carry messages by phone or in person between victims (or victims' representatives) and offenders (or their representatives). They also include one-way communications such as letters of apology from offender to victim, or letters describing a crime's impact from the victim to the offender. Perhaps the most indirect form of RJ is court-ordered restitution (which has become a substantial source of imprisonment in the US for offender failure to pay). Youth referral panels in the UK may also order restitution. When this form of RJ has been put to controlled tests, it has reduced recidivism in both adult and juvenile samples, but not consistently so (Tables 1 to 2).

Stages of the criminal process

Each of these forms of RJ has been employed in many different stages of the criminal process, and in different venues, as well as outside the CJ process altogether. RJ in schools, for example, can be used as an alternative to formal processing of young people involved in bullying. When arrests are made, RJ has been used as a diversion from criminal prosecution, as in the Canberra experiments. Prosecution in the UK has, under the Criminal Justice Act 2003, on occasion been suspended pending a "conditional caution" while the offender completes an RJ process (but only after making full admissions). When prosecuted offenders plead guilty, RJ before sentencing can provide evidence of mitigation that should normally reduce the length of imprisonment *(R v Collins,* 2003; *R v Barci,* 2003). When offenders are sentenced to community (probation) supervision, RJ can be used to determine conditions of that sentence and possible reparation to the victim. When offenders are sentenced to long-term imprisonment, they can be invited to undertake indirect or direct RJ in preparation for resettlement.

Offences and offenders

The modern use of RJ began primarily in the context of youth justice, often for such minor offences as shoplifting and vandalism. In recent years it has expanded into serious offences by adults, including robbery, burglary and assault. From the standpoint of the process, the largest distinction among offence types is the *"victimed"* versus *non-victim* offences. The latter include drink-driving or shoplifting, in which no individual who was personally harmed can meet with the offender face to face. Theories underlying RJ, such as Braithwaite (1989), logically imply that RJ should work better at reducing reoffending with victimed offences. Any interest in RJ as a policy to help victims prefers victimed crimes by definition.

This review focuses not on a global assessment of whether RJ "works" as a one-size-fits-all strategy, but rather what the evidence suggests about *what works for whom.* There is only limited evidence on the large number of possible combinations of offence type, RJ method, stage of the criminal justice process, and offender age/gender/race/prior record characteristics. The vast scope of these specific circumstances limits the extent to which any review can draw firm conclusions about "what works best". It is even possible that the differences in outcomes observed in these different categories could be due to chance, or to idiosyncratic aspects of sample selection or community characteristics. All the more reason, then, for laying out the sometimes conflicting evidence within offence types across different types of offenders, different stages of the criminal process, or different nations or cultures.

Searching for evidence

This review is based on a systematic search of the databases below from 1986 through to 2005, since the terms "restorative justice" and "conferencing" were not in use prior to 1986. Each of these databases is readily accessible online:

- C2-SPECTR
- National Criminal Justice Reference Service (NCJRS);
- Criminal Justice Abstracts;
- Sociological Abstracts;
- Criminal Justice Periodicals Index;
- Dissertation Abstracts;
- Social Science Abstracts.

The search terms to be used were "restorative *and* justice or conferenc/e/ing *with* reoffending, recidivism *and* evaluation".

Weighing and summing up the evidence

The best methods of research synthesis for such a review are subject to substantial scientific and policy debate. This review cuts through some of that debate by relying on the Cabinet Office's "PICO" model adopted from the methods of the National Institute for Health & Clinical Excellence (2006: 16): *population, intervention, comparison, outcomes*. This model is used to weigh and sum up large bodies of research evidence for guidance to medical practitioners. It encourages greater specificity in definitions of both populations and interventions. It also requires comparisons with other treatments to be used as the basis for assessing an outcome, with reasonably unbiased selection of the comparison cases.

In weighing the evidence on RJ, this review follows the Home Office (2004) adaptation of the University of Maryland's scientific methods scale (Sherman et al, 1997). This scale orders the level of internal validity, or the control of bias in drawing inferences of causation, on a five-point scale. Following the precedent of the Maryland report to the US Congress (Sherman et al, 1997) and the NICE (2006) standards, this review excludes impact evaluations on crime and victim outcomes that fall below level 3. That is, it does not consider research on RJ reasonably unbiased if it lacks direct comparisons between cases given RJ and similar cases given other treatments. Our review does, however, consider direct comparisons made between the actual recidivism of offenders given RJ to those offenders' predicted recidivism based on the OGRS2 scale, which has been validated by Home Office research on samples other than the RJ cases (see Miers et al, 2001). This method is arguably equivalent to a level 4, as demonstrated in the evaluation methods literature (eg Berk and Rossi, 1998).

Many of the UK evaluations of restorative justice compare cases in which RJ was completed with cases in which it was offered but refused, by either offenders or victims (see eg Miers et al, 2001). While such comparisons may appear to be level 3 or 4 designs, the treatment-related difference between the two groups makes any estimate of the causal effect of treatment potentially quite biased. It is not possible with such designs, no matter how many cases they may include in their samples, to eliminate the key alternative rival hypothesis: that there is something about those cases that makes consent versus refusal a confounding predictor of recidivism, in uncertain and unspecifiable ways. We excluded studies in which that method is used for estimating either offender or victim outcomes.

Similarly, many studies include only "completers" of RJ in their samples, with no data on those who were offered or initiated RJ but did not complete it (eg Vignaendra and Fitzgerald, 2006). Except in very large samples with a valid model predicting the reasons for non-completion that could be applied to a comparison group (Angrist, Imbens and Rubin, 1996), comparisons of completers with a control group not offered the treatment are inherently biased (Gorman, 2005). This applies equally to contemporary and historical controls (see eg Stone et al, 1998, which is excluded for that reason). Such studies are thus also excluded as evidence of the impact of RJ. For related reasons, correlational studies comparing offenders who do and do not get RJ (level 1) are also excluded, as well as before/after studies (level 2) that are vulnerable to regression-to-the-mean.[6]

Our key findings, summarised in Tables 1 to 5, rely on 23 reasonably unbiased point estimates of the impact of RJ on repeat offending, six estimates of effects on victims, and five estimates of effects of diversion from prosecution to RJ on offences brought to justice. The studies and their key data are listed in Tables 1 to 5 below. While all level 5 studies employed random assignment to determine whether or not a case received RJ, some of the conclusions (or what statisticians call "point estimates") are derived from subgroups of the full sample that was included in the random assignment sequence (Piantadosi, 1997: 211).

Table 1: Reasonably unbiased tests of RJ effects on repeat offending after processing for violent crime

Place, SMS (internal validity) level	Reference	Population	Intervention	Comparison	Outcome
Bethlehem, Pennsylvania, USA Level 5	McCold and Wachtel, 1998	Hispanic (51%) and white youth N = 111	Diversion to face-to-face RJ conferences, prior to victim or offender consent	Conventional juvenile prosecution	No difference in intention-to-treat analysis; high refusal rate post-random assignment
Canberra, Australia Level 5 (subgroup analysis)	Sherman, Strang, Barnes and Woods, 2006	Non-Aboriginal defendants under 30 N = 97	Diversion to face-to-face RJ conferences, with consent of offender prior to victim consent	Conventional juvenile prosecution	RJ-assigned had 84 fewer arrests per 100 offenders per year than CJ-assigned (P =.026)
Canberra, Australia Level 5 (subgroup analysis)	Sherman, Strang, Barnes and Woods, 2006	Aboriginal defendants under 30 N = 14	Diversion to face-to-face RJ conferences, with consent of offender prior to victim consent	Conventional juvenile prosecution	Subgroup sample size too small for adequate power to test effect
Indianapolis, USA Level 5	McGarrell et al, 2000	Youth N = 251	Face-to-face RJ conferences	Conventional juvenile diversion to a range of other programmes	28% rearrest rate at six months for RJ vs 34% for CJ (P <.05); effect decays by 12 months

(Continued)

Table 1: continued

Place, SMS (internal validity) level	Reference	Population	Intervention	Comparison	Outcome
Newfoundland and Labrador, Canada Level 4	Pennell and Burford, 2000	Violent families N = 32	Face-to-face RJ conferences	Conventional criminal justice and social service response N = 31	50% before/after reduction in frequency for RJ families vs 27% increase for CJ families (P =.005)
Northumbria, UK Level 5 (subgroup analysis)	Sherman, Strang, Barnes and Newbury-Birch, 2006	Female youth N = 44	Face-to-face RJ conferences in addition to final warnings by police	Conventional final warnings by police only	118 before/after fewer arrests per 100 offenders in RJ group vs 47 fewer arrests in CJ group (P =.012)
Northumbria, UK Level 5 (subgroup analysis)	Sherman, Strang, Barnes and Newbury-Birch, 2006	Male youth N = 64	Face-to-face RJ conferences in addition to final warnings by police	Conventional final warnings by police only	No RJ-CJ difference
West Yorkshire, UK Level 4	Miers et al, 2001	Young adult violence and property offenders (58% given custodial sentences) N = 153	Pre-sentence indirect, some direct mediation, requiring victim participation but rarely face-to-face; not reported to sentencing court	Offenders' own predicted recidivism rate, based on external model (OGRS2 score)	Two-year reconviction rate = 44% vs 58% predicted (P =.01)
West Midlands, UK Level 4	Miers et al, 2001	Young adult violence and property offenders (52% given custodial sentences) N =147	Pre-sentence only; offenders told mediation would be reported to court and could help reduce sentence	Offenders' own predicted recidivism rate, based on external model (OGRS2 score)	Two-year reconviction rate 44% vs 57% convicted (P =.01)
Kings County (Brooklyn), New York, USA Level 5	Davis et al, 1981	Adult felony defendants (family = 50%; acquaintance =40%; violent = 60%; property 40%) N = 465	Diversion from prosecution to direct mediation; 56% completed	Prosecution as usual: 27% conviction rate; 72% dismissed or absconded; jail sentences = 2.5%	No difference in four-month post-disposition (control absconders excepted!) rate of calling police: RJ =12%; prosecution = 13%. Arrests of victim OR defendant = 4% in both groups
Total = 10					Reductions = 6 Increases = 0 No effect = 4

Table 2: Reasonably unbiased tests of RJ effects on repeat offending after processing for property crime

Place, SMS (internal validity) level	Reference	Population	Intervention	Comparison	Outcome
Northumbria, UK Level 5 (subgroup analysis)	Sherman, Strang, Barnes and Newbury-Birch, 2006	Male youth N = 100	Face-to-face RJ conferences in addition to final warnings by police	Conventional final warnings by police only	RJ = 88 fewer arrests per 100 offenders per year before/after vs 32 fewer for CJ (P <.05)
Northumbria, UK Level 5 (subgroup analysis)	Sherman, Strang, Barnes and Newbury-Birch, 2006	Female youth N = 28	Face-to-face RJ conferences in addition to final warnings by police	Conventional final warnings by police only	Subgroup sample size too small for adequate power to test effect
Canberra, Australia Level 5 (subgroup analysis)	Sherman et al, 2006a	White youth arrested for crimes with personal victims N = 228	Face-to-face RJ conferences	Conventional juvenile prosecution	No difference
Canberra, Australia Level 5 (subgroup analysis)	Sherman et al, 2006a	Aboriginal youth arrested for crimes with personal victims N = 23	Face-to-face RJ conferences	Conventional juvenile prosecution	Comparing two years after to two years before, RJ = 288 *more* arrests per 100 offenders per year; CJ = 66 *fewer* arrests per 100 offenders per year (P =.049)
Bethlehem, Pennsylvania, USA Level 5	McCold and Wachtel, 1998	Hispanic (51%) and white youth N = 181	Face-to-face RJ conferences	Conventional juvenile prosecution	Intention-to-treat analysis shows marginally significant (P =.11) higher offending in RJ
Indianapolis, USA Level 5	McGarrell et al, 2000	Youth N = 381	Face-to-face RJ conferences, with consent of offender	Conventional diversion to a range of non-RJ programmes	RJ = 15% repeat offenders at six months, vs CJ = 27% (P <.05); difference fades by 12 months

(Continued)

Table 2: continued

Place, SMS (internal validity) level	Reference	Population	Intervention	Comparison	Outcome
Clayton County, Georgia, USA Level 5	Schneider, 1986	Youth N = 128	Court-ordered restitution	Conventional probation	RJ = 26% decline in arrest frequency vs no change in CJ (P value not reported)
Boise, Idaho, USA Level 5	Schneider, 1986	Youth N = 181	Court-ordered restitution	Eight days in jail on weekends	No difference
Oklahoma City, USA Level 5	Schneider, 1986	Youth N = 182	Court-ordered restitution	Conventional probation	No difference
Washington, DC, USA Level 5	Schneider, 1986	73% youth property offenders; 27% violent offenders N = 411	Court-ordered restitution, with consent of offender (40% dropout)	Conventional probation	Intention-to treat case RJ = 12% less arrest frequency before/after; CJ = 7% increase (P <.05)
Winnipeg, Canada Level 4	Bonta et al, 1998	Male adult property (61%) and violence(35%) offenders, accepted at a 33% rate from defence lawyer referrals, all likely to be sent to prison for at least six months N = 142	Court-ordered financial restitution and RJ face to face (10%) or by letter of apology N = 75	Matched prison inmates with similar profiles N = 67	Two-year reconviction rate for 75 RJ = 11%, for 67 ex-prison inmates = 37% (P <.05)
New Zealand Level 4	Triggs, 2005	Court-referred offenders who completed RJ (25%) N = 192	Face-to-face RJ conference with diverse participants	Offenders' own predicted recidivism rate, based on external model	No significant difference in two-year reconvictions between RJ (41%) and predicted (45%)
Total = 12					Reduction = 5 Increase = 2 Match or beat custody = 2 of 2

Table 3: Tests of the effects on repeat offending of RJ for samples of all or partially non-victim
offences

Place, SMS (internal validity) level	Reference	Population	Intervention	Comparison	Outcome
Canberra, Australia Level 5	Sherman, Strang and Woods, 2000	Drink-driving offenders caught in random breath tests N = 900	Face-to-face RJ conferences with five family members or supporters; sometimes community represented	Prosecution in court, six months' loss of driver's licence, name published in newspaper	No RJ-CJ difference in before/after difference of frequency in repeat offending
Canberra, Australia Level 5	Sherman, Strang and Woods, 2000	Youth shoplifters N = 143	Face-to-face RJ conferences with five family members or supporters; sometimes store represented	Conventional prosecution in juvenile court	No RJ-CJ difference in before/after difference of frequency in repeat offending
Indianapolis, USA Level 5	McGarrell et al, 2000	Youth public order offenders N = 143	Face-to-face RJ conferences	Conventional diversion to a range of non-RJ programmes	RJ = 28% rearrest after 12 months; CJ = 45%
Total = 3					No difference = 2 RJ decrease = 1 RJ increase = 0

Table 4: Reasonably unbiased estimates of effects of RJ on crime victim outcomes

Place, SMS (internal validity) level	Reference	Population	Intervention	Comparison	Outcome
Canberra, Australia Level 4.5	Strang, 2002	Victims of violent crime by offenders under 30, or of property crime by offenders under 18 N = 232 (Two separate RCTs combined)	Diversion to face-to-face RJ, with consent of offender prior to victim consent	Conventional prosecution in juvenile or adult court	Anger at justice process: CJ = 32% RJ = 18% Desire to harm offender: CJ = 20% RJ = 7% Preference for process: RJ = 69% CJ = 48% Satisfaction with outcome: RJ = 60% CJ = 46% (All with P =.05 or less)

(Continued)

Table 4: continued

Place,SMS (internal validity) level	Reference	Population	Intervention	Comparison	Outcome
London, UK Level 4.5	Angel, 2005	Victims of robbery or burglary N = 216 (Two separate RCTs combined)	Face-to-face RJ in addition to CJ, with consent of offender prior to victim consent	Conventional prosecution in court without RJ	Post-traumatic stress symptoms scores for: RJ = 9 CJ = 14 (P <.01)
London, UK Level 4.5	Angel, 2005	Victims of robbery or burglary N = 207 (Two separate RCTs combined)	Face-to-face RJ in addition to CJ, with consent of offender prior to victim consent	Conventional prosecution in court without RJ	Post-crime impact on employment scores for: RJ = 16% CJ = 25% (P <.12)
Canberra, Australia, and London, UK Level 4.5	Sherman et al, 2005	Eight-point estimates of male and female victims of violent and property crimes Total N = 445 (Four RCTs disaggregated by gender)	Face-to-face RJ conferences in addition to or instead of CJ, with consent of offender prior to victim consent	Conventional prosecution in court	Mean proportions desiring violent revenge against offender: RJ = 4% CJ = 14% (P <.001)
Indianapolis Level 4.5	McGarrell et al, 2000	Victims of youth offenders, latter aged seven to 14 N = 92 (Low response rates, data "descriptive")	Diversion to face-to-face RJ	Any of 23 court-ordered diversion programmes	Satisfied with how case was handled: RJ = 90% CJ = 68% Would recommend to other victims: RJ = 98% CJ = 25%
Bethlehem, Pennsylvania, USA Level 1	McCold and Wachtel, 1998	Victims of violent and property crime by offenders under 18 N = 180	Diversion to face-to-face RJ before consent of offender or victim	Conventional prosecution in juvenile court	Satisfied with the way case was handled: RJ = 96% RJ decline = 73% CJ = 79% (P <.01) Satisfied offender was held accountable: RJ = 93% RJ decline = 77% CJ = 74% (P =.05)
Total six tests summarised with 10-point estimates					In 10 of 10 estimates, victims favour RJ over CJ

Table 5: Reasonably unbiased estimates of effects of RJ on offences with victims brought to justice

Place, SMS (internal validity) level	Reference	Population	Intervention	Comparison	Outcome
Kings County (Brooklyn), New York, USA Level 5	Davis et al, 1981	Adult violent and property felony defendants N = 465	Diversion to direct face-to-face mediation	Conventional prosecution	Offences brought to justice: RJ = 56% CJ = 28% **Ratio 2:1**
Canberra, Australia Level 5	Strang et al, 1999	Defendants under age 30 charged with violent offences N = 65	Diversion to face-to-face RJ, with consent of offender prior to victim consent	Conventional prosecution	Offences brought to justice: RJ = 89% CJ = 44% **Ratio 2:1**
Canberra, Australia Level 5	Strang et al, 1999	Youth under 18 charged with property crimes against personal victims N = 126	Diversion to face-to-face RJ, with consent of offender prior to victim consent	Conventional prosecution	Offences brought to justice: RJ = 92% CJ = 27% **Ratio 3:1**
Canberra, Australia Level 5	Strang et al, 1999	Licensed drivers arrested for drink-driving N = 773	Diversion to face-to-face RJ, with consent of offender prior to victim consent	Conventional prosecution	Offences brought to justice: RJ = 99% CJ = 87% **Ratio 1.1:1**
Canberra, Australia Level 5	Strang et al, 1999	Youth arrested for shoplifting from large stores N = 87	Diversion to face-to-face RJ, with consent of offender prior to victim consent	Conventional prosecution	Offences brought to justice: RJ = 93% CJ = 18% **Ratio 4:1**
Summary Five tests					**Ratio 5:0** tests of RJ increases of offences brought to justice over CJ

Missing evidence

In assessing the prospects for a major expansion in the use of RJ, the review found no evidence of the kind that might be needed to roll out a national policy. That evidence about the effects of up-scaling RJ for widespread use – whether it would produce "collateral benefits" or harms for entire communities beyond those we can observe in studies limited to comparisons of individual cases – would include the following questions:

- Would broader use of RJ encourage more witnesses to come forward to help police solve more crimes, bringing more offences and offenders to justice by more public confidence in justice and the law?
- Would broader use of RJ encourage more offenders to accept responsibility for their offences, increasing offences brought to justice?
- If an entire community or basic command unit adopted RJ as the initial response to most crimes, would that policy weaken the general deterrent effects of the law – or strengthen compliance with the law by increasing its legitimacy?

- If RJ became more widely known and understood by the public through far more frequent use, would it attract even more victim and offender consent to participate than the substantial levels it has achieved in some pilot tests?

These and other questions about large-scale RJ could be answered with evidence generated by the scientific method, using communities as the unit of analysis. They cannot, however, be answered with evidence generated solely at the individual or case level in small-scale pilot tests. Thus the implication of this conclusion is that progress in *evidence-based* restorative justice is likely to depend on whether future testing of RJ is conducted on a neighbourhood-wide or community-wide basis.

The reasons why

One key question the Smith Institute asked us to examine is why RJ works when it does work. The short answer is that we cannot tell much from the available evidence, but there are some theories that could guide further analysis. The modern revival of RJ has been long on theory, but shorter on tests of those theories. Even when RJ itself is subjected to rigorous testing, the theories that could explain its effects are often much harder to test. This situation is not uncommon in science, as in the case of antibiotics, which cure infections for reasons that are not fully understood. Yet there is no doubt that understanding the reasons why RJ works – or doesn't – could help improve predictions and policies about when to use it or not.

A central theory about RJ highlights a massive difference from the theory of conventional justice – and also explains why conventional justice fails to deter repeat convictions far more often than not. That theory, based on "defiance theory" (Sherman, 1993), is that:

- People who commit crimes often believe, or convince themselves, that they are not acting immorally.
- RJ engages such people in a moral discussion about whether crime is wrong.
- An RJ discussion can lead offenders to redefine themselves as law-abiders, and to agree that they are not the kind of people who would do immoral things.
- That discussion would lead to the conclusion that what they did was in fact immoral, and that they should therefore not repeat such behaviour. (Whether they do anyway remains the key empirical question about this theory.)

In contrast, criminal law doctrine presumes that people know they are doing wrong, and that only fear of punishment can stop them from repeating their crime. Thus punishment is required in order to deter them (and others) from doing such wrongs. While such neoclassical theory therefore centres on *punishment,* RJ centres on *persuasion.* The aim of punishment is to enhance fear of further punishment; the aim of persuasion is to enhance moral support for voluntary obedience of the law (Braithwaite, 1989; Tyler, 1990; Sherman, 1993, 2003). A theory of obeying the law by persuasion is thus the ultimate commitment to a rule of law.

The rule of law

One frequent objection to RJ is that it may undermine the rule of law, encouraging community abuses of individual rights at the expense of universal principles and rights. This review finds no evidence for this concern. As long as RJ is conducted under the United Nations principles for RJ, the major issue for the rule of law will be one that has long plagued conventional justice as well: disparity in severity of penalty. Both RJ and CJ appear equally subject to challenges of disparities and a wide variance of discretion, as former Lord Chief Justice Woolf pointed out in his advice to judges on the testing of RJ in 2002.[7]

Any "balanced" perspective on criminal law is a subject of intense academic and public debate. Adding victims' benefits and crime prevention into the mix of criminal law offends a purely retributive view of "just desserts", leading some scholars to find RJ incompatible with traditional criminal justice. Yet those concerns are also present in CJ, with RJ seen by others as a way to help rebalance CJ itself. The evidence shows that RJ leads to more opportunities for offenders to help both victims and themselves, posing a win-win scenario more often than the zero-sum game assumed by RJ opponents (Strang, 2002: 155–191).

The major factor affecting disparity of severity is the problem of victim refusal to participate when an offender is willing. That problem, however, has been resolved in part by *R v Barci.* This case requires judges to give offenders mitigation of time in prison based on their willingness to participate in RJ, regardless of any victim's agreement to do so. Victim-absent conferences are also possible under those circumstances, which could allow the theory of RJ to be implemented in a similar fashion to what happens when victims are present.

Concerns about inconsistency in the severity of punishment associated with RJ can also be dealt with in a variety of ways, including judicial review (as in New Zealand) and good practice for insuring compliance with outcome agreements, as demonstrated by the Metropolitan and Northumbria police. It can also be managed by Crown Prosecution Service oversight, under the Criminal Justice Act 2003. These and many other solutions are possible if evidence continues to grow of the benefits to be gained from making RJ more widely available. That evidence, however, must distinguish between cases in which RJ is likely to work, have no effect, or even cause more crime.

Reliance on evidence to decide when RJ is "appropriate" can yield very different decisions from relying on theory or subjective bias. One example is the usual proposal to limit the use of RJ to "lesser" crimes, including juvenile offences, but not to allow it for "serious" crimes. Yet the evidence suggests RJ may be most effective when the crimes are most serious. For *minor crimes,* RJ is no better than CJ in reducing repeat offending among shoplifters, drink-drivers, and teenage property offenders in Canberra. For *major crimes* RJ has succeeded better than CJ in reducing repeat offending among felony defendants in New York City, violent white people under 30 in Canberra, and violent white girls under 18 in Northumbria. Banning RJ for serious crimes would destroy the chance to prevent many thousands more such offences. Nor is it clear that there is any principled basis for selectively allowing, or banning, RJ – other than the principle of harm reduction, which indicates its use with serious crime.

Predicting RJ effects on repeat crime by offenders

The question of repeat offending is often thought to be a small or limited part of the crime problem. UK evidence suggests otherwise. According to Home Office data, 76% of all persons sentenced for indictable offences in 2003 in England and Wales were people with prior convictions.[8] If prior arrests had been used, the percentage of convicted criminals who had indications of prior crime would probably have been even higher. Based on people either caught or actually punished, then, *most crime is repeat crime.*

How can we tell how much crime RJ might prevent? A reliable prediction of how RJ will affect repeat offending by offenders attending conferences must first be based on unbiased evidence. Much of the evidence about RJ, even with very large sample sizes, is uninformative for this purpose because it is plagued with the bias of *self-selection* (eg Vignaendra and Fitzgerald, 2006). This means that the kinds of offenders who complete RJ may be substantially different from those who do not, in ways that may predict their risk of repeat offending regardless of RJ. If people with lower risk of repeat offending are more likely to be offered, accept or complete RJ than people with higher risks of repeat offending, then the reason why RJ cases had less repeat offending would not be the result of RJ. The correlation with RJ would be what statisticians call a "spurious" association that reflects some third, underlying cause, rather than the effect of RJ. Much of the positive evidence on RJ suffers from this fatal flaw, especially the direct comparisons between RJ completers and RJ refusers.

Much of the evidence claiming that RJ does *not* reduce crime may suffer a different bias: the bias of measurement. Using police records on thousands of cases, for example, as the sole measure of the delivery of RJ may fail to detect an enormous variability in the content and intensity of the RJ experience. When RJ (or any programme) is rolled out quickly on a wide scale, there is a risk that many conferences will just "go through the motions" to "tick off a box", rather than treating each case as a kind of surgical procedure requiring careful advance planning, preparation and follow-up. With such heterogeneity of the RJ being delivered, the research is biased against finding any effect of "good practice" RJ, because no measurement was taken of the elements of good practice.

Randomised controlled trials (RCTs) provide the best opportunity to control both selection and measurement biases. RCTs generally remove selection bias because they first obtain consent and then assign RJ to some (but not all) of those consenting. RCTs also measure consistency of delivery of RJ, so it is clearer just what is being tested. Finally, the best RCTs analyse their data based on assignment rather than completion of RJ, so that any self-selection bias in completion is eliminated. While this procedure dilutes the effects of RJ, it maintains the capacity of the research to rule out spurious causes of a difference in repeat offending. RCTs are not the only kind of evidence that can help predict the effects of RJ on crime, but they are now available in greater abundance for RJ than for any other response to crime ever tested.

These controlled tests show that face-to-face RJ, consistently delivered by facilitators (mostly police officers) trained by the same Australian RJ training firm, has reduced repeat offending on three continents, for highly specific populations, all of which are identified by characteristics that existed before random assignment and are therefore considered by statisticians to be appropriate for subgroup analyses that produce statistically significant within-group differences by treatment:

- violent offenders under age 30 in Canberra (main effects);
- violent girls under 18 in Northumbria;
- male property offenders under 18 in Northumbria;
- property and violence offenders aged seven to 14 in Indianapolis.

Tests of other varieties of RJ, primarily court-ordered restitution or intervention of various descriptions, has also reduced crime among:

- violent families in Newfoundland and Labrador;
- adult male property and violence offenders diverted from prison in Winnipeg (and recidivism no worse than from jail for youth in Idaho);
- youth property offenders in Clayton County, Georgia;
- youth violence and property offenders in Washington, DC.

The rigorous RCT methods, however, have also found evidence that the same kind of RJ delivered by the same facilitators made little or no difference in repeat offending rates among police-selected samples of:

- property offenders under 18 in Canberra;
- violent males under 18 in Northumbria;
- property offenders under 18 in Bethlehem, Pennsylvania.

Most important, these same RCT methods have found that face-to-face RJ offered as a diversion from court causes a substantial *increase* in the frequency of arrests among a small sample of Aboriginals under 18 in Canberra arrested for property crimes, when compared with Aboriginals randomly assigned to court for similar offences. The Bethlehem findings, with many Hispanics in the sample, also veer close to significance (P =.11) in the same direction.

These findings raise important "reason why" questions about the relationship between RJ and social "marginality", with both negative and positive implications. One question is whether offenders from deeply alienated social groups, such as Australian Aboriginals or American Hispanics, will react very badly to appeals for obedience to the laws of a government they perceive as illegitimate, if they do not believe their crimes to be wrong. The same question could be raised about Islamist radicals (who believe murder in the name of God to be moral) or certain Afro-Caribbean gangs (who may see violence as part of the moral rules of a business enterprise).

The other question is whether the emotional power of RJ could be customised to engage whatever authority structure may be effective inside such alienated groups. Mobilising older Aboriginal males to attend RJ conferences, for example, could increase the perceived legitimacy of the process among such offenders – changing their minds about the morality of obeying the law more than a white police officer or white crime victim might be able to.

Insight about other reasons RJ results, in general, vary widely among different kinds of offenders can be gained from a quasi-experimental (non-RCT) study of differences in repeat offending among offenders under age 18 in South Australia. This found, controlling for other predictors of recidivism, that the lowest repeat offending rates followed conferences during which offenders showed *remorse,* and in which agreements were reached by a clearly consensual process among the people in the room (Hayes and Daly, 2003). Similar findings (Morris and Maxwell, 2005) have been reported in long-term follow-up of juvenile cases in New Zealand.

The large magnitude of the RJ effects in this evidence – both good and bad – suggests that RJ is like a powerful drug that needs to be carefully tested for specific kinds of cases before it is put into general practice. Just as penicillin can cure infections, but cannot cure cancer or diabetes, RJ can reduce crime for some kinds of offenders but not others. And just as some people are so allergic to penicillin that it can almost kill them, some offenders may find RJ so enraging or humiliating that they are provoked into committing even more crime than they would have done without RJ. This evidence might be taken as a reason to ban RJ altogether, but only one such very strong reaction has been found to date, among a small sample of Australian youth.

All interventions in medicine, or agriculture, or public health (such as vaccination programmes) cause harm under some circumstances. Yet that is rarely sufficient reason to impose a complete ban on a treatment that offers benefits under some conditions. Instead, the usual response is to predict as reliably as possible when there will be harm, and then to apply limited prohibitions of the intervention under those specific circumstances. That approach has allowed antibiotics to save millions of lives. It could also allow restorative justice to prevent millions of crimes.

Predicting RJ effects on victims

The evidence on victims is far more consistent than it is on offenders. On average, in every test available, victims do better when they participate in RJ than when they do not. Victims may report dissatisfaction in the (very infrequent) cases when offenders refuse to accept responsibility, or if offenders fail to appear at a conference as agreed, or when offenders fail to complete outcome agreements. Yet the very high rate of offender attendance, remorse and apologies in RJ conferences far outweighs these exceptions, protecting victims from being "re-victimised" during the RJ. Instead, from Canberra to London to Indianapolis, victims who go to RJ conferences report that they are glad they went. The benefits they describe include less fear of the offender, less anger at the offender, and greater ability to get on their lives.

The reductions in anger at the offender extend to victims admitting they have less desire for physical revenge against the offender after RJ than before – a result confirmed in some tests by far higher levels of desire for vengeance among victims assigned to control group status than those assigned to an RJ conference.

In London, the effects of RJ on victims of burglary and robbery include large reductions in their post-traumatic stress symptoms. Compared with victims willing to meet with willing offenders but who were not randomly assigned to RJ, victims who were assigned to (and completed) RJ reported greater ability to return to work, to resume normal daily activities, to sleep better at night and to stop their "racing thoughts". Long-term data on these victims may reveal how much RJ has improved their health, given other evidence that comparable levels of post-traumatic stress elevate risks of coronary heart disease (Kubzansky et al, 2007). That, in turn, could potentially reduce National Health Service costs in an amount sufficient to justify spending on RJ as a disease prevention strategy for crime victims.

Could RJ reduce government spending?

Healthcare for crime victims is only one of several possible avenues by which RJ could reduce government spending. Perhaps the largest opportunity is in the reduction of the prison population, especially (as Lord Woolf has suggested) in the area of short sentences. Two cases in the Court of Appeal (*Collins* and *Barci*) have already ruled that length of custody should be reduced for offenders who offer to participate in RJ. For somewhat less serious offences in which courts may be inclined to give a short custodial sentence, the addition of RJ could possibly tip the balance to keep them out of custody altogether. Even in robbery cases, London Crown Court judges have said that they had withheld a custodial sentence due to offender participation in RJ.

The possible substitution of RJ for prison is even more attractive if it would result in less crime. The reduction of reconvictions in Winnipeg (Bonta et al, 1998) with RJ as an alternative to prison provides evidence of that possibility. Even if there is merely no increase in crime, the cost savings could be achieved with zero impact on public safety. Evidence that in Boise, Idaho, youths did no worse with RJ than they did with eight days in jail is especially relevant to the debate over short sentences in the UK. At the pro rata cost of some £35,000 per year for each UK prison sentence, one offender kept out of prison for one year would cover the costs of more than 50 RJ conferences (at £25 per hour of police work for an average of 20 hours per conference, plus supervisory and overhead costs). That would equal one week of custody for each RJ conference.

Put another way, if only one in 50 RJ conferences prevented a year in custody, that alone could cover the costs of the conferences. The money for one year could thus be saved in one of two ways: by reducing sentence length, or by reducing the costs of repeat offending and reincarceration.

Another way that RJ could save money is in fees paid to lawyers by the government for appearances in court and at police stations. This would require many more defendants than at present to admit guilt in anticipation of a conditional caution involving RJ. Each admission of guilt – and diversion to RJ – could save thousands of pounds in legal fees for both defence and prosecution.

How can RJ best be delivered?

RJ has often been delivered badly in the UK by programmes operated on a take-it-or-leave-it philosophy. Courts have been asked – even in person by the Lord Chancellor – to refer cases prior to sentencing, but they did not. Victims have been sent letters inviting them to attend referral panels (on a non-negotiable date), but they did not. Prosecutors have been asked to approve cases for diversion to RJ as conditional cautioning, but they did not. Magistrates have been asked to delay sentence so that RJ conferences might be held, but they did not. RJ was there for the taking, but the current system just left it. The exception may be the youth conferencing programme in Northern Ireland, which – unlike RJ in England and Wales – is statutory. The evaluation indicates that the Northern Ireland programme works well, with cases routinely referred to RJ by criminal justice agencies as the law intends (Beckett et al, 2005; Campbell et al, 2006).

It thus appears likely that RJ programmes can be successfully run only via statutory and regulatory engineering of the criminal justice system. Statutory requirements could ultimately include an adjournment after each guilty plea to allow police to visit victims and offenders, who could then decide whether to participate in RJ. That decision could be informed by risk assessments conducted by police, who would also draw on the latest research about the kinds of cases for which RJ may be more or less effective (or could potentially backfire). Statutes could also allow or require custody suite sergeants to explain the possibility of diversion to RJ in a conditional caution if offenders admit their guilt upon arrest, which is exactly what police in Canberra were able to do without legislation. Such a practice would be contentious in the UK if seen as an "inducement", but could be cast as part of a standard information package that would be provided to all arrestees.

Other requirements could include the "best practice" methods of contacting victims face to face by knocking on doors when victims cannot be reached by phone or by post. Similar standards could be set for contacting offenders on bail, and for mobilising all participants the day before, and the day of, an RJ conference.

Most of the rigorous evidence on RJ to date is based on police administration of the RJ processes. Yet the expense of trained officers providing these services makes some police leaders reluctant to commit that expense to RJ. While there are no direct comparisons between RJ provided by police or members of other professions (with similar cases), there is a (still untested) way to reduce the cost of restorative policing. Testing police community safety officers assigned as "RJ officers" to work with a small number of sworn constables could offer a way of providing the benefits of association with police protection, as well as incorporating more community-based knowledge of the cultural dimensions of bringing together offenders and victims.

A competing viewpoint is that RJ facilitators should have no affiliation with criminal justice agencies (Roche, 2003). There is no evidence to suggest, however, that this practice can even attract substantial numbers of crime victims, let alone produce powerful reductions in offending or victim harm. The New Zealand system of social workers leading RJ conferences, for example, has a much lower victim attendance rate than the police-led programmes evaluated elsewhere (Maxwell and Morris, 1993). The best evidence for large-scale delivery of RJ, at present, is associated with police-organised and-led conferences.

More justice, less crime: a way forward

Restorative justice offers a strategy for holding more offenders accountable, with many more victims helped, with more crimes prevented, and with the costs of government reduced. The evidence so far suggests that many elements of this strategy can work with some kinds of offenders and offences. That evidence is far more extensive, and positive, than the evidence base for most national roll-outs of new criminal justice policies in any government. This conclusion would support a decision to roll out RJ as well.

Building on the promise of the evidence requires two conditions. In the short run, it requires an institutional focus for the development of RJ as a major shift in justice policy, as distinct from a minor programme on the margins. In the long run, it requires a continuing growth in the evidence of its effectiveness in order to withstand theoretically based attacks that it is not "tough" enough or may cause more crime. Both of these may be achieved by creating a stand-alone RJ agency comparable to the Youth Justice Board.

A "Restorative Justice Board" (RJB) could provide the focus and leadership for overcoming the obstacles to delivering RJ on a widespread basis in England and Wales. It could consist of five or seven members drawn from diverse constituencies concerned with justice policy, including victims, courts, police, probation, prisons, treatment professionals and the public. It could be empowered to set standards and make recommendations for statutory and policy changes. It could be given a budget to deliver two products. One would be the implementation of high-quality RJ on a much wider scale, fostered by investing the most in communities achieving the most RJ and by recommendations for statutory or other systemic changes needed to broaden access to RJ. The other focus of the budget would be research and development, investing in testing new ways to deliver RJ even in communities most challenged by crime.

This second focus of the RJB would thus be able to fill the major evidence gap found in this review: community-level impact assessments. Unlike the abundant evidence of the effect of RJ on *individual* victims and offenders, there is no evidence on how a widespread use of RJ would affect *community* rates of crime and respect for the law. In order to estimate the effects of RJ as a general (national) policy, it is necessary to conduct evaluations using neighbourhood crime rates, rather than individual offending patterns, as the unit of analysis. This review found no such tests to date. Such evidence could, however, be far more relevant to policy making than further research using individual cases as the unit of testing. Rolling out RJ right across a neighbourhood – from every stage of the criminal justice system to every civic organisation and governmental institution dealing with harms – could yield the best evidence on the effects of building a restorative society. It could also help to inform an RJB of the best practices to encourage in making funding decisions and setting standards.

Best practice for RJ

The ultimate purpose of this review is to identify "best practice" for RJ. To do that in an evidence-based way requires a focus on the two best-studied forms of RJ, face-to-face conferences and court-ordered restitution. The evidence is far from definitive, but it is at least suggestive. That suggestion is the following "best practice" in at least setting priorities for investments in RJ:

- RJ seems to work best when it is focused on the kinds of offences that have a personal victim, who can – at least in principle – be invited to meet with the offender. The major criteria for "working" in this claim include helping victims and reducing reoffending.
- RJ seems to work best when it is focused on violent crime, rather than property crime, with major exceptions: burglary victims gain reduced post-traumatic stress symptoms, and property offenders may commit less crime in future (or at least no more) if they get RJ than if they get prison.
- RJ may be best able to reduce court and imprisonment costs, as well as crime and its medical and financial impact on victims, if it is used as a form of diversion from CJ – including prosecution, or on a post-conviction basis, as a diversion from likely incarceration.

With the benefit of this evidence, and increasing dissatisfaction with the rising costs of prisons, restorative justice offers the entire UK a 21st-century alternative response to the challenge of crime in a free society.

Notes

1 All opinions and conclusions in this document are those of the authors and not of any governmental or private agencies that have funded any of the research the document reviews.
2 http://www.campbellcollaboration.org/doc-pdf/strang_restorative_prot.pdf
3 Anderson, Paul and Mann, Nyta *Safety First: The Making of New Labour* (Granta Books, 1997), p243, footnote 23).
4 Home Office, *Sentencing Statistics 2004,* table 6.2 (available at http://www.homeoffice.gov.uk/rds/pdfs05/hosb1505.pdf#search=%22sentencing%20statistics%202004%22.
5 Kelly, Walt *Pogo* (April 22, 1970) The cartoon satirises an 1813 battle report of the US Navy.
6 As a report to the Canadian government has noted, "reasonably well-designed studies of the impact of restorative justice programmes on recidivism are few" (Bonta et al, 1998: 4). For example, McCold's (1997) bibliography of 552 reports on restorative justice identified only two reports that had a comparison group and provided recidivism outcome data.
7 http://www.sas.upenn.edu/jerrylee/jrc/lordwoolf.pdf
8 Home Office, *Sentencing Statistics 2004*, table 6.2 (available at http://www.homeoffice.gov.uk/rds/pdfs05/hosb1505.pdf#search=%22sentencing%20statistics%202004%22)

References

Aber, L, Brown, J and Henrich, C *Teaching Conflict Resolution: An Effective School-Based Approach to Violence Prevention* (New York: National Center for Children in Poverty, 1999)

Angel, C *Crime Victims Meet Their Offenders: Testing the Impact of Restorative Justice Conferences on Victims' Post-Traumatic Stress Symptoms,* PhD dissertation (University of Pennsylvania, 2005)

Banton, M *The Policeman in the Community* (London: Tavistock, 1964)

Beven, J, Hall, G, Froyland, I, Steels, B and Goulding, D "Restitution or Renovation? Evaluating Restorative Justice Outcomes" in *Psychiatry, Psychology & Law* 12 (2005), pp 194–206

Bradbury, B Audit Report: *Deschutes County Delinquent Youth Demonstration Project,* Report No 2002–29 (Eugene, Oregon, 2002)

Braithwaite, J "Restorative Justice" in Tonry, M (ed) *Handbook of Crime & Punishment* (Oxford: Oxford University Press, 1998)

Braithwaite, J *Restorative Justice & Responsive Regulation* (Oxford: Oxford University Press, 2002)

Bright, P *Research into Domestic Violence & the Use of Family Group Conferences,* Fulbright Commission report (2002), posted by Hampshire Constabulary at http://www.hampshire.police.uk/NR/rdonlyres/0095EEF9-5864-478B-965A-1159FF386AFA/0/Fulbright.pdf

Burford, G and Pennell, J *Family Group Decision Making: After the Conference - Progress in Resolving Violence & Promoting Well-being: Outcome Report, Volumes 1 & 2* (St John's, Newfoundland, Canada: Memorial University of Newfoundland School of Social Work, 1997 and 1998)

Cain, M *Society & the Policeman's Role* (London: Routledge, 1973)

Calhoun, A *Calgary Community Conferencing School Component 1999 – 2000: A Year in Review* (2000) (http://www.calgarycommunityconferencing.com/r_and_eseptember_report.html)

Cameron, L and Thorsborne, M "Restorative Justice and School Discipline: Mutually Exclusive?" in Strang, H and Braithwaite, J (eds) *Restorative Justice & Civil Society* (Cambridge: Cambridge University Press, 2001)

Carr, C *Victim-Offender Reparation Programme Evaluation Report* (Inglewood, California: Centenela Valley Juvenile Diversion Project, 1998)

Chapman, B, Freiberg, A, Quiggan, J and Tait, D *Rejuvenating Financial Penalties: Using the Tax System to Collect Fines,* discussion paper no 461 (Canberra: Centre for Economic Policy Research, Australian National University, 2003)

Christie, N "Conflicts as Property" in *British Journal of Criminology* vol 17 (1977), pp 1–15

Cormier, R *Restorative Justice: Directions & Principles – Developments in Canada* (Ottawa: Department of the Solicitor General, Canada, 2002)

Crawford, A and Burden, T *Integrating Victims in Restorative Youth Justice,* Researching Criminal Justice series (Bristol: Policy Press, 2005)

Crawford, A and Newburn, T *Youth Offending & Restorative Justice: Implementing Reform in Youth Justice* (Cullompton, Devon: Willan Publishing, 2003)

Daly, K "Making Variation a Virtue: Evaluating the Potential and Limits of Restorative Justice" in Weitekamp, EGM and Kerner, H-J (eds) *Restorative Justice in Context: International Practices & Directions* (Cullompton, Devon: Willan Publishing, 2003)

Davis, R, Tichane, M and Grayson, D *Mediation & Arbitration as Alternatives to Criminal Prosecution in Felony Arrest Cases: An Evaluation of the Brooklyn Dispute Resolution Center* (First Year) (New York: Vera Institute of Justice, 1980)

Dignan, J "Repairing the Damage: Can Reparation Be Made to Work in the Service of Diversion?" in *British Journal of Criminology* vol 32, no 4 (1992), pp 453–472

Dignan, J *Understanding Victims & Restorative Justice* (Cullompton, Devon: Willan Publishing, 2005)

Dravery, W and Winslade, J *Developing Restorative Practices in Schools: Flavour of the Month or Saviour of the System?* (University of Waikato, School of Education, 2006) (www.aare.edu.au/03pap/dre03675.pdf)

Evje, A *A Summary of the Evaluations of Six California Victim Offender Reparation Programmes,* report to the California legislature submitted by the Judiciary Council of California (2000)

Fisher, R *The Design of Experiments* (Edinburgh: Oliver & Boyd, 1935)

Gehm, J "Mediated Victim-Offender Restitution Agreements: An Exploratory Analysis of Factors Relating to Victim Participation" in Galaway, B and Hudson, J (eds) *Criminal Justice, Restitution & Reconciliation* (New York: Criminal Justice Press, 1990)

Gesch, B, Bernard, S, Hammond, M, Hampson, S, Eves, A and Crowder, M "Influence of Supplementary Vitamins, Minerals and Essential Fatty Acids on the Antisocial Behaviour of Young Adult Prisoners: A Randomised, Placebo-controlled Trial" in *British Journal of Psychiatry* 181 (2002), pp 22–28

Giordano, P, Cernkovich, S and Rudolph, J "Gender, Crime and Desistance: Toward a Theory of Cognitive Transformation" in *American Journal of Sociology* 107 (2002), pp 990–1064

Gladwell, M *The Tipping Point* (Boston: Little, Brown, 2000)

Gottfredson, D "School-Based Crime Prevention" in Sherman, L, Gottfredson, D, MacKenzie, D, Eck, J, Reuter, P and Bushway, S (eds) *Preventing Crime: What Works, What Doesn't, What's Promising – A Report to the United States Congress* (Washington DC: National Institute of Justice, 1997)

Griffith, M *The Implementation of Group Conferencing in Juvenile Justice in Victoria,* paper presented at the Restoration for Victims of Crime conference convened by the Australian Institute of Criminology and the Victims Referral & Assistance Service, Melbourne (September 1999)

Hayes, H, Prenzler, T and Wortley, R *Making Amends: Final Evaluation of the Queensland Community Conferencing Pilot* (Brisbane: Griffith University, 1998)

Holdaway, S, Davidson, N, Dignan, J, Hammersley, R, Hine, J and Marsh, P *New Strategies to Address Youth Offending: The National Evaluation of the Pilot Youth Offending Teams* (London: Home Office, 2001)

Home Office *Restorative Justice: The Government's Strategy,* consultation document on the government's strategy on restorative justice (2003) (http://www.homeoffice.gov.uk/documents/rj-strategy-consult.pdf?view=Binary)

Hopkins, B *Just Schools: A Whole-School Approach to Restorative Justice* (London and New York: Jessica Kingsley, 2004)

Hoyle, C, Young, R and Hill, R *Proceed With Caution: An Evaluation of the Thames Valley Police Initiative in Restorative Cautioning* (York: Joseph Rowntree Foundation, 2002)

Hudson, C and Pring R *Banbury Police Schools Project: Report of the Evaluation,* unpublished manuscript held by the Thames Valley Police (2000)

Ierley, A and Ivker, C *Restoring School Communities. Restorative Justice in Schools Programme: Spring 2002 Report Card,* unpublished manuscript held by the School Mediation Center, Boulder, Colorado (2002)

Judge, N, Mutter, R, Gillett, T, Hennessey, J and Mauger, J *Executive Summary: From Evaluation of 30 Restorative Justice FGCs* (Essex Family Group Conference – Young People Who Offend Project, Essex County Council, 2002)

Kane, J, Lloyd, G, McCluskey, G, Riddell, S, Stead, J and Weedon, E *Restorative Practices in Three Scottish Councils*, final report of an evaluation funded by the Scottish Executive Education Department (Edinburgh: Scottish Executive Education Department, 2006)

Latimer, J, Dowden, C and Muise, D *The Effectiveness of Restorative Justice Practices: A Meta-Analysis* (Ottawa: Canadian Department of Justice, 2001)

Luke, G and Lind, B "Reducing Juvenile Crime: Conferencing vs Court" in *Crime & Justice Bulletin* no 69 (Sydney: New South Wales Bureau of Crime Statistics & Research, 2002)

Marsh, P *Supporting Pupils, Schools & Families: An Evaluation of the Hampshire Family Group Conferences in Education Project,* unpublished manuscript held by the University of Sheffield (2004)

Marshall, T and Merry, S *Crime & Accountability: Victim Offender Mediation in Practice* (London: Home Office, 1990)

Maruna, S *Making Good: How Ex-Offenders Reform & Reclaim Their Lives* (Washington, DC: American Psychological Association, 2001)

Maxwell, G and Morris, A "Family Group Conferences and Reoffending" in Morris, A and Maxwell, G (eds) *Restorative Justice for Juveniles: Conferencing, Mediation & Circles* (Oxford: Hart, 2001), pp 243–263

McCold, P and Wachtel, B *Restorative Policing Experiment: The Bethlehem Pennsylvania Police Family Group Conferencing Project* (Pipersville, Pennsylvania: Pipers Press, 1998)

McCulloch, H *Shop Theft: Improving the Police Response,* Crime Detection & Prevention Series, paper 76 (London: Home Office, Police Research Group, 1996)

McGarrell, E, Olivares, K, Crawford, K and Kroovand, N *Returning Justice to the Community: The Indianapolis Restorative Justice Experiment* (Indianapolis, Hudson Institute, 2000)

Miers, D *An International Review of Restorative Justice,* Crime Reduction Series, paper 10 (London: Home Office, Policing & Reducing Crime Unit, 2001)

Miller, W *Cops & Bobbies: Police Authority in New York & London, 1830–1870* (Chicago: University of Chicago Press, 1977)

Minnesota Department of Children, Family & Learning "In-School Behavior Intervention Grants" in *A Three-Year Evaluation of Alternative Approaches to Suspensions & Expulsions,* report to the Minnesota legislature (2002)

Moore, D and Forsythe, L *A New Approach to Juvenile Justice: An Evaluation of Family Conferencing in Wagga Wagga* (Canberra: Criminology Research Council, 1995)

Morris, A, Maxwell, G and Robertson, JP "Giving Victims a Voice: a New Zealand Experiment" in *Howard Journal* 32 (1993), pp 304–21

Morrison, B "Developing the School's Capacity in the Regulation of Civil Society", in Strang, H and Braithwaite, J (eds), *Restorative Justice & Civil Society* (Cambridge: Cambridge University Press, 2001)

Morrison, B "Restorative Justice in Schools" in Eliott, E and Gordon, R (eds) *New Directions in Restorative Justice* (Cullompton, Devon: Willan Publishing, 2005)

Morrison, B "Schools and Restorative Justice" in Johnstone, G and Van Ness, D (eds) *Restorative Justice Handbook* (Cullompton, Devon: Willan Publishing, 2006a)

Morrison, B *Restoring Safe School Communities: A Whole School Response to Bullying, Violence & Alienation* (Sydney: Federation Press, 2006b)

Morrison, BE and Martinez, M "Restorative Justice through Social and Emotional Skills Training: An Evaluation of Primary School Students", unpublished honours thesis, Australian National University, Canberra (2001)

Newburn, T, Crawford, A, Earle, R, Goldie, S, Hale, C, Masters, G, Netten, A, Saunders, R, Sharpe, K, Uglow, S and Campbell, A *The Introduction of Referral Orders into the Youth Justice System,* HORS 242 (London: Home Office, 2001)

Niemeyer, M and Stichor, D "A Preliminary Study of a Large Victim/Offender Reparation Programme" in *Federal Probation* 57 (1996), pp 48–53

Northern Ireland Office *Draft Protocol for Community-Based Restorative Justice Schemes* (2006) (http://www.nio.gov.uk/draft_protocol_for_ community_based_restorative_justice_schemes.pdf)

Nuffield, J *Evaluation of the Adult Victim-Offender Mediation Programme, Saskatoon Community Mediation Services* (Regina, Saskatchewan: Department of Justice, Saskatchewan, 1997)

Nugent, W and Paddock, J "The Effect of Victim-Offender Mediation on Severity of Reoffense" in *Mediation Quarterly* vol 12, no 4 (1995), pp 353–367

Nugent, W, Umbreit, M, Wiinamaki, L and Paddock, J "Participation in Victim-Offender Mediation Reduces Recidivism" in *Connections* Summer 1999, no 3 (1999)

Nugent, W, Williams, M and Umbreit, M "Participation in Victim-Offender Mediation and the Prevalence and Severity of Subsequent Delinquent Behavior: A Meta-Analysis" in *Utah Law Review* vol 2003, no 1 (2003), pp 137–166

Pennell, J and Burford, G "Family Group Decision-Making: Protecting Women and Children" in *Child Welfare* vol 79, no 2 (March/April 2000)

Poulson, B "A Third Voice: A Review of Empirical Research on the Psychological Outcomes of Restorative Justice" in *Utah Law Review* (2003), pp 167–203

Roy, S "Two Types of Juvenile Restorative Programmes in Two Midwestern Counties: A Comparative Study" in *Federal Probation* 57 (1993), pp 48–53

Salsburg, D *The Lady Tasting Tea: How Statistics Revolutionized Science in the Twentieth Century* (New York: Henry Holt & Co, 2001)

Schneider, A "Restitution and Recidivism Rates: Results from Four Experimental Studies" in *Criminology* vol 24 (1986), pp 533–552

Shapland, J, Atkinson, A, Colledge, E, Dignan, J, Howes, M, Johnstone, J, Pennant, R, Robinson, G and Sorsby, A *Implementing Restorative Justice Schemes (Crime Reduction Programme): A Report on the First Year,* Home Office online report 32/04 (London: Home Office, 2004) (http://www.homeoffice.gov.uk/rds/pdfs04/rdsoir3204.pdf)

Shapland, J, Atkinson, A, Atkinson, H, Chapman, B, Colledge, E, Dignan, J, Howes, M, Johnstone, J, Robinson, G and Sorsby, A *Restorative Justice in Practice: The Second Report from the Evaluation of Three Schemes* (Sheffield: Centre for Criminological Research, University of Sheffield, 2006)

Shaw, G and Wierenga, A *Restorative Practices: Community Conferencing Pilot,* unpublished manuscript held at the Faculty of Education, University of Melbourne (2002)

Sherman, L, Strang, H and Woods, D, 2000, *Recidivism Patterns in the Canberra Reintegrative Shaming Experiments (RISE)* (Canberra: Centre for Restorative Justice, Research School of Social Sciences, Australian National University, 2000) (http://www.aic.gov.au/rjustice/rise/progress/1999.html)

Sherman, L and Strang, H "Verdicts or Inventions? Interpreting Results from Randomized Controlled Experiments in Criminology" in *American Behavioral Scientist* (special issue devoted to experimental methods in the political sciences edited by Donald P Green and Alan S Gerber, Yale University), vol 47, no 5 (2003), pp 575–607

Sherman, L, Strang, H, Angel, C, Woods, DJ, Barnes, GC, Bennett, S, Inkpen, N and Rossner, M "Effects of Face-to-Face Restorative Justice on Victims of Crime in Four Randomized Controlled Trials" in *Journal of Experimental Criminology* vol 1, no 3 (2005), pp 367–395

Sherman, L, Strang, H, Barnes, G and Woods, D *Preliminary Analysis of Race, Recidivism & Restorative Justice for Victimed Crimes in Canberra,* unpublished manuscript, Lee Center of Criminology, Philadelphia, Pennsylvania (2006a)

Sherman, L, Strang, H, Barnes, GC and Newbury-Birch, D Preliminary Analysis of the Northumbria Restorative Justice Experiments, unpublished manuscript, Lee Center of Criminology, Philadelphia, Pennsylvania (2006b)

Sherman, L and Strang, H "Curing Revenge: Transforming Emotions with Restorative Justice" in Karstedt, S, Loader, I and Strang, H (eds) *Emotions, Crime & Justice,* proceedings of a conference held in September 2004 at the International Institute for the Sociology of Law, Onati, Spain (forthcoming)

Strang, H, Barnes, GC, Braithwaite, J and Sherman, L *Experiments in Restorative Policing: A Progress Report on the Canberra Reintegrative Shaming Experiments (RISE)* (Canberra: Australian National University, 1999) (http://www.aic.gov.au/rjustice/rise/progress/1999.html)

Strang, H and Sherman, L "Repairing the Harm: Victims and Restorative Justice" in *Utah Law Review* (2003), pp 15–42

Strang, H, Sherman, L, Angel, C, Woods, D, Bennett, S, Newbury-Birch, D and Inkpen, J "Victim Evaluations of Face-to-Face Restorative Justice Experiences: A Quasi-Experimental Analysis" in *Journal of Social Issues* vol 62, no 2 (2006), pp 281–306

Tilly, C *Why?* (Princeton, New Jersey: Princeton University Press, 2006)

Triggs, S *New Zealand Court-Referred Restorative Justice Pilot: Two-Year Follow-Up of Reoffending* (Wellington: Ministry of Justice, 2005)

Trimboli, L *An Evaluation of the NSW Youth Justice Conferencing Scheme* (Sydney: New South Wales Bureau of Crime Statistics & Research, 2000)

Umbreit, M "Crime Victims Confront Their Offenders: The Impact of a Minneapolis Mediation Programme" in *Research on Social Work Practice* vol 4, no 4 (1994), pp 436–447

Umbreit, M *The Handbook of Victim Offender Mediation* (San Francisco: Jossey-Bass, 2001)

Umbreit, M and Coates, R "The Impact of Mediating Victim Offender Conflict: An Analysis of Programmes in Three States" in *Juvenile & Family Court Journal* (1992), pp 21–28

Umbreit, M and Coates, R "Cross-Site Analysis of Victim-Offender Mediation in Four States" in *Crime & Delinquency* vol 39 (1993), pp 565–585

Umbreit, M, Coates, R and Kalanj, B *Victim Meets Offender: The Impact of Restorative Justice & Mediation* (Monsey, New York: Criminal Justice Press, 1994)

Umbreit, M, Coates, R and Roberts, A "The Impact of Victim-Offender Mediation: A Cross-National Perspective" in *Mediation Quarterly* 17 (2000), pp 215–229

Umbreit, M, Coates, R and Vos, B *Juvenile Victim Offender Mediation in Six Oregon Counties: Final Report* (Oregon Dispute Resolutions Commission, 2001)

Umbreit, M, Warner, S, Roberts, A, Kalanj, B and Lipkin, R *Mediation of Criminal Conflict in England: An Assessment of Services in Coventry & Leeds – Executive Summary* (Centre for Restorative Justice & Mediation, School of Social Work, University of Minnesota, 1996)

UK Select Committee of Public Accounts *Collection of Fines & Other Financial Penalties in the Criminal Justice System* (London: HMSO, 2002)

Victoria Auditor-General *Report on Ministerial Portfolios* (Melbourne, 1998)

Wachtel, T and McCold, P "Restorative Justice in Everyday Life: Beyond the Formal Ritual" in Strang, H and Braithwaite, J (eds) *Restorative Justice & Civil Society* (Cambridge: Cambridge University Press, 2001)

Walker, L "Conferencing – A New Approach for Juvenile Justice in Honolulu" in *Federal Probation* 66 (2002), pp 38–43

Willcock, R *Retail Theft Initiative: Does It Really Work?* (K2 Management Development, 1999)

Wilcox, A, Young, R and Hoyle, C *Two-Year Resanctioning Study: A Comparison of Restorative & Traditional Cautions,* Home Office online report 57/04 (London: Home Office, 2004)

Woehrle, LM *Summary Evaluation Report: A Study of the Impact of the Help Increase the Peace Project in the Chambersburg Area School District* (Baltimore, Maryland: American Friends Service Committee, 2000)

Wynne, J "Leeds Mediation and Reparation Service: Ten Years' Experience with Victim-Offender Mediation" in Galaway, B and Hudson, J (eds) *Restorative Justice: International Perspectives* (Monsey, New York: Criminal Justice Press, 1996)

Youth Justice Board for England & Wales *National Evaluation of the Restorative Justice in Schools Programme* (2004) (www.youth-justice-board.gov.uk)

Weisburd, D, Lum, C and Petrosino, A "Does Research Design Affect Study Outcomes in Criminal Justice?" in *The Annals of the American Academy of Social & Political Sciences* 578 (2001), pp 50–70

Woolf, H "Foreword" in Radzinowicz, L *Adventures in Criminology* (London: Routledge, 1999)

25 Reducing recidivism

A task for restorative justice?

Gwen Robinson and Joanna Shapland

[...]

Introduction

One of restorative justice's biggest selling points is that it offers a balanced approach to dealing with offending and its consequences. As Schiff has argued, restorative justice differs from other justice strategies, such as retribution, deterrence, rehabilitation and incapacitation, in that it is 'concerned with much more than simply what is done to or with offenders' (Schiff 2003: 330). Much of the appeal of restorative justice derives from its attempts to involve and meet the needs of victims, and sometimes other parties or stakeholders. Indeed, the current restorative justice 'boom' has been portrayed as occurring in the context of a victim's movement which has sought over a number of years to raise the profile of crime victims, highlight their needs and promote their involvement in justice processes in a number of ways (e.g. Miers 2004; see also Dignan 2005). It is thus fair to say that restorative justice is not generally considered to be an offender-centred approach.

Nonetheless, there can be little doubt that, among policy makers at least, there is growing interest in the capacity of restorative justice interventions to impact positively on rates of recidivism. This is perhaps best illustrated with reference to the increasing number of evaluative studies which have examined reoffending or reconviction rates following restorative justice interventions (e.g. Luke and Lind 2002; Hayes and Daly 2003; Mawell and Morris 2001; McGarrell *et al.* 2000; Sherman *et al.* 2000; Miers *et al.* 2001; Tyler *et al.* 2007; Wilcox *et al.* 2004). Referring to her own research on restorative conferencing in South Australia, Daly (2001a: 71) has noted that 'the conference effect everyone asks about is, does it reduce reoffending?', whilst, in the United Kingdom, the evaluators of a high-profile police-led scheme delivering restorative cautioning for juvenile offenders have observed that achieving reductions in reoffending 'for most policy-makers is the litmus test' (Hoyle *et al.* 2002: 46). Indeed, in, England and Wales, policy makers' interest in the potential of restorative justice in this regard was evident in the government's 2001 decision to provide funding to three restorative justice schemes under the auspices of its Crime Reduction Programme (Shapland *et al.* 2004; Homel *et al.* 2005), though both reducing reoffending and meeting victim needs were specified as key aims of the evaluation.[1]

This paper draws on our experience as independent evaluators of these Home Office funded schemes[2] to reflect upon the role of restorative justice as a means toward the 'end' of reducing recidivism on the part of participating offenders. The three schemes in question were run by CONNECT (in London); JRC (in London, Thames Valley and Northumbria) and REMEDI (in South Yorkshire). The schemes were designed to explore the use of restorative justice for adult offenders, including for serious offences, but, between them, the schemes delivered restorative justice in respect of both adult and youth cases and covered a range of offences, from minor offences (typically committed by young offenders) to very serious offences of burglary, robbery and violence. Offenders took part in restorative justice at different points in the criminal justice process, and included diversionary, pre-sentence and post-sentence cases (see Shapland *et al.* 2004; 2006a; 2006b). For the purposes of this article, we focus in particular on one restorative justice practice—namely conferencing—delivered by the largest of the three schemes (JRC).[3] The offences for these JRC conferences all had direct personal victims, so victims were individuals, rather than organizations or businesses.[4] In the course of this research, we (and other members of our team) observed some 280 JRC conferences and conducted a large number of post-restorative justice interviews (and some pre-restorative justice interviews) with both victims and offenders who had taken part in a restorative justice conference. JRC was set up as a randomized controlled trial experiment (RCT), primarily because such experimental methods are seen as the best way of measuring the effect on reoffending, reaching the 'gold standard' of level 5 on the Maryland Scientific Methods Scale (Sherman 1997).

We begin by considering the legitimacy of 'reducing recidivism' as a goal for restorative justice, drawing both on the theoretical literature and our own research findings. We then proceed to analyse how restorative justice might be expected to achieve crime reduction outcomes. In this section of the article, we consider the reintegrative shaming theory of Braithwaite and colleagues, as well as the broader reintegrative potential of restorative justice in respect of its role in assisting decisions to desist (Shapland *et al.* forthcoming), developing offenders' individual 'social capital' and facilitating access to sources of 'human capital' (Coleman 1988). In keeping with 'real world' analyses of restorative justice (Daly 2001a), we then move on to discuss whether the theoretical potential of restorative justice in respect of recidivism reduction is, in practice, achievable. This may provide some tentative explanations for the mixed findings of prior research on the crime reduction effects of restorative justice initiatives.

To what extent is reducing recidivism considered to be a legitimate goal for restorative justice?

As is well known, much of the restorative justice literature has tended to focus on the relationship(s) between restorative justice and criminal justice, and this has been the subject of intense debate for a number of years (e.g. von Hirsch *et al.* 2003b). Whilst some proponents have conceived or understood restorative justice as an alternative to and as a critique of retributive criminal justice, placing restorative justice in the role of a radical 'alternative paradigm' (e.g. Zehr 1990), others have conceived restorative justice in 'separatist' or 'reformist' terms (see Dignan 2005: 106). In many of these formulations, retributive criminal justice has been criticized for the dominance (some would say obsession) of its focus upon establishing guilt and apportioning blame; for the socially excluding stigma of guilt and many forms of criminal justice punishments; and for its failure to meet the needs of victims of crime.[5]

It is, therefore, perhaps unsurprising that much of the restorative justice literature eschews discussion of the legitimacy of 'traditional' criminal justice goals, such as reducing offending. The literature does, however, include some discussion of the relationship between restorative justice and the goal of offender rehabilitation—albeit that such discussions tend to reveal a degree of ambivalence. Johnstone (2002: 111) has noted that advocates have been keen to distance restorative justice approaches from notions of 'therapeutic treatment' grounded in a 'welfare model' of criminal justice; but, at the same time, there is in much writing about restorative justice an interest in bringing about rehabilitative *outcomes.* For example, having contrasted restorative justice with a 'treatment' approach, Eglash goes on to say that, for him, restorative justice is primarily about 'justice and rehabilitation for offenders' (Eglash 1977: 99). Similarly, Braithwaite makes it clear that he sees restorative justice as a means of reducing reoffending, and oriented ultimately toward the goal of crime reduction. In this vein, he discusses 'restoring offenders' in terms of reduced offending, and in one well known paper considers why restorative justice practices 'rehabilitate better than criminal justice practices grounded in the welfare model', whilst at the same time maintaining that restorative justice does *not* have rehabilitation as an aim (Braithwaite 1999: 67–9). Indeed, for Braithwaite, one of the reasons that restorative justice is better placed to rehabilitate than 'rehabilitative justice' is precisely *because* it does not have rehabilitation as an aim. 'When the criminal justice system is seen as setting out to change people', Braithwaite argues, 'that engenders reactance' (Braithwaite 1999: 68), by which he means resistance. Further, he argues, rehabilitative programmes—characterized by professionals who 'come in to do things to or for people'—are essentially stigmatic, and therefore likely to engender rather than inhibit crime (Braithwaite 1999: 68).[6]

Other advocates, however, have argued that in order to bring restorative justice into the 'mainstream', policies and practices need to address widely accepted criminal justice goals—particularly the promotion of offender rehabilitation—whilst at the same time preserving restorative justice principles (Bazemore and O'Brien 2002). But, at the same time, caution has been expressed about overemphasizing or prioritizing such a goal. For some writers, the principal problem behind such an approach is that reducing recidivism is a somewhat unrealistic goal for restorative justice (e.g. Dignan 2001; Hudson 2003; McIvor 2004). For Bazemore and O'Brien (2002), presenting restorative justice as primarily aimed at offender rehabilitation or the prevention of recidivism is inappropriate not because it is seen as an unrealistic goal per se, but rather because it diminishes the importance or salience of other goals, particularly victim-centred ones. Furthermore, they add that a focus on victim needs is; 'essential to [rj's] survival' (Bazemore and O'Brien 2002: 35).

Whilst it is difficult to generalize about the vast literature on restorative justice, it appears to us that to a large extent the problem of appearing to be overly concerned with 'offender outcomes' has been dealt with by rejecting 'rehabilitation' as an aim, but at the same time welcoming crime reduction outcomes as a 'happy side-effect' of restorative justice encounters. We would expect that, for the majority of restorative justice advocates and practitioners, the acceptance of rehabilitation and/or the prevention of reoffending as a legitimate goal would at least be qualified with reference to the needs and wishes of other stakeholders. Indeed, we agree with Johnstone, who has argued that the rehabilitation of offenders is a legitimate 'end' of restorative justice 'only insofar as it can be made compatible with the goal of achieving justice for their victims' (Johnstone 2002: 95). However, we think that many restorative justice theorists have been afflicted by a rather out-of-date conception of the possibility of victim and offender goals coexisting: they have seen benefits for offenders as potentially detracting from benefits for victims—a zero-sum game. We shall argue that, in contrast, benefits for offenders, such as reducing reoffending or rehabilitation, not only do not detract from benefits for victims, but are actually often welcomed and desired by victims.

The difficulty of reaching a conclusion about the extent to which reducing recidivism is considered a legitimate goal of restorative justice is arguably compounded by a tendency in the literature—and some restorative justice programmes—toward vague, abstract and/or ambiguous aims and objectives. Aims such as 'restoration of victims, offenders and communities' may be laudable, but they are not easily operationalized. A related issue is that restorative justice programmes have commonly been associated with multiple aims or objectives, which have not always been prioritized—or indeed shared— by all of the programme's stakeholders (e.g. see Ruddick 1989).

The three schemes that we have been evaluating had two equally weighted formal aims set by the Home Office, which provided funding: to reduce reoffending (as expressed by standard two-year reconviction rates) and to meet victim needs. We found among staff and other stakeholders involved in running the three schemes claims to be pursuing a variety of aims, which were not always clearly or similarly prioritized. In particular, it is worth noting that whilst all three of the schemes that we evaluated were funded under the Crime Reduction Programme, staff working with one of the schemes did not explicitly identify 'reducing the risk of further offending' among the three principal aims of 'their' scheme, though neither did they reject this as a legitimate aim of their work (Shapland *et al*. 2004).

In exploring *participants'* views about restorative justice, however, we found strong support for restorative justice as a vehicle for reducing reoffending. This was particularly true for conferencing, which, as we have already noted, was numerically the dominant model of restorative justice used by the three schemes in our evaluation. The final stage of JRC conferences, which all ran to a uniform pattern, turned participants' attention to outcomes and their hopes and wishes for the future. Both our observational data and the outcome agreements produced by participants in conferences[7] indicated that this final stage in conferences tended to focus much less on victims' needs than on offenders' future behaviour, and addressing offenders' problems, with a view to reducing the likelihood of further reoffending. In approximately four-fifths of the conferences that we observed, offenders' problems and strategies to prevent reoffending were discussed, whilst discussion of financial or direct reparation to the victim was rare (Shapland *et al*. 2006a). This was not because victims or their wishes were ignored but rather because victims, in common with other participants, actively wished to focus on addressing the offender's problems and so minimizing the chance of reoffending. In pre-conference interviews about why they wanted to participate in the conference, 72 per cent of victims said it was very or quite important to them to help the offender (Shapland *et al*. 2006b).

As has been suggested elsewhere, it is possible that some victims were content to waive just claims for compensation out of consideration for the need for an offender 'to be unencumbered in making a fresh start' (Braithwaite and Mugford 1994: 149). In our experience, though, such a concern was linked to an explicit desire to prevent future victimization. Thus, it was not necessarily simply the case that victims wanted to 'win the battle for the offender's soul', as Clifford Shearing put it after observing two Australian conferences in the early 1990s (see Braithwaite and Mugford 1994: 149): victims' (and their supporters') aspirations for offenders were often expressed as a desire to help or 'save' others (i.e. potential future victims) from the harm they themselves had suffered at the hands of the offender. We further observed that for many victims, an offender's stated intention to 'do something' about their offending behaviour constituted a form of reparation: it was for many victims a valuable addition to a verbal apology (Shapland *et al*. forthcoming). In our evaluation, then, the majority of victims appeared to regard the reduction of reoffending as a legitimate aim of 'their' conference, and did not regard the pursuit of such an aim as incompatible with their own needs.[8] Very similar results have been obtained in the evaluation of statutory youth conferencing in Northern Ireland—victims were not found to be vindictive, but rather to want to help offenders not to reoffend, both to decrease the likelihood of others becoming victims in the future and to help offenders to put their lives on a more useful footing (Doak and O'Mahony 2006).

Exploring the crime reduction potential of restorative justice

At the beginning of this paper, we noted the adoption in an increasing number of evaluative studies of recidivism as an outcome measure. Certainly, this would seem to suggest that there are sound theoretical grounds to connect restorative justice practices with such an outcome. It has, however, been noted that just *how* the 'end' of reduced recidivism is theoretically linked with the particular methods associated with restorative justice is not always explicit (von Hirsch *et al.* 2003a). This has prompted questions about whether the adoption of individual-level outcomes such as recidivism rates is theoretically defensible, or simply evidence of an unthinking application of 'conventional' criminal justice outcome measures to restorative justice evaluations (Kurki 2003). In this section, we move on to consider the extent to which the measurement of recidivism *is* a theoretically defensible practice, by means of a review of the relevant theoretical contributions in the restorative justice literature.

Braithwaite's 'reintegrative shaming' thesis

In theoretical terms, the clearest and best known attempt to explicate the impact of restorative justice practices on the recidivism of participating offenders lies in Braithwaite's 'reintegrative shaming' theory (RST) (Braithwaite 1989; 1993). Although Braithwaite's theory by no means underpins *all* operational examples of restorative justice, the theory has heavily influenced the development of conferencing.[9] As is well known, this model of restorative justice originated in the early 1990s in the small town of Wagga Wagga in New South Wales, Australia. Subsequently, this particular conferencing model has spread not just to other parts of Australia (most notably Canberra, where the 'reintegrative shaming experiment' (RISE) was instituted in 1995),[10] but also to the United States and the United Kingdom, where restorative cautioning for juvenile offenders was pioneered by Thames Valley police (e.g. Hoyle *et al.* 2002). RST also underpinned the model of conferencing which was adopted by the largest of the three schemes we evaluated—the Justice Research Consortium (JRC), on which we are concentrating in this article.

A key point to make about RST is that it was conceived as a theory of crime control: in other words, it is explicitly oriented toward the prevention of reoffending. Braithwaite defined 'reintegrative shaming'—in contrast to the 'stigmatic' shaming typically dispensed by the criminal courts—as 'disapproval dispensed within an ongoing relationship with the offender based on respect... shaming which focuses on the evil of the deed rather than on the offender as an irreclaimably evil person' (Braithwaite 1993: 1). Braithwaite proposed that reintegrative shaming could be an effective means of inducing guilt and eliciting remorse on the part of the offender, as well as a precursor to forgiveness, acceptance and reintegration within the law-abiding community. As Braithwaite explains in his original text, reintegrative shaming is about 'conscience-building' and can be 'a reaffirmation of the morality of the offender'. It is this new or reconstituted morality or conscience which, he argues, subsequently serves to inhibit future offending behaviour (Braithwaite 1989: 72–3).[11]

The offender's 'significant others' or 'community of care' play an important role in the theory of reintegrative shaming, in that their disapproval of the offence ('moral censure') is likely to mean more to the offender than that of a magistrate or judge, in whose esteem the offender has little or no personal investment (Braithwaite 1989: 87). But, importantly, in the context of RST, the community's 'judgement' is not a prelude to pain or retributive punishment: rather, it is intended to perform an educative and reintegrative function. The concern is to persuade offenders to *share* the community's judgment of their behaviour, and to act in future with that judgment in mind.

As Dignan (2005: 105) has pointed out, Braithwaite's (1989) original text was very offender-centred and paid little attention to the potential role of victims in processes of reintegrative shaming. However, in his subsequent work, Braithwaite acknowledged a role for the victim in the shaming process which involved drawing the offender's attention to the 'collateral damage' caused by the offence—damage which might include fear, personal injury and/or material loss (Braithwaite and Mugford 1994). Faced with the victim's personal testimony, it is argued, the offender is less likely to be able to employ 'techniques of neutralization' (Sykes and Matza 1957), which serve to minimize the harm caused by offending, and more likely to have to face up to the consequences of his or her actions.

It is this point that has led some to question whether (reintegrative) shaming is a necessary ingredient of 'successful' conferencing (in terms of reducing reoffending). In their New Zealand study of 108 young people, who participated in conferences between 1990 and 1991, Maxwell and Morris (2001; 2002) deployed multivariate analyses in an attempt to isolate the 'key' variables associated with the outcome of reduced reoffending. They found that conference-specific factors relevant to reductions in reconviction were: feelings of remorse on the part of the young offender; not being made to feel a bad person (in Braithwaite's terms, lack of stigmatic shaming); feeling involved in decision making; agreeing with the outcome; and meeting and apologizing to the victim(s).[12] Conversely, conference-specific variables which were found to be predictive of reoffending were the young person and his/her parents feeling shamed (stigmatic) and a lack of remorse on the part of the young person. In the South Australia Juvenile Justice evaluation, Hayes and Daly (2003) also found that remorse was one of two significant conference variables associated with reducing reoffending (the other being conferences rated as 'ending on a high').

Maxwell and Morris (2002) have argued that their findings provide some support for RST, particularly in respect of the negative impact of stigmatic shaming, and the positive impact of invoking remorse in young offenders. However, they question whether shaming/disapproval was *necessarily* the mechanism which invoked remorse. An alternative possibility, they argue, is that 'empathy or understanding the effects of offending on victims was the trigger' (Maxwell and Morris 2002: 280–1). This interpretation might equally apply to the findings of Hayes and Daly (2003). It is interesting to note then that more recent research and scholarship in respect of RST (Harris *et al.* 2004: 202) has ceded that hearing the victim's story might trigger the emotions of empathy and compassion in the offender, which, in turn, may trigger emotions of remorse, shame and guilt (though, they contend, this is only possible where the offender is treated with empathy). It is also important to note that though these theoretical developments postulate a time course for these changes in offender attitudes (shaming in conference— remorse—change in offending *and/or* hearing victim in conference—empathy/compassion—remorse—change in offending), their methods of retrospective interviewing of offenders and victims do not enable the proposed causal sequence(s) to be proved.

RJ and the development of social and human capital

As already noted, Braithwaite views shaming as a prelude to the reintegration of the offender. In the context of RST, reintegration tends to be represented as a largely symbolic process:

one which centres on the (re-)acceptance or 'requalification' of the offender as a law-abiding member of the community.[13] For Braithwaite, reintegration principally implies the 'decerti-fication of deviance', which, it is argued, may be underlined by the acceptance of an offend-er's apology, offers of forgiveness and/or the signing of an agreement. It may also be achieved through the offender's performance of reparative work—which may form part of such an agreement—upon which forgiveness or re-acceptance may be conditional (Braithwaite and Mugford 1994: 141).

But there are arguably other, more practical ways in which restorative justice might facilitate 'reintegration', and which might offer the potential to inhibit future offending. For example, in Bazemore's work on restorative justice with juvenile offenders, the performance of reparative work, whether to direct victims or to the wider community, is understood as a key step toward reintegration (e.g. Bazemore 1998; Bazemore and O'Brien 2002). Bazemore sees reparation as a crucial opportunity for offenders to be actively engaged—possibly for the first time—in roles that allow them to gain valuable (and valued) skills, and practice 'being competent'. According to this view, the performance of repara-tion enables offenders to see themselves—and to be seen by others—as valuable resources with something to offer the community, rather than passive recipients of 'help'. Elsewhere, this sort of process has been described as 'strengths-based rehabilitation' (Maruna and LeBel 2003; Raynor 2004).

Bazemore is also among a number of recent writers to hypothesize that restorative justice—and conferencing in particular—offers opportunities for the development of individual-level social capital[14] (Halpern 2005; Bazemore *et al.* 2000; Bazemore and O'Brien 2002; Kurki 2003). Social capital has been characterized in a number of different ways, but two definitions are particularly useful in this context. The first is provided by Bourdieu and Wacquant, who describe social capital as:

> ... the sum of the resources, actual and virtual, that accrue to an individual or a group by virtue of possessing a durable network of more or less institutionalised relationships of mutual acquaintance and recognition.
>
> (Bourdieu and Wacquant 1992: 119)

The second is provided by Coleman, who characterizes social capital as 'a resource for persons'—a facilitative aspect of social structures 'making possible the achievement of certain ends that in its absence would not be possible' (Coleman 1988: S98).

The relationship between enhancing social capital and reducing reoffending risk has been the subject of recent research in several countries on both desistance (or 'naturalistic' reha-bilitation) (e.g. Maruna 2001; Farrall 2002; Farrall and Maruna 2004) and the resettlement (or 're-entry') of ex-prisoners (e.g. Travis and Petersilia 2001; Maruna and LeBel 2003; Maruna *et al.* 2004). Both literatures have highlighted the typically low levels of (positive) social capital enjoyed by offenders, and have emphasized the key roles played by families, communities and social networks in encouraging ex-offenders to desist from offending. For example, Travis and Petersilia have argued that 're-entry activities' should take place as close as possible to the local communities to which offenders will ultimately return, because it is here that the 'positive power of social networks' can be found and exploited (Travis and Petersilia 2001: 309). Laub and Sampson (2003) highlight the importance of partners and jobs in their longitudinal study of desistance in persistent young offenders in the United States. Similarly, Farrall's (2002) research on desistance has highlighted the importance of fostering the ex-offender's social capital which, following Coleman, he defines as the productive interpersonal and social relationships which can link the ex-offender with practical resources such as homes and jobs.

In the context of conferencing, it has been argued that the potential to generate or mobilize social capital can be maximized or 'strategized' by seeking to ensure that those most closely connected to the offender are present, as well as those likely to be relevant 'resource persons' for the offender. It is also hypothesized that the possibilities for increasing social capital increase as the number of conference participants grows (Bazemore and O'Brien 2002: 51–2).

Finally, just as a restorative justice encounter offers opportunities for the development of the offender's social capital, so it can also 'set up' opportunities to develop 'human capital': namely 'changes in persons that bring about skills and capabilities that make them able to act in new ways' (Coleman 1988: S100). In other words, restorative justice can be a springboard to more overtly 'correctional' interventions, as well as more traditionally 'rehabilitative' resources such as educational and employment programmes (Bazemore and Bell 2004; Braithwaite 1999).

From theory to practice: realizing the potential?

As is well documented, evaluations of restorative justice which have included an analysis of the subsequent offending behaviour of participating offenders have yielded mixed results (for summaries, see, e.g. Luke and Lind 2002; Kurki 2003; Dignan 2005; Sherman and Strang 2007). Unfortunately, however, the majority of these evaluations have been able to shed little explanatory light on their results, due to a lack of process evaluation data (i.e. observations and/or post-restorative justice interviews with participants). In this section, we reflect on the extent to which restorative justice in the 'real world' might be capable of realizing its *theoretical* recidivism-reduction potential, and the extent to which this potential may be frustrated or problematic in practice. We conduct this analysis principally with reference to our own process evaluation—in particular, our observations of some 280 restorative justice conferences. Our discussion is structured to reflect the foregoing theoretical analysis.

Reintegrative shaming?

RST offers a plausible theoretical account of how restorative justice encounters might be expected to produce reductions in recidivism on the part of participating offenders. In this section, we reflect on its potential to bring about reductions in reoffending via conferencing.

Our first observation about RST is that it is a theory which cannot be operationalized or 'implemented' (in the context of a restorative justice event) in the same way that, say, cognitive-behavioural theory can be operationalized in an offending behaviour programme. There is arguably a paradox at the heart of reintegrative shaming as it applies to restorative justice, in that it relies on a series of carefully choreographed steps, but in the context of an encounter which is valued for the flexibility it affords participants to express themselves as they wish. This paradox is perhaps best captured in Braithwaite and Mugford's (1994) *14* conditions of 'successful reintegration ceremonies', one of which is that 'ceremony design must be flexible... so that participants exercise their process control constrained by only very broad procedural requirements' (Braithwaite and Mugford 1994: 143, 159–60). Although conferencing based on the theory of reintegrative shaming equips facilitators with a script which is designed to encourage progression through the stages outlined in the theory, such scripts are in fact quite minimal, and whilst they can effectively structure the restorative justice encounter (e.g. prompting turn-taking and posing pertinent questions to participants), scripting does not negate the fact that participants will always bring their own novel experiences and expectations to the process. So, whilst conferences are structured by a script, there is no 'dress rehearsal' and therefore no guarantee that what happens in any conference will fill the prescription of RST.

A second, related point is that RST tends to assumes that victims *will always* have suffered significantly at the hands of the offender, and seems to expect that victims should express high emotion in the context of a conference as a result. Victims are characterized by Harris *et al.* (2004) as likely to be dominated by emotions linked directly to their victimization: humiliation, shame, embarrassment and anger. However, one of the key findings of our study was that victims' reactions to victimization varied dramatically, as did the range and degrees of emotion they (and others) displayed in conferences—even though the conferences we observed were dealing with more serious offences than has typically been the case in restorative justice. Overall, 65 per cent of victims who took part in conferences that we observed were rated as having been affected by the offence 'a lot' or 'quite a lot', based on their verbal and non-verbal contributions, but we did not tend to rate conferences as highly emotionally charged affairs. Only 13 per cent of the conferences that we observed were rated as 'quite' or 'very' emotionally intense, and 42 per cent as 'not at all' emotionally intense (Shapland *et al.* 2006b). This variability in effects has been found both in victim surveys and the longitudinal work on the effects of victimization (for a review, see Shapland and Hall forthcoming).

A third problem with RST is its assumption that offenders enter a conference in a particular emotional condition: a need to *induce* the emotions of guilt and remorse, via the 'shaming' of significant others, is assumed in Braithwaite's theory (it is also, incidentally, assumed by Maxwell and Morris, albeit that, for them, remorse is not induced via shaming). Although, in later work on RST, it is acknowledged that many offenders will 'already understand before the session that they have done wrong', it is further argued that any emotions they feel 'will be vague in their mind... [and] will not yet be acknowledged shame-guilt' (Harris *et al.* 2004: 200). Yet, in our experience, many offenders came to conferences ready to openly acknowledge that they have caused harm and displaying what has variously been described as shame, remorse and/or guilt.[15] In some cases, offenders could and did not wait until the 'scripted pause' in conference proceedings which is designed to elicit an apology, opting instead to apologize at the earliest opportunity and, in many cases, on several occasions (Shapland *et al.* 2006b).[16]

This was one of a number of observations which led us to consider more carefully the 'emotional starting points' of offenders in the context of restorative justice (Harris *et al.* 2004). Another was the extent to which offenders, in the context of the conferences that we observed, engaged in what we have characterized as 'desistance talk' (Shapland *et al.* forthcoming). We propose that, for at least some offenders, a restorative justice event may be less a *trigger* for desistance than a potentially significant 'stepping stone' on a journey toward desistance on which they have already embarked.

Restorative justice and desistance processes

Desistance, or offenders stopping offending, is hard to define and operationalize, but is increasingly regarded as a process of gradually decreasing offending, rather than a sudden one-off decision not to offend again, which is immediately put into effect (Bottoms *et al.* 2004). It is also being recognized that the kinds of factors or elements which promote desistance, particularly in the sharp down-turn of the age-crime curve in the early twenties, are not always the same factors which protect against becoming strongly involved with crime in adolescence (Laub and Sampson 2003; Stouthamer-Loeber *et al.* 2004). Though the social context and practical aspects of desisting are important and have always been recognized— the 'good woman', employment and accommodation normally feature strongly—agentic elements such as taking a decision to try to desist, self-perceptions of the possibility of leading a non-offending life, and considering a possible new self and social identity are currently becoming seen as also critical (Farrall 2005; Maruna 2001; Giordano *et al.* 2002; Shapland and Bottoms 2007).

The increasing attention being paid to agentic elements in desistance makes it more important to pay attention to the possible connection between the processes involved in restorative justice events, particularly conferences, and potential cognitive and emotional processes involved in desistance (Shapland forthcoming). We do not yet have clear evidence as to the causal order between cognitive decisions to desist, identity changes and behavioural desistance (Farrall 2005), largely because most studies have used retrospective reports from desisters, with concomitant problems of people trying potentially to minimize their cognitive dissonance. One possibility is the redemption scripts found by Maruna (2001), whereby offenders come to see their past, offending life as committed by a different self. Another is that 'hooks for change' deriving from personal attachments may create identity transformation, which itself promotes offending being seen in a more negative light (Giordano *et al.* 2002). A further possibility is that desistance embodies reverberating loops of trying out, or even imagining, new possibilities for living, which themselves change the weight given to different pro-desisting and pro-criminal attachments, as well as people's self-identity: a more gradual, wavering, Matzean progression (Bottoms *et al.* 2004). Whichever occurs, however, the opportunities provided by restorative justice for offenders to meditate and talk with others about their possible future life or lives could be rare but important safe spaces for offenders intending to desist to consider the next few months of their lives and how those months could be lived.

In keeping with this hypothesis, it is notable that one of the key prerequisites of a restorative justice encounter is that the offender must consent to it. Another is that the offender must admit to the offence, and is likely to have done so 'early on' (Hayes and Daly 2003: 735). In theory, then, the presence in restorative justice encounters of offenders who have been coerced or who deny the offence ought to be a rarity. It could even be argued that voluntary conferencing (and all restorative justice theorists have said that conferencing should be voluntary) requires offenders not only to have admitted the offence, but to understand that they have committed a criminal act and so caused harm. We think, therefore, that among offenders agreeing to take part in restorative justice, there will be a significant proportion who are already thinking about desistance and whose motivation to take part is explicable with reference to a decision, or a desire, to desist.[17] This is not, of course, to deny that in some cases, offenders may have alternative, or supplementary, reasons for agreeing to take part in restorative justice. For example, it has been argued in relation to some schemes that offenders may well have instrumental reasons for participation (i.e. something to gain)— most usually when restorative justice operates pre-sentence and stands to influence the sentence of the court (e.g. Edwards 2006).

Nonetheless, we think it worth emphasizing that offenders on the threshold of a restorative justice encounter may be substantively different from those who are generally subjected to traditionally 'rehabilitative' interventions. Let us take, for example, those offenders who participate in 'correctional' offending behaviour programmes. In the majority of cases, both consent to and genuine motivation to participate in such interventions are questionable, partly because, in many cases, offenders are required to participate in programmes as a condition of a court order, and partly because eligibility tends to be determined less on the basis of motivation than on the basis of actuarially based risk assessments (Robinson 2002; Home Office 2004). To adopt the discourse of 'what works', the assessment process in respect of restorative justice is much more attuned to 'responsivity' factors (not least motivational issues) than is the typical offending behaviour programme. Put another way—and, to borrow from Valerie Braithwaite (2003)—the 'motivational posture' of an offender entering restorative justice is much more likely to be characterized by a genuine 'commitment' to the process (or perhaps the more wavering posture of 'capitulation') than are offenders shoe-horned into one of the new raft of treatment programmes on the basis that their risk profile renders them eligible.

An implication of this hypothesis in respect of RST is that rather than providing a forum for inducing the emotions of shame/guilt/remorse, a restorative justice encounter might, for at least *some* offenders, more appropriately offer one in which these emotions might be constructively expressed and/or *discharged* (Harris *et al.* 2004). This chimes with Harris's recent observation that 'reintegrative shaming may be important for reducing offending not because it results in shame, but because it provides a mechanism that assists offenders to manage their feelings of shame in more constructive ways' (Harris 2006: 343). It also links with our findings that 56 per cent of offenders said the conference had provided them with a sense of closure, whilst an additional 19 per cent said it had done so to some extent.

In this respect, it is important that a restorative justice encounter is with the victim, not just with anonymous agents of criminal justice.[18] A direct apology to the victim is a much more powerful demonstration of remorse and one which it is far more challenging for the offender to attempt than a legal representative saying that the offender is remorseful in court. Conferencing and mediation provide an opportunity to apologize both to the victim and the state (the latter in the context of acknowledging responsibility and harm for the offence). Conferencing provides an opportunity for offenders to apologize to those close to them (their supporters) in addition. Restorative justice which includes an outcome agreement about conduct in the future allows the offender to make a more substantial demonstration of that remorse, over time, through the symbolic reparation involved in turning one's life around (Shapland *et al.* forthcoming) and, in some instances, actual reparation to victims.

The notion that at least some offenders will take the opportunity to participate in restorative justice as a means of consolidating or reinforcing a decision to desist arguably also carries important implications for evaluation. One such implication is that future research on restorative justice might usefully focus on the 'motivational postures' (Braithwaite 2003) of those who agree to take part, and seek to develop a more nuanced understanding of the role of restorative justice in the broader context of an individual's offending/desistance career. Another, related point, builds on a critique of experimental evaluation designs (namely randomized controlled trials) proffered recently by Hayes and Daly (2003). They have argued that because offenders agreeing to restorative justice are likely to have 'admitted to an offense early on', they are 'similar in ways that are theoretically linked with reoffending'. Therefore, evaluations deploying RCTs (where allocation to experimental and control groups takes place following the offender's consent to restorative justice) are, to an extent, comparing like with like—and may hence find it more difficult to show significant differences between experimental and control groups than for interventions which take a heterogeneous basket of offenders on a pure 'intention to treat' basis.[19] Returning to our hypothesis, if offenders agreeing to take part in restorative justice are indeed likely to include a higher proportion of 'desistance thinkers', then we agree that evaluations deploying randomized controlled trials may struggle to discern significantly different reoffending outcomes for experimental and control groups. Including a second control group, composed of offenders who have turned down an opportunity to take part in restorative justice, may, however, be a promising strategy.

Building 'social capital'?

As already noted, the model of conferencing that we observed was underpinned by RST, and, to this end, scheme staff saw it as a priority to ensure the presence of offender support-ers as far as possible and, thanks to Home Office funding, were in a position to meet the transport costs of participants. It is perhaps not surprising, then, that in the context of our observations of restorative justice encounters, we did see examples of the mobilization or generation of social capital—that is, the apparent establishment of social connections likely to offer offenders instrumental (as well as, in many cases, emotional) support. Among these examples were some moving instances of the building of 'bonding' social capital (Putnam 2000). For example, in some cases, offenders were reunited with family members following a period of estrangement, and sometimes such reunions were characterized by explicit offers of practical help (e.g. accommodation and help finding employment). We also saw a smaller number of examples of 'bridging' social capital (Putnam 2000), such as when victims or their supporters offered similar types of help to offenders with whom they had no prior relationship.

However, working in highly individualized and urbanized communities, our schemes faced constant challenges in respect of promoting the more practical side of 'reintegration' (Van Ness and Strong 1997; Bottoms 2003). Although juvenile offenders tended to pose fewer problems in this regard, it could not always be assumed that offenders had access to—or recognized—sources of support (family or otherwise). Although, in the majority of the conferences that we observed, at least one offender supporter was present, the average number was just 1.7, and, in 7 per cent of conferences, the offender had no supporters with them (Shapland *et al.* 2006*b*). In some of these cases, it was clear that offenders had chosen not to inform potential supporters about their impending conference, for reasons of their own;[20] in others, it appeared that the offender had no sources of support available. Even where links existed and supporters were present at conferences, there was no guarantee that those individuals were willing or equipped to do the challenging work of reintegration (cf. Van Ness and Strong 1997). Thus, whilst conference organizers sought as far as possible to build a 'micro-community' around every participating offender, there could be no guaran-tees regarding the success of such a strategy in enhancing that offender's individual social capital.

The conferences that we observed also encountered numerous problems in respect of facilitating reparative activity, such that we would have to conclude that Bazemore's ideal of 'strengths-based rehabilitation' was rarely realized in the context of the restorative justice encounters that we observed. We have already noted that material reparation was not high on the agendas of the majority of victims. Nonetheless, it was not uncommon for conference participants (not only victims) to suggest that the offender might consider indirect repara-tion, in their own or the victim's community. Suggestions included voluntary work of vari-ous kinds, from 'helping elderly people' to gardening and fundraising for victims' groups, as well as suggestions that the offender might help other people like him or herself (namely other offenders). So the notion that the offender might 'give something back' was often batted around in conferences, but it rarely materialized in outcome agreements (7 per cent of conference outcome agreements included reparation of this kind: Shapland *et al.* 2006*b*). There were, however, good reasons why this potential was not realized. For many of our offenders, reparation (beyond the symbolic level) was unrealistic, either because they were serving a prison sentence or (where conferences were held pre-sentence) because they were facing one. Even where there did seem to be potential for the performance of reparative work by offenders, there was often uncertainty about how to arrange it, and concerns about 'health and safety' issues—most notably in youth conferences—tended to quash ideas about appropriate reparative activities.

Building 'human capital'?

Commenting on restorative justice in New Zealand in the late 1990s, Braithwaite argued that whilst 'the rhetoric of citizens being empowered to choose rehabilitative programs' was 'impressive', he has rarely seen it realized because there were 'no programs left to choose' (Braithwaite 1999: 69). This, he contended, was one important reason why restorative justice conferences were, in that particular context, unlikely to be having major rehabilitative effects.

In our experience, some outcome agreements included specific, time-limited requirements for the offender to try to improve his or her skills and/or qualifications. However, a lack of relevant programmes was an important issue, particularly for offenders on remand or serving custodial sentences. Although some had completed or had applied to complete programmes, many knew little about rehabilitative resources or referred to waiting lists or gaps in provision. It was not unusual for victims and other participants to voice shock or concern about the apparent lack of resources available to help offenders in prison and/or on release, particularly because, in the majority of cases, the offender's rehabilitation was the outcome in which they were most interested. Offenders' accounts of prisons rife with drugs and with long waiting lists for assessments and referrals in respect of drug issues were a source of particular consternation (e.g. see Harman and Paylor 2005; Ramsay *et al.* 2005).

However, another key sticking point in the conferences that we observed was a significant 'knowledge gap' in respect of what rehabilitative resources *might* be available across a variety of criminal justice contexts (Shapland *et al.* 2006*c*; see also Maxwell and Morris 2001: fn 7). Part of the reason for this knowledge gap was that facilitators came from a variety of professional backgrounds, such that whilst some (notably police officers and community mediators) had little or no prior recourse to such resources, others were operating in unfamiliar and/or geographically distant contexts (e.g. probation officers conducting conferences in a variety of prisons), where knowledge was limited.[21] The 'knowledge gap' problem was exacerbated by the fact that the schemes were operating in a correctional context characterized by a great deal of change in respect of the provision and availability of rehabilitative resources (Rex *et al.* 2003). The problem was further compounded by the uncertain future status of many of the offenders who took part in conferences pre-sentence. Many faced the likelihood of a prison sentence, which served to widen the 'knowledge gap' in that participants would not know where an offender might begin his or her sentence, or how frequently he or she might be moved between prison establishments. Facilitators attempted to minimize some of these problems by drawing up, in some cases, two alternative outcome agreements, intended for community-based and custodial sentencing outcomes, respectively. But significant areas of uncertainty remained. It is interesting that the two major statutory conferencing schemes for young offenders (in New Zealand and in Northern Ireland) have also faced these problems, with Northern Ireland appointing specific personnel to try to sort out relevant programmes and monitor outcome agreements (Campbell *et al.* 2006).

Conclusion

> The nirvana story of restorative justice helps us to imagine what is possible, but it should not be used as a benchmark for what is practical and achievable.
>
> (Daly 2003: 234)

We noted earlier that one of the key reasons why advocates of restorative justice have tended to play down the recidivism–reduction potential of restorative justice has been a perception that to routinely expect reductions in reoffending as an outcome of restorative justice encounters would be unrealistic. As Bazemore and O'Brien put it, 'no one should expect dramatic rehabilitative impacts from short-term conferencing encounters' (Bazemore and O'Brien 2002: 36). Dignan (2001) has similarly argued that policy makers need to retain a sense of realism about the propensity of restorative justice to contribute to crime reduction, whilst Hudson (2003: 190) agrees that '[crime] reduction is not the ground on which restorative justice should be selling itself'.

Whilst we agree with this position, we have also argued that there is a case to be made for a subtle shift in ways of thinking about the recidivism reduction potential of restorative justice. Instead of thinking about restorative justice as a new-style 'intervention'—something which is 'done to' offenders—we might be better advised to re-frame restorative justice as an opportunity to facilitate a desire, or consolidate a decision, to desist. Desistance, by definition, implies crime reduction. Those agencies which have crime reduction as their primary aim might find it helpful to start to think in terms of restorative justice as a key tool (providing, of course, that they can offer a proper service to victims as well). We have suggested that, to the extent that such encounters are voluntarily entered into by offenders, there is a high likelihood that at least some will take the opportunity to participate as a means of consolidating or reinforcing a decision to desist. For such offenders, the opportunity to express or discharge feelings of shame/guilt/remorse is likely to be more significant than exposure to 'shaming' by others. Further, access to opportunities to develop social and/or human capital may be crucial to the maintenance of momentum on the road to desistance. Looked at another way, we might argue that for such offenders, the restorative justice encounter may serve to maximize their motivation or 'responsivity' to engage with other sources of 'rehabilitative' help. But, by the same token, and to reiterate a point made above, the absence of such opportunities may be equally decisive: an intention to desist may be undone in the face of a lack of social support and/or other (appropriate) 'rehabilitative' resources.

We have argued that there are sound theoretical and empirical reasons for including the reduction of reoffending as a legitimate goal for restorative justice, but it is a goal which must be seen both in the context of other legitimate goals for restorative justice (not least victim-centred ones) and in the context of the messy and unpredictable 'real world' in which restorative justice encounters take place (Daly 2001*a*). In such a context, encounters are not choreographed, participants are not 'programmable', there are no dress rehearsals and relevant programmes may be unknown to participants or unavailable. For these reasons, the potential of restorative justice to 'deliver' reductions in reoffending—via any of the means we have discussed—will always be circumscribed. This does not, however, mean that more could not be done to help restorative justice to achieve its potential. On the basis of our own experience, there is certainly scope for improving offenders' access to 'traditional' rehabilitative resources, whether in custodial or non-custodial contexts. There is also scope to improve opportunities for reparative activities in the interests of 'strengths-based rehabilitation' (as well as the recipients of reparative 'help'). More fundamentally, in the context of offenders who have few financial or skills resources, it is important to recognize offenders doing rehabilitational work to turn their lives around, and to desist, as symbolic reparation to victims.

Acknowledgements

We would very much like to acknowledge the contribution of other members of the evaluation team (Anne Atkinson, Helen Atkinson, James Dignan, Marie Howes, Jennifer Johnstone and Angela Sorsby) and the patience and insights of the staff of the three schemes evaluated.

Funding

Home Office/Ministry of Justice.

Notes

1 For Dignan (2001), the dramatic revival in government interest in restorative justice in England and Wales is directly attributable to its perceived relevance for the government's Crime Reduction Strategy. In this context, he argues, it is no surprise that one of the primary objectives for recent evaluations of government-funded restorative justice initiatives is to examine their impact on reoffending rates.

2 The evaluation was also funded originally by the Home Office, subsequently by RDS NOMS in the Ministry of Justice.

3 Under the stewardship of Lawrence Sherman and Heather Strang, and largely replicating the methods and design used in Canberra's RISE, the Justice Research Consortium (JRC) delivered a large number of conferences in three sites: London, Thames Valley and Northumbria. Two of these sites (London and Thames Valley) targeted adult offenders only, whilst Northumbria convened conferences for both youth and adult offenders. All three sites used the same operational model, and all conferences took place in criminal justice contexts. Most took place pre- or post-sentence, whilst a smaller number were diversionary (delivered at one site in the context of a final warning or adult caution). In two sites, conferences were organized and facilitated by police seconded to the scheme; in the other (Thames Valley), conferences were convened and organized by seconded probation and prison staff, and a number of experienced community mediators who were employed on a sessional basis.

4 Our points about restorative justice conferencing below should be taken in the context of offences with individuals as victims. Both victim and offender agreed to attend the conference before preparations were made to hold it and hence victim attendance rates were very high, at over 90 per cent (see Shapland *et al.* 2006b).

5 See, e.g. Braithwaite (1989); Strang (2002).

6 Similarly, Sherman (1993) has proposed a 'defiance theory', whereby some offenders or members of groups which feel themselves antagonistic to state power may be resistant to and even fight back against any attempt by people whom they don't like or trust to tell them what to do. This would predict that such individuals will be more, not less, likely to reoffend if they are either subject to criminal justice homilies in sentencing or feel they are 'forced' to attend restorative justice (Sherman and Strang 2007). Tyler *et al.* (2007) similarly suggest that both restorative justice and criminal justice will only reduce reoffending if they embody procedural justice practices which promote the perceived legitimacy of the process for participants.

7 Outcome agreements were produced in 98 per cent of JRC conferences (n = 346) (Shapland *et al.* 2006a).

8 This argument throws into doubt practices such as excluding victims from discussion of what may happen in the future, through requiring them to leave the conference after having talked about the effects of offences upon them (Zernova forthcoming). It seems that one reason for the exclusion of victims is the adoption by facilitators of a zero-sum ideology, whereby victims' needs are assumed to be potentially incompatible with those of offenders or the overarching needs of society/their agency to reduce crime. In England and Wales, at least, this assumption does not seem to be correct for the majority of victims.

9 Dignan (2005) draws an important distinction between two types of conferencing: police-led and family group conferencing. Whilst our evaluation focused only on the first type, we have not used the term 'police-led conferencing' because not all facilitators were police officers. It should also be noted that the conferencing which we evaluated was founded on strong principles of all participants being able to say what they wished, provided they also respected others' rights to do so, and of a very non-directive role for facilitators.

10 Daly (2001b) notes that since 1993, whilst the Wagga Wagga model has spread to and proved popular in other parts of the world, it has in Australia largely been replaced by New Zealand-style family group conferencing.

11 Dignan (2005: 102) has recently argued that Braithwaite's theory of reintegrative shaming forms an important part of an emerging 'moral discourse thesis', evidence of which can be found in a variety of contemporary criminal justice practices. Central to this thesis, Dignan argues, is the idea that the offender's conscience is potentially a much more powerful weapon against deviant behaviour than is punishment, and that engaging the offender in 'normative or moralizing dialogue' can be an effective inhibitor of future offending behaviour. For Dignan, this emphasis on encouraging a moral perspective constitutes common ground for restorative justice and some contemporary 'correctional' approaches, such as cognitive-behavioural treatment, which encourages offenders to take responsibility for their actions and to acknowledge the harm caused to others. Bottoms' (2002) view that conformity (and hence learning to conform) is a far more powerful concept than using criminality as a starting point for discussions about desistance or reoffending also forms a major part of this emerging moral argument.

12 Derived from interviews with participants some years after the restorative justice event.

13 Maruna (2001: 158) similarly highlights the negotiation of moral rather than physical reintegration, referring to the notion of 'looking-glass rehabilitation' to illustrate the ways in which offender rehabilitation or reform must be negotiated through interactions between the offender and significant others.

14 Halpern (2005) explains that social capital can be understood and examined at one or more of three levels of analysis: the level of individuals (the micro level), communities (the meso level) and nations (the macro level).

15 We do, however, accept Karstedt's (2002: 306) point about the 'invisibility' of emotions: i.e. we can never objectively know whether an offender really feels shame or remorse.

16 This is not to imply that this was always the case, or that some of the offenders in our sample did not display 'defiance' (Sherman *et al.* 2003).

17 It should be noted that a substantial number of offenders, even those with substantial offending records, do show a desire to desist, even if they find it difficult to put that into practice for a while. A majority of the persistent young adult offenders in the longitudinal Sheffield Pathways out of Crime Study, for example, said they had made a definite decision to desist, though some doubted their ability to do so (Shapland *et al.* forthcoming).

18 In JRC conferences, the victim was always an individual. Offender reactions might be different were the victim to be an organization or someone representing the victim's views, as Doak and O'Mahony (2004) have shown. Offenders may perceive different victims or different kinds of victims as having different amounts of legitimacy.

19 In our evaluation, both experimental and control groups received preparation for restorative justice, and both victim and offender had to consent to take part. Essentially, therefore, the only difference was the conference event itself and any activity consequent upon the outcome agreement.

20 In one burglary conference that we observed, the offender explained that he had not invited his family, partly because of feelings of shame and partly because he wanted to shield them from the prison environment (in which he was being held on remand and in which the conference took place). The victim in this case told the offender 'You might be surprised if you talk to them....

Cutting yourself off makes it harder. I think they'd be interested in helping you'. The offender responded, 'I've not thought about it like that'.

21 An exception was conferences facilitated by a prison officer seconded within his normal work environment of Bullingdon prison.

References

Bazemore, G. (1998), 'Restorative Justice and Earned Redemption', *American Behavioral Scientist,* 41: 768–813.

Bazemore, G. and Bell, D. (2004), 'What is the Appropriate Relationship between Restorative Justice and Treatment?', in H. Zehr and B. Toews, eds, *Critical Issues in Restorative Justice.* Devon: Willan.

Bazemore, G. and O'Brien, S. (2002), 'The Quest for a Restorative Model of Rehabilitation: Theory-for-Practice and Practice-for-Theory', in L. Walgrave, ed., *Restorative Justice and the Law.* Devon: Willan.

Bazemore, G., Nissen, L. and Dooley, M. (2000), 'Mobilizing Social Support and Building Relation-ships: Broadening Correctional and Rehabilitative Agendas', *Corrections Management Quarterly,* 4: 10–21.

Bottoms, A. E. (2002), 'Morality, Crime, Compliance and Public Policy', in A. E. Bottoms and M. Tonry, eds, *Ideology, Crime and Criminal Justice: A Symposium in Honour of Sir Leon Radzinowicz.* Cullompton, Devon: Willan.

——(2003), 'Some Sociological Reflections on Restorative Justice', in A. von Hirsch, J. Roberts, A. E. Bottoms, K. Roach and M. Schiff, eds, *Restorative Justice and Criminal Justice: Competing or Reconcilable Paradigms?* Oxford: Hart Publishing.

Bottoms, A. E., Shapland, J., Costello, A., Holmes, D. and Muir, G. (2004), 'Towards Desistance: Theoretical Underpinnings for an Empirical Study', *Howard Journal,* 43: 368–89.

Bourdieu, P. and Wacquant, L. (1992), *An Invitation to Reflexive Sociology.* Cambridge: Polity Press.

——(1989), *Crime, Shame and Reintegration.* Cambridge: Cambridge University Press.

——(1993), 'Shame and Modernity', *British Journal of Criminology,* 33: 1–18.

——(1999), 'Restorative Justice: Assessing Optimistic and Pessimistic Accounts', *Crime and Justice: A Review of Research,* 25: 1–127.

Braithwaite, J. and Mugford, S. (1994), 'Conditions of Successful Reintegration Ceremonies', *British Journal of Criminology,* 34: 139–71.

Braithwaite, V. (2003), 'Dancing with Tax Authorities: Motivational Postures and Non-Compliant Actions', in V. Braithwaite, ed., *Taxing Democracy: Understanding Tax Avoidance and Evasion.* Aldershot: Ashgate.

Campbell, C., Devlin, R., O'Mahony, D., Doak, J., Jackson, J., Corrigan, T. and McEvoy, K. (2006), *Evaluation of the Northern Ireland Youth Conferencing Service,* NIO Research and Statistical Series Report No. 12. Belfast: NIO, available online at www.nio.gov.uk/evaluation_of_the_northern_ireland_youth_conference_service.pdf.

Coleman, J. S. (1988), 'Social Capital in the Creation of Human Capital', *American Journal of Sociology,* 94 Supplement: S95–120.

Daly, K. (2001a), 'Restorative Justice: The Real Story', *Punishment and Society,* 4: 55–79.

—— (2001b), 'Conferencing in Australia and New Zealand', in A. Morris and G. Maxwell, eds, *Restorative Justice for Juveniles: Conferencing, Mediation and Circles.* Oxford: Hart Publishing.

——(2003), 'Mind the Gap: Restorative Justice in Theory and Practice', in A. von Hirsch, J. Roberts, A. E. Bottoms, K. Roach and M. Schiff, eds, *Restorative Justice and Criminal Justice:Competing or Reconcilable Paradigms?* Oxford: Hart Publishing.

Dignan, J. (2001), 'Restorative Justice and Crime Reduction: Are Policy Makers Barking Up the Wrong Tree?', in E. Fattah and S. Parmentier, eds, *Victim Policies and Criminal Justice on the Road to Restorative Justice.* Belgium: Leuven University Press.

——(2005), *Understanding Victims and Restorative Justice.* Maidenhead: Open University Press.

Doak, J. and O'Mahony, D. (2006), 'The Vengeful Victim? Assessing the Attitudes of Victims Participating in Restorative Youth Conferencing', *International Review of Victimology,* 13: 157–78.

Edwards, I. (2006), 'Restorative Justice, Sentencing and the Court of Appeal', *Criminal Law Review,* Feb: 110–23.

Eglash, A. (1977), 'Beyond Restitution: Creative Restitution', in J. Hudson and B. Galaway, eds, *Restitution in Criminal Justice: A Critical Assessment of Sanctions.* Lexington, MA: Heath and Company.

Farrall, S. (2002), *Rethinking What Works with Offenders: Probation, Social Context and Desistance from Crime.* Cullompton: Willan.

——(2005), 'On the Existential Aspects of Desistance from Crime', *Symbolic Interaction,* 28: 367–85.

Farrall, S. and Maruna, S. (2004), 'Desistance-Focused Criminal Justice Policy Research', *The Howard Journal,* 43: 358–67.

Giordano, P., Cernkovich, S. and Rudolph, J. (2002), 'Gender, Crime and Desistance', *American Journal of Sociology,* 107: 990–1064.

Halpern, D. (2005), *Social Capital.* Cambridge: Polity Press.

Harris, N. (2006), 'Reintegrative Shaming, Shame and Criminal Justice', *Journal of Social Issues,* 62: 327–46.

Harris, N., Walgrave, L. and Braithwaite, J. (2004), 'Emotional Dynamics in Restorative Conferences', *Theoretical Criminology,* 8: 191–210.

Harman, K. and Paylor, I. (2005), 'An Evaluation of the CARAT Initiative', *Howard Journal of Criminal Justice,* 44: 357–73.

Hayes, H. and Daly, K. (2003), 'Youth Justice Conferencing and Reoffending', *Justice Quarterly,* 20: 725–64.

Home Office (2004), *Revised Targeting Strategy,* Probation Circular 38/2004.

Homel, P., Nutley, S., Webb, B. and Tilley, N. (2005), *Investing to Deliver: Reviewing the Implementation of the UK Crime Reduction Programme,* Home Office Research Study 281. London: Home Office.

Hoyle, C., Young, R. and Hill, R. (2002), *Proceed With Caution: An Evaluation of the Thames Valley Police Initiative in Restorative Cautioning.* York: Joseph Rowntree Foundation.

Hudson, B. (2003), 'Victims and Offenders', in A. von Hirsch, J. Roberts, A. E. Bottoms, K. Roach and M. Schiff, eds, *Restorative Justice and Criminal Justice: Competing or Reconcilable Paradigms?* Oxford: Hart Publishing.

Johnstone, G. (2002), *Restorative Justice: Ideas, Values, Debates.* Cullompton: Willan.

Karstedt, S. (2002), 'Emotions and Criminal Justice', *Theoretical Criminology,* 6: 299–317.

Kurki, L. (2003), 'Evaluating Restorative Justice Practices', in A. von Hirsch, J. Roberts, A. E. Bottoms, K. Roach and M. Schiff, eds, *Restorative Justice and Criminal Justice: Competing or Reconcilable Paradigms?* Oxford: Hart Publishing.

Laub, J. H. and Sampson, R. J. (2003), *Shared Beginnings, Divergent Lives: Delinquent Boys to Age 70.* Cambridge, MA: Harvard University Press.

Luke, G. and Lind, B. (2002), 'Reducing Juvenile Crime: Conferencing versus Court', *Crime and Justice Bulletin,* 69: 1–20.

Maruna, S. (2001), *Making Good.* Washington: American Psychological Association.

Maruna, S. and LeBel, T. (2003), 'Welcome Home? Examining the "Re-Entry Court" Concept from a Strengths-Based Perspective', *Western Criminology Review,* 4: 91–107. available online at http://wcr.sonoma.edu.

Maruna, S., Immarigeon, R. and LeBel, T. P. (2004), 'Ex-Offender Reintegration: Theory and Practice', in S. Maruna and R. Immarigeon, eds, *After Crime and Punishment: Pathways to Offender Reintegration.* Cullompton: Willan.

Maxwell, G. and Morris, A. (2001), 'Family Group Conferences and Reoffending', in A. Morris and G. Maxwell, eds, *Restorative Justice for Juveniles: Conferencing, Mediation and Circles.* Oxford: Hart Publishing.

—— (2002), 'The Role of Shame, Guilt and Remorse in Restorative Justice Processes for Young People', in E. G. M. Weitekamp and H.-J. Kerner, eds, *Restorative Justice: Theoretical Foundations.* Cullompton: Willan.

McGarrell, E., Olivares, K., Crawford, K. and Kroovand, N. (2000), *Returning Justice to the Community: The Indianapolis Juvenile Restorative Justice Experiment.* Crime Control Policy Center: Hudson Institute.

McIvor, G. (2004), 'Reparative and Restorative Approaches', in A. Bottoms, S. Rex and G. Robinson, eds, *Alternatives to Prison: Options for an Insecure Society.* Cullompton: Willan.

Miers, D. (2004), 'Situating and Researching Restorative Justice in Great Britain', *Punishment and Society,* 6: 23–46.

Miers, D., Maguire, M., Goldie, S., Sharpe, K., Hale, C., Netton, A., Uglow, S., Doolin, K., Hallam, A., Enterkin, J. and Newburn, T. (2001), *An Exploratory Evaluation of Restorative Schemes,* Crime Reduction Research Series Paper 9. London: Home Office.

Putnam, R. D. (2000), *Bowling Alone: The Collapse and Revival of American Community.* New York: Simon and Schuster.

Ramsay, M., Bullock, T. and Niven, S. (2005), 'The Prison Service Drug Strategy: The Extent to which Prisoners Need and Receive Treatment', *Howard Journal of Criminal Justice,* 44: 269–85.

Raynor, P. (2004), 'Rehabilitative and Reintegrative Approaches', in A. Bottoms, S. Rex and G. Robinson, eds, *Alternatives to Prison: Options for an Insecure Society.* Cullompton: Willan.

Rex, S., Lieb, R., Bottoms, A. and Wilson, L. (2003), *Accrediting Offender Programmes: A Process-Based Evaluation of the Joint Prison/Probation Services Accreditation Panel,* Home Office Research Study 273. London: Home Office.

Robinson, G. (2002), 'Exploring Risk Management in Probation Practice: Contemporary Developments in England and Wales', *Punishment and Society,* 4: 5–25.

Ruddick, R. (1989), 'A Court-Referred Scheme', in M. Wright and B. Galaway, eds, *Mediation and Criminal Justice: Victims, Offenders and Community.* London: Sage.

Schiff, M. (2003), 'Models, Challenges and the Promise of Restorative Conferencing Strategies', in A. von Hirsch, J. Roberts, A. E. Bottoms, K. Roach and M. Schiff, eds, *Restorative Justice and Criminal Justice: Competing or Reconcilable Paradigms?* Oxford: Hart Publishing.

Shapland, J. and Bottoms, A. (2007), 'Between Conformity and Criminality: Theoretical Reflections on Desistance', in H. Müller-Dietz, E. Müller, K.-L. Kunz, H. Radtke, G. Britz, C. Momsen and H. Koriath, eds, *Festscrift für Heike Jung,* 905–20. Baden-Baden: Nomos.

Shapland, J. and Hall, M. (forthcoming), 'What Do We Know about the Effects of Crime on Victims?', *International Review of Victimology,* 14.

Shapland, J., Atkinson, A., Atkinson, H., Chapman, B., Colledge, E., Dignan, J., Howes, M., Johnstone, J., Robinson, G. and Sorsby, A. (2006a), *Restorative Justice in Practice: Findings from the Second Stage of the Evaluation of Three Schemes,* Home Office Research Findings 274. London: Home Office.

—— (2006b), *Restorative Justice in Practice: The Second Report from the Evaluation of Three Schemes,* The University of Sheffield Centre for Criminological Research Occasional Paper 2. Sheffield: Faculty of Law, available online at http://ccr.group.shef.ac.uk/papers/pdfs/ Restorative_Justice_Report.pdf.

—— (2006c), 'Situating Restorative Justice within Criminal Justice', *Theoretical Criminology,* 10: 505–32.

Shapland, J., Atkinson, A., Atkinson, H., Dignan, J., Edwards, L., Hibbert, J., Howes, M., Johnstone, J., Robinson, G. and Sorsby, A. (forthcoming), *Does Restorative Justice Affect Reconviction? The Fourth Report from the Evaluation of Three Schemes.* London: Ministry of Justice.

Shapland, J., Atkinson, A., Colledge, E., Dignan, J., Howes, M., Johnstone, J., Pennant, R., Robinson, G. and Sorsby, A. (2004), *Implementing Restorative Justice Schemes (Crime Reduction Programme): A Report on the First Year,* Home Office Online Report 32/04. London: Home Office, available online at www.homeoffice.gov.uk/rds/pdfs04/rdsolr3204.pdf.

Shapland, M., Bottoms, T., Muir, G., Atkinson, H., Healy, D. and Holmes, D. (forthcoming), 'Perceptions of the Criminal Justice System among Young Adult Would-Be Desisters', in F. Losel, A. E. Bottoms and D. Farrington, eds, *Young Adult Offenders and the Criminal Justice System.* Cullompton: Willan.

Sherman, L. (1993), 'Defiance, Deterrence and Irrelevance: A Theory of the Criminal Sanction', *Journal of Research in Crime and Delinquency,* 30: 445–73.

—— (1997), 'Thinking about Crime Prevention', in Sherman, L., Gottfredson, D., MacKenzie, D., Eck, J., Reuter, P. and Bushway, S., eds, *Preventing Crime: What Works, What Doesn't, What's Promising,* Report to the United States Congress. Washington, DC: National Institute of Justice, available online at www.ncjrs.gov/works/.

Sherman, L. and Strang, H. (2007), *Restorative Justice: The Evidence: Report to the Smith Institute.* London: Smith Institute.

Sherman, L. W., Heather, S. and Woods, D. J. (2003), 'Captains of Restorative Justice: Experience, Legitimacy and Recidivism by Type of'Offence', in E. Weitkamp and H. Kerner, eds, *Restorative Justice in Context: International Practice and Directions.* Cullompton: Willan.

Sherman, L. W., Strang, H. and Woods, D. J. (2000), *Recidivism Patterns in the Canberra Reintegrative Shaming Experiments (RISE),* available online at www.aic.gov.au/rjustice/rise/recidivism/.

Stouthamer-Loeber, M., Wei, E., Loeber, R. and Masten, A. (2004), 'Desistance from Persistent Serious Delinquency in the Transition to Adulthood', *Development and Psychopathology,* 16: 897–918.

Strang, H. (2002), *Repair or Revenge: Victims and Restorative Justice.* Oxford: Clarendon Press.

Sykes, G. M. and Matza, D. (1957), 'Techniques of Neutralization: A Theory of Delinquency', *American Sociological Review,* 22: 664–73.

Travis, J. and Petersilia, J. (2001), 'Reentry Reconsidered: A New Look at an Old Question', *Crime and Delinquency,* 47: 291–313.

Tyler, T. R., Sherman, L., Strang, H., Barnes, G. C. and Woods, D. (2007), 'Reintegrative Shaming, Procedural Justice and Recidivism: The Engagement of Offenders' Psychological Mechanisms in the Canberra RISE Drinking-and-Driving Experiment', *Law and Society Review,* 41: 511–52.

Van Ness, D. and Strong, K. H. (1997), *Restoring Justice.* Cincinnati, OH: Anderson Publishing.

von Hirsch, A., Ashworth, A. and Shearing, C. (2003a), 'Specifying Aims and Limits for Restorative Justice: A "Making Amends" Model?', in A. von Hirsch, J. Roberts, A. E. Bottoms, K. Roach and M. Schiff, eds, *Restorative Justice and Criminal Justice: Competing or Reconcilable Paradigms?* Oxford: Hart Publishing.

Wilcox, A., Young, R. and Hoyle, C. (2004), *Two-Year Resanctioning Study: A Comparison of Restorative and Traditional Cautions, Home Office Online Report 57/04.* London: Home Office.

Zehr, H. (1990), *Changing Lenses: A New Focus for Crime and Justice.* Scottdale, PA: Herald Press.

Zernova, M. (forthcoming), *Restorative Justice: Ideals and Realities.* Aldershot: Ashgate.

26 Repair or revenge?

Heather Strang

Introduction

The momentum of the restorative justice movement over the past decade has given rise to some extravagant claims for its superiority to formal justice processes in dealing with crime. Most of those claims relate to benefits for offenders and, to a lesser extent, to communities which will profit from the lower offending rates which, it is hoped and sometimes assumed, will follow from restorative interventions. Less attention has been paid to the way victims feel about restorative programmes and many victim advocates have remained suspicious about the motivations behind such programmes, their focus, and the likely benefit to victims from taking part.

In this book I have asked whether restorative justice offers better outcomes for victims in the terms they say matter. Much more needs to be done in exploring the potentials and pitfalls of restorative justice for different kinds of victims in different kinds of circumstances, but the data gathered through the present study provide a basis upon which to build more knowledge.

This final chapter begins by retracing the course of the book. It then considers some theoretical critiques of restorative justice from the victim's perspective in the context of the empirical findings, and suggests some policy implications that may follow from the short- comings for victims of the court system. It then addresses the limitations and the strengths of the experiments from which the empirical findings are drawn, and finally suggests some future directions for research.

Summary of findings

Victims' discontents

A review of the victimological literature over the past twenty years reveals dissatisfactions widely shared by victims caught up in an adversarial justice system. However, their role was not always so debased: restorative justice has historically been the dominant paradigm of criminal justice, by which I mean that the response to crime until the rise of the modern state involved offenders making amends to their victims, so as to restore order and peace as quickly as possible and to avoid vengeful blood feuds. The diminished role for victims in criminal justice which now obtains began in Europe in the late Middle Ages as the Crown increasingly assumed the right of both adjudication and compensatory benefit for wrong-doing. This decline continued through the centuries in the West, until victims retained almost no rights in the justice process, which became exclusively a struggle between the offender and the state.

Victims have not lost their importance in the matter of bringing offenders to justice. Their co-operation is still essential in reporting offences and providing evidence in court. Nevertheless, they seem to be undervalued by every sector of the criminal justice system— police, prosecution, and the court itself—and the system remains inflexibly unresponsive to their perspective (Shapland 2000), despite more than two decades of victim movement activism [...]. Considerable effort has been made in improving victim *services* in most Western countries, but it has been argued (see, for example, Elias 1986) that the politics of victim *rights* have been captured by law-and-order forces, especially in the United States, which perceive criminal justice as a zero-sum game where the enhancement of victims' rights can be achieved only by circumscribing the rights of offenders [...].

So what is it that victims want? [...] victim research shows clearly that victims want:

- a less formal process where their views count;
- more information about both the processing and outcome of their cases;
- participation in their cases;
- fair and respectful treatment;
- material restoration;
- emotional restoration, including an apology.

It is plain that to achieve these objectives victims need the opportunity for much greater engagement with the justice system. Success has been claimed in responding to some of these issues: legislation has been passed in many countries requiring victims to be kept informed about their cases and for victim impact statements to be considered in the sentencing of offenders, while state-financed compensation arrangements now exist in many jurisdictions around the world. Yet victims still often believe they are not given the attention they deserve. An important question is whether, in terms of what victims want, the limits of the formal justice system have been reached.

The restorative justice alternative

[I] took up this question with a comprehensive examination of the theory and practice of another way of 'doing justice', restorative justice. Restorative justice is old, but only recently have ancient practices been rediscovered by the West and adapted to contemporary conditions. Dissatisfaction by both victim and offender advocates with aspects of the dominant models of criminal justice—rehabilitation and retribution—accounts in part for the interest in this third model, in which the moral, social, economic, and political contexts of crime are taken into account. Instead of offenders and offending being viewed in isolation, they are placed in a conceptual framework where the needs of victims for restoration and of communities for protection and safety are given priority as well. This 'balanced' approach aims to make the justice system more responsive to the needs of all the players (Bazemore and Umbreit 1994).

[I] discussed what is understood by the term 'restorative justice' and then described some of its forms. These include victim-offender reconciliation and mediation programmes now found in great numbers in North America and Europe, and Canadian sentencing circles, which incorporate traditional First Nation ways of responding to offenders. Also discussed were the Family Group Conferencing programmes established in New Zealand, which draw on traditional Maori strategies for resolving disputes and dealing with criminal behaviour, and the conferencing programmes developed in Australia over the past decade.

I then turned to what is known from empirical studies about the value of restorative justice in addressing the shortcomings of the adversarial justice system from the victim's point of view. Research results so far are mixed: while advantages are evident, a different set of problems sometimes arise. These include cases of increased levels of fear resulting from victims confronting their offenders, the replication of power imbalances between victims and offenders known to one another, and the excessive offender-focus of some programmes, which has at times resulted in coercion and revictimization. The chapter concludes that the next logical step is to compare in a systematic way the effectiveness for victims of the traditional formal, court-based justice system with the restorative alternative.

The Reintegrative Shaming Experiments (RISE) in Canberra were designed with victim satisfaction as a major outcome measure in comparing court with a restorative alternative in the form of a police-led programme of restorative justice conferencing. [...] a randomized controlled trial was chosen as the research protocol for RISE, despite the practical difficulties inherent in conducting field experiments of this kind, because only random assignment of subjects to treatment and control groups with equal probability ensures that prior to treatment the groups are equivalent within known statistical limits. The reason that this research design is regarded as the most rigorous of evaluation methods is its capacity to ensure equivalence, not only on known variables, but also on variables which the researcher has not considered and may not even have imagined. This means that differences which emerge between the groups may be attributed, with greater confidence than any other research design would permit, to the effect of the different treatments they have received.

In two of the four experiments the offences involved direct victims (the other two involved only indirect or unidentified victims, who were not part of this analysis). These experiments concerned middle-range property and violent crimes committed by young offenders who had made full admissions about their responsibility for the offence. All cases were serious enough that they would normally have been dealt with in court, but in the study were randomly assigned either to court or to a conference.

Ideally in testing on victims the effectiveness of the experimental treatment compared with the control treatment, the sampling frame would consist of victims randomly assigned to each treatment. However, this was not feasible because the great majority of randomly selected victims would have no identified offenders, owing to the small percentage of offences which result in an apprehension, and there could be no 'treatment' for the victim unless there were 'treatment' for an identified offender. A design involving the screening of eligible victims prior to case assignment was not employed, partly because offender recidivism was the primary outcome measure, and partly because of the extra time and expense that would have been involved. Thus, rather than a randomized controlled trial of victim effects, the study is a randomized controlled trial of offender and victim effects, where not all cases have victims. There were no significant differences between the victims assigned to conference and those assigned to court on any pre-assignment characteristic.

Structured interviews were conducted with 232 victims of property and violent crime. The interviews aimed to find out whether these victims concurred with what the literature says that victims want, and the extent to which court and conference delivered these outcomes.

Internal and external validity of the experiments are important measures of the adequacy of the design. High scores were achieved in the experiments on the key measures of treatment observation rates (90 per cent), treatment as assigned (97 per cent), and post-treatment interview response rates (89 per cent for victims and 69 per cent for offenders), so internal validity is very satisfactory. How generalizable the results are to other samples at other times or in other places—the external validity of the study—is more difficult to assess but can be tested by replicating the methodology in other locations.

Comparing court and conference

All analyses reported were conducted on the basis of treatment randomly assigned to cases, rather than the treatment victims actually experienced. […] In brief, this permits the views to be heard of victims who had expected to have a conference but it did not take place. Analysing in this way means that the findings relating to various dimensions of victim satisfaction with the conference process appear to be depressed, because those who actually experienced a conference were nearly always more positive than those assigned to a conference who did not experience it.

[I] explored the lived experiences of the property and violent crime victims who are the subject of the experiments. As expected in a randomized design, the court and conference groups were very similar in their demographic characteristics and in the amount of harm they had experienced. There was no significant difference between the groups in either experiment on age, education, sex, Aboriginality, place of birth, marital status, or employment status. On material harm, there was no significant difference between the groups in the harm suffered for property damage, loss of goods or cash, security improvements or lost wages in the case of property victims, nor in the extent of injury or associated financial costs for violence victims. These similarities give great confidence that any difference in outcomes between the treatment groups is due solely to the treatment they received.

[I] then examined the responses of all the victims to questions on the issues the literature identifies as important for victims and neglected by the formal court-based system. On some of these questions only conference data were available: too few court-assigned victims attended the disposition of their cases to question them about their opportunities for participation in their cases, whether they thought their views had been counted, or whether they felt they had been treated fairly and respectfully. On all these dimensions conference victims usually reported high levels of satisfaction.

One of the areas of persistent complaint for victims about court is the inadequate way that they are kept informed about the progress of their cases. Court victims in this study felt the same way, with many criticisms about failures in communication at every stage of the justice process. Many were amazed that their cases had progressed through the entire system without their being told anything at all. Conference victims, by contrast, needed to be consulted about both the process and the outcome of their cases because their participation was central to a successful resolution. Consequently they expressed high levels of satisfaction about the information they received.

On material restoration these victims said that they did not receive as much as they thought they should, either in court or in conference (though court victims felt this was more important than conference victims did). Few in either group received financial restitution, but conference victims more often received other forms of restitution, such as work by the offender either for them or for others.

However, the biggest differences between the groups related to emotional restoration. These were some of the notable findings:

- On safety and fear of victimization, three times as many of the court-assigned property victims and five times as many of the violence victims believed the offender would repeat the offence on them, compared with their conference-assigned counterparts. When asked whether they thought their offenders would reoffend with a different victim, their responses were also striking: more than half of both the property and violence victims whose cases were assigned to court believed this would happen, compared with only around one third of those assigned to a conference.
- Conference victims reported that their feelings of fear, anger, and anxiety fell markedly after the conference while feelings of sympathy and security rose (no comparable court data available).
- Conference victims also reported that their treatment most often had a beneficial effect on feelings of dignity, self-respect, and self-confidence. Two thirds of them reported that the conference experience had given them a sense of closure about the offence (no comparable court data available).
- Almost all victims, regardless of the offence they had suffered or their treatment assignment, believed that their offenders should have apologized to them. Four times as many conference-assigned as court-assigned victims actually received an apology.
- Most striking of all were the responses of violence victims about feelings of vengefulness and unresolved anger towards their offenders: almost half of the court-assigned said they would harm their offenders if they had the chance, compared with only 9 per cent of the conference-assigned, a compelling measure of the power of the conference to allay victims' desire for revenge.

In reviewing various measures of satisfaction […] I conclude that victims usually had a better experience with conference than with court. In answer to the question: 'you were satisfied with the way your case was dealt with by the justice system' (strongly disagree… strongly agree), significantly more of the conference-assigned victims than court-assigned victims were satisfied. An even higher proportion of those who *actually* went to a conference expressed satisfaction on this measure compared with those whose cases were dealt with in court.

But attending a conference is an inherently riskier experience: whereas many of the court victims were indifferent about what had happened in the disposition of their cases, most of the conference victims felt strongly, usually positively, but in a minority of cases very negatively. Throughout the study, it was evident that around one fifth of conference-assigned victims were unhappy with their experience. In some cases this was because, despite their being assigned to a conference, the conference never took place and victims were angry and disappointed as a result. Sometimes the cause of dissatisfaction lay in the way the conference was conducted or its aftermath. So as to learn more about the experience of the victims who were dissatisfied with their conferences, [I] concluded with a close examination of seven conferences which had gone badly wrong from the victim's point of view. The failure of conferencing for these victims turned out to be much more a failure of practice than of principle. Victims' dissatisfaction flowed mainly from the incompetent way in which the process was delivered—poor police investigation, inadequate facilitator training, poor conference organization, insufficient knowledge about the victim's role, and legitimate expectations from the process. Dissatisfaction was expressed in terms of process failures rather than negative attitudes towards the principles of restorative justice.

Zero-sum justice?

[...] I returned to the claim of many victim and offender advocates that criminal justice is a zero-sum game, in which any benefit by one side must be at the cost of the other side (win/lose). This claim has been made both about formal court-based justice and about restorative justice. I hypothesized that the restorative justice setting of conferences would provide more opportunities than court for both sides to win. This is because the restorative setting ought theoretically to provide more opportunities for emotional synergy than the court process does.

I examined the responses of victim and offender pairs (that is, the victim(s) and offender(s) involved in any one incident) to identical or reciprocal questions asked in their structured interviews. When both parties responded positively to the question, the response was rated as win/win; when both responded negatively it was rated lose/lose; and when one party was positive and the other negative it was rated as win/lose. Four areas were chosen for this study, on the basis that each provides plausible opportunities for one party to influence the other. These areas were: participation in the process; perceptions of procedural justice; perceptions of the legitimacy of the process; emotional harm and restoration.

For the dimensions of participation in the process and perceptions of procedural justice, only conference data were available: in each of these win/win occurred commonly—in around two-thirds of all cases—and win/lose infrequently (lose/lose was negligible). On legitimacy of the process, there was significantly more win/win in conference than in court and significantly more win/lose in court than in conference (again, lose/lose was negligible). On emotional harm too, there was significantly more win/win in conference than in court and significantly more lose/lose in court than conference, but similar results for both treatments in win/lose. The differences were most striking in the dimension of emotional restoration: win/win occurred here significantly more often in conference than in court—in fact, depending on the question asked, between one and a half times and four times more often—while win/lose occurred significantly more often in court than in conference (there was more lose/lose in court than conference but the difference was not statistically significant).

The analysis showed that the restorative alternative of conference was almost always more likely than court to produce a win/win result for both victims and offenders. However, it cannot be assumed that this was a consequence of their influencing each other in the same direction. It was equally possible that both parties independently reached the same view. Contingency tables were used to calculate the probability of the difference between observed and expected win/win responses being statistically significant. No difference was found for the dimensions of participation in the process, perceptions of procedural justice, legitimacy of the process, or emotional harm: in all these cases it appeared that victims and offenders independently tended towards the same views. However, on the dimension of emotional restoration there was a strong tendency in conferences for empathy felt by one party to influence the other party to feel empathy as well. The analysis revealed no evidence to support the zero-sum (win/lose) hypothesis of the rights advocates and it appears that restorative justice has the potential to allow both parties to 'win' more often than court justice does.

Critiques of restorative justice from the victim perspective

This book demonstrates that there are often substantial advantages to victims in the restorative approach. However, some principled concerns have been raised about their closer engagement in the justice process, based on jurisprudential considerations. Other objections are based on explanatory theory and can be partially answered by drawing on the empirical findings of this study.

Principled problems with focusing on harm to the victim

Ashworth (1986) argued that the restorative approach:

> ignores one cardinal element in serious crimes—the offender's mental attitude... Criminal liability and punishment should be determined primarily according to the wickedness or danger of the defendant's conduct... on what he was trying to do or thought he was doing, not upon what actually happened in the particular case. (p. 97)

Ashworth asserts that focusing on harm to the individual victim rather than the criminal intent of the offender (thus substituting the quantum of harm for the quantum of intent as the central determinant of liability and making restitution to the victim a principal goal of criminal justice) would require a major rethink of both criminal law and traditional punitive responses to these transgressions. He is concerned that sanctions agreed to in a restorative setting would not be proportionate to the severity of the offence, and that offenders who have committed similar offences would not be sanctioned in the same way.

Restorative justice does raise the prospect of a fundamental repositioning of victim and offender interests and concerns in the way we 'do justice' on the basis, as Barnett (1977) argued, that 'equality of justice means equal treatment of victims' (p. 259). But the problem may be that equal treatment of victims inevitably compromises equal treatment of offenders, and vice versa. Choosing either equality of treatment of victims or of offenders as a policy goal is bound to result in disappointingly unequal outcomes in a world where most offenders are not apprehended. The deepest inequality will remain between apprehended and unapprehended offenders, to the point where equality among those apprehended would be a comparatively trivial accomplishment, even if it could be attained. Similarly, the deepest inequality for victims is between those whose crimes are and are not solved. Dignan and Cavadino (1996) noted that only 7 per cent of offenders are caught and punished, so all victim-oriented measures that require an identified offender can benefit only a very small proportion of victims. These are the grounds for objection to restorative approaches by victim advocates such as Reeves and Mulley (2000) and Herman (2000), who fear the reallocation of scarce resources from more general forms of victim assistance. It remains true that equal justice for offenders and for victims are incompatible objectives. However, inconsistent outcomes for either victims or offenders may in fact be fairer if they are the result of genuine, undominated, consensual decision-making between all the key parties—victims, offenders, and their communities of concern. Braithwaite and Strang (2000) suggested that instead of consistency the aim should be to ensure minimum guarantees of justice for both parties instead of the impossible reconciliation of equal justice for victims and equal justice for offenders. For example, one possible compromise is to constrain unequal treatment of offenders only by a guarantee that none will be punished above a maximum specified for each offence, and to guarantee victims a hearing where their needs are considered. Another option may be the infusion of restorative justice into court-based criminal justice processing, so that agreements reached between victims and offenders in conferences may be taken into account in the sentencing of the offenders.[1]

Principled problems with focusing on private wrong rather than public interest

Another sticking point is the essentially irreconcilable and conflicting view of the public/private dimensions of crime. The restorative paradigm is based on a view of crime as not only a transgression against society but also, even perhaps primarily, a private wrong against the specific victim; further, that the principal objective of the justice system should be to focus on the repair of that private wrong. Critics object that restorative justice gives insufficient attention to the broader social dimension, that is, the harm society as a whole suffers through the harm experienced by any individual within it. For example, Ashworth (1992: 3) argued that 'the provisions of the criminal law set out to penalise those forms of wrong-doing which... touch public rather than merely private interests' and that 'punishment is a function of the state, to be exercised in the public interest' (1993: 284). This is because the state's concern is not only with the case at hand but also with the interests of other potential future victims and of the community as a whole. The complexity of the competing issues of private wrong and public interest were illustrated in a case which came before the New Zealand Court of Appeal (*R. v. Clotworthy* (1998) 15 CRNZ 651), where a beneficial conference outcome from the victim's point of view was overturned because the Court found that it contained too little consideration of the public interest in denunciation and general deterrence (see Morris and Young 2000; Mason 2000). However, this problem too may be resolved by finding a means for taking agreements reached in conferences into account in judicial sentencing.

The issue of punishment in restorative justice has recently been the subject of lively debate (see Daly 2000; Barton 2000) on whether the two concepts are irreconcilable, either on grounds of principle—that restorative processes ought never result in retributive outcomes—or on the moral and ethical grounds that punishment should remain the preserve of the state. Cavadino and Dignan (1997) supported the latter view—that punishment *per se* requires the sanction of the state or its representative with power of veto— but depart from Ashworth in arguing that the wishes of the victim of *this* particular crime should carry special weight in determining appropriate reparation. Watson *et al.* (1989) also held the view that because the offence against victims has entailed an infringement or denial of their rights in ways not shared with the general public, victims have a special status that entitles them to a say about reparation. Morris and Young (2000) describe how in New Zealand family group conferences victims and all the other participants not only discuss reparation but also take deterrence, incapacitation, denunciation, and retribution into account in deciding on the outcome. Arguably, punishment as an outcome is not irreconcilable with restorative values, provided all participants agree about the sanction and have arrived at that agreement through an uncoerced, restorative process (see Braithwaite and Strang 2000).

In balancing the personal interests of victims and the wider public interest, it is also important to remember that the restorative approach avoids the court's exclusive preoccupation with 'public interest' and provides an accessible forum for victims to participate in the disposition of their cases and secure both emotional and material restoration. And according to the theory of reintegrative shaming, the opportunities for reintegration of victims into their 'communities of care' which is provided through restorative processes is just as important as for offenders: indeed, the one is seen as an important means of accomplishing the other (Braithwaite and Mugford 1994).

Problems with victim fear

[…] I discussed some speculations about problems for victims which can result from facing their offenders in the restorative setting. Certainly the potential must be acknowledged, and much depends on the skill of the conference facilitator and other participating citizens in addressing this concern […]. However, the empirical evidence from this study is that both property and violence conference victims feel safer and less fearful of their offenders than court victims do. It seems that the opportunity to meet their offenders and make their own personal assessments is usually far more reassuring than fear-inducing, at least for these offences and these offenders. When this fails and victims are left feeling worse after a conference than they did before, it is most often because of the poor quality of the conference rather than a result of their objection to the principles of restorative justice […].

Problems with power imbalance

It remains true that to date there had been little research on how to achieve equal treatment of the disputing parties when one is much less powerful or articulate than the other. Much of this debate has centred on concerns about using restorative interventions in cases of domestic and sexual violence. Here Braithwaite and Daly (1994) have argued that victims may in fact be better served by a restorative approach than by the court because of the potential for involving more and less powerful supporters associated with each party. But Astor (1994) and Stubbs (1995, 2002), for example, believe that restorative interventions are most likely to fail and to leave women victims more vulnerable than they were before. The problem of power imbalance is not, in any case, limited to domestic violence: any dispute involving people known to each other may bring with it pre-existing power relationships, while young people in general may find themselves dominated by their elders, indigenous people by whites and so on.

There is much we need to learn about the possibilities and limitations for restorative justice in all these settings. But what we have learned from this study gives grounds for optimism: for example, women victims of offences other than domestic violence overwhelmingly reported that their conference experience was procedurally fair, that they felt able to assert and express themselves in the presence of their offenders, and that they had not been disadvantaged because of gender, age, race, or any other reason. Much of this debate must remain open to empirical investigation, rather than subjected to premature closure on purely normative grounds.

Problems with 'using' victims

[I] discussed some of the programmes used in the past which were so completely offender-focused that victims emerged from these encounters feeling angry and revictimized. Ashworth (2000) believes that the emphasis in more recent programmes on anticipated reductions in re-offending rather than on their value to victims may lead to victims being transformed from 'court fodder' under the traditional court system to 'agents of offender rehabilitation', under restorative justice. Victims' rights and support organizations also worry about this (see, for example, George 1999). Reeves and Mulley (2000) comment that initiatives introduced to give victims an enhanced role in the disposition of their cases may amount in reality to little more than new obligations. They point to the Crime and Disorder

Act 1998 in England and Wales as an example: under this Act victims have the right to be informed and consulted at almost every stage of the disposition of their cases, but they are concerned that this may be experienced as 'a burden in the form of unwanted contact with, or even responsibility for, the offender… They may feel guilty if they choose not to participate yet anxious if they do' (p. 139).

It is a shortcoming of this study that victims were not explicitly asked whether they ever felt like 'props' in the service of an offender-oriented show: indeed, this question has not yet been asked of victims in restorative interventions anywhere so it is a truly speculative issue. Nevertheless, we know that a significant minority of victims in this study felt dissatisfied with their experience. I identified some of the sources of this dissatisfaction […] when I looked at the elements of those conferences where most dissatisfaction was evident. Perhaps implicit among the problems to do with poor facilitation, insufficient preparation, unrealistic expectations, and unsatisfactory constitution of the conference (especially an unbalanced mix of victim and offender supporters) was a sense that far too much focus was placed on the offender at the victim's expense. All these problems derive from a failed understanding of what a restorative process entails. Restorative justice is not value-free: it begins with a presumption that victims have been harmed and that their restoration is a priority. It involves an ethical commitment to justice, not merely to conflict resolution. If this principle is paramount, then using victims in this damaging way is proscribed.

Policy implications

Although this analysis has concentrated on examining the comparative advantages of court and conferences for victims, it is important to look as well at where either of them absolutely fails. We have explored what the data tell us about when conferences fail victims; we need to consider too the shortcomings of court which prevail in spite of more than two decades of victim activism. In Canberra, for example, opting for principles rather than rights has not worked, even on such an apparently straightforward dimension as keeping victims informed of the progress and outcomes of their cases, a major focus of the Victims of Crime Act (1994). Victim advocates doubt the Act will ever be complied with in this regard because there, as in many other places, the justice system is not administered in a way that makes it feasible to meet this obligation.

It is possible that a full-blown rights approach, of the kind prevailing in the United States […] may be more successful in achieving what victims want. A US Department of Justice report (Kilpatrick *et al.* 1998) compared the experiences of victims in states in which legal protection of victims' rights was strong with those in states in which such protection was weak. It found that strong victims' rights laws made a difference and that victims from 'strong protection' states had better experiences with the justice system. However, there have been serious limitations to the success of even a strong rights approach: the same report found that in the states with strong protection, still more than one in four victims were very dissatisfied with the criminal justice system. Further, we must presume substantial costs in credibly enforcing a rights approach.

It may be the case that the structures of formal justice are so inflexible that their limits have been reached in terms of providing victims with better justice. What we have been exploring in the restorative alternative is a paradigm shift which bypasses the issues of marginal change and improvement in the way victims are treated, controversial as many of them have turned out to be. Restorative justice may be risky for victims because it asks more of them, but this study shows that the potential gains are considerable.

Future research

Restorative justice is a term covering a multitude of ideological, theological, and public policy principles and processes. Much has been written to clarify what the concept means, accompanied by much theorizing about its potential, but only slow progress has been made in determining empirically whether this promise can be realized.

Some would maintain that restorative justice, if it is to be successful in the mainstream of criminal justice, will have to be shown to 'work' for offenders—that it is successful in reducing recidivism and preventing crime (see, for example, Braithwaite 1998), whether alone or in conjunction with usual court-based justice. But others believe that if we can be satisfied that it is at least as successful as court justice alone on those measures, then the issue of victim satisfaction with the process becomes paramount in public policy decisions about the widespread use of restorative alternatives.

We are just beginning to piece together a knowledge base about victims and restorative justice. We know that there is some heterogeneity in their reaction to conferences. We suspect that they react differently depending on the emotional harm they have suffered: that conferences are most satisfying in absolute terms to those who have experienced much emotional harm because of the offence and have derived emotional restoration from them. Obversely, we suspect that conferences are most unsatisfying in absolute terms for those who experienced much emotional harm and who are revictimized by poor conferences which have provided no emotional restoration for them. But neither of these suspicions has been confirmed conclusively by this study. In the same vein, we suspect that victims would prefer offences with little personal content, such as the majority of shoplifting matters, to be dealt with in court, but this too has not been demonstrated conclusively: indeed, there remains a great deal we do not know about when conferences are most beneficial for victims and when the formal court response is preferable. We also know very little in a systematic way about the potential for conferencing with adult offenders or with more serious offences, including domestic and sexual violence (with the exception of the work of Burford and Pennell (1998) in Northern Canadian communities).

'An experience of justice'?

Howard Zehr (1995), a seminal thinker in restorative justice, has suggested that victims need first and foremost what he calls 'an experience of justice', an experience that he says is almost never available to them in the formal court-based system. He believes that while vengeance is often assumed to be a part of this need, that in fact vengeful feelings may more often be the result of justice denied. Findings in this study about the anger felt by victims whose conferences were never held, for example, and the desire for revenge of nearly half the victims of violence whose cases went to court, go to support this view. He also believes that because victims have experienced a fundamental disrespect for their property and their person through their victimization, what they want from justice is an experience of respect. This too accords with findings here about feelings of loss of dignity, respect, and other emotional harm caused by the offence, which were repaired for the majority of victims who had the restorative alternative of a conference.

We should be careful though in guarding against seeing victims in some 'ideal' way (Christie 1986). The 232 victims upon whose experiences and views this study is based were highly varied. Some of them fitted the stereotype of victims' rights organizations—the innocent young, the frail elderly, victims of unprovoked attacks on their right to safety and security. Others did not fit the stereotype at all, even though every victim survey shows that young males are the most victimized sector of the population. We must not be deluded into thinking that only 'ideal' victims deserve a better deal from our justice system. All of the different kinds of people who contributed to this study wanted the outcomes identified at the outset of the book: participation in their case, information, fair and respectful treatment, material and, especially, emotional restoration.

Likewise, we must be conscious of the limiting consequences of portraying crime simply as a violation of one individual by another (Wundersitz and Hetzel 1996). Young (2000) argues that it is more meaningful to see crime as typically affecting multiple victims—individuals, groups, communities, and society as a whole—in many different ways. Besides the fact that crime is often committed by organized groups, corporate entities, or the state itself (Nelken 1997; Lacey and Wells 1998), much 'street' crime also does not meet conventional views of crime as harm inflicted by one party upon another. In this study there were a number of offences for which it was impossible to identify a single victim, but which had undoubtedly caused harm; these included discharging a weapon in a public place, burglary in schools, and criminal damage perpetrated against public buildings or buses. Likewise, conspiracy, incitement, and attempted offences of various kinds are all difficult to fit within the conventional framework. Even in apparently clear-cut cases of harm-infliction such as assault, the labels of 'victim' and 'offender' may be socially constructed, which is to say 'the product of a complex interaction of personal and group perception of events and the contexts in which they take place' (Miers 1987: 9). Young suggests that in all these circumstances the formulation that 'crime involves one individual violating another, thus giving rise to a duty to repair the violation, fails rather miserably to capture the murky morality of many offender-victim interactions' (2000: 233). The flexibility of the restorative approach means that the complexities of criminal activity and of social life can be accommodated more easily than the structure of the formal justice system could ever allow, giving an opportunity for everyone affected by the crime—direct and indirect victims, offenders' 'communities of care', and the offenders themselves—to explain the harm and seek repair.

Nor should we limit our imaginations about where a restorative response to injustice is possible. Desmond Tutu (1999) has written movingly about the need of victims of South African state terror to forgive and about their extraordinary willingness to do so. He shares Hannah Arendt's belief that forgiveness actually releases the victim from revenge. Laura Blumenfeld (2002) has written movingly about her redemptive meeting with the Palestinian who tried to kill her Jewish father. The restorative approach gives victims and offenders the chance for a crucial transaction to take place—the offering of an apology and the granting of forgiveness. In this study in an Australian city we find the same reactions by victims as Tutu, Arendt, Blumenfeld, and others have found in the wider world of victims' suffering on scales almost unimaginable.

This research has explored systematically and scientifically many questions raised about the potential for restorative justice in repairing harm to victims. It does indeed offer promise for victims in delivering the justice they seek. We must be wary of claiming too much and raising expectations too far. Nevertheless, what has been learned from this study answers many of the fears of restorative justice critics and gives grounds for optimism for a better deal for victims through the restorative alternative.

Note

1 Research into the viability and effectiveness of this approach is underway in the United Kingdom (www.crim.upenn.edu/jrc).

References

Ashworth, A. (1986), 'Punishment and Compensation: Victims, Offenders and the State', *Oxford Journal of Legal Studies,* 6(1): 86–12
—— (1992) 'What Victims of Crime Deserve', paper presented to the Fulbright Colloquium on Penal Theory and Penal Practice, University of Sterling, 1992.
—— (1993), 'Some Doubts about Restorative Justice', *Criminal Law Forum,* 4: 277–299.
—— (2000), 'Victims' Rights, Defendants' Rights and Criminal Procedure', in A. Crawford and J. Goodey (eds.), *Integrating a Victim Perspective within Criminal Justice.* Aldershot: Ashgate.
Astor, H. (1994), 'Swimming Against the Tide: Keeping Violent Men out of Mediation', in J. Stubbs (ed.), *Women, Male Violence and the Law.* The Institute of Criminology Monograph Series No. 6, Sydney.
Barnett, R. (1977), 'Restitution: A New Paradigm of Criminal Justice', *Ethics: An International Journal of Social, Political and Legal Philosophy,* 87(4): 279–301, reprinted in B. Galaway and J. Hudson (eds.) (1981), *Perspectives on Crime Victims.* St Louis, Miss.: C. V. Mosby Company.
Barton, C. (2000), 'Empowerment and Retribution in Criminal Justice' in H. Strang and J. Braithwaite (eds.), *Restorative Justice: Philosophy to Practice.* Aldershot: Ashgate.
Bazemore, G. and Umbreit, M. (1994), *Balanced and Restorative Justice: Program Summary: Balanced and Restorative Justice Project.* Washington, DC: Department of Justice, Office of Juvenile Justice and Delinquency Prevention.
Blumenfeld, L. (2002), 'The Apology', *The New Yorker,* 4 March 2002.
Braithwaite, J. (1998), 'Linking Crime Prevention to Restorative Justice' in T. Wachtel (ed.), *Conferencing: A New Approach to Wrongdoing.* Pipersville, Penn.: Real Justice.
—— and Daly, K. (1994), 'Masculinities, Violence and Communitarian Control' in T. Newburn and E. Stanko (eds.), *Just Boys Doing Business.* London and New York: Routledge.
—— and Mugford, S. (1994), 'Conditions of Successful Reintegration Ceremonies: Dealing with Juvenile Offenders', *British Journal of Criminology,* 34(2): 139–171.
—— and Strang, H. (2000), 'Connecting Philosophy to Practice' in H. Strang and J. Braithwaite (eds.), *Restorative Justice: Philosophy to Practice,* Aldershot: Ashgate.
Burford, G. and Pennell, J. (1998), *Family Group Decision Making: After the Conference—Progress in Resolving Violence and Promoting Well-Being,* Outcome Report vols 1 and 2. St John's: St John's Newfoundland School of Social Work, Memorial University of Newfoundland.
Cavadino, M. and Dignan, J. (1997), 'Reparation, Retribution and Rights', *International Review of Victimology,* 4: 233–253.
Christie, N. (1986), 'The Ideal Victim' in E. Fattah (ed.), *From Crime Policy to Victim Policy.* London: Macmillan.
Daly, K. (2000), 'Revisiting the Relationship between Retributive and Restorative Justice' in H. Strang and J. Braithwaite (eds.), *Restorative Justice: Philosophy to Practice.* Aldershot: Ashgate.
Dignan, J. and Cavadino, M. (1996), 'Towards a Framework for Conceptualising and Evaluating Models of Criminal Justice from a Victim's Perspective', *International Review of Victimology,* 4: 153–182.
Elias, R. (1986), *The Politics of Victimisation: Victims,Victimology and Human Rights.* New York: Oxford University Press.
George, C. (1999), 'Victim Support's Perspective on Restorative Justice', *Prison Service Journal,* No. 123, May.

Herman, S. (1999), 'The Search for Parallel Justice', paper presented at the conference 'Restoration for Victims of Crime: Contemporary Challenges', convened by the Australian Institute of Criminology and the Victims Referral and Assistance Service, Melbourne, September.

Kilpatrick, D., Beatty, D., and Howley, S. (1998), 'The Rights of Crime Victims—does Legal Protection make a Difference?', *NIJ Research in Brief.* Washington, DC: National Institute of Justice, US Department of Justice.

Lacey, N. and Wells, C. (1998), *Reconstructing Criminal Law.* London, Butterworths.

Miers, D. (1978), *Responding to Victimisation.* Abingdon: Professional Books.

Mason, A. (2000), 'Restorative Justice: Courts and Civil Society' in H. Strang and J. Braithwaite (eds.), *Restorative Justice: Philosophy to Practice.* Aldershot: Ashgate.

Morris, A. and Young, W. (2000), 'Reforming Criminal Justice: The Potential of Restorative Justice', in H. Strang and J. Braithwaite (eds.), *Restorative Justice: Philosophy to Practice.* Aldershot: Ashgate.

Nelken, D. (1997), 'White Collar Crime' in M. Maguire, R. Morgan, and R. Reiner (eds.), *Oxford Handbook of Criminology.* Oxford: Clarendon Press.

Reeves, H. and Mulley. K. (2000), 'The New Status of Victims in the UK: Opportunities and Threats' in A. Crawford and J. Goodey (eds.), *Integrating a Victim Perspective within Criminal Justice.* Aldershot: Ashgate.

Shapland, J. (2000), 'Victims and Criminal Justice: Creating Responsible Criminal Justice Agencies' in A. Crawford and J. Goodey (eds.), *Integrating a Victim Perspective within Criminal Justice.* Aldershot: Ashgate.

Stubbs, J. (1995), ' "Communitarian" Conferencing and Violence against Women: A Cautionary Note' in M. Valverde, L. McLeod, and V. Johnson (eds.), *Wife Assault and the Canadian Criminal Justice System.* Toronto: Centre of Criminology, University of Toronto.

—— (2002), 'Domestic Violence and Women's Safety: Feminist Challenges to Restorative Justice' in H. Strang and J. Braithwaite (eds.), *Restorative Justice and Family Violence.* Cambridge: Cambridge University Press.

Tutu, D. (1999), *No Future Without Forgiveness.* London: Rider.

Watson, D., Boucherat, J., and Davis, D. (1989), 'Reparation for Retributivists' in M. Wright and B. Galaway (eds.), *Mediation and Criminal Justice: Victims, Offenders and Community.* London: Sage Publications.

Wundersitz, J. and Hetzel, S. (1996), 'Family Conferencing for Young Offenders: The South Australian Experience' in J. Hudson, A. Morris, G. Maxwell, and B. Galaway (eds.), *Family Group Conferences: Perspectives on Policy and Practice.* Sydney: Federation Press.

Young, R. (2000), 'Integrating a Multi-victim Perspective into Criminal Justice through Restorative Justice Conferences' in A. Crawford and J. Goodey (eds.), *Integrating a Victim Perspective within Criminal Justice.* Aldershot: Ashgate.

Zehr, H. (1985), 'Retributive Justice, Restorative Justice', *New Perspectives on Crime and Justice*, Occasional Papers of the MCC [Mennonite Central Committee] Canada Victim Offender Ministries Program and the MCC U.S. Office of Criminal Justice, September, Issue no. 4.

—— (1995), 'Rethinking Criminal Justice: Restorative Justice' unpublished paper for a NZ conference entitled 'Rethinking Criminal Justice: Restorative Justice' (Auckland 6/95).

Part E

Controversies and critical issues

Introduction

Restorative justice has been met in some quarters with considerable scepticism or concern. However, whilst the readings in Part E present serious challenges to its proponents, they are (perhaps with one exception) by no means hostile towards it. They raise profound questions about how we should understand and represent restorative interventions. And they suggest that there are considerable limitations and dangers in certain versions of the ideal. But, for the most part, they accept that there is considerable value in a revised and more careful development of the concept and practice of restorative justice. Part E opens with an extract from an essay by Kathleen Daly, in which she criticises the way restorative justice has been characterised and promoted by its advocates. She presents her critique as a 'debunking' of four misleading 'myths'– i.e. partial and distorted characterisations –about restorative justice. She is particularly critical of the use which proponents of restorative justice make of simplistic oppositional contrasts to describe and promote restorative justice, such as that between retributive and restorative justice. Such dichotomies, for Daly, are attempts to set up a simple bad/good opposition between the established response to crime and the response favoured by proponents of restorative justice. Whatever their rhetorical value, they have little to do with the reality of practices, such as youth conferencing, which proponents of restorative justice are seeking to promote.

In 'Responsibilities, Rights and Restorative Justice' (Chapter 28), Andrew Ashworth assesses the values and procedures of restorative justice from the perspective of the rights and responsibilities of various parties: the state, communities, victims and offenders. In the extract reproduced here he takes on the assertion, found regularly in the discourse of restorative justice, that victims should be enabled and encouraged to participate in the disposition of 'their' criminal cases. Ashworth argues against this claim on a number of grounds: the victim's legitimate interest is in compensation or reparation, and not in the form or amount of punishment inflicted upon an offender; suspects have a right to an impartial tribunal and that the victim's involvement detracts from impartiality; and the principle of proportionality of punishment to the offence is threatened by victim involvement in sentencing decisions. The thrust of these arguments is not that restorative justice is inevitably inconsistent with fundamental principles of justice, but that *many* of its values clash with these principles and therefore should be abandoned or modified. Ashworth accepts that versions of restorative justice *could* be developed which would not fall foul of what he and many others regard as basic principles of justice.

In Chapter 29, Paul H. Robinson, whilst praising restorative processes, criticises what he sees as the 'anti-justice' view propounded by many advocates of restorative justice. Robinson insists that justice means just deserts (compare this with Sullivan and Tifft in Part C). After explaining the importance of the principle of just deserts he argues that 'restorative justice' can be used in a way that conflicts with that principle and that this is morally objectionable. It also, he suggests, hinders the expansion of restorative justice to serious crimes. Robinson's advice to restorative justice advocates is to continue developing and promoting the use of restorative processes within criminal justice, but at the same time to acknowledge that they must form part of a system which rightly seeks to distribute punishment according to just deserts.

The reasons for the growth of restorative justice and the role it might play in the overall societal response to crime are analysed sociologically by Anthony Bottoms in Chapter 30. The growth of restorative justice seems to be at odds with the main direction of strategies of penal control in modern society. Its emergence and rise is therefore a puzzle requiring explanation. In his speculations about what lies behind the anomalous growth of restorative justice Bottoms links the debate about restorative justice to broader debates in the sociology of punishment and social control. Another key questions posed by Bottoms is whether the social mechanisms that lie at the heart of restorative justice interventions can work in contemporary urban societies. In addressing this question, Bottoms identifies important sociological limits to the project of replacing official criminal justice with restorative justice. Hence, he suggests a key policy issue concerns the identification of the types of case for which restorative justice is appropriate.

Chapter 31 is an excerpt from George Pavlich's short but essential book *Governing Paradoxes of Restorative Justice*. Pavlich argues that restorative justice has not made as radical a break with traditional thinking about crime and justice as its rhetoric suggests. It employs much the same vocabulary that one finds in traditional conceptions of criminal justice and uncritically adopts conservative thinking about these categories. Hence, for Pavlich, it is not surprising that restorative justice has come to operate more as an appendage to state criminal justice rather than as an alternative to it. Restorative justice defers to basic criminal justice assumptions, paving the way for its incorporation into the criminal justice system. The importance of Pavlich's argument lies in his claim that restorative justice actually fails to live up to its rhetorical claim to provide a distinctive moral compass for governance in the domain of crime because it has shown too little awareness of these contradictions; it has allowed itself to become ensnared within the language, logic and agencies of orthodox criminal justice. To the extent that Pavlich's claims are accepted, whether this fate is avoidable is an important question for the restorative justice movement.

In the final reading, Annalise Acorn explains how she became seduced by the restorative justice movement but ultimately couldn't let go of her 'moral intuition that a just response to wrongdoing often requires "throwing the book" at wrongdoers'. Acorn criticises restorative justice as a fantasy revolving around unrealistic notions about people's capacity for compassion and a selective focus on interventions with happy endings. As a number of reviewers of Acorn's work have pointed out, despite her scepticism and indeed hostility towards restorative justice, she nonetheless provides an excellent account of key aspects of its thinking and appeal. Reviewers have also claimed, however, that Acorn seriously misrepresents the nature of restorative justice and in effect attacks a straw man. Hopefully, those who work their way through this volume will be well-equipped to make up their own minds about this and other key controversies and critical issues.

27 Restorative justice

The real story

Kathleen Daly

[. . .]

Myths about restorative justice

Myth 1. Restorative justice is the opposite of retributive justice

When one first dips into the restorative justice literature, the first thing one 'learns' is that restorative justice differs sharply from retributive justice. It is said that:

1. restorative justice focuses on *repairing the harm* caused by crime, whereas retributive justice focuses on *punishing an offence*;
2. restorative justice is characterized by *dialogue* and *negotiation* among the parties; where retributive justice is characterized by *adversarial relations* among the parties;
3. restorative justice assumes that community members or organizations take a more active role, whereas for retributive justice, 'the community' is represented by the state.

Most striking is that all the elements associated with restorative justice are *good*, whereas all those associated with retributive justice are *bad*. The retributive–restorative oppositional contrast is not only made by restorative justice advocates, but increasingly one finds it canonized in criminology and juvenile justice textbooks. The question arises, is it right?

On empirical and normative grounds, I suggest that in characterizing justice aims and practices, it is neither accurate nor defensible. While I am not alone in taking this position (see Barton, 2000; Miller and Blackler, 2000; Duff, 2001), it is currently held by a small number of us in the field. Despite advocates' well-meaning intentions, the contrast is a highly misleading simplification, which is used to sell the superiority of restorative justice and its set of justice products. To make the sales pitch simple, definite boundaries need to be marked between the *good* (restorative) and the *bad* (retributive) justice, to which one might add the *ugly* (rehabilitative) justice. Advocates seem to assume that an ideal justice system should be of one type only, that it should be pure and not contaminated by or mixed with others.[1] Before demonstrating the problems with this position, I give a sympathetic reading of what I think advocates are trying to say.

Mead's (1917–18) 'The Psychology of Punitive Justice' (as reprinted in Melossi, 1998; 33–60) contrasts two methods of responding to crime. One he termed 'the attitude of hostility toward the lawbreaker' (p. 48), which 'brings with it the attitudes of retribution, repression, and exclusion' (pp. 47–28) and which sees a lawbreaker as 'enemy'. The other, exemplified in the (then) emerging juvenile court, is the 'reconstructive attitude' (p. 55), which tries to 'understand the causes of social and individual breakdown, to mend . . . the defective situation', to determine responsibility 'not to place punishment but to obtain future results' (p. 52). Most restorative justice advocates see the justice world through this Meadian lens; they reject the 'attitude of hostility toward the lawbreaker', do not wish to view him or her as 'enemy', and desire an alternative kind of justice. On that score, I concur, as no doubt many other researchers and observers of justice system practices would. However, the 'attitude of hostility' is a caricature of criminal justice, which over the last century and a half has wavered between desires to 'treat' some and 'punish' others, and which surely cannot be encapsulated in the one term, 'retributive justice'. By framing justice aims (or principles) and practices in oppositional terms, restorative justice advocates not only do a disservice to history, they also give a restricted view of the present. They assume that restorative justice *practices* should exclude elements of retribution; and in rejecting an 'attitude of hostility', they assume that retribution as a justice *principle* must also be rejected.

When observing conferences, I discovered that participants engaged in a flexible incorporation of *multiple* justice aims, which included:

1. some elements of retributive justice (that is, censure for past offences);
2. some elements of rehabilitative justice (for example, by asking, what shall we do to encourage future law-abiding behaviour?); and
3. some elements of restorative justice (for example, by asking, how can the offender make up for what he or she did to the victim?).

When reporting these findings, one colleague said, 'yes, this is a problem' (Walgrave, personal communication). This speaker's concern was that as restorative justice was being incorporated into the regular justice system, it would turn out to be a set of 'simple techniques', rather than an 'ideal of justice . . . in an ideal of society' (Walgrave, 1995: 240, 245) and that its core values would be lost. Another said (paraphrasing), 'retribution may well be present now in conferences, but you wouldn't want to make the argument that it *should* be present' (Braithwaite, personal communication).

These comments provoked me to consider the relationship between restorative and retributive justice, and the role of punishment in restorative justice, in normative terms. Distilling from other articles (e.g. Daly and Immarigeon, 1998: 32–5; Daly, 2000a, 2000b) and arguments by Duff (1992, 1996, 2001), Hampton (1992, 1998), Zedner (1994) and Barton (2000), I have come to see that apparently contrary principles of retribution and reparation should be viewed as dependent on one another. Retributive censure should ideally occur before reparative gestures (or a victim's interest or movement to negotiate these) are possible in an ethical or psychological sense. Both censure and reparation may be experienced as 'punishment' by offenders (even if this is not the intent of decision-makers), and both censure and reparation need to occur before a victim or community can 'reintegrate' an offender into the community. These complex and contingent interactions are expressed in varied ways and should not be viewed as having to follow any one fixed sequence. Moreover, one cannot assume that subsequent actions, such as the victim's forgiving the offender or a reconciliation of a victim and offender (or others), should occur. This may take a long time or never occur. In the advocacy literature, however, I find that there is too quick a move to 'repair the harm', 'heal those injured by crime' or to 'reintegrate offenders', passing over a crucial phase of 'holding offenders accountable', which is the retributive part of the process.

A major block in communicating ideas about the relationship of retributive to restorative justice is that there is great variability in how people understand and use key terms such as punishment, retribution and punitiveness. Some argue that incarceration and fines are punishments because they are *intended deprivations*, whereas probation or a reparative measure such as doing work for a crime victim are not punishment because they are *intended to be constructive* (Wright, 1991). Others define punishment more broadly to include anything that is unpleasant, a burden or an imposition of some sort; the intentions of the decision-maker are less significant (Davis, 1992; Duff, 1992, 2001). Some use retribution to describe a *justification* for punishment (i.e. intended to be in proportion to the harm caused), whereas others use it to describe a *form* of punishment (i.e. intended to be of a type that is harsh or painful).[2] On proportionality, restorative justice advocates take different positions: some (e.g. Braithwaite and Pettit, 1990) eschew retributivism, favouring instead a free-ranging consequentialist justification and highly individualized responses, while others wish to limit restorative justice responses to desert-based, proportionate criteria (Van Ness, 1993; Walgrave and Aertsen, 1996). For the form of punishment, some use retribution in a neutral way to refer to a censuring of harms (e.g. Duff, 1996), whereas most use the term to connote a punitive response, which is associated with emotions of revenge or intentions to inflict pain on wrong-doers (Wright, 1991). The term *punitive* is rarely defined, no doubt because everyone seems to know what it means. Precisely because this term is used in a commonsensical way by everyone in the field (not just restorative justice scholars), there is confusion over its meaning. Would we say, for example, that any criminal justice sanction is by definition 'punitive', but sanctions can vary across a continuum of greater to lesser punitiveness? Or, would we say that some sanctions are non-punitive and that restorative justice processes aim to maximize the application of non-punitive sanctions? I will not attempt to adjudicate the many competing claims about punishment, retribution and punitiveness. The sources of antagonism lie not only in varied *definitions*, but also the different *images* these definitions conjure in people's heads about justice relations and practices. However, one way to gain some clarity is to conceptualize punishment, retribution and punitive (and their 'non' counterparts) as separate dimensions, each having its own continuum of meaning, rather than to conflate them, as now typically occurs in the literature.

Because the terms 'retributive justice' and 'restorative justice' have such strong meanings and referents, and are used largely by advocates (and others) as metaphors for the bad and the good justice, perhaps they should be jettisoned in analysing current and future justice practices. Instead, we might refer to 'older' and 'newer' modern justice forms. These terms do not provide a content to justice principles or practices, but they do offer a way to depict developments in the justice field with an eye to recent history and with an appreciation that any 'new' justice practices will have many bits of the 'old' in them.[3] The terms also permit description and explanation of a larger phenomenon, that is, of a profound transformation of justice forms and practices now occurring in most developed societies in the West, and certainly the English-speaking ones of which I am aware. Restorative justice is only a part of that transformation.

By the *old justice*, I refer to modern practices of courthouse justice, which permit no interaction between victim and offender, where legal actors and other experts do the talking and make decisions and whose (stated) aim is to punish, or at times, reform an offender. By the *new justice*,[4] I refer to a variety of recent practices, which normally bring victims and offenders (and others) together in a process in which both lay and legal actors make decisions, and whose (stated) aim is to repair the harm for victims, offenders and perhaps other members of 'the community' in ways that matter to them. (While the stated aim of either justice form may be to 'punish the crime' or to 'repair the harm', we should expect to see mixed justice aims in participants' justice talk and practices.[5]) New justice practices are one of several developments in a larger justice field, which also includes the 'new penology' (Feeley and Simon, 1992) and 'unthinkable punishment policies' (Tonry, 1999). The field is fragmented and moving in contradictory directions (Garland, 1996; Crawford, 1997; O'Malley, 1999; Pratt, 2000).

Myth 2. Restorative justice uses indigenous justice practices and was the dominant form of pre-modern justice

A common theme in the restorative justice literature is that this reputedly new justice form is 'really not new' (Consedine, 1995: 12). As Consedine puts it:

> Biblical justice was restorative. So too was justice in most indigenous cultures. In pre-colonial New Zealand, Maori had a fully integrated system of restorative justice . . . It was the traditional philosophy of Pacific nations such as Tonga, Fiji and Samoa . . . In pre-Norman Ireland, restorative justice was interwoven . . . with the fabric of daily life . . .
>
> (1995: 12)

Braithwaite argues that restorative justice is 'ground[ed] in traditions of justice from the ancient Arab, Greek, and Roman civilisations that accepted a restorative approach even to homicide' (1999: 1), He continues with a large sweep of human history, citing the 'public assemblies . . . of the Germanic peoples', 'Indian Hindu [traditions in] 6000–2000 BC' and 'ancient Buddhist, Taoist, and Confucian traditions . . .'; and he concludes that *restorative justice has been the dominant model of criminal justice throughout most of human history for all the world's peoples'* (1999: 1, my emphasis). What an extraordinary claim!

Linked with the claim that restorative justice has been the dominant form of criminal justice throughout human history is the claim that present-day indigenous justice practices fall within the restorative justice rubric. Thus, for example, Consedine says:

> A new paradigm of justice is operating [in New Zealand], which is very traditional in its philosophy, yet revolutionary in its effects. A restorative philosophy of justice has replaced a retributive one. Ironically, 150 years after the traditional Maori restorative praxis was abolished in Aotearoa, youth justice policy is once again operating from the same philosophy.
>
> (1995: 99)

Reverence for and romanticization of an indigenous past slide over practices that the modern 'civilized' western mind would object to, such as a variety of harsh physical (bodily) punishments and banishment. At the same time, the modern western mind may not be able to grasp how certain 'harsh punishments' have been sensible within the terms of a particular culture.

Weitekamp combines 'ancient forms' of justice practice (as restorative) and indigenous groups' current practices (as restorative) when he says that:

> Some of the new . . . programs are in fact very old . . . [A]ncient forms of restorative justice have been used in [non-state] societies and by early forms of humankind. [F]amily group conferences [and] . . . circle hearings [have been used] by indigenous people such as the Aboriginals, the Inuit, and the native Indians of North and South

America . . . It is kind of ironic that we have at [the turn of this century] to go back to methods and forms of conflict resolution which were practiced some millennia ago by our ancestors . . .

(1999: 93)

I confess to a limited knowledge of justice practices and systems throughout the history of humankind. What I know is confined mainly to the past three centuries and to developments in the United States and several other countries. Thus, in addressing this myth, I do so from a position of ignorance in knowing only a small portion of history. Upon reflection, however, my lack of historical knowledge may not matter. All that is required is the realization that advocates do not intend to write *authoritative histories* of justice. Rather, they are constructing origin myths about restorative justice. If the first form of human justice was restorative justice, then advocates can claim a need to recover it from a history of 'takeover' by state-sponsored retributive justice. And, by identifying current indigenous practices as restorative justice, advocates can claim a need to recover these practices from a history of 'takeover' by white colonial powers that instituted retributive justice. Thus, the history of justice practices is rewritten by advocates not only to authorize restorative justice as the *first* human form of justice, but also to argue that it is congenial with modern-day indigenous and, as we shall see in Myth 3, feminist social movements for justice.

In the restorative justice field, most commentators focus specifically (and narrowly) on changes that occurred over a 400-year period (8th to 11th centuries) in England (and some European countries), where a system of largely kin-based dispute settlement gave way to a court system, in which feudal lords retained a portion of property forfeited by an offender. In England, this loose system was centralized and consolidated during the century following the Normal Invasion in 1066, as the development of state (crown) law depended on the collection of revenues collected by judges for the king. For restorative justice advocates, the transformation of disputes as offences between individuals to offences against the state is one element that marked the end of pre-modern forms of restorative justice. A second element is the decline in compensation to the victim for the losses from a crime (Weitekamp, 1999).

Advocates' constructions of the history of restorative justice, that is, the origin myth that a superior justice form prevailed before the imposition of retributive justice, is linked to their desire to maintain a strong oppositional contrast between retributive and restorative justice. That is to say, the origin myth and oppositional contrast are both required in telling the true story of restorative justice. I do not see bad faith at work here. Rather, advocates are trying to move an idea into the political and policy arena, and this may necessitate having to utilize a simple contrast of the good and the bad justice, along with an origin myth of how it all came to be.

What does concern me is that the specific histories and practices of justice in pre-modern societies are smoothed over and are lumped together as one justice form. Is it appropriate to refer to all of these justice practices as 'restorative'? No, I think not. What do these justice practices in fact have in common? What is gained, and more importantly, what is lost by this homogenizing move? Efforts to write histories of restorative justice, where a pre-modern past is romantically (and selectively) invoked to justify a current justice practice, are not only in error, but also unwittingly reinscribe an ethnocentrism their authors wish to avoid. As Blagg (1997) and Cain (2000) point out, there has been an orientalist appropriation of indigenous justice practices, largely in the service of strenthening advocates' positions.

A common, albeit erroneous, claim is that the modern idea of conferencing 'has its direct roots in Maori culture' (Shearing, 2001: 218, note 5; see also Consedine, 1995). The real story is that conferencing emerged in the 1980s, in the context of Maori political challenges to white New Zealanders and to their welfare and criminal justice systems. Investing decision-making practices with Maori cultural values meant that family groups (whanau) should have a greater say in what happens, that venues should be culturally appropriate, and that processes should accommodate a mix of culturally appropriate practices. New Zealand's minority group population includes not only the Maori but also Pacific Island Polynesians. Therefore, with the introduction of conferencing, came awareness of the need to incorporate different elements of 'cultural appropriateness' into the conference process. But the devising of a (white, bureaucratic) justice practice that is *flexible and accommodating* towards cultural differences does not mean that conferencing *is* an indigenous justice practice. Maxwell and Morris, who know the New Zealand situation well, are clear on this point:

> A distinction must be drawn between a system, which attempts to re-establish the indigenous model of pre-European times, and a system of justice, which is culturally appropriate. The New Zealand system is an attempt to establish the latter, not to replicate the former. As such, it seeks to incorporate many of the features apparent in whanau decision-making processes and seen in meetings on marae today, but it also contains elements quite alien to indigenous models.
>
> (1993: 4)

Conferencing is better understood as a fragmented justice form: it splices white, bureaucratic forms of justice with elements of informal justice that may include non-white (or non-western) values or methods of judgement, with all the attendant dangers of such 'spliced justice' (Pavlich, 1996; Blagg, 1997, 1998; Daly, 1998; Findlay, 2000). With the flexibility of informal justice, practitioners, advocates and members of minority groups may see the potential for introducing culturally sensible and responsive forms of justice. But to say that conferencing *is* an indigenous justice practice (or 'has its roots in indigenous justice') is to re-engage a white-centred view of the world. As Blagg asks rhetorically, 'Are we once again creaming off the cultural value of people simply to suit our own nostalgia in this age of pessimism and melancholia?' (1998: 12). A good deal of the advocacy literature is of this ilk: white-centred, creaming off and homogenizing of cultural difference and specificity.

Myth 3. Restorative justice is a 'care' (or feminine) response to crime in comparison to a 'justice' (or masculine) response

Myths 2 and 3 have a similar oppositional logic, but play with different dichotomies. Figure 27.1 shows the terms that are often linked to restorative and retributive justice. Note the power inversion, essential to the origin myth of restorative justice, where the subordinated or marginalized groups (pre-modern, indigenous, eastern and feminine) are aligned with the more superior justice form.

Many readers will be familiar with the 'care' and 'justice' dichotomy. It was put forward by Gilligan in her popular book, *In a Different Voice* (1982). For about a decade, it seemed that most feminist legal theory articles were organized around the 'different voice' versus 'male dominance' perspectives of Gilligan (1987) and MacKinnon (1987), respectively. In criminology, Heidensohn (1986) and Harris (1987) attempted to apply the care/justice dichotomy to the criminal justice system. Care responses to crime are depicted as personalized and as based on a concrete and active morality, whereas justice responses are depicted

Restorative justice	Retributive justice
Pre-modern	Modern
Indigenous (informal)	State (formal)
Feminine (care)	Masculine (justice)
Eastern (Japan)	Western (US)
Superior justice	Inferior justice

Figure 27.1 Terms linked to restorative and retributive justice.

as depersonalized, based on rights and rules and a universalizing and abstract morality. Care responses are associated with the different (female) voice, and these are distinguished from justice responses, which are associated with the general (if male) voice. In her early work, Gilligan argued that both voices should have equal importance in moral reasoning, but women's voices were misheard or judged as morally inferior to men's. A critical literature developed rapidly, and Gilligan began to reformulate and clarify her argument. She recognized that 'care' responses in a 'justice' framework left the basic assumptions of a justice framework intact . . . and that as a moral perspective, care [was] less well elaborated' (Gilligan, 1987: 24). At the time, the elements that Gilligan associated with a care response to crime were contextual and relational reasoning, and individualized responses made by decision-makers who were not detached from the conflict (or crime). In 1989, I came into the debate, arguing that we should challenge the association of justice and care reasoning with male/masculine and female/feminine voices, respectively (Daly, 1989). I suggested that this gender-linked association was not accurate empirically, and I argued that it would be misleading to think that an alternative to men's forms of criminal law and justice practices could be found by adding women's voice or reconstituting the system along the lines of an ethic of care. I viewed the care/justice dichotomy as recapitulating centuries long debates in modern western criminology and legal philosophy over the aims and purposes of punishment, e.g. deterrence and retribution or rehabilitation, and uniform or individualized responses. Further, I noted that although the dichotomy depicted different ideological emphases in the response to crime since the 19th century, the relational and concrete reasoning that Gilligan associated with the female voice was how in fact the criminal law is interpreted and applied. It *is* the voice of criminal justice practices. The problem, then, was not that the female voice was absent in criminal court practices, but rather that certain relations were presupposed, maintained and reproduced. Feminist analyses of law and criminal justice centre on the androcentric (some would argue, phallocentric) character of these relations for what comes to be understood as 'crime', for the meanings of 'consent', and for punishment (for cogent reviews, see Smart, 1989, 1992; Coombs, 1995). While feminist scholars continue to emphasize the need to bring women's experiences and 'voices' into the criminological and legal frame, this is not the same thing as arguing that there is a universal 'female voice' in moral reasoning. During the late 1980s and 1990s, feminist arguments moved decisively beyond dichotomous and essentialist readings of sex/gender in analysing relations of power and 'difference' in law and justice. Gilligan's different voice construct, though novel and important at the time, has been superseded by more complex and contingent analyses of ethics and morality.

But the different voice is back, and unfortunately, the authors who are using it seem totally unaware of key shifts in feminist thinking. We see now that the 'ethic of care' (Persephone) is pitched as the alternative to retributive justice (Portia). One example is a recent article by Masters and Smith (1998), who attempt to demonstrate the Persephone, the voice of caring, is evident in a variety of restorative responses to crime. Their arguments confuse, however, because they argue that Persephone is 'informed by an ethic of care as well as an ethic of justice' (1998: 11). And towards the end of the article, they say 'we cannot do without Portia (ethic of justice), but neither can we do without Persephone' (1998: 21). Thus, it is not clear whether, within the terms of their argument, Persephone stands for the feminine or includes both the masculine and feminine, or whether we need both Portia and Persephone. They apparently agree with all three positions. They also see little difference between a 'feminine' and a 'feminist approach', terms that they use interchangeably. In general, they normally credit 'relational justice as a distinctly feminine approach to crime and conflict' (1998: 13). They say that 'reintegrative shaming can be considered a feminine (or Persephone) theory' and that there is a 'fit between reintegrative shaming practice and the *feminist* ethic of care' (1998: 13, my italics since the authors have shifted from a feminine ethic to a feminist ethic). Towards the end of the article, they make the astonishing claim, one that I suspect my colleague John Braithwaite would find difficult to accept, that 'reintegrative shaming is perhaps the first feminist criminological theory'. They argue this is so because the 'practice of reintegrative shaming can be interpreted as being grounded in a feminine, rather than a masculine understanding of the social world' (1998: 20).

There is a lot to unpick here, and I shall not go point by point. Nor do I wish to undermine the spirit of the article since the authors' intentions are laudable, in particular, their desire to define a more progressive way to respond to crime. My concern is that using simple gender dichotomies, or any dichotomies for that matter, to describe principles and practices of justice will always fail us, will always lead to great disappointment.[6] Traditional courthouse justice works with the abstraction of criminal law, but must deal with the messy world of people's lives, and hence, must deal with context and relations. 'Care' responses to some offenders can re-victimize some victims; they may be helpful in *some cases* or for *some offenders* or for *some victims* or they may also be oppressive and unjust for other offenders and victims. Likewise, with so-called 'justice' responses. The set of terms lined up along the 'male/masculine' and 'female/feminine' poles is long and varied: some terms are about process, others with modes of response (e.g. repair the harm) and still others, with ways of thinking about culpability for the harm.

I am struck by the frequency with which people use dichotomies such as the male and female voice, retributive and restorative justice or West and East, to depict justice principles and practices. Such dichotomies are also used to construct normative positions about justice, where it is assumed (I think wrongly) that the sensibility of one side of the dualism necessarily excludes (or is antithetical to) the sensibility of the other. Increasingly, scholars are coming to see the value of theorizing justice in hybrid terms, of seeing connections and contingent relations between apparent oppositions (see, for example, Zedner, 1994; Bottoms, 1998; Hudson, 1998; Daly, 2000a; Duff, 2001).

Like the advocates promoting Myth 2, those promoting Myth 3 want to emphasize the importance of identifying a different response to crime than the one currently in use. I am certainly on the side of that aspiration. However, I cannot agree with the terms in which the position has been argued and sold to academic audiences and wider publics. There is a loss of credibility when analyses do not move beyond oppositional justice metaphors, when claims are imprecise and when extraordinary tales of repair and goodwill are assumed to be typical of the restorative justice experience.

Myth 4. Restorative justice can be expected to produce major changes in people

I have said that attention needs to be given to the reality on the ground, to what is actually happening in, and resulting from, practices that fall within the rubric of restorative justice. There are several levels to describe and analyse what is going on: first, what occurs in the justice practice itself; second, the relationship between this and broader system effects; and third, how restorative justice is located in the broader politics of crime control. I focus on the first level and present two forms of evidence: (1) stories of dramatic transformations or moving accounts of reconciliation; and (2) aggregated information across a larger number of cases, drawing from research on conference observations and interviews with participants.

Several reviewers of this article took issue with Myth 4, saying that 'advocates are less likely to claim changes in people' or that 'there is no real evidence that restorative justice of itself can be expected to produce major changes in people'. Although I am open to empirical inquiry, my reading of the advocacy literature from the United States, Canada, Australia and New Zealand suggests that Myth 4 is prevalent. It is exemplified by advocates' stories of how people are transformed or by their general assertions of the benefits of restorative justice. For example, McCold reports that 'facilitators of restorative processes regularly observe a personal and social transformation occur during the course of the process' (2000: 359) and 'we now have a growing body of research on programs that everyone agrees are truly restorative, clearly demonstrating their remarkable success at healing and conciliation' (2000: 363). McCold gives no citations to the research literature. While 'personal and social transformation' undoubtedly occurs some of the time, and is likely to be rare in a courtroom proceeding, advocates lead us to think that it is typical in a restorative justice process. This is accomplished by telling a moving story, which is then used to stand as a generalization.

Stories of restorative justice

Consedine opens his book by excerpting from a 1993 New Zealand news story:

> The families of two South Auckland boys killed by a car welcomed the accused driver yesterday with open arms and forgiveness. The young man, who gave himself up to the police yesterday morning, apologised to the families and was ceremonially reunited with the Tongan and Samoan communities at a special service last night.
>   . . . The 20-year-old Samoan visited the Tongan families after his court appearance to apologise for the deaths of the two children in Mangere. The Tongan and Samoan communities of Mangere later gathered at the Tongan Methodist Church in a service of reconciliation. The young man sat at the feast table flanked by the mothers of the dead boys.
>
> (Consedine, 1995: 9)

Consedine says that this case provides:

> ample evidence of the power that healing and forgiveness can play in our daily lives . . . The grieving Tongan and Samoan communities simply embraced the young driver . . . and forgave him. His deep shame, his fear, his sorrow, his alienation from the community was resolved.
>
> (1995: 162)

Another example comes from Umbreit (1994: 1). His book opens with the story of Linda and Bob Jackson, whose house was broken into; they subsequently met with the offender as part of the offender's sentence disposition. The offender, Allan, 'felt better after the mediation . . . he was able to make amends to the Jacksons'. Moreover, 'Linda and Bob felt less vulnerable, were able to sleep better and received payment for their losses. All parties were able to put this event behind them.' Later in the book, Umbreit (1994: 197–202) offers another case study of a second couple, Bob and Anne, after their house was burglarized a second time. He summarized the outcome this way:

> Bob, Anne, and Jim [the offender] felt the mediation process and outcome was fair. All were very satisfied with participation in the program. Rather than playing passive roles . . . [they] actively participated in 'making things right'. During a subsequent conversation with Bob, he commented that 'this was the first time (after several victimizations) that I ever felt any sense of fairness. The courts always ignored me before. They didn't care about my concerns. And Jim isn't such a bad kid after all, was he?' Jim also indicated that he felt better after the mediation and more aware of the impact the burglary had on Bob and Anne.
>
> (Umbreit, 1994: 202)

Lastly, there is the fable of Sam, an adolescent offender who attended a diversionary conference, which was first related by Braithwaite (1996) and retold by Shearing (2001: 214–15). Braithwaite says that his story is a 'composite of several Sams I have seen' (1996: 9); thus, while he admits that it is not a real story of Sam, it is said to show the 'essential features . . . of restorative justice' (Shearing, 2001: 214). This is something like a building contractor saying to a potential home buyer, 'this is a composite of the house I can build for you; it's not the real house, but it's like many houses I have sold to happy buyers over the years'. What the composite gives and what the building contractor offers us is a *vision of the possible*, of the perfect house. Whether the house can ever be built is less important than imagining its possibility and its perfection. This is the cornerstone of the true story of restorative justice, like many proposed justice innovations of the past.

Sam's story, as told by Braithwaite, is longer than I give here, and thus I leave out emotional details that make any story compelling. Sam, who is homeless and says his parents abused him, has no one who really cares about him except his older sister, his former hockey coach at school and his Uncle George. These people attend the conference, along with the elderly female victim and her daughter. Sam says he knocked over the victim and took her purse because he needed the money. His significant others rebuke him for doing this, but also remember that he had a good side before he started getting into trouble. The victim and daughter describe the effects of the robbery, but Sam does not seem to be affected. After his apparent callous response to the victim, Sam's sister cries, and during a break, she reveals that she too had been abused by their parents. When the conference reconvenes, Sam's sister speaks directly to Sam, and without mentioning details, says she understands what Sam went through. The victim appreciates what is being said and begins to cry. Sam's callous exterior begins to crumble. He says he wants to do something for the victim, but does not know what he can do without a home or job. His sister offers her place for him to stay, and the coach says he can offer him some work. At the end of the conference, the victim hugs Sam and tearfully says good luck. Sam apologizes again and Uncle George says he will continue to help Sam and his sister when needed.

Many questions arise in reading stories like these. *How often* do expressions of kindness and understanding, of movement towards repair and goodwill, actually occur? What are the typical 'effects' on participants? Is the perfect house of restorative justice ever built? Another kind of evidence, aggregated data across a large number of cases, can provide some answers.

Statistical aggregates of restorative justice

Here are some highlights of what has been learned from research on youth justice conferences in Australia and New Zealand.[7] Official data show that about 85 to 90 per cent of conferences resulted in agreed outcomes, and 80 per cent of young people completed their agreements. From New Zealand research in the early 1990s (Maxwell and Morris, 1993), conferences appeared to be largely offender-centred events. In 51 per cent of the 146 cases where a victim was identified, the victim attended the conference (1993: 118). Of all the victims interviewed who attended a conference (sometimes there were multiple victims), 25 per cent said they felt worse as a result of the conference (1993: 119). Negative feelings were linked to being dissatisfied with the conference outcome, which was judged to be too lenient towards the offender. Of all those interviewed (offenders, their supporters and victims) victims were the least satisfied with the outcome of the family conference: 40 per cent said they were satisfied (1993: 120) compared with 84 per cent of young people and 85 per cent of parents (1993: 115). Maxwell and Morris report that 'monitoring of [conference] outcomes was generally poor' (1993: 123), and while they could not give precise percentages, it appeared that 'few [victims] had been informed of the eventual success or otherwise of the outcome' and that this 'was a source of considerable anger for them' (1993: 123). Elsewhere, Maxwell and Morris report that 'the new system remains largely unresponsive to cultural differences' (1996: 95–6) in handling Maori cases, which they argue is a consequence, in part, of too few resources.

The most robust finding across all the studies in the region (see review in Daly, 2001) is that conferences receive very high marks along dimensions of procedural justice, that is, victims and offenders view the process and the outcomes as fair. In the Re-Integrative Shaming Experiments (RISE) in Canberra, admitted offenders were randomly assigned to court and conference. Strang *et al.* (1999) have reported results from the RISE project on their website by showing many pages of percentages for each variable for each of the four offences in the experiment (violent, property, shoplifting and drink-driving). They have summarized this mass of numbers in a set of comparative statements without attaching their claims to percentages. Here is what they report. Compared to those offenders who went to court, those going to conferences have higher levels of procedural justice, higher levels of restorative justice and an increased respect for the police and law. Compared to victims whose cases went to court, conference victims have higher levels of recovery from the offence. Conference victims also had high levels of procedural justice, but they could not be compared to court victims, who rarely attended court proceedings. These summary statements are the tip of the RISE iceberg. In a detailed analysis of the RISE website results, Kurki (2001) finds offence-based differences in the court and conference experiences of RISE participants, and she notes that RISE researchers' reports of claimed court and conference differences are not uniform across offence types.

Like other studies, the South Australia Juvenile Justice (SAJJ) Research on Conferencing Project finds very high levels of procedural justice registered by offenders and victims at conferences. To items such as, were you treated fairly, were you treated with respect, did you have a say in the agreement, among others, 80 to 95 per cent of victims and offenders said that they were treated fairly and had a say. In light of the procedural justice literature (Tyler, 1990; Tyler *et al.*, 1997), these findings are important. Procedural justice scholars argue that when citizens perceive a legal process as fair, when they are listened to and treated with respect, there is an affirmation of the legitimacy of the legal order.

Compared to the high levels of perceived procedural justice, the SAJJ project finds relatively less evidence of restorativeness. The measures of restorativeness tapped the degree to which offenders and victims recognized the other and were affected by the other; they focused on the degree to which there was positive movement between the offender and victim and their supporters during the conference (the SAJJ measures are more concrete and relational measures of restorativeness than those used in RISE). Whereas very high proportions of victims and offenders (80 to 95 per cent) said that the process was fair (among other variables tapping procedural justice), 'restorativeness' was evident in 30 to 50 per cent of conferences (depending on the item), and solidly in no more than about one-third. Thus, in this jurisdiction where conferences are used *routinely*[8] fairness can more easily be achieved than restorativeness. As but one example, from the interviews we learned that from the victims' perspectives, less than 30 per cent of offenders were perceived as making genuine apologies, but from the offenders' perspectives, close to 60 per cent said their apology was genuine.

The SAJJ results lead me to think that young people (offenders) and victims orient themselves to a conference and what they hope to achieve in it in ways different than the advocacy literature imagines. The stance of empathy and openness to 'the other', the expectation of being able to speak and reflect on one's actions and the presence of new justice norms (or language) emphasizing repair – all of these are novel cultural elements for most participants. Young people appear to be as, if not more, interested in *repairing their own reputations* than in repairing the harm to victims. Among the most important things that the victims hoped would occur at the conference was for the offender to hear how the offence affected them, but half the offenders told us that the victim's story had no effect or only a little effect on them.

How often, then, does the exceptional or 'nirvana' story of repair and goodwill occur? I devised a measure that combined the SAJJ observer's judgement of the degree to which a conference 'ended on a high, a positive note of repair and good will' with one that rated the conference on a five-point scale from poor to exceptional. While the first tapped the degree to which there was movement between victims, offenders and their supporters towards each other, the second tapped a more general feeling about the conference dynamics and how well the conference was managed by the co-ordinator. With this combined measure, 10 per cent of conferences were rated very highly, another 40 per cent, good; and the rest, a mixed, fair or poor rating. If conferencing is used routinely (not just in a select set of cases), I suspect that the story of Sam and Uncle George will be infrequent; it may happen 10 per cent of the time, if that.

Assessing the 'effects' of conferences on participants is complex because such effects change over time and, for victims, they are contingent on whether offenders come through on promises made, as we learned from research in New Zealand. I present findings on victims' sense of having recovered from the offence and on young people's reoffending in the post-conference period. In the Year 2 (1999) interviews with victims, over 60 per cent said they had 'fully recovered' from the offence, that it was 'all behind' them. Their recovery was more likely when offenders completed the agreement than when they did not, but recovery was influenced by a mixture of elements: the conference process, support from family and friends, the passage of time and personal resources such as their own resilience. The SAJJ project finds that conferences *can* have positive effects on reducing victims' anger towards and fear of offenders. Drawing from the victim interviews in 1998 and 1999, over 75 per cent of victims felt angry towards the offender before the conference, but this dropped to 44 per cent after the conference and was 39 per cent a year later. Close to 40 per cent of victims were frightened of the offender before the conference, but this dropped to 25 per cent after the conference and was 18 per cent a year later. Therefore, for victims, meeting offenders in the conference setting can have beneficial results.

The conference effect everyone asks about is, does it reduce reoffending? Proof (or disproof) of reductions in reoffending from conferences (compared *not only to court*, but to other interventions such as formal caution, other diversion approaches or no legal action at all) will not be available for a long time, if ever. The honest answer to the reoffending question is 'we'll probably never know' because the amounts of money would be exorbitant and research methods using experimental designs judged too risky in an ethical and political sense.

To date, there have been three studies of conferencing and reoffending in Australia and New Zealand, one of which compares reoffending for a sample of offenders randomly assigned to conference and court and two that explore whether reoffending can be linked to things that occur in conferences.[9] The RISE project finds that for one of four major offence categories studied (violent offences compared to drink-driving, property offences, shoplifting), those offenders who were assigned to a conference had a significantly reduced rate of reoffending than those who were assigned to court (Sherman *et al.*, 2000).

As others have said (Abel, 1982: 278; Levrant *et al.*, 1999: 17–22), there is a great faith placed on the conference process to change young offenders, when the conditions of their day-to-day lives, which may be conducive to getting into trouble, may not change at all. The SAJJ project asked if there were things that occurred in conferences that could predict reoffending, over and above those variables known to be conducive to lawbreaking (and its detection): past offending and social marginality (Hayes and Daly, 2001). In a regression analysis with a simultaneous inclusion of variables, we found that over and above the young person's race-ethnicity (Aboriginal or non-Aboriginal), sex, whether s/he offended prior to the offence that led to the SAJJ conference and a measure of the young person's mobility and marginality, there were two conference elements associated with reoffending. When young people were observed to be mostly or fully remorseful and when outcomes were achieved by genuine consensus, they were less likely to reoffend during an 8- to 12-month period after the conference. These results are remarkably similar to those of Maxwell and Morris (2000) in their study of reoffending in New Zealand. They found that what happens in conferences (e.g. a young person's expressions of remorse and agreeing [or not] with the outcome, among other variables) could distinguish those young people who were and were not 'persistently reconvicted' during a six-and-a-half-year follow-up period.

[. . .]

In the political arena, telling the mythical true story of restorative justice may be an effective means of reforming parts of the justice system. It may inspire legislatures to pass new laws and it may provide openings to experiment with alternative justice forms. All of this can be a good thing. Perhaps, in fact, the politics of selling justice ideas may *require* people to tell mythical true stories. The real story attends to the murk and constraints of justice organizations, of people's experiences as offenders and victims and their capacities and desires to 'repair the harm'. It reveals a picture that is less sharp-edged and more equivocal.

My reading of the evidence is that face-to-face encounters between victims and offenders and their supporters *is* a practice worth maintaining, and perhaps enlarging, although we should not expect it to deliver strong stories of repair and goodwill most of the time. If we want to avoid the cycle of optimism and pessimism (Matthews, 1988) that so often attaches to any justice innovation, then we should be courageous and tell the real story of restorative justice. But, in telling the real story, there is some risk that a promising, fledgling idea will meet a premature death.

Notes

1   Even when calling for the need to 'blend restorative, reparative, and transformative justice . . . with the prosecution of paradigmatic violations of human rights', Drumbl (2000: 296) is unable to avoid using the term 'retributive' to refer to responses that should be reserved for the few.
2   Drawing from Cottingham's (1979) analysis of retribution's many meanings, restorative justice advocates tend to use retributivism to mean 'repayment' (to which they add a punitive kick) whereas desert theorists, such as von Hirsch (1993), use retributivism to mean 'deserved' and would argue for decoupling retribution from punitiveness.
3   It is important to emphasize that new justice practices have not been applied to the fact-finding stage of the criminal process; they are used almost exclusively for the penalty phase. Some comparative claims about restorative justice practices (e.g. they are not adversarial when retributive justice is) are misleading in that restorative justice attends only to the penalty phase when negotiation is possible. No one has yet sketched a restorative justice process for those who do not admit to an offence.
4   I became aware of the term *new justice* from La Prairie's (1999) analysis of developments in Canada. She defines new justice initiatives as representing a 'shift away from a justice discourse of punitiveness and punishment toward one of reconciliation, healing, repair, atonement, and reintegration' (1999: 147), and she sees such developments as part of a new emphasis on 'community' and 'partnership' as analysed by Crawford (1997). There may be better terms than the 'old' and 'new justice' (e.g. Hudson, 2001, suggests 'established criminal justice' for the old justice), but my general point is that the retributive/restorative couplet has produced, and continues to produce, significant conceptual confusion in the field.
5   Restorative justice advocates speak of the *harm* not of the *crime*, and in doing so, they elide a crucial distinction between a civil and criminal harm, the latter involving both a *harm* and a *wrong* (Duff, 2001).
6   In response to this point, one reader said there had to be some way to theorize varied justice forms (both in an empirical and normative sense), and thus, the disappointment I speak of reflects a disenchantment with the theoretical enterprise adequately to reflect particularity and variation in the empirical social world. This is a long-standing problem in the sociological field. What troubles me, however, is the construction of theoretical terms in the justice field, which use dualisms in adversarial and oppositional relation to one another.
7   The major research studies in the region are Maxwell and Morris (1993) for New Zealand, Strang *et al.* (1999) for the ACT and the RISE project and the results reported here for the SAJJ project in South Australia. See Daly (2001) for a review of these and other studies. Space limitations preclude a detailed review of the methods and results of each study.
8   It is important to distinguish jurisdictions like South Australia, New South Wales and New Zealand, where conferences are routinely used, from other jurisdictions (like Victoria and Queensland), where conferences are used selectively and in a relatively few number of cases (although Queensland practices are undergoing change as of April 2001). When conferences are used routinely, we should not expect to see 'restorativeness' emerging most of the time.
9   Space limitations preclude a review of the definitions and methods used in the reoffending studies; rather general findings are summarized.

References

Abel, R.L. (1982) 'The Contradictions of Informal Justice', in Abel, R.L. (ed.) *The Politics of Informal Justice. Vol. 1* (New York, NY: Academic Press), pp. 267–320.

Barton, C. (2000) 'Empowerment and Retribution in Criminal Justice', in Strang, H. and Braithwaite, J. (eds) *Restorative Justice: Philosophy to Practice* (Aldershot: Ashgate/ Dartmouth), pp. 55–76.

Blagg, H. (1997) 'A Just Measure of Shame? Aboriginal Youth and Conferencing in Australia', *British Journal of Criminology*, 37:4, pp. 481–501.

Blagg, H. (1998) 'Restorative Visions and Restorative Justice Practices: Conferencing, Ceremony and Reconciliation in Australia', *Current Issues in Criminal Justice*, 10:1, pp. 5–14.

Bottoms, A.E. (1998) 'Five Puzzles in von Hirsch's Theory of Punishment', in Ashworth, A. and Wasik, M. (eds) *Fundamentals of Sentencing Theory: Essays in Honour of Andrew von Hirsch* (Oxford: Clarendon Press), pp. 53–100.

Braithwaite, J. (1996) 'Restorative Justice and a Better Future', Dorothy J. Killam Memorial Lecture, reprinted in *Dalhousie Review*, 76:1, pp. 9–32.

Braithwaite, J. (1999) 'Restorative Justice: Assessing Optimistic and Pessimistic Accounts', in Tonry, M. (ed.) *Crime and Justice: A Review of Research. Vol. 25* (Chicago, IL: University of Chicago Press), pp. 1–127.

Braithwaite, J. and Pettit, P. (1990) *Not Just Deserts: A Republican Theory of Criminal Justice* (New York, NY: Oxford University Press).

Cain, M. (2000) 'Orientalism, Occidentalism and the Sociology of Crime', *British Journal of Criminology*, 40:2, pp. 239–60.

Consedine, J. (1995) *Restorative Justice: Healing the Effects of Crime* (Lyttelton, New Zealand: Ploughshares Publications).

Coombs, M. (1995) 'Putting Women First', *Michigan Law Review*, 93:6, pp. 1686–712.

Cottingham, J. (1979) 'Varieties of Retribution', *Philosophical Quarterly*, 29, pp. 238–46.

Crawford, A. (1997) *The Local Governance of Crime: Appeals to Community and Partnerships* (Oxford: Clarendon Press).

Daly, K. (1989) 'Criminal Justice Ideologies and Practices in Different Voices: Some Feminist Questions about Justice', *International Journal of the Sociology of Law*, 17:1, pp. 1–18.

Daly, K. (1998) 'Restorative Justice: Moving past the caricatures', paper presented to Seminar on Restorative Justice, Institute of Criminology, University of Sydney Law School, Sydney, April. Available at: http://www.gv.edu.au/school/ccj/kdaly.html.

Daly, K. (2000a) 'Revisiting the Relationship Between Retributive and Restorative Justice', in Strang, H. and Braithwaite, J. (eds) *Restorative Justice: Philosophy to Practice* (Aldershot: Ashgate/Dartmouth), pp. 33–54.

Daly, K. (2000b) 'Sexual Assault and Restorative Justice.' Paper presented to Restorative Justice and Family Violence Conference, Australian National University, Canberra, July (available at: http://www.gu.edu.au/school/ccj/kdaly.html).

Daly, K. (2001) 'Conferencing in Australia and New Zealand: Variations, Research Findings and Prospects', in Morris, A. and Maxwell, G. (eds) *Restorative Justice for Juveniles: Conferencing, Mediation and Circles* (Oxford: Hart Publishing), pp. 59–84 (available at: http://www.gu.edu.au/school/ccj/kdaly.html).

Daly, K. and Immarigeon, R. (1998) 'The Past, Present, and Future of Restorative Justice: Some Critical Reflections', *Contemporary Justice Review*, 1:1, pp. 21–45.

Davis, G. (1992) *Making Amends: Mediation and Reparation in Criminal Justice* (London: Routledge).

Drumbl, M.A. (2000) 'Retributive Justice and the Rwandan Genocide', *Punishment and Society*, 2:3, pp. 287–308.

Duff, R.A. (1992) 'Alternatives to Punishment – or Alternative Punishments?' in Cragg, W. (ed.) *Retributivism and its Critics* (Stuttgart: Franz Steiner), pp. 44–68.

Duff, R.A. (1996) 'Penal Communications: Recent Work in the Philosophy of Punishment', in Tonry, M. (ed.) *Crime and Justice: A Review of Research. Vol. 20* (Chicago, IL: University of Chicago Press), pp. 1–97.

Duff, R.A. (2001) 'Restoration and Retribution.' Paper presented to the Cambridge Seminar on Restorative Justice, Toronto, May.

Feeley, M. and Simon, J. (1992) 'The New Penology: Notes on the Emerging Strategy of Corrections and its Implications', *Criminology*, 30:4, pp. 449–74.

Findlay, M. (2000) 'Decolonising Restoration and Justice in Transitional Cultures', in Strang, H. and Braithwaite, J. (eds) *Restorative Justice: Philosophy to Practice* (Aldershot: Ashgate/Dartmouth), pp. 185–201.

Garland, D. (1996) 'The Limits of the Sovereign State', *British Journal of Criminology*, 36:4, pp. 445–71.

Gilligan, C. (1982) *In a Different Voice* (Cambridge, MA: Harvard University Press).

Gilligan, C. (1987) 'Moral Orientation and Moral Development', in Kittay, E. and Meyers, D. (eds) *Women and Moral Theory* (Totowa, NJ: Rowman & Littlefield), pp. 19–33.

Hampton, J. (1992) 'Correcting Harms versus Righting Wrongs: The Goal of Retribution', *UCLA Law Review*, 39, pp. 1659–702.

Hampton, J. (1998) 'Punishment, Feminism, and Political Identity: A Case Study in the Expressive Meaning of the Law', *Canadian Journal of Law and Jurisprudence*, 11:1, pp. 23–45.

Harris, M.K. (1987) 'Moving into the New Millennium: Toward a Feminist Vision of Justice', *The Prison Journal*, 67:2, pp. 27–38.

Hayes, H. and Daly, K. (2001) 'Family Conferencing in South Australia and Re-offending: Preliminary Results from the SAJJ Project.' Paper presented to the Australian and New Zealand Society of Criminology Conference, Melbourne, February (available at: http://www.gu.edu.au/school/ccj/kdaly.html).

Heidensohn, F. (1986) 'Models of Justice: Portia or Persephone? Some Thoughts on Equality, Fairness and Gender in the Field of Criminal Justice', *International Journal of the Sociology of Law*, 14:3–4, pp. 287–98.

Hudson, B. (2001) 'Victims and Offenders.' Paper presented to the Cambridge Seminar on Restorative Justice, Toronto, May.

Kurki, L. (2001) 'Evaluation of Restorative Justice Practices.' Paper presented to the Cambridge Seminar on Restorative Justice, Toronto, May.

La Prairie, C. (1999) 'Some Reflections on New Criminal Justice Policies in Canada: Restorative Justice, Alternative Measures and Conditional Sentences', *Australian and New Zealand Journal of Criminology*, 32:2, pp. 139–52.

Levrant, S., Cullen, F.T., Fulton, B. and Wozniak, J.F. (1999) 'Reconsidering Restorative Justice: The Corruption of Benevolence Revisited?', *Crime and Delinquency*, 45:1, pp. 3–27.

McCold, P. (2000) 'Toward a Holistic Vision of Restorative Juvenile Justice: A Reply to the Maximalist Model', *Contemporary Justice Review*, 3:4, pp. 357–414.

MacKinnon, C. (1987) *Feminism Unmodified* (Cambridge, MA: Harvard University Press).

Masters, G. and Smith, D. (1998) 'Portia and Persephone Revisited: Thinking about Feeling in Criminal Justice', *Theoretical Criminology*, 2:1, pp. 5–27.

Matthews, R. (1988) 'Reassessing Informal Justice', in Matthews, R. (ed.) *Informal Justice?* (Newbury Park, CA: Sage), pp. 1–24.

Maxwell, G. and Morris, A. (1993) *Family Victims and Culture: Youth Justice in New Zealand* (Wellington: Social Policy Agency and the Institute of Criminology, Victoria University of Wellington).

Maxwell, G. and Morris, A. (1996) 'Research on Family Group Conferences with Young Offenders in New Zealand', in Hudson, J. *et al.* (eds) *Family Group Conferences: Perspectives on Policy and Practice* (Monsey, NY: Willow Tree Press), pp. 88–110.

Maxwell, G. and Morris, A. (2000) 'Restorative Justice and Reoffending', in Strang, H. and Braithwaite, J. (eds) *Restorative Justice: Philosophy to Practice* (Aldershot: Ashgate/Dartmouth), pp. 93–103.

Mead, G.H. (1917–18) 'The Psychology of Punitive Justice', *American Journal of Sociology*, 23, pp. 577–602.

Melossi, D. (ed.) (1998) *The Sociology of Punishment: Socio-structural Perspectives* (Aldershot: Ashgate/Dartmouth).

Miller, S. and Blackler, J. (2000) 'Restorative Justice: Retribution, Confession and Shame', in Strang, H. and Braithwaite, J. (eds) *Restorative Justice: Philosophy to Practice* (Aldershot: Ashgate/Dartmouth), pp. 77–91.

O'Malley, P. (1999) 'Volatile and Contradictory Punishment', *Theoretical Criminology*, 3:2, pp. 175–96.

Pavlich, G.C. (1996) *Justice Fragmented: Mediating Community Disputes under Postmodern Conditions* (New York, NY: Routledge).

Pratt, J. (2000) 'The Return of the Wheelbarrow Men or, The Arrival of Postmodern Penality?', *British Journal of Criminology*, 40:1, pp. 127–45.

Shearing, C. (2001) 'Punishment and the Changing Face of the Governance', *Punishment and Society*, 3:2, pp. 203–20.

Sherman, L.W., Strang, H. and Woods, D.J. (2000) *Recidivism Patterns in the Canberra Reintegrative Shaming Experiments (RISE)* (Canberra: Centre for Restorative Justice, Australian National University) (available at: http://www.aic.gov.au/rjustice/rise/ recidivism/index.html).

Smart, C. (1989) *Feminism and the Power of Law* (London: Routledge).

Smart, C. (1992) 'The Women of Legal Discourse', *Social and Legal Studies*, 1:1, pp. 29–44.

Strang, H., Sherman, L.W., Barnes, G.C. and Braithwaite, J. (1999) *Experiments in Restorative Policing: A Progress Report to the National Police Research Unit on the Canberra Reintegrative Shaming Experiments (RISE)* (Canberra: Centre for Restorative Justice, Australian National University) (available at: http://www.aic.gov.au/rjustice/rise/index.html).

Tonry, M. (1999) 'Rethinking Unthinkable Punishment Policies in America', *UCLA Law Review*, 46:4, pp. 1751–91.

Tyler, T.R. (1990) *Why People Obey the Law* (New Haven, CT: Yale University Press).

Tyler, T.R., Boeckmann, R.J., Smith, H.J. and Huo, Y.J. (1997) *Social Justice in a Diverse Society* (Boulder, CO: Westview Press).

Umbreit, M. (1994) *Victim Meets Offender: The Impact of Restorative Justice and Mediation* (Monsey, NY: Criminal Justice Press).

Van Ness, D. (1993) 'New Wine and Old Wineskins: Four Challenges of Restorative Justice', *Criminal Law Forum*, 4:2, pp. 251–76.

Von Hirsch, A. (1993) *Censure and Sanctions* (New York, NY: Oxford University Press).

Walgrave, L. (1995) 'Restorative Justice for Juveniles: Just a Technique or a Fully Fledged Alternative?', *The Howard Journal*, 34:3, pp. 228–49.

Walgrave, L. and Aertsen, I. (1996) 'Reintegrative Shaming and Restorative Justice: Interchangeable, Complementary or Different?' *European Journal on Criminal Policy and Research*, 4:4, pp. 67–85.

Weitekamp, E. (1999) 'The History of Restorative Justice', in Bazemore, G. and Walgrave, L. (eds) *Restorative Juvenile Justice: Repairing the Harm of Youth Crime* (Monsey, NY: Criminal Justice Press), pp. 75–102.

Wright, M. (1991) *Justice for Victims and Offenders* (Philadelphia, PA: Open University Press).

Zedner, L. (1994) 'Reparation and Retribution: Are they Reconcilable?', *Modern Law Review*, 57:March, pp. 228–50.

28 Responsibilities, rights and restorative justice

Andrew Ashworth

[. . .]

Rights and responsibilities of the victim

It is common for those writing on restorative justice to insist that all parties 'with a stake in the offence' ought to be able to participate in the disposition of the case, through a circle, conference, etc. (e.g. Llewellyn and Howse, 1998: 19). The victim certainly has 'a stake', and Christie's (1977) assertion that the 'conflict' in some sense 'belongs' to the victim has become a modern orthodoxy among restorative justice supporters (e.g. Morris and Maxwell, 2000: 207, who write of 'returning the offence to those most affected by it and encouraging them to determine appropriate responses to it'). The approach has ancient roots (Braithwaite, 1999: 1–2 for a summary and references), although the growing awareness of the existence of secondary victimization (e.g. Morgan and Zedner, 1992 on child victims) demonstrates the complexity of the issues arising.

The politico-historical argument is that most modern legal systems exclude the victim so as to bolster their own power. Originally the state wanted to take over criminal proceedings from victims as an assertion of power, and what now passes for 'normal' is simply a usurpation that has no claim to be the natural order. My concern is not to dispute this rather romantic interpretation of criminal justice in early history (Daly, 2000 does this splendidly; also Johnstone, 2001: ch. 3) but rather to raise three points of principle which have a bearing on the nature and extent of victims' rights: the principle of compensation for wrongs, the principle of proportionality, and the principle of independence and impartiality.

The first point of principle is the most direct of all in its target. What I want to argue is that the victim's legitimate interest is in compensation and/or reparation from the offender, and not in the form or quantum of the offender's punishment. The distinction between punishment and compensation is not widely appreciated: when a court fines an offender £300 for careless driving in a case where death resulted (but where there was no conviction for the more serious offence of causing death by dangerous driving), newspapers will often report comments such as 'my son's life has been valued at just £300'. However, the size of the fine will usually be related to the offender's culpability (and financial resources), and will not be a 'valuation' of the loss. Compensation for loss, from whatever source, is a separate matter. It may not require a separate civil case: English criminal courts are required to consider ordering the offender to pay compensation to the victim or victim's family, so far as the offender's means allow. However, in many cases the offender will not have the funds to pay realistic compensation. It is now recognized as part of the state's responsibility for criminal justice that it should provide a compensation fund for victims of crimes of violence, at least (see Ashworth, 1986 and, on the current scheme, Miers, 1997). This is not to deny that victims primarily have a right to compensation from the offender: that is clear on legal and moral grounds, if not always practical.

The key question is whether the victim's legitimate interest goes beyond reparation or compensation (and the right to victim services and support, and to proper protection from further harm), and extends to the question of punishment. It would be wrong to suggest that the victim has no legitimate interest in the disposition of the offender in his or her case, but the victim's interest is surely no greater than yours or mine. The victim's interest is as a citizen, as one of many citizens who make up the community or state. In democratic theory all citizens have a right to vote at elections and sometimes on other occasions, and to petition their elected representatives about issues affecting them. If I am an ardent advocate of restorative justice or of indeterminate imprisonment for repeat offenders, I can petition my MP about it, or join a pressure group. Just because a person commits an offence against me, however, that does not privilege my voice above that of the court (acting 'in the general public interest') in the matter of the offender's punishment. A justification for this lies in social contract reasoning, along the lines that the state may be said to undertake the duty of administering justice and protecting citizens in return for citizens giving up their right to self-help (except in cases of urgency) in the cause of better social order. This returns to the earlier argument about the state's responsibility, and to the 'rule of law' values of impartiality, independence and consistency in the administration of criminal justice.

This principle is not opposed by all those who advocate a version of restorative justice. Thus Michael Cavadino and James Dignan (1997) draw a strong distinction between the victim's right to reparation and the public interest in responding to the offence. In their view it is right to empower victims to participate in the process which determines what reparation is to be made by the offender, and reparation to the victim should be the major element of the response. In serious cases some additional response (punishment) may be considered necessary, and they then insist on a form of limiting retributivism in which proportionality sets upper and lower boundaries for the burdens placed on offenders (and also serves as a default setting for cases where a conference or circle proves impossible or inappropriate). It is a matter for regret that few restorative justice theorists refer to Cavadino and Dignan's attempt to preserve as many of the values of restorative justice as possible whilst insisting upon principled limits. They rightly see the distinction between compensation and punishment as crucial, even though their proportionality constraints are looser than many desert theorists would require, and they regard victim involvement as a value to be enhanced where possible. 'Victim personal statements' must now be taken into account by English courts before sentencing: Edna Erez claims that 'providing victims with a voice has therapeutic advantages' (1999: 555; cf. Edwards, 2001), but findings from the English pilot projects indicated no great psychological benefits to participant victims and some evidence of disillusionment (Sanders *et al.*, 2001: 450).

The second point of principle concerns proportionality. Sentencing is *for* an offence, and respect for the offender as a citizen capable of choice suggests that the sentence should bear a relationship to the seriousness of the offence committed. To desert theorists this is axiomatic: punishment should always be proportionate to the offence, taking account of harm and culpability (von Hirsch, 1993: ch. 2), unless a highly persuasive argument for creating a class of exceptional cases can be sustained. It is a strong criticism of deterrent sentencing and of risk theory that they accord priority to predictions and not to the seriousness of the offence committed: von Hirsch and Ashworth (1998: chs 2, 3). The proportionality principle is not the sole preserve of desert theorists: on the contrary, versions of it are widely accepted as limiting the quantum of punishment that may be imposed on offenders, whether as a major tenet of the Council of Europe's recommendation on sentencing (1993: para. A4) or as an element in Nicola Lacey's communitarian approach to punishment (Lacey, 1988: 194). Other important functions of the proportionality principle are that it should ensure consistency of treatment among offenders, and that it should give protection against discrimination, by attempting to rule out certain factors from sentencing calculations. It is not being suggested that existing sentencing systems always pursue these principles successfully, but it is vital that they be recognized as goals and efforts made to fulfil them.

The principle of proportionality goes against victim involvement in sentencing decisions because the views of victims may vary. Some victims will be forgiving, others will be vindictive; some will be interested in new forms of sentence, others will not; some shops will have one policy in relation to thieves, others may have a different policy. If victim satisfaction is one of the aims of circles and conferences, then proportionate sentencing cannot be assured and may be overtaken in some cases by deterrent or risk-based sentencing. Two replies may be anticipated. First, it may be argued that in fact the involvement of victims assures *greater* proportionality (Erez and Rogers, 1999; Erez, 1999; cf. Sanders *et al.*, 2001: 451): the actual harm to the victim becomes clear, and in general victims do not desire disproportionate sentences. But these are aggregative findings, whereas the point of the principle is to ensure that in no individual case is an offender liable to a disproportionate penalty. A second reply would be to concede that victim involvement should be subject to proportionality limits, so that no agreement reached in a circle or conference should be out of proportion to the seriousness of the offence. The significance of this concession depends on the nature of the proportionality constraint. There is a range of possible proportionality theories: desert theory requires the sentence to be proportionate to the seriousness of the offence, within fairly narrow bands (von Hirsch, 1993: chs 2 and 4), whereas various forms of limiting retributivism recognize looser boundaries. Michael Tonry, for example, argues against the 'strong proportionality' of desert theorists and in favour of 'upper limits' set in accordance with a less precise notion of proportionality (Tonry, 1994). Among restorative justice theorists, Braithwaite refers to 'guaranteeing offenders against punishment beyond a maximum' (1999: 105), but it is unclear whether his 'guarantee' adopts as much of proportionality theory as Tonry seems prepared to accept, and whether it imposes similar constraints or even less demanding ones. Most restorative justice theorists would insist that one of their objectives is to reduce levels of punitiveness, not to increase them; but some questions will be raised below about the contours of the 'background' penal system which is envisaged for cases where restorative justice processes fail or are rejected.

The third point is that everyone should have the right to a fair hearing 'by an independent and impartial tribunal', as Article 6.1 of the European Convention on Human Rights declares. This right expresses a fundamental principle of justice. Under the European Convention it applies to the sentencing stage as much as to trials. Do conferences and other restorative processes respect the right? Insofar as a victim plays a part in determining the disposition of a criminal case, is a conference 'independent and impartial'? The victim cannot be expected to be impartial, nor can the victim be expected to know about the available range of orders and other principles for the disposition of criminal cases. All of this suggests that conferences may fail to meet the basic standards of a fair hearing, insofar as the victim or victim's family plays a part in determining the outcome.

Most restorative justice supporters will be unimpressed with this, because the argument simply assumes that what has become conventional in modern criminal justice systems is absolutely right. But the issue of principle must be confronted, since it is supported by the European Convention, the International Covenant on Civil and Political Rights and many other human rights documents. One reply from restorative justice supporters might be that the required 'impartiality' and 'objectivity' produce such an impersonal and detached tribunal as to demonstrate exactly what is wrong with conventional systems, and why they fail. But that reply neglects, or certainly undervalues, the link between independence, impartiality and procedural justice. Might it be possible to sidestep the objection by characterizing conferences and other restorative justice processes as alternatives to sentencing rather than as sentencing processes, and therefore not bound by the same principles? This might be thought apposite where any agreement reached in the conference or circle has to be submitted for approval by a court, and where the offender may withdraw from the conference and go to the court at any time.

This is an appropriate point at which to question the reality of the consent that is said to underlie restorative justice processes and outcomes. The general principle is that 'restorative processes should be used only with the free and voluntary consent of the parties. The parties should be able to withdraw that consent at any time during the process' (UN, 2000: para. 7). This suggests that the offender may simply walk out and take his or her chances in the 'conventional' system. However, the result of doing so would usually be to propel the case into a formal criminal justice system that is perceived to be harsher in general, or that the offender may expect to be harsher on someone who has walked away from a restorative justice process. On some occasions, then, as in plea-bargaining (Sanders and Young, 2000: ch. 7; Ashworth, 1998: ch. 9), the 'consent' may proceed from a small amount of free will and a large slice of (perceived) coercion. Where the 'consent' is that of young people, and it is the police who explain matters to them, the danger of perceived coercion may be acute (Daly, 2001). The United Nations draft principles attempt to deal with some of these issues, by providing that failure to reach agreement or failure to implement an agreement 'may not be used as a justification for a more severe sentence in subsequent criminal justice proceedings' (UN, 2000: paras. 15, 16). But it is right to remain sceptical of the reality of consent, from the offender's point of view.

Returning to the right to an independent and impartial tribunal, is it breached if the victim makes a statement about sentencing, written or oral, to the court or other body that is to take the sentencing decision? This refers to statements that go beyond a victim impact statement, and are not limited to the issue of compensation. The ruling of the European Commission on Human Rights in *McCourt* v. *United Kingdom* (1993) 15 EHRR CD110 may be taken to suggest that such a statement on sentence could prejudice the impartiality of the tribunal, but this might be thought to go too far, not least because defendants have the right to make a 'plea in mitigation', in which their lawyers usually argue against certain outcomes and (sometimes) for a certain sentence. A stronger argument here is to return to the principles of compensation and of proportionality, discussed above, and to assert that the victim's view as to sentence should not be received because it is not relevant. Consider the case of *Nunn*, where the defendant had been sentenced to four years' imprisonment for causing the death of a close friend by dangerous driving. When Nunn's appeal against the sentence came before the Court of Appeal, the court had before it some lengthy written statements by the victim's mother and sister, recognizing that some punishment had to follow such a terrible offence, but stating that their own grief was being increased by the thought of the victim's close friend being in prison for so long. They added that the victim's father and other sister took a different view. In the Court of Appeal, Lord Justice Judge said this:

> We mean no disrespect to the mother and sister of the deceased, but the opinions of the victim, or the surviving members of the family, about the appropriate level of sentence do not provide any sound basis for reassessing a sentence. If the victim feels utterly merciful towards the criminal, and some do, the crime has still been committed and must be punished as it deserves. If the victim is obsessed with vengeance, which can in reality only be assuaged by a very long sentence, as also happens, the punishment cannot be made longer by the court than would otherwise be appropriate. Otherwise cases with identical features would be dealt with in widely differing ways, leading to improper and unfair disparity, and even in this particular case . . . the views of the members of the family of the deceased are not absolutely identical. (*Nunn* [1996] 2 Cr. App. R. (S) 136, at p. 140; see also *Roche* [1999] 2 Cr. App. R. (S) 105)

This statement captures the principles well.[1] Neither one victim's forgiveness of an offender, nor another's desire for vengeance against an offender, should be relevant when the community's response to an offence (as distinct from compensation) is being considered. The plea in *Nunn* was for leniency in the outcome, as also in the New Zealand case of *Clotworthy* (see Braithwaite, 1999: 87–8). There are other cases where victims and their families campaign for severity, some with a very high profile (e.g. the case of Thompson and Venables, convicted at the age of 11 of the murder of James Bulger, whose family campaigned, with considerable support from the mass media, in favour of prolonging the imprisonment of the offenders). In dismissing an application by James Bulger's father for judicial review of the tariff set by the Lord Chief Justice, the Queen's Bench Divisional Court noted with approval that Lord Woolf had invited the Bulger family to make representations about the impact of their son's death on them, 'but had not invited them to give their views on what they thought was an appropriate tariff' (*R v. Secretary of State for the Home Department, ex parte Bulger, The Times*, 16 February 2001).

The above discussion of the three principles of compensation for wrongs, of independent and impartial tribunals, and of proportionality of sentence, suggests that the substantive and procedural rights of victims at the stage of disposal (sentence) ought to be limited. This should apply whether the rights of victims are being considered in the context of restorative justice or of a 'conventional' sentencing system. The rights of victims should chiefly be to receive support, proper services, and (where the offender is unable to pay) state compensation for violent crimes. There are arguments for going further, so as to achieve some measure of victim participation: this would require the provision of better and fuller information to victims, and the objective would be to enable some genuine participation in the process of disposal 'without giving [victims] the power to influence decisions that are not appropriately theirs' (Sanders *et al.*, 2001: 458). This would be a fine line to tread, as the debate following the decision of the US Supreme Court to allow victim impact statements in capital cases demonstrates: *Payne v. Tennessee* (1991) 111 S Ct 2597, discussed by Sarat, 1997.

Exploring the 'default setting': when restorative justice runs out

Although some restorative justice practitioners and writers express themselves as if there are no aspects of criminal justice with which restorative justice could not deal, most are realistic enough to recognize that provision must be made for some cases to be handled outside restorative justice processes. We have noted that Cavadino and Dignan provide for a 'default system' to deal with cases in which a circle or conference does not prove possible, perhaps because the necessary consents are not forthcoming. Certain writers make much stronger claims for the ability of restorative justice to handle a wide range of disputes in criminal justice, schools, industry, and business regulation (e.g. Wachtel and McCold, 2001). But even some of those recognize that there must be some form of 'background system' in place (Braithwaite, 1999). If one adds together the groups of offenders for whom such a system may be needed – those who refuse to participate in restorative justice, or whose victims refuse to participate,[2] or who have failed to comply with previous restorative justice outcomes – the numbers might be considerable. It has been argued above that some restorative justice processes themselves are incompatible with principles of justice on independence, impartiality, proportionality, and so on. How does the 'default' or 'background' system measure up to these principles?

Braithwaite explains his background system by reference to this enforcement pyramid, developed in relation to regulatory enforcement (1999: 61) [Figure 28.1]. The idea is that one starts with restorative justice at the base of the pyramid. It may be tried more than once. If it clearly fails, then one would move to an 'active deterrence' strategy, which Braithwaite distinguishes carefully from the 'passive deterrence' described in most of the punishment literature (see Ayres and Braithwaite, 1992: ch. 2). To have this kind of deterrence in the background helps restorative justice to work, in Braithwaite's view. Nonetheless, he warns that:

> The problem is that if deterrent threats cause defiance and reactance, restorative justice may be compromised by what sits above it in a dynamic pyramidal strategy of deterrence and incapacitation . . . The challenge is to have the Sword of Damocles always threatening in the background but never threatened in the foreground.
>
> (Braithwaite, 1999: 63–4)

From the point of view of principle, this approach is troubling. It seems that, once we leave the softly, softly world of restorative justice, offenders may be delivered into raging deterrent and incapacitative strategies, with rogue elements like Uncle Harry calling the shots

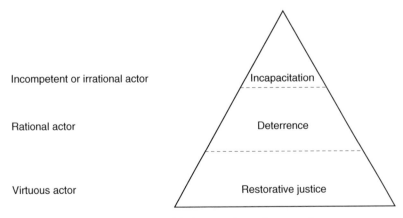

Figure 28.1 Braithwaite's 'pyramid of restorative enforcement'.

(see the remarkable paragraphs in Braithwaite, 1999: 66–7, on Uncle Harry), and with only the vaguest of gestures towards 'guaranteeing offenders against punishment beyond a maximum' (*ibid*: 105). When Philip Pettit and John Braithwaite state that, in pursuit of the goal of 'community reassurance', sentencers should take account of 'how common that offence has become in the community' and 'how far the offender is capable of re-offending again' (1993, excerpted in von Hirsch and Ashworth, 1998: 326), the glass becomes very dark, and the excesses of the 'risk society' seem to beckon.

Braithwaite and Pettit (1990: ch. 7) would answer that current maximum penalties should provide the guarantee in the first instance, and that there should then be a 'decremental strategy' of lowering those maxima progressively so as to reduce levels of punitiveness. But statutory maximum sentences are often very high, and certainly much higher than most proportionality theorists (including Tonry's looser approach to limits) would accept. It is also countered that desert-based critics are not paying attention to the difference between the usual run of consequentialist theories based on ('passive') deterrence and incapacitation, and the meaning of those strategies within a 'republican' framework which respects the dominion of each individual (Braithwaite and Pettit, 1990). We should not find these aspects of Braithwaite's restorative justice theory threatening, it is contended, if we looked at the practical meaning of the pyramid of enforcement and took account of the emphasis on penal parsimony in a republican system. But it is not enough to proclaim penal parsimony and yet to give such prominence, even in a 'background system', to deterrent and incapacitative strategies. What types of deterrent strategy are permissible, within what kinds of limits? What forms of incapacitation? To what extent does the background system permit, nay encourage, sentencing on the basis of previous record rather than present offence? The answers to these questions about restorative justice and recalcitrant offenders remain unclear (see von Hirsch and Ashworth, 1998: 317–35), but the need for firm safeguards against undue severity does not disappear if a system is labelled 'restorative'. Penal history yields plenty of examples of apparently benign policies resulting in repressive controls.

Conclusions

It has been argued that, despite the decline of statism and the rise of neo-liberal and 'advanced liberal' programmes for the responsibilization of other agencies of security, it should still be acknowledged to be a fundamental role of the state to maintain a system for the administration of justice and to ensure that proper standards of procedural protection are applied. It is recognized that there have been and are failures of state-led criminal justice, just as there have been and are manifest failures of states to deliver security (Garland, 2001: ch. 5). The growth of restorative justice schemes is encouraged by both these phenomena. However, it should remain the responsibility of the state towards its citizens to ensure that justice is administered by independent and impartial tribunals, and that there are proportionality limits which should not only constrain the measures agreed at restorative justice conferences etc. but also ensure some similarity in the treatment of equally situated offenders. If the state does delegate certain spheres of criminal justice to some form of community-based conference, the importance of insisting on the protection of basic rights for defendants is not diminished.

Many of the innovations urged by restorative justice advocates ought to be tested and evaluated – the effect on victims and on offenders of face-to-face meetings, the value of apologies, the effect on victims and offenders of reparation agreements, the effect on victims and offenders of victim participation in conferences, and so forth. Too often, however, enthusiasm for such processes leads proponents either to overlook the need for safeguards, or to imply that they are not relevant. The steps being taken to develop standards for restorative justice processes are important in this respect (see UN, 2000; Braithwaite [2002]), but they must be accompanied by a re-examination of deeper issues. In order to ensure that there is no deficit of procedural justice or human rights, it was argued above that governments must retain a primary role, that community-based processes and outcomes should be scrutinized closely, and that the proper role of the victim in criminal justice processes should be reappraised. Thus any restorative justice processes for offenders who might otherwise go to court should (a) be led by an independent and impartial person;[3] (b) be required to submit its decisions for court approval; (c) allow the participation of the victim, the offender, and their families or significant others; (d) make provision for access to legal advice before and after any restorative justice processes, at a minimum (Council of Europe, 2000, para. 8; cf. UN, 2000: para. 12); (e) focus on apology and on the appropriate reparation and/or compensation for the offence; and (f) be required to respect relevant principles, such as not imposing on the offender a financial burden that is not means-related. If, contrary to the argument here, a restorative justice conference is permitted to make proposals for community restoration or other responses going beyond reparation to the individual victim(s), there should be clear and circumscribed proportionality limits for those measures. However, the practical implications of 'restoration of the community' call for closer examination than they have hitherto received.

Criticisms of this kind seem to leave many restorative justice practitioners baffled, however. They may protest that restorative justice processes are not about punishment anyway; that all the safeguards are about offenders, not victims; and that in practice restorative justice encounters no problems about undue severity, etc. On the first point, Kathleen Daly (2000) rightly calls for caution among those restorative justice advocates who claim not to be in the punishment business but to be engaged in constructive and non-punitive responses to wrongdoing. Even if one were to adopt a narrow definition (that only measures intended to be punitive count as punishment), many restorative justice outcomes satisfy that definition inasmuch as they are known to impose obligations or deprivations on offenders: Johnstone, 2001: 106–10; cf. Walgrave, 2001. The argument that such obligations or deprivations proceed from full consent is, as we have seen, unconvincing. So far as the bias of rights towards offenders is concerned, it must be conceded that most human rights documents do not incorporate victims' rights into their framework – although there are well-known (separate) declarations of victims' rights. This imbalance ought to be rectified, but only after focusing on the arguments presented above. The third point (the absence of severity) may be generally true, since most of those interested in promoting restorative justice seem to oppose penal severity; but attention was drawn above to Braithwaite's 'background system', and even within restorative justice clear limits are important to prevent violations of rights behind a mask of benevolence. Once it is conceded that restorative justice cannot deal with absolutely all criminal cases, the relationship between the formal system and any restorative justice processes must be carefully crafted so as to avoid inequities. This third point is particularly important where enthusiasm for restorative justice leads a government to 'parachute' elements of restorative justice into a system suffused with rather different principles and practices, as has been done with youth justice in England and Wales (Morris and Gelsthorpe, 2000; Ball, 2000).

Notes

1 The *Nunn* case also points to the practical problem arising where two or more victims have different views on the proper response to the crime. A further complication would be where there is a disagreement between the victim and the community representatives over outcome (cf. Law Commission of Canada, 1999: 38), although this should be resolved on the basis that the victim's interest lies in reparation and compensation whereas the state's (or community's) interest lies in measures going beyond that.
2 Some RJ schemes are prepared to proceed with a conference in the absence of the victim, which expands the role of the facilitator or coordinator: see, e.g. Daly (2001) on South Australia.
3 This raises the question of police-led conferences, used in England in certain types of case (Young, 2001). Braithwaite asks 'whether there is something wrong in principle with the police facilitating a conference. Does it make the police investigator, prosecutor, judge and jury?' (1999: 99). He never answers the question of principle, and instead points out the need to have someone assume the role of facilitator, and suggests that police involvement might have beneficial effects on police culture. But the question of principle must surely be answered by stating that this is wrong. It is not appropriate for the police to take on what is a quasi-judicial role, when they are so heavily involved in investigations. More strongly, it is inappropriate for the police to be involved in any 'shaming' of offenders (cf. Cunneen, 1997 and Blagg, 1997 with Braithwaite, 1997). It is insufficient to reply that offenders who have misgivings can withdraw their consent: as stated above, the 'consent' in these situations may take a severely diluted form. This critique is, of course, no less applicable to the ongoing practice of police cautioning of adults.

References

Ashworth, A. (1986) 'Punishment and Compensation: State, Victim and Offender', *Oxford Journal of Legal Studies*, 6, pp. 86–122.

Ashworth, A. (1998) *The Criminal Process* (2nd edn) (Oxford: Oxford Univesity Press).

Ayres, I. and Braithwaite, J. (1992) *Responsive Regulation: Transcending the Deregulation Debate* (New York, NY: Oxford University Press).

Ball, C. (2000) 'The Youth Justice and Criminal Evidence Act 1999: A Significant Move towards Restorative Justice, or a Recipe for Unintended Consequences?', *Criminal Law Review*, pp. 211–22.

Blagg, H. (1997) 'A Just Measure of Shame? Aboriginal Youth and Conferencing in Australia', *British Journal of Criminology*, 37:4, pp. 481–501.

Braithwaite, J. (1997) 'Conferencing and Plurality: Reply to Blagg', *British Journal of Criminology*, 37:4, pp. 502–6.

Braithwaite, J. (1999) 'Restorative Justice: Assessing Optimistic and Pessimistic Accounts', *Crime and Justice: A Review of Research*, 25, pp. 1–110.

Braithwaite, J. (2002) 'Setting Standards for Restorative Justice', *British Journal of Criminology*, 42, pp. 563–77.

Braithwaite, J. and Pettit, P. (1990) *Not Just Deserts* (Oxford: Oxford University Press).

Cavadino, M. and Dignan, J. (1997) 'Reparation, Retribution and Rights', *International Review of Victimology*, 4, pp. 233–71.

Christie, N. (1977) 'Conflicts as Property', *British Journal of Criminology,* 17:1, pp. 1–15.

Council of Europe (1993) *Consistency in Sentencing* (Recommendation R (92) 18) (Strasbourg: Council of Europe).

Council of Europe (2000) *Mediation in Penal Matters* (Recommendation R (99) 19) (Strasbourg: Council of Europe).

Cunneen, C. (1997) 'Community Conferencing and the Fiction of Indigenous Control', *Australia and New Zealand Journal of Criminology,* 30, pp. 297–320.

Daly, K. (2000) 'Restorative Justice: The Real Story.' Unpublished paper presented to Scottish Criminology Conference (www.gu.edu.au/school/ccj/kdaly.html).

Daly, K. (2001) 'Conferencing in Australia and New Zealand: Variations, Research Findings and Prospects', in Morris, A. and Maxwell, G. (eds) *Restorative Justice for Juveniles: Conferencing, Mediation and Circles* (Oxford: Hart Publishing).

Edwards, I. (2001) 'Victim Participation in Sentencing: The Problems of Incoherence', *Howard Journal of Criminal Justice,* 40, pp. 39–54.

Erez, E. (1999) 'Who's Afraid of the Big Bad Victim? Victim Impact Statements as Empowerment and Enhancement of Justice', *Criminal Law Review,* pp. 545–56.

Erez, E. and Rogers, L. (1999) 'Victim Impact Statements and Sentencing Outcomes and Processes: The Perspectives of Legal Professionals', *British Journal of Criminology,* 39:2, pp. 216–39.

Garland, D. (2001) *The Culture of Control: Crime and Social Order in Contemporary Society* (Oxford: Oxford University Press).

Johnstone, G. (2001) *Restorative Justice* (Cullompton: Willan Publishing).

Lacey, N. (1988) *State Punishment* (London: Routledge).

Law Commission of Canada (1999) *From Restorative Justice to Transformative Justice* (discussion paper) (Ottawa: Law Commission).

Llewellyn, J.J. and Howse, R. (1998) *Restorative Justice: A Conceptual Framework* (Ottawa: Law Commission of Canada).

Miers, D. (1997) *State Compensation for Criminal Injuries* (London: Blackstone).

Morgan, J. and Zedner, L. (1992) *Child Victims* (Oxford: Oxford University Press).

Morris, A. and Gelsthorpe, L. (2000) 'Something Old, Something Borrowed, Something Blue, but Something New? Comment on the Prospects for Restorative Justice under the Crime and Disorder Act', *Criminal Law Review,* pp. 18–30.

Morris, A. and Maxwell, G. (2000) 'The Practice of Family Group Conferences in New Zealand: Assessing the Place, Potential and Pitfalls of Restorative Justice', in Crawford, A. and Goodey, J. (eds) *Integrating a Victim Perspective within Criminal Justice* (Aldershot: Ashgate).

Pettit, P. with Braithwaite, J. (1993) 'Not Just Deserts, Even in Sentencing', *Current Issues in Criminal Justice,* 4, pp. 222–32.

Sanders, A., Hoyle, C., Morgan, R. and Cape, E. (2001) 'Victim Impact Statements: Can't Work, Won't Work', *Criminal Law Review,* pp. 447–58.

Sarat, A. (1997) 'Vengeance, Victims and Identities of Law', *Social and Legal Studies,* 6, pp. 163–84.

Tonry, M. (1994) 'Proportionality, Parsimony and Interchangeability of Punishments', in Duff, A. *et al.* (eds) *Penal Theory and Practice* (Manchester: Manchester University Press).

United Nations (2000) *Basic Principles on the Use of Restorative Justice Programmes in Criminal Matters* (www.restorativejustice.org/.ents/UNDecBasicPrinciplesofRJ.htm).

von Hirsch, A. (1993) *Censure and Sanctions* (Oxford: Oxford University Press).

von Hirsch, A. and Ashworth, A. (eds) (1998) *Principled Sentencing: Readings on Theory and Policy* (Oxford: Hart Publishing).

Wachtel, T. and McCold, P. (2001) 'Restorative Justice in Everyday Life', in Strang, H. and Braithwaite, J. (eds) *Restorative Justice and Civil Society* (Cambridge: Cambridge University Press), pp. 114–29.

Walgrave, L. (2001) 'On Restoration and Punishment', in Morris, A. and Maxwell, G. (eds) *Restorative Justice for Juveniles* (Oxford: Hart Publishing), pp. 17–40.

Young, R. (2001) 'Just Cops Doing "Shameful" Business? Police-Led Restorative Justice and the Lessons of Research', in Morris, A. and Maxwell, G. (eds) *Restorative Justice for Juveniles* (Oxford: Hart Publishing), pp. 195–226.

29 The virtues of restorative processes, the vices of "restorative justice"

Paul H. Robinson

This Symposium is important for its ability to make better known the great benefits in the use of restorative processes. Below, I try to summarize some of the many promising achievements of those processes, by which I mean to include such practices as victim-offender mediation, sentencing circles, and family-group conferences to name just the most common. While many people refer to such processes by the name "restorative justice," that term and its originators, in fact, have a more ambitious agenda than simply encouraging their use. But that agenda is not one that the frontline practitioners of restorative processes necessarily share. It is primarily an anti-justice agenda, which prompts impassioned opposition. In this brief Article I try to explain why this is so and why it need not be so. I argue that restorative processes can and should be used more widely in ways entirely consistent with doing justice, and that the best thing for the restorative processes movement would be to publicly disavow the anti-justice agenda of the restorative justice movement.

I. The virtues of restorative processes

First, let me speak to the virtues of restorative processes. Frankly, it is hard to see why anyone would oppose such practices. They have the potential to change an offender's perspective – to make them fully appreciate the human side of the harm they have done – which can change their behavior when an opportunity for crime arises in the future. They also have the potential to deter offenders. That is, to the extent that there is some discomfort to having family and friends brought together to discuss one's wrongdoing, the social discomfort and the risk to social relations can stimulate offenders to avoid wrongdoing in the future. Restorative processes also provide an important mechanism of norm reinforcement. The concern of the people present makes clear to the offender – and to everyone present – the validity and importance of the norm violated. It is a unique opportunity for each person to see that *other* people share the norm, and it is that reinforcement that makes the norm stronger in the community. The power of such social influence on conduct ought not be underestimated. Social science studies increasingly suggest that it is the force of such social influence, more than the threat of official sanction by the criminal justice system, that induces law-abidingness. What could be better than a process that advances several crime control mechanisms at the same time: rehabilitation, deterrence, and norm reinforcement?

Finally, the restorative processes advance other valuable interests, beyond those normally held to be the charge of the criminal justice system: providing restitution to the victim (normally the charge of civil tort law); giving victims a direct involvement in the disposition process, thereby providing an emotional sense of restoration and justice done; and putting a human face on the offender, thereby reducing the victim's generalized fear of victimization and perhaps giving the victim some appreciation of how the circumstances may have brought the offender to commit the offense.

Other articles in this Symposium give us specific evidence and illustrations of the value of restorative processes. William Nugent reports a nine percent reduction in recidivism.[1] This is quite impressive when one considers how small the investment of resources is in restorative processes as compared to other programs that typically do little better. Barton Poulson finds that restorative processes do much more than reduce recidivism.[2] I note of particular importance its effect in making people feel better about the adjudication system – feeling that it is more fair and more likely to give an appropriate sanction[3] – because these effects can build the moral credibility and legitimacy of the system, which can produce its own significant crime control benefits.

As hinted above, social science data suggests the great power of social influence in gaining law-abidingness. Criminal law is not irrelevant to this influence: If law can earn a reputation of moral authority with the community, it can to some extent harness this power. John Darley and I suggest two kinds of mechanisms by which criminal law can have an effect.[4] First, it can help shape – build up or tear down – social norms. We have recently seen such norm shifting, as in the increasing opposition to domestic violence and drunk driving and decreasing opposition to same-sex intercourse. These changes did not come about *because* of changes in criminal law, but criminal law changes played an important role in reinforcing the change in norms. Second, the criminal law can directly influence conduct in those instances in which the moral status of the conduct is ambiguous. Thus, it may not be initially obvious that insider trading or computer hacking are condemnable acts, but a criminal prohibition from a morally credible criminal justice system can signal that they are. Of course, neither of these mechanisms can work to give law power to alter conduct unless it has moral credibility with the community it seeks to influence. And it is for this reason that the criminal law gains in crime control effectiveness by heeding the community's shared intuitions of justice, for its dispositions will then reinforce its reputation as a moral authority rather than undercut it. Ultimately, then, the ability of restorative processes to build the criminal law's moral credibility and legitimacy can give the law a greater ability to gain compliance.

Finally, there seems to be little downside to the use of restorative processes. If in some cases there could be an increased danger to victims from an unrepentant offender learning more about the victim, organizers can screen out such cases. The only real risk, then, is that the restorative processes will not work – that they will not give the full payoff that is their potential. But that is no reason not to try them.

II. The vices of restorative justice

With this enthusiasm for *restorative processes,* how can I be opposed to restorative justice when such processes are its central feature? Answer: Because of what "restorative justice" adds to restorative processes.

It is clear that many advocates of restorative processes use the term "restorative justice" as if it were interchangeable with restorative processes. But the literature by the leaders of the restorative justice movement make clear that they conceive of restorative processes not simply as a potentially useful piece of, or complement to, the criminal justice system, but as a *substitute* for it.[5] Further, restorative justice ideally would ban all "punishment," by which is meant, apparently, banning all punishment based on just deserts. (The restorative justice advocates concede, as they must, that in practice participants in restorative sessions commonly bring to bear their own intuitions of justice in sorting out an acceptable disposition, but the restorative justice ideal is forgiveness and reintegration, not deserved punishment.) Bowing to what they see as the demands of reality, the restorative justice advocates reluctantly direct the use of deterrence mechanisms if restorative processes fail, and incapacitation mechanisms if deterrence fails.[6] But giving offenders the punishment they deserve – no more, no less – is rejected as never an appropriate goal.[7]

The centrality of this anti-justice view is expressed in the movement's name: restorative justice. The point of the naming exercise is to present restorative processes as if they were a form of doing justice. But, of course, these kind of word games only work so far. Calling something "justice" does not make it so. The term "justice" has an independent meaning and common usage that cannot be so easily cast aside: "reward or penalty as deserved; just deserts."[8] The naming move can create confusion, and perhaps that is all the leaders of restorative justice want at this point: time to get a foothold in common practice before it becomes too obvious that their restorative *justice* program is in fact anti-justice. But such word-trickery is not likely to be sufficient for gaining longer-term or wider support. For that, they must face the anti-justice issue squarely and persuade people, if they can, that people ought no longer care about doing justice.

It is this anti-justice agenda that restorative justice adds to restorative processes and that I find objectionable, somewhat odd, and potentially dangerous. (In this Article, I use the term "restorative justice" to include the more ambitious, anti-justice agenda, and the term "restorative processes" to refer to just the processes themselves.)

III. Giving restorative justice priority over deterrence and incapacitation

Let me look separately at the two components of restorative justice's proposed program: (1) giving restorative justice priority over deterrence and incapacitation, and (2) barring punishment based on justice.

As to the first, I am highly skeptical of the effectiveness of deterrence as a distributive principle. No doubt having some kind of sanctioning system has some deterrent effect. But the notion that we can construct distributive rules that will optimize deterrence is, I suspect, unrealistic. Offenders simply are not likely to alter their conduct because the law formulates a liability rule one way or another.[9] In any case, deterrence as a distributive principle often produces results that a just society ought not tolerate.

As for incapacitation as a principle for distributing liability and punishment, I concede that it does work. One can prevent offenders from committing most offenses by keeping them in prison. However, as I have argued elsewhere, using the criminal justice system for such preventive detention purposes is bad for both detainees and for society, for such a system is both unfair to detainees – detaining even when there is little preventive justification and confining under inappropriately punitive conditions – and is inefficient and ineffective in protecting society.[10]

So I am inclined to let these distributive programs fend for themselves in response to restorative justice claims for superiority. I am happy to have them replaced.

Before moving on, however, I should say I am not sure I understand the restorative justice arguments for why it should take priority over these distributive principles. The restorative justice perspective on deterrence is particularly confusing. The proposal is that restorative justice should be used first, and repeatedly, until it is clear that it cannot work, and only then should the system resort to deterrence. Of course, by turning first to restorative justice, repeatedly, deterrence has already been sacrificed. The signal to potential offenders is that they will be given repeated chances to escape the threatened deterrent sanction. That message cannot be undone when the system finally does "turn to deterrence," upon a failure of restorative justice.

I will let the deterrence advocates press these arguments. My real opposition to restorative justice is based on its conflict with just punishment.

IV. Restorative justice vs. just punishment

First, let me define what I mean by distributing punishment according to justice – for the restorative justice proponents seem inclined to caricature notions of just desert. (I understand the appeal of the move: if one can make the alternative a monster, then restorative justice looks more attractive. But that kind of distortion only tends to signal weakness in one's own theory.) Here is what I mean by doing justice: Giving a wrongdoer punishment according to what he deserves – no more, no less – by taking account of all those factors that we, as a society, think are relevant in assessing personal blameworthiness.[11] Justice, then, requires that, in assessing an offender's blameworthiness, we must take account of not only the seriousness of the offense and its consequences but also the offender's own state of mind and mental and emotional capacities, as well as any circumstances of the offense that may suggest justification or excuse. Indeed, a rich desert theory would take account of many facets of what can happen during restorative processes. Genuine remorse, public acknowledgment of wrongdoing, and sincere apology can all, in my view, reduce an offender's blameworthiness—and, thereby, the amount of punishment deserved.[12]

It is a peculiar view of just desert to see it as "degrading to both its subject and its object,"[13] as the restorative justice proponents suggest. How many times have we seen on the television news the bereaved family of a victim – ordinary people with good hearts – express their often tearful relief that justice has finally been done. Frankly, I do not know of anyone (other than restorative justice proponents) who would think of the family members as degrading themselves by taking relief in justice being done. That certainly is not the way most societies judge the feeling.

Restorative processes can provide some wonderful benefits, but they can also create serious injustices and failures of justice if used in a way that systematically conflicts with doing justice – where offenders are given more punishment, or less punishment, than their wrongdoing deserves. That does not mean that we must avoid restorative processes. It only means that we must use them in a way that does not conflict with doing justice – something that I will suggest later *can be done* easily for a *full range of cases.*

Let me flesh out this relation between restorative justice and justice by addressing three questions:

A. Does restorative justice conflict with doing justice?
B. Why is such conflict objectionable?
C. Can restorative processes be used in a way that does not conflict with doing justice?

A. Does restorative justice conflict with doing justice?

It is more than obvious that restorative justice *can* conflict with doing justice. That does not need much discussion. I can imagine a devoted Jew finding it in her heart to "take the great opportunity for grace to inspire a transformative will"[14] to forgive Dr. Mengele for his ghastly concentration camp experiments on her and her family. But few would think justice was done if that meant Dr. Mengele was free to skip away to a happy life, even if he genuinely apologized to her.

Another obvious problem is the potential disparity in treatment of identical offenders committing identical offenses. Every "sentencing circle" will have a different cast of characters. Having the offender's punishment depend not on his personal blameworthiness but rather on the chance collection of persons at the circle is objectionable in itself, whatever the disposition in the case.

The discussions in this Symposium by David Dolinko and Stephen Garvey provide persuasive illustrations of just how inconsistent restorative justice can be with doing justice.[15]

While it seems clear that restorative justice *can* seriously conflict with doing justice, I think I would be more cautious than most in predicting that the use of restorative processes necessarily will conflict. John Darley and I have researched lay intuitions of justice and found a surprising amount of agreement among laypersons, over a wide range of situations and cutting across most demographic variables.[16] Thus, when people in a restorative process session are sorting out what they think is an acceptable disposition, their intuitions are likely to track those of the larger community, especially as the sentencing circle is made larger. No doubt some members will tend to be more harsh in their demands and some more lenient, but typically there will be general agreement as to what factors affect the offender's blameworthiness and how they affect it, and the harsh and the lenient sentencers will average out across the group. Indeed, I might predict that a sentencing circle would be more likely to track the shared intuitions of justice of the community than would a single sentencing judge.

But I remain uneasy about a sentencing circle operating without articulated guidelines, for some of the reasons addressed by Robert Weisberg.[17] Even for the fair-minded person, it is easy to be distracted by the particular characteristics of the offender at hand and hard to stand back and put this case in the larger perspective of other cases. There is too much danger for participants left without articulated guidelines to be influenced, perhaps unconsciously, by things such as how similar or different this offender is from themselves. What would be better than pure ad hoc decision-making would be articulated guidelines that captured the larger community's shared intuitions of the principles of justice, to provide at least a benchmark that could inform the sentencing circle's discussions. (On the other hand, it is also my view, as many of you know from my dissent from the United States Sentencing Commission guidelines, that badly-drafted guidelines can do more harm than good.[18])

My ultimate conclusion, then, is that the use of restorative processes might or might not conflict with doing justice, depending upon how they are structured. That is, one could use restorative processes in a way that would *guarantee* failures of justice, and that is just what true restorative justice proponents appear to want: Specifically, to require disposition by restorative processes where the dispositional options available are inadequate to satisfy the demands of justice. In fact, from what I can tell from the restorative justice literature, it is this justice-frustrating effect of restorative processes that is thought of by its proponents as being one of its most important virtues.

B. Why is the conflict of restorative justice with doing justice objectionable?

For those who believe that "doing justice" is a value in itself, the question is rhetorical. Neither the value of doing justice nor the harm of conflicting with justice needs further explanation or independent justification.

For crime control utilitarians, doing justice has traditionally been thought of as suboptimal in reducing crime, or at least as less effective than the mechanisms of deterrence and incapacitation. But crime control utilitarians *ought* to be interested in doing justice (in the sense of having the criminal justice system distribute liability and punishment according to the intuitive principles of justice shared by the community) because, as noted above, social science data suggests that the criminal law can harness the great power of social influence to gain law-abidingness if it can earn a reputation of moral authority and legitimacy with the community.[19] By distributing punishment that conflicts with the demands of doing justice, restorative justice ultimately undercuts the system's crime control effectiveness.

Let me also speak to those persons who care neither about doing justice for its own sake nor about crime control, but rather in something more ethereal such as promoting forgiveness for its own sake. I would advise the devoted Jew in her forgiveness of Dr. Mengele that, despite all the virtues of forgiveness that have been expressed by advocates for restorative processes, there is more at stake in how we deal with Dr. Mengele than just this victim's forgiveness.

First, the harm of most criminal offenses spreads to persons beyond the immediate "official victim." Many Jews not part of Dr. Mengele's experiments may nonetheless feel victimized by him. Indeed, criminal law is unique in embodying norms against violation of societal, rather than personal, interests. All crimes have society as their victim, not merely a single person. Further, not all victims may be as forgiving as the one at hand. Are the feelings of many to be overlooked because of the forgiveness of a few? Are the societal norms that protect us all to be undercut because of the forgiveness of the victim at hand?

Second, many people believe that forgiveness is appropriate only after a wrongdoer accepts full responsibility for his wrongdoing and fully atones for it. Being remorseful, by itself, is not full atonement. Atonement is not achieved simply by making restitution, but may require suffering beyond restitution, a suffering the acceptance of which will show the person's acceptance of the wrongfulness of his actions. Indeed, the offender who does not expect and accept his just punishment may be seen as one who does not understand or accept the wrongfulness of his conduct.[20] Finally, it is not entirely clear to me that the *personal* virtue of forgiveness can be an effective operating principle for a society. One can admire and encourage forgiveness, and believe that it is a personal virtue that ought to guide people in their daily lives, yet also conclude that those who have the responsibility to build a better society – where victims as well as wrongdoers can live fruitful lives – must leave forgiveness to the realm of personal virtue.

[...]

V. Can present restorative processes be expanded to include a full range of cases while remaining true to justice?

Can the use of restorative processes be expanded to serious offenses and remain consistent with desert? This is a particularly important question because, according to the empirical results Heather Strang and Lawrence Sherman report, it may be that restorative processes have their greatest benefit in the most serious cases.[21]

I believe such expansion is possible in a way that is consistent with justice. How can this be done? First, as is obvious from the previous discussion, if the seriousness of the authorized dispositions by restorative processes are increased, the kinds of cases dealt with could be widened. Some people will be hesitant to give serious sentencing authority, such as imprisonment, to a restorative process body, no matter what an offender's veto power. But one can conceive of versions of restorative processes that include judicial participation and/or include guidelines that structure discretion.

A second point may be the most important for expanding restorative processes. Consider for a moment the demands of justice: justice cares about *amount, not method* of punishment. Thus, one could impose deserved punishment through any variety of alternative methods without undercutting justice – fine, community service, house arrest, curfew, regular reporting, diary keeping, and so on – as long as the total punitive "bite" (the "punishment units") of the disposition satisfies the total punishment the offender deserves, no more, no less.[22]

This characteristic of justice has two important implications for restorative processes. First, because all forms of sanction can give rise to "punishment credit," good-faith participation in restorative processes can count toward satisfying the required punishment, at least to the extent of the personal suffering that it produces. No doubt there is discomfort in attending a meeting where family and friends have gathered to discuss one's wrongdoing. Second, restorative processes may provide an effective means for sorting out just how the total punishment units called for are best "spent" – *i.e.*, restorative processes may be a particularly effective means of fashioning a disposition from among the wide variety of available methods, that will best advance the interests of restoring the victim, the offender, and society.

Finally, as has been noted above, the problem of limitations on the dispositional authority of restorative processes is relevant only in instances where such restorative processes are used as the dispositional process – that is, where it is substituting for the criminal justice system or becoming the dispositional mechanism for that system. This is equally true when restorative processes are used for serious offenses. Where such processes are only complementary to the criminal justice system – where they operate parallel to criminal justice – there is no reason for any limitation on their use, for there is no danger that justice will be undercut. (One might worry that if restorative processes were an entirely complimentary rather than a substitute system, offenders might have little motivation to participate. But one could have the criminal justice system look to and take account of the restorative processes disposition in setting the criminal justice sentence.)

VI. Conclusion

Ultimately, my reaction to restorative justice – the theory of restorative justice, not the practice of restorative processes – is one of puzzlement, for this reason: What makes restorative processes work is the emotional need of the participants – a victim's or participant's sense of satisfaction or release in justice being done or, on occasion, an offender's sense of atonement from a just result. Yet it is this same emotional need – inherent in human nature – that restorative justice is so quick to reject outside of the restorative process.

Imagine the people who have attended a sentencing circle one day, who the next day read in their morning newspaper a story of a twenty-two year old who runs on foot from police when police spot him in a car he has failed to return to its owner. During the police chase, an officer on foot is killed by an officer driving a patrol car. The offender is convicted of murder under the felony-murder rule and sentenced to forty years imprisonment.[23] The readers are likely to be offended by this result; it violates their collective notions of what the offender deserves. (Empirical studies confirm that people typically see such cases of accidental killings in the course of a felony as tantamount to manslaughter at most, not murder.[24]

Indeed, in this case it is not even clear that people would see the offender in such a case as having much, if any, causal accountability for the death.[25]) Yet this is apparently irrelevant to the restorative justice proponents. If the restorative process does not work – assume the dead police officer's family is of a very unforgiving sort – the restorative justice proponents would defer to deterrence, and the felony-murder rule makes good sense under a deterrence theory; deterrence is the primary basis on which it is justified. Why wouldn't the restorative justice proponents, sensitive as they are to the importance of people's feelings about justice; enthusiastically support attempts to track shared community intuitions of justice as the criminal justice system's distributive principle? How can the feelings of those at the sentencing circle be so legitimate and so central the day before, but now so irrelevant?

Or imagine that our sentencing circle members the next morning read the story of an unrepentant Nazi concentration camp officer who, it is decided, will not be prosecuted because he is now elderly and no longer a danger – classic incapacitation analysis. Our sentencing circle people are offended: They see a failure of justice in this disposition. Yesterday their collective views were central, but today their views are irrelevant, something the criminal justice system should ignore? Restorative justice tells us to follow the principle of incapacitation, which lets the Nazi officer go free because there is no danger of future crime to be avoided by his incarceration, rather than to look to doing justice.

To summarize my proposal, it is this: Use restorative processes as much as possible, as either complementary to the criminal justice system or as a dispositional process within it. Where restorative processes are used as the dispositional process, the sanctioning options made available ought to be sufficiently serious to allow justice to be done. This can be done either by limiting the use of restorative processes to cases where deserved punishment is not great – as is typically done today – or by increasing the punishment available to restorative processes. In the latter case in particular, articulated guidelines are desirable, as would be a "punishment units" system that allows the restorative processes greater unfettered discretion in determining the method of punishment than in determining its amount.

Notes

1 *See* William Nugent et al., *Participation in Victim-Offender Mediation and the Prevalence and Severity of Subsequent Delinquent Behavior: A Meta-Analysis*, 2003 Utah L. Rev. 137, 163.
2 *See* Barton Poulson, *A Third Voice: A Review of Empirical Research on the Psychological Outcomes of Restorative Justice*, 2003 Utah L. Rev. 167, passim.
3 *See id.* at 192–93. Also recall Kathy Elton's moving accounts – such as her story about the Christmas presents stolen by a neighborhood youth, which frightened so many, but which, in the end, produced a positive good of greater understanding and closer relationships – of how restorative processes could work so effectively on so many levels. Kathy Elton & Michelle M. Roybal, *Restoration, A Component of Justice*, 2003 Utah L. Rev. 43, 53 n.57.
4 *See* Paul H. Robinson and John M. Darley, *The Utility of Desert*, 91 NW. U. L. Rev. 453, 471–77 (1997).
5 *See, e.g.*, John Braithwaite, *A Future Where Punishment Is Marginalized: Realistic or Utopian?*, 46 UCLA L. Rev. 1727, 1746 (1999) (classifying restorative justice as competing with punitive justice).
6 *Id.* at 1742.
7 Consider the 1998 New Zealand case of Patrick Clotworthy, who inflicted six stab wounds upon an attempted robbery victim, which collapsed a lung and diaphragm and left the victim badly disfigured. *See* John Braithwaite, *Restorative Justice: Assessing Optimistic and Pessimistic Accounts*, 25 Crime & Just. 1, 87–88 (1999) (discussing *Clotworthy*); *see also* The Queen v. Patrick

Clotworthy [1998], available at http://www.restorativejustice.org.nz/Judgements%20Page.htm (providing texts of opinions and sentencing notes for case). At a restorative conference organized by Justice Alternatives, the victim agreed to a disposition of a suspended prison sentence, two hundred hours of community work, and a compensation order of $15,000 to fund his cosmetic surgery. *See* Braithwaite, *supra*, at 87–88. Justice Thorburn of the Auckland District Court entered the disposition agreed upon at the conference. *See id.* (also noting that Court of Appeal ultimately quashed disposition and entered sentence of four years in prison and $5,000 compensation).

Requiring the offender to pay the victim $15,000 for the needed surgery seems entirely appropriate, but such a sanction hardly reflects the extent of the punishment the offender deserves for so vicious an attack. Even if the offender were allowed to stay out of prison long enough to earn the $15,000, why would it not be appropriate for him to spend his weekends in jail, or to serve a term of imprisonment after the compensation had been earned? Restorative justice proponents like John Braithwaite support the disposition and decry the fact that it was later quashed, noting that the victim subsequently committed suicide for reasons unknown. The suicide is obviously tragic, but it does not alter the fact that the original disposition failed to do justice. Indeed, many would see the restorative conference as a second victimization—a desperate victim must agree to forgo justice in order to rid himself of the disfiguring scar the offender caused. It is a case of an offender benefitting from his own wrongdoing. That restorative justice proponents support such a disposition seems only to confirm their anti-justice orientation.

8   Webster's New World Dictionary of the American Language 766 (2d ed. 1970).
9   *See* Paul H. Robinson and John M. Darley, Does Criminal Law Deter? A Social Science Investigation 3 (forthcoming 2003); Paul H. Robinson and John M. Darley, *The Role of Deterrence in the Formulation of Criminal Law Rules: At Its Worst When Doing Its Best*, 91 Geo. L.J. (forthcoming 2003).
10 *See* Paul H. Robinson, *Punishing Dangerousness: Cloaking Preventive Detention as Criminal Justice*, 114 Harv. L. Rev. 1429, 1446–47 (2001) (arguing that using criminal justice system for preventive detention is ineffective and unfair).
11 There are two sources of data for determining what is relevant to desert – moral philosophy and empirical studies of a community's shared intuitions of justice – but for present purposes I do not believe that the difference between them is significant. I have written elsewhere about these differences. *See* Paul H. Robinson and Michael T. Cahill, Law Without Justice (forthcoming 2004).
12 I do not know that retributivists as a group would agree with this; I offer it only as my own view.
13 *See* Braithwaite, *supra* note 5, at 1742.
14 *See* Braithwaite, *supra* note 7, at 1–2.
15 *See generally* David Dolinko, *Restorative Justice and the Justification of Punishment*, 2003 Utah L. Rev. 319, 331–34 (noting that restorative justice may give similar offenders disparate treatment); Stephen P. Garvey, *Restorative Justice, Punishment, and Atonement*, 2003 Utah L. Rev. 303, 306–08 (distinguishing harms from wrongs and arguing that restorative justice repairs harms but ignores wrongs).
16 *See* Paul H. Robinson and John M. Darley, Justice, Liability, and Blame: Community Views and the Criminal Law *passim* (1995).
17 Robert Weisberg, *Restorative Justice and the Danger of "Community,"* 2003 Utah L. Rev. 343, 370–71.
18 *See* Sentencing Guidelines for United States Courts, Dissenting View of Commissioner Paul H. Robinson on the Promulgation of Sentencing Guidelines by the United States Sentencing Commission, 52 Fed. Reg. 18,046, 18,121 (May 13, 1987).
19 *See* Tom Tyler, Why People Obey the Law 108 (1990); Robinson & Darley, *supra* note 4, at 471–77. This represents a different kind of "hybrid" distributive principle from that which Erik Luna has discussed. *See* Erik Luna, *Punishment Theory, Holism, and the Procedural Conception of Restorative Justice*, 2003 Utah L. Rev. 205, 225–27. Here there are no trade-offs between utility and doing justice. Rather, the greatest utility is found in a justice distribution of liability and punishment, or at least in a distribution according to a community's shared intuitions of justice.

20 In fact, genuinely remorseful offenders will think their just punishment is *less* than that actually deserved, for this reason: The offenders' genuine remorse reduces their blameworthiness for the offense, yet offenders cannot expect or insist that their remorse reduce their punishment, any more than they can expect or insist on forgiveness. To insist on a mitigation for remorse is to undercut the sincerity of the remorse itself. Thus, the punishment discount for remorse will always be a pleasant surprise to the genuinely remorseful offender.

21 *See* Heather Strang and Lawrence W. Sherman, *Repairing the Harm: Victims and Restorative Justice*, 2003 Utah L. Rev. 15, 40.

22 I have written about such a proposal. Paul H. Robinson, *Desert, Crime Control, Disparity, and Units of Punishment*, in Penal Theory and Practice: Tradition and Innovation in Criminal Justice 93, 99–104 (Anthony Duff et al. eds., 1994).

23 This is the *McCarty* case from South Chicago. *See* Paul H. Robinson, Criminal Law Case Studies 1–5 (2nd ed. 2002); Paul H. Robinson, Teacher's Manual for Criminal Law Case Studies 13–14 (2nd ed. 2002).

24 *See* Robinson and Darley, *supra* note 16, at 169–81.

25 *See id.* at 181–89.

30 Some sociological reflections on restorative justice

Anthony Bottoms

John Braithwaite is a master of the arresting aphorism. In his comprehensive 1999 review of the research literature on restorative justice, there are several examples of this; but here I want to focus on just two. First, Braithwaite tells us, 'restorative justice has been the dominant model of criminal justice throughout most of human history for all the world's peoples' (Braithwaite, 1999: 2). Secondly, in the abstract of his paper it is claimed that 'for informal justice to be restorative justice, it has to be about restoring victims, restoring offenders, and restoring communities' (Braithwaite, 1999: 1).

In dictionary definition, an aphorism is 'a concise pithy saying that expresses a truth' (Longman, 1984). In my view, both of the sayings I have quoted qualify as aphorisms under this definition, because they both—to some extent—'express a truth'. Those truths, however, require a good deal of contextualisation before they can be fully understood. Moreover, the fact that a saying expresses *a* truth does not mean that it necessarily expresses the whole truth, and I shall argue that neither of these sayings does so (although the second comes closer to doing so than does the first). The remainder of this chapter can be read, in one sense, as an elaboration of and commentary on Braithwaite's two aphorisms, and their relevance for our contemporary understanding of restorative justice.

Most of human history has been lived in what we now call pre-modern societies. Braithwaite's first aphorism is, therefore, another way of saying that restorative justice (RJ) is the dominant model of criminal justice in pre-modem societies. This reminds us of the fact that contemporary advocates of RJ have quite frequently used pre-modern societies as exemplars, arguing for example that such communities generally 'handled their own conflicts, and their primary aim was to make peace between the conflicting parties' (Johnstone, 2002: 12). Some consideration of traditional justice in pre-modern societies might therefore assist us in understanding more fully at least some features of RJ in contemporary societies.

But if RJ (or something like it) was an important form of justice in many pre-modern societies, it has certainly not been dominant in the criminal justice systems of modern Western states from the Renaissance onwards. Yet, as everyone knows, even in such states it has in the last quarter-century enjoyed a significant revival. Some careful sociological reflection on the reasons for this revival would therefore seem to be an important issue for those like myself who are interested in the sociology of contemporary criminal justice systems.

While Braithwaite's first aphorism focuses our attention on these historical and macro-sociological issues, his second aphorism raises a different, and more micro-oriented, set of considerations. 'For informal justice to be restorative justice, it has to be about restoring victims, restoring offenders, and restoring communities'. But, in this saying, what does 'restoring a community' or 'restoring a victim' actually mean? And, assuming that such phrases do mean something (as I shall argue that they do), then by what *social mechanisms* are these 'restorations' accomplished?

The topics raised in the preceding three paragraphs constitute the core subject matter of this chapter. To develop them, the remainder of the chapter is divided into four sections. In the first section, a classic early paper on the themes of RJ is reanalysed. Then, secondly, two of the intellectual roots of the RJ movement are examined: these are what might be described as the 'wisdom of pre-modern societies' argument, and the argument that civil methods of dispute resolution are preferable to criminal ones. In the third section, the social mechanisms of RJ are explored, in pursuit of the questions as to whether—and, if so, how—RJ can 'restore' victims, offenders and communities. These various discussions then pave the way for a final section on RJ in contemporary societies, in which a number of questions are raised, including the reasons for the revival of RJ in the last quarter century, the structural location of RJ in contemporary penal systems, and whether the social mechanisms of RJ can be expected to work effectively in contemporary advanced economies.

I. Revisiting a classic article

I shall begin by discussing Nils Christie's (1977) celebrated paper 'Conflicts as Property', described by Braithwaite (1999: 5) as 'the most influential text of the [contemporary] restorative tradition'. This article was originally delivered as a public lecture on a formal occasion, and as one of those who was on the platform that day,[1] I have naturally retained a strong personal interest in the paper, and its subsequent influence.[2]

A key strategy in Christie's paper was to introduce, at an early stage, a description of a civil case from a small village in the Arusha province of Tanzania, about the disposition of property after an engagement to be married had been broken. It rapidly becomes clear to the reader that this case is presented as a kind of normative ideal, an example of the kind of process that Christie wishes to advocate. In describing the case,[3] the following matters were especially emphasised:

(a) The two litigating parties were in the centre of the room, and at the centre of everyone's attention. Others, including relatives and friends but also a general audience, were present, but they did not take over (p 2). The case was thus, very obviously, focused upon the parties' own conflict; and that conflict had not in any sense been taken away ('stolen') from the parties by lawyers or by State professionals (p 4).

(b) The court hearing was very much a community occasion. No reporters attended; their presence was unnecessary because 'most grown-ups from the village and several from adjoining ones were there' (p 2). There was some oral participation from this wider audience, with 'short questions, information or jokes' (p 2). This participation 'crystal-lised norms and clarified what had happened', but without taking over the case from the main parties. The proceedings were described by Christie as a 'happy happening', with 'fast talking, … smiles, eager attention, not a sentence… to be lost' (p 2).

(c) The 'judges, three local party secretaries, were extremely inactive'.[4] They are described as 'obviously ignorant with regard to village matters', whereas all the other people in the room were 'experts' on such matters (p 2).

(d) It was 'not by chance that the Tanzanian case was a civil one', because 'full participation in your own conflict' (for Christie, a desirable attribute) 'presupposes elements of civil law' (p 3).

In sociological language, what is being described here is a *gemeinschaft* society settling a conflict. As Anthony Giddens (1990: 102) has pointed out, in such a society, typically, much emphasis and trust will be placed upon kinship relationships; upon the 'thick' social relations of people who live close together and know many aspects of one another's business; and upon tradition.

Later in his paper, Christie explicitly advocates for Western societies a 'model of neighbourhood courts' (p 10). Such courts would be strongly victim-oriented (p 10). They would also have an 'extreme degree of lay-orientation', so that both lawyers and behaviour experts would be viewed with suspicion, and 'if we find them unavoidable in certain cases or at certain stages [of the process]', it will still be necessary 'to get across to them the problems they create for broad social participation' (p 12).[5] The neighbourhood courts 'would represent a blend of elements from civil and criminal courts, but with a strong emphasis on the civil side' (p 11).

Christie is fully aware that his choice of an opening example from a Tanzanian village context is not accidental. The 'lack of neighbourhoods' in contemporary Western urban societies, he concedes, could be one of several significant 'blocks' against the establishment of the system of neighbourhood courts that he advocates. In response to this problem, Christie says he has only two weak arguments to offer (p 12). The first is that the death of real neighbourhood-based communities in modern societies 'is not complete'. The second is that his proposed neighbourhood courts are themselves intended as a 'vitaliser for neighbourhoods'; that is to say, neighbourhood courts would themselves, it is hoped, help to keep close-knit neighbourhoods alive.

In this key foundational text, then, RJ is explicitly linked to a particular kind of macro-social organisation deemed to be desirable, and that social organisation is fairly clearly of a *gemeinschaft* character. Christie, however, is under no illusions that *gemeinschaft* communities are plentiful in the neighbourhoods of modern cities. Since 1977, RJ has proliferated, but there is little or no evidence of it having been a 'vitaliser for neighbourhoods'. The reasons for its expanding influence must therefore lie elsewhere than in the sphere of neighbourhood *gemeinschaft*, a point to which I shall return in the final section.

But while Christie is explicit about the optimum macro-social context for his proposed neighbourhood courts, he is silent on meso-social structural contexts. Interestingly, however, a good illustration of the importance of such issues can be found in an earlier anthropological study by Gulliver (1963) of indigenous social control among the Arusha, the selfsame tribal group from whom Christie drew his Tanzanian example. According to Gulliver, in traditional Arusha society there were three distinct meso-structural sub-systems, respectively based on residence, lineage and age-set, and the existence of these separate sub-systems could significantly affect the procedures used in disputes.[6] Moreover, in a society where disputes could not be settled by the decision of independent arbiters [...],[7] litigants with equivalently strong cases did not always achieve similar outcomes: rather, 'the degree of convergence between normative standards... and the details of actual settlements [could] vary considerably, according to the relative distribution of bargaining power between the two parties' (p 300). Bargaining power, not surprisingly, was intimately linked to the three sub-systems of Arusha society: '[t]he composition and strengths of the two conflicting parties in a dispute, [and] the identification of leaders and the scope of their influence ... , are... direct functions of the sub-systems of Arusha society' (Gulliver, 1963: 301).

Gulliver's fieldwork was conducted in 1956–1958, and it is of course possible that some aspects of Arusha dispute settlement had altered by the time that Christie wrote, twenty years later (though radical change seems unlikely in a rural society, even in a pre/post-independence context: see n 4). However, the main point to be made is not specific to the empirical details of Arusha society, but rather the more general issue that in examining dispute-settlement processes in pre-modern societies, meso-structural questions (including issues of intra-societal power) need to be considered. This general point was well documented twenty years ago by Sally Merry (1982) in her literature review on mediation practices in non-industrial societies. Merry argued that some Western scholars had 'misunderstood the process of mediation' in such societies, 'focusing on its consensual and conciliatory qualities and ignoring the very important role of coercion and power' that was linked to the meso-structural context (Merry, 1982: 20). In the light of Merry's evidence, Maureen Cain (1988: 56) subsequently took the view that Christie, and writers like him, had fallen into the trap of constructing a 'romantic idealization of pre-capitalist (but non-feudal) forms' of legal or quasi-legal decision-making. These are harsh words; whether they are justified is an issue to be explored further as the argument of the chapter unfolds.

II. 'Civilisation' and the 'wisdom of pre-modern societies'

It can be plausibly argued that the intellectual roots of the modern RJ movement derive originally from two principal sources.[8] The first of these was a realisation that, as Marjery Fry (1951: 124) put it in an early text (and using now outdated language) 'in primitive societies [the] idea of "making up" for a wrong done has wide currency', so that we should perhaps 'once more look into the ways of earlier men, which may still hold some wisdom for us. [9] The second principal intellectual inspiration of the RJ movement derived from writers who argued that most crimes are an attack *on the individual victim*[10] (rather than the State or the community at large), and that the victim has been sidelined (if not completely displaced) in the modern Western criminal trial, where it is the State (and not the victim) that brings proceedings against the alleged offender. A key way of returning the victim to her/his rightful centre-stage position is therefore to reconceptualise the proceedings as primarily *civil* rather than *criminal* proceedings (sometimes described, in a deliberate *double entendre,* as a process of 'civilisation'). It is interesting that Christie's (1977) influential early article contains elements of both of these intellectual roots of the contemporary RJ tradition.

In this section, I shall briefly consider aspects of both these intellectual derivations, and I shall argue that neither is unproblematic for contemporary RJ advocates. I shall begin with the so-called 'civilisation thesis'.

1. The 'civilisation' thesis

The 'civilisation' thesis[11] can be dealt with fairly briefly, and I will discuss the thesis in what seems to me to be its most persuasive form, namely that propounded by Louk Hulsman (1981, 1982, 1986) in the 1980s.[12] Hulsman points out that, in contemporary societies, only a proportion of events which fit the official legal definitions of crimes such as 'theft' and 'assault' are dealt with by the criminal justice system, even where the identity of the offender is known. Instead, many of these events are dealt with informally in families, schools, workplaces, social clubs, among local neighbours, and so on. Not infrequently, the processes for handling such events have a restorative element within the group in question: as Johnstone (2002: 59) puts it, they are handled 'without the state's involvement and with an emphasis on recompense and contrition rather than punitive suffering'.

Hulsman's argument is thus that restorative justice already exists informally (or indigenously) in many places in contemporary societies, and hence there is significant scope for developing it. All we have to do is to extend our horizons and realise that many more acts defined as 'crimes' could be dealt with in a similar informal fashion, or if necessary by the civil law. As he explicitly states in one of his articles, he has (like Christie) a strong preference for dispute resolution by those directly involved, ie the perpetrator and the victim, with settlements aimed at 'concrete restitution' (Hulsman, 1982: 45). He further complains that, from this perspective, the criminal justice system is seriously deficient:

> Conflicts which occur in society between persons or groups are defined in the penal system not in terms of the parties involved, but rather in terms of the regulations (criminal legislation) and the organisational requirements of the system itself. The parties directly involved in a conflict can exert little influence on the further course of events once a matter has been defined as criminal and as such has been taken up by the system... [Moreover] if we compare 'criminal events' with other events there is—on the level of those directly involved—nothing which distinguishes those 'criminal' events *intrinsically* from other difficult or unpleasant situations [such as] matrimonial difficulties... serious difficulties at work and housing problems... Nor are they singled out to be dealt with in a way differing radically from the way other events are dealt with.
>
> (Hulsman 1981: 153–4, emphasis in original)

Hulsman's account is sociologically very useful in drawing attention to much 'hidden' informal justice even in countries with advanced economies. His normative thesis—that this approach should be extended, even to the point of abolition of the criminal justice system (Hulsman, 1991)—is of course much more controversial, and I shall not deal with it here.[13] Rather, I shall highlight two more general issues that arise from the 'civilisation' thesis.

The first issue is the extent to which RJ-type processes in contemporary societies should involve the wider community (however that concept is defined) as well as the direct participants. For Hulsman (1981: 157), one of the attractions of civil procedures is that the parties 'can to an important extent define the problem submitted to [the] system, and in the end they are not forced into a specific settlement of their conflict by the civil law judgement. They remain in a context of negotiation ... '. Perhaps arising out of such thinking, many of the early practical experiments in RJ took the form of victim-offender mediation (see, eg Marshall and Merry 1990); but, as Johnstone (2002: 151) points out, this led to something of a backlash, where 'many who were sympathetic towards the ideas of restorative justice which arose from these experiments nevertheless criticised such... mediation for being too "private" and for failing to involve the community'. It would seem that this 'private' versus 'community' debate is a continuing point of tension within the RJ movement, and it is worth exploring a little further.

In an important phrase, Braithwaite (2000a: 122) has described contemporary restorative justice as based on 'individual-centred communitarianism'. Both halves of this phrase are significant. Frequently occurring motifs in the RJ literature are the central role to be given to the parties directly involved ('participating in their own disputes' etc), and the weakness of traditional criminal justice in sidelining the victim. Hence, it is argued, the individual parties are crucial to RJ processes. Yet the importance of 'the community' is also frequently invoked, certainly in the literature on so-called 'family group conferencing', but also by 'civilisation thesis' writers such as Hulsman (see, eg Hulsman, 1981: 154–8).[14] So, what exactly should be the relative weight given to 'individuals' and 'communities' in the 'individual-centred communitarianism' of RJ; and what justifies these relative priorities? There is no clear or agreed answer. In a more formal sociological vein, one can also note, vis-à-vis the so-called 'civilisation thesis', that in contemporary societies civil proceedings are essentially *gesellschaft*-type law, while—from Christie onwards—RJ advocates have tended to emphasise many *gemeinschaft*-type elements within RJ processes.[15] There are significant conceptual tensions here.

The second general issue arising from the 'civilisation thesis' is related to the first. Nils Christie (1977: 8) makes clear that one of the things he is seeking, in his 'model of neighbourhood courts', is a set of *opportunities for norm-clarification.* This would constitute no less than 'what we might call a political debate in the court' about what facts are relevant to the decision, and ultimately about what should be done. For example, what if a petty thief steals from the owner of a big house? Or what if 'the other party is an insurance company, or if his wife has just left him, or if his factory will break down if he has to go to jail... or if he was drunk ... ? There is no end to it. Any maybe there ought to be none' (p 8). Whether Christie is aware of it or not, there is a marked similarity between these comments and some aspects of traditional Arusha dispute-settlement practice.[16] But if, in a modern context, matters of the kind that Christie describes are to be left to the parties involved to debate and decide in individual cases, then any hopes of consistency in decision-making vanish, and the principle of equal treatment before the law seems to be fatally compromised. As Johnstone (2002, p 146) shrewdly points out, Christie's agenda here has 'quite radical implications... which, when they become clear, are unlikely to appeal much to most mainstream advocates of restorative justice'. Christie seems to want endless normative/political debates; more mainstream advocates often see RJ as an effective instrument for consolidating and strengthening community normative standards.

In summary, then, detailed examination of the 'civilisation thesis' quickly exposes real uncertainties and disagreements within the RJ movement. What about the other strand in the original intellectual roots of RJ, the alleged 'wisdom of the pre-moderns'?

2. Wise pre-moderns?

The 'pre-modern' strand of contemporary RJ thinking has recently been usefully discussed in a textbook by Johnstone (2002: ch 3). Johnstone particularly focuses on Navajo peacemaking processes because of their prominence in the RJ literature, especially in North America.

Navajo peacemaking has some marked similarities to the Arusha civil case that Christie (1977) described, with the major difference that the 'peacemaker' or mediator (an apparently high-status individual) plays a significantly more proactive and interventionist role than the judges did in that case.[17] To quote Johnstone (2002: 45–6):

> The *naat'aanii*-peacemaker calls on the interested parties—the victim and the perpetrator and their families and clan relations—to participate in a meeting in which the aim is to resolve the dispute between them... [At the meeting, victims] have an opportunity to state what happened and to vent their feelings about it. The accused person then has an opportunity to speak. Frequently, they will put forward excuses or justifications. One of the purposes of the process appears to be to expose the weakness or unacceptability of the excuses which people habitually use to justify unacceptable behaviour such as drink-driving and spouse-abuse. To achieve this, the plausibility of excuses are assessed, not by lawyers through Western methods of cross-examination, but by people who know the wrongdoer intimately and who will use their intimate knowledge of the wrongdoer to expose the frailty of their excuses... The group, *led by the peacemaker,*

will then seek to construct a reparative plan of action. This search is guided by principles drawn, not just from legal precedents (in the Western sense), but from a rich range of traditional [teachings].

(Emphasis added)

According to Johnstone, some RJ advocates (and he cites examples) go on to claim that:

Navajo peacemaking is a virtually universal process found among nearly all aboriginal groups and in all pre-modern societies. There is an implication that Navajo peacemaking represents a natural, authentic form of justice, a form abandoned by modern western societies in favour of a more 'artificial' system of state punitive justice.

(Johnstone 2002: 44)

This claim, of course, is not dissimilar to (although more specific and more provocatively stated than) John Braithwaite's claim about restorative justice being 'the dominant model of criminal justice throughout most of human history' (see the introduction to this chapter).

So, what we have here is a kind of foundational myth about the 'naturalness' of RJ, based on the alleged universality or near-universality of RJ-type principles in pre-modern societies. To return to the dictionary definition of an aphorism, however (see the introduction to this chapter), while there is *some* truth in these claims, the claims are, without serious question, both overstated and decontextualised.

The alleged near-universality of RJ-style dispute settlement is quickly refuted by any serious look at the literature of legal anthropology. As Simon Roberts puts it in his classic textbook, in different stateless societies the 'approved means of handling disputes... are extremely varied' (Roberts 1979: 116). For example:

In some societies it is recognized that quarrels *should* be resolved through talk rather than by fighting, ostracism or sorcery. In others no particular value is attached explicitly to talking but it may be used alongside other methods of handling disputes. Elsewhere different values prevail, demanding as a matter of honour some direct physical response to many types of wrong and resulting in the identification of conciliatory gestures with weakness. In the last case retaliatory violence may represent the likely reaction to a wrong, and where further injury is inflicted this may in turn lead to sustained fighting between kinsmen and co-residents of the principals.

(Emphasis in original)

It is also clear from the relevant literature that, where conciliatory ('peacemaking') discussions are found in a given pre-modern society, they are sometimes set within a range of other procedures and sanctions that are much less obviously 'restorative'. Moreover, even within reconciliatory/restitutive processes, individuals may be 'coerced into settlements by the prestige of the mediator and the threat of sanctions, both secular and supernatural' (Merry, 1982: 28).

To illustrate these last points, I shall discuss in some detail Joan Ryan's (1995) recent anthropological study of the Dogrib hunter-gatherer tribal group (part of a larger community known as the 'Dene people') in the Canadian Northwest Territories. An important part of the purpose of Ryan's research was to recover (through oral accounts) how indigenous Dene traditional justice worked—what the rules were, how children were socialised to obey rules, what happened when someone broke the rules, and so on (see especially Ryan, 1995: 33–4, 57–8).[18]

In traditional Dogrib society, there was no single mechanism of justice. The most serious offences were dealt with by banishment from the tribe, which 'was essentially a death sentence', because in the Dene territory (close to the Arctic Circle) no-one 'could survive out on the land on his own for long' (p 58). At the other end of the scale of seriousness, minor offences (such as a small theft) were dealt with by ridicule and shaming, which was intended to act as a deterrent (p 33).

Between these extremes came the intermediate offences. Some of these might be dealt with by the local camp *k'àowo* (each camp had a *k'àowo,* who was an assistant to the overall tribal leader or *yabahti*). An example might be theft of an animal from a trap; here the *k'àowo* would speak what are described as 'harsh words' to the thief, who would also 'be asked to acknowledge the theft and to return the fur (or another of equal value) to the person from whom it had been stolen' (p 34).

If the offender refused to comply with the *k'àowo's* requirements, he would then be required to be 'put in the circle'. The same procedure would also be adopted for offences which the *k'aowo* considered too serious for him to deal with by himself. Here we reach the full RJ element within Dene traditional justice.

The 'circle' consisted of the whole local Dogrib community, presided over by the *yabahti* (tribal leader) and senior men and women of the tribal group. Joan Ryan (1995) describes the procedure as follows:

> The offender was kept |in the circle] until he or she admitted guilt,[19] at which point the senior people and leadership would give the person 'harsh words'. These words usually restated the rules and how the person should have behaved. They also made reference to the harm done to individuals and/or the group. Once the harsh words were spoken, the gathering shifted to discussing how the individual might make things better. People arrived at consensus about what the person might do to restore harmony [with the victim and within the community], compensate the victim, and end the matter.
>
> When the solution was proposed, the offender agreed to do what the elders had indicated would make things right. If the person did not agree, then the gathering [might decide] that he must leave the community since he would not follow the rules. [But] banishment was rare because few young people had the courage, or lack of respect, to 'break the words' of the elders.
>
> Once [the offender had carried out what was considered appropriate to restore harmony], no further action was taken and no further mention of the offence was made.
>
> (A composite of passages at pp 57–8 and p 34 of Ryan (1995))

Ryan's perception of these processes is that 'the offender is not punished. Rather, the group demands that he or she face the victim, that restitution be made, that reconciliation start' (p 91). However, although in her view there is no punishment, Ryan is in no doubt that the processes described could be perceived as coercive, and indeed seemed to produce a deterrent effect:

> In all our accounts, people said that they feared the discipline of their parents, they feared the power of the *yabahtis,* they feared 'harsh words'... As well, the reality of being shamed by all those gathered if one ended up in the circle, caused many people to think seriously before committing an offence.
>
> (Ryan, 1995, p 58)

Additionally, Ryan (1995: 90–1) makes clear that there are a number of similarities—though not, of course, total similarity—between the traditional Dogrib procedure and the modern Canadian criminal trial. (The person accused of committing a wrong act is arraigned before a community tribunal, who may take harsh measures against him/her, and so on.)

Three points are of special interest about this account. First, restorative processes exist, but they are heavily buttressed by other processes (notably, the very real threat of banishment—hardly a 'restorative' sanction), in a way that must significantly affect the dynamics of the 'circle' process itself. Secondly, to use Emile Durkheim's (1893) celebrated distinction, traditional Dogrib society was apparently a society characterised more by *mechanical solidarity* than by *organic solidarity*.[20] In such societies, it is the group that is all-important, and any individual is secondary to the group. It is thus very noticeable that, in Ryan's account, although the end-results of the circle procedure are restitution and reconciliation, prior to that it is the elders who dominate the proceedings, acting essentially *on behalf of the victim(s)*, as well as on behalf of the community at large. The victim her/himself plays a somewhat passive role in the proceedings, so that this version of RJ, unlike those described by Christie and Hulsman, is apparently not in any serious sense akin to civil proceedings. This leads directly to the third key observation, which is that in Dogrib traditional justice the elders (or chairs of the circle) are anything but inactive. All members of the circle are invited to participate, but it is the elders who dominate.

Two problems of sociological explanation arise directly from Ryan's account of Dogrib traditional justice. First, why are Dogrib penalties harsher, and their procedures less individualistic and more collective, than those often described for other societies? The answer to this question is almost certainly related to the fact that this was a hunter-gatherer society living in harsh physical circumstances. Under such conditions—according to other anthropological studies—'everything depends on the cohesion and co-operation of a group', so the group acts in a collective way to protect itself, because of 'the value that must be attached to relationships of mutual reliance' (Roberts, 1979: 98).

The second problem for explanation concerns the use of restitutive and reconciliatory techniques even for quite serious offences, and even in a society that is not afraid (where necessary) to use harsh sanctions such as banishment. At first sight, it seems surprising that offences falling just short of the seriousness threshold for banishment could nevertheless be dealt with by a restitutive procedure where, once the agreed restitution had been made, 'no further action was taken and no further mention of the offence was made' (Ryan 1995: 34). But, on further reflection, the reasons for this are not hard to discern. As Chris Hann (2000: 145) puts it:

> In a small-scale society where [direct enforcement options such as a prison system) are not available, the payment of compensation to the victim of a crime is likely to be more important than punishment. Reconciliation is especially important where the contesting parties have necessarily to continue sharing the same economic resources, to be part of a cooperative community in daily life.

This indeed seems to be the principal reason why settlement-directed talk, reconciliation and restitution is widespread (but by no means universal) in pre-modern societies. I shall return to the significance of this point when discussing the social mechanisms of RJ in the next section of this chapter.

Finally, what main conclusions can be drawn from this brief analysis of the 'wisdom of the pre-moderns' argument? I would suggest the following:

- Pre-modern societies are significantly more varied in their dispute-resolution procedures and sanctions than some RJ advocates have suggested.
- Reconciliatory/restitutive processes are nevertheless widespread in pre-modern societies, particularly because of the absence of direct enforcement mechanisms (which are much more readily available in contemporary societies), and also the imperative need for reconciliation in small-society contexts where people have to continue to live in close proximity to one another in a functioning economic and social community.
- Reconciliatory/restitutive processes always occur within the particular macro- and meso-structural contexts of the given society. These contexts can, however, vary quite widely as between different pre-modern societies, with consequential differences for dispute settlement. (For an instructive contrast, compare Gulliver on the Arusha with Ryan on the Dogrib; the former has significantly more complex substructures).
- Despite the genuinely reconciliatory nature of dispute-settlement procedures in many pre-modern societies (see second point above), it remains the case that within such procedures there is frequently a strong degree of social pressure, so that 'individuals may be coerced into settlements by the prestige of the mediator and the threat of sanctions' (Merry, 1982: 28). The precise form of such social pressure is strongly linked to the social structural context of the particular society (see third point above), but coercive forces of various kinds can readily be identified in societies as different as the Dogrib and the Arusha.[21]
- As noted earlier in this chapter, contemporary RJ advocates tend to put forward a version of RJ based on 'individual-centred communitarianism' (see eg Braithwaite, 2000a; Christie, 1977), but some pre-modern societies were significantly more collectively-oriented than this model suggests (see the Dogrib example).
- In using examples from pre-modern societies in pursuit of contemporary RJ policy-formation, there is a particular need for care in generalising about the role of the president of the tribunal.[22] Even in this brief discussion, we have encountered very varied styles of chairperson activity, ranging from the inactive bystander (Christie on the post-colonial Arusha) to the respected and powerful mediator between individuals within a context of shared community norms (accounts of Navajo peacemakers) to dominant figures concerned above all with collective cohesion (Ryan on the Dogrib). In more comprehensive legal-anthropological accounts of dispute settlement in pre-modern societies, such as that of Roberts (1979), a similar range of roles can be found. This issue, of course, is linked to the tensions between 'individual' and 'community' emphases in RJ (already discussed in the context of the 'civilisation thesis'), since more collectively-oriented societies tend to assign stronger roles to those presiding over dispute-settlement procedures.

I noted earlier Maureen Cain's (1988; 56) claim that Nils Christie (1977) had constructed a 'romantic idealization of pre-capitalist (but non-feudal) forms' of legal or quasi-legal decision-making. After a more detailed examination of pre-modern societies, it can be seen that there is some truth in such a characterisation, and that a similar tendency to idealisation of the pre-modern still exists among some RJ advocates (see some of the comments made by RJ advocates about the near-universality of processes akin to Navajo peacemaking). Despite this tendency, there remains some validity to claims—such as that by Braithwaite with which I began this chapter—about the widespread existence of processes of reconciliation and restitution in pre-modern societies. Those processes, however, vary widely in different pre-modern societies (see the third and sixth summary points above); and the widespread existence of reconciliatory/restitutive processes in such societies is itself connected to certain features of such societies which are either not present or not prominent in contemporary advanced urban societies (see the second and fourth point above). As Sally Merry (1982) argued twenty years ago, there is therefore no easy line of normative argument that can be drawn from reconciliatory/restitutive processes in pre-modern societies to the advocacy of RJ (or equivalent procedures) in contemporary societies. Contemporary societies will be considered more fully in the final section of this chapter, but first it is necessary to take a closer look at the social mechanisms of 'restoration'.

III. Apology and the social mechanisms of 'restoration'

I began this chapter with John Braithwaite's aphorism that 'for informal justice to be restorative justice, it has to be about restoring victims, restoring offenders, and restoring communities'. In looking more closely at this saying, we can begin by noting that if victims, offenders, or communities are to be 'restored', then it would seem that there must be some *social mechanism* that will restore them. Hedstrom and Swedborg (1996) have argued persuasively that sociologists need always to develop 'explanations that systematically seek to explicate the generative mechanisms that produce observed associations between events' (p 281), and if that is correct, then we need to ask ourselves what 'generative mechanisms' might produce an observed association between RJ procedures and/or sanctions, and the subsequent 'restoration' of the victim, the offender, or the community.

I shall begin this task by considering the community, bearing in mind that communities always consist of individuals in relationships, those relationships taking place within social structures and cultural contexts. Given this background, the most appropriate way for a social scientist to use the terminology of post-RJ 'community restoration' is, I would suggest, to speak of *a restoration of prior social relationships in a community, within an understood structural and normative framework.* Since many advocates of RJ claim that this is precisely what it can achieve, and since such a claim is not (see below) a meaningless statement,[23] then it can be regarded as a testable hypothesis that the processes of RJ can in some way act as 'generative social mechanisms' to restore prior social relationships in communities. In saying this, it is explicitly assumed for present purposes that both the victim and the offender belong to the same social/moral community, although their direct personal linkage within that community might be tenuous (thus, while some offenders and victims might be linked through the 'thick' social relations of family members, or the 'thinner' relationships between, say, work colleagues or members of a social club, others might simply be residents of a town or village who barely know each other, but are both embedded in meaningful social networks which connect elsewhere within a functioning social/moral community).

So how might RJ 'restore prior social relationships' within such a context? It is at this point that we need to give special attention to one central feature of RJ processes, namely *the apology.* Almost all accounts of RJ emphasise the desirability of the apology as a prelude to meaningful reparation and reconciliation; and empirically, the evidence from the RISE randomised experiment in the Australian Capital Territory suggests that victims receive apologies far more often in RJ conferences than they do in courts (by a factor of six or seven to one: see Braithwaite, 1999: 24). Sociologically speaking, then, can the apology (followed usually by some restitution) be plausibly represented as a generative social mechanism that can potentially lead to the restoration of prior social relationships in a community (as defined above)?

In my view, the answer to this question is a straightforward affirmative. To understand why, we need to examine the pioneering monograph on the sociology of apology by Nicholas Tavuchis (1991)—a text that is sometimes cited in the RJ literature (see eg Braithwaite, 1999: 44; Johnstone, 2002: 135) but one that (to my knowledge) has rarely been carefully analysed in that literature. Tavuchis examines the apology from two distinct but complementary perspectives. The first of these relates to the *social-structural context* of the apology, and here the key point is that the apology:

> speaks to an act that cannot be undone, but that cannot go unnoticed without compromising the current and future relationship of the parties, the legitimacy of the violated rule, and the wider social web in which the participants are enmeshed.
>
> (p 13)

As we shall shortly see, every word of that formulation is important. Tavuchis's second perspective shifts our attention away from this 'social scaffolding of apology', and instead looks towards its 'experiential dynamics' (p 120). In the fully-accomplished apology, it is argued, we have first a *call* for an apology from the person(s) who regard themselves as wronged, or from someone speaking on their behalf; then the *apology* itself; and finally an expression of *forgiveness* from the wronged to the wrongdoer (p 20). Each of these moves can be emotionally fraught; thus, the whole apologetic discourse is (on both sides) 'a delicate and precarious transaction' (p vii). Yet it is important to emphasise that a successfully accomplished apology can have 'almost miraculous qualities' (p 6). This last point is explained as follows:

> no matter how sincere or effective, [an apology) does not and cannot *undo* what has been done. And yet, in a mysterious way and according to its own logic, this is precisely what it manages to do.
>
> (p 5, emphasis in original)

To understand more fully the 'social scaffolding' and the 'experiential dynamics' of the apology, let us take a closer look at three issues: the social background, the dyadic quality of apologetic discourse, and the allegedly 'miraculous qualities' of the successful apology. This approach can be regarded, in Max Weber's (1949) terminology, as the development of an ideal-typical analysis of a successful apology.[24]

(i) The background: In the ideal-typical apology, the parties already have some kind of relationship, even if that relationship is, at a personal level, tenuous and indirect (see above). But a social norm is violated, and so a 'moral imperative' (p vii) compels the wronged person to take note of that breach and to call for an apology. (The alternative is simply to forget the incident, but in any serious social/moral community, with pretensions to maintain an effective 'positive morality',[25] this is not a sustainable option.) The call for the apology therefore simultaneously:

- draws attention to the prior shared social relationships and understandings within the community;
- emphasises that the act complained of is a departure from the accepted positive morality of the group, and cannot be ignored if the legitimacy of the relevant moral rule is to be upheld; and

- potentially looks forward to a social situation where, after the apology has been offered, there will be a restoration of a prior state of relations between the parties, and within the community more generally (note the key word 'restoration' here).

In other words, both prior social relationships in community, and the accepted positive morality of the group, are deeply embedded as background characteristics (or part of the framework) of the ideal-typical apology.

(ii) The structure of the apologetic discourse: Tavuchis emphasises, rightly in my view, that the ideal-typical apology is essentially dyadic in its nature. That it to say, while supporters of the two key parties may have much to offer by way of advice, support, censure, and so forth, at the end of the day it is those two parties who are the central players in the drama, and no-one can displace them in that role if the apologetic discourse is to be really meaningful: one must express genuine regret and remorse for an act that has breached a shared moral code, and the other must forgive.[26] Only in this way can prior social relationships be 'restored', although (see below) this process itself requires continual emotional work by the parties.

(iii) The allegedly 'miraculous qualities' of successful apologies: Why does a successfully accomplished and accepted apology seem 'miraculous'? It seems so because, in one sense, nothing at all has happened (except that some words have been exchanged); and yet in another sense, everything has changed. The apology, as Tavuchis repeatedly emphasises, does not (and indeed cannot) annul the wrong that has occurred; but the *pain* and the *regret* of the sincere apology (often a difficult matter for the offender to express), followed by the equally difficult act of forgiveness offered (perhaps uncertainly) by the wronged person, have the power to effect a social transformation. The complex experiential dynamics of apology can therefore be 'a prelude to reunion and reconciliation' (p 22), even though that process of reconciliation might encounter further emotional difficulties on both sides before it is fully accomplished. We are not far here from Braithwaite's (1999: 2) aspirational words about RJ at its best: 'Crime is an opportunity to prevent greater evils, to confront crime with a grace that transforms human lives to paths of love and giving'.

To bring these points down to earth, consider a hypothetical case, that of a seriously wrong act committed by one party to a 'thick' social relationship, directly against another party (say, an adult son, with a close relationship with loving parents, committing an act that seriously wrongs his mother). Reflecting on such a scenario, we quickly realise that a true apology has much to offer. The reason for this resides in the dual facts of (i) the shared commitment to a particular social group (in this case, the family unit) *and* (ii) a genuine shared belief in the importance of the moral rule that has been broken. Given a real social/moral community of this kind, often an apology offers by far the best hope of repairing the social/moral breach, and paving the way for the resumption of something like the previous set of relationships. Those few words of apology may seem to the hypothetical Martian observer to be nothing; but to the participants they can be everything, especially if backed up by practical action to put right—so far as possible—the wrong caused by the original action. This, in a nutshell, is the sociological explanation of the 'miracle' of the successful apology: it is a social mechanism that can help to transcend breaches of the normative order within a given group or community, and to begin to restore prior relationships within that community. The key to its success lies squarely in the normative and relational realms.

I have focussed so far on 'community restoration', deliberately leaving aside Braithwaite's apparently wider agenda when he spoke of 'restoring victims, restoring offenders and restoring communities' (see above). At first blush, talk of 'restoring victims' or 'restoring offenders' might seem to have a somewhat mystical ring to it, and it is not at all clear how one could identify the generative social mechanisms that might lead to such 'restorations'. However, I would suggest that these ideas are again best considered in relational terms. How can victims, having suffered a perhaps traumatic shock, be brought again into something like their prior set of social relationships and activities, regaining their self-esteem and the confidence to live their lives without undue anxiety? How can offenders, having been/rightly censured (perhaps severely) for their offence, nevertheless be reintroduced into society so that they—and the society—may 'move on' after the offence? So understood, these apparently more individualistic kinds of 'restoration' may also be understood within the framework I have previously suggested, namely the 'restoration of prior social relationships in a community, within an understood structural and normative framework'.[27]

The preceding discussion has deliberately been conducted on the basis of two explicit assumptions: first, that we are speaking of the ideal-typical apology; and second, that the victim and the offender are part of the same social/moral community (although perhaps with only a tenuous or indirect relationship within that community). It is time to address the question of what difference it makes if either or both of these assumptions is not instantiated in a given case.

We have seen that, for Tavuchis (1991), the ideal-typical apology is essentially dyadic in its nature. It follows that, where third parties become involved, there are potential complications; and these can include, according to Tavuchis, 'eliciting and exacerbating latent anger, self-righteousness, moral indignation, and, most perniciously, the development of a punitive atmosphere' (p 52). Hence, an apology forced out of someone by a group of others encircling him and threatening to beat him up is a long way from the ideal-typical apology.[28] The presence of third parties, however, does not necessarily have such pernicious effects, and the best kind of third party is a true mediator, who is 'a kind of moral stand-in or surrogate, a necessarily temporary social actor', (p 66), who can assist the parties towards genuine apology and reconciliation. These issues highlight the delicate balancing act that is required of chairpersons of RJ-style tribunals in contemporary societies, where the offender has broken the criminal law. As the experience of pre-modern societies attests, the involvement of third parties (such as mediators), and a degree of social pressure or coercion, do not in themselves preclude a sincere and eventually socially effective apology. Nevertheless, the presence of such factors certainly might not assist the emergence of really genuine apologetic discourse, perhaps especially in contemporary societies where the parties are not necessarily members of the same social/ moral community.

Which brings us to our second explicit assumption in the discussion to this point; namely, the assumption that the victim and the offender are part of the same moral/social community. On this issue, Gulliver's (1963: 263) study of indigenous Arusha dispute settlement contains a finding with significant admonitory resonance for the contemporary RJ movement:

> Most serious disputes occur between people who are directly and fairly closely related to one another in one or more ways—members of a single lineage, or of a single parish,… etc… Arusha indigenous procedures are on the whole able to deal with these relationships because the procedures themselves arise out of the social sub-systems in

which these relationships operate. 'Unrelated' people[29] are less likely to come into serious dispute; but when they do, indigenous procedures are cumbersome and not altogether efficient. Injuries may have to be tolerated under the circumstances because of the difficulty, perhaps impossibility, of taking useful action.

The reasons for this finding are interesting. One reason relates to the previously-quoted comment by Chris Hann (2000: 145) about reconciliation being 'especially important where the contesting parties have necessarily to continue… to be part of a continuing community in everyday life'; by definition, this consideration is much less relevant for 'unrelated' than for 'related' parties. Secondly, in 'unrelated' cases the linkage to the moral/social attachments and structures in the society is necessarily weaker; in a society like the Arusha, this may make a formal dispute settlement procedure harder to convene,[30] and any settlements reached harder to enforce. The general implication is that, where the offender and the victim are not part of the same moral/social community, the genuine apology—and the social mechanisms of reconciliatory justice more generally—may be significantly harder to orchestrate. This obviously raises questions about RJ mechanisms in the anonymous urban societies of the contemporary world, and this is an issue to which we must return in the final section of this chapter.

Finally, we should return again foursquare to Braithwaite's aphorism, with which this discussion began ('for informal justice to be restorative justice, it has to be about restoring victims… (etc)'). In the light of the analysis in this section, we can now see that Braithwaite has formulated a very demanding test. What he is saying is that informal justice (say, a family group conference) is one thing, but true *restorative* justice (in my preferred formulation, justice that will restore social relationships in community) is quite another matter. In other words, just because a given part of a particular criminal justice system claims that it is running a 'restorative cautioning system' (or whatever), it does not follow, for Braithwaite, that this system truly is 'restorative'—that is, restoring relationships through the kinds of generative social mechanisms explored in this section. Given the complexity and the often fraught emotional character of the process of ideal-typical apology, it would in fact not be at all surprising if officially-sponsored 'restorative justice schemes' in contemporary societies sometimes succeeded, but sometimes failed to deliver the kind of 'restoration' to which Braithwaite aspires; and, to his credit, John Braithwaite (1999) clearly recognises this. We shall explore these issues further as we move to an analysis of RJ in contemporary societies.

IV. Restorative justice in contemporary societies

In this final section, I shall first discuss the view that RJ is an apparent anomaly in contemporary penality, and then go on to consider sociological reasons for the rapid growth of RJ in recent decades, an analysis which includes some discussion of the structural location of RJ in contemporary societies. Finally—and building on the analysis in the preceding sections—I shall assess the extent to which we can expect the truly 'restorative' elements of the mechanisms of RJ to be routinely delivered in contemporary societies.

1. The anomaly of RJ in contemporary penality

Contemporary sociologists have developed, as one of their main preoccupations, an extensive discourse and set of theorisations about, for example, 'globalisation', 'late modernity' or 'post-modernity', 'the risk society' and so forth (see for example Harvey, 1989; Giddens, 1990 and 1991; Beck, 1992; Beck et al 1994; Lash and Urry, 1994; Bauman, 1997; Lupton, 1999). Criminologists, also, have become interested in applying such theoretical ideas to a wide variety of topics. To take just one example, Ericson and Haggerty's (1997) *Policing the Risk Society* sees contemporary public police services as primarily information-brokers in a knowledge-based society, where they co-ordinate activities with, for example, the insurance and private security services. Even so-called 'community policing' is, these authors argue, really 'risk communication policing', providing a basis for risk management, that is, the pre-identification of, and subsequent containment of, risks seen as undesirable.

In the specifically penal sphere, rather similar arguments have been developed about the so-called 'new penology' (Feeley and Simon, 1992, 1994), and anyone interested in the correctional services must now actively engage with the impact of managerialism upon those services (see for example James and Raine, 1998). Quite sophisticated tools of risk assessment are now routinely deployed in the penal sphere (Robinson, 2002). Additionally, one of the most astonishing features of the penal scene in many countries at the end of the twentieth and the beginning of the twenty-first century is the apparently inexorable rise of prison populations. All this has led David Garland, one of the leading writers on the sociology of punishment, to entitle his recent book *The Culture of Control* (Garland, 2001). Nor finally, in this brief inventory of contemporary penality, must one forget the growing importance of human rights protections enforced by the law, well exemplified by the very significant impact of the European Convention on Human Rights on various aspects of criminal justice in the United Kingdom.

Every one of these various issues seems rather remote from the main preoccupations of RJ. Unquestionably, RJ is now an international movement, and in a number of countries it has come to have a significant influence on mainstream criminal justice policies. This has been achieved from a position of almost complete marginality of quarter of a century ago. Yet, in achieving its phenomenal growth, RJ has remained predominantly small-scale and communitarian in its preferred operating style, with—for example—usually only at best a very marginal role for lawyers[31] and other professionals, and certainly very little use of such late modern devices as risk assessment profiles. Neither RJ practitioners, nor most academics sympathetic to RJ, show any sustained interest in the issues of 'managerialism' and 'risk' in relation to criminal justice,[32] and even the legal protections arising from human rights conventions are on occasion downplayed. In all these respects, the RJ movement has remained faithful to the wariness of 'experts' (both legal and behavioural), and to the preference for ordinary people to have a direct say in their own conflicts, expressed by Nils Christie (1977) a quarter of a century ago. But, equally, all this makes RJ distinctly *anomalous* in contemporary penality, in the sense that RJ has genuinely grown in influence in the last quarter-century, yet this has occurred within a penal policy context that in many ways seems to operate on a set of assumptions very different from its own. If this analysis is correct, then the apparently 'anomalous' growth of RJ in contemporary societies requires serious sociological attention.

2. The appeal and growth of RJ in contemporary societies

Why, then, has RJ's influence spread so rapidly, especially given the apparently inauspicious context (see above)? Any answer to this question must be, in part, speculative, but a number of possibilities can, I think, be reasonably suggested.

(i) The appeal of the gemeinschaft in late modern societies: Kamenka and Tay (1980a), influential writers on the sociology of law, have identified three major types of law in Western societies. These types, they emphasise, are not necessarily evolutionary, and indeed all three types are often co-present in a given legal system. Their analysis, although perhaps over-schematic, can I think help us in our task of explanation.

The first of the three types is *gemeinschaft*-type law, which 'takes for its fundamental presupposition and concern the organic community' (p 19). By contrast, *gesellschaft*-type law takes for its fundamental presupposition and concern the individual, who is 'theoretically— for the purposes of law—free and self-determined, limited only by the rights of other *individuals'* (p 19, emphasis in original). In the third type of law, so-called 'bureaucratic-administrative law', the presupposition and concern is 'neither an organic human community nor an atomic individual, it is a non-human ruling interest, public policy, or ongoing activity, of which human beings are subordinates, functionaries or carriers' (p 19).[33]

In the contemporary world, it is often not at all difficult to discern each of these three kinds of law in operation on a co-present basis in a given legal jurisdiction. For example, in the sphere of criminal justice one might find, in a particular jurisdiction, a Human Rights Act (or equivalent) enshrining basic legal rights and freedoms for individuals (*gesellschaft*-type law); together with risk-based legislation on parole release, or on the community-based monitoring of sex offenders (bureaucratic-administrative law); together with provisions for restorative justice conferences for certain categories of persons who have admitted offences *(gemeinschaft*-type law).

Of the three legal types, individualized *gesellschaft*-type law is in an important sense the foundation-stone of legal rules in any modern liberal-democratic state. But a central problem for such states is that *gesellschaft*-type law 'is not attuned, in its underlying individualism, to the fact of social interconnection and inter-dependence, or to the supra-individual require-ments of social activities and social living' (Kamenka and Tay, 1975: 140). These supra-individual requirements, insofar as they are properly within the province of law at all, must therefore be provided either by *gemeinschaft*-type or by bureaucratic-administrative law, or by some mixture of the two. In practice, however, in contemporary societies there *is a tendency for bureaucratic-administrative values and arrangements to be favoured* for such purposes, since 'the necessary structure, the resources and control in a world of atomic individuals not shaped in and by coherent [social] institutions, can only be provided by the State', or by other organisations acting ostensibly in the public interest (Kamenka and Tay, 1980b: 108).[34] Hence, in criminal justice systems, the rapid development of 'managerialism' and of 'risk' paradigms, which are undoubtedly predominantly bureaucratic-administrative in their approach, and are designed to meet the 'supra-individual requirements of 'social activities and social living' in late modern societies (see further, Bottoms, 1995; Bottoms and Wiles, 1996).

This analysis, however, whilst prioritising the bureaucratic-administrative approach to 'supra-individual requirements', nevertheless allows us to see why there might be, in modern legal arrangements, something of a hunger for *gemeinschaft*-type approaches, as policies that could help to provide, at a minimum, 'a certain humanising cosmetic for bureaucratic practice' (Kamenka and Tay, 1975: 142), and perhaps substantially more than that. Such a hunger for the *gemeinschaft* could of course be purely nostalgic (the hankering after a lost world of 'thick' social relationships and neighbourhood-based communities), but it could also be, in part, completely genuine (the search for an organic rather than a bureaucratic approach to at least some supra-individual requirements within modern legal systems).

Such considerations would be consistent with the rise of RJ arrangements in a globalised, risk-oriented, bureaucratic-administrative world. But if this approach to explanation has any validity, then two things follow. First, on this view RJ conferences (or their equivalents) are not—contrary to Christie's (1977) original vision—in any serious sense organisations that will be a 'vitaliser for neighbourhoods', but rather organisations that are allowed to exist in certain spaces of late modern societies where it is thought that a *gemeinschaft* approach might have some value (as an addition to the bureaucratic-administrative and *gesellschaft* approaches that are elsewhere dominant in criminal justice). And secondly, if the first proposition is correct, then it will be worth paying some serious attention to those 'structural spaces' where, in practice, RJ seems to be most often allowed to flourish in contemporary societies. The most obvious such 'structural space', empirically speaking, clearly lies in the field of youth justice:[35] it follows, therefore, that our search for explanation needs to consider why youth justice is seen as a particularly appropriate site for RJ approaches.

(ii) Victims and moral clarification: Sociologically speaking, the RJ movement can unquestionably be read as part of the 'victimological turn' in criminal justice policies in many jurisdictions since about 1960—a movement that has seen a host of innovations such as increases in victim compensation, victim impact statements, 'Victim Charters' and the like. Such movements can be, and have been, analysed in detail on a country-by-country basis, notably in the distinguished work of Paul Rock (1986,1990). But for present purposes, perhaps a more macro-level, broad-brush explanation is of greater relevance to an understanding of the international growth of RJ.

Possibly the most interesting contribution in this regard has come from the Dutch criminologist Hans Boutellier (1996, 2000). In contemporary societies, sources of social trust typically shift from traditional, localised social groups and communities to a more individualised and technologically-based set of social arrangements. These developments tend to produce moral individualism and some moral relativism, which in turn mean that the criminal law 'cannot be legitimised any more by the self-evident moral cohesion of the community' (Boutellier, 1996: 15). Moreover, and as Durkheim (1901) long ago indicated, such moral shifts result in changes in the way in which we see crimes in contemporary societies—the crime is less often seen as an offence against the State (or collectivity), and more often as against the individual victim. In such a social context, the victim and his or her suffering can and does tend to become the organising focus for a new moral code that is simultaneously more individualistic and more concrete than its predecessors. Members of contemporary societies (especially younger members) can see the point of a moral code based on preventing the sufferings of a flesh-and-blood victim more easily then they can relate to the abstract violation of a traditional collective norm. Giving the victim a prominent role in the courtroom (or its equivalent) may therefore be a way of helping to 'find a criterion that draws a line on moral relativism and pluralism' (Boutellier, 1996: 15). RJ, on this reading, is therefore attractive as a social policy because it helps to provide an element of *normative clarification* in a morally changing society, struggling to develop a new 'positive morality' (Hart, 1963) for our times. (On morality, crime and criminal justice, see further Bottoms, 2002.)

In short, RJ, on this view, can be seen as helping to provide an attractive form of *moral clarification* and *moral pedagogy* (based on the suffering of the victim) to contemporary penal policymakers. And if that view is correct, then it becomes much easier to see why RJ has become structurally focussed especially on juveniles, the traditional subjects of moral pedagogy. The focus on juveniles also links back to the first possible explanation (based on the work of Kamenka and Tay), because juveniles are one group of offenders who many people would wish to see treated within a *gemeinschaft,* rather than a bureaucratic-administrative, policy approach.

A final comment may be made on Boutellier's thesis. His proposal is that there is a contemporary shift in perception of the nature of crimes, now seen less often as the violation of an abstract moral principle, and more often as a harm to a specific victim. Such a shift in perception, of course, would not only produce a 'victimological turn' in criminal justice, it would also encourage a shift away from perceiving incidents necessarily as 'crimes' at all. In other words, the previously-discussed 'civilisation thesis' might itself in part be the product of the kind of social changes to which Boutellier has drawn attention.

(iii) The questionable legitimacy of courts: In its origins, the RJ movement had links not only with the 'victim movement' but also with the 'informal justice' movement (on which see eg Abel, 1982; Matthews, 1988). Important reasons for the growth of the informal justice movement are well captured by Merry (1982: 17), in a passage that reminds one of Hulsman's emphasis on 'naturally occurring' restorative justice processes:

> The increasing urbanism, transiency, and heterogenity of American society in the twentieth century has undermined informal dispute settlement mechanisms rooted in home, church, and community and increased the demand for other means of dealing with family, neighbor, and community disputes. However, many legal experts argue that the formality of the courts, their adherence to an adversary model, their strict rules of procedure, and their reliance on adjudication render them inappropriate for handling many kinds of interpersonal quarrels arising in ongoing social relationships.

Since the early 1980s, the informal justice movement has lost some of its impetus,[36] though RJ has not. But the RJ movement, like the informal justice movement, has gained part of its strength from the perceived deficiencies of the courts. These deficiencies have also been more fully exposed owing to some macro-social developments to which we must now turn.

Those who have lived through the second half of the twentieth century in Western societies have witnessed a sustained period of economic growth, yet also the decline of manufacturing industry in most countries, as such goods can now be produced more cheaply in the low wage economies of developing societies. The apparent paradox of manufacturing decline despite sustained growth is explained, of course, by a massive switch into service industries in most Western economies, and by the stimulation of demand (through advertising and the like) for luxury goods, and for leisure and personal services. This rapid development of a *consumer* rather than a *producer* economy (to adopt the usual shorthand phrase) has cultural as well as economic consequences (see generally Lash and Urry 1994). In a service-led, consumer-oriented society, consumers have realised that they can make their demands assertively where they consider that the product is not up to standard. As is well known, they have learned to make such demands not only in their private purchasing, but also in relation to public sector organisations such as schools, the police and (in Britain) the health service.

Two key issues that public organisations have had to address in response to these developments are demands for the enhanced *accountability* of professionals (who are no longer afforded the automatic deference that they once were); and, on occasion, demands for *lay participation* in decision-making. The growth of RJ appears to fit well with these sociological trends, since RJ typically uses a primarily lay and participatory forum, and tends to have a suspicion of professionals. Hence, it is not surprising that on the question of *procedural justice*—as developed in the work of Tom Tyler (1990) and others—both the RISE and the SAJJ research evaluations in Australia have produced very high ratings of satisfaction, among both offender and victim participants in RJ conferences, on questions such as having a proper chance to have one's say, and being treated with respect within the forum. In the RISE study, ratings for the conference samples on these variables were consistently higher than those for the court sample [...].

These matters undoubtedly help to explain the worldwide growth of RJ, yet they perhaps do not explain it fully. For the advocates of RJ, it is ultimately what Kathleen Daly (2002) has called the *restorative justice* elements of RJ (that is, the possibility of really engaging with and influencing the other party) that is substantially more important than the *procedural justice* elements of participation and so forth, important though these also are. Moreover, the 'participation/accountability' approach seems to offer little by way of explanation as to why RJ has become structurally concentrated in the youth justice sector. On balance, therefore, it seems likely that the doubtful legitimacy of courts in the contemporary era has been a contributory factor, rather than a major force, in the rapid development of RJ in the last quarter-century.

(iv) Political contexts of contested legitimacy: As is well known, the first jurisdiction to incorporate restorative justice processes into its justice system in a really major way was New Zealand with its 'family group conferences' (see Maxwell and Morris, 1993). It is sometimes asserted that family group conferences are a replication of Maori indigenous (pre-colonial) practice, but this is not the case (Maxwell and Morris, 1993:4). Kathleen Daly (2002:63) tells the story briefly:

> conferencing emerged in the 1980s, in the context of Maori political challenges to white New Zealanders and to their welfare and criminal justice systems. Investing decision-making practices with Maori cultural values meant that family groups (whanau) should have a greater say in what happens, that venues should be culturally appropriate, and that processes should accommodate a mix of culturally appropriate practices. New Zealand's minority group population includes not only the Maori but also Pacific Island Polynesians. Therefore, with the introduction of conferencing, came awareness of the need to incorporate different elements of 'cultural appropriateness' into the conference process. But the devising of a (white, bureaucratic) justice practice that is *flexible and accommodating* towards cultural differences does not mean that conferencing is an indigenous justice practice.

(Emphasis in original)

Rather similar stories can be told for other jurisdictions. The Canadian 'sentencing circles', for example, are an attempt to provide a sentencing context that will be more culturally appropriate for the Canadian indigenous peoples.[37] In the rather different political context of Northern Ireland, following the so-called 'peace process' and the Good Friday Agreement of 1998, a formal Review of the Criminal Justice System was set up, designed to be acceptable to both principal communities (Unionist/Loyalist and Nationalist/Republican) in the jurisdiction. That review recommended the general development of RJ approaches for juvenile offenders, and the formal integration of RJ principles into the official juvenile justice system (Northern Ireland Office, 2000: chs 9 and 10), and subsequently these recommendations were accepted by the U.K. government (Northern Ireland Office, 2001).

What all the above jurisdictions share is the presence of a minority group of a significant size that has, over time, become significantly alienated from the official criminal justice system in the light of a colonialist or quasi-colonialist history. In each case, RJ processes now seem attractive to policymakers as a way of trying to heal past conflicts and wrongs, and to incorporate greater awareness of differing cultural traditions into the criminal (and especially juvenile) justice systems. It is not hard to see that such developments draw on at least two important features of RJ: these are, first, the reconciliatory elements in RJ philosophy; and secondly, the element of 'normative clarification' sometimes present in RJ-style fora, to which Christie (1977) drew attention long ago (see earlier section). This 'normative clarification' dimension, however, has its own dangers in a situation of seriously contested legitimacy, because the official policymakers' gesture of setting up RJ processes—within a State formation still dominated by the previous majority group—can easily be attacked as being insufficiently aware of cultural differences, insufficiently aware of the depth of the 'legitimacy deficit' (Beetham 1991) that the majority community's past actions have engendered, and so forth. Exactly such responses have sometimes been encountered in all of the jurisdictions mentioned above. Despite these continuing tensions, there seems little doubt that a political context of seriously contested legitimacy is, in the contemporary world, a powerful motivating factor (along with the other factors already discussed) that makes more likely—although, of course, not inevitable—the establishment of RJ-type processes.

(v) The new regulatory state: John Braithwaite (2000b) has proposed a very interesting additional explanatory suggestion concerning the rise of RJ. This suggestion arises out of the political science literature, and can be regarded as potentially complementary to some of the earlier explanations discussed, notably explanations (i) and (ii) above.

Braithwaite follows Osborne and Gaebler (1992) in distinguishing between two possible approaches to the exercise of State power in society, namely 'rowing' (where, as in a rowing boat, the State does the principal work) and 'steering' (where, like a coxswain, the State provides direction, but the 'rowing' is done by others, notably private firms, voluntary agencies and local communities). In a somewhat overschematic, but nevertheless very heuristically useful discussion, Braithwaite suggests that in the last two hundred years we have witnessed three different types of State formation: *first,* the 'nightwatchman state', where 'most of the steering and rowing was done in civil society'; *secondly,* the Keynesian state, where the State did 'a lot of rowing, but was weak on steering civil society'; and *third* the new 'regulatory state', 'which holds up state steering and civil society rowing as the ideal' (Braithwaite, 2000b: 233). The shift from Keynesian to regulatory politics has involved massive privatisation of former State functions (from nationalised industries to policing and prisons), but also a pattern of insisting that individuals and groups should make provisions for their own welfare (a process sometimes described as 'responsibilisation'). Yet, in thus withdrawing from previous 'rowing' functions, the State has frequently set up 'regulators' whose task is to ensure that the public interest is protected: hence, the State offers a strong 'steering' guideline to markets and to civil society in the 'new regulatory state'.

From this perspective, contemporary RJ procedures—where, typically, people are asked to settle their own conflicts under the guidance of a State-appointed mediator or chairperson—can be viewed as an 'important manifestation of the new regulatory state in criminal justice' (Braithwaite, 2000b: 227). However, Braithwaite is uneasy about a policy of total State withdrawal in this area (save for the provision of the mediator), since he argues that in contemporary societies 'restorative justice founders when the welfare state is not there to support it' with appropriate services to victims and offenders (Braithwaite, 2000b: 233). He therefore concludes that what we should aspire to is a new regulatory state that is strong on steering, *combined with* a strong market economy and with 'communities in civil society that are... strong on both steering and rowing' (including indigenous dispute settlement), *combined with* State retention of certain 'Keynesian' rowing functions as a support to markets and to civil society.

Braithwaite's interesting analysis does, I believe, further help to explain the revival of some RJ-style practices in contemporary societies. As presented by Braithwaite, however, the analysis is somewhat less successful in explaining what I called (earlier in this section) the anomaly of the rise of RJ in the predominantly managerialist and control-oriented penal systems of contemporary Western societies (since many of these developments look distinctly like State 'rowing'). A possible development of Braithwaite's argument would, however, be to see the criminal justice in the era of the regulatory state as having a dual focus: a coercive, 'rowing-based', risk-focussed State criminal justice system for more serious and persistent criminality, and a delegation to local communities of the process, of dealing with non-persistent, low level criminality.[38]

(vi) Overview: As I indicated at the beginning of this subsection, any answer to the question 'why has the influence of R] spread so rapidly?' must be, in part, speculative, and I do not claim that the preceding analysis is in any sense definitive. Nevertheless, I think it is reasonable to claim that, at least on a preliminary basis, many of the explanations suggested here have some potential validity. RJ sceptics, in particular, need to come to terms with these matters, for their implication is that there are in contemporary advanced-urban societies some apparently plausible reasons for the revivication of RJ-related ideas. Policymakers, too, could perhaps benefit from considering some of the specific reasons that 1 have outlined, and reflecting upon how they relate to the development (and potential development) of RJ processes in their particular jurisdiction.

3. The mechanisms of RJ in contemporary societies

Sally Merry (1982: 34), in her literature overview of mediation processes in pre-industrial societies, offered a warning about the simple transplantation of mediation practices from one social context to another:

> The efficacy of mediation depends on the existence of a cohesive, stable, morally integrated community whose powers of informal social control can be harnessed to informally achieved settlements... [But in contemporary America) disputants are rarely embedded in a close, cohesive social system where they need to maintain cooperative relationships. Even when disputants come from the same neighborhood, unless they are integrated into a unitary social structure their conflicts in one relationship do not have repercussions for others.

The potential importance of this issue had, of course, already been raised by Christie (1977) in his landmark early paper (though with little precision about the social mechanisms involved). As we have seen, Christie's proposed solution was to try to revivify 'thick' social relationships in the neighbourhoods of contemporary cities; but there is little evidence that this has occurred. Not surprisingly, therefore, scepticism about the viability of RJ processes within contemporary urban contexts is a topic that has resurfaced fairly regularly in the RJ literature (see eg the recent textbook discussion in Johnstone, 2002: ch 3). RJ advocates tend to deal with this issue by offering three counter-arguments:

> *First,* while 'thick' social ties have diminished in contemporary societies, the nature of a globalised economy means that we are all now more socially interdependent with a larger number of other people than was the case in traditional societies; *Secondly,* and relatedly, that while communitarian relationships *in neighbourhoods* have diminished, non-geographic relationships (fostered by the easy communication afforded by developments such as email) and 'communities of fate' (Braithwaite, 2000b) have flourished. Accordingly, for example, 'one cannot withdraw from the disapproval of one's international professional community by moving house' (Braithwaite, 1993:14); *Thirdly,* that the communitarianism of RJ is an 'individual-centred communitarianism that can work in a world of weak geographical communities', because it 'looks for community on many and any bases that can be built around a single person' (Braithwaite, 2000a: 122); and everyone has at least some community ties that can be used in support of RJ processes.

There is, of course, some prima facie merit in all of these arguments. However, the real issue is whether the *social mechanisms* of RJ (exemplified *par excellence* in the apology) can work in contemporary urban societies. Certainly they can work in international professional relationships and the like (see the second point above), but this is of very limited relevance to street crime, most perpetrators of which are anything but globalised in their social relationships (see Wiles and Costello, 2000). 'Interdependence' (see the first point) is in itself of very little significance; the issue is whether, in contemporary societies, adequate meso-social structures exist to support RJ-type approaches, and the social mechanisms on which successful reconciliation depends, and it is not obvious that globalised interdependence helps at all in these respects. Hence, at least for dealing with street crime, it is the third of the above arguments that is crucial. Here, the central point seems to be that while indeed *some* (perhaps vestigial) element of 'community' can be built around almost every single person, that 'community' might or might not be a strong enough social-structural base to make the social mechanisms of RJ work effectively.

If all this is correct, a corollary would seem to be that one would expect detailed empirical examinations of RJ in contemporary societies to show a very mixed picture, with (for example) apologies sometimes being received as sincere and sometimes not; sometimes a real meeting of hearts and minds among the participants, sometimes not; and so on. And that is, indeed, exactly what the current empirical evidence seems to show. [...] (see also Daly, 2002).

V. Conclusion

Finally, I shall offer seven brief conclusions that can, I believe, reasonably be derived from the analysis in this chapter.

First, there seem to be some good sociological reasons for the growth of RJ in contemporary societies. Policymakers (and RJ sceptics) should take these matters seriously.

Secondly, for a number of reasons (including mainstream developments in contemporary penal systems, and the kinds of generative social mechanisms on which successful RJ depends) it is extremely unlikely that, in contemporary societies, RJ will ever completely replace existing criminal justice systems.

Thirdly, there remains among RJ advocates a significant lack of agreement as to whether the 'individual-centred communitarianism' of RJ should primarily offer a 'civil justice' or a more 'communitarian' vision of RJ.

Fourthly, the social mechanisms on which RJ depends work less well in contemporary than they do in traditional societies, because of the different social-structural context; hence, a 'blanket' delivery of RJ (to all cases in a given category) is always likely to achieve modest and/or patchy results in contemporary societies.

Fifthly, a version of informal RJ will always exist alongside the official criminal justice system, in families, schools, and so on (see the analysis by Hulsman).

Sixthly, and taking into account the previous five conclusions, a key policy debate (which has as yet barely begun) is that contemporary societies should start to consider seriously the kinds of case for which we might wish to develop formal RJ-type responses (and why), and the kinds of case in which we would prefer to retain standard criminal justice processes. For the kinds of case that we might wish to develop RJ approaches, we will need to specify the relative degree of emphasis on the 'private' and the 'communitarian' elements (a matter that might of course vary between different kinds of case).

Seventhly, in all these policy debates, we should always hold at the forefront of our minds the social mechanisms that apparently underpin successful social reconciliations, and the social structures that best support these social mechanisms.[39]

Notes

1 'Conflicts as Property' was originally delivered on 31 March 1976 as the Foundation Lecture of the Centre for Criminological Studies at the University of Sheffield. As the first Director of the new Centre, I had the pleasure of proposing the vote of thanks at the conclusion of the lecture.

2 The subsequent major influence of Christie's paper would have been predicted by very few of those who first heard it. It was initially regarded as an extremely interesting intellectual argument, but one that was unlikely to have much subsequent practical impact. How wrong first impressions can be!

3 Christie gives no reference to indicate from what source he drew his description of this case.

4 The unexplained reference to 'party secretaries' suggests that this is a post-independence case (independence from colonial rule was achieved in Tanganyika in 1963); hence Cain (1988: 53) refers to Christie's article as describing a 'post-colonial African community moot'. However, by being inactive the judges were, in a new context, remaining essentially faithful to the traditions of indigenous Arusha dispute-settlement, where there were 'no third parties recognised as having authority to resolve a dispute by decision, [so] settlement has to be by compromise reached through negotiation' (Roberts, 1979: 133). See further, n 7 below.

5 Christie (1977:10–11) envisages a four-stage process for his proposed neighbourhood courts: (i) fact-finding about the incident; (ii) the victim's situation is considered in detail, including possible compensation and other assistance to her/him (first by the offender, and then by the wider community); (iii) possible punishment of the offender in *addition to* his/her restitutive actions to the victim; and (iv) possible social assistance to the offender. Christie is willing to consider the possible introduction of lawyers and behaviour experts into some of these stages (lawyers in stage (i); behaviour experts in stages (ii) and (iv)), but his underlying attitude is that 'experts are as cancer to any lay body' (p 11).

6 As Roberts (1979:129) summarises Gulliver's evidence: 'Arusha do not live in well-defined villages, but in homesteads located here and there across... arable lands... divided up into... geographical units which Gulliver describes as "parishes"'. But, unlike many pre-modern societies, residential groupings do not necessarily coincide with patrilineal descent groups; rather 'the homesteads of members of a given lineage are likely to be scattered all over Arusha country'. Since 'age-sets' (groups of persons of similar age who go through initiation rites together) are also important in traditional Arusha society, the social structures of that society have 'three distinct sub-groupings' [residence; lineage; age-sets], a feature that can have 'important consequences in the event of a dispute' (including giving the litigant 'a choice of forum before which disputes can

be taken' (p 129), the principal options in the event of a public dispute being the 'parish assembly' and a lineage-based moot: Gulliver, 1963:174).

7 See generally Gulliver (1963: ch 10). Neither in parish assemblies nor in moots (see note 6 above) were there any independent judges. Gulliver (1963: 228–9) notes however that there were several accepted 'general principles of proper behaviour' at these gatherings, including: (i) a degree of spatial separation of the disputants and their supporters; (ii) the right of each disputant to argue his/her case fully; and (iii) the presence of high-status 'spokesmen, counsellors (or) other notables' to support each party, these 'notables' being crucial to the maintenance of good order. ('Though avowedly on opposite sides in the dispute, they are generally ready to ally together against unruly behaviour, lengthy irrelevancies, and persistent contumely. It is only by their willingness together to maintain orderly discussion that an assembly can carry on its work adequately': p 229).

8 I am grateful to Jim Dignan for this insight. It should be emphasised: (i) that the claim relates only to *principal* sources, and there were others (eg elements of Christian thought); and (ii) the claim relates only to the *origins* of the RJ movement, ie to the period preceding John Braithwaite's important book on reintegrative shaming (Braithwaite, 1989), which greatly influenced many later developments in RJ.

9 Marjery Fry's claim here relates only to financial restitution, but a similar claim was later made in broader senses by RJ advocates.

10 See for example the claim made in Zehr's very influential book *Changing Lenses* that even property crimes such as burglary, vandalism and car theft are essentially attacks on personal security, and are experienced as such: 'Crime is in essence a violation: a violation of the self, a desecration of who we are, of what we believe, of our private space. Crime is devastating because it upsets two fundamental assumptions on which we base our lives: our belief that the world is an orderly, meaningful place, and our belief in personal autonomy. Both assumptions are essential for wholeness' (Zehr, 1990: 24).

11 Hulsman (1982: 46) defines the 'civilisation' thesis as 'an approach in which the compensatory model of civil law (by adaptation of civil procedure) is extended to areas in which it docs not yet operate'.

12 For other early contributions broadly within the 'civilisation' tradition, see Cantor (1976) and Barnett (1977).

13 Hulsman's core approach is illustrated in the quotation above by the phrase 'on the level of those directly involved, nothing... distinguishes these "criminal" events *intrinsically* from other difficult or unpleasant situations'. For desert theorists such as von Hirsch (1993), this is to ignore the crucial element of societal censure.

14 It could be argued that victim-offender mediation projects are almost wholly individualistic, with little of a communitarian dimension. However, as Marshall and Merry (1990) make clear in their discussion of early projects of this kind in England, part of the philosophy of victim-offender mediation is that 'citizens generally ("the community") should be cncouraged to play an active part in crime prevention and local social control' (p 6). Later, the same authors argue that, for example, 'as they become known as "experts" in mediation, the staff of such projects inevitably get asked to help train others in such techniques, even beyond the sphere of victim-offender mediation. In their work with corporate victims who suffer repeated crime, for instance, schemes could promote discussion of how to cope with the problem more constructively, and, through meetings with offenders, help to formulate ways of preventing it... All the schemes [studied] seem to be making some headway in these respects' (pp 209–10). Thus, while in these projects there was little direct community involvement in the formal mediation processes (pp 206–8), a communitarian dimension clearly remained, not least at an aspirational level.

15 On *gemeinschaft*-type law and *gesellschaft*-type law, see the fuller discussion later in this chapter of the work of Kamenka and Tay (1975, 1980a, 1980b).

16 As Gulliver (1963: 299–300) puts it: 'Arusha are inclined to view each new dispute as a unique phenomenon, to the solution of which the ideal norm and past precedent provide only the initial basis for negotiation'. Thus, Arusha dispute processes 'have a nature which can be characterised as mainly political rather than judicial'.

17 On mediators in small-scale societies, see Merry (1982). As she comments: 'mediators are respected, influential community members with experience and acknowledged expertise in settling disputes... they are experts in village social relationships and genealogy, bringing to the conflict a vast store of knowledge about how individuals are expected to behave toward one another as well

as about the reputations and social identities of the particular disputants... To flout [a mediator's] settlement is to defy the moral order of the community' (Merry, 1982: 30).

18 Ryan's concerns, in undertaking this research, were not only academic but also policy-oriented; that is, they were focussed on how the research team's findings about traditional justice 'might provide some directions and new ideas for the Dene to take back responsibility for their own ways of social control now' (Ryan, 1995; xxviii). These policy issues were addressed by Joan Ryan in her speech to a public meeting on restorative justice held at the University of Toronto in May 2001, linked to the discussions leading to this book.

19 As Ryan several times emphasises, there is no concept of a 'not guilty' plea in Dogrib justice. However, 'no action is taken against an individual unless people are sure that something wrong has been done by the individual which affects the safety and well-being of the collective' (Ryan, 1995: 91).

20 As Lukes (1973: 149) explains (quoting liberally from the original), Durkheim saw mechanical solidarity as ' "a solidarity *sui generis* which... directly links the individual with society"; it "arises from the fact that a number of states of consciousness (*conscience*) are common to all the members of the same society". It can be strong "only to the extent that the ideas and dispositions common to all the members of the society exceed in number and intensity those which pertain personally to each of them".' Societies with organic solidarity are more internally differentiated, and have a more elaborate division of labour. In such societies '"the individual depends upon society because he depends upon the parts which compose it", while society is "a system of different and special functions united by definite relations". It presupposes that individuals "differ from one another"... [and so, in such societies] "the yoke we submit to is infinitely less heavy than when the entire society weighs on us, and it leaves much more room for the free play of our initiative"' (Lukes, 1973: 153).

21 For a full discussion of coercion in traditional Arusha dispute-settlement, see Gulliver (1963: ch 11).

22 In contemporary RJ debates, disagreement sometimes arises about the appropriate role of the president(s) of a tribunal. For example, in the so-called Referral Orders established in the English youth justice system by an Act of 1999, some young offenders are mandatorily 'referred' from the Youth Court to a so-called 'Youth Offending Panel', a forum with intendedly restorative justice features. This panel consists of three community representatives, and some have argued that this constitutes an over-heavy community representation, for example by comparison with the New Zealand family group conferences (on which see Maxwell and Morris, 1993).

23 Indeed, it should be recalled that Ryan's evidence suggests this is what is actually achieved among the Dogrib: once an agreed restitution had been made, 'no further action was taken and no further mention of the offence was made' within the community (Ryan, 1995: 34).

24 As Frank Parkin (1982: 28) explains: 'Ideal-types are conceptual abstractions that we employ in trying to get to grips with the complexities of the social world. Weber properly points out that we cannot grasp social phenomena in their totality. Patterns of behaviour and institutional forms like capitalism, or Protestantism, or bureaucracy, are each composed of a large number of inter-connected elements, both normative and structural. In order to comprehend any such institution or social formation it is necessary to reduce it to its core components. We do this by singling out and accentuating the central or basic features of the institution in question and suppressing or downgrading those features that could be considered marginal to it'.

25 The term 'positive morality', first used by nineteenth century utilitarians, was helpfully revived by HLA Hart forty years ago (see MacCormick, 1981: ch 4). Hart defined 'positive morality' as 'the morality actually accepted and shared by a given social group'; by contrast, he suggested that 'critical morality' refers to 'the general moral principles used in the criticism of actual social institutions including positive morality' (Hart 1963: 20).

26 Even in collective societies such as the Dogrib, note the language used by Joan Ryan (1995: 91): 'the group demands that [the offender] face the victim, that restitution be made, that reconciliation start'. There is very strong collective pressure here, but also a recognition that meaningful apology and reconciliation is ultimately dyadic: The offender must 'face the victim', and only in this way can reconciliation 'start'.

27 It should be noted that, once again, these formulations do not necessarily presuppose that the offender and the victim have any direct relationship. As before, however, it is assumed for present

purposes that both the offender and the victim belong to the same identifiable moral/social community.

28 For a worst-case scenario of this kind in a criminal justice context, see the description by Karp (1998) of the coerced apologies ordered by courts in some American jurisdictions, in some cases combined with debasement gestures such as requiring the defendant to make the apology while on his hands and knees.

29 Gulliver deliberately places inverted commas around the word 'unrelated'. As he explains elsewhere, among the Arusha everyone is structurally related to all other people through the patrilineal descent system; nevertheless 'those who live more than a few miles apart and whose patrilineal link is relatively remote, may be said for practical purposes to be "unrelated"' (Gulliver, 1963: 258).

30 Among the Arusha in the 1950s this led to 'unrelated' people not infrequently taking their case to the courts of the colonial power (Gulliver, 1963: 266, 204ff), notwithstanding that the Arusha in general regarded these courts as 'alien-imposed institutions' which were over-formal, and in which they lacked faith (pp 273–4).

31 For example, the recent English legislation concerning 'Referral Orders' (sec n 22 above) expressly excludes state-assisted legal aid from being available in the Youth Offender Panel proceedings.

32 An important exception here is John Braithwaite, whose work on restorative justice in relation to 'the new regulatory state' (Braithwaite, 2000b) is considered later in this chapter.

33 Kamenka and Tay (1980a: 19–20) explain this more fully by reference to laws and regulations relating to railways. 'The (*Gesellschaft-*) law concerning railways is oriented toward the rights of people whose interests may be infringed by the operation of railways or people whose activities may infringe the rights of the owners or operators seen as individuals exercising individual rights, *(Bureaucratic-administrative)* regulations concerning railways take for their primary object the efficient running of railways or the efficient execution of tasks and attainment of goals and norms set by the authorities and taken as given. Individuals as individuals are the object of some of these regulations but not their subject: they are relevant not as individuals having rights and duties as individuals, but as part of the railway-running process and its organization, as people having duties and responsibilities. Such people are seen as carrying out roles, as not standing in a "horizontal" relation of equivalence to the railway organization or to all their fellow-workers, but as standing in defined "vertical" relations of subordination and sub-subordination. The relation of the bureaucratic to people as subjects and not objects is never direct but mediated through the policy, plan or regulations that purport to have human needs as well as technical requirements for their foundation.'

34 Writing in the early 1980s, Kamenka and Tay did not appreciate the extent to which the State would in the near future withdraw from the direct provision of the 'structure, resources and control' of which they speak, in favour of a more regulatory role. On this, see further subsection (v) below.

35 Almost all contemporary jurisdictions that have developed RJ-style approaches have developed them more quickly and extensively for juveniles than they have for adults.

36 Part of the reason for this loss of impetus probably lies in the decline in the influence of socialism since about 1990, and the linkage of socialist analyses with some aspects of the informal justice movement (see eg Cain, 1988). For an account of optimism and pessimism in the informal justice movement of the 1980s, see Matthews, (1988).

37 Restorative justice has also expanded rapidly in the various Australian jurisdictions, mostly but not exclusively in a juvenile justice context (see Daly and Hayes, 2001). However, while there are of course serious anxieties in Australia about the social exclusion of the aboriginal communities, and the over-representation of aboriginals in the criminal justice system, the rise of RJ in Australia— unlike the parallel process in New Zealand—mostly seems not to have occurred in direct response to aboriginal 'political challenges to white [settlers] and to their welfare and criminal justice systems' (Daly, 2002: 63).

38 More than any other writer, Braithwaite (1999) has additionally drawn attention to the importance of RJ mechanisms in dealing with white-collar and corporate crime in contemporary societies. These developments, of course, fit extremely well with the 'regulatory state' thesis that Braithwaite (2000b) has also advanced; but they are not the principal concern of the present chapter.

39 I am most grateful to Jim Dignan for several clarificatory discussions, and for his comments on an earlier draft of this chapter. The chapter has also benefited from my conversations with Kathleen Daly, John Braithwaite and Paul Crosland. Of course, none of these colleagues should be held responsible for the final product.

References

Abel, RL (ed) (1982) *The Politics of Informal Justice,* 2 vols (Academic Press, New York).

Barnett, R (1977) 'Restitution: A New Paradigm of Criminal Justice' 87 *Ethics* 279–301.

Bauman, Z (1997) *Postmodernity and its Discontents* (Polity Press, Cambridge).

Beck, U (1992) *Risk Society: Towards a New Modernity* (Sage, London).

Beck, U, Giddens, A and Lash, S (1994) *Reflexive Modernization* (Polity Press, Cambridge).

Beetham, D (1991) *The Legitimation of Power* (Macmillan, London).

Bottoms, AE (1995) 'The Philosophy and Politics of Punishment and Sentencing' in C Clarkson and R Morgan (eds), *The Politics of Sentencing Reform* (Clarendon Press, Oxford).

—— (2002) 'Morality, Crime, Compliance and Public Policy' in AE Bottoms and M Tonry (eds), *Ideology, Crime and Criminal Justice* (Willan Publishing, Cullompton, Devon).

Bottoms, AE and Wiles, P (1996) 'Crime and Insecurity in the City' in C Fijnaut, J Goethals, T Peters and L Walgrave (eds), *Changes in Society, Crime and Criminal Justice in Europe: vol I: Crime and Insecurity in the City* (Kluwer Law International, Antwerp).

Boutellier, H (1996) 'Beyond the Criminal Justice Paradox' *European Journal on Criminal Policy and Research* 4(4) 7–20.

—— (2000) *Crime and Morality: The Significance of Criminal Justice in Post-Modern Culture* (Kluwer Academic, Dordrecht).

Braithwaite, J (1989) *Crime, Shame and Reintegration* (Cambridge University Press, Cambridge).

—— (1993) 'Shame and Modernity' 33 *British Journal of Criminology* 1–18.

—— (1999) 'Restorative Justice: Assessing Optimistic and Pessimistic Accounts' 25 *Crime and Justice: A Review of Research* 1–127.

—— (2000a) 'Survey Article: Repentance Rituals and Restorative Justice' 8 *Journal of Political Philosophy* 115–31.

—— (2000b) 'The New Regulatory State and the Transformation of Criminology' 40 *British Journal of Criminology* 222–38.

Cain, M (1988) 'Beyond Informal Justice' in R Matthews (ed), *Informal Justice?* (Sage Publications, London).

Cantor, G (1976) 'An End to Crime and Punishment' 39 *The Shingle* (Philadelphia Bar Association) 99–114.

Christie, N (1977) 'Conflicts as Property' 17 *British Journal of Criminology* 1–15.

Daly, K (2002) 'Restorative Justice: The Real Story' 4 *Punishment and Society* 55–79.

Daly, K and Hayes, H (2001) *Restorative Justice and Conferencing in Australia* (Trends and Issues in Crime and Criminal Justice No 186) (Australian Institute of Criminology, Canberra).

Durkheim, E (1893) *De la Division du Travail Social* (Alcan, Paris) English translation: *The Division of Labour in Society* (Macmillan, Basingstoke 1984).

—— (1901) 'Deux Lois de l'Evolution Penale' 4 *L'Année Sociologique* 65–95. English translation: 'The Evolution of Punishment' in S Lukes and A Scull (eds), *Durkheim and the Law* (Martin Robertson, Oxford 1983).

Ericson, RV and Haggerty, KD (1997) *Policing the Risk Society* (Clarendon Press, Oxford).

Feeley, M and Simon, J (1992) 'The New Penology: Notes on the Emerging Strategy of Corrections and its Implications' 30 *Criminology* 449–74.

—— (1994) 'Actuarial Justice: The Emerging New Criminal Law' in D Nelken (ed), *The Futures of Criminology* (Sage, London).

Fry, M (1951) *Arms of the Law* (Victor Gollanez, London).

Garland, D (2001) *The Culture of Control* (Oxford University Press, Oxford).

Giddens, A (1990) *The Consequences of Modernity* (Polity Press, Cambridge).

—— (1991) *Modernity and Self-Identity* (Polity Press, Cambridge).

Gulliver, PH (1963) *Social Control in an African Society: A Study of the Arusha* (Routledge & Kegan Paul, London).

Hann, C (2000) *Social Anthropology* (Hodder and Stoughton, London).

Hart, HLA (1963) *Law, Liberty and Morality* (Oxford University Press, London).

Harvey, D (1989) *The Condition of Postmodernity: An Enquiry into the Origins of Cultural Change* (Basil Blackwell, Oxford).

Hedstrom, P and Swedborg, R (1996) 'Social Mechanisms' 39 *Acta Sociologica* 281–308.

Hulsman, LHC (1981) 'Penal Reform in the Netherlands: Part 1—Bringing the Criminal Justice System under Control' 20 *Howard Journal of Penology and Crime Prevention* 150–59.

—— (1982) 'Penal Reform in the Netherlands: Part II—Reflections on a White Paper Proposal' 21 *Howard Journal of Penology and Crime Prevention* 35–47.

Hulsman, LHC (1986) 'Critical Criminology and the Concept of Crime' 10 *Contemporary Crises* 63–80.

—— (1991) 'The Abolitionist Case: Alternative Crime Policies' 25 *Israel Law Review.*

James, A and Raine, J (1998) *The New Politics of Criminal Justice* (Longman, London).

Johnstone, G (2002) *Restorative Justice: Ideas, Values, Debates* (Willan Publishing, Cullompton, Devon).

Kamenka, E and Tay, AES (1975) 'Beyond Bourgeois Individualism: The Contemporary Crisis in Law and Legal Ideology' in E Kamenka and RS Neale (eds), *Feudalism, Capitalism and Beyond* (Edward Arnold, London).

—— (1980a) 'Social Traditions, Legal Traditions' in E Kamenka and AES Tay (eds), *Law and Social Control* (Edward Arnold, London).

—— (1980b) '"Transforming" the Law, "Steering" Society' in E Kamenka and AES Tay (eds), *Law and Social Control* (Edward Arnold, London).

Karp, DR (1998) The Judical and Judicious Use of Shame Penalties' 44 *Crime and Delinquency* 277–94.

Lash, S and Urry, J (1994) *Economies of Signs and Space* (Sage Publications, London).

Longman, (1984) *Longman Dictionary of the English Language* (Longman, Harlow, Essex).

Lukes, S (1973) *Emile Durkheim: His Life and Work* (Allen Lane The Penguin Press, London).

Lupton, D (1999) *Risk* (Routledge, London).

MacCormick, N (1981) *H. L. A. Hart* (Edward Arnold, London).

Marshall, T and Merry, S (1990) *Crime and Accountability: Victim/Offender Mediation in Practice* (HMSO, London).

Matthews, R (1988) 'Reassessing Informal Justice' in R Matthews (ed), *Informal Justice?* (Sage Publications, London).

Maxwell, G and Morris, AM (1993) *Family, Victims and Culture: Youth Justice in New Zealand* (Social Policy Agency and Victoria University of Wellington, Wellington, NZ).

Merry, SE (1982) 'The Social Organization of Mediation in Nonindustrial Societies: Implications for Informal Community Justice in America' in RL Abel (ed), *The Politics of Informal Justice: vol 2, Comparative Studies* (Academic Press, New York).

Northern Ireland Office, (2000) *Review of the Criminal Justice System in Northern Ireland* (The Stationery Office, Belfast).

—— (2001) *Criminal Justice Review: Implementation Plan* (The Stationery Office, Belfast).

Osborne, D and Gaebler, T (1992) *Reinventing Government* (Addison-Wesley, New York).

Parkin, F (1982) *Max Weber* (Ellis Horwood, Chichester and Tavistock Publications, London).

Roberts, S (1979) *Order and Dispute: An Introduction to Legal Anthropology* (Penguin Books, Harmondsworth, Middlesex).

Robinson, G (2002) 'Exploring Risk Management in Probation Practice: Contemporary Developments in England and Wales' 4 *Punishment and Society* 5–25.

Rock, P (1986) *A View from the Shadows: The Ministry of the Solicitor General of Canada and the Making of the Justice for Victims of Crime Initiative* (Clarendon Press, Oxford).

—— (1990) *Helping Victims of Crime: The Home Office and the Rise of Victim Support in England and Wales* (Clarendon Press, Oxford).

Ryan, J (1995) *Doing Things the Right Way: Dene Traditional Justice in Lac La Martre, NWT* (University of Calgary Press and Arctic Institute of North America, Calgary).

Tavuchis, N (1991) *Mea Culpa: A Sociology of Apology and Reconciliation* (Stanford University Press, Stanford, California).

Tyler, TR (1990) *Why People Obey the Law* (Yale University Press, New Haven, Connecticut).

von Hirsch, A (1993) *Censure and Sanctions* (Clarendon Press, Oxford).

Weber, M (1949) *The Methodology of the Social Sciences* (Free Press, New York).

Wiles, P and Costello, A (2000) *The 'Road to Nowhere': The Evidence for Travelling Criminals* (Home Office Research Study No. 207) (Home Office, London).

Zehr, H (1990) *Changing Lenses: A New Focus for Crime and Justice* (Herald Press, Scottdale, Pennsylvania).

31 Justice anew?

George Pavlich

In 1832, a Member of the British Parliament, one Thomas Babington Macaulay, is reputed to have uttered these telling words: 'People crushed by law,' he warned, 'have no hopes but from power. *If laws are their enemies, they will be enemies to law.*'[1] He thus intoned the importance of 'incorporating' new groups into law, subordinating all parties to state power. Since his time, the terms of different 'incorporations' of new subjectivities have been orchestrated by law's ability to predefine limited conceptual horizons, mentalities that render particular incorporations practicable. Successive historical waves of legal reform suggest an irregular yet astonishingly robust quality to legal hegemonies – even though describing the situation as absorption by stealth might accord too hypostatised an identity and agency to 'law', legal fields do display a chameleon-like ability to assimilate even the most determined of contenders to justice. Restorative justice has proved to be, despite the critical promise of its early incarnations, no match for that capricious old fox which is assembled under the banner of criminal justice. By virtue of the diverse replications of the *imitor* paradox, through which restorative justice both governs and is governed, restorative governmentalities have fallen prey to the faint incorporations of criminal justice empires. This book has alluded to various governmental nuances of such subtle integration and absorption.

Yet it is important to stress that there may be little hope of escaping some degrees of incorporation, some measure of the *imitor*'s paradoxical environment. It is all a question of the magnitude of the assimilation, or conversely of the limitation placed on being smothered by the entwining tentacles of dominant institutions of justice at work. Levels of incorporation may be part and parcel of all attempts to burst the sphere of presently dominant justice, to pierce its encompassing meaning horizons in order to calculate justice anew. We are, after all, locally produced subjects who face our times temporally, address what is to come as a future, or as promises fashioned using significations that themselves trace – are constitutive of us and our – present meaning constellations.

With this in mind, the work of restorative justice and its governmentalities should not be narrated as a simple merger with criminal justice. Indeed, the promise to work beyond adversarial images of justice is deeply attractive to many. And the spirit that traces so many of the processes deployed in the restorative name bears the promise of an alternative vision of justice aspiring to challenge the punitive, guilt-seeking, violent, pain-inflicting practices of justice calculated around criminal law and philosophies of the *lex talionis*. This aspiration, particularly evident in the informal justice lineage […], pledged to resist the cascading flows of adversarial criminal justice. There is, to put it another way, a degree of resistance in this call for alternation, even if it predicated itself upon the very concepts it seeks to transcend.

That restorative justice's iridescent aspiration to pursue such alternatives should have dimmed in direct proportion to its exceptionally successful expansion into criminal justice arenas, such that even its leading lights now question their earlier allegiances to a distinctively different, substitute justice[2] should not diminish the tangible resistances exacted from its rise (Fitzpatrick, 1988). That degrees of resistance may now be unnecessarily, if severely, curtailed is not to say that the pursuit is without its resistances, without openings to idioms beyond the courtroom. Indeed, it may well be that working out of restorative justice's *imitor* paradox, one can glimpse renewed possibilities for calculating justice outside criminal law's conceptual horizons.

Five implications of the *imitor* paradox

Discussion […] has located the different contours of the *imitor* paradox by which restorative justice advocates simultaneously pledge allegiance to an alternative to criminal justice, invoking different values (traditions) and processes of justice; yet their options rest ultimately upon key aspects of existing criminal justice systems. As we have seen, in all the areas discussed – harm, victims, offenders, community – this paradox is reproduced. In each sphere of its program, restorative advocates claim radically different visions of justice from criminal justice arrangements whilst ultimately deferring to, and relying on, the latter's key assumptions. As noted too, by drastically limiting the meaning of 'alternative' to criminal justice so that it becomes less a matter of replacement and more a question of complementing, restorative advocates are in danger of compromising the popular appeal that legitimated restorative justice as a different approach in the first place. Let us here turn to five important implications of sustaining this paradox within restorative justice governmentalities under these headings:

- political appeal;
- the impossible structure of restorative justice;
- restorative justice's parasitic identity;
- recalibrating justice ethically; and
- promises of justice to come.

Political appeal

One of the most immediate implications of the paradox within restorative justice governmentalities has to do with the political advantages of clinging to potentially opposing conceptual ideas in current horizons. Perhaps one of the most important reasons for restorative justice's dramatic rise of late has to do with its ability to appeal simultaneously to differing interests. On the one hand, it appeals to people of various shades of contemporary political opinion by claiming to provide a radical alternative to the state's criminal justice system. This assertion is appealing to those on the left because of deep-seated concerns about the capitalist state's ability to yield any just institutions. It simultaneously appeals to 'libertine' politicians on the right because of their neo-liberal calls to roll back the state and enable the privatisation/deregulation of as many welfare state functions as possible. Furthermore, by claiming to complement existing criminal justice institutions, restorative governmentalities appeal to social democrats in search of democratic enhancements of existing state institutions. At the same time, the quest to complement criminal justice arrangements with potentially cost-saving measures appeals to politicians looking for ways to show that they are doing something valuable about a seemingly intractable 'crime problem', with maximum administrative efficiency and minimal cost. It also appeases concerns about the potential for dissent generated by radical alternative propositions to the existing status quo.

Consequently, the *imitor* paradox renders restorative justice attractive to diverse groups, spreading its appeal broadly across the political spectrum. What is yielded in analytic integrity, conceptual clarity and the ethical commitment to an alternative is gained in popular political appeal and the ability to install restorative processes widely within existing arrangements. There is thus much political mileage to be gained from maintaining the paradox and ensuring that its opposing poles are sustained. It should also allude to some costs of maintaining the paradox. For one, as noted, it disallows critical questioning which moves beyond the assumptive universes that sustain both restorative and criminal justice governmentalities. In essence, this sacrifice has turned proponents away from their initial ethical motivations and the quest for alternatives to purportedly flawed criminal justice values, traditions and governmental practices. The restorative promise to provide a vastly different way of conceptualising justice has, in effect, been traduced by sustaining a paradox that enables political accommodations to the current status quo. In the process, the identity of restorative justice as a discrete regulatory practice is blurred, and increasingly is incorporated into its supposed opposite. As such, we now confront a residual, complementary governmentality that serves the very criminal justice its rationales and processes were meant to replace.

The impossible structure of restorative justice

The paradoxical ways in which restorative governmentalities are framed and deployed have generated an identity defined in relation to the justice institutions it claims to oppose. It exists by virtue of claims to simultaneously exceed and remain within the terms of criminal justice. It is both inside and outside, friend and foe, dependent and independent, of criminal justice. But these polar terms give a sense of schism at the heart of the identity that is both this and not this, that and not that, at the same time. As a result, there is a profound impossibility at the heart of the identity; an identity fissured around a breach that pulls it in two opposing directions.

Restorative justice is thus impossible. Its quest to exceed criminal justice demands that it does so with a requisite *ecstasis*, a requisite moving beyond the stasis of present legally calculated horizons of justice. However, were it to do that, then restorative justice might have to jettison its defining governmental edifice that revolves around notions like crime, offender, victim, and other stanchions of criminal jurisprudence. On the other hand, if it clings to the latter, then it must betray the quest to exceed criminal justice calculations. This is an impossible bind that paradoxically enables something like the restorative governmentalities we have described to emerge. Restorative justice is thus structured around the impossible. Ironically, the impossible structure of restorative justice makes possible something like the governmental logic, experience and techniques that we have encountered. In this respect, the impossible lies at the very heart of restorative justice; it is the very foundation upon which the paradoxical identity of restorative justice has over the past few decades been built.

It is important to note a point of clarification. Saying that restorative justice is structured on impossible grounds is not to say that it is impossible in the sense that it does not, or cannot, exist. Rather, it is to say that the governmentality's current identity has been made possible precisely because of an impossible, paradoxical trace that lurks as a constitutive dimension of its emergence. We are not dealing with, say, a timeless, stable, fixed, necessary, absolute or independent identity (there is no such thing). Restorative justice is instead contingently constituted on the basis of an impossible aporia that highlights the more or less arbitrary historical performances that bring sequences of sometimes quite disparate events to coalesce around the name 'restorative justice'. If nothing else, I take this realisation to emphasise the non-absolute, non-necessary, undetermined, finite and transient arrival of restorative justice governmentalities. Their impossible structure betokens the finitude of restorative justice calculations, and the brazenly laudable attempts to exceed the identity of criminal justice.

Restorative justice's parasitic identity

If the structure of impossibility challenges the sense of restorative justice as a necessary, singular identity, the *imitor* paradox compromises any quest for those aspiring to exceed criminal justice to arrive as a fully autonomous identity. However, it may be that restorative justice's close attachments to criminal justice institutions have contingently narrowed its alternative claims to justice; during the course of its relatively short history, restorative justice has made itself vitally dependent upon criminal justice assumptions and categories to identify itself (for example, on the basis of 'crime', 'victim', 'offender', etc). As such, and as Braithwaite notes:

> Restorative justice is most commonly defined by what it is an alternative to. Juvenile justice, for example, is seen as seesawing back and forth during the past century between justice and a welfare model, between retribution and rehabilitation. Restorative justice is touted as a long-overdue third model or a new 'lens'... a way of hopping off the see-saw....
>
> (2002: 10)

The inability to define restorative justice absolutely may not be so much a failure as a feature of language. As Derrida (1976, 1995) notes, signs always defer to other signs for meaning, leaving us without the ability to close off language absolutely and underscoring its dynamic contingency. The meaning of any identity may well then rely constitutively on its absence, on systems of '*differance*' (with the 'a') through which signs refer to others to create a 'presence', a being. However brief and oversimplified these statements might be, they at least highlight this point: there are ontological consequences produced by given systems of differance, by the ways in which signs defer to one another in a given discourse. The way in which signs are assembled to generate meaning constellations is deeply consequential for how we come to live our lives.

However, this means that so long as restorative justice defines itself through systems of differance that defer to basic criminal justice assumptions, thereby entrenching its dependence on the latter, the degree to which it is able to exceed such assumptions is unduly truncated. This suggests again that an alternative calculation of justice need not position itself as a servant of state criminal justice decrees.

By seeking to complement criminal justice, and deferring to fundamental criminal justice assumptions for its being, restorative justice renders itself *parasitic* upon existing criminal justice arrangements (see Woolford and Ratner, 2003). This has profound ramifications for the identity (and existence) of restorative justice, betraying a deep-seated ontological dependence on current criminal justice arrangements. There may well be reciprocal dependencies, but criminal justice governmentalities appeal to a far wider system of differance, and so maintain a broader identity formation (eg, by engaging jurisprudence, criminology, penology, criminal justice, law, sociology, political science, etc). In restricting restorative initiatives to being relevant, complementary, and so on, restorative justice has allowed its calculations to depend constitutively upon its supposed opposite.

Furthermore, an alternative that defines itself in relation to, and uses the concepts of, the very approach it seeks to replace is either a parasitic or a non-distinct venture. So long as restorative justice defines itself as a complement to criminal justice, it cannot exist without the latter. It certainly cannot replace criminal justice, for that would imply an independent identity capable of accomplishing such a replacement. Were it actually to overcome criminal justice, restorative justice would lose the discursive anchor against which it has defined itself, to which its key linguistic concepts defer. Without criminal justice, in short, the self-defined complement would lose its meaning – quite literally, its structure of differance would disappear. Its systems of deferring would be lost, rendering the current 'restorative justice' governmentalities meaningless. In other words, one might say that a governmental-ity which defines itself as an appended alternative would have no meaning whatsoever without the anchoring concepts that it serves.

Restorative justice as an alternative in this sense is unattainable because it constitutes its identity largely by deferring to the very (criminal justice) institutions it seeks to replace, reform, alter, etc. Were those institutions to change, a goal many proponents actively pursue, restorative justice would be left without the founding auspices of its current identity, without traces for its sign constellations to defer. By building its identity on not being criminal jus-tice, restorative proponents have left themselves little room for autochthonous enunciation. Any claim to an identity in excess of the state's criminal justice is paradoxically made by deferring to its underlying assumptions, predicating restorative justice upon the very thing that it is supposed to alter. Ironically, this again confirms that the quest for a restorative justice as an independent alternative to criminal justice is impossible, and it is that very impossibility which sustains the possibility of restorative governmentalities as 'complemen-tary alternative' to existing criminal justice structures.

However, were restorative significations to erect themselves in relation to sign constella-tions beyond criminal justice system governmentalities, one could expect a very different vision of justice to emerge. The claim to being an alternative would also resound to a far larger extent beyond, in excess of, existing structures. So, the distinction to bear in mind is not that of restorative versus criminal justice; instead it is restorative and criminal justice versus a justice that is yet to arrive. That is, if the aim is to seek ways of enunciating alternatives to existing rationales and practices of governing in the name of justice, then it is perhaps best to situate criminal and restorative justice not in opposition, but as similar sort of calculations of justice. It is not that justice is calculated either as restorative restitution or criminal retribution, but rather that together these interlocking paradigms form one pole of what potentially could be opposed to a new horizon of justice with very different concepts and ideas. The quest would, no doubt, involve notions of justice beyond both restorative and criminal governmentalities.

This recognition is acknowledged by restorative justice literatures where the sharp divisions between restorative justice's victim-centred, problem-resolution approach and the state's (alleged) retributive focus on punishing guilty offenders is challenged. Several commentators, for example, note that punishment is by no means absent from restorative processes (Daly, 2003b: 363–66).[3] Even Braithwaite's famous 'reintegrative shaming', while clearly meant as a corrective to destructive (non-integrative) punishments, necessarily entails degrees of punishment.[4] The basic point of the debate is this: despite claims to the contrary, retribution and punishment are not absent from restorative control horizons.[5]

In addition, both restorative and criminal justice sometimes defer to medical model notions of healing when approaching 'crime'.[6] Furthermore, it is not at all clear that restorative and restitutive practices are absent from criminal law (Woolford and Ratner, 2003; Walgrave, 1999). Zehr (2003) acknowledges the significance of civil law and notes that fines provide a model for restitutive justice.[7] The point echoed through all of these debates is the homologous overlaps between restorative and criminal justice.

If restorative justice is parasitically built on the foundations of already existing criminal responses to crime, can it nonetheless establish a unique niche? Perhaps there is a trade-off between legitimating restorative justice as a substitute for failing criminal justice initiatives and the quest to serve that system. Being relevant to existing governmental contexts may compromise the spirit of trying to develop an alternative that redresses key problems with existing criminal justice approaches. Remaining relevant and calculating justice anew is an impossible trade-off, but it may also suggest the possibility of recalibrating justice in a rather different way – as always a promise yet to come.

Recalibrating justice ethically

Within restorative governmentalities, we are implored to imagine a new paradigm of justice, a new way of dealing with crime. However, when justice is approached through ethical languages within restorative governmentalities, it is often seen through particular theological lenses (eg, Consedine, 1995; Zehr, 1990). These lenses have helped to frame restorative justice as a value and set of processes, such as its role in 'healing the harm' of crime. In addition, problem-solving, future-directed restorative practices defer to a version of the medical model and the very criminal justice assumptions they claim to replace. Restorative governmentalities here relocate discussions of justice outside moral and ethical languages. This all too often leads proponents to embrace technicist, administrative and even managerial reasons to explain the intrinsic value of restorative justice as something to pursue. In turn, the *imitor* paradox – despite calls to envisage restorative justice as requiring a change of moral paradigms – may be read as signalling a virtual retreat from any ethical meaning horizons.

Doubtless, there would be a profit to recovering an ethical language that addresses justice not as an ontological (existing) absolute entity that is manifest through institutions declaring themselves as just. The pursuit of discourses that exceed both restorative and dominant legal frameworks of justice might approach the idea of justice, not as an ontology which declares what is essential to, or absolutely proper for, justice; instead, it might evoke ethical precepts to grapple with the undetermined, infinite and never fully present moments in which the name of justice is called upon to deliver subjects from one sort of being to another. We should recall that ethics is possible precisely when there are undetermined, inessential choices at stake. Where life is fully determined, there is no choice, and so no ethics. The language of ethics becomes possible because of the radical undecidability of given moments.

So, instead of gathering concepts to 'discover' justice as ontology with fixed, essential characteristics, one could imagine justice as a never closed, never fully calculable, open and infinite idea that promises new ways to be with others. Derrida (1992) elaborates upon such an open-ended notion of justice.[8] Although this is not the place to pursue his thought in any detail, suffice to note that he begins with a seemingly curious, but profoundly significant, statement: 'There is no such thing as justice.' It does not exist as such. When someone declares 'I am just', or 'this process is just', they thereby mistake justice for an ontology, as something which exists, and so lose sight of its ethical, undecidable, never fully present meaning horizons. Justice is never an absolute entity, a reality or even a definable ideal to which our institutions might strive. Justice instead implies:

> non-gathering, dissociation, heterogeneity, non-identity with itself, endless inadequation, infinite transcendence. That is why the call to justice is never, never fully answered. That is why no one can say 'I am just'. If someone tells you 'I am just', you can be sure that he or she is wrong, because being just is not a matter of theoretical determination.
>
> (Derrida, 1997: 17)

If anything, justice is an incalculable, non-definable idea that forever calls us from the mists of what is to arrive. Related to Kant's transcendental ideas, it is always projected beyond as an infinite promise that can never finitely arrive. Justice emerges as an incalculable promise, but nevertheless one that requires calculations to be made in its name; law and restorative justice are two such calculations, but neither is ever entirely just, for justice always extends beyond a specific reckoning.

It is thus important to approach local calculations of justice with a sense of disquiet, remaining vigilant to their inevitable dangers and open to other possible computations. This underscores the importance of opening up to the arrival of unexpected events, ideas, and thereby preventing any image of justice from declaring itself as necessary, or as intrinsically better than any other. In the uneasy comforts of such decrees resides a spectre of totalitarian formations. So, one may insist upon a primary responsibility to what lies outside, what is other to, a given calculation of the just. This ethical formulation of justice implies a sense of justice that welcomes alterity, and never portrays the present as necessary; any given present is always constituted by its connection with what is absent. It also understands justice to constantly recalculate the borders of present limit formations.

With this different ethical horizon, it becomes possible to recalibrate justice in precepts that exceed restorative and criminal justice computations. Although it would reverse the spirit of the foregoing to declare with certainty what any specific calibration ought – necessarily – to be, one could nevertheless attend to another more relevant matter: what can one learn from the *imitor* paradox by way of calculating justice without deferring to key criminal justice precepts?

Just promises, anew?

As we have seen, the *imitor* paradox revolves around at least four key assumptions within criminal justice horizons: *crime*, *victim*, *offender* and *community*. These bind the governmentality to the everyday concepts of an ethos. But if the aim is to formulate calculations in excess of current justice horizons, it may be useful to work a way through the impossibilities of the *imitor* paradox, to erect sign constellations in excess of its conceptual foundations. In an ethos so centrally defined through the above categories, from its culture to everyday practice, the task may appear to some as laughably absurd. Can justice really be imagined without crime, victims, offenders or communities? However, it is precisely the silent crevasses of impossibility that allegations of absurdity mask, the cleaving transition from one meaning constellation to another, which is raised as a question here. For, not quite three centuries ago, let us recall, the thought that such precepts would ordain themselves as exclusive organisers of the just might have raised similarly incredulous guffaws. Extending the laughter of the ages, it may be poignant to allude to potential calculations of an ecstatic aspiration to justice, without deferring centrally to such founding concepts. Any attempt to puncture pervasive meaning horizons of restorative and criminal justice, using new frameworks to calculate the promise of justice differently, should be mindful of not replicating the *imitor* paradox *as far as possible.*

By way of an opening to other horizons, the following paragraphs might be read as cautionary remarks about the kind of justice that could be at stake. For example, [...] allude to the central place that legal definitions of crime play in criminal justice calculations and – even if by default – restorative governmentalities. One might ponder the implications for restorative justice as an alternative practice were its proponents to follow through with their critiques of crime, and perhaps even reject legal formulations of crime as the basis of the harms wrested upon victims, offenders and communities. What effects would developing calculations of justice without crime have on the processes used to deploy an alternative justice?

The very prospect is not quite as outlandish as those ensconced in cultures of crime may take it to be; a battery of critical criminologists have long argued that definitions of what constitutes a crime are always the fluid outcomes of socio-political struggles, as opposed to self-evident reflections of a pre-defined 'reality'.[9] From this vantage, the political processes that define 'crime', that bring the concept into being, are as consequential as the processes that lead to the creation of specific criminal identities in local contexts. To accept these human decisions as fundamental or primordial categories is itself a political decision; moreover, it is one made in favour of, and as a support for, the current legal status quo.

What might such calculations of justice entail? Of course, there are many possible variants – for example, one might evoke diverse experiences of *injustice* (as opposed to crime) as the most immediate and basic call to justice. Calculations of justice would be evoked when an injustice is experienced; it is then that subjects – 'singularly plural, or plurally singular' (Nancy, 2000) – do often turn to the idea of justice in search of new ways to be with others. Thus, one might frame calculations of justice directly around, say, immediate experiences of injustice as defined in local contexts. No doubt, the spectre of vigilantism appears though this enunciation, not unlike restorative justice (see Roche, 2003), occasioning the need for further calibrations of how to address these logically and procedurally. This makes clear that responding to locally framed injustice could be accomplished in all sorts of ways, and through diverse institutions (Pavlich, 2000). This need not exclude either criminal or restorative justice processes in all instances, but it would radically limit the inordinate privilege that both have managed to secure in contemporary justice terrains. The aim would be to seek calculations of justice that do not take for granted, or accept in large measure,[10] legal formulations of crime as the necessary mobilising event for justice. This sort of calculation would also emphasise the need to develop an apposite politics of crime, harm and injustice – the terms of which would have to be developed in far more detail.

Additionally, one might consider the prospect of resisting an ethos that emphasises individual victim and offender identities in its calibrations of justice. [...], the idea of empowering victims of crime *as individual victims* may be tenable in particular cases. However, if one's aim is to transcend the victim identity, to enable those who have been disabled by injustice, is the obligation to assume an individual victim identity always most apposite? As noted too, to what extent is it possible to empower a disempowered – even if temporarily so – identity? What about the political resources and possibilities that might be available to collective consolidations, for those who suffer as a consequence of the interactive effects of broader political envelopes? Very often conflicts, or injustices at local or broader levels, allow – even if for fleeting moments – almost invisible power formations to surface. Wresting the embedded power formations out of their shelters, enabling subject resistance to respond in whatever guise is politically feasible in context, and not obliging all to accept individual victim identities, implies a calculation of justice in excess of that which pervades current legal horizons.

Similarly [...], there may be some purchase in not, as a matter of course, accepting legal definitions of the guilty offender. In some cases, it may well be appropriate to generate the offender identity, perhaps in the relatively smaller proportion of violent injustices. Yet there should never be complete closure around the political environments that define offenders, or indeed isolate perpetrators of injustice. From the moment of accusation, from the moment cultural resources mobilise rituals that decide who are strangers in their midst, who is to be designated a perpetrator of harm, who is to make amends, one might well seek to develop an open politics which enables a dialogue to direct itself back to the means of accusation, as well as the basis upon which an accusation is made. Tying accusation to promises of justice is precisely the sort of politics that is at stake here.

On top of this, one might work out of the *imitor* paradox [...] to worry about calculating justice with reference to a closed community deployed in large measure by state formations, or whose strength is tied to the active participation of (individual) crime victim and offender identities. Seeking to surpass the totalitarian dangers associated with, or at least not avoided by, such closure, one might focus on the open-ended spirit of spontaneous mutual solidarity that traces many different quests for community. One problem is how this spirit is betrayed by approaching the community as something essentially fixed, definable and so potentially closed.

The question 'what is community?' implies (ironically, given the open appearance of the question) the prior existence of community and reduces the ethical question of how we could be with others to a question of ontological necessity (ie, how, given our human nature, we *must* live with one another). Eschewing this ontological question, a different calculation of justice could instead redraft a response to injustice by asking how it could be possible to exist thus, and seeking new ways to be with others. This ethical meaning horizon could, perhaps, align with quests for a community that never is, that never arrives (eg, Nancy, 1991; Agamben, 1993), but I am more inclined to trace the spirit though other allegorical images – such as Derrida's concept of hospitality (Pavlich, 2004, 2002b). Regardless, the calculation of justice may be tied to experiences of injustice within a given collective formation, and the ethical quest to seek styles of living in ways not attached to perceived injustices, to face up to the constitutive responsibility of being differently with others.

Even this hesitant attempt at opening to a different promise of justice begins with its own paradoxical attachments to past legacies and concepts. Perhaps this is inevitable to some degree when framing something new, when seeking new institutions. Derrida put the matter thus:

> The paradox in the instituting moment of an institution is that, at the same time that it starts something new, it also continues something, is true to the memory of the past, to a heritage, to something we receive from the past, from our predecessors, from the culture. If an institution is to be an institution, it must to some extent break with the past, keep the memory of the past, while incorporating something absolutely new.
>
> (Derrida, 1997: 6)

If this book has been an avid attempt to open up to justice anew, it is equally an attempt to be true to a memory of the past, to promises of justice that beckon ceaseless beyond the horizons of time. One could begin with the promise of another existence, traced by an obdurate glow of just promises that exceed what we have come to be.

Notes

1 In Harvie and Matthew (2000: 5); emphasis added.
2 For example, Zehr notes: 'In my earlier work, I often drew a sharp contrast between the retributive framework of the legal or criminal justice system and a more restorative approach. More recently, however, I have come to believe that this polarization may be somewhat misleading' (2002: 58). He calls for attempts to isolate areas of similarity and collaboration between the two approaches.
3 Daly argues thus: 'Reverence for and romanticization of an indigenous past slide over practices that the modern "civilized" western mind would object to, such as the variety of harsh physical (bodily) punishments and banishment. At the same time, the modern western mind may not be able to grasp how certain "harsh punishments" have been sensible within the terms of a particular culture (Daly, 2003b: 367). She notes further: 'Is it appropriate to refer to all of these practices as "restorative"? No, I think not. What do these practices in fact have in common? What is gained, and more importantly, what is lost by this homogenizing move?' (Daly, 2003b: 368).
4 Taking this further, Levrant *et al.* show just how far coercion and 'getting tough' mentalities are integrated into restorative justice practices; without due process safeguards, they worry that restorative justice has the potential to 'increase the punitiveness of the social control imposed on offenders' (1999: 371). Furthermore, although naked vengeance may offend restorative values, a degree of contrition for 'crimes' committed, often with punitive intent, is expected of participants in conferences. On a related tack, Duff (2002) argues that rehabilitative forms of punishment *should* be part of any restorative efforts.
5 Likewise, and by contrast, one may challenge the view that criminal law is only – or even primarily – retributive, devoid of restorative elements. In many ways, this is a view of criminal law overly influenced by classical criminological perspectives. No doubt, Beccaria's (1963) age-old classical tenets remain relevant to some degree in neo-classical revivals and current 'get tough on crime' ethos. However, the residual influence of equally influential positivist criminological approaches remains evident in contemporary criminal justice systems. One could, for example, refer to the focus on rehabilitation, correctionalist, and disciplinary responses to crime (Pfohl, 1994; Foucault, 1977). Drawing on medical models, positivist criminologists view crime as a legal reflection of prior 'norms'; 'criminals' commit crime because of biological, genetic or psychological traits. It is worth noting that for positivists the appropriate response to crime is to diagnose and 'treat', or set about healing, underlying pathologies. Such healing language is certainly related to talk of healing so firmly entrenched within restorative discourses. Hence, one may see why Bazemore and O'Brien (2002) would think it possible to find a 'restorative model of rehabilitation'. Finally, restorative processes are not devoid of rules and expectations, just as criminal justice systems are not devoid of significant degrees of discretion. See Gelsthorpe and Padfield (2003) and Ashworth (1998).
6 Notwithstanding Braithwaite (2002: 3) and Johnstone's (2002: 5) astute warnings about seeing restoration as a new version of rehabilitation.
7 Johnstone too notes that: '...it is highly likely that many criminalisable events are already being interpreted and handled within a restorative justice framework, ie they are handled with the state's involvement and with an emphasis on recompense and contrition rather than punitive suffering. It is indeed likely that, in social practice, restorative justice is more the norm, and stayed punitive justice the exception' (2002: 59). In a related way, one could argue that criminal justice systems are mostly focused on restitution when dealing with first-time offenders (hence the emphasis, for example, on diversion and community service programs). All such points make clear that the restitutive-retributive distinction alleged by many restorative justice proponents is much less clear than one might take from many accounts.
8 See also Lyotard and Thébaud (1985) and Pavlich (1996a: Chapter 2).
9 See Milovanovic (2002), Pavlich (2001), Christie (2000), Taylor (1999) and generally Hinch (1994).
10 Of course, merely referring to crime legitimates its standing to some degree but, by rendering it marginal to a calculation, the balance of signing forces is shifted.

434   *George Pavlich*

References

Agamben, Giorgio, 1993, *The Coming Community*, Minneapolis, MN: University of Minnesota Press.

Ashworth, Andrew, 1998, *The Criminal Process*, Oxford: OUP.

Bazemore, Gordon and O'Brien, Sandra, 2002, 'The Quest for a Restorative Model of Rehabilitation', in Walgrave, Lode (ed), *Restorative Justice and the Law*, Cullompton: Willan, pp. 31–67.

Beccaria, Cesare, 1963, *On Crimes and Punishments*, Indianapolis, IN: Bobbs-Merrill.

Braithwaite, John, 2002, *Restorative Justice and Responsive Regulation*, Oxford: OUP.

Christie, Nils, 2000, *Crime Control as Industry: Towards Gulags, Western Style*, New York: Routledge.

Consedine, Jim, 1995, *Restorative Justice: Healing the Effects of Crime*, Lyttleton, NZ: Ploughshares.

Daly, Kathleen, 2003b, 'Restorative Justice: The Real Story', in Johnstone, Gerry (ed), *A Restorative Justice Reader*, Cullompton: Willan, pp. 361–72.

Derrida, Jacques, 1976, *Of Grammatology*, Baltimore, MD: Johns Hopkins UP.

Derrida, Jacques, 1992, 'The Force of Law: The "Mystical Foundation of Authority"', in Cornell, Drucilla, Rosenfeld, Michel, Carlson, David and Benjamin, Neil (eds), *Deconstruction and the Possibility of Justice*, New York: Routledge, p. 409.

Derrida, Jacques, 1995, *Points...: Interviews, 1974–1994*, Stanford, CA: Stanford UP.

Derrida, Jacques, 1997, *Deconstruction in a Nutshell: A Conversation with Jacques Derrida*, New York: Fordham UP.

Duff, Antony, 2002, 'Restorative Punishment and Punitive Restoration', in Walgrave, Lode (ed), *Restorative Justice and the Law*, Cullompton: Willan, pp. 82–100.

Fitzpatrick, Peter, 1988, The Rise and Rise of Informal Justice', in Matthews, Roger (ed), *Informal Justice?*, London: Sage, p. 214.

Foucault, Michel, 1977, *Discipline and Punish: The Birth of the Prison*, New York: Pantheon.

Gelsthorpe, Loraine and Padfield, Nicola (eds), 2003, *Exercising Discretion: Decision-Making in the Criminal Justice System and Beyond*, Cullompton: Willan.

Harvie, Christopher and Matthew, Colin, 2000, *Nineteenth-Century Britain: A Very Short Introduction*, Oxford: OUP.

Hinch, Ronald Owen, 1994, *Readings in Critical Criminology*, Scarborough, Ont: Prentice Hall Canada.

Johnstone, Gerry, 2002, *Restorative Justice: Ideas, Values, Debates*, Cullompton: Willan.

Levrant, Sharon, Cullen, Francis T, Fulton, Betsy and Wozniak, John F, 1999, 'Reconsidering Restorative Justice: The Corruption of Benevolence Revisited?', *Crime and Delinquency* 45:3–27.

Lyotard, Jean François and Thébaud, Jean-Loup, 1985, *Just Gaming*, Minneapolis, MN: University of Minnesota Press.

Milovanovic, Dragan, 2002, *Critical Criminology at the Edge: Postmodern Perspectives, Integration and Applications*, Westport, CT: Praeger.

Nancy, Jean-Luc, 1991, *The Inoperative Community*, Minneapolis, MN: University of Minnesota Press.

Nancy, Jean-Luc, 2000, *Being Singular Plural*, Stanford, CA: Stanford UP.

Pavlich, George, 1996a, *Justice Fragmented: Mediating Community Disputes under Postmodern Conditions*, London: Routledge.

Pavlich, George, 2000, *Critique and Radical Discourses on Crime*, Aldershot: Ashgate/Dartmouth.

Pavlich, George, 2001, 'The Force of Community', in Braithwaite, John and Strang, Heather (eds), *Restorative Justice and Civil Society*, Cambridge: CUP, pp. 56–68.

Pavlich, George, 2002b, 'Deconstructing Restoration: The Promise of Restorative Justice', in Weitekamp, Elmar and Kerner, Hans-Jürgen (eds), *Restorative Justice: Theoretical Foundations*, Cullompton: Willan, p. 350.

Pavlich, George, 2004, 'What are the Dangers as Well as the Promise of Restorative Justice?', in Zehr, Howard and Toews, Barb (eds), *Critical Issues in Restorative Justice*, New York: Criminal Justice Press, pp. 173–84.

Pfohl, Stephen J, 1994, *Images of Deviance and Social Control: A Sociological History*, New York: McGraw-Hill.

Roche, Declan, 2003, *Accountability in Restorative Justice*, Oxford: OUP.

Taylor, Ian R, 1999, *Crime in Context: A Critical Criminology of Market Societies*, Boulder, CO: Westview.

Walgrave, Lode, 1999, 'Community Service as a Cornerstone of a Systematic Restorative Response to (Juvenile) Crime', in Bazemore, Gordon and Walgrave, Lode (eds), *Restorative Juvenile Justice: Repairing the Harm by Youth Crime*, New York: Criminal Justice Press.

Woolford, Andrew and Ratner, RS, 2003, 'Nomadic Justice: Restorative Justice on the Margins of Law', *Social Justice* 30: 177–94.

Zehr, Howard, 1990, *Changing Lenses: A New Focus for Crime and Justice*, Scottdale, PA: Herald.

Zehr, Howard, 2002, *Fundamental Principles of Restorative Justice*, Intercourse, PA: Good Books.

Zehr, Howard, 2003, 'Retributive Justice, Restorative Justice', in Johnstone, Gerry (ed), *A Restorative Justice Reader*, Cullompton: Willan, pp. 69–82.

32 The seductive vision of restorative justice

Annalise Acorn

When I first encountered "restorative justice," I was filled with enthusiasm. Restorative justice took a positive, forward-looking approach to crime. It focused on repair instead of punishment, on healing the wounds of injustice instead of inflicting further retributive suffering.[1] It conceptualized crime as the wrongful violation, not of an impersonal set of rules, or an abstract notion of "the state," but of individual victims.[2] It was concerned with the humanity of both victim and offender, and sought to restore the dignity of each by reintegrating both into respectful and healthy communities. It saw the community as the source of resolution of conflict.[3] Restorative justice seemed to hold a credible promise of something that had always appeared too illusive to hope for: a reconciliation of meaningful – even strict – accountability for wrongdoing with compassion for both victim and perpetrator.[4] I was powerfully drawn to restorative justice in many of these particulars. I was persuaded by its rejection of our cultural obsession with punishment as satisfying proxy for justice; its critique of our faith in imprisonment as necessary and sufficient assurance that justice has been done;[5] its claim that punishment as imprisonment is gratuitously cruel and counterproductive.[6] Most importantly, however, I was persuaded that our conflation of justice with punishment as imprisonment – or as any pure infliction of suffering on the wrongdoer – belied an impoverished, shallow, unsophisticated, and ultimately empty understanding of justice itself.[7] Llewellyn and Howse's claim that "there is no positive value for justice in the *very fact* of the perpetrator's suffering or sacrifice of well-being" sounded right.[8] Understanding justice as the creation of relations of reciprocal respect seemed a far fuller and more enlightened understanding than the crude and brutal equation of justice with punishment. I became convinced that our obsession with retribution had created, and was serving to perpetuate, habits of mean-spiritedness that were doing untold damage in every facet of our lives, from international conflicts to our most intimate micro-interactions. In place of this nasty and destructive retributive obsession, restorative justice offered an array of spiritually expansive ideals. It conceived wrongdoing in terms of wrong-relation and justice in terms of "right-relation."[9] Drawing on the spiritually sumptuous ideas of Martin Buber, restorative justice envisioned an escape from our bondage in so many "I-It" relationships. It envisioned justice as the repair of the world; the struggle toward ever more sustaining "I-Thou" relationships. Justice, then, was to be found in an authentic experience of mutuality, reciprocity, and regard between and among individuals. In place of the spiteful aspiration to inflict suffering on the wrongdoer as a means of achieving justice, restorative justice offered a loving aspiration to heal the damage of the wrong and to repair the injury to the relationship between the victim and the perpetrator. Such healing was to be supported and sustained by a community committed to mutual equality and respect. In place of the bleak procedural labyrinths of traditional legal institutions, restorative justice offered immediate and dramatic encounters between victims and offenders.[10] It offered both victims and offenders an experience of justice as a personal achievement.[11] Justice would no longer be imposed from on high but would be imaginatively and actively created and enacted by individuals and communities.[12] We would no longer look for justice in the substance of judicial decisions, jury verdicts, or prison sentences. We would expect and demand to find justice in relationships.[13]

I was enticed by all these wholesome carrots held out as alternatives to the sinister stick of retribution. It seemed so right-headed to organize the energy of our sense of justice around these far more positive goals: renewal of the victim's dignity, security, and sense of belonging in community; the perpetrator's contrition, his coming to accept the validity of shared norms prohibiting harmful conduct, his active participation in helping to repair the harm to the victim; and, ultimately, through this process of accountability and repair, the social redemption of both victim and perpetrator and their return – without stigma – to a position of acceptance and participation in the community.[14]

The point of justice (along with the point of a career devoted to justice) would no longer be merely the infliction of retaliatory suffering. Nor would it even be the piecing back together of some banal *status quo ante*.[15] Instead, the goal of justice might become something far more worthy of devotion. Restorative justice could also be seen as an approach to crime that was working toward social justice and the broader goals of the creation of relations and communities of mutuality, respect, peace, harmony, and equality.[16] And, though this idealized goal of right-relation might always elude our grasp, and though we might be forever stuck in an agonistic struggle toward this idealized conception of justice, at least, with right-relation as the target of justice, we could be confident we were aiming at something genuinely desirable and worthwhile. We could be certain that justice – not only in its abstract understanding, but in its day-to-day applications in the resolution of specific wrongdoing – was at least on the trail of something indisputably good, something indisputably connected with the pursuit of peace and with the creation of sustaining communities and relationships. This promised no small gain given that the value of the pursuit of criminal justice in the form of ever-longer prison sentences seemed so utterly doubtful.

The rhetoric of restorative justice speaks very personally to the listener, and I was aware that my attraction to it had some very personal pulls. First, my own weariness of feminist rage exhaustion was significant. The feminist commitment to anger and to a retributive sense of what was needful to bring about greater equality for women in areas such as sexual assault, domestic violence, pornography, and sexual harassment was becoming a heavy emotional and energetic burden. Many of the feminist stars in the academy were skilful rhetoricians of rage.[17] Being a legal feminist seemed to require emulation of those performances and, as a result, negotiating the difficult terrain of the negative emotions of justice: anger, resentment, vengefulness, and bitterness.[18] To be publicly committed to eliminating injustice caused by sexism in the law often meant incurring the risk that others would instantly collapse one's persona into the toxic trope of the angry feminist. At the same time, within the feminist community, a pose of anger, at the very least, was necessary lest one be seen as lax in one's feminist commitments.[19]

And, in all good conscience, it was cowardly and complacent to refuse to participate in the anger to which gender injustice gave rise. The retributive sentiments of feminism were often rightly fuelled by compelling evidence that the system was set up so that men could and did "get away with it." Exercise of police and judicial discretion sympathetic to accused men and dismissive of victimized women and children made convictions hard to come by in cases of private violence. The only available antidote to this bias in favour of the accused seemed to be to advocate that more credence be given to women and child victims and harsher penalties be dealt out to male offenders.

Restorative justice seemed to offer a better alternative. It was committed not only to holding offenders accountable, but also to repairing relations and to establishing communities capable of supporting practices of equality and respect. Feminist retributivism, while it perhaps offered justice to women on some level, also seemed to entail ever more gender animosity.[20] Restorative justice, by contrast, seemed to promise something better than mere retribution.[21] It potentially offered better solutions to the intractably complex problems of intimate violence. It aimed at hard-nosed accountability for male offenders as well as at the possibility of improved, more respectful, more harmonious gender relations in the future. Perpetrators of sexual assault, child sexual abuse, and domestic violence would be forced to look their victims in the eye and acknowledge the damage they had done rather than simply hiding behind aggressive defence counsel or bitterly doing time without acknowledging responsibility. Perpetrators would suffer genuine shame about their conduct, but restorative institutions would channel the energy of that shame toward better futures for both victim and offender.[22] Thus restorative justice, accompanied by genuine community support for victims, was perhaps a better means of ensuring accountability as well as effective deterrence.

My attraction to restorative justice was also motivated by the malaise that afflicts many lawyers, law professors, judges, and other actors in the legal system: weariness of squabble in general. Not propelled by any first-order thirst for revenge, stuck in that sorry niche of the world set up to manage the energy of other people's resentment, and, worse still, knowing that the legal system, even when it does deliver on its own terms, never really delivers a particularly satisfying experience of justice, we can fall prey to a dejected disgust with our own endeavour. We are encumbered by a guilty awareness that the usual rights and remedies afforded – imprisonment, fines, probation, conditional sentences – all too often fail to fulfill the aspirations behind victims' decisions to participate in the criminal process.[23] Even when, on those rare occasions, the court's pronouncement of a guilty verdict inspires the victim to burst out with a victorious "Hooray!" the celebration seems somehow artificial and hollow – relief masquerading as satisfaction. Or perhaps the outcry is itself an attempt to grasp in the last moment some more immediate encounter, some catharsis of genuinely relational gloating, that the process of adjudication has failed to deliver. This lacklustre sense of what the present system has to offer by way of experiential justice inspires a longing for something more. To be able, then, to approach the endeavour of justice with a sense that, at least theoretically, one might be able to offer something as seductive and rich as encounter and experiential justice-in-relation seemed to lend a new-found nobility to the task.

If, as Martin Buber claims, "All actual life is encounter,"[24] then institutions of justice, set up to facilitate the possibility of actual encounter, would surely yield a more life-giving conception of justice than institutions that do all they can to prevent encounter. Or as restorative justice advocate John Braithwaite puts it: The restorative movement is attractive because it is "to justice as jazz is to music."[25] Restorative justice seemed to have a freer form and deeper soul than do our traditional institutions.

Moreover, restorative justice seemed to offer hope to those who recognized the importance of, and felt a need to participate in, the legal process but who also claimed no desire to deal in the currencies the system has to offer. For those victims who cared more about apologies than imprisonment – those who weren't interested in seeing the offender punished but who would have been gratified by the offenders' acknowledgment of responsibility, expression of remorse, and making of meaningful reparation – restorative justice offered the possibility of principled participation in institutions of justice.[26] Likewise, restorative justice seemed to offer an important alternative for victims uninterested in punishment but deeply concerned as responsible citizens to try to ensure that the offender would not go on to victimize others.

Thus the tremendous appeal of restorative justice seemed to lie primarily in its validation of my own and other peoples' dissatisfaction with a legal system that depersonalizes, desiccates, and fetishizes justice in a way that deprives people of meaningful experiences of justice *in relation.* Restorative justice was appealing because, while it offered to put the doing back into doing justice, it did not at the same time validate the impulse toward revenge.[27] It held out a refreshing optimism that the desire for revenge – though not the desire for a personal experience of actively participating in bringing about justice – is a product of our reluctance to use our imaginations to envision other ways of creating accountability in the victim-offender relationship.[28] Restorative justice respected the desire for a personalized experience of justice as an individual and relational achievement, and it set the imagination to the task of envisioning positive, nonviolent ways of creating that experience.[29]

Perhaps we were not hardwired for revenge after all. Perhaps, by strengthening connections between compassion, equality, mutuality, reciprocity, and respect, on the one hand, and justice, on the other, we could be true to our need for justice while ending cycles of retributive suffering. Vengeful longings would, therefore, gradually be replaced with desires for the experience of respectful relation.[30] Successful practices and supporting discourses of justice-as-repair would become mutually reinforcing in their pedagogical and practical effects.

Along with being drawn into the theory of restorative justice, I was also moved by its success stories. I was inspired by stories of the proceedings of the South African Truth and Reconciliation Commission, by moments in which victims and perpetrators of the most horrific crimes of apartheid faced one another across a table and recounted the unimaginable suffering of their victimization, recounted the details of their crimes, and struggled, however ambivalently, however painfully, to work toward an understanding of how to move forward together into a more humane society.[31] Likewise, I was amazed by compelling stories of victims of sexual abuse who have been able to encounter their abusers, speak their suffering, and educate their abusers about the harm caused by their conduct. Some victims had clearly received benefits from such encounters. They had obtained information about the details of the abuse that they had repressed and had been able to set out strict guidelines to be followed by their offenders in assuring that the offenders would not interfere in the victims' lives again.[32] Others had benefited simply from the experience of hearing their abuser accept blame. I was moved also by stories of healing restorative encounters between murderers and the surviving loved ones of their victims.[33]

One of the most powerful aspects of these stories was the degree to which their focus on "encounter" showed an astute awareness of the mysterious exclusivity in the relation between victim and perpetrator.[34] Restorative practices seemed singularly capable of accessing and redirecting the energy of that sinister intimacy – bringing it out in the open and enlisting it in the service of justice and right-relation. It brought the tie between victim and offender out of the closets of shameful and mutual stigma and into the open, where it could be seen, heard, and healed.[35]

Some skeptical anxieties

Eventually, however, I began to experience twinges of doubt. I had a niggling but persistent embarrassment about my willingness to be seduced by the restorative justice movement.

And the embarrassment grew as my commitment to an intellectual defence of restorative justice seemed to be pushing me into more and more situations where I was answering too many difficult questions about the viability of restorative justice with rhetorical platitudes about right-relation, mutuality, equality, and respect.

Inasmuch as I was drawn to this project of trying to find a nicer way of doing justice, as much as I tried to effect the necessary conceptual uncoupling of justice and punishment and to effect the necessary new coupling of justice and right-relation, I couldn't quite do it. I remained unable to let go of my moral intuition that a just response to wrongdoing often requires "throwing the book" at wrongdoers, with equal emphasis on the "throwing" and the "book." Justice persisted in being bound up with both violence and consistency. Compensatory *schadenfreude* for victims and nasty comeuppance for wrongdoers still felt just. Moreover, "the book" (by which I mean the ideal of the rule of law) and its commitment to consistency, predictability, precision, and universal application also continued to have compelling and even essential connections to any sane and workable notion of justice.[36] Thus the restorative aspiration to divorce justice from reciprocal infliction of suffering, along with its faith in context supersensitivity, which sees the shape of relational justice as ever springing from the particulars of this victim, this wrongdoer, and this community, caused me considerable anxiety. Perhaps justice just wasn't nice. And perhaps it had to be tied to a notion of fairness which held that a just response to wrongdoing required some kind of parity in the consequences of wrongdoing among perpetrators of the same kind of wrong.[37]

Thus I became concerned that, in my enthusiasm for restorative justice, I was indulging in what Jonathan Allen so aptly calls the "wishful thinking (or at least, not very thoughtful wishing)" of restorative justice.[38] I began to feel that there was a shamefully Panglossian aspect to the whole restorative justice movement for which someone, though most likely not the advocates of restorative justice, would have to pay.[39]

I also identified an element of hypocrisy. I discovered that I felt this discomfort most intensely when I stopped thinking about the beauty of the ideas; stopped luxuriating in the voyeuristic moral gratification of looking on at the allegedly healing encounters of others; and started to think about whether in my own life and my own conflicts I was really willing to sign up for restorative encounters and restorative solutions. There was something troubling about my own hesitancy and about my lack of confidence in my own willingness and ability to apply the theory to myself. Restorative justice seemed just fine for other people, for harms I had not suffered, but when it came to *me,* restorative justice wasn't what I wanted. I did not feel competent as an advocate for restorative justice because I doubted both my ability to repair relationships marred by wrongdoing and my commitment to doing so.

Of course, I was not alone in thinking that if I wanted to promote restorative justice I would have to be able to claim a few impressive restorative successes of my own. Most advocates of restorative justice are aware of their obligation to "walk the talk." The territory of envisioning grand-scale social, communal, and relational transformations for the better generally comes with a recognition that (like analysts who must submit to analysis) advocates of restorative justice need to have a track record of successful healing and transforming in their own lives and relationships. Van Ness and Strong in their book *Restoring Justice* write:

> A hallmark of restorative justice must be ongoing transformation: transformation of perspective, transformation of structures, transformation of people. It begins with transformation of ourselves, for we too have recompense to pay, reconciliation to seek, forgiveness to ask, and healing to receive. We look not only for justice "out there," but

must turn the lens on ourselves as well – on our daily patterns of life and on our treatment of and attitudes toward others. Restorative justice is an invitation to renewal in communities and individuals as well as procedures and programs. Transformation of the world begins with transformation of ourselves.[40]

Similarly, Michael Hadley concedes that restorative justice "requires all of us to come to grips with who we are, what we have done, and what we can become in the fullness of our humanity."[41]

So the primary optimism is about the possibility of recompense, reconciliation, forgiveness, and healing in the context of the criminal offender-victim relationship. The application of this optimism to oneself is an earnest and well-meaning nod to the problems of hypocrisy that the primary optimism creates.

Thus the stumbling block for me came with my recognition of my own inability to put myself forward with a straight face as a competent participant in reconciliation, healing, and forgiveness. On the one hand, it was clear to me that my zeal for restorative justice was springing, in part, from an essentially romantic desire to get in on this starry-eyed notion of right-relation that restorative justice was so sanguine about. Surely, if it could happen for murderers and the survivors of their victims, it could happen for me in my troubled relationships fraught with petty, low-stakes conflicts and trivial insults. Surely, I too could participate in and experience reciprocal, mutual, and compassionate justice-in-relation.

Of course, it wasn't as if there were no "right-relations" in my life. Taking an honest stock of things, so long as I didn't go too far in idealizing this notion of right-relation, I could reasonably say that some of my relationships were pretty much "right." But in looking at the right ones, it was also clear that they tended to have a number of other characteristics, such as: spontaneous affinity, shared purpose, shared interests, shared history, absence of a history of serious wrongdoing, mutual commitment to respectful engagement, and the investment of much (richly rewarded) time and effort, sensitivity, and hard work, with no small assistance from affection, humour, and fun. So these were the precious right ones. These were the ones that could plausibly be thought of in terms of some kind of "I-Thou" mutuality.

But there were lots of wrong ones too – lots of relationships that were marred by resentment, wrongdoing, bitterness, and small-minded pettiness on all sides. And what struck me, in reflecting on these relationships, was that I was far less cheery about the possibility for recompense, reconciliation, forgiveness, and healing in the context of these – my own comparatively trivial, low-stakes – "wrong relations" than I was in the context of relations between murderers, burglars, sexual abusers, even the most heinous of war criminals, and their victims. Something had to be seriously wrong here. Reflecting on the trivial problems in my botched relations, it was evident that, in most cases, I did not have the will or desire necessary to repair them. Moreover, reparation did not seem either likely or possible even if sought with the best of intentions. In any event, why not save my energy for those pretty-much-right relationships that were not marred by any of these difficulties but nevertheless required lots of time and devotion to maintain? Wrong-relations seemed to have a kind of incorrigibility to them that made the project of repair a waste of time. So I had to admit that I personally was not up for sinking my energy into relational transformations.

How, then, was I to avoid the pessimism prompted by my own experience? And how was I to square this pessimism with the feel-good optimism about healing that had been induced in me by reading, rather than living, tales of restorative justice in the contexts of apartheid, ethnic cleansing, assault, rape, murder, robbery, and criminal negligence causing death?

Here I permitted my thoughts to follow a troubling trail: Could it be that right-relation stood a better chance of being restored when the wrongs to be overcome were big rather than trivial? Restorative justice advocate John Braithwaite says: "The more evil the crime the greater the opportunity for grace to inspire a transformative will to resist tyranny with compassion."[42] So perhaps the wrongs that marred the rightness of *my* relations were too subtle – they just didn't constitute sufficiently jarring events – to serve as the powerful blast-off needed to propel a journey into wholeness and healing.

My thoughts strayed to a singularly wrong relation in my life. I thought to myself: "Perhaps if I were to break into her house and, well, I probably couldn't bring myself to actually assault her but let's say maybe I could just steal her TV or her stereo. Might we not then be forced into a cathartic and ultimately transformative encounter? And propelled by its momentum, might we not be flung out of this terrible lock of hostility and into healing and right-relation? Might we not then embark, with the support of a respectful community, upon a restorative journey toward equality, right-relation, and mutual respect for each other's dignity?" Heaven knows, there did not appear to be any other way forward. So, perhaps crime was the answer.

This curious logic got me more than a little worried. And what troubled me most was that I was not *exactly* misapplying the theory. The rhetoric of restorative justice *was* evoking a fantasy of idealized harmony in relationships between victims and perpetrators of crime – often purely injury-generated relationships – and not even remotely desired by either party, least of all by the victim. But the rhetoric of transformation, healing, repair, love, compassion, equality, and respect in the context of victim-wrongdoer relations was shamelessly bypassing the obvious: that relationships marred by big wrongs and serious violations *have* to be more difficult to fix than relationships marred by petty wrongs and trivial insults and annoyances. Moreover, this rhetoric was bypassing the perhaps even more incontrovertible fact that harmony, mutuality, equality, reciprocity, and respect are hard won even in our most significant and well-intentioned relationships. The achievement of relations of equality and respect in the context of those core everyday relationships – the ones we put so much of our energy and intelligence into maintaining, the ones that receive the food, water, and sunshine of our spontaneous affection and desire – are themselves so painstakingly difficult and uncertain in success. So how can we – without hypocrisy – embrace a notion of justice grounded in a vision of right-relation, mutuality, reciprocity, equality, and respect between victims and perpetrators of unthinkable, unforgivable evils?

Thus confused, I turned to Derrida for help. His discussion of forgiveness offers one possible answer to this question. Justice-as-reconciliation can be seen as anticipating or requiring forgiveness,[43] and impossibility is, for Derrida, at the core of the very concept of forgiveness. If you don't have a grand-scale wrongdoing that defies the possibility of forgiveness, then it's not merely that you are in the minor leagues of forgiveness; you aren't even playing the game: "If one is only prepared to forgive what appears forgivable… then the very idea of forgiveness would disappear… From which comes the aporia, which can be described in its dry and implacable formality, without mercy: forgiveness forgives only the unforgivable. One cannot, or should not forgive; there is only forgiveness, if there is any, where there is the unforgivable. That is to say that forgiveness must announce itself as impossibility itself."[44] Forgiveness is a logical possibility only in respect of the inexpiable, unforgivable wrong that defies even the attempt to imagine a proportionate response. It does not require the contrition or apology of the wrongdoer or the possibility of punishment.[45] Nevertheless, Derrida commends forgiveness to us (or to those who have the opportunity to forgive: the victims of unforgivable wrong) as a worthy existential challenge. Worthy, it appears, primarily because of its richness as a paradoxical puzzle. Forgiveness is an impressive – possibility-defying – exercise of existential willpower. The audacious impossibility of forgiveness goads one to dare to try it. Forgiveness is a conceptual "attractive nuisance" (like the running bulldozer parked next to the school yard) for a paradox-crazed sensibility like Derrida's. It appeals as an exhilarating form of ethical bungee jumping.

Derrida's insights give us some sense of the potential intuitive appeal attaching to the idea that horrendous wrongs are, on some level, easier to repair and restore than trivial ones. There is no existential glory in forgiving the forgivable. Forgiveness of the unforgivable appeals because of its impossibility and its unquestionable status as a breathtaking achievement. Thus the worse the wrongdoing is, the greater is the power of the paradox of forgiveness to goad us into trying – if, like Derrida, we are inclined that way. The unavailability of a proportionate response likewise recommends forgiveness as a way out of an otherwise immobilizing conundrum.[46] Forgiveness of the unthinkably egregious has more drama and is worth the effort because, if successful, it clearly counts as seriously impressive ethical and existential muscle flexing. Forgiveness of the garden variety crimes and misdemeanours of ordinary life is too low stakes to have any existential cachet. In Derrida's formulation, such wrongs don't even give rise to the opportunity to forgive. So why bother? Thus we see how it is possible to conclude that repair and reconciliation as effected between victims and perpetrators of horrific crimes are potentially more attainable than repair and reconciliation between the victims and perpetrators of commonplace wrongs. Forgiveness of the unforgivable evokes the possibility of existential sainthood. Forgiveness of the forgivable is too mediocre to have any really compelling payoff for the victim.

Thus it might be that restorative justice – insofar as it is seen as a challenge to forgive – would have more appeal in relation to unimaginable atrocities than in relation to run-of-the-mill wrongdoing. Yet Derrida is quick to point out that "one could never, in the ordinary sense of the words, found a politics or law on forgiveness."[47] As Derrida rightly notes, for example, the South African Truth and Reconciliation Commission was founded on a legal category of amnesty completely distinct from any notion of forgiveness.[48] It was Desmond Tutu who later urged South Africans and the world to reinterpret the process in terms of the Christian vocabulary of repentance and forgiveness. But forgiveness, especially in Derrida's formulation, cannot be a matter of justice. It is a "hyperbolic ethics," an "ethics beyond ethics"; it is the unthinkably supererogatory.[49] Thus it is outside the realm of justice.

Moreover, in Derrida's formulation, forgiveness – superdemanding though it may be – is, in some senses, not as demanding as restorative justice. Forgiveness for Derrida seems to be primarily an inner state, constituted by a once-off leap of will. But restorative justice requires something more. If forgiveness is a necessary element of restorative justice, it is only instrumentally so.[50] The significance of forgiveness to restorative justice lies in its possible contribution to the ultimate restorative goal of right-relation – that is, a lived relationship of mutual equality and respect. Most restorative justice advocates see repentance and forgiveness as important parts of the process toward right-relation; but it is right-relation, not forgiveness, that is equated with justice. Thus to achieve justice-as-repair, one must actually persevere in the relationship with the offender and work toward something better. This expectation is a constitutive element of restorative justice no matter what kind of wrong we are dealing with. Thus, even if Derrida helps us to see how forgiveness as an ethical feat might have greater allure the worse the wrongdoing, once we add the requirement of working things out in the relation between victim and perpetrator, we are thrown back on our initial puzzle. Why would one do it unless committed to an ethic of self-sacrifice and saintliness? And how can a system of justice be structured around a general demand for such supererogatory patience and devotion from victims?

The question of expenditure of resources alone would seem to rule out restorative justice as a viable possibility.[51] The resources, care, and attention that serious and workable institutions of restorative justice would have to bestow on relationships either generated or marred by criminal violation would be enormous. When the right-relations that we have the good luck to create take so much of our time and energy, why would we sink a necessarily far greater amount of time and energy into the wrong ones? Why would anyone pour so many resources into these least promising of relations? Why would victims want to expend their time and energy on a bad and unwanted relationship that they would prefer to erase from their lives?[52]

Though I have difficulty coming up with positive answers to these questions, it is apparent to me that the problem with my skepticism here may be merely my own moral failing. Restorative justice may well be for people who are much more patient than I; more committed to peace, healing, and harmony; less curmudgeonly; more pious; more morally inclined toward the endeavour of working things out for the sake of building community; more willing to persist with people who have wronged them. Yet (and I hope there is no self-righteousness in this claim), if the success of restorative justice is contingent upon consistently finding participants (victims, offenders, and community members) who are significantly more morally patient than I, then it is in some considerable trouble – and not because I am morally good but because neither am I a moral monster. I am pretty much the run of the moral mill. Yet restorative justice seems to anticipate that it will be drawing its participants (including its offenders) from the ranks of the morally supererogatory. I am worried about how such a system is to protect the interests of victims and even (although to a lesser extent) the interests of perpetrators of crime. I am concerned about a system of justice that asks victims in particular to take on the onerous task of working things out in relation to their offenders. But I am also worried about a system that purports to be able to deliver caring and compassionate assistance in effectively healing the admittedly terrible wounds suffered by offenders, wounds that go some way toward explaining the participation of offenders in wrongdoing.

Consider the following example. Restorative justice proponent Herman Bianchi tells a story of two young men who had brutally assaulted a cab driver.[53] The assault left the victim permanently confined to a wheelchair. The assailants were arrested. While awaiting trial, however, they became extremely remorseful and very much wanted to make reparations to the victim. Their lawyer suggested that they write the victim a letter. They then wrote to the victim, offering to take care of him for twenty-five years as compensation for the harm they had done. The victim did not answer the first letter, so the perpetrators wrote to him again. The victim was initially very skeptical about the offer, but the victim's friends were enthusiastic and persuaded him to accept, assuring him that the offenders "will do their utmost to make your life bearable." The victim was convinced by his friends' arguments and accepted the offer.

Bianchi celebrates the agreement as a restorative move from damage to repair, from wrong-relation to right-relation, from wrongdoing to true penitence and meaningful accountability: "This is now a wonderful case as it should be. This is divine justice. Now, just do it!" However, the perpetrators, whom we are to assume are not particularly wealthy, would not be able to care for their victim were they in jail, so the agreement needed ratification from the judge. But the judge refused, finding that the victim's consent did not obviate the need for punishment; other potential assailants needed to be taught a lesson. Bianchi laments the judge's refusal to grant a stay of proceedings against the two offenders and to allow the agreement to be put into practice. He also bemoans the refusal of our system to support this restorative solution, arguing that the default solution that our system offers – the offenders go to prison, and the victim is supported by the state in an institution – exacerbates and perpetuates the damage to all concerned. Bianchi's position seems compelling enough. At a glance, the plan seems to be a perfect example of restoration of balance in the relation between victim and perpetrator.

Now, the story as told does not give us any explanation of what it would mean for the perpetrators to "take care of" the victim for twenty-five years, and it asks us to assume that the victim accepted the offer without any further clarification – apart from the interpretation offered by his friends (who had presumably never met the perpetrators) that the offenders meant to "do their utmost to make his life bearable." In all events, we can assume that the arrangement would require extensive close contact between the perpetrators and the victim. Depending on the degree of the victim's disability, he might need something close to twenty-four-hour care, which would most likely require that the perpetrators live with the victim.

As Bianchi's research demonstrates, this kind of response to crime has its historical precedents.[54] Feuding cultures provide interesting support for the basic idea that meaningful reparations can be made when a wrongdoer voluntarily agrees to care for the victim or the victim's dependents.[55] This idea also gleans some historical support from the work of William Ian Miller. Miller notes that in medieval Iceland wrongdoers would commonly agree to foster one or more of the victim's children as a means of pacification. Miller describes an incident in the sagas where "Sturla forced his young son on a man who had sold him wormy meal."[56] By fostering children belonging to a victim, the wrongdoer was relieving the victim of the financial burden of feeding the child. Significantly, he was also symbolically accepting a one-down status in relation to the victim since, in the context of medieval Icelandic culture, "he who fosters another's child is always considered the lesser man."[57] Yet even in a culture where such fosterage was an accepted means of offering reparation and effecting reconciliation, Miller notes that the practice must give us a pang of anxiety about the fate of the poor child. How could this father so cavalierly send his son into the house of the man who was his enemy? Yet Miller concludes with the assurance that nothing in the sagas suggests that such children were treated at all like hostages: "The children, it seems, were treated no differently than any other child would have been."[58] Means of caring for children were already in place in the households; thus the foster children could simply take up an equal place with the other children.

This arrangement seems all very nice. But can we apply this cheery picture to our case of the disabled man and his two assailants? Imagine living for even one week as a disabled person in the same space as the two men who have caused your misery by brutally assaulting you – with men who have no skills in the care of the disabled, whose general "life skills" are likely to be less than optimal, and for whom your presence can only be an annoying and possibly painful reminder of their guilt. I fear that the outcome of this story, even at its most optimistic, would likely resemble the predictable tale of the well-meaning person who, in a rush of compassion, decides to care for an abandoned puppy only to find weeks later that it is far too much to handle and that its presence has become a source of overwhelming frustration and hostility. Even if some extraordinary victim might wholeheartedly take on the risks of such a vulnerable life, can we, in good conscience (and could this cab driver's friends in good conscience), support a system that would encourage the subjection of victims to this kind of intense intimacy with those who have harmed them? How can we endorse a system of justice that rests on the prediction that equality, mutuality, reciprocity, and respect will be achieved in such relationships?

It is doubtful that the fosterage practised by such a profoundly communal people and culture as that of medieval Iceland can really serve as an adequate precedent or inspiration for similar practices in modern society. Nor does a relationship as hopelessly unpromising as that between the victim and the wrongdoers in Bianchi's story provide a stable foundation for the creation of a more cohesive community. There is no good reason to feel any less anxious about the fate of the disabled man's living in such prolonged intimacy with his assailants than we might about the fate of the Icelandic children going off to be cared for in the houses of their parents' enemies.

Before leaving this anecdote, let's consider it from a slightly different angle. Let's imagine that the perpetrators were very wealthy men. And let's then imagine that instead of extending this imprecise offer "to take care of him for twenty-five years," the perpetrators made a very precise, and indeed far better, offer of, let's say, three million dollars to provide the victim with professional home care for life, compensation for pain and suffering, and so forth. Now one would assume that, under our present system, if such a payment were made spontaneously by the perpetrators, this gesture would figure as a mitigating factor in a judge's determination of the appropriate criminal punishment. But to conclude that the offer of monetary compensation should completely extinguish the state's obligation to proceed with the criminal charges (which Bianchi's story seems to entail) would collapse the present system of a dual civil action and criminal prosecution into a single civil action. As long as the perpetrators were in a position to pay compensation, they would be excused, as it were, from criminal prosecution. But what if the perpetrators were not in a position to pay compensation, which would seem to be the case in the story as told? It appears that the restorative solution would then also collapse the criminal prosecution into a civil action but would allow the impecunious offender to pay by working for the victim.

This arrangement, of course, is an ancient practice tried and true. It is found, for example, in the Bible, the laws of Hammurabi, and Roman law. It is called debt-slavery.[59] Where an offender was unable to pay compensation to a victim or to pay a debt owed to a creditor, he was made to fulfill the obligation by handing over the only thing he did have: his body and its labour. In other words, he became the slave of the victim or creditor. We can easily read the story of the cab driver and his assailants in a similar light. Presumably, any agreement to be ratified by the judge would have to provide for the consequences of breach. The perpetrators could not simply decide after a year or two that they didn't much like the arrangement and preferred not to look after the victim. One would assume that if the perpetrators were to default on the agreement, the criminal jurisdiction would be resurrected, and the perpetrators would either honour the agreement or go to jail. It would appear, then, that what is being promoted in the story is an arrangement between victim and perpetrators in which either the perpetrators continue to work for the victim or suffer incarceration.

We should also note that such an arrangement, if universalized, would give rise to a significant disparity in the treatment of rich and poor offenders. The present system, of course, has wealth disparity to be sure. Things like quality of representation, prosecutorial zeal, and judicial sympathy are not distributed evenly across class lines. But, to the extent that our system prosecutes them at all, it potentially makes the rich pay twice: once by subjecting them to criminal punishment and again by requiring them to pay civil damages to compensate their victims. Under our system, the impecunious offender can pay only once through criminal punishment. The story of the cab driver and his assailants, inasmuch as it is being offered as a model for a system of justice, would risk a different and significant inequity between rich and poor. The story writ large would give rise to a system that treated poor offenders more harshly than their wealthy counterparts. The repentant rich would be able to pay up without doing time, but the penitential poor, those without the option of paying-up, most likely would have to do time either as the employee/caretaker of the victim or in prison.

Given these difficulties, why does Bianchi's story remain nevertheless so oddly persuasive and even moving? I suggest that the appeal of this story depends largely on the judge's rejection of the plan.[60] The momentum of the story takes our imaginative focus off the details of what such an arrangement would really be like for the victim and the perpetrators. It is only because we give superficial imaginative consideration to the rejected restorative fantasy that we find the overall vision of restorative justice in the story persuasive.

Admittedly, not all or even most restorative solutions anticipate this kind of ongoing intimate bond (or bondage) between victim and offender. Yet the theory, in its idealization of equality and respect in the relationship between victim and offender, and many of the testimonial success stories of restorative justice tend to envision some kind of amiable optimality in the victim-offender relation. The concepts of mutuality, reciprocity, healing, equality, and respect to be achieved between victim and offender may be staggeringly vague and open to many divergent conceptions, but all these conceptions reach toward a vision of shared satisfaction between victim and offender.[61]

The seductive vision of restorative justice seems, therefore, to lie in a skilful deployment – through theory and story – of cheerful fantasies of happy endings in the victim-offender relation, emotional healing, closure, right-relation, and respectful community. Yet, as with all seductions, the fantasies that lure us in tend to be very different from the realities that unfold.[62] And the grandness of the idealism in these restorative fantasies, in and of itself, ought to give us pause.

Moreover, the contexts in which restorative justice is most vigorously and successfully promoted are the same contexts in which other powerful emotional pulls are inducing us to, as Jonathan Allen again aptly puts it, "confuse aspiration with prediction."[63] Enthusiasm about restorative justice thrives best in contexts already conducive to optimistic fantasy. For example, South Africans of all races experienced a heady idealism at of the end of the apartheid regime. There was an exuberant sense that South Africa, newly freed of the yoke of apartheid, would surely become a country of unprecedented cultural richness, economic prosperity, and political enlightenment. This exuberance, in part, inspired the wave of willingness to go along with the vision of justice offered by the Truth and Reconciliation Commission. The shared anticipation of a glorious new era of national flourishing opened South Africans to an understanding of justice that was sunny and forward-looking. Apartheid had been a long and shameful yesterday, and to focus national energy on punishing its past might destroy the possibility of the brilliant tomorrow just beyond the horizon.

This mood factor also surfaces in our assessment of other contexts in which restorative justice might be appropriate. Consider, for example, two common settings in which restorative justice is advocated: Aboriginal and juvenile crime. Take the Aboriginal context first. The restorative justice movement in Aboriginal contexts is bound up with both the political push toward Aboriginal self-government and a more general renaissance of traditional Aboriginal culture.[64] The distant Aboriginal past evokes a spiritually enlightened culture that fosters harmonious interconnections between people and nature.[65] The recent Aboriginal past represents oppression and pollution by a spiritually inferior white culture that privileged acquisition and egoism over shared purpose and relationship. The Aboriginal future promises a proud renewal of traditional values and practices. Thus, in the Aboriginal context, as in South Africa, restorative justice is supported by an atmosphere of shared anticipation of a soon-to-be-celebrated future. Optimism that Aboriginal peoples are on their way out of a toxic condition of oppression – a condition that contributed significantly to high crime rates in Aboriginal communities – supports the idea that healing of relations between victim and offender is an appropriate and viable response to wrongdoing.

In the context of juvenile crime, youth itself supports an optimistic focus on the future. We are more willing to see the wrongdoing of the young as attributable to lack of maturity rather than to actual malevolence or viciousness. The juvenile criminal's whole life stretches out before him. We are reluctant to abandon hope either for the possibility of spontaneous change of a young offender's ways or for their improvement through better education and socialization.[66] To presume that a young offender doesn't deserve a chance to make amends seems culpably cynical – just as it seems culpably naive to give adult offenders the benefit of the same set of doubts. The fairness of this disparity in our assessment of the young and the older is beside the point. Youth puts us in the optimistic mood necessary for restorative justice.[67] It opens us up to the idea that the appropriate response to wrongdoing is to try to educate offenders about the harm they have done, attempt to engender a compassionate response both in offenders for their victims and in victims for their offenders, and give the young every reasonable chance to redeem themselves.

Again the emotional pulls that render us susceptible to optimistic fantasy and aspiration do not necessarily map onto the practical conditions that would make restorative healing and repair more likely. The probability of the success of restorative justice seems to depend primarily upon the character and resources of the offender.[68] Restorative justice is possibly the perfect solution to crime where the offenders have the capacity for serious critical self-reflection, the resources and ability to repair the damage caused, and a bona fide desire, along with sufficient self-command, to behave respectfully in their relations with their victims and their communities in the future. It is difficult to imagine how one could isolate particular contexts or types of crime in which one was likely to find a critical mass of these good bad guys capable of transformation and participation in relations of equality and respect.[69] Moreover, it would seem that in promoting restorative justice at the theoretical level and in seeking victims' consent to restorative processes at the practical level, we are asking victims to wager that their particular offenders fall into this category of redeemable rogues capable of taking responsibility for their actions and making meaningful amends.

Of course, there are many more factors beyond just the character of the offender that will influence the success or failure of restorative justice: whether the damage is reparable, whether the victim is amenable to forgiveness, whether the victim supports the goal of re-establishing the worth of the offender or continues to desire the offender's suffering. Yet, at the end of the day, the primary control over the success or failure of restorative justice seems to lie in the hands of offenders. Nevertheless, the credibility of restorative justice is absolutely contingent upon its ability to deliver some version of its promise of equality, respect, mutuality, reciprocity, and healing in the relation between victim, offender, and community.

Notes

1 Van Ness and Strong, *Restoring Justice,* 2nd ed., 49.
2 Sharpe, *Restorative Justice,* 3.
3 Christie, "Conflict as Property."
4 Pollard, "Victims and the Criminal Justice System," 11–12.

5 Zehr, *Changing Lenses,* 34.
6 Bianchi, *Justice as Sanctuary,* 35; Braithwaite, *Crime, Shame, and Reintegration,* Ch. 2, "The Dominant Theoretical Traditions: Labelling, Subculture, Control, Opportunities and Learning Theories"; Van Ness and Strong, *Restoring Justice,* 2nd ed., 7; Zehr, *Changing Lenses,* Ch. 3, "The Offender."
7 Llewellyn and Howse, "Institutions for Restorative Justice," 357, and *Restorative Justice,* 37–41.
8 Llewellyn and Howse, "Institutions for Restorative Justice," 376, emphasis in the original.
9 Heyward, *Staying Power,* 16–17. Heyward uses the phrase "right-relation" to explain Martin Buber's concept of I and Thou. See also, for example, Buber's discussion of relationality in *I and Thou,* 69–72; Umbreit, *Handbook of Victim Offender Mediation,* xxxi, Item 5.
10 Van Ness and Strong, *Restoring Justice,* 2nd ed., 55.
11 For a persuasive account of the benefits of restorative justice on this score – especially with respect to victim inclusion in the process – see Pollard, "Victims and the Criminal Justice System."
12 See Christie, "Between Civility and State."
13 We can turn to Michael L. Hadley's introduction to *The Spiritual Roots of Restorative Justice* for a classic statement of restorative justice: "Restorative justice, with its principles of repentance, forgiveness, and reconciliation, is instead [of a quick fix] a deeply spiritual process. It is never the easy way out; neither for the offender, the victim, or the community. It requires all of us to come to grips with who we are, what we have done, and what we can become in the fulness of our humanity. It is about doing justice as if people really mattered; it addresses the need for a vision of the good life, and the Common Good. To borrow the title of a recent study the restorative approach is concerned with restoring the moral bond of community" (9).
14 As Pollard notes, the present system usually requires victims and perpetrators to deal with their respective difficulties in isolation ("Victims and the Criminal Justice System," 7).
15 Llewellyn and Howse, "Institutions for Restorative Justice," 375; Llewellyn, *Restorative Justice,* 2.
16 Braithwaite, "Restorative Justice and Social Justice."
17 Mary Daly, *Gyn/Ecology*; Dworkin, *Intercourse,* MacKinnon, *Toward a Feminist Theory of the State.*
18 Robert Solomon argues that these negative emotions have been given too short shrift in our understanding of justice, that we have been too quick to disown the energy of their affective force toward justice, and that we have privileged the relationship between justice and those kinder gentler emotions like compassion and empathy. But this analysis appears unaware that certain struggles for justice – particularly gender justice – are powerfully and inextricably identified with anger and vitriol. See Solomon, *A Passion for Justice,* Ch. 6, "The Cultivation of Justice and the Negative Emotions."
19 On feminism and the politics of resentment, see Elshtain, "Politics and Forgiveness," 44. See also Martin, "Retribution Revisited."
20 On the question of whether love is threatened by an increase in justice in an intimate relationship, see Okin, *Justice Gender and The Family,* 28 et seq. Okin rejects Michael Sandel's idea that love is a higher virtue than justice and his claim that moves toward greater love can sometimes threaten love, shared purpose, and spontaneous affection (*Liberalism and the Limits of Justice,* 31 et seq.).
21 For a feminist discussion of restorative justice as an alternative to retributive justice for violence against women, see Martin, "Retribution Revisited."
22 Braithwaite, *Crime, Shame, and Reintegration.*
23 Jurevic, for example, notes: "When I practiced law, the legal remedies I was able to offer and procure for my clients often did not bring significant or meaningful change to their lives. The abused wife who received custody of her children would return with an illegal eviction notice or a problem with receiving public benefits or a dispute concerning access visits. Training students to enter the legal profession seemed like adding to the problem, and my attempts at introducing alternative perspectives on dispute resolution were often met with questions such as 'What does this have to do with The Law,' or 'How will this help me get Articles?' Researching issues such as the Stolen Generations or Domestic Violence was becoming unsatisfying given the constraints imposed by legal thought, theory, and language. I, like many other lawyers, felt little joy when contemplating anything legal" (*"What's Love Got to Do With It?"* prologue).
24 Buber, *I and Thou,* 62.
25 Braithwaite, *Restorative Justice and Responsive Regulation,* 10.

26 Van Ness and Strong, *Restoring Justice,* 1st ed., 152; Zehr, *Changing Lenses,* 28; Umbreit, "Crime Victims Seeking Fairness Not Revenge."

27 Kerruish, *Jurisprudence as Ideology,* 17, 172. In many ways, Valerie Kerruish's critique of rights provides a sophisticated foundation for restorative justice. Kerruish argues that like the fetishist who replaces the lover with a shoe, our legal system puts rights in place of the experience of respect in relationship. See herein Chapter 3, "Three Precarious Pillars of Restorative Justice," Section 1, "Malleability of the Meaning of Justice."

28 Llewellyn and Howse, "Institutions for Restorative Justice," 376. See also Nietzsche, *On the Genealogy of Morals,* 14.

29 Zehr, *Changing Lenses,* 42.

30 See, for example, Fatić's discussion of restorative justice as a "trust encouraging" institution and the possibility of creating a pacifist culture through institutions of restorative justice *(Punishment and Restorative Crime-Handling,* 222–23).

31 *ABC Nightline,* 1 January 1999; *All Things Considered,* 13 December 1996; *All Things Considered,* 15 April 1996. See, generally, *Truth and Reconciliation Commission of South Africa Report* and "Truth, the Road to Reconciliation: Official Truth and Reconciliation Commission Website," <http://www.truth.org.za/index.htm> (6 June 2002).

32 Evers, "A Healing Approach to Crime." This understanding of the role of restorative justice as a means of conclusively putting an end to relations between victims and perpetrators of sexual assault goes against Heyward's discussion of right-relation as paradigmatically erotic. It essentially adopts the idea that sometimes right-relation can and should mean no relation. See herein Chapter 5, "'Lovemaking is Justice-Making': The Idealization of Eros and the Eroticization of Justice."

33 *Ideas,* "Justice as Sanctuary," with Herman Bianchi, Part 1, Canadian Broadcasting Corporation Radio Program; Umbreit, *Handbook of Victim Offender Mediation*: "One of the most powerful and perhaps most controversial expressions of the transformative qualities of empowerment and recognition has been consistently observed in the small but growing application of mediation and dialogue between parents of murdered children and the murderer" (8–9).

34 Evers, "A Healing Approach to Crime," 46, It is sometimes only the perpetrator who has the information necessary to assist the victim with healing; that is, the perpetrator is the only source of information about the details of the abuse in cases where the victim has repressed memories of it. Likewise the perpetrator is the only one in a position to give an unqualified acknowledgment of reality of the abuse and an absolute assurance that it was not the fault of the victim. This is not to say that others cannot assist the victim with understanding that the abuse was not her fault. However, victims report being particularly affected by the statements of wrongdoers to that effect.

35 For a discussion of the shared stigma of victims and offenders, see Van Ness and Strong, *Restoring Justice,* 2nd ed., 101. See also La Prairie, "Developments in Criminal Law and Criminal Justice," 581.

36 For a discussion of the requirement of the lack of consistency in restorative justice, see Delgado, "Goodbye to Hammurabi," 759.

37 See Ashworth, "Some Reservations about Restorative Justice," and "Responsibilities, Rights and Restorative Justice."

38 Allen, "Balancing Justice and Social Utility," 317.

39 It is interesting to note that Voltaire's *Candide* can be retrospectively read as a critique of the present new-age movement. So many ideological staples of the new-age movement (by which restorative justice is tremendously influenced, not to mention fuelled), in particular the idea that everything that happens is rightly construed as being somehow for the good, are fully formulated in the character of Dr. Pangloss and subsequently ridiculed. But the Western intellectual history of new-age hyperoptimism is far older than the movement itself seems to be aware.

40 Van Ness and Strong, *Restoring Justice,* 2nd ed., 249.

41 Hadley, *The Spiritual Roots of Restorative Justice,* 9.

42 Braithwaite, *Restorative Justice and Responsive Regulation,* 3. Braithwaite attributes the insight to Aug San Suu Kyi and the Dalai Lama.

43 See, for example, Biggar: "The ultimate of fulfilment of justice is reconciliation … and … reconciliation requires forgiveness." He uses this formulation, however, to conclude that in this world, "full justice in the case of murder is impossible, since the victim, being dead, cannot forgive" (ed., *Burying the Past,* 18).

44 Derrida, *On Cosmopolitanism and Forgiveness,* 32–3.

45 See Arendt, *The Human Condition*. Both Arendt and Derrida stress that punishment and forgiveness are not in opposition to one another. Arendt writes: "The alternative to forgiveness, but by no means its opposite, is punishment, and both have in common that they attempt to put an end to something that without interference could go on endlessly. It is therefore quite significant, a structural element in the realm of human affairs, that men are unable to forgive what they cannot punish and that they are unable to punish what has turned out to be unforgivable" (241).

46 Again here *Arendt* would disagree with Derrida to say that the impossibility of proportionate punishment entails the impossibility of forgiveness *(The Human Condition,* 241).

47 Derrida, *On Cosmopolitanism and Forgiveness,* 39.

48 Ibid., 42. See *Truth and Reconciliation Commission of South Africa Report,* vol. 1. The commission's mandate with respect to amnesty is to facilitate "the granting of amnesty to persons who make full disclosure of all the relevant facts relating to acts associated with a political objective" (55). So the criteria for amnesty are disclosure and political purpose. Neither apology nor remorse were conditions of amnesty under the terms of the Truth and Reconciliation Commission.

49 Derrida, *On Cosmopolitanism and Forgiveness,* 35–6.

50 For example, Umbreit writes: "Although forgiveness may be an outcome of the dialogue for some, it is not the goal of the program. To recognize the humanity of the person who took the life of your child is not easy but can be done. To want that person as well as yourself to heal and therefore to become better at living nonviolently is understandable and attainable. But to forgive the individual for what she or he has done requires almost superhuman effort" *(Handbook of Victim Offender Mediation,* 286).

51 In *Justice as Sanctuary,* Bianchi acknowledges the huge difficulties of adopting time-consuming restorative practices in our time-is-money culture (117).

52 Llewellyn and Howse, "Institutions for Restorative Justice," 378–79. Restoration must take place in the relationship between victim, offender, and the community.

53 *Ideas,* "Justice as Sanctuary," with Herman Bianchi, Part 2, Canadian Broadcasting Corporation Radio Program.

54 See Bianchi, *Justice as Sanctuary,* Ch. 5, "Sanctuary," in which he reviews historical precedents for restorative justice drawn from ancient, medieval, and early-modern practices.

55 Boehm, *Blood Revenge,* 136; Miller, *Bloodtaking and Peacemaking,* 122–24, 171–74; Hasluck, *The Unwritten Law in Albania;* marriage was another means of pacification (257). Interestingly, we also see this idea being put forward in the epic film *Gandhi,* where Gandhi's advise to a penitent Hindu wishing to make amends for violence done to Muslims was that the man should take an orphan Muslim child and bring it up as though it were his own.

56 Miller, *Bloodtaking and Peacemaking,* 172.

57 Ibid.

58 Ibid.

59 For a discussion of debt-slavery, see Miller, *Bloodtaking and Peacemaking,* 29, 75, 129, 148–49.

60 It's interesting that the persuasiveness of stories advocating restorative justice often rests on the wrong-headed rejection of imagined restorative solutions whereas the persuasiveness of stories critiquing revenge often rests on the presence of botched and unsatisfying revenge.

61 While restorative justice advocates will often say that the victim and offender need not be friends, most restorative case studies or vignettes end up with some sense of friendship and affection between the victim and offender. Take, for example, Braithwaite's description of the relation between a teenager who burned down the school library and the school's headmaster after a restorative conference. The boy's father remarks: "To be honest with you I couldn't see that this would do any good, and have wondered if it might make things worse… but isn't it wonderful to see those two chatting away like the best of friends" *(Restorative Justice and Responsive Regulation,* 9). All three of Umbreit's case studies in *The Handbook of Victim Offender Mediation* end with affirmations of friendship between victim and offender. The first ends with the robber, Jim, inviting the victims, Bob and Anne, over for dinner; "The meeting was scheduled two months later at Jim's home, with a mediator present. Jim offered to cook lasagna. Bob and Anne quickly indicated their interest" (90). The second case study ends with the victim of car theft, Tom, offering unconditional support to the offender, Josh. "Tom gave Josh his home telephone number and told Josh he would be available any time of the day or night if Josh needed to talk, needed support, or for any reason at all. Josh's eyes filled with tears as he thanked each one of them. He said he couldn't believe that they could care so much for him after what he had done to them" (97). The final case study ends

with the offenders hugging the victim. "As the mediators closed the session, most of the parents and young people [the offenders] came over to hug Barbara [the victim] and offer words of encouragement" (104).

62 Of course, it is also true that retributive justice is grounded in fantasies of the satisfaction of vengeance. See Miller, "In Defence of Revenge" and "Clint Eastwood and Equity." Interestingly, however, restorative critiques of vengeance are often built upon a combination of concrete examples of botched revenge and fantasized examples of restorative healing.

63 Allen, "Balancing Justice and Social Utility," 317.

64 Dinnen, "Restorative Justice in Papua New Guinea"; Kwochka, "Aboriginal Injustice"; La Prairie, "Developments in Criminal Law and Criminal Justice" and "Some Reflections on New Criminal Justice in Canada"; Ross, "Restorative Justice"; Yazzie, "Hozho Nahasdlii."

65 Umbreit, *Handbook of Victim Offender Mediation,* 5.

66 Umbreit, "Holding Juvenile Offenders Accountable" and "Restorative Family Group Conferences"; Umbreit and Coates, "Multicultural Implications of Restorative Juvenile Justice."

67 Umbreit and Bradshaw, however, report that victims are about as satisfied with victim-offender mediation when the offender is an adult as they are when the offender is a juvenile. The authors use the study to argue that restorative justice should be expanded into the area of adult crime ("Victim Experience of Meeting Adult vs. Juvenile Offenders").

68 It is interesting to note that Braithwaite's initial theories about reintegrative shaming were fleshed out in the context of corporate crime, where the loss and the means to repair tended to be primarily financial and where offenders would be more likely to have financial means of making amends. See Braithwaite, *Crime, Shame, and Reintegration,* Ch. 9, "Reintegrative Shaming and White Collar Crime," 124.

69 A more thorough-going retributivist would say that even the bona fides of the contrition of the offender and his capacity to change for the better would still be insufficient and that a righting of the balance through intentional infliction of suffering on the offender is absolutely necessary to justice. On the idea that restorative justice sees offenders as good people who do bad things, see Sharpe, *Restorative Justice,* 12.

References

Allen, Jonathan. "Balancing Justice and Social Utility: Political Theory and the Idea of a Truth and Reconciliation Commission." *University of Toronto Law Journal* 49 (1999): 315–55.

Arendt, Hannah. *The Human Condition.* Chicago: University of Chicago Press, 1958.

Aristotle. *"Nicomachean" Ethics.* Translated by David Koss. Oxford: Oxford University Press, 1986.

Ashworth, Andrew. "Some Reservations about Restorative Justice." *Criminal Law Forum* 4, 2 (1993): 277–99.

Barton, Charles K.B. *Getting Even: Revenge as a Form of Justice.* Chicago: Open Court, 1999.

Bianchi, Herman. *Justice as Sanctuary: Toward a New System of Crime Control.* Bloomington: Indiana University Press, 1994.

Biggar, Nigel ed. *Burying the Past: Making Peace and Doing Justice after Civil Conflict.* Washington, DC: Georgetown University Press, 2001.

Boehm, Christopher. *Blood Revenge: The Anthropology of Feuding in Montenegro and Other Tribal Societies.* Lawrence: University Press of Kansas, 1984.

Braithwaite, John. *Crime, Shame, and Reintegration.* Cambridge: Cambridge University Press, 1989.

——. "Restorative Justice and Social Justice." *University of Saskatchewan Law Review* 63, 1 (2000): 185–94.

——. *Restorative Justice and Responsive Regulation.* Oxford: Oxford University Press, 2002.

Buber, Martin. *I and Thou.* Translated by Walter Kaufmann. New York: Simon and Schuster, 1970.

Christie, Nils. "Conflict as Property." *British Journal of Criminology* 17, 1 (1977): 1–15.

——. "Between Civility and State." In *The New European Criminology: Crime and Social Order in Europe,* edited by Vincenzo Ruggiero, Nigel South, and Ian Taylor, 119–24. London: Routledge, 1998.

Daly, Kathleen. "Diversionary Conferencing in Australia: A Reply to the Optimists and Skeptics." Paper presented to the American Society of Criminology Annual Meeting, Chicago, November 1996. <http://www.gu.edu.au/school/ccj/kdaly.html> (15 May 2002).

——."Restorative Justice: Moving Past the Caricatures." Paper presented to the Seminar on Restorative Justice, Institute of Criminology, University of Sydney Law School, April 1998. <http://www. gu.edu.au/school/ccj/kdaly.html> (22 August 2000).

——. "Restorative Justice in Diverse and Unequal Societies." *Law in Context* 17, 1 (1999): 167–90.

——. "Revisiting the Relationship between Retributive and Restorative Justice." In *Restorative Justice: From Philosophy to Practice*, edited by John Braithwaite and Heather Strang, 33–54. Aldershot: Dartmouth, 2001. <http://ww.gu.edu.au/school/ccj/kdaly.html> (5 February 2002).

——. "Restorative Justice: The Real Story." *Punishment and Society* 4, 1 (2002): 55–79.

Daly Mary. *Gyn/Ecology: The Metaethics of Radical Feminism.* Boston: Beacon Press, 1990.

Delgado, Richard. "Goodbye to Hammurabi: Analysing the Atavistic Appeal of Restorative Justice." *Stanford Law Review* 52 (2000): 751–75.

Derrida, Jacques. *On Cosmopolitanism and Forgiveness.* Translated by Mark Dodey and Michael Hughes. Thinking in Action series. London: Routledge, 2001.

Dickens, Charles. *Little Dorrit.* Oxford: Oxford University Press, 1982 [1857].

Dinnen, Sinclair. "Restorative Justice in Papua New Guinea." *International Journal of the Sociology of Law* 25 (1997): 245–62.

Duff, Anthony. *Punishment, Communication, and Community.* Oxford: Oxford University Press, 2001.

——. "Restoration and Retribution." In *Restorative Justice and Criminal Justice: Competing or Reconcilable Paradigms?* edited by A. Von Irsch et al., 43–60. Oxford: Hart Publishing, 2003.

Elshtain, Jean Bethke. "Politics and Forgiveness." In *Burying the Past: Making Peace and Doing Justice after Civil Conflict,* edited by Nigel Biggar, 40–56. Washington, DC: Georgetown University Press, 2001.

Evers, Tag. "A Healing Approach to Crime." *The Progressive* 62, 9 (1998): 30.

Fatić, Aleksandar. *Punishment and Restorative Crime-Handling: A Social Theory of Trust.* Aldershot: Avenbury, 1995.

Hadley, Michael L. "Multifaith Reflections on Criminal Justice." In *The Spiritual Roots of Restorative Justice,* edited by Michael L. Hadley, 1–29. Albany: State University of New York Press, 2001.

Hasluck, Margaret Masson Hardie. *The Unwritten Law in Albania.* Cambridge: Cambridge University Press, 1954.

Heyward, Carter. *Touching Our Strength: The Erotic as Power and the Love of God.* San Francisco: Harper, 1989.

——. *Staying Power: Reflections on Gender, Justice, and Compassion.* Cleveland: Pilgrim Press, 1995.

Johnstone, Gerry. *Restorative Justice: Ideas, Values, Debates.* Cullompton: Willan, 2002.

Jurevic, Linda. *"What's Love Got to Do With It?" Addressing Spirituality within the Context of Transformative Mediation.* L.L.M. thesis. University of Melbourne. June 2000.

Kerruish, Valerie. *Jurisprudence as Ideology.* London: Routledge, 1991.

King, Jr., Martin Luther. *Stride Toward Freedom: The Montgomery Circle.* New York: Harper and Row, 1958.

La Prairie, Carol. "Developments in Criminal Law and Criminal Justice: Conferencing in Aboriginal Communities in Canada: Finding Middle Ground in Criminal Justice." *Criminal Law Forum* 6 (1995): 576–99.

——. "Some Reflections on New Criminal Justice in Canada: Restorative Justice, Alternative Measures and Conditional Sentences." *The Australian and New Zealand Journal of Criminology* 32, 2 (1999): 139–52.

Llewellyn, Jennifer J., and Robert Howse. *Restorative Justice: A Conceptual Framework.* Discussion paper prepared for the Law Commission of Canada. 1998.

Llewellyn, Jennifer J., and Robert Howse. "Institutions for Restorative Justice: The South African Truth and Reconciliation Commission." *University of Toronto Law Journal* 49 (1999): 355–88.

MacKinnon, Catherine A. *Toward a Feminist Theory of the State.* Cambridge: Harvard University Press, 1989.

Martin, Dianne L. "Retribution Revisited: A Reconsideration of Feminist Criminal Law Reform Strategies." *Osgoode Hall Law Journal* 36 (1998): 151–88.

Miller, William Ian. *Bloodtaking and Peacemaking: Feud, Law, and Society in Saga Iceland.* Chicago: University of Chicago Press, 1990.

——. "Clint Eastwood and Equity: The Virtues of Revenge and the Shortcomings of Law in Popular Culture." In *Law and the Domains of Culture*, edited by Austin Sarat and Thomas Kearns, 161–202. Ann Arbor: University of Michigan Press, 1998.

——. "In Defense of Revenge." In *Medieval Crime and Social Control*, edited by Barbara A. Hanawalt and David Wallace, 70–89. Minneapolis: University of Minnesota Press, 1999.

Niebuhr, Reinhold. *The Nature and Destiny of Man.* New York: Scribner, 1964.

——. *Love and Justice: Selections of the Shorter Writings of Reinhold Niebuhr.* Cleveland: World Publishing, 1967.

Nietzsche, Friedrich. *On the Genealogy of Morals.* Translated by Walter Kaufmann. New York: Random House, 1989.

Nussbaum, Martha C. "Compassion: The Basic Social Emotion." *Social Philosophy and Polity* 13, 1 (1996): 27–58.

Okin, Susan Moller. *Justice, Gender, and the Family.* New York: Basic Books, 1989.

Pollard, Charles. "Victims and the Criminal Justice System: A New Vision." *The Criminal Law Review* [2000]: 5–17.

Sandel, Michael J. *Liberalism and the Limits of Justice.* 2nd ed. Cambridge: Cambridge University Press, 1982, 1998.

Sharpe, Susan. *Restorative Justice: A Vision for Healing and Change.* Edmonton: Edmonton Victim-Offender Mediation Society, 1998.

Solomon, Robert C. *A Passion for Justice: Emotions and the Origins of the Social Contract.* Lanham, Maryland: Rowman and Littlefield, 1995.

Teitel, Ruti G. *Transitional Justice.* Oxford: Oxford University Press, 2000.

Truth and Reconciliation Commission of South Africa Report. Vols. 1–10. Capetown: CTP Book Printers, 1998.

"Truth, the Road to Reconciliation: Official Truth and Reconciliation Commission Website." <http://www.truth.org.za/index.htm> (6 June 2002).

Umbreit, Mark S. "Crime Victims Seeking Fairness Not Revenge: Toward Restorative Justice." *Federal Probation* 3 (1989): 53–7.

——. "Holding Juvenile Offenders Accountable: A Restorative Justice Perspective." *Juvenile and Family Court Journal* 46, 2 (Spring 1995): 31–42.

——. *Handbook of Victim Offender Mediation.* San Francisco: Jossey-Bass, 2001.

Umbreit, Mark S., and William Bradshaw. "Victim Experience of Meeting Adult vs. Juvenile Offenders: A Cross-National Comparison." *Federal Probation* 61, 4 (1997): 33–40.

Umbreit, Mark S., and Robert B. Coates. "Multicultural Implications of a Restorative Juvenile Justice." *Federal Probation* 63, 2 (December 1999): 44–51.

Van Ness, Daniel W., and Karen Heetderks Strong. *Restoring Justice.* 1st ed. Cincinnati: Anderson Publishing, 1997.

——. *Restoring Justice.* 2nd ed. Cincinnati: Anderson Publishing, 2002.

Voltaire. *Candide.* Boston: Bedford, 1999 [1759].

Yazzi, Robert. "'Hozho Nahasdlii': We Are Now in Good Relations: Navajo Restorative Justice." *Saint Thomas Law Review* 9 (1996): 117–24.

Zehr, Howard. *Changing Lenses: A New Focus for Crime and Justice.* Scottdale: Herald Press, 1990.

Index